COMMENTARY ON THE SCHEDULED CASTES AND THE SCHEDULED TRIBES (PREVENTION OF ATROCITIES) ACT, 1989

The daring publisher, Universal Law Publishing Company, among the foremost in the law publishing field and progressive in venturing to bring out rare legal literature of avant garde *character has rightly enriched the* corpus juris *of India*

Justice V R Krishna Iyer
Random Reflections, page 14

PREFACE

The development of cultural and civilizational process of the entire human race, from antiquity to present day, cannot be encompassed and understood in a single frame, because the basic elements governing the process of such development depends on so varied individual complexities in different regions that it is most difficult to understand it through one pattern. Normally these elements could be cited as geographical, economic or religious etc. which affect formation of cultures and the societies.

When we look at the Indian scenario, we find a unique pattern of process of development. After Aryan invasion of Indian peninsula it was conqueror and conquered relationship with the aborigines which became a governing element for cultural development, and which in the end resulted in formation of an institution, generally called as 'caste system', where practice of "Untouchability" was the most important consequential product. Such system and practice of "Untouchability" could not be found in any other society throughout the world.

The institution had become so strong that it persistintly went on unabated for centuries and ages, but during freedom struggle Gandhian prudence recognised it as a biggest hurdle in making of a free and modern India. That was the reason why Gandhi vehemently insisted for complete 'abolition' and eradication of this evil of "Untouchability".

The historical causes and facts of this rare Indian phenomenon had been explained in the "Introductory" to this commentary.

However, the framers of the Indian Constitution had taken a cue and incorporate provisions of abolition of "Untouchability" under article 17 of the Constitution. To discharge the obligations provided under article 35 of the Constitution, the Parliament enacted a law in the year 1955, declaring practice of "Untouchability" in any form to be a penal offence (which later became Protection of Civil Rights Act, 1955).

The "Statement of Objects and Reasons" of the Scheduled Castes and the Scheduled Tribes (Prevention of Atrocities) Act, 1989 itself had accepted failure of the previous enactments and laws in this behalf, to contain, rather than abolish completely, the evil of victimization of members of Scheduled Castes and the Scheduled Tribes. Thus the present enactment came into being, but instead of using the word "Untouchability" the new enactment used the word "Atrocity", which different Courts have justified on various grounds. The effort may be compared to the enactment of 'anti slavery' laws in some countries.

The scheme of this commentary, though had to follow the sequential scheme of the Act of 1989, presents a comparative study of other penal statutes with a view to fully explain the interpretations of used words, phrases, expressions, underlying principles, scope and procedures; besides, different kinds of punishments as well as compensations as has been provided in the Scheduled Castes and Scheduled Tribes Rules of 1995. The work is a reason based analytical commentary with the latest case law.

Every effort has been made so that problems faced by professional lawyers, prosecutors and the Courts in day-to-day work may be redressed while dealing with Scheduled Castes and Scheduled Tribes cases. Appendices 1 and 2 have been added to explain fully the important Rules as well as the matters related with 'practices and procedures', that too with the latest case law.

While commenting on various principles, such as provided minimum and maximum punishments etc., I tried to present comparative views given by experts in their studies under the subjects of Penology, Victomology and Criminology, which had become well accepted International norms. I hope this kind of effort would culminate in formation of independent thought through which balanced opinions would emerge.

Even utmost caution cannot gaurantee an absolute product, because the man who makes no mistakes usually does not make anything. Thus, I apologize to the esteemed users of this commentary, in anticipation of such mistakes, which might have crept in. Suggestions, even in form of criticism are welcome.

Banda, (U.P.) **YAWER QAZALBASH**

November 2012 Advocate

CONTENTS

INTRODUCTION

THE SCHEDULED CASTES AND THE SCHEDULED TRIBES (PREVENTION OF ATROCITIES) ACT, 1989

Chapter I
PRELIMINARY

Chapter II
OFFENCES OF ATROCITIES

Chapter III

EXTERNMENT

Chapter IV
SPECIAL COURT

Chapter V

MISCELLANEOUS

TABLE OF CASES

A

E

F

G

H

K

P

R

S

V

W

Y

INTRODUCTION

SYNOPSIS

1. General Introduction

After attaining independence, "People" of this country opted for a secular democracy to secure to all its citizens: justice – social, economic and political; liberty of thought, expression, belief, faith and worship; equality of status, and to promote among them all fraternity for the unity of the Nation. Article 15 of the Constitution also prohibited all kinds of discriminations on grounds of "religion, race, caste, sex or place of birth."

So far so good. Some sincere and earnest efforts were made by the Government of India to discharge their constitutional obligations to secure justice, liberty and equality of status for the members of Scheduled Castes and the Scheduled Tribes, who comprised a sizable number among Indian population, but all their endeavour failed due to various reasons, most notable of them all was inherited legacies and the mind-set culminated in last few thousand years.

In the early days of independent Indian democracy, Protection of Civil Rights Act, 1955 (commonly called as 'untouchability' law) was passed, when it was found that the then provisions of existing Indian Penal Code were not sufficient. Many other laws and rules were either promulgated or amended to abolish the vice of untouchability as well as forced or bonded labour as criminal offences. But of no avail as is evident from the first paragraph of "Statement of Objects and Reasons", of the Act, which is as follows:

> "Despite various measures to improve the socio-economic conditions of the Scheduled Castes and the Scheduled Tribes, they remain vulnerable. They are denied number of civil rights. They are subjected to various offences, indignities, humiliations and harassment. They have, in several brutal incidents, been deprived of their life and property. Serious crimes are committed against them for various historical, social and economic reasons."

After admitting failure of efforts taken until 1989 in this behalf, the said "Statement of Objects and Reasons," for a need to bring the special legislation which also mentions about the reactions of "vested interests" as:

> "2. Because of the awareness created amongst the Schedule Castes and the Scheduled Tribes through spread of education, etc., they are trying to assert their rights and this is not being taken very kindly by the others. When they assert their rights and resist practices of untouchability against them or demand statutory minimum wages or refuse to do any bonded and forced labour, the vested interests try to cow them down and terrorise them. When the Scheduled Castes and the Scheduled Tribes try to preserve their self-respect or honour of their women, they become irritants for the dominant and the mighty. Occupation and cultivation of even the Government allotted land by the Scheduled Castes and the Scheduled Tribes is resented and more often these people become victims of attack by the vested interests. Of late, there has been an increase in the disturbing trend of commission of certain atrocities like making the Scheduled Caste persons eat inedible substances like human excreta and attacks on and mass killings of helpless Scheduled Castes and Scheduled Tribes and rape of women belonging to Schedules Castes and Scheduled Tribes."

In the above mentioned circumstances prevailing among the Indian society, the "Statement" justified the "special Legislation: to check and deter 'special crimes' committed by "non-Scheduled Castes and non-Scheduled Tribes." It was also found necessary to define "atrocity", and also to provide "higher punishments for committing such atrocities". Besides, it was also felt necessary to provide stringent measures and specific preventive and punitive measures to protect the Scheduled Castes and the Scheduled Tribes. The special legislation has emphatically asserted to provide adequate relief, assistance and rehabilitation to the victims of atrocities.

The Bill (Act) was not found lacking in providing all the objectives mentioned in the said "Statement." Whatever had been left, the Rules, framed under section 23 of the Act in the year 1995 by the Central Government (besides formation of a National Commission for Scheduled Castes and Scheduled Tribes had been constituted as a watchman to ascertain that provisions are being followed strictly) completed the objectives. These exercises and efforts by all concerned had brought in wonderful results. No doubt, the part played by lower and higher Judiciary cannot be ignored when the achievement of said 'objectives' is under discussion. The Act of 1989 was repeatedly challenged for its various provisions being discriminatory and as such unconstitutional, but every time its constitutionality was upheld, sometimes on very solid reasons and grounds, but sometimes, it is submitted, on not so solid grounds or reasons. (These decisions would be discussed in detail in the foregoing pages).

However, cause for "atrocities" and "serious crimes" committed against the Scheduled Castes and the Scheduled Tribes is admittedly "historical". (last sentence of paragraph 1 of the "Statement of Objects and Reasons").

2. Historical Perspective

For our purpose the Indian history would start from the point of time when Aryans invaded India and fought with the aboriginals. Some of the aboriginals were pushed towards southern parts, some fled to hills and some were captured. The actual date of this invasion is in obscure antiquity, but some estimates have been made since scholars find some written materials. Thus, on this basis, history of ancient India has been broadly divided in two phases,—Vedic period, which begins with around 1500 B.C and extended upto around 200 B.C, while the second phase starts from the end of first phase (around 200 B.C.) to the advent of Muslim conquest (around 1000 AD) or may be regarded as coming down to present era. The other Sanskrit scholars place this date as 2000 B.C. but it is considered too high.[1]

However, one fact may be safely inferred: when the ten books (later on called ten Mandalas in single volume by Vedaa-Vyas) of Rg-Veda were revealed, Aryans must have been well settled in India. Proof is that the Avestan language had been changed a little bit, but not considerably, which was brought with the Aryans from parts of Central Asia. This gestation period might have taken at least few centuries.

The word "Aryan" itself means 'kinsmen', though there were many tribes among them. The Sanskrit literature of upper parts of first 'phase' show notable results is "law", besides astronomy and medicine etc., but all these subjects were dealt generally in secular manner, because of notion of general 'kinsmanship' among different Aryan tribes, who were settled in different clusters, each of which was called "Pur".

The population of these "Purs", comprised of Aryans as well as "Anaryans". These 'Anaryans' were the captured aboriginals.

2.1 Beginning of Caste System

The Aryans and the 'Anaryans' were differentiated on the basis of their colours (which in Sanskrit is "Varna"). The aboriginals were described as "black" (Krsna) or "Dasa Colour" in contrast with Aryan Varna.

1. For further details please see present author's book "Word of God" p. 59 *et seq.*

The members of conquered race who were captured were given name of "Dasyu", which later on became "Das". In the early days, when the Rg-Veda came into being it was within the area between Kabul and Jamuna, but later on the term "Aryavarta" (land of Aryans) was devised, which lies between Himalyas and the Vindhy range. As new territories were captured by Aryans, more and more aboriginals,—Anaryas, (non-Aryans) or *Dasyus* were brought under subjugation.

In course of time when the subjugation became complete, these *Dasyus* comprised the lowest Caste, and later on they were called *Sudras*.

Rg-Veda describe the *Dasyus* as non-sacrificing, unbelieving and impious. In two passages, these people were also mentioned as phallus-worshippers, though, Aryans themselves adopted this form of worship in due course of time.[1]

Rg-Veda, the first of the four, also gives some indications to the other castes, not in so many words, though. The "five tribes" among Indian Aryans have frequently been mentioned. The tribes mentioned in two passages are: Purus, Turvasas, Yadus, Anas and Druhyus.

The most north-westerly tribe was also mentioned as Gandharis, who may be judged from the given description as breeders of sheep. Atharva-Veda also mention a tribe, settled in north-west of Aryan settlements, called Mujavats. Different places of abodes as well as other circumstances were mentioned about the Aryan established settlements, such as – their *inter se* rivalry, wars and coalitions.

Two important names, *viz.*, that of king Sudas and that of Bharatas have been mentioned among Vedic tribes, but later literature like Aitareya Brahmana and Manu ignored those names. It had been so because the original Vedic tribes merged or intermingled into various nations with new names in the altered circumstances of mode of life. Kurus belonged to race of Bharata, from whom the name of Mahabharat was derived, the great war fought with Purus.

One hymn (iii: 33) describes Sudas and Bharatas came to rivers Vipas and Sutudri accompanied by Visvamitra. Another hymn (iii: 53) mentions that previously Visvamitra has been chief priest of Sudas, but then he went with Bharatas. Yet another hymn (vii: 33) says that Bharatas were defeated by Sudas with help and invocation of Vasistha, who became rival and successor of Visvamitra. Two names of Bharatas, *i.e.*, Devasravas and Devavata has also been mentioned (hymn iii: 23), belonging to a region, which was later called the holy land of "Brahmanism", under the twin names of Brahmavarta and Kuruksetra.

Till the time when Atharva-Veda was completed, the names of original Aryan five tribes were rarely mentioned, instead, new names like Magadhas (Bihar) or Angas (Bengal) were mentioned, indicating that till then Aryans had spread to the delta of Ganges. The Brahmanas, the commentaries written on Vedas mentioned newer and newer names, while in few cases old names were distorted. For instance Yadus had become Yadava, as has been mentioned in epic of Mahabharata, or the old Krivis had become Pancalas etc.

---

1. "A history of Sanskrit Literature"- by Arther A. MacDonell; Pub. Motilal Banarsidas, Del, 1962 p. 130. Prof. MacDonnel was Professor of Sanskrit at Oxford and written the book in 1898.

Above discussion had taken place to give a broader picture of the society which was gradually formed on the basis of split or intermingling of original tribes or their combinations among Aryans in early days. The tribes (Jana) were settled in a number of settlements (Vis) which was spread in several villages (Grama).

Whatever be their internal contradictions or disputes for political reasons, the Vedic Aryans were collectively conscious of their race, language and religion. As far as classes or castes were concerned, they recognised only Aryans and non-Aryans (Anarya), and the sole basis of this division was on the basis of colour (Varna).

Patriarchal family system was prevalent generally, among whom noble and royal families were given credence. The form of government was monarchical, therefore when a ruler was to be elected from the districts (Vis) of tribes, the choice of person was not limited to noble families.

Whether the king was elected or had attained the honours through heredity, his prime duty was to protect the people; and, to offer sacrifice on behalf of his tribe. But on the occasions of battles and wars, the sacrifices were offered by the priests who were employed by him.

Each and every tribe had a family of singers, who composed hymns which were sung on the occasion of sacrifices to Gods. But out of these singers, the one who was appointed by the king to officiate him at the time of sacrifices etc., was called "Purohit".

2.2 *Brahmanic Hierarchy*

When the Rg-Veda was in process of coming and its older portions were written, which also was the period of king Sudas and Vasistha, the caste system had not emerged as such. But it is also a fact that there had been three classes in the society: the warrior class (normally to which the king belonged), the priestly class and the 'Anaryas' (Dasyus or Dasas).

Most important point is that the priesthood had not become hereditary till then anywhere. The Aryan tribes settled in Punjab had assumed and transformed these classes into castes. In fact in the Madhyadesa, Brahmanic caste system grew up and flourished and due to this reason people of this region considered people of north-west as semi-barbarians because of the reason that they had not established that system.

In the early days of priesthood, they received liberal gifts *i.e.*, gold, cows, chariots, clothes etc., at the will of their patrons and because of this priests would praise the deeds of their patrons, specially on the occasion of wars, alongwith the praises given to Gods. But as the Brahmanic order established, the liberality of the patrons had become a duty.

In almost every major religion of the so-called West, the priestly class had developed similarly in one way or the other and exercised considerable amount of influence or sometimes achieved political power among their own societies. Torah and Talmud confirms development and existence of a priestly class (called Kahans) among Jews, who would pray and make sacrifices and also that they would be maintained by the respective religious societies to their own standards.

Roman emperor Constantine, after slaughtering thousands of Christians, had established a permanent Papal seat at Vetican in 325 AD. The Catholic church in the Middle Ages had assumed great political power through religion, though became a class in themselves who even controlled the writs of the kings in Europe, but the said posts were never hereditary.

After advent of Islam, its tenets enshrined in Quran, though emphatically prohibited to make classes or castes among Muslim Ummah and consider every member on equal footing (Masawat), some people had tried everything to denounce this pillar (Masawat) of religion. Quran mandates that no person or member of Ummah would be discriminated on the basis of financial, political, or any other kind of status. Thus the king and the slave can stand side-by-side to pray. Against that some people made a criteria of being a Quraish to become a caliph. Or some people do not allow non-Sayyads to wear black turban etc.[1]

Compared to emergence of priesthood in other religions, a unique hierarchical system emerged in India. When fully established, Brahmins assumed supreme status and position in society. The complexity of the system was contained in hereditary assumption of caste in which a person was born, not seen in any other society. Even sacred learning was restricted to Brahmins, and it had become a monopoly as a birth-right.

In other societies, main power was vested in the hands of princes or the warriors in early days. That would certainly mean that the power belonged to physical force. But in India intellectual supremacy prevailed over physical force. Because of this reason the emergence of caste system, Brahmins remaining on top, is a very unique phenomenon. It had been fully understood that for enhancing intellectual levels, learning was necessary, therefore Dharm-Shastra (Smritis) prohibited other castes from learning Vedas, specially the Shudras were prohibited strictly from even listening the hymns of Vedas.

2.3 The Four Castes

In the early days of Aryan conquests, every member of the race was a soldier and a civilian as well. But once the conquests gave *Aryans* complete dominance in northern India, period of inactivity started, except on the occasions of a sudden attack or occasional uprising of Anaryas (the aboriginals). On those occasions, help had came from the families of lesser tribes, who had intermingled under some warrior of repute in one time. This separate class took care of attacks or uprisings, so that the traders and agriculturists continued their work uninterrupted.

At the same time religious ceremonies were becoming more and more complex as newer concepts (adopted from the aboriginals) were merging with the original concepts of Aryans. Besides, it was felt that ancient texts had to be preserved by cramming.

Due to these full-time occupations three classes emerged in Aryan society, which inevitably separated according to their respective trades, while the Sudras were added as a fourth.

---

1. For other details please see present author's book "Principles of Muslim Law", Alld.

These four classes existed and were established in the period when the independent parts of Yajur-Veda and later parts of Atharva-Veda (book VIII to XIII) were written. Even the last Mandal (Chapter) of Rg-Veda mentions four castes (X:90) by name.

A question may strike the mind: how and why the three classes of the single race (Brahman, Chattri and Vaishya) had so separated from each other, that they were not only prohibited from inter marrying but even eating together or touching the eatables of one another?

The rigid confinement of one caste, where others were and are excluded, was perhaps developed on the basis of old traditions, customs and practices of treating Dasyus or Dasas (the aboriginals) in the earliest days of advent of Aryans. The Brahmins had gradually assumed highest status and position in society and found it fit to make rules for others the same way, to treat a member of caste made lower (according to gradation formulated by Brahmans) to them. In that way they remained supreme to all the three castes lower to them.

One important point must also be mentioned here. A reader may assume that all the members of Scheduled Castes and Scheduled Tribes living in present day India are aboriginals. This is not simply correct, though very few of them may be maintaining their purity. In the first place various sub-castes among Scheduled Castes and Scheduled Tribes are product of admixture of races, and others are product of conversions to Buddhism and Jainism during 2nd century B.C. and seventh century A.D., and then reconversion to "Brahmanic order" in or after the 7th century A.D. (The matter would be discussed in foregoing pages).

3. Smriti – Generally

To understand the coded law as to religion, specially the rules governing caste-system in India, it is important to understand Smritis, which are collection of rules, procedure and the laws.

Smriti, means 'memory', which are the later works on religious traditions and laws derived from ancient sages on the basis of memory. They are also considered legal treatises and Codes. The Vedas have been claimed to have come through Sruti (the revelation), while the Sutras belonging to sphere of tradition and customs are Smriti, which are claimed to be remembered.

Gautam (not Lord Buddha) had written that Smriti is the main part of religion, that is why Smritis are included in "Dharm Shastra". Gautam had not mentioned any Smriti writer except Manu, but he had mentioned the "Dharm Shastra".

But later on various Smriti writers have been mentioned and in total, it is said, there were about 100 Smritis written by different writers. Out of these 100, only 18 are recognised as main Smriti writers, while others were considered as their deputies. Some of prominent main writers were, – Manu, Brahaspati, Dakcha, Gautam, Yam, Angira, Yogishwar, Parashar, Samvart, Vishnu. Narad, Vishwamitra, Kashyap, Vyas, Kautilya, Vasisth and Yana etc. were others who have been mentioned.[1]

---

1. Dharm Shastra Ka Itihas: by Bharatratn Maha Mahopadhyaya, Dr. Pandurang Waman Kane, Vol. 1, p 41, Published by UP Hindi Sansthan, M.G. Marg, Lucknow.

As far as Western scholars, who have worked on Sanskrit literature, are concerned, name of Sir William Jones (1746-1794) comes in forefront. He was the first to indulge in the literary activity in India and founded Asiatic Society of Bengal in 1784. He published translations of Shakuntala in 1789, followed by translation of "Code of Manu", which he rightly called a law-book in Sanskrit.

4. Offences and Punishments in Smrities

Certain classes of offences have been described in detail and sometimes defined, for which punishments were also provided by Smriti law. One important point to be noted here is that the acts or omissions declared to be an offence did not had a universal application to all members of society uniformly. So was the case with the provided quantum of punishments. It was so because the legislation was based on class or Varna principles and offenders were punished according to the caste they belonged. It becomes a natural inference that the 'Sudras' had to take the brunt of punishments most excessively.

There were some special rules made for 'Sudras', as for instance they were forbidden from listening Vedas, and if any 'Sudra' intentionally found doing so, his ears had to be filled with molten lac.[1] In case a 'Sudra' recited a Vedic text, he was punished in a way that his body had to be split[2]. A 'Sudra' was punished to death if he tried to boast an equal status with upper castes.[3] The very concept of crime depended not upon its gravity but the status of the offender.

Sir William Jones mentioned in the preface about the code of Manu as, "It is a system of despotism and priest craft, both indeed limited by law, but artfully conspiring to give mutual support, though with mutual checks; it is filled with strange conceits in metaphysics and natural philosophy, with idle superstitions, and with a scheme of theology most obscurely figurative, and consequently liable to dangerous misconception, it abounds with minute and childish formalities, with ceremonies generally absurd and often ridiculous; the punishments are partial and fanciful, for some crimes; dreadfully cruel, for others reprehensively slight; and the very morals, though rigid enough on the whole, are in one or two instances (as in the case of light oaths and of pious perjury) unaccountably relaxed:................"

Sir William Jones has calculated period of Manu as 880 B.C, while the Indian writer Pandurang Waman Kane mentions period of Manu as 200 to 100 BC which must be wrong, because this is the period after the Ashoka the great, when majority of the Indian population was converted to Buddhism or Jainism. In such a hostile period works like Manu Smriti, tending to promote "Brahmanic order" cannot be presumed to have come into being.

Justice demands that work of Manu should be appreciated on other counts. As said above Manu Smriti was one of the earliest codes, thus it was inevitable that he emphasised on the natural principles of what anthropologists call, – Moral Laws, which has also been recognised by modern genetic scientists, after they have found 'moral-gene' in human genome.

1. Gautam Dharma Sastra XII: 4.
2. Gautam Dharma Sastra XII: 5.
3. Gautam Dharma Sastra XII: 6.

However, the Smrities in general, and Manu in particular, have conceptualized the crime as,—(a) abuse and defemation; (b) assault and battery; (c) theft, robbery and misappropriation of property; (d) adultery; and (e) gambling.

Manu has also provided some rules of procedure and of evidence through which the king himself, or persons appointed by him had to impart justice. That way, he had given concepts of judicial system. But he was very specific about the judges appointed by the king. They must belong to either of the three upper castes, and not in any case a Sudra be appointed by the king to impart justice or allowed to sit on judge's or administrative seat and a Brahmin who is even for name sake a Brahmin should be preferred.[1]

5. Punishments Provided by Different Smrities

Smriti laws in general seem to be antithesis of the rule enshrined in article 14 of Indian Constitution, *i.e.,* equality before law. Different punishments have been provided for the same offence committed, whether minor or major.

5.1 Punishments for Minor Crimes

If a Chatriya abuses a Brahmin, he would be fined 100 Karsapanas, but where a Brahmin abuses a Chatriya, he would be fined only 50, if Brahmin abuses Vaishya, fine would be twenty-five, and nothing would be paid by a Brahmin when he abuses a Sudra.[2]

If a Sudra abuses a Sudra, the amount of fine is twelve Panas. In general when higher caste person abuses one belonging to lower caste, fine is of six Panas.[3]

Against Gautam, Manu provides a fine of 12 Panas for abusing a Sudra, though, but has provided a very harsh punishment to a Sudra when he insults a twice-born person. He prescribes cutting of tongue, and inserting in his mouth hot iron rod.[4] Also that if a Sudra tries to teach religion to Brahmins, the king has been directed to pour hot oil in Sudra's mouth and ears.[5]

5.2 Punishments for Sexual Crimes

Smriti law does not generally relate adultery with a married woman, but unmarried woman have also been included. One important point is that adultress was also made liable for punishment. If a woman of a higher caste has indulged in sexual act with a lower caste man, king has been directed to get the adulteress devoured by dogs at a public place.[6] No doubt the Smriti has differentiated between a willing and un-willing woman.

Kautilya states that when a Brahmin woman was outraged by a Chatriya, the man should be fined with his costliest property, in case of a Vaishya, his entire property to be confiscated, but if he is a Sudra, he should be burnt alive. When a

1. Manu Smriti VIII, 20, (21).
2. Gautam Dharma Sastra XII, 8 to 31.
3. Vishnu V, 35, (36).
4. Manu VIII, 270, (271).
5. *ibid* VIII, 272.
6. Gautam Dharma Sastra XXIII, 14.

person commits adultery with a woman of lower caste, he should be degraded to that caste, but a Sudra in any case would get death.[1] Other Smrities also provide death penalty by burning to Sudras as for the same act.[2]

When a Brahmin male commits adultery for the first time with a woman of same caste, he would be ordered to perform one quarter of penance prescribed for an out-caste.[3]

Manu has provided many punishments for corrupting a maiden (cutting of two fingers with fine) or even lesbian practices have been provided with punishments.[4]

5.3 Major Crimes and Punishments in Smriti

Theft and robbery have been seriously taken by Smriti la as an offence. Manu prescribes a punishment for cutting the limb of the thief.[5]

Though Gautam sets-in a principle that if a learned man commits a crime, the punishment should be very much enhanced.[6] But unfortunately the said enunciated principle has been time and again contradicted. Brahmins have been treated very leniently while provisions of awarding punishments were invoked. He himself has asserted that death punishments should not be given to Brahmins, and they should be given immunity.[7] Likewise Vishnu[8] and Narada have asserted firmly that a Brahmin should not be killed even if he has been found guilty of committing all kinds of offences.[9]

Manu has emphatically mentioned that there is no greater crime (sin) on earth than to slay a Brahmin, therefore a king must never think of killing a Brahmin.[10] He prescribed that in case a Brahmin has to be punished, the Brahmin should be externed, his entire property should be given to other Brahmins and some marks are to be engraved on his head.

For murder, many rules had been formulated. In case a Chatriya is killed, the offender has to give 1000 cows to the Brahmins, hundred for murder of Vaishyas and 10 for murder of a Sudra. This process is for expiation of the *sin*, but the prevalent rule – eye for an eye applied, that means for murder, the offender was awarded death penalty, except in cases where it was found that the murder took place in self defence.[11] In a nutshell Vishnu puts it – "Great criminals should be put to death."

1. Kautilya's, Arthasastra, IV Chapter XIII.
2. Vasisth Dharm Sastra XXI, 1; Gautam Dharm Sastra XXIII, 15.
3. Apastamba Dharma Sutra
4. Manu Smriti VIII, 365 to 370.
5. ibid VIII, 334.
6. Gautam Dharma Sastra VII, 12, 13 and 17, XII.
7. ibid.
8. Vishnu V, 2, (3).
9. Narad Smriti V, 36.
10. Manu Smriti VIII 380-381, also see IX 238 and V, 134.
11. For further details see "History of Dharma Shashtras", by P.V. Kane or scores of other books like Manu Smriti by Chamanlal Gautam, Pub. By Sanskrit Sansthan, Bareilly, U.P., etc.

5.3.1 The Consequences of Discriminatory Law

It does not need much stronger grasping power to infer that what would have become the condition of lower castes since the advent of Smriti laws specially of the so-called Sudras. Besides the above mentioned discrimination in treatment by the judicial and law enforcing agencies, in whatever shape they might have existed, these Sudras had to suffer common social discrimination. They were untouchables, and in some cases were forced to walk on the roads having a bell in hand, so that from the sound of bell, incoming high-caste people may know their presence and keep themselves out of their body shadows. Naturally their lives should have been very hard to live.

In that scenario advent of Buddhism, around 400 BC, and also Jainism proved to be a boon, where all humans were treated equal and no class or caste was allowed to be formed. In the early days of Buddhism the mass conversions were prevented, but in due course of time when Ashoka the great embraced Buddhism after Kalinga war around 200 BC, that religion became a State religion and people became free to convert without interference from within, the result was – mass conversions took place.

Lucky for them, for many powerful kings followed Ashoka in religion and practices. This process had continued upto 7th century A.D. Harshwardhan was the last powerful Buddhist king in the series, but after his death in 7th century A.D., the Buddhistic empire disintegrated. In these eight or nine centuries, the lower castes of yester-years had been living peacefully as respectable members of the society who enjoyed equal rights, at least socially.

But after the disintegration of Buddhist empire (not in the stricter sense) Adi Shankaracharya started a movement, commonly called by historians as "Bhakti Movement" in 7th century A.D. itself to re-establish Brahmanic order by re-converting all those who had previously been converted to Buddhism or Jainism from the Brahmanic order.

Adi Shankaracharya rightly thought that for achieving his objective a State-power was necessary. He convinced a great number of people from his creed and they collectively established a Brahmin kingdom in Punjab, headed by a Brahmin king named Dahir. Adi Shankaracharya had established four centres (called Peethas) to promote Brahmanic religion (or Sanatan Dharma, where Sanatan simply means old), and he alongwith his disciples started the process of re-converting those who had once converted to Buddhism and Jainism, a few centuries ago. Bringing back a great chunk of population was not an easy task. Sacred threads (Janaiwa) were loaded on carts and animals and each and every village was visited, all the times Dahir's army accompanied them for protection and also to use force, if necessary, for re-conversions.

By and by village after village started to re-convert to Brahmanic order through process of "purification" (Sudhikaran), which was often done by force. That is why historians mark 7th century A.D. as downfall of Buddhism and Jainism and revival of Brahmanism.

But during the process few new problems were created, as is the case with every movement and its aftermath. *Firstly*, use of force by Dahir's army to help make re-conversions on a larger scale, which continued to the extent of some 'atrocities' to sustain the re-converted people to remain in the fold. This use of force and, in some cases 'atrocities' created a feeling of hatred and averseness among newly converted people towards kingdom of Dahir, with whose help all the conversions were made. That was the reason why, when first Muslim attack by Mohammad Bin Qasim was made in 712 A.D., many Indian people helped and fought with Mohammad Bin Qasim, so that kingdom of Dahir may be finished. Result was inevitable, Dahir was killed in the battle. But the movement continued some-how or the other.

Secondly, these re-conversions created another problem. The members of original four castes, who did not convert to Buddhism or Jainism then and remained as aboriginals as to the castes, refused to accept re-converted people to be brought into their fold. For quite some time these re-converted people remained in confusion, but in due course they formed their own classes or sub-castes, which exist to the present day. That is the reason why innumerous sub-castes are recorded in Indian society.

5.3.2 Castes During Later Periods

Around 1000 A.D. Muslims took over the governance in India. After 7th century A.D. to tenth century there was enough time to stabilize the re-converted population to the castes' fold. When Muslims took-over the reigns, it was none of their business to interfere in the religious affairs of majority Hindu population, because it could create a political turmoil, which no ruler would like to happen in his domain. Besides, the upper-castes in the majority always remained in close contacts with the rulers, for they required a workforce who were educated, having intellect and learning and rulers found Chatriyas for army and Vaishyas for stability of business and financial conditions of their kingdom. Perhaps, due to these complex reasons, Muslim rulers looked other way when they saw the pathetic conditions of the lowest castes, which had also bifurcated into various sub-castes during the "Bhakti Movement" reconversion.

If looked from another angle, the reason of overlooking the atrocities and the discriminatory practices and customs in caste-system, perhaps the Muslim rulers overlooked because that convinced a great number of majority to convert to their own religion, *viz.*, Islam, where equality of social status (Masawat) is one of the basic tenets. When a Hindu was converted to Islam in those periods, he or she got, firstly equal status (where he was not considered untouchable etc.) among Muslim society, and secondly, the convert became nearer to power, though it might have been a mere feeling. As rulers were Muslims no body was in a position to oppose such conversion.

The situation was same in or around 1000 A.D. and afterwards which prevailed in or around 200 B.C., when Ashoka the great made Buddhism as State religion and large-scale conversions took place defying the "Varn-Vewastha."

A very similar situation could be gathered from pages of Modern Indian History. When the British empire was established, a large number of majority Indians converted themselves to Christianity. British rulers adopted same policy as that of Muslim rulers towards overlooking and sometimes deliberately neglecting the abrogation of "civil right" of some of the majority population, root cause of which was caste-system.

Though, a marked change in the strict implementation of Smriti law could be seen during Muslim or British period, but the mindset and treatment of lower castes created such discriminatory atmosphere that whenever such a member got an opportunity, he or she converted to other religions (Buddhism or Jainism in first phase, Islam in second phase and to Christianity in the third phase).

Even in modern times persons of imminence like Dr. Bhimrao Ambedkar (formerly a Dalit) had embraced Buddhism.

The process is continuing and for that reason some States (Gujarat) had to legislate an "anti-conversion" law.

6. Victimology and Compensations to Victims in Context of SC/ST Act

In the earliest stages of human history concept of State emerged on the sole basis of protection of individual and administration of justice, civil as well as criminal. The objective of a welfare state is to protect rights of an individual and thereby the society at large.

The individual, when subjected to one of various kinds of crimes, is called a victim, becomes subject-matter of protection for which the State was initially constituted. It is expected of a welfare State to stand at the side of victim, that is why by fiction the State also becomes victim. Thus state had to function as protective and restitutive entity. In protective duty State has to see that the wrongdoer is being punished, and for discharging the other duty, it is expected that State had to render some help to the victim, sometimes in pecuniary terms.

The offender and the victim both are the individuals and are members of the society as well. Previously the victim was considered as a witness for the State to find and prosecute the offender, but in the whole process gradually the victim was left on his own. The State had made laws and rules for such situations providing that the victim could indulge himself to file civil suit for obtaining damages for the criminal wrong the offender has inflicted on him.

On the other hand the State found satisfaction in conviction of offenders, on the dictum that "a criminal must pay his debt to the society."

But in the modern era, criminal lawyers and criminologists found that there is a public responsibility for the victims of crime, and a "retributive theory" was formulated which influenced the administration of justice systems, particularly in the West, and later on shifted to "reformative theory". All these principles were formulated for the benefit of the offenders, who, as it was considered that, would ultimately benefit the society. But the victim was let alone to curse his fate.

For maintaining a balance between conflicting interests of State, the offender and the victim, it was found necessary to ensure justice to the victim, by way of restitution to his original position, as far as possible, and to pay compensation. Therefore lately the "restitutive theory" was developed.

6.1 History of "Restitutive Theory"

In old days, the injured or killed persons were given a legal right to appropriately get an exact vengeance from the offender or from his kin, this legal concept was later on converted to provide an option to the victim or his kin to accept "blood-money", instead of persuing the feud further, which would eventually make suffer other individuals of the society or endanger its peace. The value of money was set according to the status of man which was called "wer" and the compensation was "wergild" or "bot". Apart from these there was also a penal fine to the king which was called "wite".[1] But it was not called a rule of law of crime, as it was from law of torts.

The "Anglo-Saxons" that way recovered these payments in the form of compensation or damages. This was also termed as "self-help justice."

In thirteenth century A.D., the self-help justice had taken another shape; *viz.*, the king or the State started receiving payments in criminal cases and the victim was left with an option to file a civil suit for compensation to the wrong he suffered. It was so because by then the State had assumed exclusive right to punish the wrong-doers. During nineteenth century some criminologists started advocating strongly to pay compensation and restitution to victims, on the ground that victims were "public responsibility".

The "Social Contract Theory" forwarded by Hobbes, Locke and Rousseau stipulates that people agreed to live in a society on the condition that society would give them protection and a happy life, therefore it was a duty of society and the State to look after the welfare of the people. For securing the protection of people, the State constituted a criminal justice system. The negligence and inefficiency of State allow some individuals to deviate from the agreed behaviour for various reasons. No doubt State punishes such wrong doers, according to the parameters and the manner provided under the constitution, other Penal laws in general and of course special laws legislated (as SC/ST Act 1989 and Rules, 1995).

6.2 Real Concept of Victimology and its Development

After the end of Second World War, criminologists realized that to understand the crime and its origin, it is necessary to study the criminal-victim relationship. In that way 'victimology' was developed as a branch of criminology.

The criminologists started to understand the crime from victim's point of view and that way the victims were made center of study.

The offender-victim relationship and victim's share in causation of crime, when deeply examined, helps in developing the ways to protect the victim before the actual commission of crime. This kind of study also helps to actually stop perpetration of crime from where it emanates (various preventive measures have been incorporated in the Act of 1989 and Rules of 1995).

Attention was diverted towards it, because after Second World War, the frequency of all kinds of crime had taken dangerous dimensions the world over. At the behest of United Nations first international conference on 'victimology' was held at Jerusalam in the year 1973, which was followed by another at Bastan in 1976 and since then extensive studies were conducted for the problems of victims, required legal proceedings and for entitlement of victims to receive compensations.

1. The Ancient Law, by H.S. Maine (1861).

The outcome of studies, discussions and seminars, it was found necessary to define the 'victim' first, because the victims could be of various categories, *i.e.,* victims of natural disasters, victims of bad living conditions or victims of negligent acts which caused accident etc., and these cannot be brought under the study of criminology.

In 1985 the 7th U.N. Congress in Milan included the topic, "Victims of Crime" in its agenda and during the discussion recognised officially the scope and study of victimology. They defined the victims as those persons, individually or collectively, who have suffered harm physically, mentally or emotionally, economic loss or impairment of fundamental rights through acts or omissions that are in violation of "criminal laws" operative within the country, including the laws prescribing criminal abuse of power.

The above definition is quite exhaustive which brings in its scope not only victims of crime of abuse of political or economic power, but also the victims of social "atrocities" due to established classes or "castes".

One important suggestive objective of the resolution was to find out all possible solutions to the problems of the victims by focusing on the areas of "law reforms".

Though it has not been mentioned in the "Statement of Objects and Reasons" of the Scheduled Castes and Scheduled Tribes (Prevention of Atrocities) Act, 1989, but it appears that, the 1985 U.N. resolution was the motivating force for bringing in the legislation. (It would be discussed in detail later).

6.3 General Problems of Victims and Remedies in SC/ST Act and Rules

Victims of crime face problems of various kinds, but members of Scheduled Castes and Scheduled Tribes face some additional problems as compared to general victims of crime. Therefore special provisions were required to provide for eradication of those problems. Additionally, special remedial measures were also required. Few of such problems are cited below:

6.3.1 Economic Strain

When a family becomes a victim in cases where its sole bread earner was killed or incapacitated in such a way that he becomes disabled, the dependent members of the family need economic help. The Act of 1989 and Rules 1995 made under Scheduled Castes and Scheduled Tribes Act provide wide ranging relief to such victims of crime and atrocity. Rules 10, 11 and 12 *etc.,* and Annexures 1 and 2 provide a variety of measures for giving economic compensation.

6.3.2 Displacement of Victims

In case of individual or collective acts of crimes and 'atrocities', generally the victims of crimes are forced to leave their ancestral dwelling places out of fear and reocurrence of crime. The Act of 1989 and the Rules very specifically provide for rehabilitation of victims. Not only that the Rules provide at all levels appropriate officers to monitor the situation on regular basis and even declaring the area as atrocity prone, besides taking all possible measures to prevent any further crime, including ordering removal or externment of all nuisance mongers from the area or imposing collective fines.

6.3.3 Social Stigma

Generally the victim of any crime face brunt of the society, but specially in rape or other such kind of crimes related with sex, the victim and her family faces grave problems. It is true that State cannot return the honour or the dignity of the victim, but it is possible to provide solace to the victim in two ways – by punishing the wrongdoer; and, by compensating the victim in monitory terms. Apart from taking these two recourses, the Scheduled Castes and Scheduled Tribes Act, 1989 had provided some indirect measures so that the offenders of 'atrocities' are so reciprocally humiliated that the victim gets solace.

S. Murlidhar has rightly said that Basic Principles of Justice for Victims of Crime and Abuse of Power recognized four major componants of the rights of victims of crime as:

(a) Access to justice and fair treatment
(b) Restitution
(c) Compensation
(d) Assistance.[1]

Some of the criminologists apprehended that the victims of crime if being further victimized by the criminal justice delivery systems, they may refuse to co-operate, and in that case the whole system would automatically fail. Therefore, caring, protecting and compensating the victims of crime are very necessary. Long delays, indifferent attitudes and further victimization, sometimes deter victims of crime not to approach police for reporting occurrence of rapes, etc.

For these reasons, the Scheduled Castes and the Scheduled Tribes Act, 1989 and the Rules framed thereunder had tried to make a separate skeleton of administrative machinery and also a watchdog to monitor and review the situation at least twice a year on higher levels, so that further victimization of victims may be avoided, if not completely eradicated. Section 4 of the Act provides punishment to 'public servants' who are found negligent in performing their duties in this behalf.

7. Concepts of Compensation to Victims

The concepts of legally providing for compensation to victims of crime was not a product of 20th century. The concept could be traced to antiquity. In old Greek city, states, developed concept for paying compensations to victims of crime was in vogue. Manu Smriti also made provisions for the same. (Chapter VIII: 287, 288 etc),. In old Arabia and as such under Islamic law very specific provisions could be found for such compensations.

If we go even deeper in the history of human civilization, we can find the said provision even when there existed no rule of law or authority to enforce the payment of compensation to victims. In that era the victims themselves tried to realize the compensation from the wrongdoers through brute force himself or by the help of other members of society. That process naturally adopted attack or other kinds of threats to do so. After this era, the societies, in form of tribes

1. "Rights of Victims in the Indian Criminal Justice System", by S. Murlidhar, Pub. Journal of the National Human Rights Commission 88 Vol. 2 (2003).

or clans, had developed a rule according to which victims were supposed to be collective responsibility of the society. Later on, the king took this responsibility.

In modern era the United Nations had taken the initiative through adopting a resolution by its General Assembly in 1985 *(Supra)*, through which following "Basic Principles" were set:

(1) A victim's right was recognised who was found entitled, for the suffered harm to be treated by a well defined mechanism of Justice so that he or she may get prompt redressal.

(2) Offenders were made responsible for fair restitution to the victims or to their families. This restitution should be made part of punishment by law in criminal cases.

(3) In cases where, the compensation could not be made available to the victims from the resources of the offenders, the State should give monetary compensation and restitution to the victim. For this purpose a National Fund be set up by the member States.

As could be seen, it is the direction of the 'U.N. Resolution' that either the offender or the State or both should pay compensation to the victims.

Arnould Bonneville had collected many views in this regard of pioneers of Criminology[1].

It was suggested that "victim should be legally entitled to receive a part of the proceeds from work done by culprit during detention". Accordingly New Zealand, U.K., USA and Australia had legislated various laws in the past to provide compensations to victims through various ways, including in the first place, State pays the compensation to the victim for immediate redressal, and thereafter recovering the sum from the guilty offender.

8. Specific Special Provisions of SC/ST Act and Rules as to Compensation and Restitution

The Rules framed under section 23 of the SC/ST Act, 1989 very specifically mention in Rule 12(4),(5) and (6) that it is duty of District Magistrate or Sub-Divisional Magistrate or any other Executive Magistrate for making "arrangements for providing immediate relief in cash or in kind or both to the victims of atrocity, their family members and dependents according to the scale as in Schedule annexed to" those rules (Annexture 1 read with Annexture II).

The Annexture 1 categorically specify the amounts for each and every acts of crime (atrocities) mentioned in section 3 of the Act or elsewhere.

All the compensatory amounts mentioned (or the materials supplied to victims) are the responsibility of State; and, the Act or the Rules do not generally involve the offenders to participate in the payment of such compensation for items mentioned in Annexure 1 to Rules of 1995.

The eligibility to receive those compensation amounts etc., has been restricted only to the members of Scheduled Castes and Scheduled Tribes. Besides, no conditions have been imposed for the eligibility. (Please also see Appendix 1).

---

1. "Arnould Bonneville" in Mannheim, Pioneers in Criminology (Second Ed., 1972).

9. Eligibility and Computation of Compensation Rules in General Law

General rules of Victimology recommend that all victims of crime are entitled to compensation ideally, but this process had to take place in a phased manner (over a period of years), depending on the resources of the State. In case where death has taken place, the eligibility of dependents and the menthod of computation may stipulate the need, the living standards etc., of victim. The method of computation depend's on multiplication of annual loss of earnings by the deceased or other victim's work-like expectancy, while deducting the personal expenses.

Furthermore to avoid double compensation, it is also considered whether the victim is getting benefits from any other schemes or sources, such as insurance or Workman's Compensation etc.

Though, general rules of victimology recommend compensation to victims of crime, irrespective of the fact whether the offender is convicted or acquitted, but these general rules also do recommend some pre-conditions such as that either compensation should be reduced or the order to pay compensation amount should be cancelled where:

(a) the victim does not co-operate in the process of prosecution (becoming a hostile witness),

(b) the victim has failed in his or her duty to divulge correct informations, or given almost wrong informations (for the objective of getting compensation),

(c) the victim being a criminal himself, having a criminal record and due to his own criminal conduct the crime was committed.

The above mentioned rules of general victimology had not been considered while, the draft of the Act or Rules was prepared, perhaps on the assumption that the Scheduled Castes and Scheduled Tribes are a hapless lot who have been persecuted for thousands of years and they need help by all means.

10. Other Legislation Providing Compensation to victims

India as well as other countries of the world had legislated a variety of provisions for empowering the courts to award compensation to victims of crime, and in some cases it had been made part and parcel of conviction orders.

These legislations may be used in addition to whatever has been provided under the provisions of the Scheduled castes and Scheduled Tribes Act, 1989.

10.1 Indian Legislations

The Compensatory Philosopy in criminal jurisprudence is not new in the arena of criminal justice system in India. The legislature had provided for compensation to the victims of crime in various enactments, such as: (a) Criminal Procedure Code, 1973; (b) Probation of offenders Act, 1958; and (c) Indian Constitution.

10.1.1 Provisions Under Cr.PC.

Sections 237, 250, 357, 358 and 359 of Criminal Procedure Code, 1973, deal with compensation to victims in one way or the other.

Section 357 Cr.PC. empowers a Court to order whole or part of imposed fine to be paid to any person as "compensation for any loss or injury caused by the offence" [section 357 (i)(b)]. The incorporation of this provision was a positive gesture towards the victims of crime on one hand and on the other recognition of compensation philosophy in criminal jurisprudence. Prior to this provision the compensations were claimed under *torts* or other civil legislations.

Similarly section 358 Cr PC provides for payment of compensation to victims who had been "groundlessly arrested". Section 359 Cr PC provides similar rule regarding payment of compensation to the complainants who was found victimized by the accused.

Supreme Court had observed in this regard as: "this power of court to award compensation is not ancillary to other sentences but it is in addition thereto. This power was intended to do something to reassure the victim that he/she is not forgotten in the criminal justice system."[1]

Courts are free to award to the victims of Scheduled Castes and Scheduled Tribes compensation under sections 357, 358 and 359 Cr PC but these provisions of the Code have following limitations:

(i) Court cannot impose and award compensation in cases of acquittal,

(ii) If substantive sentence has been imposed, the quantum of compensation is limited because the amount cannot exceed the amount of imposed fine,

(iii) the awarded compensation can only be paid if the ordered fine has been realized, and in cases were fines cannot be realized for whatever reasons, victim gets nothing.

(iv) The amounts of fines to be imposed are subject to limited amounts provided under provisions of Indian Penal Code, which were fixed about hundred and fifty years ago, which inevitably are inadequate.

(v) The Court has to consider the alternative remedy by the victim for recoverable compensation from the civil court.

10.1.2 Probation of Offenders Act

Section 19 of Scheduled Castes and the Scheduled Tribes (Prevention of Atrocities) Act, 1989 bars provisions of Probation of Offenders Act, 1958 to be applicable to the convicted person, who is above age of eighteen years and found guilty of having committed an offence under the Act. Thus, further discussions in this regard would be irrelevant.

10.1.3 Constitutional Provisions

Indian people chose that independent India would be a 'welfare State' and on this principle the provisions of Indian Constitution were formulated after due and extensive debates. State was made responsible for ensuring safety and security of its citizens. Fundamental rights of citizens were guaranteed under Part III of the Constitutions. Under Article 21 life and liberty of all citizens have been declared to be most precious right'.

The Apex Court, while trying to develop compensatory jurisprudence, has asserted that as the right of life and liberty is available to the accused, it is also available to the victim as well. But the majority of decisions had come where due

1. *Hari Krishnan and State of Haryana* v. *Sukhbir Singh*, AIR 1988 SC 2127: 1989 Cr LJ 116: JT 1988 (3) SC 711.

to negligent acts of the sovereign some person was detained illegally and court found it fit to order for payment of compensation. Cases of victims of crime are different.

There cannot be two opinions about the victimization of members of Scheduled Castes and the Scheduled Tribes at the hands of so-called upper castes in the Hindu Varna Vewastha. Therefore, by all philosophical and practical rules of compensatory jurisprudence the provided compensation for such victims are fully justified, unless, of course, it was found that some fraud had taken place to illegally obtain the provided compensation.

11. Hate Crimes and Special Law

Webster's Legal Dictionary defines 'hate crime' as, "a crime motivated by bias against a group identified by race, religion, sexual orientation, or other group characteristic, or a crime in which the victim is chosen because of perceived membership in such a group, *States may impose extra penalties for such crimes.*"

The last phrase of the definition justifies a special legislation where the defined 'hate crimes' are in vogue.

The phenomenon is not new and could be observed all over the world from very old times. Romans killed more than ten thousand Christians, Europeans trying to settle in America killed native 'American Indians' or Nazis killed thousands of Jews are few instances from the West.

As has been described earlier in the preceding paragraphs, the Aryan's aversion and hatred of aboriginal Indians could be traced to the present day, though the aboriginals presently seen as Scheduled Castes and Scheduled Tribes, also include some of the original Aryan lot, who were considered in the lowest caste due to various reasons, but they were hated.

Smriti laws, as has been mentioned before, specifically divided the Indian society in four Varnas and the lowest of them all has been the subject of persecution throughout and lived for ages without any rights. Smriti law even very strictly prohibited them from educating themselves.

It would not be just if one does not mention the initial efforts by the British to eradicate menace of hatred and assertion of same rights to Scheduled Castes and Tribes, though on a limited scale. As said before, despite the fact that it was not their policy to indulge themselves in social conflicts of Indian society, thus such indulgence had come in a very limited and localised sphere. After all the process had begun when some laws were enacted in this regard. Some of these are: The Madras Removal of Civil Disabilities Act, 1938 (Act XXI of 1938), Removal of Civil Disabilities Act, 1943 (Mysore Act XLII of 1943), Orissa Removal of Civil Disabilities Act, 1946, Bombay Harijan (Removal of Social Disabilities) Act, 1946 (Bombay Act X of 1946) etc.[1]

When India became independent and its Constitution came into existence, it was felt that enough is enough and persecution of the lower classes to the extent of tradition of 'untouchability' had to go, Indian Parliament passed Protection of

1. All the mentioned legislations were repealed by section 17 (Schedule) of Protection of Civil Rights Act, 1955.

Civil Rights Act, 1955, though it took 22 years to frame rules under the said Act that is in the year 1977. (Constitution abolished untouchability).

These few legislations and some provisions of Indian Constitution had helped this persecuted lot to get themselves educated, due to which awareness and awakening came for demanding their due rights suppressed for thousands of years.

These demands of rights and assertions for self-respect were not taken very kindly by others. The causes for enacting a special law has been given in "Statement of Objects and Reasons" of the Scheduled Castes and the Scheduled Tribes (Prevention of Atrocities) Act, 1989. Para 2 reads as:

> "2. Because of the awareness created amongst the Scheduled Castes and the Scheduled Tribes through spread of education, etc., they are trying to assert their rights and this is not being taken very kindly by the others. When they assert their rights and resist practices of untouchability against them or demand statutory minimum wages or refuse to do any bonded and forced labour, the vested interests try to cow them down and terrorise them. When the Scheduled Castes and the Scheduled Tribes try to preserve their self-respect or honor of their women, they become irritants for the dominant and the mighty......... Of late, there has been an increase in the disturbing trend of commission of certain atrocities.........". etc. etc.

When the Indian situation is compared with the situations and the circumstances of other countries, historically or otherwise, the Indian situation is found to be unique. In Roman or Nazi cases in the past, or in the present era the ethnic cleansing in Bosnia, the hatred was directed against members belonging to other religions or even races, but in Indian scenario the directed hatred and consequential crimes are directed against the members of same religion and race.

Till date the Indian battle for eradication of 'hate crimes' are 'caste' specific and laws have been enacted to combat caste discrimination. But other religious groups are awaiting to see similar enactment or laws so that they may be spared from 'hate crimes' unwantedly thrust upon them.

The Communal Violence Bill, 2005, proposed after the Gujarat carnage and at the backdrop of communal violence against Christians, is yet to be put before the Parliament. Recently some of the provisions have been diluted, when the reactionary forces objected to certain provisions. However, the Bill if sees the light of the day would be second effort to combat 'hate crimes' in the long going battle.

12. Criticisms and Drawbacks of SC/ST Act, 1989 and the Rules, 1995

Despite the intent, good faith and the spirit behind the passage of the Scheduled Castes and the Scheduled Tribes (Prevention of Atrocities) Act, 1989 and the Rules framed thereunder, there are some people who criticize the provisions sometimes on the basis of genuine, and sometimes on not so sound reasons.

In the early stages the Act was constitutionally challenged but it was upheld to be constitutionally valid by Full Benches of different High Courts. A Full

Bench of Rajasthan upheld the Act in the year 1993[1], and again a Full Bench of Allahabad had done the same in 1995[2].

(1) As a criticism it was said, "however with the passage of time some perversions, transgressions, *mala fides* and the like started in its application and it started being used for settling personal scores by the members of Scheduled Castes or a Scheduled Tribes against a member of upper caste in offices, factories and in other establishments. The stringent provisions of the Act started terrorizing others and there was exponential growth in the number of cases under this Act."[3]

The above mentioned article also cited a case from Rajasthan High Court[4] wherein the court sounded a word of caution to prosecution for complaints under the Act, because provisions of the Act have been blatantly misused with a view to vindicate one's personal vendetta against members of different caste, because caste rivalries are very much prevalent.

(2) Sub-clauses (1) and (2) of section 3 of the Act starts with words: "whoever, not being a member of a Scheduled Caste and the Scheduled Tribe, –" though exclude the said members mentioned therein, but include the rest of Indian population, which certainly include Muslims, Christians, Jews, Parsis etc., etc. Incidentally it may be mentioned that Islam, Christianity, Judaism etc., had always been very sternly opposed to any class (caste) system of any type and as such their mind-set never allow the members of these religions or communities to consider any other member of society to be lower than or higher than himself.

Above mentioned phrase and the prefix to section 3 of the Act could have been more diligently constructed.

(3) Severity of punishments provided for various offences, though, have been upheld constitutionally by many courts, but some defy the rules formulated by penology.

(4) Logically payments of compensations provided under the Rules is duty of State which is bound to make restitution to the victim on the ground that it has broken the 'contract' by not preserving the life and limb of its citizen, but it has been also found world over that too much fraud had taken place for obtaining such compensations. Experiences of Northern Ireland have been cited in such contentions relating to frauds for unlawful claims. In our own country unlawful claims are made in different insurance schemes, undoubtedly indicate tendencies towards misuse of the lawful provisions for unlawful pecuniary gains. The Act or the Rules has no provisions to restrict the misuse.

---

1. *Jai Singh* v. *Union of India*, 1993 Cr LJ 2705 (FB) (Raj): AIR 1993 Raj 177: 1993 (1) Raj LW 157.
2. *Mata Sewak Upadhyay* v. *State of Uttar Pradesh*, 1995 JIC 1168 (All) (FB): 1996 (1) East Cr C 97 (All) (FB).
3. "Atrocities Prevention Law – Purpose and Perversion", by R.C. Chaturvedi, Pub in 2006 Cr LJ (Journal) 78.
4. *Bishanlal* v. *Hargovind*, RLW 2000 (3) (Raj) 1680.

THE SCHEDULED CASTES AND THE SCHEDULED TRIBES (PREVENTION OF ATROCITIES) ACT, 1989

(33 of 1989)

[11th September, 1989][1]

An Act to prevent the commission of offences of atrocities against the members of the Scheduled Castes and the Scheduled Tribes, to provide for special courts for the trial of such offences and for the relief and rehabilitation of the victims of such offences and for matters connected therewith or incidental thereto.

Be it enacted by Parliament in the Fortieth Year of the Republic of India as follows:

SYNOPSIS

1. The Title of the Act

Generally speaking titles of the Acts may be of three kinds, *viz.* short, long and full title. The short title of a statute is like identification mark which may be used for reference as a name, and which, according to the adopted practice in history of legislations, is being mentioned in section 1(1) of each and every statute. The heading of section 1 of each statute is; "short title..........", and that clearly indicates the short title or name from which it would be referred and called. The legislature names the statute in a similar way as an author names his book, who

---

1. Received the assent of the President on September, 11, 1989, and published in the Gazette of India, Extra, Pt. II, section 1 dated 12 September 1989, Sl No. 39.

   Came into force on 30-1-1990, *vide* S.O. 106(E), dated 29th January, 1990.

is the creator of and fully knows the contents of the book and the implications. For instance, short title of the statute under discussion is "the Scheduled Castes and the Scheduled Tribes (Prevention of Atrocities) Act, 1989."

On the other hand the long title is usually given in the beginning of every statute which signify the objective, the need or purpose for which that particular statute was being legislated. The example in the present case is the long title which has been mentioned above ("An Act to prevent............"). This long title gives some details of described provisions, its objectives and also how these objectives would be achieved.

When the short and long titles are clubbed together and read in combination, it may determine the scope and purview of the statute, through which intention of the legislature may be gathered.

It had been a settled law that the title of an Act is part of the Act itself, therefore it has been held legal and legitimate to use the title for purposes of interpretation of the Act as a whole and also for ascertaining its scope.

There may arise two different conditions in this regard, *i.e.*, firstly the title of the statute may be short and ambiguous, but the Act as a whole is clear and unambiguous, and secondly in the reverse case to the first. As per Baray J.: if the statute is clear and unambiguous, no reference can be made to the title of the Act. Besides, according to one opinion, the title cannot be taken for granted as conclusive intent of the legislature[1].

The policy and purpose of a given provision or measure may be deducted from the long title and the Preamble of an Act.[2] Whatever might be value of title and the Preamble, when used as an aid to find out the construction of the statute, they undoubtedly throw light on the intent, design and purpose of the legislation and indicate scope of the provision.[3]

Supreme Court in its decision of *Manoharlal* v. *State (Supra)* has also put a word of caution in the way that, though for exploring the purpose, scope and policy of the legislation it may be looked into, but they do not control the express provisions of the Act.

But on the other hand, where the provisions are ambiguous and difficulties are faced by the courts in deducting the real purpose of a provision of the Act, it is permissible to take help from the title and the preamble of the Act[4].

2. Preamble – Generally

Unless and until one understands the Preamble of a statute, the underlying provisions could not be understood on a better footing. A Full Bench decision of the Rajasthan High Court dealt with the issue and observed that the Preamble of a statute is part of the Act and is an admissible aid to the construction of the statute. The Preamble is expected to express the scope, object and purpose of the

1. Statutory Constructions, by Sutherland, 3rd Ed, Vol. II, p. 344.
2. *Manohar Lal* v. *State of Punjab*, AIR 1961 SC 418: (1961) 1 Cr LJ 570: (1961) 2 SCR 343.
3. *Poppatlal Shah* v. *State of Madras*, 1953 Cr LJ 1105: 1953 SCJ 369: AIR 1953 SC 274.
4. *Minerva Talkies, Bangalore* v. *State of Karnataka*, AIR 1988 SC 526: 1988 (1) SCJ 208: 1988 Supp SCC 176.

Act more comprehensively than the long title. It may recite the ground and cause of making the statute, the evils sought to be remedied or the doubts which may be required to be settled[1].

Preamble of a statute signify the matter of a policy that is why it lies within the exclusive domain of the appropriate legislature. The Courts are not concerned with that the process of judicial review is primarily confined to the validity and not the need for the Act. Courts are there to see whether the statute conforms to the provisions of the Constitution. In search for fairness the court cannot ignore the policy, which is given in the Preamble.[2]

But against that there are limitations to this rule, – that Preamble is an aid in understanding the provisions of any Act. If the meaning of a certain section or provision is clear, Preamble cannot be referred, because it does not control the unambiguous meaning of the enactment.[3] Therefore if the language of the Act is clear and admits no ambiguity, it cannot be permitted that the 'Statement of Objects and Reasons' is used to extract some desired meaning[4]. The reason is simple, and it being that any narrow or technical interpretation of the provisions would certainly defeat the legislative policy. Therefore, the court must keep this policy in mind while it is interpreting a statute.[5]

Though, on one hand it may be said that Preamble or the 'Statement of Objects and Reasons' clearly signify public policy from which intention of the legislature can be gathered, but in a landmark judgment Supreme Court has observed as: "the concept of public policy is, however, illusive, varying and uncertain." It has also been described as 'untrustworthy guide', 'unruly horse' etc.. The Bench of Apex Court had cited *Egerton* v. *Brownlow,* (1853) 4 HLC 1, wherein it was observed:

"Public Policy is a vague and unsatisfactory term and calculated to lead to uncertainty and error, when applied to the decision of legal rights; it is capable of being understood in different senses; it may, and does, in its ordinary sense, mean 'political expediency' or that which is best for the common good of the community; and in that sense there may be every variety of opinion, according to education, habits, talent and dispositions of each person, who is to decide whether an act is against public policy or not. To allow this to be a ground of judicial decision would lead to the greatest uncertainty and confusion. It is the province of the system and not the lawyer, to discuss, and of the Legislature to determine what is best for the public good and to provide for it by proper

---

1. *Jai Singh* v. *Union of India,* 1993 Cr LJ 2705 (FB) (Raj): AIR 1993 Raj 177: 1993 (1) Raj LW 157.
2. *Simranjit Singh Mann* v. *Union of India,* 2002 Cr LJ 3368: 2003 (1) All Cri LR 170: ILR (2002) 2 P&H 575.
3. *Mansha Singh Dhaman Singh* v. *State of Punjab,* AIR 1960 Punj 317: 62 Punj LR 1: ILR (1960) Punj 589; also see *Miss Maria Antonica Rodrigues* v. *B.R. Baliga,* AIR 1967 Bom 465: 69 Bom LR 41: 1967 Mah LJ 249.
4. *Govind Saran Ganga Saran* v. *Commissioner of Sales Tax,* AIR 1985 SC 1041: 1985 Tax LR 2917: 1985 13 STL 111.
5. *Kameshwar Singh Srivastava* v. *IVth Addl. Distt. Judge, Lucknow,* AIR 1987 SC 138: (1986) 4 SCC 661: 1987 (1) SCJ 84; *Lal Agarwal* v. *Jagdish Narain,* (2000) 1 SCC 31.

enactment. It is the province of the Judge to expound the law only; the written from the statutes; the unwritten or common law for decisions of our predecessors and of our existing Courts, from text writers of acknowledged authority, and upon the principles to be clearly deducted from them by sound reason and inference; not to speculate upon what is the best, in his opinion, for the advantage of the community........... They have become a part of law, and we are therefore bound by them, but we are not thereby authorised to establish as law, everything which we may think for the public good........"[1]

A Full Bench decision of Patna High Court had adopted a middle course, by observing—"Though the history of the legislation may not lead to a definite conclusion to find out the correct meaning of an expression but at times it may be usefully employed for interpreting the meaning of the statute. Similarly Statements of Objects and Reasons cannot control the actual words used in the statute, yet it may be referred to for the purpose of ascertaining the conditions prevailing at the time, which necessitated the making of law."[2]

As is evident from above discussions it could very well be gathered that the title and the Preamble extends to the whole of the State, whether in the limited sense or not. When elaborations or interpretation has to be done of a certain provision in the main body of the statute, it has to be borne in mind that the title or the Preamble or both do not control the provisions of the statute but may help in understanding the same.

The importance of use and scope of title and Preamble has increased in the recent past, because courts have started refusing to adhere to the 'golden rule',—according to which Judges and lawyers were allowed to interpret the statute according to grammatical and ordinary sense of the words used at a particular place, unmindful of the intention of the Legislature, consequently leading to the wrong result. It is so because dictum is that it is the Legislature which is empowered by law to amend the Act and the Courts should not intervene in innovative interpretation. The days of 'golden rule' have gone and now the courts have started looking into 'intention' of the Legislature or the 'purpose' for which the statute was enacted. Presently the new approach is to look at the statute in a framework and as a whole. Thus, now principles are not considered abstract and separated from the objects of the Legislation.[3]

It was further observed by Apex Court in the same case that this new approach may be used in adventurous way, in the sense that this approach enlarges the discretion of the courts in the matters of interpretation, and warned that the Courts should abstain themselves from substituting their own notions of legislative intentions. This new approach, they further went on, implies power of choice only where different meanings in the constructions are available.

---

1. *P. Rathinam Nagbhusan Patnaik* v. *Union of India,* 1994 Cr LJ 1605 (SC): AIR 1994 SC 1844: 1994 AIR SCW 1764.
2. *In the matter of Reference made by Shri Ravi Nandan Sahay, Sessions Judge, Patna,* 1993 Cr LJ 2436 (FB): 1993 (3) All Cri LR 205: 1992 (1) BLJ 231.
3. *Kehar Singh* v. *State (Delhi Administration),* AIR 1988 SC 1883: 1989 Cr LJ 1: (1988) 3 SCC 609(SC).

3. Preamble of SC/ST Act

After quoting Preamble's text *in verbatim* (para 10), his Lordship similarly quoted Statement of Object and Reasons of the Scheduled Castes and the Scheduled Tribes (Prevention of Atrocities) Act, 1989 (para 11), it was observed: "The Preamble of a statute is a part of the Act and is admissible aid to construction. Although not an enacting part, The Preamble is expected to express the scope, object and purpose of the Act more comprehensively than the long title. It may recite the ground and cause of making the statute, the evils sought to be remedied or the doubts which may be intended to be settled", in the Full Bench decision of Rajasthan High Court, when the constitutional validity of the Act of 1989 was under challenge.[1]

The Bench further observed, "Reading the preamble of the present Act, it would be found that it had been enacted to prevent the commission of atrocities against the members of Scheduled Castes and the Scheduled Tribes. It is this intention which has to be kept into account while interpreting the various sections of the Act".[1]

As Indian Courts follow English law while dealing with the principles in general, it would not be out of order to mention their contention about the use of preamble. It seems to be the crux.

"The Preamble may now be regarded like the title, as part of the statute for the purpose of explaining, restraining or even extending enacting words, but not for the purpose of qualifying or limiting express provisions couched in clear and unambiguous terms."[2]

Around these concised qualifications of Preamble, most of explanation, elaborate or short, are extracted.

4. Other Aids Which Help Interpretations

Apart from and in addition to the title, Statement of Object and Reasons and the Preamble, there are many other aids through which Courts world over try to interpret a statute where there seems an ambiguity in the language applicable to the given facts or circumstances which differ from case-to-case.

The process of application of enacted laws is an age old exercise, and in this process multiple rules have automatically come up for interpretation of a statute, or also of construction, and through these rules the courts seek to ascertain the meaning of the statute. Though apparently it would look that constructing a statute and interpreting the same are different things, but in a sense they are connected with each other, though not strictly. By 'interpretation' it is conceived that one is trying to find out the actual sense of the word, which the author wanted to convey and wanted to be understood in the same way as was the intention of the author.

Whereas the construction is drawing of conclusion, respecting subjects that are beyond the direct expression of the text from elements known from and given in

1. *Jai Singh* v. *Union of India*, 1993 Cr LJ 2705 (FB) (Raj): AIR 1993 Raj 177: 1993 (1) Raj LW 157.
2. Halsbury's Law of England, 2nd Edn, Vol. XXXI, para 558.

the text and conclusions which are in the spirit, though not within the letter of law.[1]

The courts use following additional aids for interpretation:—

4.1 Heading of Sections

In modern statutes each and every section has a heading prefixed to it, which is considered as a preamble of that particular section. It was held that, though the heading of sections do not control the plain words, but if there is any doubt in the interpretation of the words in the section, heading certainly helps. The Apex Court had cited Maxwell (On Interpretation of Statutes' 10th Edn. p. 50) as: "The headings prefixed to sections or set of sections in some modern statutes are regarded as preambles to those sections."[2]

The same rule of interpretation applies to the titles of the chapters. The Scheduled Castes and the Scheduled Tribes (Prevention of Atrocities) Act, 1989, has been divided into five chapters, and each chapter has its own heading. Accordingly these headings should be considered as preambles to the respective chapters.

As the Act of 1989 did not use the marginal notes, as has been used in other enactments, therefore there is no need to enter in such discussion. However, same rule applies to it, though there is some difference of opinion on the point.

4.2 *Extrinsic Aids*

The expression 'extrinsic aids', denote the proceedings of the legislature or, the speeches made, for or against, when the Bill of the statute in question was put before the House of Parliament for its passage into law. During this stage, a debate takes place and in the course, the Bill might have gone through, radical changes. The entire process, speeches or the changes etc., do not form part of the Bill or the final product which emerges as law.

Therefore it is sound logic that these proceedings or the speeches should not be allowed to be used when some provisions, words or the expressions are to be interpreted. The rules of interpretation have rightly excluded the said process from consideration, on the ground that: firstly all the process, including the speeches, do not form the part of the Bill which was voted upon by the members; and, secondly as it is inevitable that the debate may contain some materials which are contradictory or irrelevant to the final product which had been passed into law by the majority. Hence it is never safe to allow these as aids for interpretation.

On the basis of above mentioned reasons various Indian as well as foreign courts have made all the proceedings before the passage of the Bill to be inadmissible for use as an aid.

---

1. *Nasirkhan Nivaskhan Pathan* v. *District Development Officer, Bharuch*, AIR 2002 Guj 143 (FB): 2002 AIHC 1313: 2001 (3) Guj LH 133.
2. *Bhinka* v. *Charan Singh*, 1959 Cr LJ 1223 (1229) (SC): AIR 1959 SC 960: 1959 All Cri R 337; *Frick India Ltd.* v. *Union of India*, AIR 1990 SC 689: (1990) 1 SCC 400.

But, Supreme Court has given some latitude, while observing and holding that statement of the Minister who moved the Bill can be looked upon for ascertaining object and purpose for which the legislation has been enacted.[1]

In yet another judgment, Supreme Court had held that Reports of the committee which preceded the enactment of a legislation, reports of the Joint Parliamentary Committee, report of a commission set up for collecting information leading to the enactment are permissible external aids to construction. In its opinion, if the Parliament had taken these 'reports' in consideration, why the courts should not be permitted to use them for knowing the intention of the legislature and the objects of the Act. Therefore the "Rule of Exclusion" cannot be invoked, which deprives the courts of substantial and illuminating aid and material to the construction and consequently interpretation. It was further observed that the words and expressions used in a statute take their colour from the context in which they appear, therefore it is permissible to refer to dictations to find out the meaning of the word.[2]

The Apex Court has also held that objects and the purposes which were recommended by the Law Commission in its Report, but was not discussed in the Parliament, it would be inferred that those objects were accepted by the Parliament, therefore the court could very well use it.[3]

4.3 *Proviso, Explanation, Illustrations, Exception, Qualifying Clause and Saving Clause*

The Scheduled Castes and the Scheduled Tribes (Prevention of Atrocities) Act, 1989, did not use Proviso, *Explanation, Illustration, Exception,* Qualifying Clauses or the Saving Clauses in the body and the text of present statute, therefore it would be superfluous to discuss their value in and use for purposes of interpretations.

However, some reasons may be mentioned why these items of construction, specially in a penal statute like the Act under discussion, were not used. Whether these items were considered as surplusages when the said Act was 'constructed' or drafted, or, whether those items were kept out of scene deliberately to affect the scope of the provisions? The question could be answered by Courts when it is put before them.

Barket Ali Zaidi J., while discussing a controversy in drafting of statues observed that it could have been avoided if section 156(3) Cr PC had been drafted in a more explicit manner; cited a couplet from Frances Bienniom as:

"I am the Parliamentary Draftsman. I composed the country's Laws. And of Half the litigation. I am undoubtedly the cause."[4]

Generally the penal statutes use provisos, explanations, illustration and qualifying clauses to extend or limit the scope of the provisions to which these

1. *P.V. Narsimha Rao* v. *State (CBI/SPE),* 1998 Cr LJ 2930 (SC): 1998 AIR SCW 2001: AIR 1998 SC 2120.
2. *R.S. Nayak* v. *A.R. Antulay,* 1984 Cr LJ 613 (SC): AIR 1984 SC 684: (1984) 2 SCC 183.
3. *Moideenkutty Haji* v. *Kunhikoya,* AIR 1987 Ker 184 (FB): 1987 Cr LJ 1106 (Ker) (FB): ILR (1987) 2 Ker 123.
4. *Sukhwasi* v. *State of Uttar Pradesh,* 2008 Cr LJ 472 (All) (DB).

items were enclosed at the time of construction or drafting of a statute. In absence of these items it is the discretion of the interpretor to dilute or enhance the gravity of – say an offence or punishment. More flexibility of the language, words or expressions is being provided.

For instance, the expression: ".......in any place within *public view*," used under section 3(1)(x) of the Act was not elaborated through any means, neither the "public view" was defined, therefore it has been interpreted by various courts that, though insults or an intent to humiliate a member of Scheduled Castes or Scheduled Tribes may have been "intentionally" done, but if it was not "within public view", the act is not covered under the provisions of the Act of 1989. In other words, intentionally insulting or intimidating such members in a room or secluded place, would constitute no offence under the Act. It may also be added, that "public" defined elsewhere does not comprise presence of one or two persons.

4.4 *Punctuation*

It was observed in a very old case[1] that before 1849 no punctuations normally appeared in the Acts on the Rolls of Parliament in England, therefore the Court held that punctuation could not be relied on in those cases, but in India, no unpunctuated statutes are found in original Statute Book, thus there is no reason why the punctuation may be disregarded.

A better and cogent rule is that punctuation is part of the legislation therefore it may be considered at the time of interpretation of the Act, but with the limitation that such exercise should not be adopted to distort or defeat the purpose of the legislation. But where intent and purpose of legislature does not look certain, then punctuation may be used as an aid for interpretation.

4.5 *Use of Dictionaries as Aids*

One famous exegesist of religious scripture had rightly said that meaning of words are like colours of 'rainbow', and it is the interpretor's choice to choose one colour out of those seven colours which rather suits him. Each and every word has been in most cases, attributed by multiple meanings in dictionaries and job of exegesist is almost similar to that of interpretor of statutes in legal arena. In a similar footing rules of exegesis have also been formulated.

However, it is always safe to keep the context in mind for which the word was selected and used, because same word may mean different things in diverse contexts. The value of words in legal arena are most precious when compared to its value in literature etc., because here they may make vast difference to an individual or the society as a whole. Therefore it becomes very important to adhere to the strict rules for interpreting a statute through meanings of a particular word.

In determining the meaning of a particular word in a statute, it is permissible to take into account external aids, such as dictionaries, previous legislations or decided cases.[2]

1. *Blanche Somerset Taylor* v. *Charles, George Bleach,* ILR 39 Bom 182 (189): AIR 1915 Bom 50.
2. *Henrietta Muir Edward* v. *Attorney General for Canada,* AIR 1930 PC 120: 58 Mad LJ 300: 1930 AC 124.

Modi J. had observed: "Under our system of law, by words we are governed; we must be governed and ought to be governed by words but it has to be remembered that words divorced from underlying idea which they are designed to convey will be empty vehicles and in order to gather the meaning of words we have to view them as a whole in a particular context."[1]

Therefore it becomes necessary that, as a word is capable of various meanings provided by a dictionary, no arbitrary selection and mechanically applying it to the statute can be made permissible. Meanings given in the dictionary of a particular word are no doubt helpful in understanding its meaning in the general sense, but any or many meanings given in the dictionaries cannot control the meaning of the word of statute, where scheme or purpose of the statute is some what different.

Each word of a statute is important because Parliament does not use any word without meaning something. The Parliament does not waste its breath unnecessarily.[2]

When general words follow particular and specific words of same nature, they must be construed as taking their meaning from the specific words which precede them and must be restricted to the same genus. This is the well-known rule of *ejusdem generis.*[3]

4.6 Various Other Aids

Besides above mentioned aids, there are a lot of other aids which courts the world over have allowed to be used for interpretation of statutes, such as foreign and national decisions of Courts, use of same words or expressions in other statutes etc. etc. (which may be gathered from any text book on construction and interpretations of Statutes).

But most important of them all, and for purpose of present discussion, it is the use of previous enactments on similar subject for proper interpretation. It may be pointed out here that all the legislations mentioned below belong to 20th century. Before this era no such legislations could be found, though in the early periods of British rule, they were fully aware of the situation, but perhaps for political reasons, they kept quiet.

Following is the list of previous similar enactments as to the Act of 1989:

5. Very Early Acts which were Repealed by Section 17 of Protection of Civil Rights Act, 1955

(1) The Bihar Harijan (Removal of Civil Disabilities) Act, 1949 (Bihar Act XIX of 1949),

(2) The Bombay Harijan (Removal of Social Disabilities) Act, 1946 (Bombay Act X of 1947),

(3) The Bombay Harijan Temple Entry Act, 1947 (Bombay Act XXXV of 1947),

1. *Hiranand* v. *Umaid Raj,* AIR 1973 Raj 120: 1973 Raj LW 32: 1973 Ren LJ 441.
2. *Utkal Contractors and Joinery Pvt. Ltd.* v. *State of Orissa,* AIR 1987 SC 1454 (1460): JT 1987 (3) SC 466: (1987) 3 SCC 279.
3. *Thakur Amar Singhji* v. *State of Rajasthan,* AIR 1955 SC 504: 1955 SCJ 523: (1955) 2 SCR 303; *Lila Vati Bai* v. *State of Bombay,* AIR 1957 SC 521: 1957 SCA 465: 1957 SCJ 557.

(4) The Central Provinces and Berar Scheduled Castes (Removal of Civil Disabilities) Act, 1947 (Central Provinces and Berar Act, XXIV of 1947),

(5) The Central Provinces and Berar Temple Entry Authorisation Act, 1947 (Central Provinces and Berar Act, XLI of 1947).

(6) The East Punjab (Removal of Religious and Social Disabilities Act, 1948 (East Punjab Act, XVI of 1948).

(7) The Madras Removal of Civil Disabilities Act, 1938 (Madras Act XXI of 1938).

(8) The Orissa Removal of Civil Disabilities Act, 1946 (Ori Act XI of 1946).

(9) The Orissa Temple Authorisation Act, 1948 (Ori Act, XI of 1948).

(10) The United Provinces Removal of Social Disabilities Act, 1947 (UP Act XIV of 1947).

(11) The West Bengal Hindu Social Disabilities Act, 1948 (WB Act, XXXVII of 1948)

(12) The Hyderabad Harijan Temple Entry Regulation 1358F (No. LV of 1358 Fasli).

(13) The Hyderabad Harijan (Removal of Social Disabilities) Regulation 1358F (No. LVI of 1358 Fasli).

(14) The Madhya Bharat Harijan Ayogta Nivaran Vidhan, Samvat 2005 (MB Act, No. 15 of 1949).

(15) The Removal of Civil Disabilities Act, 1943 (Mysore Act XLII of 1943).

(16) The Mysore Temple Entry Authorisation Act, 1948 (Mysore Act, XIV of 1948).

(17) The Saurashtra Harijan (Removal of Disabilities) Ordinance (No. XL of 1948).

(18) The Travancore-Cochin Removal of Social Disabilities Act, 1125K (TC Act VIII of 1125).

(19) The Travancore-Cochin Temple Entry (Removal of Disabilities) Act, 1950 (TC Act XXVII of 1950).

(20) The Coorg Scheduled Castes (Removal of Civil and Social Disabilities) Act, 1949 (Coorg. Act I of 1949).

(21) The Coorg Temple Entry Authorisation Act, 1949 (Coorg. Act II of 1949).

6. Other early Enactments of Parliament

(1) The Scheduled Area (Assimilation of Laws) Act, 1951 (Act XXXVII of 1951).

(2) The Scheduled Area (Assimilation of Laws) Act, 1953 (Act XVI of 1953).

(3) The Scheduled Castes and Scheduled Tribes Orders (Amendment) Act, 1956 (Act LXIII of 1956).

(4) The Scheduled Castes and Scheduled Tribes Orders (Amendment) Act, 1976 (Act 108 of 1976).

(5) The Constitution (Scheduled Castes) Orders (Amendment) Act, 1990 (Act 15 of 1990).[1]

---

1. *Punjab Rao* v. *D.P. Meshram*, AIR 1965 SC 1179: 1965 (2) SCJ 725: (1965) 1 SCR 849 – It was held that what the Constitution (Scheduled Castes) Order [clause (3)] contemplates is that for a person to be treated as one belonging to a Scheduled Caste within the meaning of Order, he must be one who professes either Hindu or Sikh religion. Please also see 'Appendix'.

7. The Protection of Civil Rights Act, 1955 (Act 22 of 1955)

7.1 The Protection of Civil Rights Rules, 1977

Originally the Act was passed in the name of "The Untouchability (Offences) Act, 1955" (Act 22 of 1955) but the name was substituted through section 2 of Amending Act (106 of 1976 which came in force w.e.f. 19-11-1976).

The Protection of Civil Rights Act, 1955 was enacted to prescribe punishment for the preaching and practice of "Untouchability, for the enforcement of any disability arising therefrom and for matters concerned therewith.

The Protection of Civil Rights Act, 1955 was in force since 1955 itself but no rules were framed thereunder till 1977. In 1976 the Act was amended, and on 19-11-1976 section 16B was inserted which empowered the Central Government to frame rules.

The "Statement of Objects and Reasons" of the Scheduled Castes and the Scheduled Tribes (Prevention of Atrocities) Act, 1989, in the end of para 2 states: "under the circumstances, the existing laws like the Protection of Civil Rights Act, 1955, and the normal provisions of the Indian Penal Code have been found to be inadequate to check these crimes." Therefore the present Act, as a special legislation had become necessary to be enacted.

According to Sutherland: "Statutes are considered to be in *pari materia* – to pertain to the same subject-matter – when they relate to the same person or thing, or to the *same class of persons* or things, or have the *same purpose or object*........... To be in *pari materia*, statutes need not have been enacted simultaneously or refer to one another."[1]

All authors who are supposed to be authorities on the subject of statutory construction and interpretation agree that different legislations and enactments with similar objects and on the same subject may be used to interpret one another. This is a well-settled principle which is accepted by courts the world over. The words, phrases or expressions had already been interpreted under one such similar legislation, may be used to understand and interpret while dealing with another similar provision.

Words are after all used merely as vehicles to convey an idea, so words naturally have to be construed as to fit in with the idea which emerges on a consideration of the entire context. Each word is only a symbol which may stand for one or number of objects.[2]

Again it is also a cardinal principle of construction of statute that a penal statute should never be constructed so as to narrow the words of the statute to the exclusion of cases which those words in their ordinary accepted meaning would comprehend.

As such when two penal Acts are enacted in the same field, " one dealing with special law, then in case of inconsistency between the two, the special law will prevail. When two enactments are passed one later than the other, then

---

1. Statutory Construction, by Sutherland, Vol. 2, p. 535.
2. *Deputy Chief Controller of Imports and Exports, New Delhi* v. *K.T. Kosalram*, 1971 Cr LJ 1081 (SC): AIR 1971 SC 1283: 1971 SCD 99.

it becomes a business for the courts to consider the exact effect of the latter enactment to see whether they can wholly or in part stand together."[1]

North J. observed: "The provisions of an earlier Act may be revoked or abrogated in particular cases by a subsequent Act, either from the express language used being addressed to the particular point, or from implication or inference from the language used".[1]

This assertion is based on the assumption that when the legislature enacts a subsequent Act on the same subject-matter on which a previous legislation exists, it ponders and peruses on each and every word, hence there cannot be any anomaly.

In case one statute enacts something in general terms, and afterwords another statute is passed on the same subject, which although expressed in affirmative language, introduces special conditions and restrictions, the subsequent statute will usually be considered as 'repealing by implication' the former, on the ground that 'will of the Parliament must always prevail.' In that way the special Acts (like SC/ST Act) will prevail, but the extent to which the special Acts would override the general law, or create exceptions would depend upon the terms of the enactment in question.

If same expressions in many parts of the same enactment exists, it would be presumed that both carry same meaning. To this presumption, though, a word of caution has been issued, as that the same words used at many places even within one enactment proper approach is to apply sufficient reason while extracting same meaning because it is not necessary that the words used in one part of the legislation may have been used in the same sense. But ordinarily same meaning may be extracted, unless the context or object require otherwise.[2]

When it is found that in a previous Act a section was not well drafted, then it was held that Court is entitled to look at the later legislation on the same subject to see if light can be thrown upon the meaning. "subsequent legislation on the same subject may be looked to in order to see the proper construction.........."[3]

It was observed that it is well-known principle of interpretation of statutes that use of same words in similar connection in a later statute gives rise to a presumption that they are intended to convey the same meaning as was given to the earlier statute. When once certain words in an Act have received a judicial approval for that construction and the legislature has repeated them, the legislature must be taken to have used them according to the meaning which a court of competent jurisdiction had given to them.[4]

---

1. *Antaryami Patra* v. *State of Orissa*, 1993 Cr LJ 1908 (1913): 1993 (75) Cut LT 803: 1993 (1) Ori LR 464 [citing (1887) 36 Ch D 573 in Re Williams by North J.]
2. *Shamrao Vishnu Parulekar* v. *District Magistrate, Thana*, 1957 Cr LJ 5 (SC): AIR 1957 SC 23: 1956 SCC 504; *Kamleshwar Singh* v. *Dharamdeo Singh*, 1957 Cr LJ 879 (Pat) (FB): AIR 1957 Pat 375: 1957 BLJR 527; 1962 Cr LJ 59: 1962 Cr LJ 449.
3. *Sher Khan* v. *State*, 1958 Cr LJ 1261 (All) (FB); law on this point was stated by Lord Sternadale in *Cape Brandy* v. *Inland Revenue Commrs.*, (1921) 2 KB 403: 90 LJ KB 461: 37 TLR 402 and approved in 1928 in *Ormond Investment Co.* v. *Betts*, 1928 AC 143: 97 LJ KB 342: 13 Tax Cas 400.
4. *Bansidhar* v. *Seema*, 1992 Cr LJ 1562: (1992) I DMC 353: 1992 (2) Hindu LR 40 [1964 Cr LJ 724 (SC) was followed]

A few rules about the aids of construction and interpretation of statute have been discussed here in brief. There had been a series of legislations (mentioned above) to eradicate the menace of 'untouchability' and 'atrocities' on the Scheduled Castes and the Scheduled Tribes. In course of this presentation occasions would arise on almost every step to assess the meanings of all relevant expressions used in the previous Act and Rules (Protection of Civil Rights Act, 1955). Sometimes help has to be taken from the interpretations given by various courts on similar provisions of old Act.[1]

8. General and Special Enactments

The Scheduled Castes and the Scheduled Tribes (Prevention of Atrocities) Act, 1989 is a "special Legislation" as has been specifically mentioned in Statement of Objects and Reasons. Therefore, there is no doubt about it being a special statute. Section 20 of the Act specifically mendated that the provisions of the Act, shall "Override other laws". Even customs and usages or any instrument having effect by the same have been covered under this section.

Substantive and procedural law have been divided into two categories, *i.e.*, General law and Special law. Indian Penal Code deals with general offences, while the Scheduled Castes and the Scheduled Tribes (Prevention of Atrocities) Act, 1989 was enacted specially to deal with the special crimes in special circumstances, because the "existing laws like Protection of Civil Rights Act, 1955 and the normal provision of Indian Penal Code have been found to be inadequate" to check the atrocities committed by "non-Scheduled Castes and the non-Scheduled Tribes."

The special legislation was brought in "to provide for higher punishments for committing such atrocities", though the provisions of Indian Penal Code also deal with almost similar provisions and prescribe punishments, but Indian Penal Code is general law.

Occasionally questions come before courts, whether general law would be applicable or the special law should be applied in the given situation under scrutiny, when the facts of the case seemed to attract provisions of both types of laws in force. In such circumstances there is consensus of judicial opinion that special law would prevail.

8.1 Act of 1955 and Act 1989 are Penal Statutes

The term "penal statute" if used without any qualifications becomes ambiguous. If a perticular Act contains command, prohibitions or contravention that has been declared by the Act some kind of penalty then it is a penal statute. In a wider sense a penel Act, includes every statute creating an offence against State whatever be the nature of penalty or offence, declared by State for violating some prohibition in the public interest.

It was stated that: "No doubt all penel statutes are to be construed strictly that is to say, the Court must see that the thing charged as an offence is within the plain meaning of the words used, and must not strain the words on any notion

1. For further detailed study on the rules of construction and interpretation, various authoritative text books on the subject may be consulted.

that there has been slip, that there has been *casus omissus*, that the thing is so clearly within the mischief that it must have been intended to be included and would have been included if thought of."[1]

A penal statute, its understanding and interpretation can only be determined and construed when intention of those who made it has been ascertained. Once that has been fully understood, its correct interpretation becomes possible. Finding the intention of Legislature to interpret is a general principle, but when it comes to penal statutes and applied there as such, it is said that it has to be applied in more stricter sense, as it may affect lives of people and may determine between innocence and guilt of persons involved. The requirement of strict construction is that the language should be so construed that no case shall fall within it which does not come within the reasonable interpretation.

The rule of strict construction is based on the tenderness of law for the rights of citizens. Power of providing punishments vests in Legislature, while a court can only define a crime and ordain its punishment.

To constitute a crime the statute must use clear language, and it is basic principle that a penal statute should give the person of ordinary intelligence a reasonable opportunity to know what is prohibited, so that he may act accordingly. It should issue a warning. It is insisted that the Court and the person charged should understand that the act was an offence under the plain meaning of the words of a penal statute. Both the Acts under discussion has done the same thing.

In the antiquity realms, the Indian Hindu Society had developed a system, which was completely established till Muslims or Britishers came on the scene, where religion and law were so welded with each other that later rulers found themselves at complete loss to separate them for various and complex reasons. Britishers, lately showed some courage and enacted some penal laws in this connection ('atrocities') for local areas.

But when independent Indian republic was formed which adopted the Constitution, its Art. 15 specifically 'prohibited' any kind of discrimination on grounds of religion and "caste" etc. be subjected to any "disability, liability, restriction" to have an "access" to all places used by others. Article 17 of Indian Constitution emphatically "abolished" the "untouchability" and provided the disability arising out of untouchability "shall be an offence punishable according to law."

Article 35(a)(ii) mandatorily imposed a responsibility to enact laws "for prescribing punishment for acts" which were declared as offences in that Part (Part III).

Thus it had become a prime duty of the Parliament to enact law providing "punishment" for prohibiting discrimination (atrocities) and 'untouchability'.

It was held by Supreme Court that the thrust of Act 17 is to liberate the society from blind and ritualistic adherence and traditional beliefs which lost all legal

1. Judicial Committee in The Gauntlet, 1872 LRPC 184 (191), cited in *M. Narayan Nambiar* v. *State of Kerala*, (1963) 2 Cr LJ 186 (SC): AIR 1963 SC 1116: 1963 (2) SCJ 582.

or moral base. It seeks to establish new ideals for society – equality to "Dalits," bringing them at par with general public, absence of disabilities, restriction or prohibition on grounds of caste and religion and opportunities in the stream of national life. It was further observed that in interpreting the Protection of Civil Rights Act, 1955, the Judge should be cognizant to and always peep at the constitutional goals and purpose of the Act.[1]

It was held by a Full Bench that Article 17 places the word "Untouchability" in inverted commas; accordingly the subject-matter of the Article is not untouchability in its literal sense but the practice as it has developed historically in India. The Bench observed that Art. 17 is similar to the 13th Amendment of the Constitution of United States which abolished slavery and empowered the Congress to enforce the abolition by appropriate means. The Bench went on further as they observed that the Scheduled Castes and the Scheduled Tribes Act, 1989 is a legislation falling within the field of Articles 17 and 35(a)(ii) of the Constitution. It is self operating for anybody indulging in any of the activities committing offence should be liable for punished.[2]

Another Full Bench had observed that once an act is declared as an offence within the meaning of Art. 17, the Parliament has exclusive power to prescribe punishment for such offence, and is under constitutional obligation to declare the act as an offence. Parliament alone to prescribe the punishment for acts declared offences under Article 17.[3]

Article 17 read with Article 35(a)(ii) of Indian Constitution has created a new and special offence ("Untouchability"), not known to the West and the English law. On this basis special provisions, offence and punishments arising therefrom were constructed in the Scheduled Castes and the Scheduled Tribes (Prevention of Atrocities) Act, 1989. Chapter II of the Act of 1989 deals with such special provisions of "Offences of Atrocities". They are to override the general provisions on the basis of applicability of maxim, *generalibus specialia derogant*.'[4]

It was a very intelligent move on the part of drafters of Indian Constitution that they made the provisions of declaring "untouchability" as abolished in Art. 17 and later in article 35 made it obligatory on the Parliament to enact penal laws in this regard as mentioned above. These provisions, when clubbed together five years later, culminated in passage of the Untouchability (Offences), Act, 1955 (which later on became Protection of Civil Rights Act) providing for punishment who practiced "untouchability".

The concept of punishment came out of the instinct of vengeance whether in expression or out of desire. It has become an instrument of public justice. It is being inflicted by one group in a corporate capacity or authority upon a member of the same group with sanction of law; and, it involves pain and suffering to the punished by design and justified according to some values.

1. *State of Karnataka* v. *Appa Balu Ingale*, 1993 Cr LJ 1029 (SC): AIR 1993 SC 1126: 1993 AIR SCW 337.
2. *Jai Singh* v. *Union of India*, 1993 Cr LJ 2705 (FB) (Raj): AIR 1993 Raj 177: 1993 (1) Raj LW 157.
3. *Mata Sewak Upadhyay* v. *State of Uttar Pradesh*, 1995 JIC 1168 (All) (FB): 1996 (1) East Cr C 97 (All) (FB).
4. *State of Rajasthan* v. *Gopi Kishan Sen*, AIR 1992 SC 1754: 1992 AIR SCW 1958: 1992 (6) Serv LR 726 (only for the maxim).

After the establishment of kingship, punitive reaction for law-breaking became a public matter, and wrongs were viewed as crimes.

Various theories were developed for punitive reactions as punishment.

Section 2 of Indian Penal Code, 1860 says: "Every person shall be liable to punishment under this Code and not otherwise for every act or omissions contrary to the provisions thereof, of which he shall be guilty within India."[For further details please see comments under section 3(2)]

8.2 Stringent Punishments

The SC/ST Act of 1989 has sanctioned five kinds of punishment, namely – (i) death, (ii) imprisonment for life, (iii) imprisonments (iv) fine (including collective fines) (v) forfeiture of property under Chapter II of the Act. Entire Chapter III deals with another and sixth type of punishment in form of "Externment", and punishment of imprisonment in case of non-compliance of order of 'externment'. The punishment of 'externment' is akin to the punishment of "transportation" once incorporated under the Indian Penal Code as an approved form. In ancient nations this kind of punishment was very favourite. In Rome and Greek nations this punishment had sanction of law. Even in ancient India "Desh Nikala" (externment or expiation) was a recognised form of punishment. Manu and other Smriti writers have frequently proposed such kind of punishment not only to others, but even to Brahmins, when they were found to be violating a law which attracted death penalty.

As far as penalty of death is concerned, it is most dreaded punishment which has remained under debate for a long time the world over and a large number of U.N. member States have already abolished death penalty from their penal laws. Even in India there is a tendency to restrict penalty of death to 'rarest of rare cases'. The question of abolishing or retaining the death sentence has been extensively debated by criminologists, jurists and Human Rights Organisations, but the answer to the question depends on the view and approach one takes about the punishment itself. Perhaps all the concerned would never agree to make a consensus.

The concept of punishment is initially based on 'rule of retaliation' which was considered as a means of incapacitation or *membrun pro membro,* – an eye for an eye and a tooth for a tooth. This was an accepted doctrine in every society.[1]

What to say of ancient societies, the so-called civilized societies in the modern world still believe in the said rule. Punishments provided under anti-terrorism or the like laws in Western legislations of all major 'powers' provide punishments not only 'an eye for an eye', but 'an eye for both the eyes', to create fear psychosis.

The harsher and more stringent punishments may be justified in special circumstances and unique type of crimes which become inversely proportional to the gravity of crime (or offence) committed, but the exercise certainly negates the idealistic approach that stringent punishments appeals only to vulgar minds which are primitive, brute or barbaric and have no place in a civilized or advanced society.

1. Bentham's Rationale of Punishment Vol. I, p. 83.

The punishment of mutilation or corporal punishment by various means is the part and parcel of some systems of criminal justice, which has been branded as barbaric and cruel by those who have considered themselves modern on the basis that they have already passed the changing phases of morality. These very people have established prisons where the prisoners were treated worse than those whom they call savages and barbarians – not while punishing the guilty – but those who have not yet faced trials. It proves that planks of civilizational advancement or philosophical approach towards harsher or stringent punishment, calling it with various names, is a hypocrisy.

At the bottom of all sociological thinking is the fundamental human nature, which never changes, irrespective of surrounding circumstances through which a child becomes a man and part of a particular society placed in a civilizational slot.

Time and again it has been rationally and practically proved that reformatory or other such kinds of theories developed on the basis of philosophical thoughts are not workable. This is so because till date philosophy has not finally settled an issue in any field.

Whenever a situation arises, which is peculiar in nature the criminal justice systems suggest and accordingly legislations are passed providing harsher and stringent punishments for acts which are advocated for eradicating the 'evil', forgetting altogether their previous stands for Human Rights or claims of intellectual refinement according to which they consider themselves to be an elevated and advanced society. The entire Western society is presently passing through this phase of double standards.

One point which comes out of the above discussion is that the harsher and stringent punishments are necessary when one wants genuinely and in good faith to eradicate, to check and to deter crimes of a particular nature. No doubt there cannot be an arithmetical formula to measure a wrong-doing and its reciprocal punishment, but a stringent punishment for an illegal act may be said, which reason and common sense tells, that a particular punishment is beyond the proportion of the wrong, illegal and a criminal act.

The punishments provided under the provisions of the Scheduled Castes and the Scheduled Tribes (Prevention of Atrocities) Act, 1989, may be branded as harsh or stringent but they have left a grand-impact on the Indian society. Even lax government officials were not spared. Section 4 provides for "punishment for neglect of duties" by public servants. These stringent punishments had deteriorated the infliction of 'atrocities' in just about two decades actually and factually, which had not been made possible in about three thousand years. In that sense the 'special legislation' has done a special job.

9. Some Special Procedures Under the Act

The Scheduled Castes and the Scheduled Tribes (Prevention of Atrocities) Act, 1989 alongwith the Rules of 1995 contains some special procedures to be adopted for ensuring prevention, repetition and making stringent provisions to be implemented for eradicating atrocities. One of the grounds pleaded in the *Mata Sewak Upadhaya's* case *(supra)* for challenging the Constitutional validity of the Act of 1989, was that Rules were not framed (till then) under the Act. Though, the Full Bench of Allahabad High Court had rejected the plea, but Rules were framed the same year (1995).

Section 23(2) stipulates that the Rules framed by the Central Government must by put before both Houses of the Parliament and have an approval from the Houses. That means the framed rules have also assumed nature of a legislation. In other words the Rules of 1995 are part and parcel of the Act of 1989.

For further consolidating and ensuring the implementation of the Act of 1989, President of India in exercise of his powers conferred by sub-clause (f) of clause (5) of Article 338A of the Constitution, made Rules 2005 for constituting "The National Commission for the Scheduled Tribes (Specification of Other Functions) Rules, 2005.[1] Later on "Rules of Procedure of the National Commission for Scheduled Castes were made.[2]

Apart from constituting 'Special Court' and 'Special Public Prosecutor', the Act of 1989 has provided other precautionary measures to be implemented by Government officials, of which a regular monitoring would be done at the highest level of administrative machinery of respective State from time-to-time Specific procedure has been laid down by the Act and the Rules.

Procedure for minute things, like lodging of First Information Reports (FIRs) have been covered, despite the fact that such provisions are contained in section 154 *(et sq)* of Cr. P.C. But the Procedure laid down by Rule 5 in this behalf is a combination of Provisions of Criminal Procedure Code, 1973 and Police Regulations of various States. Same is the position of procedure provided for 'investigation' or 'spot inspections'. In that sense those procedures have become special for the special legislation. (Details could be found at appropriate places in foregoing pages of this commentary).

10. Uses and Misuses of Provisions

The object, purpose and the cause for enacting the Scheduled Castes and the Scheduled Tribes (Prevention of Atrocities) Act, 1989 and Rules 1995 was noble, to eradicate the vice of Indian Society, but voices are coming from within that in some cases the provisions are being misused for various complex reasons. That means, that how well purposeful and *bona fide* intentions might be, the laws may go wrong and out of track. But it also means that legislatures should not be criticized for enacting such laws.

One other example may be mentioned here, as to how a good law may go wrong. Section 498A of Indian Penal Code, 1860 was enacted and inserted in the Code through an amendment to prevent 'cruelty' to married women by her husband and in-laws. The object and purpose was noble, but recently Supreme Court had to refer the matter to law Commission of India to study and suggest some amendments in section 498A so that, "harassment" of "husbands" and their

---

1. *Vide* S.O. 1175(E), dated 23rd Aug., 2005, published in the Gazette of India, Extra., Pt. II, section 3(ii), dated 24th Aug, 2005.
2. *Vide* GSR 414(E), dated 25th March, 2009, published in the Gazette of India, Extra, Pt. II, section 3(i), dated 15th June, 2009.

families may be prevented, because the Apex Court found large-scale misuse of the said provision.

In the early days of its inception, the provisions of Act of 1989 were challenged to its constitutionality, but these were upheld by different Benches of Courts. However, as the provisions were put to test of time, it was found that some perversions, transgressions or *mala fides* had started creeping in the application of these provisions.

In the similar way the provisions of the Scheduled Castes and the Scheduled Tribes (Prevention of Atrocities) Act, 1989, were used for the prime purpose of settling scores with non-Scheduled Castes or non-Scheduled Tribes members, usually of Hindu society, in villages, offices or other places of work. In the process complainants are also benefited through receiving 'compensation' money provided under the Rules of 1995, which in some cases are in substantive amounts.[1]

---

1. Annexure I, Schedule, appendend to the Rules, 1995 provide amounts to be paid for various crimes committed by others.

Chapter I
PRELIMINARY

1. Short title, extent and commencement.—(1) This Act may be called the Scheduled Castes and the Scheduled Tribes (Prevention of Atrocities) Act, 1989.

(2) It extends to the whole of India except the State of Jammu and Kashmir.

(3) It shall come into force on such date[1] as the Central Government may, by notification in the Official Gazette, appoint.

SYNOPSIS

1. Analogous Law

The words "Scheduled Tribes" were first used by Symon Commission which was appointed in the year 1931. In Census of 1931 these castes were given name of "Exterior Castes" Britishers also called these classes as "Dipressed Classes". In the year 1935 a "Schedule" was prepared in which people from these classes were listed and as such name of "Scheduled Castes" came into being. Later on Indian Constitution adopted these expressions.

On May 8th, 1955 Indian Parliament passed the Untouchability (Offences) Act, 1955 (Act XXII of 1955), Section 1(i) of which was amended later by Amending Act (106) of 1976 and "the Untouchability (Offences) Act" was substituted as "the Protection of Civil Rights Act".[2]

---

1. Came into force on 30-1-1990, *vide* S.O. 106(E), dated 29th January, 1990.
2. The Untouchability (Offences) Act, 1955 came into force on 1-6-1955, S.R.O. 1109, D/-23-5-1955 printed in Gazette of India, 1955, Extra, Pt. 2, section 2 p. 971. The Act was extended to Union territories of Goa, Daman and Diu – Regn XII of 1962 (w.e.f. 26-1-1963), Dadra and Nagar Haveli–Regn VI of 1963 (w.e.f. 1-7-1965) and Pondicherry – Regn VII of 1963 (w.e.f. 1-10-1963);

   The Amending Act No. 106 of 1976: Section 2 inserted words in the Preamble – before word practice, - "preaching and practice......." was inserted. The same Amending Act's section 3 substituted the title of the Act through amendment in section 1(1).

The Act of 1955 also repealed 21 enactments on the same subject matter through section 17. These repealed enactments have been mentioned in the "Schedule" appended to the Act of 1955. (The entire list of 21 Acts have been given under the comments on preamble.)

The 'Statement of Objects and Reasons' of Act of 1955 admitted that: "It is not possible to define untouchability, therefore, the scheme of the draft Bill is to make express provisions with respect to the more common forms of untouchability which are practiced in India."

In this connection the Parliament had also passed Constitution (Scheduled Castes) Order Act, 1950 and thereafter – Constitution (Scheduled Castes) (Union Territories) Order Act, 1951, and thereafter the Scheduled Castes and Scheduled Tribes Orders (Amendment) Act, 1976 (Act 108 of 1976) and then Constitution (Scheduled Castes) Orders (Amendment) Act, 1990.

Above mentioned (Constitution Scheduled Castes and Scheduled Tribes) Order, Acts and their amendments were made in the form of an Act of Parliament for purposes of adjusting parliamentary and assembly constituencies and census, through inclusion in and exclusion from the lists of Scheduled Castes and Scheduled Tribes, certain castes and tribes by amending the lists from time-to-time.

2. Applicability of Act to Castes

For purposes of the Scheduled Castes and the Scheduled Tribes (Prevention of Atrocities) Act, 1989, above mentioned Orders and their latest amendments are very crucial because the lists *determine the difference between the victim and the culprit*. Difficulties arise when in one State or Union Territory particular caste may be declared as Scheduled Caste, while in another State it may belong to upper caste.

For example: In the 'Schedule', Part IX-Madhya Pradesh, at serial No. 2 'Bagri' has been mentioned; similarly Part XV-Rajasthan 'Bagri' has been mentioned at Serial No. 4, as such 'Bagris' are declared Scheduled Caste in M.P. and Rajasthan, but in Uttar Pradesh they are considered as Thakurs (upper caste).[1] Therefore victimization of Bagris in M.P. and Rajasthan would amount to "atrocity" and provisions of Act of 1989 would be attracted, additionally they would be entitled to the benefits of compensations and reservation etc., provided and contained in the Rules 1995. On the other hand, in U.P if a complaint is lodged by some Scheduled Castes or Scheduled Tribe person against a Bagri, he or she would be tried under the provisions of the Act of 1989 by a Special Court, constituted in this behalf. That makes a lot of difference.

There are a lot more such castes which have been declared through the 'Schedule' of Scheduled Castes and Scheduled Tribes Order Acts in one State as such while in other States they were excluded from the list.

Applicability of provisions of Act of 1989 and Rules 1995 depends exclusively on these lists provided by the (Order) Act of 1950 (including Amendments).

1. The Scheduled Castes and Scheduled Tribes Orders (Amendment) Act, 1976. Please see the 'Schedule'.

What clause (3) of the Constitution (Scheduled Castes) Order, 1950 contemplates is that for a person to be treated as one belonging to a Scheduled Caste within the meaning of the Order he must be one who profess either Hindu or Sikh religion.[1]

As the inclusion or the exclusion of a certain caste from the 'Scheduled' list makes a lot of difference for the members of that particular caste – as they may or may not get 'reservations' in jobs, besides being declared a victim or culprit under provisions of SC/ST Act, – a great number of litigations come up before the Courts for declaration of a certain caste for such inclusion in the 'list'. In some cases revision of the "select list" is made at the time of reconstituting the constituencies and amending the Act accordingly. These exercises of revisions in the 'select lists' for giving effect to 'reclassification' in the Act was declared legal [1983 lab IC 1721: ILR (1983) 2 Ker 578 (DB)]. This power of inclusion in or exclusion from the list vests in the Parliament. State Government is not competent to notify a caste or a tribe as S.T. State Govt. cannot include "Wanjara" as part of genus "Sugali". [1995 Lab IC 219 (AP)].

Some non-listed caste members often try to take benefit of even printing mistakes in the 'list', so that their caste may be considered as part of the 'Schedule'. In such an instance, "Lohar" was printed in the list of Hindi version of the Act. Supreme Court specifically ruled that Lohar is a backward class and Court cannot declare it to be a Scheduled Caste. It was further observed that Lohar community was wrongly included as Scheduled Tribe in Hindi version of the Act and the Court shall take judicial notice of only English version of the Act, which is authoritative[2]. [Scheduled Castes and Scheduled Tribes Orders Act, 1950 as well as Amending Acts and the Scheduled lists have been given at the end of this presentation].

3. SC/ST Act of 1989 – A consolidating Legislation

Combined study of 'Statement of Object and Reasons', preamble and the title mentioned in section 1(1) clarify beyond doubt that intention of the legislature was to consolidate the provisions prescribed in the past for protection, abolition, victimization, commission of atrocities and of course relief and rehabilitation of members of Scheduled Castes and Scheduled Tribes. It was clearly mentioned that "existing laws like the Protection of Civil Rights Act, 1955 and the normal provisions of Indian Penal Code" are not sufficient to deal with the ongoing situation. Therefore the Scheduled Castes and the Scheduled Tribes (Prevention of Atrocities) Act, 1989 had consolidated various offences declared as crime by Indian Penal Code, 1860 and Protection of Civil Rights Act, 1955, the provisions of compensation, relief and rehabilitation provided elsewhere, like various Criminal law amendment acts in existence. Not only some new crimes were created but new kinds of punishments were also formulated in form of collective fines or externment etc. These new forms were consolidated with the old ones.

For procedural part, the Act of 1989 has consolidated provisions of Criminal Procedure Code, 1973, while prescribing some procedure of its own, which could be named as 'special procedure' because the Act is a 'special Act'.

---

1. *Punjab Rao* v. *D.P. Meshram*, AIR 1965 SC 1179: 1965 (2) SCJ 725: (1965) 1 SCR 849 (at 1184).
2. *Nityanand Sharma* v. *State of Bihar*, AIR 1996 SC 2306: 1996 AIR SCW 782: (1996) 3 SCC 576.

Most striking feature in the exercise of this consolidation is incorporation of section 4 and section 22 of the Act. Generally it is the practice of legislatures the world over that when a special legislation is enacted for eradicating, prohibiting or even fighting an evil in the society, where it is inevitable to provide for harsher punishments, State keeps its employees immune from the actions taken which the courts may find not justified. In criminal jurisprudence such over-enthusiastic action, sometimes going beyond the limits of legality, are called 'impunity'.

Section 4 of the Act of 1989 is an antithesis to this general practice. But for purposes of consolidation section 22 was enacted so that those employees who function in 'good faith' would remain immune, but in presence of section 4, the burden of proving 'good faith' would naturally be on the charged employee.

However, the process of consolidation has helped to enact one legislaticn to modify various provisions in a single Act to meet the objective.

4. Extent of Territory

Sub-clause (2) of section 1 makes and mandates the territorial extent of provisions of the Act to "whole of India" except the State of Jammu and Kashmir. After States Reorganization Act, 1956 (37 of 1956) by virtue of Constitution (Seventh Amendment) Act, 1956, India is a Union of States, territories of which comprise, *firstly* the territories of all States, *secondly* the Union territories, and thirdly such other territories as may be acquired.

Section 18 of Indian Penal Code, 1860 defines India as:

> 18. "India"- "India" means the territory of India excluding the State of Jammu and Kashmir.

Article 1(3) of the Constitution, "the territory of India shall comprise—

(a) the territories of the States;

(b) the Union territories specified in the First Schedule; and

(c) such other territories as may be acquired.

Section 3 of General Clauses Act, 1897, and other Acts define the territory of India in the like manner.

The Scheduled Castes and the Scheduled Tribes (Prevention of Atrocities) Act, 1989 is a substantive law and its extent to the "whole" of Indian territory shall certainly include to the extent of "territories" as stipulated by International law, according to which:

4.1 Territorial Waters

Hyde in his International Law says – "There has long been a disposition on the part of the some publicists of distinction to advocate an extension of three marine miles as the limit of territorial waters" (vol. 1 pp 465 and 466).

According to Oppenheim, the territory of a State, under International Law, consists in the first place of the land within its boundaries, and to this must be added the sea coast and certain waters which are adjacent to its land boundaries. These waters are of two kinds – national and territorial. Thus territorial waters are extended to and includes waters in bays, gulfs and straits.

Around the Indian Coasts a lot of islands are situated, with substantial populations, in some cases comprising of Scheduled Castes and Scheduled

Tribes. The Act of 1989 would extend its application if the island, according to International law, is considered territory of India.

4.2 Ships

The confines of a ship, wherever it may be, at high seas of international waters or otherwise, it is considered the "territory" of the State to which it belongs. Ships belonging to other States but stationed on territorial coasts of a particular State become the "territory" of that State. This rule, applies to all kinds of ships, whether private or public or armed etc.

Therefore any offence committed on an Indian ship, wherever it may be could be tried in India by Special Court.

4.3 Aircraft

Similar rule applies to the aircrafts registered in India. They are Indian "territory" to which provisions of the Act are applicable.

4.4 Depth of Earth and Air

Depth of Earth from its center to surface and from the surface to the 'firmament', the column of air is the "territory" of the State. This rule is based on the principle: *Cujus est solum, ejus est usque ad infero,* meaning who is the owner of the soil, it is his even to the firmament, and to the center of the planet Earth.

4.5 Procedural law for Offence Outside Territory

From the discussion above it has been clear that the expression "whole of India" in section 1(2) of the Act of 1989 includes ships etc., which may be territorial limits otherwise stipulated. In case an offence has been committed on a ship at high seas or aircraft, provisions of section 188 of Cr PC 1973 would be applicable.

Section 188, Cr PC reads as— "188. Offences Committed outside India – When an offence is committed outside India,—

(a) by a citizen of India, whether on high seas or elsewhere; or
(b) by a person, not being such a citizen, on any ship or aircraft registered in India,

he may be dealt with in respect of such offence as if it had been committed at any place within India at which he may be found:

Provided that, notwithstanding anything in any of the preceding sections of this chapter, no such offence shall be inquired into or tried in India except with the previous sanction of Central Government."

5. Section 1(3) "Come into Force" and "Notification"

As has been mentioned that the Scheduled Castes and the Scheduled Tribes (Prevention of Atrocities) Act, 1989, though received the assent of the president on Sept. 11, 1989 and the next day *i.e.,* on Sept. 12, 1989 it was published in the Gazette of India (Extra, Part II, Section 1, Serial No. 39), but it did not come into force till 30th Jan. 1990. As a general mode it is usual to give effect to any law it is published in the Official Gazette. It is a settled law that, unless otherwise stated, a law and a notification will come into force immediately upon its being published in the Official Gazette.

Same is the position of Rules of 1995 framed under section 23 of the Act, 1989[1]. Though, previously, the Scheduled Castes and the Scheduled Tribes (Prevention of Atrocities) Act, 1989 was challenged for vires of the Act on various grounds, one of the ground for its challenge was that Rules, were not framed (till then), before the Full Bench of Allahabad High Court. (Later on Rules were produced by Addl. Solicitor-General and on that Court contention was disposed). But on this count and arguments forwarded as to the 'notifications' issued by the State Government, the Bench had dealt in detail the validity of the 'notification' in question (of August 2, 1989). It was argued that the notification does not indicate as to when "it will come into force and, therefore it is a mere statement of fact and not 'law' within the meaning of Art. 13 of the Constitution".[2]

Various provisions of the Act of 1989 as well as the Rules framed thereunder empower State Government to issue notifications. It was also argued before the Full Bench that law making powers cannot be handed over to the executive on the principle "that one who makes the law, can amend the same and none else." Both these contentions were rejected by the Bench.[3]

In *Sanjay Dutt's* case the similar matter was raised before the Supreme Court, as to whether a notification may be issued by Government without the specific delegation of power by the Act of Parliament (The TADA Act). It was held that it has to be inferred by reading the enactment as a whole keeping in view its objects.[4]

Thus the two notifications published in Gazettes of India on 12th September, 1989 (Sl. No. 39) and on 29th January, 1990 are justified.

The words used in a particular 'notification' must be read as such and not in any other manner, that is the normal rule.[5]

6. Section 1(3) "Central Government.......... Appoint"

The word 'appoint' would also mean 'specified' or 'authorise', as all these words are equivalent as held by Kerala High Court, citing Black's 'Law Dictionary' (sixth Edn.), wherein meaning of 'appoint' has been mentioned as – to assign authority to a particular use, task, position or office, and likewise word 'authorise' means to empower or to give a right or authority to act or effective legal power.[6]

Therefore the Central Government was required to 'appoint' two things, – the 'date from which the Act would come into force', and secondly 'who would notify in the Official Gazette', or in other words who would be specially

1. *Vide* G.S.R. 316(E), dated 31st March, 1995, published in the Gazette of India, Extra, Pt II, section 3(i), dated 31st March, 1995.
2. *Mata Sewak Upadhyay* v. *State of Uttar Pradesh*, 1995 JIC 1168 (All) (FB): 1996 (1) East Cr C 97 (All) (FB).
3. *ibid.*
4. *Sanjay Dutt* v. *State through C.B.I., Bombay*, 1994 AIR SCW 3857: 1995 Cr LJ 477: (1994) 5 SCC 410.
5. *Hari Chand Aggarwal* v. *Batala Engineering Co. Ltd.*, AIR 1969 SC 483: 1969 Cr LJ 803: (1969) 2 SCR 201.
6. *R. Balakrishna Pillai* v. *State of Kerala*, 1999 Cr LJ 1286 (Ker) (1291): ILR (1999) 1 Ker 639: 1999 (1) Ker LJ 383.

empowered to do so. This empowerment implies a special selection of a particular person for conferment of the power. This special empowerment may be for selected specified person or a post may be specified. In other words a special empowerment for issuing the notification may be for a person by name or by virtue of their office or by their official title.

7. Supreme Court on section 1

Supreme Court, in one of its landmark judgments, has very diligently thrown light on the contents of section 1 as: "The thrust of Art 17 and the Act is to liberate the society from blind and ritualistic adherence and traditional beliefs which lost all legal or moral base. It seeks to establish new ideal for society – equality to the Dalits, at par with general public, absence of disabilities, restrictions or prohibitions on grounds of caste or religion, availability of opportunities and a sense of being a participant in the main stream of national life."[1]

Though, the above comments and observations were made while dealing with section 1 of Protection of Civil Rights Act, 1955, but the situation also applies to the present Act of 1989.

The Apex Court further observed:

> "In interpreting the Act the judge should be cognizant to and always keep at the back of his/her mind the Constitutional goals and the purpose of the Act and interpret the provisions of the Act in the light thus shed to annihilate untouchability; to accord to the Dalits and the Tribes, right to equality, social integration a fruition and fraternity a reality."[1]

2. Definitions.—(1) In this Act, unless the context otherwise requires,—

(a) "atrocity" means an offence punishable under section 3;

(b) "Code" means the Code of Criminal Procedure, 1973 (2 of 1974);

(c) "Scheduled Castes and Scheduled Tribes" shall have the meanings assigned to them respectively under clause (24) and clause (25) of article 366 of the Constitution;

(d) "Special Court" means a Court of Session specified as a Special Court in section 14;

(e) "Special Public Prosecutor" means a Public Prosecutor specified as a Special Public Prosecutor or an advocate referred to in section 15;

(f) words and expressions used but not defined in this Act and defined in the Code or the Indian Penal Code (45 of 1860) shall have the meanings assigned to them respectively in the Code, or as the case may be, in the Indian Penal Code.

---

1. *State of Karnataka* v. *Appa Balu Ingale,* AIR 1993 SC 1126: 1993 Cr LJ 1029 (1040) (SC): 1993 AIR SCW 337.

(2) Any reference in this Act to any enactment or any provision thereof shall, in relation to an area in which such enactment or such provision is not in force, be construed as a reference to the corresponding law, if any, in force in that area.

SYNOPSIS

1. Analogous Law
2. Underlying Principle
3. Section 2(1)(a) – "Atrocity
4. Section 2(1)(b) – "Code"
5. Section 2(1)(c) – "Scheduled Castes and Scheduled Tribes"
6. Who Belongs to Scheduled Castes
7. Section 2(1)(d) – "Special Court"
8. Section 2(1)(e) – "Special Public Prosecutor"
9. Section 2(1)(f)
10. Section 2(2) of SC/ST (Prevention of Atrocities) Act, 1989
11. Interpretation Clause Under Rules of 1995

1. Analogous Law

Except for the term "atrocity", all the terms and expressions have frequently been used in various other legislations, specially the 'special' ones. Some of the expressions were used in the previous Acts of the Parliament which may be said to be the predecessors of the Scheduled Castes and the Scheduled Tribes (Prevention of Atrocities) Act, 1989.

Section 2 of the Act of 1989 is the elaborate interpretation clause, which was incorporated in the Act to become a key so that the definitions, explanations and the meaning may be adhered to while interpreting various previsions of the Act, distributed throughout the Act as well as the Rules.

However, terms like "Code", "Special Court" and "Special Public Prosecutor" have been defined and used in Prevention of Corruption Act, 1988, POTA 2002 (now repealed) or the like special enactments, and various courts have repeatedly interpreted from various angles these terms. Term "Scheduled Castes and Scheduled Tribes" had been used since[1] the inception of the Constitution and various Constitution Orders Acts, alongwith the amendments, are in vogue for declaring these Castes and Tribes for census, constituting Parliamentary or Assembly constituencies or for other purposes.

2. Underlying Principle

Incorporating an interpretation clause, for defining various words and terms used in the Act is the normal practice of legislature. Whether it is a criminal legislation or otherwise such a clause is always present. Once Sir James Stephen had suggested during proceedings of the Council in 1860; during discussion on interpretation clause of Indian Penal Code, that the interpretation clause (chapter in that case) had to be incorporated to prevent Judges from misunderstanding the legislation.

It is also true that such clauses may not provide explanations and definitions for all cases indiscriminately, but only those cases are considered where in the

1. Symon Commission used expression "Scheduled Tribes" in 1935, then in the same year a listed 'Schedule' was prepared by the then British rulers who called the listed persons as "Scheduled Castes".

opinion of legislators difficulties may arise. Section 6 of Indian Penal Code, 1860, explains that "every definition of an offence, every penal provision" shall be understood accordingly. Thus any act or omission, when it seems to constitute an offence under the Act of 1989, it has to be looked that it is within the four corners of the definitions.

Unlike the provisions of Indian Penal Code, 1860, the Scheduled Castes and the Scheduled Tribes (Prevention of Atrocities) Act, 1989 does not provide exceptions (or explanations), except one – that the provisions of the Act of 1989 are not applicable to members of Scheduled Castes or Scheduled Tribes, even the public servants belonging to this group has been excluded under section 4 from the ambit of the Act.

Besides, it is a generally accepted principle that all the explained and defined terms bear same meaning, wherever and in whatever context it may be. Therefore, if a term has been used in one sense at a particular place, it must be considered that it ought to have been used in the same sense at other place or places.

The above principle of common law is based on the two maxims:

Inclusio unius est exclusio alterious, words must be given same meaning as the legislature had intended, unless, by doing so, any repugnancy would be created in the subject or context.

The interpretation clause should not be taken as a substitution of a group of words for another, or strictly defining the word, considering the meaning given to apply in all circumstances of different cases. In defining the words in the interpretation clause, legislature declares what may be conceived and comprehended within the term, provided the circumstances require otherwise. Thus it should not be understood that the meaning provided by the interpretation clause should apply in all cases, in spite of the fact that the given meaning would control and explain the meaning in the section, where the given word was used.

That is the reason why words "unless the context otherwise requires" or the like, are generally inserted in the interpretation clause of almost every statute.

Whether the words like, "unless the context otherwise requires" have been inserted in a statute or not, though SC/ST Act of 1989 specifically uses the phrase, they are implied to be present where they were not prefixed to the interpretation clause, the defined terms used in various sections of the statute are being taken to have narrower meanings and sometimes taking a wider character.

The meaning assigned in the definition clause would not apply when the word appears in a subject or context which makes the application of the definition impossible or repugnant to the meaning of the context in which the word was found to have been used. But in doing so these are limitative which does not permit to go beyond the Act and apply definitions of other Acts.

3. Section 2(1)(a) – "Atrocity"

The term "atrocity" was not used in the entire genus of enactments brought by the Indian Parliament in the past, or precisely from the date when the constitution was adopted by the 'People of India'. Thus it is a new term.

Oxford Dictionary and Thesaurus defines "atrocity" as: wicked or cruel act; while the synonyms are given as cruelty, enormity, evil, offence, crime and outrage (p 42).

In Webster's Third International Dictionary, one of the meanings assigned to word "atrocity" is, "the quality of state of being atrocious", and the word 'atrocious' has been ascribed following meaning:

"(1) marked by or given to extreme wickedness;
(2) marked by or given to extreme brutality or cruelty;
(3) outrageous; violating the bounds of common decency; uncivilized, barbaric;
(4) extremely painful, marked by intense distress;
(5) of such a kind as to fill with fright or dismay." (page 139)

Section 2(1)(a) does not in fact define "atrocity", but simply mentions: "atrocity" means an offence punishable under section 3.

The word "atrocity" also finds a place in the title of the Act of 1989, which indicates the nature of the enactment and also intention of the Legislature.

While describing the meanings given to the word "atrocity" by Webster's Third International Dictionary as well as the word defined in section 2(1)(a), a Full Bench of Rajasthan High Court observed: "If we were to have the meanings of these words in mind while interpreting section 3 of the Act, we would find that each one of the acts contemplated by section 3 is atrocious and the aim at punishing the persons who are found guilty of the same......... The Act was enacted to prevent the commission of offences of atrocities."[1]

Irony of the situation is that along with the word 'atrocity', section 2(1)(a) also uses two other words, "offence" and "punishable". The Preamble of the Act starts with words: "An Act to prevent the commission of offences of atrocities..........". The word "atrocity" has also been used in the title of the Act. Section 2(n) of Criminal Procedure Code, 1973 defines: "offence" means any act or omission made punishable by any law for the time being in force........". Section 40 of Indian Penal Code, 1860 also defines word "offence".

As could be seen that one of the meanings of word "atrocity" is given as "offence", therefore using the same words twice for defining "atrocity" seems to be superfluous.

But in a very old case Madras High Court, following its own previous decision, tried to examine, whether term "offence" under the Indian Penal Code may cover "offences" under other Acts, such as Indian Railways Act or Martial Law Regulations. It was held that the term used in IPC does not include offences in other Acts. Thus it was held: "The rule of Strict Construction is followed in the case of Penal Statutes as well as fiscal statutes. According to Maxwell, "The paramount object in construing the penal as well as other statutes is to ascertain the legislative intent, and the rule of strict construction is not violated by

1. *Jai Singh* v. *Union of India*, 1993 Cr LJ 2705 (FB) (Raj) (2713): AIR 1993 Raj 177: 1993 (1) Raj LW 157.

permitting the words to have their full meaning or the more extensive of the two meanings that best effectuate the intention of legislature."[1]

4. Section 2(1)(b) – "Code"

Section 20 of the Scheduled Castes and the Scheduled Tribes (Prevention of Atrocities) Act, 1989 bars application of any other law for the time being in force. Section 18 and section 19 of the Act specifically bars operation of section 438 and section 360 of Criminal Procedure code, 1973. Besides section 6 of Act provides application of certain provisions of Indian Penal Code, 1860.

Apart from these specific provisions made applicable to the provisions of the Act of 1989, there are some other provisions which provide a different procedure as has been provided by the Cr PC, such as in regard to Special Court, Special Public Prosecutor, Security for keeping peace and preventive measures (Chapter VIII Cr PC), for attachment and forfeiture of property (Chapter VII-A Cr PC) etc.. The Act of 1989 has provided its own procedure, through its own provisions or through Rules of 1995.

Rule 3 provides 'precautionary and preventive measures, supervision of prosecutions, importantly rule 5 provides how information to police would be given and recorded etc. (FIR S. 154 *et sq* of Cr PC), spot inspections (rule 6) and the mode of 'investigation' and by whom it would be done (rule 7).

The rule framing powers were given to the Central Government by section 23 of the Act of 1989, which also mandates to put the framed Rules before both the Houses of the Parliament and accordingly approved by it, thus the Rules so framed almost assume statute of an enactment or legislation, short of assent by the President.

However, the procedures laid down by the Act of 1989 or Rules of 1995 for specific purposes are limited and not exhaustive. Therefore application of provisions of Criminal Procedure Code, 1973 cannot be avoided. Therefore procedures provided by Criminal Procedure Code, 1973 have to be applied, unless these provisions have been expressly, excluded; or, by necessary implication.[2]

The procedure during the trial before the Special Court have to be controlled by provisions of Cr PC, likewise during the investigation etc., provisions of Cr PC would be applicable. This was the reason why the "Code" has been defined in the interpretation clause of Act of 1989.

When a question arose before a Special Court to decide in respect of its powers, it was held that the Special Court has to be treated as Court of original criminal jurisdiction, therefore the court has all the powers as any other Court of original criminal jurisdiction has, which have been provided under the Cr PC, except where it is specifically excluded by the Special Act.[3]

---

1. *Aydrooss* v. *Emperor*, AIR 1923 Mad 187: 24 Cr LJ 360 and *Re Purvaantur* v. *Anthamy*, AIR 1925 Mad 239.
2. *Vivek Gupta* v. *CBI*, (2003) 8 SCC 628.
3. *A.R. Antulay* v. *Ramdas Sriniwas Nayak*, AIR 1984 SC 718: 1984 Cr LJ 647 (SC): (1984) 2 SCC 500. (excluding the power to take direct cognizance without committal proceedings).

5. Section 2(1)(c) – "Scheduled Castes and Scheduled Tribes"

Section 2(1)(c) defines and almost narrows down the meaning of Scheduled Castes and the Scheduled Tribes as has been assigned to them respectively under clause (24) and clause (25) of Article 366 of the Constitution. Clause (24) and clause (25) of Article 366 of Constitution of India reads as follows:

> (Article)" 366 Definitions.—In this Constitution, unless the context otherwise requires, the following expressions have the meanings hereby respectively assigned to them, that is to say—
>
> (24) "Scheduled Castes" means such castes, races or tribes or parts of or groups within such castes, races or tribes as are deemed under Art. 341 to be Scheduled Castes for the purposes of this Constitution;
>
> (25) "Scheduled Tribes" means such tribes or tribal communities or parts of or groups within such tribes or tribal communities as are deemed under Article 342 to be Scheduled Tribes for the purpose of this Constitution;"

Section 2(1)(c) of the Act of 1989 only refer clauses (24) and (25) of Article 366 of the Constitution, but as seen above both of these clauses of Art. 366 again refer to Art. 341 and Art. 342 respectively and for completely understanding the definitions of or recognizing the actual members who may claim to comprise Scheduled Castes and Scheduled Tribes. As such Art. 341 and 342 of Constitution have been given below.

(Art) "341 Scheduled Castes.— (1) The President may with respect to any State or Union territory, and where it is a State, after consultation with the Governor thereof, by public notification specify the castes, races or tribes or parts of or groups within castes, races or tribes which shall for the purposes of this Constitution be deemed to be Scheduled Castes in relation to that State or Union territory, as the case may be.

(2) Parliament may by law include in or exclude from the list of Scheduled Castes specified in a notification issued under clause (1) any caste, race or tribe or part of or group within any caste, race or tribe, but save as aforesaid a notification issued under the said clause shall not be varied by any subsequent notification."[1]

(Art.) "342. Scheduled Tribes.— (1) The President may with respect to any State or Union territory, and where it is a State, after consultation with the Governor thereof, by public notification, specify the tribes or tribal communities or parts of or groups within tribes or tribal communities which shall for the purposes of this Constitution be deemed to be Scheduled Tribes in relation to that State or Union territory, as the case may be.

(2) Parliament may by law include in or exclude from the list of Scheduled Tribes specified in a notification issued under clause (1) any tribe or tribal community or part of or group within any tribe or tribal community, but save

---

1. See the Constitution (Scheduled Castes) Order, 1950, published as C.O. 19 dated 10-8-1950, in Gaz India 1950, Part II, section 3, Ext, p 163; and the Constitution (Scheduled Castes) (Union Territory) Order, 1951, published as C.O. 32, dated 20-9-1951, in Gaz India 1951, Pt II, section 3, p. 1198 (please see the Apendices). Please also see Repealing and Amending Act 1988 (19 of 1988), section 2, Sch 1 (31-3-1988), which repealed Schedules I and II.

as aforesaid a notification issued under the said clause shall not be varied by any subsequent notification."[1]

"Scheduled Castes" (but not the Scheduled Tribes) has also been defined under section 2(db) of Protection of Civil Rights Act, 1955. Besides, section 2(e) and (f) of the Scheduled Castes and Scheduled Tribes Orders (Amendment) Act, 1976 (108 of 1976) also define the said castes and the Tribes as referred under Art. 341 and Art. 342 of the Constitution.

6. Who Belongs to Scheduled Castes

Clause (3) of the Constitution (Scheduled Castes) Order, 1950 provides that a person claiming to be treated as a member of Scheduled Caste must be one who professes Hindu or Sikh religion. Because of this Buddhists were held not to be treated as members of Scheduled Castes within the meaning of section 2(db) of Protection of Civil Rights Act, 1955 [AIR 1979 Bom 282 (284)]. But on the contrary, a special mention is made of the Sikh religion, which has to follow that the word "Hindu" had been used in the narrower sense for the orthodox Hindu religion under which caste systems are recognised and as such injunctions are issued for clear cut distinction.[2]

For determining a particular caste to be declared as such under Art. 341 of the Constitution, one has to look at the notification issued by the President in this behalf, which mention State-wise lists.[3]

But difficulties came up before courts when a member of a particular caste want to be declared as a member of Scheduled Caste which is not mentioned in the State-wise lists of the notification. For instance Supreme Court clarified that the term "Bhovi" includes the "Vodda" community, although the same was not added to the list mentioned in Schedule. In that case it was held that question of issuing any fresh certificate to the petitioner by any authority does not arise as it was not necessary, because he would automatically qualify for inclusion in the S.C. Category. [ILR 1996 Kant 718 (722)]. Or in another case it was held that persons belonging to "Kotegar" community are of Scheduled Caste, but "Kotegar and Metri" are synonymous terms of same caste and not caste by name *"Kotegar Metri"*. (AIR 1986 Kant 237).

In *Bhaiya Lal* v. *Harikishan Singh*'s cases (Supra), Supreme Court observed that the notification refers to Chamar, Jatav and *Mochi*, therefore, to decide the dispute, the Election Tribunal can only ascertain whether or not the appellant was a Chamar, Jatav or Mochi. The appellant belonged to "Dohar" caste, and claimed that it was a sub-caste of Chamar, that cannot be accepted. Supreme Court specifically held that such kind of enquiry cannot be made permissible, having regard to provisions of Article 341. But in another case Supreme Court

1. See the Constitution (Scheduled Castes) Order, 1950, C.O. 22 dated 6-9-1950, Gaz India 1950, Pt II, section 3, Extra., p. 597, as amended from time-to-time; Constitution (Scheduled Tribe) (Union Territories) Order, 1951, C.O. 33, dated 20-9-1951, Gaz India, 1951, Pt II, section 3, Extra., p. 1198G. Later on amended in 1956, by Amendment Act, 1956 (63 of 1956). Both the orders of Scheduled Castes and the Scheduled Tribes were consolidated by Scheduled Castes and the Scheduled Tribes Orders (Amendment) Act, 1976 (108 of 1976).
2. *Punjab Rao* v. *D.P. Meshram*, AIR 1965 SC 1179 (1184): 1965 (2) SCJ 725: (1965) 1 SCR 849.
3. *Bhaiya Lal* v. *Harikishan Singh*, AIR 1965 SC 1557: 1966 (2) SCJ 77: (1965) 2 SCR 877.

decided a question as to whether non-specified caste *"Mochi"* may be included in mentioned caste *"Chamar"*.[1]

In normal circumstances the word "profess" used in the Presidential Order would mean that a person openly profess by all declared means that the person is a Hindu (or Sikh), but if he converts to another religion and declare that he had ceased to be belonging to the old religion as a result of his conversion, commonsense says that the person should be deprived of the benefits. But Bombay High Court had observed that Bhil Tribe is a Scheduled Tribe in Maharashtra and as such included in the Schedule of Scheduled Castes, Scheduled Tribes Order (Amendment) Act, 1971, and if a Bhil after conversion to Christianity maintains the tribal ways of life in all matters he will continue to remain a tribal (AIR 1984 Bom. 392: 1984 Mah LJ 432). In later cases other High Courts followed suit and various judgments have come in which converts to Christianity were given status of Scheduled Castes or Tribes. [For further details please see note (2) 'Scope' under section 3.]

7. Section 2(1)(d) – "Special Court"

The weight of the definition under section 2(1)(d) of the Scheduled Castes and the Scheduled Tribes (Prevention of Atrocities) Act, 1989, has been shifted to section 14 of the Act, as it is described to mean "a Court of Session specified as Special Court in section 14".

Sections 14 and 20 of the Act of 1989, when read together, exclude application of provisions of other laws which are in force for the time being. Section 4(2) of Criminal Procedure Code, 1973 stipulates as: "All offences under any other law shall be investigated, inquired into, *tried,* and *otherwise dealt with* according to the same provisions, but subject to any enactment for the time being in force regulating the manner or place of investigating, inquiring into, trying or otherwise dealing with such offences."

Besides section 5 of Cr PC, in its "Saving" clause says: "nothing contained in this Code shall, in the absence of a specific provision to the contrary, effect any special or local law....... or any *special jurisdiction* or *power conferred*........."

Section 2(1)(d), or for that matter section 14 of the Scheduled Castes and the Scheduled Tribes (Prevention of Atrocities) Act, 1989 or any provision of the Act or Rules provide for the procedure or otherwise dealing with the proceedings and jurisdiction of Special Court which remains a Court.

In these circumstances it was held that sections 2(1)(d), section 14 and the section 20 of the Act of 1989 have not taken away the procedure laid down under sections 4 and 5 of Cr PC, as no procedure for trial of offences under the Act has been provided or laid down. Due to these reasons the general procedure has to be followed by the Special Court by virtue of provisions of sections 4 and 5 of the Cr PC. [(1997) 3 Chand Cri C 453: (1993) 1 Chand LR (Civ and Cri) 148 (157) (P&H)]

(Please also see notes and comments under section 14.)

---

1. *Parsram* v. *Shivchand,* AIR 1969 SC 597: (1969) 1 SCC 20: (1969) 2 SCR 997.

8. Section 2(1)(e) – "Special Public Prosecutor"

Section 2(1)(e) contemplates the meaning of the Special Public Prosecutor to be taken as has been specified in section 15 of the Act. Section 15 of the Act empowers State Government to specify a Public Prosecutor or appoint an advocate of seven years of standing in practice as a Special Public Prosecutor for every Special Court, by issuing a notification to this effect.

In the normal circumstances the Public Prosecutors on the pay-roll of the State Government do not work in Court of Sessions, but here the State Government has been given an option to "specify" one Public Prosecutor already on its pay-roll, or appoint an advocate who has been in practice as an advocate for seven years, as a Special Public Prosecutor for each Special Court.

(Please also see notes and comments under section 15).

9. Section 2(1)(f)

Sub-Clause (f) of clause (1) of section 2, the interpretation and defining section of the Scheduled Castes and the Scheduled Tribes (Prevention of Atrocities) Act, 1989, has given a blatant latitude to include the definitions of the "words and expressions used but not defined" in the Act and generally defined by Criminal Procedure Code, 1973 as well as Indian Penal Code, 1860 shall have the meanings assigned to them in said two enactments. The only restriction put forward by this clause is that those words or the expressions which have been defined in section 2 of the Act (or the Rules) would be interpreted according to definitions and meanings assigned therein. In such a case the definitions of Cr PC or the IPC, as the case may, shall not be used.

10. Section 2(2) of SC/ST (Prevention of Atrocities) Act, 1980

The first phrase of section 2(2) ("Any reference in this Act to any enactment or........") legitimatized the references of other enactment which have been mentioned in the Act of 1989. For instance, section 16 of the Act provides for imposition of collective fine by the State Government in certain area, refer to section 10A of the Protection of Civil Rights Act, 1955, for "imposition and realisation" of such collective fine.

The second part of the clause (2) of section 2 of the Act contemplates in relation to a certain area, where the provisions of the other enactment "is not in force", would be construed to be in force. There are a lot of enactments which declare some area or areas under which provisions of such enactments may apply, but perhaps it is not intention of section 2(2) to encompass all such Acts and their provisions, because there are such Acts in vogue, as Terrorist Affected Areas (Special Courts) Act, 1984 or Disturbed Areas Act, etc., etc.. Such enactments also provide for the provisions to control a certain "area", but for completely different reason or cause.

11. Interpretation Clause under Rules of 1995

Section 23 of the Act of 1989 had empowered the Central Government to make rules for carrying out the purpose of the Act. Important thing about this rule making process, as has been provided under section 23(2) of the Act was that these framed rules had to be put and approved by both the Houses of the Parliament after due discussions and deliberations. Thus short of assent of the

President, these framed rules almost assume status of an enactment and these Rules have to be read with the provisions of the Act.

Because of these reasons when the Scheduled Castes and the Scheduled Tribes (Prevention of Atrocities) Act, 1989 was challenged for its Constitutionality and vires before the Full Bench of Allahabad High Court in *Mata Sewak Upadhaya's* case (supra), it was one of the pleas taken by the petitioners that rules were not framed (till the filing of the writ petition), but during the final argument, Mr. Tulsi representing the State had produced the framed Rules 1995, therefore the plea was rejected by the Full Bench.

Rule 2 of Rules 1995[1] deals with the "Definitions" and Rule 2(h) says:

> "words and expressions used herein and not defined but defined in the Act shall have the meanings respectively assigned to them in the Act". This clause of Rule 2 (approved by both Houses of the Parliament stipulates that the definitions given under section 2 of the Act of 1989 be read with the definitions provided by the Rule 2.

Rule 2 of Rules of 1995 defines words, "Act", "Dependent", "identified area", "Non-Government Organisation", "Schedule", "Section" and "State Government".

The definitions of words and the expressions given under Rule 2, though not exhaustive but limited, give some explanations to the provisions of the Act of 1989. For example: Section 2(2) of the Act of 1989 provides for the construing of an "area" for purposes of application of provisions of other enactment, but the "area" has not been explained by the said section. Rule 2(c) specifically explains about the "identified area" as: "such area where State Government has reason to believe that atrocity may take place or there is an apprehension of reoccurrence of an offence under the Act or an area prone to atrocities."

---

1. *Vide* G.S.R. 316(E), dated 31st March, 1995, published in the Gazette of India, Extra., Pt II, Sec. 3(i), dated 31st March, 1995.

Chapter II

OFFENCES OF ATROCITIES

3. Punishments for offences of atrocities.—(1) Whoever, not being a member of a Scheduled Caste or a Scheduled Tribe,—

(i) forces a member of a Scheduled Caste or a Scheduled Tribe to drink or eat any inedible or obnoxious substance;

(ii) acts with intent to cause injury, insult or annoyance to any member of a Scheduled Caste or a Scheduled Tribe by dumping excreta, waste matter, carcasses or any other obnoxious substance in his premises or neighbourhood;

(iii) forcibly removes clothes from the person of a member of a Scheduled Caste or a Scheduled Tribe or parades him naked or with painted face or body or commits any similar act which is derogatory to human dignity;

(iv) wrongfully occupies or cultivates any land owned by, or allotted to, or notified by any competent authority to be allotted to, a member of a Scheduled Caste or a Scheduled Tribe or gets the land allotted to him transferred;

(v) wrongfully dispossesses a member of a Scheduled Caste or a Scheduled Tribe from his land or premises or interferes with the enjoyment of his rights over any land, premises or water;

(vi) compels or entices a member of a Scheduled Caste or a Scheduled Tribe to do 'begar' or other similar forms of forced or bonded labour other than any compulsory service for public purposes imposed by Government;

(vii) forces or intimidates a member of a Scheduled Caste or a Scheduled Tribe not to vote or to vote to a particular candidate or to vote in a manner other than that provided by law;

(viii) institutes false, malicious or vexatious suit or criminal or other legal proceedings against a member of a Scheduled Caste or a Scheduled Tribe;

(ix) gives, any false or frivolous information to any public servant and thereby causes such public servant to use his lawful power to the injury or annoyance of a member of a Scheduled Caste or a Scheduled Tribe;

(x) intentionally insults or intimidates with intent to humiliate a member of a Scheduled Caste or a Scheduled Tribe in any place within public view;

(xi) assaults or uses force to any woman belonging to a Scheduled Caste or a Scheduled Tribe with intent to dishonour or outrage her modesty;

(xii) being in a position to dominate the will of a woman belonging to a Scheduled Caste or a Scheduled Tribe and uses that position to exploit her sexually to which she would not have otherwise agreed;

(xiii) corrupts or fouls the water of any spring, reservoir or any other source ordinarily used by members of the Scheduled Castes or the Scheduled Tribes so as to render it less fit for the purpose for which it is ordinarily used;

(xiv) denies a member of a Scheduled Caste or a Scheduled Tribe any customary right of passage to a place of public resort or obstructs such member so as to prevent him from using or having access to a place of public resort to which other members of public or any section thereof have a right to use or access to;

(xv) forces or causes a member of a Scheduled Caste or a Scheduled Tribe to leave his house, village or other place of residence,

shall be punishable with imprisonment for a term which shall not be less than six months but which may extend to five years and with fine.

(2) Whoever, not being a member of a Scheduled Caste or a Scheduled Tribe,—

(i) gives or fabricates false evidence intending thereby to cause, or knowing it to be likely that he will thereby cause, any member of a Scheduled Caste or a Scheduled Tribe to be convicted of an offence which is capital by the law for the time being in force shall be punished with imprisonment for life and with fine; and if an innocent member of a Scheduled Caste or a Scheduled Tribe be convicted and executed in consequence of such false or fabricated evidence, the person who gives or fabricates such false evidence, shall be punished with death;

(ii) gives or fabricates false evidence intending thereby to cause, or knowing it to be likely that he will thereby cause, any member of a Scheduled Caste or a Scheduled Tribe to be convicted of an offence which is not capital but punishable with imprisonment for a term of seven years or upwards, shall be punishable with imprisonment for a term which shall not be less than six months but which may extend to seven years or upwards and with fine;

(iii) commits mischief by fire or any explosive substance intending to cause or knowing it to be likely that he will thereby cause damage to any property belonging to a member of a Scheduled Caste or a Scheduled Tribe, shall be punishable with imprisonment for a term which shall not be less than six months but which may extend to seven years and with fine;

(iv) commits mischief by fire or any explosive substance intending to cause or knowing it to be likely that he will thereby cause destruction of any building which is ordinarily used as a place of worship or as a place for human dwelling or as a place for custody of the property by a member of a Scheduled Caste or a Scheduled Tribe, shall be punishable with imprisonment for life and with fine;

(v) commits any offence under the Indian Penal Code (45 of 1860) punishable with imprisonment for a term of ten years or more against a person or property on the ground that such person is a member of a Scheduled Caste or a Scheduled Tribe or such property belongs to such member, shall be punishable with imprisonment for life and with fine;

(vi) knowingly or having reason to believe that an offence has been committed under this Chapter, causes any evidence of the commission of that offence to disappear with the intention of screening the offender from legal punishment, or with that intention gives any information respecting the offence which he knows or believes to be false, shall be punishable with the punishment provided for that offence; or

(vii) being a public servant, commits any offence under this section, shall be punishable with imprisonment for a term which shall not be less than one year but which may extend to the punishment provided for that offence.

SYNOPSIS

1. Analogous Law

Section 3 of the Scheduled Castes and the Scheduled Tribes (Prevention of Atrocities) Act, 1989 is being analogous to sections 3, 4, 5, 6, 7, 7A and 10 of Protection of Rights Act, 1955, difference being that Act of 1989 has added some new offences and some new culprits on whom the provisions of the Act would be applicable,— such as public servants in general who try to fabricate evidence against the members of Scheduled Castes and the Scheduled Tribes.

Secondly, the punishments provided under section 3 of the Act of 1989 is much harsher and stringent as compared to the provisions of punishments for similar acts under various sections of Protection of Rights Act, 1955[1]. In 1965 Government of India appointed a Committee on untouchability etc., under the chairmanship of Shri L. Elavaperumal. The Committee submitted its report in 1969, in which it made certain recommendations for plugging the loopholes, and specially making the penal provisions more stringent.

Some of the recommendations of the committee were given effect in the Bill for the Amending Act (Act 106) of 1976.

In fact the present Act of 1989 had consolidated the penal acts and the provided punishments arising therefrom, in the Act of 1955, and section 3 of Act of 1989 became the final product of the long experimental process. Because of this 'Statement of Objects and Reasons' of the Act of 1989 says: "the existing laws like the Protection of Rights Act, 1955 and the normal provisions of the Indian Penal Code have been found to be inadequate to check these crimes."

2. Scope, Extent and Applicability

Though the word "Untouchability" was not used in body of the Scheduled Castes and the Scheduled Tribes (Prevention of Atrocities) Act, 1989, Supreme Court referred to that practice by observing as, "looking to the historical background relating to the practice of 'untouchability' and the social attitudes which lead to the commission of such offences against Scheduled Castes and Scheduled Tribes......"[2]

Following the line Karnataka High Court held that the offences which are enumerated under section 3 are offences which to say the least, denigrate members of Scheduled Castes and Scheduled Tribes in the eye of society, and prevent them from leading a life of dignity and self-respect. Such offences are committed to humiliate and subjugate such members with a view to keeping them in a state of servitude. These offences constitute a separate class and cannot be compared with offences under the Penal Code.[3]

Dealing with the scope, extent and applicability of section 3 of the Scheduled Castes and the Scheduled Tribes (Prevention of Atrocities) Act, 1989, different Courts have tried the subject matter and in the process some difference of opinion

1. Protection of Civil Rights Act, 1955 was previously and originally named as Untouchability (Offences) Act, 1955. The title of the Act was changed through Amending Act of 1976.
2. *State of Madhya Pradesh* v. *Ram Krishna Balothia,* 1995 Cr LJ 2076 (SC): AIR 1995 SC 1198: 1995 AIR SCW 1267: JT 1995 (1) SC 310.
3. *Bapu Gouda* v. *State of Karnataka,* 1996 Cr LJ 1117 (Kant) (1118): ILR 1995 Kant 3586: 1996 (1) Kant LJ 111.

have also come up, which is evident from the following observations on deciding the question,— whether in a given case and under specific circumstances the victim should be considered member of a Scheduled Caste or a Scheduled Tribe, as the case may be?

In one case, facts were that the victim had alleged that rape was committed on her, who claimed to be a member of a Scheduled Tribe named "Kondho". The court found the evidence of the victim as contradictory, besides admitting that she belonged to Telegulu caste, of which she did not possess any certificate showing her to be Kondho, the court found that the victim did not belong to Kondho caste, hence provisions of section 3 of the Act of 1989 cannot be attracted.[1]

A petitioner claimed himself to be Hindu, but in cross-examination he admitted that his son-in-law was John Babu, whose marriage with her daughter was performed according to Christian customs. The petitioner had also admitted that his father's name was Anandam who was also Christian. The court observed "Except denying the suggestion that he is not a Hindu, the petitioner did not explain as to how he is not a Christian, when both his father and daughter were Christians". The Court expected a proof from the petitioner *(onus)* how he continued to be a Hindu, therefore it was held that initiation of proceedings against the accused under section 3 of the Act were without any basis.[2]

In another case Kerala High Court observed that 'status' of the victim has to be taken into consideration, which is not conferred on the basis of religion they profess but on the basis of community to which they belonged, for the purpose of application of provisions of the Act of 1989. Change of religion by a member of Scheduled Tribe by embracing Christianity, would not deprive him of their status and benefit as a member of Scheduled Tribe. It was held that provisions of the Act (section 3) would still be applicable.[3]

In a Full Bench case of Bombay High Court, it was held that for offences of atrocities committed under section 3 of the Act, the complainant need not to disclose the caste of accused and this would not render the complaint to be quashed.[4]

Yet again it was held that where the parents of the victim originally belonged to the community which was considered as the Scheduled Tribe but later on they embraced Christianity and the victim was born from them thereafter; in the circumstances the victim cannot be treated as a member of Scheduled Tribe. As such no offence under section 3 would be attracted in her case.[5]

---

1. *Dasarathi Sahukar* v. *State*, 2007 Cr LJ 3445 (Ori) (DB): 2007 (37) OCR 802.
2. *Papatla John Veeranna* v. *State of Andhra Pradesh*, 2003 Cr LJ 2204 (AP) (2205): 2003 (2) Andh LT (Cri) 474 AP: 2003 (3) Rec Cri R 489.
3. *Rosamma Thomas* v. *Circle Inspector of Police, Tripunithura*, 1999 Cr LJ 1666 (Ker): ILR (1999) 2 Ker 520: 1999 (1) Ker LJ 413: 2000 (1) JIC 915 (Ker).
4. *Pushpa Vijay Bonde* v. *State of Maharashtra*, 2009 Cr LJ 3204 (Bom) (FB): 2009 (79) All Ind Cas 293: 2009 (2) Bom CR (Cri) 32: 2009 (4) Rec Cri R 936.
5. 1996 AIHC 5513 (5514) Ker.

A very academic discussion had taken place on the point of scope and applicability of provisions of SC and ST (PoA) Act, 1989 when a question was raised before Madras High Court. The facts were that in the FIR it was mentioned that the accused abused the complainant Tehenmozhi in her caste name. The complainant who belonged to a Scheduled Caste, married Haridoss, who belonged to "Hindu Yadhava" community by registering their marriage in Registrar's office. The petitioner Kaliyaperumal was the uncle of Haridoss. It was argued on behalf of the accused petitioner that the complainant had become his relative and one of the members of his family and even if the petitioner has used filthy language against the complainant in caste name, the provisions of the Act could not be attracted. The contention was that when a woman of Scheduled Caste marries a person belonging to Backward Class community, she becomes the member of Backward Class community to which her husband belonged.

It was held that marriage does not create conversion of caste as the complainant had acquired the status of a Scheduled Caste by her birth right and as such did not lose her right of prosecuting under the relevant sections of the SC/ST Act, merely on the ground that she married a person who belonged to Backward Class community.[1]

It is interesting to note here that a similar question was raised before Supreme Court, though in a different reference; as it was: "whether a lady marrying a Scheduled Caste, Scheduled Tribe or OBC citizen, or one transplanted by adoption or any other voluntary act, *ipso facto*, becomes entitled to claim reservation under Art. 15(4) or 16(4), as the case may be?"

While answering the question the Apex Court observed that the constitutional provisions have been intended for the advancement of socially and educationally backward citizens, cannot be defeated by including candidates by allowance or any other mode of joining the community. The observations (relevant portions) are:

> "Therefore persons who by birth belong to Scheduled Caste, Scheduled tribe or Backward classes alone are entitled to the benefit.......... By marriage, adoption or any other device, *viz.*, by procuring "false social status certificates, they are not eligible to avail of protective discrimination......."
>
> "Therefore, when a member is transplanted into the Dalits Tribe and OBCs he/she must of necessity also undergo some handicaps, be subject to same disabilities, disadvantages, indignities or sufferings so as to entitle the candidate to avail the facility of reservation........ Acquisition of the status of Scheduled Caste etc., by voluntary mobility into these categories would play fraud on the Constitution......."[2]

Where the offence was committed on the ground that the injured or the deceased belonged to Scheduled Caste or the Scheduled Tribe, or cases in which question was relating to the property, the provisions of SC and ST Act cannot be

1. *Kaliya Perumal* v. *State*, 1998 Cr LJ 1467 (Mad): 1998 (2) APLJ (Cri) 49: 1998 (2) Rec Cri R 562; Please also see *Rosamma Thomas* v. *Circle Inspector of Police, Tripunithura*, 1999 Cr LJ 1666 (Ker): ILR (1999) 2 Ker 520: 1999 (1) Ker LJ 413: 2000 (1) JIC 915 (Ker).
2. *Valsamma Paul* v. *Cochin University*, AIR 1996 SC 1011: 1996 AIR SCW 492: (1996) 3 SCC 545.

invoked unless the condition has been satisfied, namely – whether the injured/ deceased belonged to Scheduled Caste or Scheduled Tribe but in any case the assailant should not belong to such caste or the Tribe. [(1992) 3 Andh. LT 509 (573)].

In another instance two parties at the spot claimed fishing rights on a tank, not knowing each other. The accused addressed the complainants by their Tribe's name, it was held, firstly, that the address was not made as an intentional insult, and secondly it was not in the "public view", therefore it was not sufficient to make out an offence under section 3(1)(x) of the Act. [For further details on "public view"-please see notes on section 3(1)(x)]. The most important observation was made as – special and stricter provisions have been made in the Act, hence it is duty of the prosecution to examine the case more carefully. They have to be vigilant for avoiding any possibility of the Act "being misused for harassment of the citizens" Registration of the offence under the Act is not sufficient only because the complainant belonged to Scheduled Caste. "Such a mechanical exercise of authority has to be deprecated. The courts have, to see immediately after a case is brought to it whether an offence under the Act is purely made out......."[1]

3. Section 3 of the Act 1989 – Generally

Section 2 of the Act defines "atrocity": means offences punishable under section 3 of the Act. In providing offences and punishments, section 3 of the Act overlap many other existing laws and enactments existing in the statute book. This is not the only anomaly with the Scheduled Castes and the Scheduled Tribes (Prevention of Atrocities) Act, 1989, but many other laws, even obsolete and outdated ones, co-exist with each other, which pose a remarkable task for the judiciary to indulge in developing interpretative techniques to keep the letter and spirit of law.

The rule of strict construction of penal statutes was formulated with the object of keeping balance of principle, under which rights of individuals are guarded on one hand and on the other, the principle is being followed and for that reason the power of punishment is vested in the legislature. The function of Courts remains restricted to define offence, or crime, its gravity and accordingly the punishment is determined.

3.1 Offence

Section 2(1)(a) of the Scheduled Castes and the Scheduled Tribes (Prevention of Atrocities) Act, 1989 defines "atrocity" in a similar manner as "offence" has been defined under section 40 of Indian Penal Code, 1860 as: "………the word "Offence" denotes a thing made punishable by this Code". Section 2(1)(a) of the Act of 1989 confines the extent of the "atrocity" to be an offence which has been mentioned as offences under section 3 of the Act. The other provisions which provide for punishments of various kinds (as section 4 etc.), are not being covered under the ambit of word "atrocity". Therefore for wider application of definition of "offence", help has to be taken from elsewhere.

---

1. *Karan Singh* v. *State of Madhya Pradesh*, (1992) Andh LT 509 (573): 1992 Cr LJ 3054 (MP); please also see (on the same point) *Bishanlal* v. *Hargovind*, RLW 2000 (3) (Raj) 1680.

For yet other wider definition of the word "offence" we have to refer section 2(n) of Criminal Procedure Code, 1973, which says: "Offence" means any act or omission made punishable by any law for the time being in force and includes any act in respect of which a complaint may be made under section 20 of the Cattle-trespass Act, 1871."

The definition of "offence" provided by Cr PC covers the other offences and punishments prescribed by other provisions contained in other sections of the Act of 1989, apart from the offences and the punishments thereof provided under section 3 of the Act.

But the measures taken under sections 10, 16 or 17 of the Act of 1989 are not offences, though the liable persons may be arrested, fined, externed or put under other legal mandated liabilities. It is so because unless there is a declared offence, there can be no prevention.

Under the English law the word "offence" has been used in yet wider sense, as it includes treason, felonies and misdemeanours, often termed as 'misprisons' The 'misdemeanours' or the 'misprisons' include all crimes and offences, not being treason or felonies, for which punishment of fine or imprisonment has been provided. It is not that use of word "offence" is foreign to English law. It was observed by Collins J. that "*prima facie* an offence is equivalent to a crime."[1]

Whereas "continuing offence" would mean an offence that continues from moment to moment without any interruption or break. The offence in question must continue without requiring any act on the part of offender to keep it continuing in its existence. That particular offence would come to an end only when the offender does an act to terminate it. The 'continuous offence' is akin to and should be interpreted in the same manner as "continuing breach of contract" has been construed.

3.2 Quantum of Penalty

Section 3 of the Scheduled Castes and the Scheduled Tribes (Prevention of Atrocities) Act, 1989 provides following kinds of punishments:

(1) Death [section 3(2)(i)]
(2) Imprisonment for life and with fine
(3) Imprisonments of various descriptions of terms, which shall not be less than six months (in some cases not less than one year) and with fine
(4) Forfeiture of property
(5) Fine, including collective fines (section 16)
(6) Externment

Punishment is a device through which the State enforces its laws by declaring certain acts or omissions as forbidden. There are various kinds and forms of punishments, but they are always correlated to law enforcement by the State.

The underlying principle of punishment is that the violator of law is put to the suffering in person or property by sanction of law. Generally the measure put forward by the crime or created offence is the gravity and the circumstances or

1. *Derbyshire Coal Co.* v. *Derby*, (1896) 2 QB 57 (58).

the seriousness under which the violation of law had occurred. Another factor which is considered is measure of guilt as the measure of punishment. But in any case the punishment must fit the crime.

Bentham considered prevention of mischief as the sole object of punishment.[1] Others consider retribution as the chief object of punishment, because it is so desired by the aggrieved person. With the progress of ideas it has developed along with the progress of the society and the retribution concept had receded in the background, and provocation of crime along with reforms of criminal became the accepted object. The theory of revenge had also taken a back seat. Notwithstanding what Plato had said, public as well as personal sentiments practically demand that person who has made others to suffer should himself be put to suffering. But again this may be said that this idea inherits an element of revenge, whatever meager it might be. The other and remaining part in such an idea may be said to be moralistic, to which courts are not concerned. The courts while punishing someone, governed by two aspects – the nature of the act which has been created as a crime (offence), and breach of legislated law.

3.2.1 Measure of Punishment

Prevention of crime or a particular class of crimes, is the sole and well accepted object of punishment. The general rule of criminal jurisprudence concerning punishments is that: punishments should be made as moderate as is the object of a penal legislation.

According to Bantham's view (which was followed in scores of very old English cases) was that, punishment in excess is apt to defeat its own object by producing a reaction of popular feeling, as experience has shown (also in the present case). Where a person has been put in prison in pursuance of an order of punishment for a longer time than it is necessary, or his property is forfeited etc., is not only bad for the individual himself, but a civil society should consider it as cruelty, besides being cumulative economic loss to the society in general.

It is also a rule of common-sense that the provided punishment must be directly proportional to the degree of the prohibited committed act in a particular circumstance. We have seen the punishments provided by 'Code of Manu' (as well as other Smrities, mentioned in the early pages of this presentation) were violative of this proportionality. In some cases very severe punishments were provided for such acts, which in the modern era cannot be conceived as an offence at all (for instance, pouring of molten lead in the ears if a Sudra hears words of Vedas, etc.). Some may justify such kind of punishments as the product of very primitive society.

But one thing which is evident is that, due to disproportionality of those provided punishments the penal system had degenerated to its lowest ebb, resulting in sufferings of Scheduled Castes and the Scheduled Tribes for centuries altogether.

As far as Manu's Code is concerned it was an extreme, and few people think that stringent punishments provided under section 3 (and others) of the

1. Principles of Penal Law, Vol. 1, p 396.

Scheduled Castes and the Scheduled Tribes (Prevention of Atrocities) Act, 1989 can be said to be another reciprocal extreme by the standards fixed in this behalf in the present times.

Three standards can be fixed for measuring reciprocality or proportionality of criminal act *vis-à-vis* punishment:

(i) gravity of the act,

(ii) the time scale according to prevalence of a particular form of crime,

(iii) circumstances.

A particular statute provides the maximum penalty as punishment indicates the gravity of crime. This is the normal rule which presumes that while providing the maximum penalty for a particular crime, the legislature has measured and considered the balance in the reciprocality and proportionality between the gravity of the created crime and thus provided maximum punishment.

Secondly, as the prime object of punishment is prevention of crime, therefore measure of punishment must vary from time-to-time and the circumstances (iii). The severe punishment may be very appropriate at a given time, which may become unnecessary or uncalled for in other times and other circumstances.

Quite substantial time has lapsed since the Act of 1989 was enforced, and it is also seen that stringent and harsher punishments provided by the Act had worked satisfactorily resulting in generating enormous confidence in the protected class on one hand and on the other diluting the aggressive attitude of perpetrators of 'atrocities'. Therefore, would not it be a good idea to amend the Act, as far as quantum of punishments are concerned.

3.2.2 Punishments Subject to Court's Discretion

Legislature provides maximum limits of punishment for a particular offence, and rest is left to the discretion of courts. In case the Court finds that committed offence falls short of the maximum degree of gravity, it may aportion the maximum provided punishment to that extent. In the eyes of court, which is dependent on the given circumstances of each case, the gravity may fluctuate from minimum possible to greater or maximum degree, because amount of severity may differ from the circumstances of each case.

Generally the penal statutes, while providing punishment for a certain offence write: "shall be punishable with imprisonment for a term which may extend to.......... years, or fine or both."

Such a phrase gives latitude and complete discretion to courts to choose a portion of the provided maximum limits, while convicting an accused. This is so because the legislature had given the maximum limits of imprisonment for a particular offence, and the word "extend" gives courts the discretion and choice. It is true that the limits for use of courts' discretion cannot be fixed either by the law or precedents of courts themselves, because it depends on the facts and circumstances of each case.

The main criteria for limiting or extending the limits or sentence depends on two sane principles – namely on one hand the extent of period of imprisonment must be such that it may serve as a deterrent to others for prevention of crime, and on the other it should be moderate and reciprocal to the gravity. The presiding Judge decides the proportionality between the committed offence and the penalty according to the nature of facts, seriousness and circumstances etc. Nobody can provide a complete list of factors upon which considerations may be made for determining the amount of punishment, or develop a mathematical formula to measure gravity versus penalty ratio.

Not that, where the situation demands, the Courts never shirk from the responsibility and award maximum provided sentences. For instance, where the law has given two options to the court, either to award life imprisonment or the death penalty, Courts normally use first option using their discretion, but in "rarest of rare cases" they also award death penalty.

3.2.3 Punishments provided under section 3 of SC & ST Act

From the very beginning and since its coming into force, whenever the Scheduled Castes and the Scheduled Tribes (Prevention of Atrocities) Act, 1989 was constitutionally challenged before various High Courts and the Supreme Court, a common point of challenge was the stringent punishments provided by the Act, but the plea was set aside on various grounds and such provisions were upheld.

In an old case it was held that the punishment is in itself an evil which can only be justified by its effects in deterring the offender from committing the offence in future, besides deterring others by putting an example by such punishment. Thus punishment must be so maximum which will produce both of these effects.[1]

Though, the punishment provided by section 3 of the Act of 1989 have repeatedly been constitutionally upheld, but it is a fact that these provisions have restricted and confined the discretion of courts. For all the created offences under section 3(1), the prescribed punishment uses phrases like: "may extend to five years and with fine", but the phrase – "........... imprisonment for a term which shall not be less than six months......." abridges the discretion of courts. Similarly, section 3(2)(viii) and section 5 of the Act of 1989 provide the minimum limit as one year instead of six months provided elsewhere.

Sections 3, 4, 5, 6, 7 and 7A of Protection of Civil Rights Act, 1955 also provided the terms of punishment "of not less than one month", or in some cases minimum amount of fine has also been fixed. It was held, "the section prescribes a statutory minimum period of sentence and also a statutory minimum quantum of fine..........." therefore no discretion has been left with the court which is bound to impose sentence and also the fine.[2] But in other case where the lower court had imposed a fine of Rs 2 only, the High Court enhanced the amount of fine from Rs. 2 to Rs. 250.[3]

The study of human behaviour shows each individual is unique as far as his or her mental attitude in relation to society is concerned. No doubt the environment of individual under which he was brought up plays a considerable part. In that sense only a day's or few days imprisonment to an honorable man will have fair

1. *Mst. Nanhi Gond* v. *Emperor*, AIR 1927 Nag 221: 28 Cr LJ 493 (1927 Nag).
2. *State of Karnataka* v. *Annappa*, 1992 Cr LJ 158: ILR 1991 Kant 3220: 1991 (2) Kant LJ 8; also see *Mata Sewak Upadhyay* v. *State of Uttar Pradesh*, 1995 JIC 1168 (All) (FB): 1996 (1) East Cr C 97 (All) (FB) (1191).
3. (1976) 2 Kant LJ 457.

and more deterrent effect on the life of such individual, than long or very long periods of imprisonments would do on others.

The element of cruelty can be said to be inseparable part of any kind of punishment, therefore in the present civilized countries the focus has shifted from vengeful (based on cruelty) punishments to reformative types. The chief purpose of such reformation is that the socially misfit offenders could be transformed into an asset for the society.

Various systems were devised for reformation of criminals, and out of many pardon was one. But the Act of 1989 has again blocked the discretion of the courts through the provisions of section 19 of the Act, wherein it was provided that provisions of section 360 of Cr PC and Probation of Offenders Act, 1958 shall not apply to any person above the age of eighteen years when he was found guilty of an offence committed under the Act.

No doubt the Act of 1989 was enacted for achieving a 'special objective' – eradicating atrocities inflicted on members of Scheduled Castes and the Scheduled Tribes. About 22 years have elapsed and it seems the stringent provisions of the Act has done wonders during this long period, alongwith the provisions of "reservations" provided to such members in jobs, including political forums. The rapid economic growth and 'special' protection provided by various enactments, including the Act of 1989 has also increased the instances of its misuse as well as reactions from the other quarters.

Perhaps time has come to amend the Act of 1989 as far as stringency of the provided punishments are concerned, at least some dilution is need of the hour. The situation was recognised by Government of Uttar Pradesh, when it was headed by a member of Scheduled Castes as Chief Minister and in consequence a Government Order No. 92 M.M./6, Pu-3-2002-25-P/2002 dated 12 June, 2002 was issued. Para 22 of the said G.O. stipulates that some people for the purpose of defaming the Government get (false) cases registered under the provisions of the Scheduled Castes and the Scheduled Tribes (Prevention of Atrocities) Act, 1989 by using a member of such caste to get their scores settled with others. Therefore all the government agencies, including the police were ordered to prevent the misuse of the provisions of the Act and register such cases only after preliminary enquiry. The said order presumably would apply to even cases of rape or other heinous crimes. (Copy of the G.O. has been given in the Appendices).

3.3 Mens Rea

According to the rules of Common law *mens rea* is an essential ingredient of a criminal offence. There may be exceptions to this rule, besides, some statute may exclude *mens rea* from its ingredients, but in such cases the statute must expressly exclude it.

It was observed by Supreme Court that when the object of the statute is to promote welfare activities or to eradicate a grave social evil, is by itself not decisive of the question whether the element of guilty mind excluded from the ingredients of an offence.[1]

1. *Ravula Hariprasada Rao* v. *State*, AIR 1951 SC 204: 1951 SCJ 296: 1951 SCR 322; *Sarjoo Prasad* v. *State of Uttar Pradesh*, AIR 1961 SC 631: 1961 (2) SCA 456: (1961) 3 SCR 324; *Nathulal* v. *State of Madhya Pradesh.*, AIR 1966 SC 43: 1966 Cr LJ 71: 1966 (2) SCJ 421.

When offences mentioned in clauses (i) to (xv) under section 3(1) of the Act of 1989, the requirement of *mens rea* could be found to be present only in clauses (ii), (x) and (xi), and in the rest of the clauses the ingredient is missing. But in clauses (i) to (vii) of section 3(2) the most of the prescribed offences made *mens rea* as an essential part. Here a question may arise, if Parliament had deliberately omitted the most essential ingredient of *mens rea* in creating some offences mentioned in sub-section (1) of section 3 of the Act of 1989, why it was not mentioned expressly? However, a Full Bench of Allahabad High Court while dealing with the question held that: "Parliament did not think it necessary to make *mens rea* a necessary requirement of all the offences which is so normally required in other offences." It was observed that the Parliament is well aware that the accused persons go scot free due to legal quibblings in the courts and, therefore, from the ingredients of such offences, *mens rea* is omitted.[1]

In another case[2], Subba Rao J. delivering the dissenting judgment, cited scores of authorities and text books for deciding the point that where there is a statutory crime then, whether or not the element of *mens rea* is an essential ingredient? Following citations were made:

"In Russell on Crime, 11th Edn., Vol. I, it is stated at page 64:

> '........... there is a presumption that in any statutory crime the common law mental element, *mens rea*, is an essential ingredient."

On the question how to rebut this presumption, the learned author points out that the policy of the Courts is unpredictable. I shall notice some of the decisions which appear to substantiate the author's view. In Halsbury's Laws of England, 3rd Edn, Vol. 10, in para 508 at page 278, the following passage appears:

> 'A statutory crime may or may not contain an express definition of the necessary state of mind. A statute may require a specific intention, malice, knowledge, wilfulness, or recklessness. On the other hand, it may be silent as to any requirement of *mens rea*, and in such a case in order to determine whether or not *mens rea* is an essential element of the offence, it is necessary to look at the objects and terms of the statute."

This passage also indicates that the absence of any specific mention of a state of mind as an ingredient of an offence in a statute is not decisive of the question whether *mens rea* is an ingredient of the offence or not; it depends upon the object and the terms of the statute. So too, Archbold in his book on Criminal Pleading, Evidence and Practice, 35th Edn., says much to the same effect at page 48 thus:

> "It has always been a principle of the common law that *mens rea* is an essential element in the commission of any criminal offence against the common law........... In the case of statutory offences it depends on the effect of the statute. There is a presumption that *mens rea* is an essential ingredient in a statutory offence, but this presumption is liable to be

1. *Mata Sewak Upadhyay* v. *State of Uttar Pradesh*, 1995 JIC 1168 (All) (FB): 1996 (1) East Cr C 97 (All) (FB) (1191).
2. *State of Maharashtra* v. *Mayer Hans George*, AIR 1965 SC 722: (1965) 1 Cr LJ 641: (1966) 1 SCR 123.

displaced either by the words of the statute creating the offence or by the subject matter with which it deals."

'Coming to Indian decisions the Judicial Committee in *Sri Nivasa Mall* v. *Emperor*,[1] through Lord Du Pareq, approved the view expressed by Goddard C.J., in *Brend* v. *Wood*[2], observing: "Their Lordships agree with the view which was recently expressed by the Lord Chief Justice of England, when he said : 'It is in my opinion of the utmost importance for the protection of the liberty of the subject that the Court should always bear in mind that, unless the statute either clearly or by necessary implication, rules out *mens rea* as a constituent part of a crime, a defendant should not be found guilty of an offence against the criminal law unless he has got a guilty mind."

Summing up the discussion, Subba Rao J. in his dissenting judgment, concluded that; "the law on the subject relevant to the present enquiry may briefly be stated as follows. It is a well-settled principle of common law that *mens rea* is an essential ingredient of a criminal offence. *Doubtless a statute can exclude that element, but it is a sound rule of construction, adopted in England and also accepted in India to construe a statutory provision creating an offence in conformity with the common law rather than against it unless the statute expressly or by necessary implication excluded mens rea.* To put if differently, there is a presumption that *mens rea* is an essential ingredient of a statutory offence; but this may be rebutted by the express words of a statute creating the offence or by necessary implication. But the mere fact that [*the object of a statute is to promote welfare activities or to eradicate grave evil is in itself not decisive of the question whether the element of guilt is excluded from the ingredients of the offence.*] It is also necessary to enquire whether a statute by putting a person under strict liability helps him to assist the State in the enforcement of law: can he do anything to promote the observance of the law? A person who does not know that gold cannot be brought into India without a licence or is not bringing into India any gold at all cannot possibly do anything to promote the observance of the law. *Mens rea by necessary implication can be excluded from a statute only where it is absolutely clear that the implication of the subject of a statute would otherwise be defeated and its exclusion enables those put under strict liability by their act of omission to assist the promotion of law.* The nature of *mens rea* that will be implied in a statute creating an offence depends upon the object of the Act and the provisions thereof."[3]

By the above discussion it is clear that, though, *actus non facit reum nisi mens sit rea* is the cardinal doctrine of criminal jurisprudence but the legislature is empowered to create offences which consist solely in doing an act, without any intention or implied intention.

While dealing with the cases under section 3 of the Scheduled Castes and Scheduled Tribes (Prevention of Atrocities) Act, 1989, the court are often confronted with two types of questions relating to *mens rea,* intention or

---

1. AIR 1947 PC 135: 49 Bom LR 688: ILR 26 Pat 460.
2. 62 TLR 462: 175 LT 306: 110 JP 317
3. *State of Maharashtra* v. *Mayer Hans George*, AIR 1965 SC 722 (731): (1965) 1 Cr LJ 641: (1966) 1 SCR 123.

knowledge of the accused – namely (i) whether the main act constituting the criminal offence under the Act was intentional; and (ii) whether the accused had knowledge that the victim against whom the criminal act was done, was a member of Scheduled Caste or a Scheduled Tribe:

When the criminal acts prescribed under section 3 of the Act of 1989 were done which are covered under clauses (ii), (x) and (xi), where intention is one of the provided ingredients, generally the second instance (above mentioned) would apply; but, when an act is done not covered under such clauses, the question of intention would be presumed. A Division Bench had held that in a case of kidnapping and rape, there was no evidence to the effect that the offence was committed on the ground, that it was with knowledge and reason that the victim was a member of Scheduled Caste or a Scheduled Tribe, therefore accused were not liable under section 3 of the Act of 1989.[1] Similarly, simply addressing a person by his caste without any intention to insult does not constitute offence under the Act.[2]

In *Mata Sewak Upadhaya's case* Palok Basu and I.S. Mathur JJ. (Supra), in their majority judgment observed that offences will be made out under section 3 of the Act only if they are committed with the intention or necessary knowledge for the main offence, and in clear words, it must be established that the accused had knowledge regarding the victim belonging to Scheduled Caste/Scheduled Tribe, and that the offence was committed for that reason. But in a separate judgment Om Prakash J. held that knowledge on the part of the accused relating to the victim that he belonged to a Scheduled Caste or a Scheduled Tribe is presumed in the offences enumerated in section 3 of the Act.

It was held that unless the offence is committed with the knowledge that the injured or the deceased was a member of Scheduled Caste or Scheduled Tribe, the provision of the Act cannot be invoked.[3]

Going a step further M.P. High Court held that mechanical exercise of registration of a case by police, merely because complainant party belonged to Scheduled Caste cannot be allowed.[3]

But on the other hand it is clear that the legislature can create offence where *mens rea* may not be an ingredient, such as in Explosive Act or Food Adulteration Act, where mere possession of certain objects is crime without any *mens rea*.

3.4 Special and General Law

Section 41 of Indian Penal Code, 1860 defines: "special law" is a law applicable to a particular subject whereas section 42 of the same Act also defines "local law". It is well-settled that when there is a conflict between 'special law' and general law (as the IPC), the 'special law' will prevail.

But there is still another distinction. In the first instance a distinction may be made between a 'special law' and a 'local law' or general law, but in the second

---

1. *Tutu* alias *Bijaya Kumar Patnaik* v. *State of Orissa*, 2008 Cr LJ 3424 (Ori) (DB).
2. *Pappu Singh* v. *State of Uttar Pradesh*, 2002 Cr LJ 1251 (All) (1252): 2001 (3) All Cri R 2702: 2002 (46) All LR 586; 1998 Cri LR (Raj) 304.
3. *Karan Singh* v. *State of Madhya Pradesh*, (1992) Andh LT 509 (573): 1992 Cr LJ 3054 (MP).

instance, a distinction has to be made between an enactment which had created a new offence with a particular penalty and another Act seeking to enlarge the scope of the similar offences and the penalties thereof. An example could be cited for the first instance, the distinction between Excise Act, Opium Act, Cattle Trespass Act and SC & ST Act and Indian Penal Code; while for the second, a distinction between Protection of Civil Rights Act, 1955 and the Scheduled Castes and the Scheduled Tribes (Prevention of Atrocities) Act, 1989.

Another point which is worth mentioning here is that if an Act does not create a very new offence, but only a new kind of punishment, as was seen in the case of old and now repealed Whipping Act could not be said as 'special law', because it did not create any new offence, but only provided additional penalty to the already existing ones.

The 'Statement of Objects and Reasons' of the Scheduled Castes and the Scheduled Tribes (Prevention of Atrocities) Act, 1989, itself declares the Act to be a "Special Legislation". On the other counts there is no doubt that the Act of 1989 is a 'special law'. Since long, even Evidence Act was declared to be a 'special enactment' and accepted as such by various courts[1], though the said Act did not create any new offence. (For further details on the point please see "Introductory')

Section 3 and IPC:—Section 20 of The Scheduled Castes and the Scheduled Tribes (Prevention of Atrocities) Act, 1989 provides that, "the provisions of this Act shall have effect notwithstanding anything inconsistent therewith contained in any other law for the time being in force.........". As such the provisions of the Act would override other laws, as the heading of the section 20 prescribes.

It is a general rule that if a specific punishment has been provided by a Special Act, it would apply in preference to the general punishment provided in Indian Penal Code. But where the Special Act does not provide any such specific provision, the general law of the land would apply. This situation is applicable where the provisions of Special Act and the General Act are in conflict.

But for this applicability, there are two restrictions: (i) if it appears from the whole frame of the Special Act that it was intended to be complete in itself and the penalties can be enforced which have been prescribed by it. In such case the court cannot frame simultaneous charges and, (ii) any person cannot be punished twice *i.e.*, under the Special Act provisions as well as provisions contained in the general penal statute, because it would hit principle of double jeopardy. (for further details please see notes under section 20).

Section 3 and Cr PC:—Sections 18 and 19 of The Scheduled Castes and the Scheduled Tribes (Prevention of Atrocities) Act, 1989 have specifically barred the application of provisions of sections 438 and 360 of Criminal Procedure Code 1973, similar provisions were made under section 16A of Protection of Civil Rights Act, 1955.

Section 2(1)(b) defines "Code" to mean as Code of Criminal Procedure, 1973. Thus in other matters such as framing charges and procedure applied to trial etc., provisions of Cr PC would *mutatis mutandis* apply. According to one contention

1. *Emperor* v. *Fauzdar*, AIR 1933 All 440; *Hakim Khuda Yar* v. *Emperor*, AIR 1940 Lah 129: 41 Cr LJ 591 (Lah).

the Act of 1989 has only defined "atrocity" and not the "offence", which has been defined by Cr PC, hence accordingly Cr PC would override the provisions of the Act, according to sections 4 and 5 of Cr PC. It would be interesting to see when matter comes up before a court for decision. (For further details please see notes and comments under sections 18 and 19 of the Act and 'Introductory').

3.5 Private Complaint and section 3 of the Act

When a complaint was filed by a member of Scheduled Caste for two different incidents and she was not aware as well whether the police, had registered her case or not, it was held that there was no question as to call a report from the police under section 210 Cr PC. Importantly it was held that there is no bar of taking cognizance after the examination of complainant and the witneses have been completed under sections 200 and 202 of Cr PC. On the plea that the accused also belonged to Scheduled Caste, court declined to pass any order on the ground that no material was present before the court to this effect and the question can be decided only after the trial.[1]

Two important points were decided by another Bench,—namely, firstly that the Magistrate has no jurisdiction to take cognizance of a private complaint under section 3 of the Act of 1989 and only Special Judge is empowered to take such cognizance; and, secondly application of provisions of 197 Cr PC have to be strictly followed where the accused person was a public servant and was discharging his duty at the relevant time.[2] (Please also see Appendix II).

4. FIR under section 3 of the Act

To roll the wheels of the criminal justice system, it is necessary to lodge a 'first information report' with the police. A general procedure has been provided in Chapter XII of Cr PC 1973, comprising 25 sections (including 164A, 166A and 166B), for lodging/recording of FIR and a process followed thereafter. This chapter of the Code of Criminal Procedure governs the procedure to be followed by police when a 'first information report' has been lodged, in connection with commission of a cognizable or non-cognizable offence, declared by the legislature in a general or special law. But the first information reports 'lodged' under section 3 of the Act of 1989 would be governed by Rule 5 of the Scheduled Castes and the Scheduled Tribes (Prevention of Atrocities) Rules, 1995, and not by section 154 Cr PC which deals with "Informations in cognizable cases." Rule 5 reads as follows:

> "5. *Information to Police Officer in-charge of a Police Station.*—(1) Every information relating to the commission of an offence under the Act, if given orally to an officer in-charge of a police station shall be reduced to writing by him or under his direction, and be read over to the informant, and every such information, whether given in writing or reduced to writing as aforesaid, shall be signed by the persons giving it, and the substance thereof shall be entered in a book to be maintained by that police station.
>
> (2) A copy of the information as so recorded under sub-rule (1) above shall be given forthwith, free of cost, to the informant.

1. *Vidavaluru Balaramaiah* v. *State of Andhra Pradesh*, 2003 Cr LJ 3192 (AP): 2003 (1) Andh LT (Cri) 420 AP: 2004 (1) Rec Cri R 882.
2. *Dinakrushna* v. *Sunanda Behera*, 2003 Cr LJ (Supp) 5102: 2003 (12) All Ind Cas 71: 2003 (2) Ori LR 492; 1996 MPLJ 141 (FB).

(3) Any person aggrieved by a refusal on the part of an officer in-charge of a police station to record the information referred to in sub-rule (1) may send the substance of such information, in writing and by post, to the Superintendent of Police concerned who after investigation either by himself or by a police officer not below the rank of Deputy Superintendent of Police, shall make order in writing to the officer in-charge of the concerned police station to enter the substance of that information to be entered in the book to be maintained by that police station."

First parts of clause (1) and clause (3) of section 154 Cr PC have been copied *in verbatim* in sub-rules (1) and (3) of rule 5, while sub-rule (2) is the replica of sub-section (2) of section 154 Cr PC. Wordings in the later parts of sub-rules (1) and (3) have been changed. In latter part of sub-rule (1) of rule 5, the form prescribed by the State Government has been omitted to make it universal, as the forms prescribed by different State Governments in the country which are generally prescribed in the Police Regulations of the respective State, require different kinds of informations to be entered in the said format. For instance, U.P. Police Regulation in Para 97 (Part II Chapter X) mention: "Whenever information relating to the commission of a cognizable offence is given to an officer in-charge of a police station the report will immediately be taken down in triplicate in the check receipt book for reports of cognizable offences (Police Form No 341).............". Similar provisions exist in either Police Regulations or other circulars issued by the department and prescribing forms in this behalf.

In sub-rule (3) of the Rules of 1995, the words "not below the rank of Deputy Superintendent of Police" have been substituted for the words "by any police officer subordinate to him, in the manner provided by the Code, and such officer shall have all the powers of an officer in-charge .....". This substitution has to be made because the rule 7 of Rules of 1995 specifically allow "a police officer not below the rank of a Deputy Superintendent of Police to investigate the case." Therefore part played by "Officer in-charge of a Police Station", ends after he or she reduce, or got it to be reduced in writing the informations received relating to the commission of an offence under the Act of 1989, in the book maintained at the police station.

Though, the process of recording the FIRs are being governed by rule 5 of Rules of 1995, and not by section 154 Cr PC, but for other anomalies the rules laid down by different Courts in the country would apply. As FIR requires to contain basic prosecution case[1]. The answer to the question whether the FIR in a given case has been lodged belatedly or not is always a question of fact and has to be answered considering the delay in lodging of the FIR and the explanations furnished. There can be no mathematical computation of the time taken in lodging of the FIR. Court has to take into account whether the reason given for the delay was cogent or not and whether the delay was inordinate delay[2]. The FIR did not disclose any fact about presence of members of 'public' hence the accused was granted anticipatory bail:[3] (Please also see Appendix 1).

---

1. *Manoj* v. *State of Madhya Pradesh*, AIR 1999 SC 1403: 1999 (2) Crimes 329 (SC): 1999 Cr LJ 2095.
2. *State* v. *Joseph Mingal Koli*, (1997) 2 Crimes 228 (Bom).
3. *Mahesh Sakharam* v. *State of Maharashtra*, 2009 Cr LJ 3831 (Bom) (3833): 2009 (5) AIR Bom R 214: 2009 (2) Bom CR (Cri) 867.

5. Investigation under section 3 of the Act of 1989

Detailed procedure for investigation has been provided under the provisions of Chapter XII of Code of Criminal Procedure, 1973, starting from section 157 onwards.

But Rules of 1995, framed under the powers conferred under section 23 of the Scheduled Castes and the Scheduled Tribes (Prevention of Atrocities) Act, 1989, provide "special" procedure for appointment of "Investigating Officer" under Rule 7, which reads as follows:

> "7. *Investigating Officer.*—(1) An offence committed under the Act shall be investigated by a police officer not below the rank of a Deputy Superintendent of Police. The investigating officer shall be appointed by the State Government/Director-General of Police/Superintendent of Police after taking into account his past experience, sense of ability and justice to perceive the implications of the case and investigate it alongwith right lines within the shortest possible time.
>
> (2) The investigating officer so appointed under sub-rule (1) shall complete the investigation on top priority basis within thirty days and submit the report to the Superintendent of Police who in turn will immediately forward the report to the Director-General of Police of the State Government.
>
> (3) The Home Secretary and the Social Welfare Secretary of the State Government, the Director of Prosecution, the officer in-charge of Prosecution and the Director General of Police shall review by the end of every quarter the position of all investigations done by the investigating officer."

Sub-rule (1) of Rules of 1995 provide that investigations must be conducted by a police officer not below the rank of Deputy Superintendent of Police in respect of offences committed under section 3 of the Act of 1989. If the investigations were conducted by a Circle Inspector of Police, it was held to be illegal and it was quashed.[1]

The provisions of Rule 7 of Rules of 1995 is mandatory. Some other special legislations like Prevention of Corruption Act also provide similar mandatory provisions so that the offences committed under those special enactments must be investigated by officers of higher ranks, specially mentioned to have jurisdiction to investigate. But Supreme Court has observed in a case under PC Act:

> "......... that the function of investigation is merely to collect evidence and any irregularity or even illegality in the course of collection of evidence can scarcely be considered by itself to affect the legality of the trial by an otherwise competent Court of the offence so investigated. In *H.N. Rishbud and Inder Singh* v. *State of Delhi,* (1955) 1 SCR 1150: AIR 1955 SC 196: 1955 Cr LJ 526, it was held that an illegality committed in the course of investigation

1. *Tutu @ Bharatendu Balang* v. *State of Orissa,* 2003 Cr LJ 722: 2002 (23) OCR 31: 2002 (2) Ori LR 184; also see *D. Ramalinga Reddy @ D. Babu* v. *State of Andhra Pradesh.,* 1999 Cr LJ 2918 (AP) (2919): 1999 (2) Andh LD 572: 1999 (2) Crimes 343.

does not affect the competence and jurisdiction of the Court for trial and where cognizance of the case in fact been taken and the case has proceeded to terminating the invalidity of the proceeding investigation does not vitiate the result unless miscarriage of justice has been caused thereby. When any breach of the mandatory provisions relating to investigation is brought to the notice of the Court at an early stage of trial the Court will have to consider the nature and extent of the violation and pass appropriate orders for such reinvestigation as may be called for, wholly or partly, and by such officer as it considers appropriate with reference to the requirements of section 5A of the Prevention of Corruption Act.........."[1]

In a rape case under the Act, the investigation was conducted by inspector of police who had filed charge-sheet and the Session Judge convicted the accused under section 376 IPC, read with section 3(2)(v) of Scheduled Castes and the Scheduled Tribes (Prevention of Atrocities) Act, 1989, for imprisonment for life.

A question was raised before the Division Beach involving Rule 7 of Rules of 1995, as to whether it is mandatory that the investigation must have been done by a police officer not below the rank of Deputy Superintendent of police, while that case was investigated by a police inspector. Considering the facts and the evidence recorded, it was held that offence under section 376, IPC has been proved, but the claim of the victim being a member of the Scheduled Caste not proved due to contradictory evidence hence, application of provisions of section 3(2)(v) not proved and consequently the mandatory provision of Rule 7 was not attracted[2].

Where the investigation was made by a Circle Inspector of Police under Protection of Civil Rights Act, 1955, but at the time of filing of the charge-sheet it was found that the case falls under the provisions of SC and ST (PoA) Act, hence the charge-sheet was filed by Assistant Commissioner of Police, this was questioned before the High Court. It was held that the filed charge-sheet was on the basis of investigation by the Circle Inspector, who was not competent to investigate the case under the Act due to a bar under Rule 7, and it was a violation as such.[3]

Under an offence registered under sections 341/323/34 IPC, read with section 3 of the Act of 1989, the police inspector conducted raid on the houses of the petitioners and got them declared absconders by the Court. The petitioners, while having obtained an order from the High Court regarding their bail on surrender, moved the District Court to recall the order of cognizance but the District Court declined to recall the order. They went to High Court, again it was held that the raids and the accused shown as absconders was not investigation which was illegally conducted in contravention to Rule 7, and as such the order of cognizance was set aside.[4]

---

1. *A.C. Sharma* v. *Delhi Administration*, 1973 Cr LJ 902: AIR 1973 SC 913: 1973 All Cri R 104.
2. *Dasarathi Sahukar* v. *State*, 2007 Cr LJ 3445 (Ori) (DB): 2007 (37) OCR 802.
3. *M. Niranjan Reddy* v. *State of Andhra Pradesh*, 2000 Cr LJ 3125 (AP): 2000 (2) Andh LT (Cri) 164; *Pentakota Rao* v. *State*, (1999) 1 Andh LT (Cri) 236.
4. *Pradeep Pradhan* v. *State of Orissa*, 2005 Cr LJ 1859 (Ori): 2005 (28) All Ind Cas 360: 2005 (2) Crimes 413.

5.1 Delay in Investigation

Rule 7(2) of rules framed under the Act and approved by both the Houses of the Parliament as provided under section 23 of the Act, provides that the investigating officer appointed under sub-rule (1) of rule 7 shall complete the investigation "within thirty days and submit the report to the Superintendent of Police who in turn will immediately forward the report to the Director-General of Police of the State Government."

Sub-rule (3) of Rule 7 further complicates the matter, wherein Home Secretary, Social Welfare Secretary of the State Government, Director of Prosecution the officer in-charge of Prosecution and the Director-General of Police are required to review the position of all investigations at the end of every quarter.

Provisions of sub-rules (2) and (3) seem to be incomplete and vague. The word "report" used in sub-rule (2) cannot be construed and equated with the same word used in section 101 Cr PC. The word "report" in sub-rule 2 perhaps refer to charges-sheet or the 'final report' mentioned in section 173 of Cr PC, because the word used here referred to a "report" at the completion of the investigation, that too within thirty days.

Sub-rule (2) of Rule 7 is silent what would happen to it after such "report" has been forwarded to the Director General of Police of the State *via* Superintendent of Police concerned. Perhaps it is expected that the charge-sheet or the final report as the case may be, after the investigation has been completed, would be sent to the Court concerned having jurisdiction.

However, the provisions of section 167(2)(a)(ii) of Cr PC would be applicable for purposes of bail, in case the charge-sheet has not been put before the Court concerned within the stipulated period. It is so because all the other provisions of Cr PC relating to investigation, such as examination of witnesses (sections 160 and 161) or 'Search' (section 165) etc., are applicable to the investigations under section 3 of the Act.

6. Cognizance of Offence under section 3 of the Act

The word 'cognizance' has neither been defined by the Act of 1989 nor the Code of Criminal Procedure, 1973. Section 190 of Cr PC provides how the Courts (Magistrates) should take cognizance and how it would be dealt with.

Section 14 of the Scheduled Castes and the Scheduled Tribes (Prevention of Atrocities) Act, 1989 provides for establishment of a "Special Court" in each district throughout the country "to try the offences under this Act."

In the early stages when the Act of 1989 came into force some confusion prevailed as to who was competent to take cognizance of offences committed under section 3 of the Act. But gradually the well accepted position was developed by the Courts.

In one such case a Judicial Magistrate took cognizance of offences punishable under various sections of the Indian Penal Code as well as under section 3 of the Scheduled Castes and the Scheduled Tribes (Prevention of Atrocities) Act, 1989, on 23-10-1992. The matter of taking cognizance was agitated before the High Court on the ground that Magistrate was not empowered to take cognizance of offences under section 3 of the Act, neither the Magistrate had any jurisdiction in the matter. The court also considered another question, whether the Special Court constituted under the Act of 1989 can deal with the offences punishable under various provisions of Indian Penal Code as well. The law on this point had already been settled that the special court is not only empowered and has jurisdiction to try the offences under section 3 of the Act of 1989, but also offences committed under other enactments in the same transaction. Therefore the accused may be tried in the same proceedings and for that purpose, no order of commitment by the Magistrate is necessary. If the Magistrate is satisfied that *prima facie* materials exist to show commission of offences punishable under the Act of 1989, he should return the case for presentation to the proper court with an endorsement to that effect.[1]

It was held that this being the correct position of law that the Magistrate has no jurisdiction to take cognizance and proper course for him was to return the complaint for presentation to the proper Court.[2] [This finding was later reversed by Supreme Court[3]].

But later on the position had changed through decisions of various High Courts in the country including a Full Bench of Kerala High Court and endorsed the view taken by the Court, mentioned above. This Full Bench of Kerala H.C. was later on overruled by Supreme Court.[3] Not this Full Bench decision but all the decisions which ruled that the Special Court is a Court of original Jurisdiction and empowered to take direct cognizance were overruled and it was held that Special Court cannot take cognizance without the case being committed to it under section 193 Cr PC by a Magistrate.

A Division Bench of A.P. High Court discussed the matter in detail and even dissented from the view taken by the Full Bench of Kerala High Court, and accepted the decision approved by Supreme Court. The Division Bench held that the Charge-sheet should be filed in the court of concerned Magistrate of the First Class for securing committal of the accused to the Court of Sessions constituted as *Special Court* under the Act of 1989. One more aspect was clarified relating to the offences committed under section 3 of the Act, as well under the Indian Penal Code. The Division Bench sat to decide the question referred under section 395(2) Cr PC, as to whether the Special Court, which had taken cognizance of offences under the Act of 1989 and even made some progress in the case, can proceed and complete the trial in view of observation made by Supreme Court in *Mohammad Safi* v. *State of West Bengal*.[4] which was:

"Whether the proceedings would become *null* and *void* in cases where cognizance of the offences was taken contrary to the prohibition in section 193 Cr PC.........."[5]

1. *Pratap Chandra Barik* v. *State of Orissa*, 1999 Cr LJ 562 (Ori): 1998 (15) OCR 98; also see *Bandaru Venkata Swami* v. *State of Andhra Pradesh*, 2001 Cr LJ 1889: 2000 (2) Andh LT (Cri) 84.
2. *ibid.*
3. *Gangula Ashok* v. *State of Andhra Pradesh*, 2000 Cr LJ 819 (SC): AIR 2000 SC 740: 2000 AIR SCW 279.
4. AIR 1966 SC 69: 1966 Cr LJ 75.
5. *In Re: Referring Officer, Addl. District and Sessions Judge, Srikakulam*, 2000 Cr LJ 3422 (AP) (DB): 2000 (1) Andh LT (Cri) 388.

Overruling the Full Bench [*Hareendran* v. *Sarada*, 1995 AIHC 4552: (1996) 1 Andh. LJ (Cri) 162 (Ker (FB)], Supreme Court held that Special Court mentioned in the Scheduled Castes and the Scheduled Tribes (Prevention of Atrocities) Act, 1989, cannot take cognizance of any offence without case being committed to that as provided under section 193 Cr PC.[1]

Before the decision in *Gangula Ashok's* case (Supra) came, a very confusing situation was prevailing in the country, as different High Courts in the country were delivering contradictory opinions on the point of jurisdiction of Special Court to take cognizance. Different reasons were given to emphasise respective point of views. (The available decisions have been discussed here)

In another case, Jharkhand High Court compared provisions of section 3 of the Act of 1989 and section 190 Cr PC, where the Magistrate took cognizance on the protest application at the submission of 'final report' by the investigating officer. The accused forcibly took Adivasi girl in a car and tried to rape her. The case was investigated by Dy. Supdt. of Police, who was competent to investigate, but in the end submitted a 'Final report'. The Chief Judicial Magistrate thereafter took cognizance on the basis of materials available in the case diary and issued notice to the accused. It was held that order of Magistrate taking cognizance was proper and legal.[2]

7. Constitutionality of section 3 of the Act

Time and again constitutionality of section 3 of the Scheduled Castes and the Scheduled Tribes (Prevention of Atrocities) Act, 1989 as a whole was challenged before different High Courts and the Supreme Court. The points of agitations for declaring the Act as unconstitutional were based on various grounds, which are discussed below.

7.1 Articles 15, 17, 35 and 46 and the Act

It was argued that the Act of 1989 is based on caste, hence violative of Article 15(1) and it cannot be saved by Art. 15(4) provided as an exception. Art 15(1) injucts the State from discriminating against any citizen on ground of religion, race, caste, sex, place of birth or any of them, and that the Act creates two groups of people on caste basis, therefore it is a caste legislation. The Act could have been saved under Article 15(4), if only it had been legislated for the 'advancement' of the Scheduled Castes and the Scheduled Tribes, but instead the Act is a punitive legislation, therefore the Act does not serve any purpose for the 'advancement' of such group.[3]

It was observed that Art. 17 of the Constitution prescribes the 'untouchability' as an offence and Art. 35, with *non-obstinate* clause which overrides all other

1. *Gangula Ashok* v. *State of Andhra Pradesh*, 2000 Cr LJ 819 (SC): AIR 2000 SC 740: 2000 AIR SCW 279; endorsing the view taken in *Meera Bai* v. *Bhujbal Singh*, 1995 Cr LJ 2376 (MP) (DB): 1995 (3) Rec Cri R 125; *Pappu Singh* v. *State of Uttar Pradesh*, 1995 Cr LJ 2803 (All) (2804): 1995 All LJ 1037: 1994 (3) Cur CriR 1947; *Jhagru* v. *State*, (1993) 1 Crimes 643 (Pat); *Jyoti Arora* v. *State of Haryana*, 1998 Cr LJ 2662 (P&H): 1997 (24) Cri LT 672: 1998 (4) Crimes 643: (1998) 2 All Cr LR 73.
2. *Deepak Kumar Lal* v. *State of Jharkhand*, 2006 Cr LJ 299 (Jhar): 2005 (27) All Ind Cas 226: 2004 (3) BLJR 2027.
3. *Mata Sewak Upadhyay* v. *State of Uttar Pradesh*, 1995 JIC 1168 (All) (FB): 1996 (1) East Cr C 97 (All) (FB).

provisions of the Constitution, makes it obligatory to the Parliament to make laws declaring offences and punishments thereof under Part III of the Constitution. Therefore offences of 'atrocities' provided under section 3(1) and (2) of the Act stem from the enforcement of disability arising out of untouchability.[1]

Similarly, Art. 46 in Part IV mandates that the state shall promote the economic and educational interests of weaker sections of people and protect them from social injustice and exploitation. Thus the provisions of the Act of 1989 is being saved by Art. 15(4) and are fully constitutional.[1]

The provision for offences enumerated in section 3 of the Act of 1989 is actually meant for purpose of achieving its object *viz.*, inhuman sufferings and exploitation of socially downtrodden, and as such, is for the advancement of the members of the Scheduled Castes and the Scheduled Tribes. The legislature has jurisdiction and authority to make such provisions, by exercising powers under Act 15(4) of the Constitution. Therefore the Act is protected under Art. 15(a) of Constitution[2].

It was observed by another Court that Art. 17 of the Constitution was "self-operating" and if read with Art. 35(a)(II), the irresistible conclusion follows that untouchability has been abolished and its practice in any form is forbidden. And the present legislation (Act of 1989) falling within the field of this provision. The word 'untouchability' is to be understood in its historical sense and not in grammatical sense. (*Devarajiah* v. *B. Padamma*, AIR 1958 Mys 84). The Art. 17 is similar to 13th Amendment of the Constitution of the United States of America which abolished slavery and empowered Congress to enforce the abolition by appropriate means (like Art. 35). The Congress was empowered to enact statutes to penalize the offenders.[3]

7.2 Legislative Competency of Parliament to Enact Act of 1989

When the legislative competency of Parliament was challenged, the Court observed that Art. 35 and Art. 17 both falling in Part III of the Constitution and are self-contained. Art. 35, notwithstanding anything contained in the Constitution, empowers the Parliament to prescribe punishments for the acts which are declared to be offences under Part III. But for Articles 17 and 35, the legislative power in respect of officers relating to the enforcement of disability arising out of untouchability would have been determined under Art. 246 which confers legislative power, read with Lists I, II and III in 7th Schedule. For the offence declared under Art. 17, there is no need to take recourse to Art. 246 and Lists I, II and III in the 7th Schedule. Article 17 itself declares untouchability as an offence, while Art. 35 confers power exclusively to the Parliament to prescribe punishment for the acts which are declared to be offences under Part III, besides Art. 35 further obligates upon the Parliament to make laws for punishment for

1. *Mata Sewak Upadhyay* v. *State of Uttar Pradesh*, 1995 JIC 1168 (All) (FB): 1996 (1) East Cr C 97 (All) (FB).
2. *Dr. Ram Krishna Balothia* v. *Union of India*, 1994 Cr LJ 2658 (MP) (DB): AIR 1994 MP 143: 1994 MPLJ 644 (This DB was reversed on another point by SC, *State of Madhya Pradesh* v. *Ram Krishna Balothia*, 1995 Cr LJ 2076 (SC): AIR 1995 SC 1198: 1995 AIR SCW 1267: JT 1995 (1) SC 310.
3. *Jai Singh* v. *Union of India*, 1993 Cr LJ 2705 (FB) (Raj): AIR 1993 Raj 177: 1993 (1) Raj LW 157.

the acts enumerated in Part III, immediately after the commencement of the Constitution. Art. 17 abolishes "Untouchability", therefore the onerous task is entrusted to the Parliament to punish guilty persons suitably. Because of these reasons Parliament alone is competent and also responsible for enacting the Act of 1989[1].

It was further held that the Act of 1989 made by the Parliament is otherwise valid, and does not cross over the limits imposed by Part III of the Constitution, thus cannot be declared *ultra vires*. The argument is not correct, as Articles 245(1) and 246 confer power on the Parliament to make laws with regard to matters enumerated in the List I of the 7th Schedule of the Constitution under the field conferred, the Parliament has supremacy and its powers are only limited by:

(1) The fundamental rights guaranteed by part III of the Constitution.
(2) The distribution of powers *i.e.,* the limitation imposed by the Entries in the Union List on which the Union may legislate.
(3) Mandatory provisions of the Constitution which imposed limitations upon the powers by Articles 286, 301 and 303.

It was also observed that court may have its own views on a particular matter but it cannot question the wisdom of Parliament. If a legislation is within the competence of Parliament, and does not infringe Part III of the Constitution, it has to be accepted. The judicial process does not lay where the Parliament has exclusive jurisdiction.[2]

7.3 *Whether section 3 is discriminatory or Violative of Article 14*

It was argued that section 3 of the Act of 1989 treats the accused differently from that of members of Scheduled Castes and the Scheduled Tribes. The two types of accused may be namely, (i) belonging to Scheduled Castes and the Scheduled Tribes; and, (ii) not belonging to that class. When the accused belonging to these two groups commit one and the same offence jointly which is an offence of atrocities under the Act of 1989, then the accused belonging to the latter category will be subjected by a Special Court to severe punishment and the other accused belonging to the former category will be subjected to a lessor punishment under the Penal Code. In short, the Act was challenged as such to be violative of Article 14 of the Constitution.

Supreme Court had interpreted Article 14 in *Shri Ram Krishna Dalmia* v. *Justice S.R. Tendulkar*[3], as:

> "It is well-established that while Article 14 forbids class legislation, it does not forbid reasonable classification for the purpose of legislation. In order, however, to pass the test of permissible classification, two conditions must be founded on an intelligible differential which distinguishes persons or things that are grouped together from others left out of the group; and
>
> (2) that differentiation must have a rational relation to the objects sought to be achieved by the statute in question. The classification may be founded on different basis, namely, geography or according to objects or

---

1. *Mata Sewak Upadhyay* v. *State of Uttar Pradesh*, 1995 JIC 1168 (All) (FB): 1996 (1) East Cr C 97 (All) (FB).
2. *Jai Singh and others*, 1993 Cr LJ 2705: AIR 1993 Raj 177: 1993 (1) Raj LW 157 (Raj) (FB).
3. AIR 1958 SC 538: 1958 SCA 754: 1959 SCJ 147.

occupation or the like. What is necessary is that there must be a nexus between the basis of the classification and the objects of the Act under consideration."

Starting from *Maneka Gandhi* v. *Union of India*[1] case Supreme Court has been reading something more in Article 14 of the Constitution. "Equality" and "arbitrariness" are sworn enemies to each other, as one belong to rule of law while the other to the whim and caprice of the absolute monarch. When an act becomes arbitrary, only then that act violates Art. 14.

The offences of atrocities as has been enumerated in section 3 of the Act of 1989 are committed by a specified group against the other specified group. This classification was declared to be valid and there being no arbitrariness.[2]

The offences enumerated under section 3 of the Act of 1989 are offences which denigrate members of Scheduled Castes and the Scheduled Tribes in the eyes of society, and to prevent them from leading a life of dignity and self-respect. These offences constitute a separate class and cannot be compared with offences under the Penal Code. Therefore these offences cannot be said as violative of Articles 14 of the Constitution. As well as the offences prescribed under section 3(1) arise out of the practice of "untouchability".[3]

When it was argued that there is a hostile discrimination in-between the persons belonging to caste Hindu and those who did not. It was held that what has been prescribed by section 3 is "that caste Hindu should not indulge in activities which may be considered as having not treated the Shudras or persons of Scheduled Tribes of unequal level."[4] [For further details please see comments on section 3(1)]

7.4 Omission of **Mens Rea** *in Section 3 – Arbitrary*

It was argued that *mens rea* is an essential ingredient of a criminal offence (already discussed in detail previously), and its absence from some of prescribed offences enumerated in section 3 of the Act of 1989, is inconsistent to the criminal jurisprudence, therefore it being arbitrary for that reason thus liable to be struck down.

Answering the question, the court observed – "can an offence be termed and will that be liable to be struck down on the ground of *mens rea* being omitted?", the Bench further observed: untouchability is not a separate institution by itself; it is a corollary of the institution of the caste system of Hindu society. It is an attitude on the part of a whole group of people, K. Ramaswami J. in his separate but concurring judgment in the *Appa Balu Ingle*[5] had observed, "..........It is an attitude to regard Dalits as pollutants: inferior and out caste. It is not founded on *mens rea*."

1. AIR 1978 SC 597: (1978) 1 SCC 248: (1978) 2 SCR 621.
2. *Mata Sewak Upadhyay* v. *State of Uttar Pradesh*, 1995 JIC 1168 (All) (FB): 1996 (1) East Cr C 97 (All) (FB); also see 1997 (1) East Cri C 328: 2 BLJR 1029 (Pat)
3. *State of Madhya Pradesh* v. *Ram Krishna Balothia*, 1995 Cr LJ 2076 (SC): AIR 1995 SC 1198: 1995 AIR SCW 1267: JT 1995 (1) SC 310; (Reversing *Dr. Ram Krishna Balothia* v. *Union of India*, 1994 Cr LJ 2658 (MP) (DB): AIR 1994 MP 143: 1994 MPLJ 644.
4. *Jai Singh* v. *Union of India*, 1993 Cr LJ 2705 (FB) (Raj) (2713): AIR 1993 Raj 177: 1993 (1) Raj LW 157.
5. *State of Karnataka* v. *Appa Balu Ingale*, 1993 Cr LJ 1029 (SC): AIR 1993 SC 1126: 1993 AIR SCW 337.

Parliament saw that despite existing provisions of Act of 1955, the offences continued unabated as these punishments fell short and proved ineffective and to give more teeth, the Parliament enacted Act of 1989 to curb the increasing menace. It was observed that the Parliament was of the view that the whole object of the enactment would be defeated if *mens rea* is made a necessary ingredient of the prescribed offences. Besides, in fact *mens rea* was omitted in few of the offences under section 3(1), but most of the offences mentioned in section 3(2) of the Act of 1989 contains *mens rea* as a necessary condition. Therefore it would be appropriate to hold that the Parliament had delibertely excluded *mens rea* from few offences under section 3(1) of the Act.[1]

7.5 Providing Minimum Punishment – Arbitrary

Section 3 of the Scheduled Castes and the Scheduled Tribes (Prevention of Atrocities) Act, 1989 was constitutionally challenged on the ground that offences under clauses (i), (ii), (iii) and (vii) of section 3(2) of the Act are void being arbitrary, inasmuch as minimum punishment is prescribed thereunder.

Whereas under clause (i) punishment of imprisonment for life with fine or punishment of death, as the case may be, is prescribed, under clause (ii) and (iii) minimum punishment for six months imprisonment has been provided. Under clause (vii) minimum punishment of one year imprisonment is provided.

Minimum punishment is not provided for the first time while enacting the said Act, but several enactments, which are punitive in nature, provide minimum punishment. Under section 302 IPC the minimum punishment is imprisonment for life for committing murder. It is for the legislature to decide the quantum of punishment. Once a legislature is competent to legislate about the offences and the punishments, then it may provide a punishment depending on the gravity of the offence, and no offence can be declared void on the ground of excessive punishment, which is exclusively in the domain of the legislature, court said.

The Court also observed that this argument is in complete disregard of Art. 35(a)(ii) of the Constitution, which stipulates and mandates that the Parliament should discharge its duties for providing punishments for offences under Part III of the Constitution. Therefore minimum punishments provided under clauses (i), (ii), (iii) and (vii) of section 3 of the Act are the result of constitutional mandate, and cannot be said to be arbitrary or void.[1]

7.6 Providing Severe Punishments – Arbitrary

The Act of 1989 was challenged for providing severe punishments for offences mentioned in section 3 and on the ground that the punishments should have been made in accordance with the degree of moral blameworthiness.

It was observed that Judges' task, after all, is to do justice and see how the punishment is related to justice, except by asking whether it deserved or not. If punishments were to be based purely on theories of deterrence and reformation and the question of what the accused deserved were to be eliminated, would not the concept of justice be eliminated too? The courts constantly act on the assumption, that the punishment must be appropriate to guilt.

1. *Mata Sewak Upadhyay* v. *State of Uttar Pradesh*, 1995 JIC 1168 (All) (FB): 1996 (1) East Cr C 97 (All) (FB).

Denning J. observed: "The punishment inflicted for grave crimes should reflect the revulsion felt by the great majority of citizens of them. It is mistake to consider the object of punishment as being deterrent or reformative or preventive and nothing else. .... The ultimate jurisdiction of any punishment is not that it is deterrent, but it is the emphatic denunciation by the community of crime........"

In fact different Judges impose punishment differently and even the same Judge is not always consistent in his 'sentencing'. There cannot be agreement among Judges as to what criteria ought to be fixed or taken while a sentencing decision is given. The court was answering thus an argument that section 3 of the Act of 1989 has provided severe punishment for most trivial acts.

The Bench further went on that the maxim, *de minimus non curat lex* is applicable to criminal cases and the courts would not forget to take into account the said maxim while passing sentences for the offences committed under the said section, hence apprehension of some of the counsel that even in cases of most trivial nature severe punishment would be awarded, has no substance. As such sections 3 and 4 of the Act of 1989 cannot be held *ultra vires*.[1]

7.7 Vagueness of Procedure and Provisions to Hold the Act Void

The Act of 1989 was constitutionally challenged on the ground that unlike Terrorist and Disruptive Activities (Prevention) Act, 1987 (TADA) and Narcotic Drugs and Psychotropic Substances Act, 1985, there is no provision under the Act of 1989 to take cognizance for offences under section 3, therefore the said provision is vague and as such void.

In reply, the Bench observed that section 193 of Cr PC states that except as otherwise expressly provided by the Code or by any other law for the time being in force, no Court of Sessions shall take cognizance of any offence as a court of original jurisdiction, unless the case has been committed to it by a Magistrate. (Since then several Courts upheld this procedure – please see the head-note 'Cognizance')

A second point raised on the Act of 1989 for it being void on the basis of vagueness, was that the Act is a fraud on the Constitution, as no provision enabling the Special Courts under the Act to take cognizance of offences under section 3(1) of the Act has been made to ensure speedy trial and that the accused persons subjected to Special Courts under the Act are left at the mercy of the Magistrate, who is in seize of committal proceedings. Unless committal proceedings are over, the proceedings of the Special Court cannot begin and that may considerably delay the trial before the Court of Sessions. Special Courts are being constituted under section 14 of the Act of 1989, which are also bound to ensure speedy trial, but in fact, there will be no speedy trial, as the Special Court is not competent to take cognizance of offences enumerated under section 3 of the Act, unless the case is committed to Special Court by a Magistrate.

The Bench, though accepted that if the Special Courts under the Act, were given power to take cognizance of the offences under section 3 of the Act

1. *Jai Singh* v. *Union of India*, 1993 Cr LJ 2705 (FB) (Raj) (2713): AIR 1993 Raj 177: 1993 (1) Raj LW 157.

directly, the trial would have been speedier, but, the Bench observed that there is no legitimacy in such an argument that in absence of such power there will be no speedy trial at all. A Magistrate cannot delay the committal proceedings whimsically. A Magistrate is expected to act as expeditiously as possible and, therefore, the apprehension of delayed committal proceedings is unfounded. Conferment of power to Special Court to take cognizance directly would have been an ideal situation as has been given under TADA and Narcotic Act, and it was suggested that, earlier the better, Parliament should amend section 14 to this effect to ensure speedy Trial. But in absence of such powers of Special Courts that cannot be stretched to the extent that Parliament played a fraud on the Constitution by not conferring power to Special Court to take direct cognizance. Therefore the argument that absence of control of Special Court on committal proceedings thereby ensuring speedy Trial and hence arbitrary has to be rejected.

As to False Proceedings under section 3(viii):—The third point raised as to the vagueness of provision of section 3(1)(viii), which says – "(viii) institutes false, malicious or vexations suit or criminal or other legal proceedings against a member of a Scheduled Caste or a Scheduled Tribe;". An argument was forwarded that the Act is arbitrary and vague for the reason that it does not give any guidance or guideline whether proceedings for the offences envisaged by clause (viii) of section 3(1) can be taken up only after conclusion of the false, malicious or vexatious suit or criminal or other proceedings against the member of a Scheduled Caste or a Scheduled Tribe, and whether the Special Court can hold a parallel enquiry as to the falsity of the suit or criminal or other legal proceedings when such suits or the proceedings are already pending before the Competent Court.

In reply to this contention, the Hon'ble Bench conceded to the opinion given by the counsel representing the Union of India, who opined that proceedings in connection with such offences will be taken up before the Special Court only after the suit or other legal proceedings are concluded and where that court found the suit or other legal proodings were false, malicious or vexatious only then the Special Court may proceed under section 3(1)(viii). In the end plea was rejected.[1]

7.8 Plurality of Offences and Trial under section 3

It was argued before the Bench that if accused commits various offences in the same transaction, some of which may not be covered under atrocities described under section 3 of the Act of 1989 and for which the Special Court is empowered to take cognizance, then multiple trials cannot be avoided. To obviate split, trials for instance under the provisions of U.P. Gangster and Anti-Social Activities (Prevention) Act, 1986, the Special Court is empowered to try allied offences as well. But section 14 of the Act of 1989 allows the Special Court to take cognizance of offences committed only under the Act. Such analogous provision has not been made under the Act, therefore it being vague and unworkable and liable to be struck down.

It was observed that section 218(1) of the Code of Criminal Procedure envisages the rule that for every distinct offence there shall be a separate charge

1. *Mata Sewak Upadhyay* v. *State of Uttar Pradesh*, 1995 JIC 1168 (1193) (All) (FB): 1996 (1) East Cr C 97 (All) (FB).

and every such charge shall be tried separately. For convenience sake, the rule has been diluted, inasmuch as section 220(1) Cr PC provides that if in one series of acts so connected together as to form the same transaction, more offences than one are committed by the same person, he may be charged with and tried at one trial for every such offence. Section 223(d) Cr PC permits that persons accused of different offences committed in the course of same transaction may be charged and tried together. Section 193 Cr PC declares that except as otherwise provided expressly, no Court of Sessions shall take cognizance of any offence as a court of original jurisdiction unless the case has been committed to it by a Magistrate under the Code. The Special Court under section 14, being the Court of Sessions and will continue to be so despite designated as a Special Court under section 14 of the Act of 1989, will, therefore, proceed to decide the case which has been committed to it. There being sufficient guidelines on the joinder of charges and for combining them in a single trial, a case of offences in plurality cannot be made out. Thus there is no ambiguity and unworkability for section 14 of the Act.[1]

7.9 Compounding of Offences under the Act

The offences which were created for the Protection of Civil Rights Act, 1955 were, though, provided lessor punishments, were held to be non-compoundable.

Earlier Madras High Court held that when the affected parties themselves come before the court and were prepared to compound the offence, there is no reason why the court should not accept the same.[2]

But later on a Division Bench of Karnataka High Court, dissenting from single Judge Bench of Madras (ibid), held that offences alleged *per se* are not compoundable even with the permission of the Court, because of the simple reason that neither the Special Act nor section 320 Cr PC make the offences compoundable either with or without permission of the Court. Once State prosecutes a person for contravention of provisions of certain act, thereafter the individuals who were responsible for initiating action by police, could not, without the reference to the State which indeed is *de jure*, possibly ask the Court to free the accused of the charges, without the reference being made to the State.[3]

Same opinion was given by MP High Court that the offences cannot be covered under section 320 Cr PC.

7.10 Bail under Section 3 of the Act

(Please see comments under section 18 and Appendix 2)

7.11 Presumption of Knowledge of Accused About the Caste of Victim

Section 3 of the Act of 1989 was challenged as to its validity on the ground that prior knowledge on the part of accused of the fact that the victim belongs to a Scheduled Caste or a Scheduled Tribe has not been made necessary, and it is not so made an ingredient of the offences of atrocities under section 3, therefore the same is void.

1. *Mata Sewak Upadhyay* v. *State of Uttar Pradesh*, 1995 JIC 1168 (1196-97) (All) (FB): 1996 (1) East Cr C 97 (All) (FB).
2. *Dhanraj* v. *State*, 1986 Cr LJ 284 (Mad): 1985 Mad LW (Cri) 81.
3. *State* v. *Kudligere Hanumanthappa*, 1992 Cr LJ 832: 1991 (1) Kant LJ 622; *State* v. *Kapoore*, 1983 Cr LJ (NOC) 15.

The Bench conceded that prior knowledge of the accused of the fact that victim belonged to Scheduled Caste or a Scheduled Tribe has not been expressly stated as an ingredient in any of the clauses of section 3. Rejecting the submissions of State as to the powers of the Parliament to enact special enactments in special circumstances etc., the Bench held that the knowledge on the part of accused of such fact is nothing but a mental state of the accused and that knowledge could be "presumed". The Bench observed: "......... it will be more reasonable to hold that a presumption was raised under section 3 so far as knowledge on the part of the accused is concerned, because it would be easier for the accused to prove that an offence of atrocity under section 3 of the Act was not committed by him with the knowledge that the victim belonged to a Scheduled Caste or a Scheduled Tribe."

It is submitted that such an analogy would put a burden on the accused to prove his innocence and that would be against all the basic and cardinal rules of criminal jurisprudence. Besides, presuming an inherent "presumption" embodied in the ingredients of section 3 of the Act would defy rules of interpretation of statutes. In the first place if existence of an inherent embedded presumption was presumed, then the accused's rights of rebuttal of such presumption was discussed referring to the ruling given by Supreme Court in *Sanjay Dutt* v. *State through CBI, Bombay* case[1], which was decided on the point of express presumption provided under section 5 of TADA and burden of proof arising therefrom. Secondly, presuming existence of such a presumption under section 3 of the Act of 1989 would shift the burden of proof from prosecution to the accused.

7.12 Some other views on the Knowledge of the Accused

A few Full Benches might have upheld the constitutionality of section 3 of the Act of 1989 on various points but section 3 is silent about the prior knowledge of the accused about the victim belonging to the Scheduled Caste or the Scheduled Tribe at the time of committing the offence. Two persons on a road or at any other public place might indulge in some sort of acts which may constitute offences under section 3, while both of them not knowing each other from before, but in case the victim belonged to Scheduled Caste or Scheduled Tribe, a case may be registered under section 3 against the other.

Sometimes it is alleged that taking the advantage of being such members, they try to harass others by lodging reports with the authorities. Supreme Court has observed: "........ Court proceeding ought not to be permitted to degenerate into a weapon of harassment or persecution. ....The ends of justice are higher than the ends of mere law.........."[2]

Mr. Madhusudan Tripathi, has mentioned an interesting illustration in his 'article' published in the Journal Section of Cr LJ 2011.[3] He states: "*A*, a member

1. 1994 AIR SCW 3857: 1995 Cr LJ 477: (1994) 5 SCC 410.
1. *State of Karnataka* v. *L. Muniswamy*, AIR 1977 SC 1489: 1977 Cr LJ 1125: (1977) 2 SCC 699.
2. "Provisions of section 3(2) of SC & ST (PA) Act are unconstitutional, where a Member at ST/SC's is himelf aggressor and was cross case is Registered against him" – By Madhu Sudhan Tripathi, Retired Government Counsel (Cr), Azamgarh. Journal Section p 205, 2011 Cr LJ 207. (he mentioned perhaps a real case still pending in District Court).

of higher class, not member of SC/ST caste going on his way driving his own car reaches a point in a densely populated area of a city. The road was overburdened rather jammed. On query be came to know that some miscreants in drunken condition are realizing 'Rangdari' from the passerby at the rate of Rs 10 from two-wheeled vehicles and 20 to 50 from 4-wheeled vehicles. He also stopped his car and was driving slowly. The miscreants came to him and asked Rs 50 which was denied. In drunken condition miscreants started abusing him and fired upon him, damaging his car and caused firearm injuries to the owner. None of the parties were knowing each other, nor even their caste and creed. The time of incident was 8.30 PM., distance from the police station ½ k.m. .... SHO and C.O. found no injuries on the bodies of the miscreants who were working under guidance of the son of M.L.A. of ruling party........" Case was registered against the owner of the car, while he was forced to get his cross case registered on the orders of C.J.M. under section 156(3) Cr PC. According to the said author, the miscreant, who was found to be belonging to Scheduled Caste, should not have got the privilage of section 3 of the SC/ST Act because no case of 'atrocity' is made out and thus according to him, Constitutional provision of Art 14 fails. After mentioning this, plight of Brahmins was also mentioned, who were working in the State as "Safaiwala", while the "members of SC and ST caste have joined crime" etc. As such he claims that the "entire Act is against the letter and spirit of fraternity clause of the Preamble of our Constitution."

One may cogently say that such writings are coming in reaction to the loss of power enjoyed by upper castes till the passage of the Act of 1989, but it is also true that in some cases the provisions of the Act are being misused. The Full Bench in *Mata Sewak's* case (Supra) has admitted and observed: "Abuse has to be checked up by constant vigilance and monitoring of individual cases."

The same caution was given by the Government Order (G.O) No 92 M.M. Chai-Pu-3-2002-25 P/2002 dated 12 May 2002, issued by the previous BSP government of Uttar Pradesh, to prevent the misuse of the provisions due to which reactions are generated.

7.13 Juvenile Offenders Trial

If it is found that a Juvenile had committed an offence, he had to be tried by Juvenile Court. There is no theory imported into the Act, and the thrust is to protect and develop the juvenile. A Juvenile cannot be sent to general prison. For this reason the court observed that Parliament had totally excluded the jurisdiction of ordinary courts for juvenile offenders, or the jurisdiction is ousted to any other courts.

While, on the other hand Act of 1989 deals with the crimes aganist members of Scheduled Castes and the Scheduled Tribes. The aim is to give protection to the victims of atrocities. Act of 1989 is *not concerned with the offenders* who perpetrate crime against such members. For this protecting purpose section 20 of the Act was enacted to give an overriding effect. The Division Bench was of the opinion that overriding power "cannot be extended to nullify the provisions" of Juvenile

Act. Therefore it was held that 15-year old accused had to be tried by Juvenile Court and not by Special Court.[1]

8. Comments on section 3(1) of the Act, – The Common Starting Phrase

Section "3. Punishments for offences of atrocities.—

(1) Whoever, not being a member of a Scheduled Caste or a Scheduled Tribe.-"

8.1 Introduction Generally

Exactly similar Phraseology of words in the same sequence has been used in the starting statements of sub-clause (1) as well as sub-clause (2) of section 3 of The Scheduled Castes and the Scheduled Tribes (Prevention of Atrocities) Act, 1989.

If generally analysed, the words of expression as a whole indicate two important enumerations,—namely,

(a) the created offences and punishment arising therefrom enumerated under section 3 of the Act of 1989, are not applicable to the members of Scheduled Castes and the Scheduled Tribes; and

(b) the provisions of section 3 of the Act encompass the entire Indian population, irrespective of any caste, creed or religion, except the members of the Scheduled Castes and the Scheduled Tribes.

However, the matter would be more clear when we break-up the words of the whole expression and try to understand the meaning.

8.1.1 "Whoever"

Grammatically word 'who' is interrogative pronoun, while the word 'whoever' is relative pronoun, which, according to Oxford Dictionary and Thesaurus, means "the or any person(s) who" (page 883). The Shorter Oxford English Dictionary (Vol. 2, p 2543) explains the word "whoever" as *"any one who, any who"*. The meaning given in Webster Comprehensive Dictionary, International Edn., (Vol. 2 at page 1437), is given: "anyone without exception" and "any person who".

Supreme Court held that "whoever" includes any person, including a partnership firm, a company or other body corporate or any association of persons.[2]

As could be seen, almost every meaning given by different sources of the word 'whoever', word 'person', is included in the meaning. The General Clauses Act (X of 1897) under section 3 defines the word 'person' as has been defined under section 11 of Indian Penal Code, 1860.

When meanings and definitions to the words – 'whoever' and 'person', are compared it could be easily found that word 'whoever' indicates a wider meaning than the word 'person'. Hence the legislature preferred the word

---

1. *In re: Sessions Judge*, 1995 Cr LJ 330 (Ker) (DB): 1994 (2) Ker LJ 122: 1994 (2) Ker LT 157; *Antaryami Patra* v. *State of Orissa*, 1993 Cr LJ 1908 (1913): 1993 (75) Cut LT 803: 1993 (1) Ori LR 464 – Dissented.

2. *Rai Bahadur Seth Shreeram Durgaprasad* v. *Director of Enforcement*, AIR 1987 SC 1364: 1987 Cr LJ 1123 (SC): (1987) 3 SCC 27.

'whoever' instead of 'person' in the starting phrase of both the starting statements of section 3 of the Act of 1989.

The word 'whoever' may include anybody or any person, including a child. Other penal statutes have also used the word 'whoever' to include variety of offenders under the ambit of respective enactments. Madras High Court, while dealing with a case under Tamil Nadu Prevention of Dangerous Activities of Boot-leggers, Drug Offenders, Forest Offenders, Goondas, Immoral Traffic Offenders and Slum Grabbers Act (14 of 1982), had held that a child below 16 years of age cannot be termed as "Goonda" and cannot be subjected to the provisions of the Act, though the penal sections starts with 'whoever'.[1]

Only three sections of the Act of 1989 start with the word 'whoever', which are sections 3, 4 and 5. The rest of the sections, where some kind of punishment has been provided, use words like-'a person' or 'any person' etc.

8.1.2 "not being a member of Scheduled Caste or a Scheduled Tribe"

This portion of the starting and opening statement of section 3(1) of the Act of 1989, in fact could be said as an excepting clause, through which the legislature has intentionally and deliberately excluded all the members of the Scheduled Caste and the Scheduled Tribe from the ambit of offences of 'atrocities', created and enumerated under section 3. That means no member of Scheduled Castes or the Scheduled Tribes could be made an accused or charged under the provisions of section 3 of the Act, even if that member has been found to have committed such an offence singly or in connivance with others against the co-members of the said category or community.

Perhaps, the legislature had presumed that all the members of the Scheduled Castes and the Scheduled Tribes would function cohesively and in unison in whatever situation or circumstances they are. In the similar manner section 4 of the Act of 1989 excludes all "public servants" from any penal action, except members of Scheduled Castes or the Scheduled Tribes, functioning as public servants, if found guilty of wilful neglect of duties required to be performed by him under the Act.

This presumption, that the whole community of Scheduled Castes and the Scheduled Tribes would function as a unit in unison and guard the rights and interests, besides desisting individually from committing acts of 'atrocities' against co-members, is against basic human nature and rationale. Human history is a witness, for most of the exploiters, persecutors and exploited and persecuted belonged to the same community. When some of the members of one community become economically and politically strong, they first start to persecute (even to the extent of inflicting atrocities) their own community and lot.

Apart from this, the 'lists' annexed to The Scheduled Castes and Scheduled Tribes Orders Act (including all the Amending Acts) itself is a proof of diversity among the said community or the class. In this situation the presumption that all of them would function in unison or cohesion cannot be conceived. From the very early days the Scheduled Caste members of a particular sub-caste had

1. *Ramachandran* v. *Inspector of Police,* 1994 Cr LJ 3722: 1994 (2) Mad LW (Cri) 585.

treated members of other sub-castes differently, even observing untouchability among themselves, and what to say of Scheduled Tribe members.

8.1.3 Opening Words of section 3(1) when read Collectively

Collectively reading the opening phrase, consisting of 13 words, of sub-clause (1) of section 3 [also of sub-clause (2) of the same section], no two meanings or inferences could be drawn. It does not need an expert of English language to draw an inference by the collective reading that two distinct classes have been made among the Indian population,- *viz.* members of Scheduled Castes and the Scheduled Tribes comprising one group and the rest of the Indian population, irrespective of caste, creed or religion etc. In other words it may be said that it is members of Scheduled Castes and the Scheduled Tribes versus the rest of Indian population.

The Act of 1989 thereby considered the 'extremely diverse population of India' as an opposing unit for purposes of inflicting and committing 'atrocities' on such members. Various Courts have ruled throughout the life of 'Protection of Civil Rights Act, 1955', as well as the Scheduled Castes and the Scheduled Tribes (Prevention of Atrocities) Act, 1989 the offences and the punishments created therefrom are sourced from Article 17 of the Constitution of India, which had 'abolished' the vice of "Untouchability", and Art. 35 mandated for providing punishment. In *Jai Singh's* case, the Full Bench (Supra) has emphatically held that The Scheduled Castes and the Scheduled Tribes (Prevention of Atrocities) Act, 1989 "is a legislation falling within the field" of Arts 17 and 35(9)(11) of the Constitution. Nevertheless the *inter se* practice of 'untouchability' among different Scheduled Caste communities has not been mentioned.

8.2 "Rest of Indian Population"

The natural inference is, that the 'rest of Indian population', who, "not being a member of a Scheduled Caste or a Scheduled Tribe" are being presumed to be compulsorily practicing "Untouchability" and consequently committing offences of 'atrocities' enumerated under section 3 of the Act.

A substantial portion of Indian population consists of Muslims, Christians, Buddhists, Jews and Parsees. There is a very strict prohibition among these religious groups for practicing 'untouchability'.

Whenever the Act of 1989 was constitutionally challenged before different Courts on the ground that: "there is a hostile discrimination in between the persons belonging to caste Hindu and those who did not" (*Jai Singh* v. *Union of India*[1]; or, "that the Act of 1989 creates two groups of people on caste basis is nothing but a caste legislation and hence is violative of Art. 15(1)" (*Mata Sewak Upadhyay* v. *State of Uttar Pradesh*[2] etc. etc., it was held that such offences arise out of "practice of untouchability" and "caste polarization is bound to be there because offences arising from untouchability are committed by a section of society against another" (para 24); and, caste Hindu are made punishable under the Act of 1989.

---

1. 1993 Cr LJ 2705 (2713) (Raj) (FB): AIR 1993 Raj 177: 1993 (1) Raj LW 157.
2. 1995 JIC 1168 (1181-82) (All) (FB): 1996 (1) East Cr C 97 (All) (FB).

A very pertinent question would arise: when it has become a settled law that the Act of 1989 is a legislation falling in the field of Arts 17 and 35 to abolish "Untouchability", whether those religious communities, making an essential ingredient of 'rest of Indian population', among whom practice of "untouchability" has been very strictly prohibited by 'personal law' can be brought under the ambit of provisions of section 3 of the Act of 1989?

Question was raised, though a little bit differently, before a Division Bench of M.P. High Court. It was "argued that section 3 operates against Muslims and Christions who are not believers of caste system".[1] Answering the question, the DB avoided holding a specific answer, but simply referred a Supreme Court decision in which it was observed, that "caste system has penetrated other religious and dissentient Hindu sects to whom the practice of caste should be anathema and today we find that practitioners of other religious faiths and Hindu dissentients are sometime as rigid adherents to the system of caste as the conservative Hindus."[2]

9. Question of Caste and "Untouchability"

Above mentioned observations of Hon'ble Justice O. Chinnappa Reddy of Apex Court in *K.C. Vasanth Kumar* v. *State of Karnataka*[2] case reveal truth as far as development of caste system is concerned. Muslims have lived with Hindus for more than one thousand years. When Al-Baruni came to India, he described situations in the country around 950 AD in his book "Al-Hind". (Published by Book Trust of India)

Buddhism was an Indian product and one of the causes of large scale conversion to Buddhism for more than two thousand years, particularly in early days of Buddhism, was the caste system in "Brahmanic Order". Even in recent times many members of Scheduled Castes and the Scheduled Tribes, including personalities like Dr. Ambedkar converted to Buddhism. It was so because Buddhism defied caste system, as Lord Buddha said that nobody becomes respectable or degraded due to his or her birth.

Among Muslims, "Masawat" is followed as a cardinal principle of that religion, and considered one of the pillars of Islam, which envisages that all the members of human race and the Muslim community (called Ummah) has equal rights in the eyes of God. The principle comes as an strict command from Quran and Sunnat and its violation, in any way, is considered greatest sin.[3]

Torah, Bible and Avesta- the religious scriptures of Jews, Christians and Parsees command similar kind of equality and equal status to every member of the community as well as human race.

But despite all these commands, at least Muslims in India have developed a limited kind of caste system among themselves, though, it may be said to be a

1. *Dr. Ram Krishna Balothia* v. *Union of India*, 1994 Cr LJ 2658 (MP) (DB): AIR 1994 MP 143: 1994 MPLJ 644 (Though it was Reversed by SC, *State of Madhya Pradesh* v. *Ram Kishna Balothia*, 1995 Cr LJ 2076 (SC): AIR 1995 SC 1198: 1995 AIR SCW 1267: JT 1995 (1) SC 310, on other point).
2. *K.C. Vasanth Kumar* v. *State of Karnataka*, AIR 1985 SC 1495: 1985 Supp (1) SCR 352: (1985) Supp SCC 714.
3. For other details please see present author's book "Principles of Muslim Law" Pub. Modern Law House, Alld.

unique phenomena among Indian Muslims, but it is very much present here, perhaps as a contagious decease. But despite such limited castiest concept no Muslim practices untouchability of the kind which was abolished by Article 17 of the Constitution.

According to Arther A. MacDonell[1] development of caste system in ancient India was a unique phenomena, alien to other religious communities of the world. This system had degenerated to the practice of "untouchability", and due to which large scale conversions of lower castes took place when Buddhism and Jainism came to fore. The process continued till 7th century A.D., That is why 7th century is called as: "downfall of Buddhism and Jainism and revival of Brahmanism". After this Muslims started coming to India (since 712 AD) and in due course Muslims also accepted the influence, resulting in practicing the caste system among themselves. But it may also be emphatically said that despite practicing the caste system, they never allowed the practice of 'untouchability' to penetrate their fold even for a limited purposes.

10. Question of "Untouchability" Among Non-Hindus

Following a system of caste is one thing and practicing "Untouchability", as envisaged and "abolished" under Article 17 of Indian Constitution is another.

The observations of Hon'ble Justice O. Chinnappa Reddy (Supra) were made because the question was not put before the Apex Court properly. It was argued that: "Section 3 of the Act also operates against Muslims and Christians who are not believers of caste system" (Supra).

As of now it has become a settled law that section 3 or for that matter other provisions of the Act of 1989 is not a caste legislation, and it falls within Arts. 17 and 35 of Constitution to abolish 'untouchability'.

The question before the court should have been raised: whether provisions of section 3 (etc.) may be made operative against Muslims, Christians, Jews, Parsees and Buddhists, who neither believe in nor practice "untouchability"?

Buddhist have been included in the question because a court had held that Buddhist cannot be treated as members of Scheduled Castes[2] and as such outside the ambit of opening clause of section 3 of the Act of 1989, because they constitute 'rest of Indian population'. In fact, '*Explanation*' to section 3 of Protection of Civil Rights Act, 1955 says "......... persons professing the Buddhist, Sikh or Jain religion or persons professing the Hindu religion in any of its forms or developments including Virashavias, Lingayats, Adivasis, followers of Brahmo, Prarthna, Arya Samaj and the Swaminarayan Sampraday shall be deemed to be Hindus."

Indian Muslims might have (wrongly) divided themselves amongst different castes, – such as Syeds, Pathans, Julahas (weavers), Kunjras, Quraisis etc. but "untouchability" has never been practiced among them. Ghalib, in his famous 19th century letter (published) had written and mentioned about Kunjra, Qasai etc., and that proves that casts' presence in Delhi of those days. But neither the

1. "A History of Sanskrit Literature" by Arther A. MacDonell, published by Motilal Banarsidas pp. 16, 28, 113, 129.
2. AIR 1979 Bom 282: 1979 Bom CR 309.

old literature nor the present observations show that there was or is any concept or practice of "untouchability" among Muslims.

It could be commonly seen in India every where, that even those who are being considered as untouchables among Hindu community generally, are being treated by Muslims in not that capacity.

Out of scores of examples one may be mentioned here. When Sharqi dynasty kings were ruling in Ruhailkhand region, Jaunpur being as its capital, wholesale conversion to Islam of "Domar" (as mentioned at No 32 in Part XVIII of The Scheduled Castes & Scheduled Tribes Orders Act), community took place and they were given a new name – "Lalbegi" (also mentioned at No. 52 in the said Part of the said Act). The 'Lalbegi' community could still be found in substantial numbers in Jaunpur, Varanasi, Pratapgarh etc., and due to migrations could be found at any place throughout the country.

From the very beginning some of the members of 'Lalbegi' community had abandoned but some continued scavenging jobs. In spite of this the members of 'Lalbegi' community were never prevented from entering a mosque or praying in the same formation of lines of prayers. These community members were allowed to eat at the same "Dastarkhan" (A piece of long cloth on which collective eating takes place). In fact nobody from the Muslim community even thought of preventing these members from entering mosques or other dwelling places. Caste is not a criterion, but cleanliness of a common Muslim is the condition in which he may enter a mosque etc. Even a Syed, the highest caste considered among Indian Muslims, if becomes unclean would not enter a mosque.

The above example (like many) would prove that there is no practice or concept of "Untouchability" among Indian Muslim, hence it becomes imperative to keep them out of ambit of the Act.

Comments

Section 3(1)(i) "forces a member of a Scheduled Caste or a Scheduled Tribe to drink or eat any inedible or obnoxious substance;"

SYNOPSIS

1. The Elements Essential
2. Scope
3. Relief and Compensation

1. The Elements Essential

To prove an offence under section 3(1)(i) of The Scheduled Castes and the Scheduled Tribes (Prevention of Atrocities) Act, 1989, are:

(a) that the accused are other than a member of Scheduled Caste or a Scheduled Tribe, whereas the victim must be such a member;

(b) use of force of any kind is a must;

(c) use of force by accused to compel member of Scheduled Caste or a Scheduled Tribe to drink or eat any inedible or obnoxious substance;

(d) mere such attempt would constitute the offence, because there is no indication from the language of the clause that when such member actually drinks or eat the said substance only then the offence would be constituted; and

(e) element of *mens rea* is not present, as has been observed in *Mata Prasad Upadhaya's* case (supra) can be presumed.

2. Scope

Though, clause (i) of sub-section 1 of section 3 has created a different kind of offence as had been enumerated in sections 3 to 7A of Protection of Civil Rights Act, 1955, which declare various forms of enforcement of disabilities arising out of untouchability (1998 Cr LJ 760). The offence created in the present clause is an aggravated form, where use of force is an essential ingredient, because here an act of 'atrocity' has been covered and not the disability.

Therefore the two kinds of offences, as mentioned above, cannot be said to be overlapping each other and both may co-exist. However, no such case as mentioned and covered in the clause has been reported yet.

3. Relief and Compensation

In "Annexure" to the Schedule attached to the rules of 1995, at serial No. 1 it has been provided that: "Rs. 25,000 or more depending upon the nature and gravity of the offence to each victim and also commensurate with the indignity, insult and defamation suffered by the victim."

The State Government would pay this amount through D.M., S.D.M or other magistrate as provided under Rule 12(4).

Comments

Section 3(1)(ii) "acts with intent to cause injury, insult or annoyance to any member of a Scheduled Caste or a Scheduled Tribe by dumping excreta, waste matter, carcasses or any other obnoxious substance in his premises or neighbourhood;"

SYNOPSIS

1. Elements
2. "Injury"
3. "Insult"
4. Analogous Law
5. Scope
6. Amount of Relief

1. Elements

The elements essential to prove a charge under section 3(1)(ii) of the Act of 1989 are:

(a) that the accused must belong to the 'rest of Indian population', and not being a member of Scheduled Caste or a Scheduled Tribe;

(b) acts mentioned must be with "intent", hence *mens rea* is an essential ingredient,

(c) the intention must be with the object "to cause injury, insult or annoyance to member of a Scheduled Caste or a Scheduled Tribe";

(d) the acts covered and restricted as "dumping excreta, waste matter, carcasses or any other obnoxious substance in his premises or neighbourhood."

2. "Injury"

In Webster's Legal Dictionary, the meaning of injury has been given as: "any harm to an individual or entity through conduct regarded by the law as wrongful, including bodily injury, mental suffering, harm to reputation, property damage, financial loss, or deprivation of legal right".

3. "Insult"

The Oxford Dictionary and Thesaurus, mentioned the meaning of the word 'insult' as "abuse scornfully, treat with indignity, offend self respect etc. of". In the Chambers Twentieth Century Dictionary the meaning of word 'insult' has been given as "to assail, to triumph insolently or exultantly or; to treat with indignity or contempt, to affront; to make and attack, to behave with boastful insolence; abuse."

4. Analogous Law

It is interesting to note that clauses (b) and (d) of sub-section (1) of section 7 of Protection of Civil Rights Act, 1955 also uses words "injures, annoys" and "insults or attempts to insult" in connection with Scheduled Castes and the Scheduled Tribes, and in relation with creating offences arising out of "untouchability".

It is noteworthy that section 7(1)(d) makes an attempt to insult, on the ground of 'untouchability', to a member of the Scheduled Castes to be an offence. For this reason the attempt has been included in the essential ingredients of the present clause of the Act of 1989. Secondly because, the language of the section 3(1)(ii) allows that natural inference.

5. Scope

It was observed that the word 'insult' in the legal parlance means to treat with offensive disrespect or to offer indignity to a person. The significance attached to the word used would depend on the facts and circumstances of each case, the occasion and the manner in which the words are used, or the act has been done, against the person. Any act or speech meant to hurt the feelings or self-respect of another or treat the person with insolence or contempt by words or action amount to an insult.[1]

A careful reading of the clause shows that intention regarding the acts done to constitute the offence must be to cause injury, insult or annoyance to a member of Scheduled Caste or a Scheduled Tribe. There may be a general dumping ground near the house of such a member and simply dumping some obnoxious substance etc., would not constitute an offence. The prosecution has to prove the intention *(mens rea).*

In Mata Sewak Upadhyay v. *State of Uttar Pradesh*[2] case (supra) it was held that under section 3(1)(ii) "*mens rea* has been made necessary. So that a person having no intention to cause injury, insult or annoyance......... by dumping may not be unnecessarily punished."

6. Amount of Relief

As has been mentioned under section 3(1)(i) before.

---

1. *Baste Subrayalu* v. *Robert Mariadassou*, 1987 Cr LJ 272 (274) (Mad HC): 1986 Mad LW (Cri) 329.
2. 1995 JIC 1168 (1189) (All) (FB): 1996 (1) East Cr C 97 (All) (FB) (para 55).

Comments

Section 3(1)(iii) "forcibly removes clothes from the person of a member of a Scheduled Caste or a Scheduled Tribe or parades him naked or with painted face or body or commits any similar act which is derogatory to human dignity;"

SYNOPSIS

1. Scope
2. Relief Amount

1. Scope

Removal of clothes, parading him naked or painting the face or body of a person for purposes of insulting or degrading him, is a peculiar and "unusual feature in our country". Not only the public but often police indulges in such activities when they arrest some accused who had committed a ghastly crime and the general public approves it.

Naturally such acts are being committed to others 'forcibly' to make it derogatory to such person.

In *State* v. *Ram Krishna Balothia*'s case (Supra), Supreme Court had held that the offences which are enumerated under section 3 are offences to denigrate members of Scheduled Castes and the Scheduled Tribes in the eyes of society and to prevent them to lead life of dignity and self-respect. These offences constitute a separate class and cannot be compared with offences provided elsewhere.

It is also noteworthy that to signify or identify a victim from the Scheduled Caste or a Scheduled Tribe, word "him" has been used throughout different clauses of section 3. The word "him" denotes a masculine gender and singular number. If it is contended that female victims were kept outside the ambit of section 3, perhaps it would be said that word "him" includes "her" or "them" etc..

2. Relief Amount

At serial No. 3 in the 'Annexure 1' to the 'Schedule' attached to Rules 1995, the payment to be made to the victim, 25% when the charge-sheet has been sent to court; and 75% when the accused are convicted by the lower court.

Comments

Section 3(1)(iv) "wrongfully occupies or cultivates any land owned by, or allotted to, or notified by any competent authority to be allotted to, a member of a Scheduled Caste or a Scheduled Tribe or gets the land allotted to him transferred;"

Language of the clause is simple and convey a direct meaning, without any need for any explanations, except that *mens rea* has not been mentioned, though, it may be presumed.

Under Rule 15(b), while providing that the concerned State Government shall make a contingency plan, provides for "allotment of agricultural land and house, sites", which is subject to a strict monitoring (Rules 16 and 17) by the State, and at local level (by Administration) to ensure that such members get the allotted land. Under Rule 12, the Superintendent of Police, District Magistrate, Sub-Divisional Magistrate and any other Executive Magistrate are made responsible to ensure the implementation of the provisions and if they are found negligent they are liable to be punished under section 4 of the Act. Perhaps that is the reason why no cases have been reported under section 3(1)(iv).

Comments

Section 3(1)(v) "wrongfully dispossesses a member of a Scheduled Caste or a Scheduled Tribe from his land or premises or interferes with the enjoyment of his rights over any land, premises or water;"

SYNOPSIS

1. Ingredients
2. "Wrongfully Dispossesses"
3. Possession of Land or Premises Must Belong to Such Member
4. Enjoyment of Right Interfered
5. Investigation under section 3(1)(v) of the Act
6. Amount of 'Relief' and Compensation

1. Ingredients

The essential ingredients of clause (v) of sub-section (1) of section 3 of the Act of 1989, are:

(a) wrongful dispossession of land or premises;

(b) the land must belong to such member by title or by any other legal means;

(c) even interference in the free enjoyment of land, premises or water, has been made an offence under the Act;

(d) the lawful owner of the land, premises or water must be a member of Scheduled Caste or a Scheduled Tribe.

2. "Wrongfully Dispossesses"

It was observed that "there has to be actual dispossession from the land or premises, belonging to the members of the category of Scheduled Castes or Scheduled Tribes or interference with the enjoyment thereof. Unless this part of the section is met out, there cannot be any prosecution for commission of the said offence, much less conviction. Thus the requisite condition is either dispossession or interference of enjoyment of his rights over the land, premises or water. This is the most essential ingredient which must be proved.[1]

But when accused agreed to sell his land to the accused and delivered the possession and thereafter the accused forcibly entered upon the land and damaged the crops and started tilling, it was held by Apex Court that the accused were liable for conviction under section 3(1)(v), because the complainant was wrongfully dispossessed.[2]

3. Possession of Land or Premises Must Belong to Such Member

For securing a conviction under section 3(1)(v), the prosecution, for the first cause is required to prove that the accused has wrongfully dispossessed a member of Scheduled Caste or a Scheduled Tribe from his land or premises. A

---

1. *Devisingh* v. *State of Madhya Pradesh*, 2003 Cr LJ 147 (MP) (148): 2003 (1) MPHT 24: 2002 (4) MPLJ 490.
2. *Kashiben Chhaganbhai Koli* v. *State of Gujarat*, 2009 Cr LJ 1156 (SC): 2009 AIR SCW 695: (2008) 16 SCALE 145.

wrongful dispossession presupposes positive and *de facto* possession. Unless a man is shown to be in actual physical possession of the property, he cannot be dispossessed. Even if there is a sale deed and on it an order of mutation has been passed in favour of the complainant, he had to prove that he was in possession to constitute an offence under section 3(1)(v) of Act.[1]

Where according to the complaint, the complainant had himself alleged that he and his father had some agricultural land in village which was let out for cultivation to others on rent and as such delivered the possession of the land. It was held that no offence is made out.[2]

When a person was in possession of the land, before it was allotted to the complainant and there was no evidence that the land was in possession of the complainant, it was held that offence of criminal trespass could be made out. Mere occupation, even if illegal, cannot amount to criminal trespass, thus accused cannot be said to have dispossessed the disputed land, and offence cannot be made out under section 3(1)(v).[3]

4. Enjoyment of Right Interfered

When it was alleged in the FIR that the accused assaulted the complainant, a member of the Scheduled caste and also asked him to leave his field, it was held that accused had interfered with the enjoyment of right of the complainant over the land in question, as such an offence under section 3(1)(v) of the Act of 1989 could be made out and order for framing the charge cannot be quashed.[4]

Accused was charged that he had closed the water drain of the complainant by putting stones and waste earth, but it was nowhere suggested in the charge when the accused had been filling the drain with earth, murum and stones, and also when it was done. Prosecution has also failed to prove the possibility of the said drain being filled-in therefore it was observed that the accused cannot be held guilty of the offence under section 3(1)(v) of the Act.[5]

The complainant was interested in disposing of the land and the accused was offering a lesser price than the demanded price of the land in question. For this reason it could not be said that the accused was either dispossessing or interfering with the enjoyment of rights of such member over the land. No offence could be made out under section 3(1)(v) of the Act of 1989.[6]

5. Investigation under section 3(1)(v) of the Act

When the offence committed under section 3(1)(v) was investigated by a Sub-Inspector of Police, who took up the investigation and recorded the statements of witnesses, and thereafter the charge-sheet was filed by Deputy Superintendent

1. *Janggu alias Shobhit* v. *State of Madhya Pradesh,* 2000 Cr LJ 711 (MP): (2000) 1 Crimes 7: 1999 (2) MPLJ 474; also see 1989 SC Cri R 108.
2. 1991 Cri LR (Raj) 336.
3. *State of Rajasthan* v. *Dipti Ram,* 2001 Cr LJ 3910 (Raj): 2001 (4) Rec Cri R 765.
4. *Yashwant* v. *State of Maharashtra,* 2003 Cr LJ 2765 (Bom): 2003 (8) All Ind Cas 717: 2003 (4) Bom LR 590; but also see *State of Rajasthan* v. *Dipti Ram,* 2001 Cr LJ 3910 (Raj): 2001 (4) Rec Cri R 765 *(ibid).*
5. (1996) 4 All Mah LR 34 (38): (1997) 1 Cur Cri R 20 (Bom).
6. *Devisingh* v. *State of Madhya Pradesh,* 2003 Cr LJ 147 (MP): 2003 (1) MPHT 24: 2002 (4) MPLJ 490.

of Police, only verifying the charge sheet and the investigation done by his subordinate officer, it was held that the process was illegal vitiating the trial. Consequently the conviction was set aside.[1]

6. Amount of 'Relief' and Compensation

For sub Clauses (iv) and (v), the amount of relief provided by the 'Schedule' ('Annexure 1') attached to the Rules of 1995, is: "At least Rs 25,000 or more depending upon the nature and gravity of the offence. The land/premises/water supply shall be restored where necessary at Government Cost. Full payment to be made when charge-sheet is sent to the Court."

Comments

Section 3(1)(vi) "Compels or entices a member of a Scheduled Tribe to do 'begar' or other similar forms of forced or bonded labour other than any compulsory service for public purposes imposed by Government;"

SYNOPSIS

1. Analogous Law
2. To do 'Begar'
3. Payment of Compensation and Relief

1. Analogous Law

Section 7A of Protection of Civil Rights Act, 1955 also deals with "Compulsory labour" meaning thereby to "do begar". Though, the provision mentions a few kinds of jobs like-scavenging, sweeping, removing carcass or flay any animal etc., but has also included "social or economic boycott" in the meaning of the term "compulsion".

The provisions of this clause of section 3 are in clear words and better format, when compared to the similar but limited form provided under section 7A of Protection of Civil Rights Act, 1955, wherein the *"Explanation"*, reads as "For purpose of this section, "compulsion" includes a threat of social or economic boycott."

2. To do "Begar"

The word 'begar' is not simply "forced or bonded labour'. The word had a historical importance and had been in use for centuries among Indian society. The word actually means that a person is forced physically to work without any wages or remuneration. In the times of tyrant kings, and lately during the British rule, the Zamindars used to grab people by using force physically or by implied threats to work for which no wages were paid.

In the present Indian society perhaps it is impossible to compel some body "to do begar", and probably that is the reason why no cases have been reported by any law Journal of repute.

3. Payment of Compensation and Relief

"At least Rs. 25,000 to each victim, payment of 25% at FIR stage and 75% on conviction in the lower Court." "Annexture 1" Schedule attached to the SC/ST Rules, 1995.

---

1. *Ambati Vykunta Rao* v. *State*, 2003 Cr LJ (NOC) 241 (AP): (2003) 1 Andh LT (Cri) 340; *Mansingh Baburao Garud* v. *State of Maharashtra*, 2011 Cr LJ (NOC) 444 (Bom).

Comments

Section 3(1)(viii) "forces or intimidates a member of a Scheduled Caste or a Scheduled Tribe not to vote or to vote to a particular candidate or to vote in a manner other than that provided by law;"

The offence created under this clause of section 3(1) relates to other practices, which have otherwise been declared as offences under provisions of People' Representation laws as well Indian Penal Code (Section 17-IC, 171F). But those overlapping offences do not specifically cover members of Scheduled Castes and the Scheduled Tribes. In the present clause a special offence has been created to this effect, so that the election offences may be brought under the definition of "atrocity", when they are committed against members of Scheduled Castes and the Scheduled Tribes.

Comments

Section (1)(viii) "institutes false, malicious or vexatious suit or criminal or other legal proceedings against a member of a Scheduled Caste or a Scheduled Tribe;"

SYNOPSIS

1. Ingredients
2. "Institutes"
3. "False, Malicious or Vexatious Suit or Criminal or other Legal Proceedings"
4. Falsehood Must be Intentional
5. Knowledge of Falsehood
6. "Other Legal Proceedings"
7. Offence Under the Clause May Arise at the End of Proceedings
8. "Relief Amount"

1. Ingredients

It was observed that there are two basic ingredients of this offence, Firstly, there must be a suit or criminal or any other legal proceeding against any such member, and Secondly, such suit or criminal or any other legal proceedings so instituted must be false, malicious or vexatious.[1]

The essential ingredients and meaning of words of clause (viii) of section 3(1) of the Act are—

2. "Institutes"

Means "initiate (inquiry etc.)", according to Oxford Dictionary and Thesaurus. Naturally the word initiate implies some overt act which could start and roll the wheel of legal system of any kind. If some person simply boastingly threats to file a suit or lodge a FIR against anybody (in the present case a member of SC or ST), whether on genuine or on false, malicious and vexatious facts or reasons, it must not be considered as the initiation or 'institution' of any legal proceeding. The proceedings must be actually initiated.

3. "False, Malicious or Vexatious Suit or Criminal or other Legal Proceedings"

The clause correspond to some extent to section 211 IPC, which, though has been restricted to criminal proceedings only, whereas the present clause encompass "suits" as well as other legal proceedings. Both the offences may overlap and can be simultaneously committed and charged.

1. *Rajat Kumar Bandyopadhyay* v. *State of West Bengal*, 2009 Cr LJ 3360 (Cal) (3362): 2009 (3) Cal HN 383: 2009 (3) Cal LT 246.

False means untrue; malicious means arising from malice or ill will or a desire to do harm; whereas, the word vexatious means lacking sufficient grounds for action and seeking only to annoy the defendant. These are the meanings of the said words as given by Dictionaries.

4. Falsehood Must be Intentional

Though, *mens rea* has not been mentioned expressly in the said clause but according to the decisions of various courts it would be presumed that the institution of false, malicious or vexatious suit or criminal or other legal proceedings must be presumed. That presumption would imply that only institutions of those suits or criminal or other kind of legal proceedings would be covered which were instituted intentionally and knowing them to be false, malicious or vexatious. In case some fact has been mentioned in such proceedings by the accused on the misinformation or wrong legal advise, that would not constitute the offence under the clause.

5. Knowledge of Falsehood

Knowledge and belief by a person instituting a suit, criminal or other proceedings against such member is essence of criminality. If a person did not know the truth respecting the facts mentioned in such proceedings, which he believed to be true, or due to mistake and defective observation he mentioned them, he cannot be roped under the 'clause'. Thus three degrees of knowledge of facts could be mentioned: (i) a fact known to be false, (ii) a fact believed to be false, and (iii) a fact not believed to be true.

Falsity must be known to the person who is instituting or initiating the proceeding against such member of SC or ST, for otherwise he might have believed it to be true at the time of instituting the proceedings and later on he came to know the truth.

Knowledge may be an outcome of an observation which becomes conscious knowledge of a fact, which again is result of an inference. The knowledge, gained through this process of observation and inference could be believed to be true by the observer. Therefore it becomes a very intricate process to prove falsehood, but in any case the prosecution is duty-bound to prove that the proceedings initiated or instituted was on false, malicious and vexatious grounds. Simply mentioning or proving a contradictory fact, mentioned by the accused elsewhere, and by comparing the other facts, falsity cannot be proved, because it is possible that the other fact mentioned by the accused elsewhere could have been false and the facts in question might have been true.

6. "Other Legal Proceedings"

The institution of suit or criminal proceedings could be confined to judicial proceedings, but 'other legal proceedings' equally applies to a proceeding before a public servant or an institution authorised by law. For instance a forest officer is empowered to hold an inquiry into an offence connected with the forest, and initiating any proceedings, based on false facts or grounds would be covered under the clause.

7. Offence Under the Clause May Arise at the End of Proceedings

Any offence and charge under clause (viii) of section 3(1) of SC and ST (PoA) Act could only be slapped against any person who had instituted a suit, criminal or other legal proceedings against a member of Scheduled Caste or a Scheduled Tribe, only when the said proceeding comes to an end and when it was found that the 'proceeding' was instituted with false, malicious or vexatious intention, and not before.

It was held by a Division Bench that mere filing of a writ petition would not constitute any offence under the clause. The offence can be made out only after disposal of the proceedings even an adverse remark was by the Bench, as it was observed that registration of an offence during pendency of such proceeding amounts to abuse of process of the Court.[1]

8. "Relief Amount"

[See in the last of Comments under next sub-clause (ix) as both are same].

Comments

Section 3(1)(ix) "gives, any false or frivolous information to any public servant and thereby causes such public servant to use his lawful power to the injury or annoyance of a member of a Scheduled Caste or a Scheduled Tribe;"

SYNOPSIS

1. Analogous Law
2. Scope
3. Meaning of Words
   - 3.1 "Public Servant"
4. "Gives any false or frivolous information"
5. "Information"
6. Different Forms of Information
7. Voluntary or Involuntary Informations
8. Ingredients of Constituting Offence
9. Relief Amount

1. Analogous Law

The clause (ix) of section 3(1) of the Act of 1989, contains almost similar provisions as has been provided under section 182 of Indian Penal Code, 1860. But in the present case "injury or annoyance has been restricted to members of Scheduled Caste or a Scheduled Tribe, instead of "any person" used in the Code, which inevitably cover all.

2. Scope

In addition to word "false" another word "frivolous" has been inserted. Dictionary meaning of word "frivolous" is not only serious, shallow or silly, but it certainly creates a situation which is other than the 'false'. A "frivolous information" may not be absolutely antidote to truth, but it cannot be put in the category of total 'falsehood'. An information may not be serious or shallow etc., but its contents may be based on some part of or element of truth.

The said clause is based on the principle which describe that class of offences which accrue on the accused when he tries to deter pubic servants from the path of their lawful duties. The misleading information given to a public servant, not only becomes a cause of 'injury or annoyance' to a member of a Scheduled Caste or a Scheduled Tribe, but also becomes a waste of time, energy and money on the part of State.

1. *Abdul Rasheed Siddiqui* v. *State of Madhya Pradesh*, AIR 1995 MP 138 (140) (DB): 1994 Jab LJ 394: 1994 MPLJ 578; also see *Ms Shamim Modi* v. *Sudha Chaudhary, DM Betul*, 2008 Cr LJ (NOC) 1185 (MP) (DB); *Rajat Kumar Bandyopadhyay* v. *State of West Bengal*, 2009 Cr LJ 3360 (Cal) (3362): 2009 (3) Cal HN 383: 2009 (3) Cal LT 246.

The applicability of section 3(1)(ix) of the Act of 1989 was explained as that for instance, when an information was given to police by falsely charging a member of Scheduled Caste of having committed an offence, and that false information was given so that the public servant (police officer) could use his lawful powers for causing injury to the aggrieved person. Otherwise the police officer or other public servant may also become an accused on such basis. In such a case Bar under section 195 of Cr PC could not be attracted when an offence under section 3(1)(ix) of Act of 1989 is being alleged. Besides, the Scheduled Caste member cannot be restrained from lodging a FIR against the accused, complaining that accused had gone to police for falsely implicating him in an offence of murder for which he had spent long period in jail. Bar under section 195 would not come into play.[1]

3. Meaning of Words

3.1 "Public Servant"

'Public servant' has not been defined in the Scheduled Castes and the Scheduled Tribes (Prevention of Atrocities)Act, 1989, but the expression 'public servant' has been defined in section 21 of Indian Penal Code, 1860, and also under section 2 of Prevention of Corruption Act, 1988. (For these definitions and detailed discussion, please see comments under section 4).

4. "Gives any False or Frivolous Information"

The words 'false' and 'frivolous' have been explained before (under the comments cn previous clause). A pre-condition is that such false or frivolous information must be given to a public servant and there must be a positive act of giving such information. Withholding any information or giving such false and frivolous information to a person other than a public servant would not constitute an offence.

5. "Information"

The word "information" has been used here in its widest sense as stipulating a communication of any intelligence or purported knowledge of facts, importantly that must be in the nature of accusation to a member of Scheduled Caste or a Scheduled Tribe, and, importantly again, which is capable of causing "injury or annoyance" to such member. It is not sufficient that the accused had reason to believe the information to be false, or even that he did not believe it to be true. To constitute the offence it must be proved that accused must have a positive knowledge or belief that such information was false.[2]

But giving informations to public servants in different circumstances may or may not be brought under the ambit of clause (ix) of section 3(1) of the Act. For instance a genuine information of the criminal activities of such a member, for which that member would naturally suffer 'injury or annoyance', cannot be brought under the ambit of the present clause.

---

1. *Ram Babu Dixit* v. *State of Uttar Pradesh*, 2009 Cr LJ (NOC) 677 (All) (DB); also see *B.H. Ismail* v. *State*, 2009 Cr LJ (NOC) 428 (Kant).
2. *Sukhdeo Singh* v. *State*, 1961 All Cr R 312.

6. Different Forms of Information

The process of giving informations to public servants may be varied. Some person may give informations during recording of his statement in defence during a criminal trial; informations may be given to the answers of questions of an investigating officer; informations may be given by an advocate on behalf of his client in pleadings during civil, criminal or revenue proceedings; *'pairokars'* of jailed persons mentioning some informations in affidavits filed before different Courts; some informations may be divulged by any person to a public servant when it is requested; or it may be given in form of a petition to some authority, who happen to be a public servant. But every such information must be false and frivolous and against some member of a Scheduled Caste or a Scheduled Tribe, to attract provisions of this clause.

7. Voluntary or Involuntary Informations

Giving "false and frivolous information" so that the lawful powers of a public servant may be invoked to cause some injury or annoyance to a member of Scheduled Caste or a Scheduled Tribe, simply gives a reason to infer that such information giving act must be an intentional and voluntary act. Though intention or *mens rea* has not been expressly incorporated in the language of the clause, but it should be presumed to be present, according to various decisions of the Courts.

In that sense, the situation of stipulation between the present clause and provisions of section 182 IPC is slightly different.

But, an intricate question may arise: whether answers to questions, in course of a departmental enquiry or otherwise, if found false and frivolous later on, and against such a member, would that be brought under the ambit of the present 'clause' of the section 3? The answer of this question should be in the negative, because the answers to the questions in the inquiry are involuntary in the first place, as the questioned person is bound to answer the question, and secondly such answers to the questions must be regarded as an explanation, might be given in his defense. Same thing could be said about statements recorded under section 161 Cr PC during an investigation, as its use, otherwise for purposes of proving omissions or contradictions, has been restricted by section 162 Cr PC. But lodging a FIR on false or frivolous facts against a member of Scheduled Caste or a Scheduled Tribe would certainly constitute an offence under the present clause of section 3.

But the criminality under the clause would only depend on the element of *mens rea,* which according to observations of Courts has to be presumed under offences under section 3.

The informations given in various kinds of pleadings etc., submitted to Courts also do not come under the ambit of clause, if found false or frivolous, because it cannot be said to have been given to cause the court to do something or use its lawful power to the injury or annoyance to such member, though such information giving person may be prosecuted under other provisions of law.

8. Ingredients of Constituting Offence

Main ingredients of clause (ix) of the section 3(1) of the Scheduled Castes and the Scheduled Tribes (Prevention of Atrocities) Act, 1989 are:

(i) A person must give false or frivolous information;

(ii) that information must be given to a public servant and nobody else;

(iii) that information must be such that it causes public servant to act and use his lawful power in consequence thereof;

(iv) such use of lawful power by the public servant on false or frivolous information, must result in injury or annoyance;

(v) such injury or annoyance must have been caused to a member of Scheduled Caste or a Scheduled Tribe, and nobody else.

In *Mata Sewak's* case (Supra) it was clearly held that in the clauses of section 3 of the Act, where express intention has not been mentioned, it may be presumed. Therefore the false or frivolous information must be given to secure the illegal power by a public servant. The criminality would depend upon the probability of action taken on such information by the public servant with the given and provided result.

The object and intention of the legislature to enact clause (ix) of the section 3 is that members of Scheduled Caste etc., should not be subjected to injury or annoyance on account of false informations to the public servants, who ought to be misled. The offence would not be complete unless on such false or frivolous information the public servant acts due to which such member is subjected to injury or annoyance.

9. Relief Amount

For sub-clause (viii) and (ix) above, the Schedule in "Annexure 1" to the SC/ST Rules, 1995 provide: "Rs 25,000 or reimbursement of actual legal expenses and damages or whichever is less after conclusion of the trial of the accused".

Comments

Section 3(1)(x) "intentionally insults or intimidates with intent to humiliate a member of a Scheduled Caste or a Scheduled Tribe in any place within public view;"

SYNOPSIS

Clause (x) of section 3(1) of the Scheduled Castes and the Scheduled Tribes (Prevention of Atrocities) Act 1989, is one of the most frequently used atrocitious offence and a great number of cases had come and are coming before courts.

1. Ingredients

Apex Court has observed that the complaint under section 3(1)(x) must contain:

(i) "that the accused-appellant was not a member of the Scheduled Caste or a Scheduled Tribe......";

(ii) the complainant "was intentionally insulted or intimidated by the accused";

(iii) such intentional insult or the intimidation was "with intent to humiliate" such member; and

(iv) this intentional insult or intimidation with an intent to humiliate must be in a place within "public view".[1]

2. "Criminal Intimidation"

Has been defined in section 503 IPC which reads as under:

> "Whoever threatens another with any injury to his person, reputation or property, or to the person or reputation of any one in whom that person is interested, with intent to cause harm to that person, or to cause that person to do any act which he is not legally bound to do, or to omit to do any act which that person is legally entitled to do, as the means of avoiding the execution of such threat, commits criminal intimidation".

And "Insult" means – abuse scornfully; treat with indignity or offend self-respect.[2]

3. Analogous Law

Section 7(1)(d) of Protection of Civil Rights Act, 1955 reads as:

> Section 7(1)(d) "insults or attempts to insult on the ground of "untouchability" a member of a Scheduled Caste"[3];

(Besides above mentioned *see section* 503 IPC)

4. Comparing Provision of section 7(1)(d) of PCR Act, 1955 and section 3(1)(x) of SC/ST Act

In a case where cognizance was taken by the Special Judge for trial of the accused for offences under section 3(1)(x) of The Scheduled Castes and the Scheduled Tribes (Prevention of Atrocities) Act, 1989, as well as section 7(1)(d) of Protection of Civil Rights Act, 1955. The allegation was that when the petitioner was contesting election, and during course of speech, the petitioner made some remarks about the complainant and his caste, deliberately to insult intentionally in public view, thus committed an offence under section 3(1)(x) of SC and ST Act of 1989. It was further alleged by the complainant that the conduct of the petitioner also amounted to practicing untouchability or an action arising out of untouchability and thereby committed an offence under section 7(1)(d) of Protection of Civil Rights Act, 1955. For both the alleged offences the special Judge took cognizance against that petitioner who prayed for quashing of the order.[4]

---

1. *Gorige Pentaiah* v. *State of Andhra Pradesh*, 2009 Cr LJ 350 (SC): 2008 AIR SCW 6901: (2008) 12 SCC 531, also see 1991 Cr LR (Raj) 583.
2. *Baste Subrayalu* v. *Robert Mariadassou*, 1987 Cr LJ 272 (274) (Mad HC): 1986 Mad LW (Cri) 329.
3. Clause (d) of section 7(1) of Protection of Civil Rights Act, 1955 was inserted by Act 106 of 1976.
4. *E. Krishnan Nayanar* v. *Dr. M.A. Kuttappan, Member, Kerala Legislative Assembly*, 1997 Cr LJ 2036 (Ker): ILR (1997) 2 Ker 837: 1997 (1) Ker LJ 280.

It was submitted by the petitioner that alleged statement had been made in absence of complainant, hence offence under section 3(1)(x) of Act of 1989 is not made out. Secondly it was argued that the statement was not an intentional insult, but only a reference to the conduct of the complainant in the Assembly and not about his caste but an incident, thus no offence under section 7(1)(d) of Act of 1955 was made out. Against that it was argued that presence of the complainant was not necessary and the use of word "Harijan" was enough to show intentional insult.

It was observed that in the complaint it was alleged that the petitioner uttered those words with a view to encourage his audience to practice untouchability but none of such thing was mentioned in the complaint, hence, the court felt that there is no justifications for initiating criminal proceeding.[1]

5. Applicability

For applicability of section 3(1)(x) of the Act of 1989, it was observed that two kinds of "insults" have been mentioned under section 3(1): one mentioned and defined under clause (ii) and the other defined under clause (x) of the said section. A combined reading of the two clauses shows that under clause (ii) insult can be caused to a member of Scheduled Caste or a Scheduled Tribe by dumping excreta, waste matter, carcasses or any other obnoxious substance in his premises or neighbourhood, and such acts need not necessarily be done in presence of the person insulted. And insult under clause (x) can be caused to the person insulted only if he is present in view of the expression "in any place within public view." It was in the court's opinion the words "within public view" are referable only to the person insulted. By avoiding to use words "within public view" in clause (ii), the legislature has created two different kinds of offences relating to insult caused to such members, stipulating his absence and in his presence by the words. With the result that the insulted person must be present to constitute an offence under clause (x) of section 3, because the words used in the clause are not "in public place", but "within public view", which means public must view the person being insulted for which he must be present.[1]

6. Calling By Caste Name

The Scheduled Caste and the Scheduled Tribe (Prevention of Atrocities) Act, 1989 was enacted to prevent the commission of offences of atrocities against the members of the Scheduled Castes and the Scheduled Tribes; to provide for Special Courts for trial of such offences, and for the relief and rehabilitation of the victim of such offences and for matters concerned therewith.

There are various ingredients in section 3(1)(x) of the Act of 1989, which have to be necessarily mentioned in the complaint to constitute the offence under this provision. Simply calling any person by caste name does not attract provisions of the Act. In the instant case the petitioner was even not aware about the caste of the complainant. Thus it was held that "merely calling some one by his caste does not attract the provisions of the Act".[2]

1. *E. Krishnan Nayanar* v. *Dr. M.A. Kuttappan, Member, Kerala Legislative Assembly*, 1997 Cr LJ 2036 (Ker): ILR (1997) 2 Ker 837: 1997 (1) Ker LJ 280.
2. *Chandra Poojari* v. *State of Karnataka*, 1998 Cr LJ 53 (54) (Kant): 1998 (2) Cur CriR 129: 1997 (4) Kant LJ 81.

But in another case it was found that, it is not merely calling a person by caste name but also, as was mentioned in the FIR, that the accused petitioner abused the complainant in her caste name in filthy language, thereby causing insult and intimidation to her, it was held that the FIR cannot be quashed on the ground that no offence was made out.[1]

Complainant was waiting for a bus and accused were playing football which hit the complainant. It was observed that act of accused was not intentional but accidental, and, *secondly* during the event if the accused called the complainant as *"Chamarin"*, only shows that the accused did not intend to insult or intimidate the complainant.[2]

But use of words "pallan", 'pallayal', 'paraparayan' with intent to insult, an offence under the provision would constitute the offence.[3]

When words of abuse attributed to the accused are "idiot" and "nonsense" uttered against a member of Scheduled Caste, who filed a complaint against the accused, it was held that these words have no reference to the community and from those "words it cannot be inferred that the intention or intimidation are with reference to the community to which complainant belonged".[4]

It was also held that if an accused is charged under section 3(1)(x) of the Act and the Court framed charges, there is no indication that insult to the member of Scheduled Caste or a Scheduled Tribe has been meted out, and that insult etc., should have been in public view.[5]

Merely addressing samebody by her caste name, calling her *"Chamarin"* is no offence, if such act of calling was without intention to insult or intimidate her.[6]

In a preferred revision it was prayed that the accused may be discharged under sections 323, 504, 506 IPC and 3(1)(x) of SC/ST Act. It was observed that on the basis of FIR and the statement of 161 Cr PC it is established that on the exhortation of one accused other persons had caused *'mar peet'* with the complainant and also had humiliated him by making aspersion about his caste and also threatened him to kill. The court found sufficient materials in the case diary, hence it was held that the lower court had wrongly discharged the accused, as there was sufficient ground to proceed against them and a case is made out from the facts on record.[7]

7. "Within Public View"

Supreme Court had observed that: "........ calling a member of the Scheduled Caste *'Chamar'* with intent to insult or humiliate him in a place *within public view* is certainly an offence under section 3(1)(x) of the Act. Whether there was intent

1. *Kaliya Perumal* v. *State*, 1998 Cr LJ 1467 (Mad): 1998 (2) APLJ (Cri) 49: 1998 (2) Rec Cri R 562.
2. 1998 Cr LR (Raj) 304 (305).
3. *Arumugam Servai* v. *State of Tamil Nadu*, 2011 Cr LJ 2899 (SC).
4. *Ravindra Kumar Mishra* v. *State of Madhya Pradesh*, 1995 Cr LJ 3060 (MP) (3061): 1995 (2) Cr CJ 590: 1995 MPLJ 645.
5. *Rakesh Kumar* v. *State*, 2001 WLC (Raj) UC 736.
6. *Pappu Singh* v. *State of Uttar Pradesh*, 2002 Cr LJ 1251 (All) (1252): 2001 (3) All Cri R 2702: 2002 (46) All LR 586; 1998 Cri LR (Raj) 304; and *Ajai Kumar* v. *State*, 2001 ACC 920.
7. *Gaurav Agarwal* v. *State of Uttar Pradesh*, 2009 Cr LJ 4491 (All): 2009 (5) ALJ 456: 2009 (66) All Cri C 552.

to insult or humiliate by using the word *'Chamar'* will of course depend on the context in which it was used."[1]

The complainant was standing near a car parked at the gate of the premises, which was held to be place within public view, since the gate of a house is a place within public view. Though, the Court went on, that it could have been a different matter had the alleged offence been committed inside a building, which could not be a place within public view. "Even if the remark is made inside a building but some members of the public are there (not merely relatives or friends) then also it would be an offence since it is in public view. We, must, therefore not confuse the expression 'place within public view' with the expression 'public place'......... ordinarily mean a place which is owned or leased by the Government........."[2]

The words used in clause (x) are not "in public place" but "in public view" which means public must view the person being insulted, for which he must be present". And no offence on the allegations under the section gets attracted if the insulted person is not present.[3]

For constituting an offence under section 3(1)(x) of the Act, the offence should occur in presence of public or atleast utterances should be audible to members of public. The word "public" would include members of public, already in the locality as residents as well as visitors from outside. "The members of family or the resident-servant" cannot be treated as members of public. It was observed that the material on record show that at the time of incident neither there was presence of public nor it was heard by neighbours, thus no offence is made out under section 3(1)(x).[4]

Complainant must prove certain words uttered by the accused which were alleged as offensive, neither eye-witnesses were produced, instead the eye-witness appeared for defence. It was held that the accused was entitled to acquittal.[5]

Offence under section 3(1)(x) contemplates presence of the complainant, though the words were uttered in a public meeting. Thus it was held that the alleged insult was not made in public view as he was not present there.[6]

In short, to attract the provisions of section 3(1)(x), it is necessary that the insult or the intimidation must be done at a place in public view.[7]

---

1. *Swaran Singh* v. *State,* 2008 Cr LJ 4369 (SC): 2008 AIR SCW 5758: (2008) 8 SCC 435; also see *Asmathunnisa* v. *State of Andhra Pradesh,* 2011 Cr LJ 2594 (SC).
2. *Swaran Singh* v. *State,* 2008 Cr LJ 4369 (SC): 2008 AIR SCW 5758: (2008) 8 SCC 435.
3. *Asmathunnisa* v. *State of Andhra Pradesh,* 2011 Cr LJ 2594 (SC); also see *Arumugam Servai* v. *State of Tamil Nadu,* 2011 Cr LJ 2899 (SC).
4. *Mahesh Sakharam* v. *State of Maharashtra,* 2009 Cr LJ 3831 (Bom) (3833): 2009 (5) AIR Bom R 214: 2009 (2) Bom CR (Cri) 867.
5. (1996) 2 Rec CriR 641 (MP)
6. *E. Krishnan Nayanar* v. *Dr. M.A. Kuttappan, Member, Kerala Legislative Assembly,* 1997 Cr LJ 2036 (Ker): ILR (1997) 2 Ker 837: 1997 (1) Ker LJ 280.
7. *Govind Das* v. *State of Orissa,* (2000) 1 Ker LJ (NOC) 43 (SC); *Binoy* v. *State of Kerala,* (2001) 1 Ker LJ 64: 2001 Cr LJ 112; *Bishanlal* v. *Hargovind,* RLW 2000 (3) (Raj) 1680.

8. Intention of Utterances Covered

The accused had simply addressed the complainant with the words "*Chamariya*" but "did not use ugly words relating to his caste." It was held that "it cannot make out the offence punishable under section 3(1)(x) of the Act", because "simply addressing a person by his caste without any intention to insult or intimidate does not constitute the offence under this section."[1]

But answering a question, whether mere calling of caste name with the intention to insult or humiliate can be gone into at the initial stage of the proceeding, the court ruled that the FIR cannot be quashed as it was initial stage at which intention could not be established.[2]

9. Cases Not in "Public View"

To constitute an offence under section 3(1)(x) when insult or intimidation has been done in a place within public view, but when the things had transpired in a office of a company. There was no material to show that the office was visible to public at large, hence no offence under the said section was made out.[3]

Accused was principal of college where complainant was working as teacher. Action was taken against the complainant for illegalities committed by him including misbehaving with girl students as well as female staff. Complainant alleged that when he went to the chamber of principal to ask about the notice issued to him the accused abused him in his caste name in her chamber and in front of two friends of the complainant. It was observed that the alleged event had taken place inside the chamber and out of public view, therefore no offence could be made out.[4]

In a delayed complaint it was alleged that the accused called the complainant by caste name, but there was no disclosure in the complaint that the occurrence had taken place in public view. Besides, it was shown that the accused was not aware of the caste of the complainant. Therefore it was held that merely calling somebody by caste name does not attract provisions of the Act and none of the requirements of section 3(1)(x) were satisfied. The courts also citied approvingly a decision of same court in Criminal P. 1449/95, *B.N. Channegowla* v. *State of Karnataka*, dated 27-1-1997, wherein it was held: "It is also stated that all these words were uttered in the private chamber of the petitioner and not in public view and no other person was present," thus no offence.[5]

When the entire occurrence had taken place inside and "within the bounded area of the house of the complainant and not in any place within public view", no offence under the provisions of the Act is made out.[6]

---

1. *Pappu Singh* v. *State of Uttar Pradesh*, 2002 Cr LJ 1251 (All) (1252): 2001 (3) All Cri R 2702: 2002 (46) All LR 586; 1998 Cri LR (Raj) 304; but also see 2011 Cr LJ 2899 (SC) (Supra).
2. *Rosamma Thomas* v. *Circle Inspector of Police, Tripunithura*, 1999 Cr LJ 1666 (Ker): ILR (1999) 2 Ker 520: 1999 (1) Ker LJ 413: 2000 (1) JIC 915 (Ker).
3. *Alka A. Misra* v. *J.P. Shoke*, 2003 Cr LJ 1333 (Bom): 2003 (9) All Ind Cas 666: 2003 All MR (Cri) 207.
4. *Suryakanta Ramesh Ajmera* v. *State of Maharashtra*, 2011 Cr LJ 1803; *Dr. Narendra Bhojram Patil* v. *State of Maharashtra*, 2010 Cr LJ 2762 (Bom): 2010 All MR (Cri) JS 38: 2010 (3) AIR Bom R 243.
5. *Chandra Poojari* v. *State of Karnataka*, 1998 Cr LJ 53 (Kant): 1998 (2) Cur Cri R 129: 1997 (4) Kant LJ 81.
6. *Gorkhi Ram* v. *State of Haryana*, 2006 Cr LJ 4385 (P&H) (4386): 2006 (4) Rec Cri R 356.

10. Quashing of Proceedings under section 482

Supreme Court justified quashing of the proceedings under section 3(1)(x) under the powers given to High Courts under section 482 Cr PC. It was observed that when abuse of process leading to injustice is found, the High Court would be justified in invoking its inherent powers provided under section 482 Cr PC, while there was no specific provision in the statute which abrogates this inherent power, and quashing the complaint. A complaint was lodged under section 3(1)(x) alleging use of filthy language against a person who was not present and it was admitted in the FIR. Basic ingredients was found by the court missing, hence it was observed that the filing of complaint was unjust.[1]

11. Framing of Charges may be Challenged

It was alleged by the complainant that when she had gone to the Government quarter of the accused on the first floor, for purpose of asking her wages, the accused called her *"Saali Dhobin"*. It was observed that the place cannot be said to be "within public view". With the result, it was held that in the circumstances order for framing of charge of intentional intimidation in public view was not proper nor there was any ground for framing the charge.[2]

12. Suggested Caution

V.S. Kokji J. had observed: "Before leaving this case, I consider it to be my duty to point out that these days several cases are being registered by the police under the Atrocities Act without carefully considering whether the offence under the Act is made out or not. As special and stricter provisions have been made in the Act, it is duty of the prosecution to examine the case more carefully. They have to be vigilant for avoiding any possibility of the Act being misused for harassment of the citizens who have not committed any offence under the Act.........."[3]

The same kind of caution was issued by a G.O. issued by Uttar Pradesh Government (mentioned earlier).

Various articles have also appeared in so many law journals, indicating that, though, the Act was legislated for a good cause, but with the passage of time some perversions and *mala fides* have crept in its application and often the provisions are being used for settling scores.

13. Disclosing Caste of Accused in FIR – Whether Necessary

Several Benches, including a Division Bench of Bombay High Court had earlier ruled that every complaint or the FIR registered under the provisions contained under section 3, must mention the caste of the accused because of its opening statements states so[4]. Because of this Bombay High Court constituted a Full Bench to decide the matter. The Full Bench held that merely because the caste of the accused was not mentioned in the FIR, it cannot be quashed. The Bench

1. *Asmathunnisa* v. *State of Andhra Pradesh*, 2011 Cr LJ 2594 (SC); *Mohd Nisarul Haq* v. *State*, 2011 Cr LJ 2755 (Jhar).
2. *Suhail Fasih* v. *State of Uttar Pradesh*, 2012 Cr LJ (NOC) 177 (All).
3. *Karan Singh* v. *State of Madhya Pradesh*, (1992) Andh LT 509: 1992 Cr LJ 3054 (3056-57) (MP).
4. *Manohar M. Kulkarni* v. *State of Maharashtra*, 2005 Cr LJ 4653: 2006 (37) All Ind Cas 611: 2006 (1) Bom CR (Cri) 778; and *Anant Vasantlal Sambre* v. *State of Maharashtra*, writ pet. No. 49 of 2001 decided on 20-4-2001 (Both cases were overruled by the Full Bench of Bom HC.)

further went on that during the course of investigation facts may be ascertained as to the caste of the accused and a proper step could be taken.[1]

14. Constitutionality of section 3(1)(x)

Provisions of section 3(1)(x) of The Scheduled Caste and the Scheduled Tribe (Prevention of Atrocities) Act, 1989 were declared legal, valid and constitutional because the Parliament had enacted this provision to prevent atrocities provided under Arts. 17 and 35 of the Constitution.[2]

Another Bench of M.P. High Court observed that validity of the section 3 cannot be faulted on the ground that it operates against Muslims and Christians who do not believe in Caste system.[3] (Please also see under the headline constitutionality of section 3 in the earlier part)

15. Applicability of section 3(1)(x) on Conversion

There seems to be a difference of opinion between different Courts, whether a person who had converted to Christianity may take benefit and protection of section 3 of the Act and initiate the proceeding thereunder.

Madras and Kerala High Courts are of opinion that if the victim originally belonged to Scheduled Caste or a Scheduled Tribe, his or her conversion or marriage would not deprive him or her of that status and benefit, and the provisions of section 3 would still be applicable in that case.[4]

While A.P. High Court is of the view that proceedings under section 3 of the Act cannot be initiated by a person belonging to Christian community by conversion.[5]

16. Section 3(1)(x) and section 482 Cr PC

High Court, in its exercise of its inherent powers provided under section 482 Cr PC, can interfere with the order of taking cognizance, where it appears from the facts of the case mentioned in the complaint that no case was made out under the provisions of the Scheduled Castes and the Scheduled Tribes (Prevention of Atrocities) Act, 1989, as the occurrence had not taken place in public view.[6]

But when the FIR was lodged under section 3(1)(x) of the Act on the ground that accused abused the complainant in her caste name in filthy language causing insult and intimidation to her the High Court would not make enquiries into the truth of the allegations in exercise of powers under section 482 Cr PC, thus FIR cannot be quashed.[7]

---

1. *Pushpa Vijay Bonde* v. *State of Maharashtra*, 2009 Cr LJ 3204 (Bom) (FB): 2009 (79) All Ind Cas 293: 2009 (2) Bom CR (Cri) 32: 2009 (4) Rec Cri R 936 (overruling above mentioned two cases of the same Court).
2. *K.C. Ravindran Pillai* v. *Union of India*, 1997 Cr LJ 1231 (Ker): 1997 (1) Crimes 566: 1996 (2) Ker LT 1016.
3. *Ram Krishna Balothia* v. *Union of India*, 1994 Cr LJ 2658: AIR 1994 MP 143: 1994 MPLJ 644; also see *Mata Sewak Upadhaya* v. *Union of India* (Supra).
4. *Rosamma Thomas* v. *Circle Inspector of Police, Tripunithura*, 1999 Cr LJ 1666 (Ker): ILR (1999) 2 Ker 520: 1999 (1) Ker LJ 413: 2000 (1) JIC 915 (Ker); *Kaliya Perumal* v. *State*, 1998 Cr LJ 1467 (Mad): 1998 (2) APLJ (Cri) 49: 1998 (2) Rec Cri R 562.
5. *Papatla John Veeranna* v. *State of Andhra Pradesh*, 2003 Cr LJ 2204 (AP) (2205): 2003 (2) Andh LT (Cri) 474 (AP): 2003 (3) Rec Cri R 489.
6. *Chandra Poojari* v. *State of Karnataka*, 1998 Cr LJ 53 (Kant): 1998 (2) Cur Cri R 129: 1997 (4) Kant LJ 81; *Asmathunnisa* v. *State of Andhra Pradesh*, 2011 Cr LJ 2594 (SC).
7. *Kaliya Perumal* v. *State*, 1998 Cr LJ 1467 (Mad): 1998 (2) APLJ (Cri) 49: 1998 (2) Rec Cri R 562.

The Apex Court had guided that, though no hard and fast rule can be laid down in regard to inherent powers provided under section 482 Cr PC for quashing the proceedings of lower courts, but the power should be used sparingly and carefully and it can be used only in situations laid down in section 482 as to prevent abuse of process of law, which is one of the consideration for use of such powers under the Act.[1]

In dealing with another case under section 3(1)(x) the Apex Court had held that correctness of allegations in FIR cannot be seen into by High Court under use of provisions of its inherent powers (section 482 Cr PC), it has to be seen whether on perusal of FIR *prima facie* is made out or not.[2]

17. Section 3(1)(x) and Revision

When the adduced evidence shows that no case can be made out under section 3(1)(x) of the Act against the accused, thus the finding recorded by Special Judge was declared perverse as conviction was based without any evidence. It was held that perverse finding of fact can be interfered with in the revision, petition and the revision succeeded.[3]

18. Section 3, Private Complaint and section 197 Cr PC

A private complaint was filed under section 3 of the Act against a public servant before a Magistrate, who had taken cognizance of the case. The complainant's shop was demolished by Chairman Municipal Board and who also abused her husband saying him "Dhoba". A final report was submitted by I.O., the Dy. S.P., but Magistrate after conducting an enquiry under 202 Cr PC, took cognizance under section 3(1)(x) of the Act.[4]

It was held that the Act of 1989 empowers Special Judge to take cognizance of offences under section 3 of the Act, and not the Magistrate, who has no jurisdiction to take cognizance of offence or act upon complaint under section 3 of the Act. Besides the accused was discharging official duty at the time of alleged occurrence, hence the accused was a public servant and it was required by section 197 Cr PC that a previous sanction was necessary before taking cognizance of such complaint. On this ground also the cognizance ought not to be taken.[5] The decision was based on the old notion, which was overruled by Apex Court in *Gangula State of Andhra Pradesh* case[6]. Now it is the settled law that Magistrate is empowered to take cognizance of offences under section 3 of the Act.

It is submitted that Court of Special Judge constituted under the Act of 1989 is also a Court of Sessions, and the Magistrate is empowered to adduce and record

1. *Gorige Pentaiah* v. *State of Andhra Pradesh*, 2009 Cr LJ 350 (SC): 2008 AIR SCW 6901: (2008) 12 SCC 531.
2. *Swaran Singh* v. *State*, 2008 Cr LJ 4369 (SC): 2008 AIR SCW 5758: (2008) 8 SCC 435.
3. *Gulab Khawal* v. *Hiraji*, 2006 Cr LJ 3451; *Pappu Singh* v. *State of Uttar Pradesh*, 2002 Cr LJ 1251 (All) (1252): 2001 (3) All Cri R 2702: 2002 (46) All LR 586; 1998 Cri LR (Raj) 304; but also see *Ram Chander* v. *State of Uttar Pradesh*, 2002 Cr LJ 1253 (All): 2002 (92) Fac LR 213: 2002 (1) LLJ 907; 2004 Cr LJ (NOC) 356 (Raj).
4. *Dinakrushna* v. *Sunanda Behera*, 2003 Cr LJ 5102 (Ori) (Supp)): 2003 (12) All Ind Cas 71: 2003 (2) Ori LR 492.
5. *Dinakrushna* v. *Sunanda Behera*, 2003 Cr LJ (Supp) 5102: 2003 (12) All Ind Cas 71: 2003 (2) Ori LR 492; 1996 MPLJ 141 (FB); *Udhab* alias *Udhab Charan Kar* v. *Guru Bindhani*, 1994 Cr LJ 3815: (1994) 78 Cut LT 865: 1994 (7) OCR 656; *Vidavaluru Balaramaiah* v. *State of Andhra Pradesh*, 2003 Cr LJ 3192 (AP): 2003 (1) Andh LT (Cri) 420 AP: 2004 (1) Rec Cri R 882.
6. 2000 Cr LJ 819 (SC): AIR 2000 SC 740: 2000 AIR SCW 279.

evidence under sections 200 and 202, Cr PC for offences triable by sessions, and after adducing such evidence in private complaints the Magistrate concerned is required to commit the case to Sessions Court. Besides presently it has become a settled law that the Special Court constituted under the Act cannot take cognizance of offence under the Act directly. The Special Court is required to take cognizance only after case has been committed to it by Magistrate, complying with the requirements of section 193 Cr PC. The position of ruling in *A.R. Antulay* v. *Ram Das Srinivas Nayak*[1] was different, and the correct position has been given in *Gangula Ashok's* case (supra).

19. Amount of Relief

Provided under rule 12(4) of SC, ST Rules, 1995 and scale as has been mentioned in the Schedule attached therewith at Serial No 10: "upto Rs 25,000 to each victim depending upon the nature of the offence. Payment of 25% when charge-sheet is sent to the Court and rest on conviction."

Section 3(1)(xi) "assaults or uses force to any woman belonging to a Scheduled Caste or a Scheduled Tribe with intent to dishonour or outrage her modesty;"

SYNOPSIS

1. Analogous Law
2. Meaning of Words – Section 349, 350, 351 and 354 of IPC – Defines
3. "Assault"
4. "Uses Force"
5. "Dishonour or Outrage her Modesty"
6. Offence under 3(1)(xi) and section 354 IPC
7. Attempt to Commit Offence
8. Section 3(1)(xi) and Rule 7
9. Section 3(1)(xi) and Provisions of Cr PC
10. Relief Amount

1. Analogous Law

A new kind of offence has been created through section 3(1)(xi) of The Scheduled Castes and the Scheduled Tribes (Prevention of Atrocities) Act, 1989, which is also a combination of various sections of Indian Penal Code, 1860. Section 349 IPC defines "force", section 350 IPC defines "Criminal force", section 351 IPC defines "Assault" and section 354 IPC provides punishment for "Assault or Criminal force to woman with intent to outrage her modesty".

Because the Act of 1989 did not define the above mentioned words, their meanings or for their likely interpretations, it would be better to mention those definitions etc.

2. Meaning of Words – Sections 349, 350, 351 and 354 of IPC – Defines

A person is said to use force to another if he causes motion, change of motion, or cessation of motion to that other, or if he causes to any substance such motion, or change of motion, or cessation of motion as brings that substance into contact with any part of that other's body, or with anything which that other is wearing or carrying, or with anything so situated that such contact affects that other's sense of feeling:

Provided that the person causing the motion or change of motion, or cessation of motion, causes that motion, change of motion, or cessation of motion in one of the three ways hereinafter described:

---

1. AIR 1984 SC 718: 1984 Cr LJ 647 (SC): (1984) 2 SCC 500.

First.—By his own bodily power.

Secondly—By disposing any substance in such a manner that the motion or change or cessation of motion takes place without any further act on his part, or on the part of any other person.

Thirdly—By inducing any animal to move, to change its motion, or to cease the move.

Section 350. 'Criminal Force.—Whoever intentionally uses force to any person, without the person's consent, in order to the committing of any offence, or intending by the use of such force to cause, or knowing it to be likely that by the use of such force he will cause injury, fear or annoyance to the person to whom the force is used, is said to use criminal force to that other.

Illustrations (a to h given)

Section 351. Assault.—Whoever makes any gesture, or any preparation intending or knowing it to be likely that such gesture, or preparation will cause any person present to apprehend that he who makes that gesture or preparation is about to use criminal force to that person is said to commit an assault.

Explanation.—Mere words do not amount to assault. But the words which a person uses may give to his gesture or preparation such a meaning as may make those gestures or preparations amount to an assault.

Illustrations [(a) to (c) given]

Section 354. Assault or Criminal force to woman with intent to outrage her modesty.—Whoever assaults or uses criminal force to any woman intending to outrage or knowing it to be likely that he will thereby outrage her modesty, shall be punished with imprisonment of either description for a term which may extend to two years, or with fine, or with both.[1]

3. "Assault"

Section 3(1)(xi) of the Act of 1989 starts with and can be read with the opening phrase of the section 3(1), which would make it – "Whoever not being a member of Scheduled Caste or a Scheduled Tribe 'assaults'.........." etc.

The sub-section 3(1)(xi) contains the element of 'intention in such assault, whereas the definition under 351 IPC even makes an attempted assault to be covered under the definition. An assault stipulated an act or attempt of unlawful violence with intention to use force criminally.

Under English Law, 'assault' has been distinguished from 'battery'. Assault is a threat to inflict unlawful force by one person to another. The crime has been said to have been completed if the person has made an intentional such kind of gesture which an onlooker may anticipate that a threatened force was about to be applied, though it may not have actually been applied. That is why under English law a threat to kiss is not a dangerous act. But in Indian society there are different perceptions, and even touching back of a woman is considered dangerous and outrageous. There must be some overt act.

1. Madhya Pradesh has made an amendment by inserting section 354A "Assault or use of Criminal force to woman with intent to disrobe her" – M.P. Act No. 14 of 2004 (w.e.f. 2-12-2004.

On the other hand a mere gesture or threat which is not in the slightest degree executed, could constitute assault. It will depend on the different circumstances, such as distance of the two persons involved where the threat cannot possibly be executed.

It would be a good defence for the accused to prove that the acts did not constitute an offence under section 3(1)(xi) when the acts were accidently occurred, or where the parties were major and the occurrence took place with due consent. It should always be born in mind that without use of criminal force or violence offence of assault cannot be constituted.

According to established American view, a battery is consummation of the assault, while assault is wilful touching the person of another aggressively, or by some substance put in motion by him for touching the other person in a sexual way, without the consent of other (Webster's Legal Dictionary p. 17).

4. "Uses Force"

'Force' is a very wide term and it is being used in various meanings in different subjects. For instance in Physics, four kinds of 'forces' govern the entire matter in the cosmos, which is beyond the scope for the present discussion. (they define it differently).

The definition given under section 349 IPC of 'force' is outcome of English phrase – *"vi et armis"*, which means an exertion of energy, producing a change in other things, making one as subject and the other as object. But we are here concerned with the use of force between two human beings, the other of whom must be a woman belonging to a Scheduled Caste or a Scheduled Tribe.

In the context the other word which could be used along with the word 'force' would be 'criminal', so that an offence may be constituted under section 3(1)(xi) of the Act.

5. "Dishonour or Outrage her Modesty"

Generally preserving honour and modesty of women is a rule of morality law and the object is to keep decency intact in society. For the general law such acts as outraging modesty of woman through assault or using criminal force has been declared as an offence by Indian Penal Code.

"Modesty" implies a quality of being 'modest'. In regard to women, the word "modesty" means decorous in manner and conduct, scrupulously chaste and shrinking from indecency. Whereas word 'decency' means propriety of behaviour, what is required by good taste or delicacy, avoidance of obscene language and gesture and of undue exposure of person and the repectability.[1]

But a question would naturally come to mind: whether a woman who do not possess above mentioned qualities, can be called modest, or whether an act against such kind of women may be brought under the ambit of criminal law when their modesty has been alleged to be outraged? Answer is in the negative, because the question has to be decided on the facts of each case, as there is no abstract conception of 'modesty' which can be applied to all cases.

---

1. The Oxford and Webster's dictionaries.

An infant female child of 6 or 7 months does not have any sense of modesty or possesses the qualities as aforementioned. If somebody tries any wrong to such a child, (often cases come before the courts), the accused should be held responsible for the offence, despite the fact that the child had neither the modesty nor honour. In the same sense the modesty of an unfortunate adult prostitute may be outraged under certain circumstances.

Section 10 of Indian Penal Code, 1860 defines woman as: "the word 'woman' denotes a female human being of any age." For the purpose of section 3(1)(xi) it must be added to this definition that the "woman" must belong to Scheduled Caste or a Scheduled Tribe.

But it is also interesting to note what amounts to "dishonour or outraging the modesty" of a woman? These acts may be covered under numerous forms, and which may also depend on the prevailing customs and practices among a particular community. The Scheduled Tribes living in different parts of country have various such customs, which may look very outrageous to city people but it may be nothing for them. Permitted acts in festival of Holi, marriage or with some related women may be nothing at special occasions, but during ordinary days such acts may become dishonour or an outrage. It is so because such acts on special occasions are presumed to be done with consent.

The outrageous acts must, again be intentional, whereas an inadvertent mistake or a circumstance, it may be indicated that the act was outrageous, though, but it would not become a punishable offence under the Act, if there was no intention. For instance, during a travel in a crowded bus or a train it may happen that some lady may be touched due to lack of space or movements of bodies in sync with the movement of the vehicle. This would not automatically become an offence, unless a clear intention is proved.

In one instance accused was a total stranger to the woman at the time when the alleged occurrence took place, where the accused caught hold of a lady belonging to Scheduled Caste. Witnesses allegedly saw the incident from a long distance of 440 yards. The Court refused prosecution of the accused and he was released.[1]

6. Offence under section 3(1)(xi) and section 354 IPC

An act of assaulting or using force to any woman who belongs to Scheduled Caste or a Scheduled Tribe with the intention to dishonour or outrage her modesty is a punishable offence under section 3(1)(xi). It would be immaterial to consider that such act is also punishable under any other provision of Indian Penal Code. The offence under section 3(1)(xi) of the Act of 1989 is an aggravated form of offence under section 354 IPC.[2]

1. *Nazeeruddin* v. *State of Andhra Pradesh*, 1999 Cr LJ 1773: 1999 (1) APLJ (Cri) 19: 1999 (1) Andh LD 685; *Peedikandi Abdulla* v. *State of Kerala*, 1998 Cr LJ 2758: 1999 (1) Crimes 660: 1998 (4) Cur Cri R 339; *Ram Prashad* v. *State of Madhya Pradesh*, 1997 Cr LJ 1846 (1847): 1997 (2) Cri CJ 70: 1997 (3) Rec Cri R 425.
2. *Vidyadharan* v. *State of Kerala*, 2004 Cr LJ 605 (SC): AIR 2004 SC 536: 2003 AIR SCW 6511; also see *Thana Ram* v. *State of Rajasthan*, 1996 Cr LJ 502 (Raj): 1994 (1) Raj LR 519: 1994 (2) Raj LW 326; *Kailas Govind Wadekar* v. *State of Maharashtra*, 2010 Cr LJ 2752 (Bom): 2010 (3) AIR Bom R 211: 2010 (2) Bom CR (Cri) 709, but also see *Sanjay Das* v. *State of Madhya Pradesh*, 2011 Cr LJ 2095; *Dwarika Rai* v. *State of Jharkhand*, 2011 Cr LJ (NOC) 168; *State of Rajasthan* v. *Bhanwar Lal*, 2011 Cr LJ (NOC) 429 (Raj).

7. Attempt to Commit Offence

Accused was alleged to have taken Adivasi girl forcibly in car, but a final report was submitted by the police on the ground that the case was false. Thereafter the Magistrate took cognizance. It was found by the Court that there is no absurdity and a *prima facie* case was made out. It was not necessary to consider protest application by the Magistrate and order of taking cognizance was proper.[1]

8. Section 3(1)(xi) and Rule 7

When an offence has been committed against a woman belonging to the Scheduled Caste or a Scheduled Tribe, the provisions of Rules of 1995, framed under The Scheduled Caste and the Scheduled Tribe (Prevention of Atrocities) Act, 1989 have to be strictly followed; meaning thereby that the investigation of the case must be conducted by a police officer not lower than Deputy Superintendent of Police, who has been specified under Rule 7 of Rules of 1995.

If the investigation was not conducted by the specified officer under rule 7, the trial shall be declared as vitiated.[2]

But when an investigation was conducted by Sub-Inspector of Police, where the accused were convicted under sections 341 IPC and 3(1)(xi) of the Act of 1989, it was held that the trial was vitiated as far as the conviction relates to section 3(1)(xi). However Court further held that there was clear evidence showing that the woman victim was wrongfully restrained by accused, therefore accused were liable for conviction under section 341 IPC.[3] (Please also see Investigation, mentioned previously).

9. Section 3(1)(xi) and Provisions of Cr PC

A private complaint filed by a victim whose modesty was allegedly outraged. She was not aware of the fact, whether police had registered a case or not in respect of one of the incidents. The Court observed that a report under section 210 Cr PC cannot be called as it cannot be said that investigation was in progress. It was held that Magistrate was competent to take cognizance after recording statements under sections 200 and 202 Cr PC. It was also observed that Magistrate can take cognizance and try two different incidents in a single complaint under section 218 Cr PC, considering both to be in one transaction. And, lastly the court refused to quash the proceedings under the Act of 1989 under section 482 Cr PC, on the ground that the accused also belonged to Scheduled Caste hence he cannot be tried under the Provisions of the Act of 1989, holding that the last plea would be decided after the trial.[4]

---

1. *Deepak Kumar Lal* v. *State of Jharkhand*, 2006 Cr LJ 299 (Jhar): 2005 (27) All Ind Cas 226: 2004 (3) BLJR 2027.
2. *T. Hanmanthu* v. *State of Andhra Pradesh*, 2004 Cr LJ 4087 (AP): 2005 (1) Crimes 627: 2005 (1) Cur Cri R 65; *Mansingh Baburao Garud* v. *State of Maharashtra*, 2011 Cr LJ (NOC) 444 (Bom).
3. *D. Ramalinga Reddy @ D. Babu* v. *State of Andhra Pradesh*, 1999 Cr LJ 2918 (AP) (2919): 1999 (2) Andh LD 572: 1999 (2) Crimes 343.
4. *Vidavaluru Balaramaiah* v. *State of Andhra Pradesh*, 2003 Cr LJ 3192 (AP): 2003 (1) Andh LT (Cri) 420 AP: 2004 (1) Rec Cri R 882.

10. Relief Amount

Please see at the last of 'Comments under section 3(1)(XII) as same amount has been given in the Schedule.

Section 3(1)(xii) "being in a position to dominate the will of a woman belonging to a Scheduled Caste or a Scheduled Tribe and uses that position to exploit her sexually to which she would not have otherwise agreed;"

SYNOPSIS

1. Ingredients

Ingredients of Section 3(1)(xii) were mentioned by a Division Bench in the following manner:

"(i) the offender must be a person who is not a member of Scheduled Caste or a Scheduled Tribe.

(ii) he be in a position to dominate the will of a woman belonging to a Scheduled Caste or a Scheduled Tribe.

(iii) the said position was used to exploit the woman sexually, to which she would not have otherwise agreed."[1]

2. Meaning of Words

Two positions were explained. In order to attract the application of provisions of section 3(1)(xii), sexual exploitation must have taken place, and that too, because of the offender's position of dominance. It was also observed that the word "otherwise" is significant, which clearly points out that this "exploitation" was with agreement of the helpless woman, which she would not have agreed but for the offenders' position of dominance. It is also significant to note that expressions used in section 3(1)(xii) uses word "agreed" and "exploit sexually", and not "consent" and "rape".[1]

Word "exploit" means to make an illegitimate use of, to utilise for one's own ends, treat selfishly as more workable material to make capital out of it. To have "carnal knowledge of woman" by use of position of dominance, is sexual exploitation, if the victim would not have agreed to the act, but for the position. Words 'consent' and 'agreement' are not etymologically different. The expression "would not have otherwise agreed" conveys that the agreement would not have been there, but for the position of the dominance. In short it is not free and voluntary consent.[1]

---

1. *Panibhushan Behera* v. *State of Orissa*, 1995 Cr LJ 1561 (Ori) (1568): 1995 (3) Crimes 537: 1995 (1) Ori LR 151.

3. Conditions of Applicability of section 3(1)(xii)

There can be following conditions under which provisions of section 3(1)(xii) would apply:

(i) The victim woman must belong to either a Scheduled Caste or a Scheduled Tribe.

(ii) The offender must not belong to a Scheduled Caste or Scheduled Tribe.

(iii) The offender must hold a dominating position by any means or circumstances.

(iv) The position of dominance must be such that the will of the woman of Scheduled Caste or a Scheduled Tribe has become defunct due to the position of offender.

(v) The position of dominance must be used to exploit such woman sexually.

(vi) The "agreement" of such woman must be subject to that dominating position of offender.

(vii) In other circumstances such woman would not have "agreed" to get her sexually exploited by the offender.

4. Legal Meanings of Expressions

Being in a Position to Dominate the Will

The expression "being in a position to dominate the will" of a woman clearly signify a condition, a circumstance or combination of circumstances. The word "will" and "consent" refer here to same condition and act of mind in general sense and both of them are functions of volition. The word "will" is not susceptible to variations, while word "consent" may be susceptible to variations, such as a subsequent 'consent'.

The word "will" is a faculty of mind which gives discretion to a person to decide whether to do or not to do a certain thing. The "will" also implies determination in taking decisions consciously or in cognition.

5. Circumstances

Various kinds of instances and circumstances may be cited when the discretionary faculty of mind of a woman may be dominated, which could be said to dominate the will of a woman. But for fulfilling the requirements of section 3(1)(xii) it would certainly not include those conditions of mind of the woman where she has lost her consciousness by some means, such as in sleep, under hypnotic trance or under influence of drugs etc. It is so that the section 3(1)(xii) requires dominance of "will", which should be a state of mind where the woman is fully in control of her consciousness and "will" to agree (or consent) or not, but for the reason of dominating factor, she agrees to get her exploited which in free conditions or circumstances "she would not have otherwise agreed".

A tribal woman was promised that the upper caste boy would marry her and for that reason she lived with him for five months and when she became pregnant, the boy deserted her. Accused boy was found guilty of an offence under section 3(1)(xii) on the ground that he dominated the will of the woman and he also used his position to exploit her sexually, assuring her that he would marry her.[1]

---

1. *Gujula Satyanarayana Reddy* v. *State of Andhra Pradesh*, 1997 Cr LJ 948 (949-50) (AP): 1996 (3) Andh LD 406: 1996 (4) Cur Cri R 455.

It is submitted that the object of the Act of 1984 was to protect and to prevent "atrocities" on Scheduled Castes and the Scheduled Tribes. It was nowhere stated in the judgment that the accused, though belonging to an upper caste, lived with the victim on the ground of inflicting atrocities on the woman. *Secondly*, the "will" of the woman was not dominated, because she was free to deny her sexual exploitation in the first instance and could have told him to get married first, and till then she would not allow him to touch her. Thus it was a free consent. It would be clear from the facts of following case.

In a similar case, it was alleged that a class teacher of a tribal girl committed rape on the promise of marrying her. Complaint was lodged only when pregnancy was shown. It was observed by a Division Bench that evidence showed that the victim willingly and with full consent had sexual intercourse with accused. The Bench set aside the conviction under section 3(1)(xii) of the Act of 1989, on the ground that there was no question of exploitation or dominating of will of victim girl can arise, as she had sexual intercourse with the accused with full consent.[1]

6. Objections on Applicability

The woman, who alleged rape did not mention in the complaint that the offence was committed against her because she was a member of Scheduled Caste. On this ground, accused raised the question of jurisdiction of Special Court. The Court observed that the question was not raised before the charge was framed. The questionable inherent jurisdiction cannot be raised before High Court under section 482 Cr PC after the charge was framed by the Special Court. Raising the objection subsequently would only cause unavoidable delay in proceedings. The petitioner was a landlord and the woman was working in his field when occurrence happened. It was observed that the petitioner was in advantageous position due to her poverty, and that is why the rape was committed.[2]

7. "Exploit Her Sexually"—Burden of Proof

According to above mentioned conditions of applicability of provisions of section 3(1)(xii), it must be proved that the molested women must belong to Scheduled Caste or a Scheduled Tribe and on the ground of which they were molested. Accused cannot be prosecuted for atrocities on Scheduled Caste woman, just because the woman was molested by the accused.[3]

Prosecution must establish, before requesting a conviction under the provisions of section 3 of The Scheduled Castes and the Scheduled Tribes (Prevention of Atrocities) Act, 1989, that the ingredients of the section have been proved beyond reasonable doubt. It was observed that the burden is certainly

1. *M.C. Prasannan* v. *State*, 1999 Cr LJ 998 (Cal) (DB): 1999 (1) Cal HN 123: 1999 (1) Cal LT 458; also see *Amar Bahadur Singh* v. *State*, 2011 Cr LJ 1921 (SC); *Dinesh Jaiswal* v. *State of Madhya Pradesh*, 2010 Cr LJ 1917 (SC): AIR 2010 SC 1540: 2010 AIR SCW 1606; *Abbas Ahmad Choudhary* v. *State of Assam*, 2010 Cr LJ 2060 (SC): 2010 (2) AIR Kant R 503: 2010 AIR SCW 1917; *Jafar* v. *State*, 2010 Cr LJ (NOC) 780 (All).
2. *Naga Bhixam* alias *Bhixapathi* v. *State of Andhra Pradesh*, 1996 Cr LJ 2400 (AP): 1996 (2) APLJ 239: 1996 APLJ (Cri) 263.
3. *Karan Singh* v. *State*, 2004 Cr LJ (NOC) 352 (P&H): 2004 (3) Rec Cri R 827.

on the prosecution in this respect as is in any other criminal case. The victim of rape belonged to a Scheduled Tribe. It was not proved by the prosecution that accused was "not a member of a Scheduled Caste or a Scheduled Tribe. The prosecution ought to have investigated into this aspect and obtained a certificate from the authorities as to the community to which the accused belongs and the fact whether he is a member of a Scheduled Caste or a Scheduled Tribe." As no evidence was adduced by the prosecution to show "that the accused committed rape on PW 1 on the ground that she is a member of Scheduled Tribe. ...... The cause for the offence must contain an element of racial prejudice".[1]

"Exploit" means to make an illegitimate use of; to utilize for one's own ends etc., as has been mentioned above. "Exploit her sexually" would mean that sexual act or intercourse was performed not out of free consent.

The Immoral Traffic Act also uses expression "sexual exploitation". This Act first was enacted in 1956 in pursuance to the International Convention to which India was a signatory, but since then the Act had been amended twice, *i.e.*, in 1976 and then in 1986. The Amending Act of 1986 had changed the title of the Act from "Suppression" to "Prevention". In the old definition of prostitution given in section 2(f) was as: "the act of a female offering her body for promiscuous sexual intercourse for hire". This definition has now been changed as: "*sexual exploitation* or abuse of persons for commercial purposes".

The important ingredient of prostitution, mentioned by the old definition as "promiscuous sexual intercourse" has now been replaced by two requirements of exploitation or abuse of the person, and secondly the abuse of exploitation should be for commercial purposes. It is crystal clear under the expression "sexual exploitation", not an *iota* of free will or free consent could be included. Thus the expression "sexual exploitation" would include such a sexual intercourse where consent is absent and in other words it is "rape". Therefore, whether or not the woman belongs to a Scheduled Caste or a Scheduled Tribe, it has to be proved that there was no free consent, irrespective of the facts and circumstances that the offender was holding a position of dominance.

8. Section 3(1)(xii) and sections 375, 376 IPC

In majority of cases when it is found that an accused has been charged and complained under section 3(1)(xii) of The Scheduled Caste and the Scheduled Tribe (Prevention of Atrocities) Act, 1989, he is simultaneously also charged under section 376 IPC etc.. Indian Penal Code, 1860 defines 'Rape' under section 375.

Though the word 'rape' has not been specifically used in the body of section 3(1)(xii) of the Act, but according to above discussion the expression "exploit her sexually" stipulates sexual intercourse without express consent. Further the last expression, just after the previous one, "to which she would not have otherwise agreed", confirms the absence of express consent for such sexual intercourse. Consequently the said expressions are elaborations of the definition of rape given in the Code of 1860, which is:

---

1. *M. Ramachandran* v. *State of Kerala*, 1996 Cr LJ 3566 (3569) (Ker) (DB): ILR (1996) 2 Ker 511: 1996 (1) Ker LJ 378; *Karan Singh* v. *State of Madhya Pradesh*, 1992 Cr LJ 3054 (MP).

"375. *Rape.*—A man is said to commit "rape" who, except in the case hereinafter excepted, has sexual intercourse with a woman under circumstances falling under any of the five following descriptions:

First.—Against her will.

Secondly.—Without her consent.

Thirdly.—With her consent, when her consent has been obtained by putting her in fear of death, or of hurt.

Fourthly.—With her consent, when the man knows that he is not her husband, and that her consent is given because she believes that he is another man to whom she is or believes herself to be lawfully married.

Fifthly.—When or without her consent, when she is under sixteen years of age.[1]

Explanation.—Penetration is sufficient to constitute the sexual intercourse necessary to the offence of rape.

Exception.—Sexual intercourse by a man with his own wife, the wife not being under fifteen years of age, is not rape."

It is said that, "rape or Raptus is when has a carnal knowledge of a woman by force and against her will". The essential words in an indictment for rape are *'rapuit & carnaliter cognovit'*. Literally the word 'rape' means a forcible seizure and ravishment of a woman without her consent or against her will.

It is not the question of honour of only women in case of rape but it has also become honour of her relatives which arouse in such a manner at times that feelings of retaliation and often revenge had resulted in bloodshed during long human history.

Accused willing to marry prosecutrix, above 16 years of age and belonging to Scheduled Caste but the marriage was refused by her inmates, then the complaint was lodged. Prosecutrix also was found 142 days foetus inside her. It was held that they were intimate and no offence, under the Act or 376 is made out.[2]

9. Difference Between Sexual Exploitation and Rape

As mentioned above the body of text of section 3(1)(xii) of the Act of 1989 does not use the word 'rape' but it uses the expression "exploit her sexually", therefore it is necessary to understood between the two, though, apparently both may seem to bear same meaning.

In the first place it may be mentioned that for constituting an offence of rape, universal definition given under section 375 IPC, alongwith its conditions, explanation or even exception may be referred. The offence of rape is confined

1. Age of consent mentioned originally in clause 'fifth' was "ten years". It was raised to "12 years" by section 1 of the Criminal Law (Amendment) Act X of 1891, and then it was again raised to "14 years" by section 2 of the Amending Act XXIX of 1925, and finally to "16 years" by section 3 of the Amending Act XLII of 1949.

   In the Exception "12 years" were raised to "13 years" by Amending Act of 1925 (above), and to "15 years" by section 3 of Amending Act, 1949 (above).

2. *Dinesh Kumar* v. *State*, 2012 Cr LJ 228; also see *Radhu* v. *State of Madhya Pradesh*, 2007 AIR SCW 5845: AIR 2007 SC (Supp) 847: 2007 Cr LJ 4704; *Alamelu* v. *State*, AIR 2011 SC 715; *Chandra Mohan alias Bunti* v. *State of Haryana*, 2011 Cr LJ 898 (P&H).

in these parameters. While the expression 'sexual exploitation' is a more wider term, which, though may include rape, but it may also take other forms. For elaborating the point it would be better to cite the explanations referred to by Webster's Legal Dictionary (As has been perceived in America):

> "generally, the crime of forcing or causing a person to submit to sexual intercourse, whether vaginal, oral or anal against her will, or when consent is obtained by unfair and unlawful means (as by putting a drug in a drink), or under circumstances in which the person is incapable of giving legally valid consent (as with a person who is unconscious or underage). The terminology for such offences, the exact range of conduct covered by term used – such as 'rape', 'sexual imposition' or 'sexual assault' varies from state to state."[1]

Thus it is clear that the terminologies used for such offences cover a range of conduct and forms of acts connected with sexual activity.

The third clause attached to section 375 of IPC partially applies to section 3(1)(xii), because the expression – "being in a position to dominate the will of a woman" stipulates every other possibility and eventuality beyond "putting her in fear of death, or of hurt". Many facts of the cases have been cited in the preceding paragraphs where the offender was found to dominate the will of the woman due to economic, social or other reasons.

Therefore all unlawful acts concerning sexuality which are beyond 'outraging modesty' [covered under section 3(1)(xi)] and even if short of 'rape' may be covered under the ambit of section 3(1)(xii) of the Act. ('Rape' itself would certainly included). It would depend on the circumstances of each case and no fixed lines could be strictly drawn.

Secondly, section 3(1)(xii) of the Act does not use the expression "without her consent" as has been used in the second clause of section 375 IPC. Neither the present section used words "against her will". If we, for the purpose of understanding, draw attention to the text of section 3(1)(xii) of the Act of 1989 as: "being in a position to dominate the will of a woman........... exploit her sexually to which she would not have otherwise agreed", the last phrase is indicative of a condition of, say duress or compulsion on the part of woman. It would also cover the state of "against her will" and "without her consent". (also implied one).

On the other hand phrase: "not have otherwise agreed" in section 3(1)(xii) of the Act stipulates full consciousness of the woman concerned who is presumed to be a normal person, because in case of a weak intellect or unconscious woman, question of her 'agreeing' cannot arise. A woman must be in full possession of her senses and reason, besides capable of exercising her own volition otherwise she cannot be said to have "agreed". The terms "will" and consent are both functions of mind arising out of volition and discretion. Similarly "agree" or 'not to agree' is a state which stipulates that after application of reason and pros and cons have fully been weighed some final decision has been taken to 'agree' or 'not to agree'. (rules of age put apart).

1. Webster's Legal Dictionary p. 217-18. Also describe the kinds as: 'Date rape', 'acquaintance rape', 'marital rape', 'spousal rape' and 'statutory rape'.

Thirdly, in rape cases which had come up for trial and decision, often a question arises that whether the circumstances shown may lead to presume a consent on the part of woman (of course if she is not minor). Hundreds of hypothetical situations may be created where it would become difficult to decide whether it was a free or implied consent or an apparent or forced consent by reason of duress etc. (Please see Russell on Crime, 11th Edn, Vol. 1, pp 794 *et sq*). In all cases where no resistance was caused by woman may not be taken as implied consent. The offence under section 3(1)(xii) would stipulate that an apparent consent and consequential submission has taken place because the ravisher is "being in a position to dominate the will of a woman" must exist. For that reason consent under section 3(1)(xii) and consent under sections 375 or 376 IPC should be understood differently.

Section 3(1)(xii) assumes that submission without resistance must be found to exist. As consent is the fundamental ingredient of rape, which decides the act to be legal or criminal, difference between consent and submission is important. Every consent is followed by submission, but if the situation is conversed, as to be presumed under the created offence of section 3(1)(xii), every submission would not become consent, it would rather constitute 'compulsion'.

Correct situation described under section 3(1)(xii) of the Act may be gathered from an observation of Hon'ble Tek Chand J. – "A mere act of helpless resignation in the face of inevitable compulsion, quiescence, non-resistance, or passive giving in, when volitional faculty is either clouded by fear or vitiated by duress, cannot to be deemed to be 'consent' as understood by law".[1]

10. Norms for Relief

For clause (xi) and (xii) under 'Annexure' 1 of Schedule [see Rule 12(4)] attached to the Scheduled Caste and the Scheduled Tribes (Prevention of Atrocities) Act, 1995, it has been provided at Serial No. 12 that Rs. 1,20,000 has to be paid "to each victim of offence, 50% of the amount may be paid after medical examination and remaining 50% at the conclusion of trial".

This amount of compensatory relief is paid by the Government. The amount of Rs. 1,20,000 has been fixed both in cases where the modesty of the woman has been outraged or she is being sexually exploited as mentioned in clauses (xi) and (xii) of section 3 of the Act.

Section 3(1)(xiii) "corrupts or fouls the water of any spring, reservoir or any other source ordinarily used by members of Scheduled Castes or the Scheduled Tribes so as to render it less fit for the purpose for which it is ordinarily used:,"

SYNOPSIS

---

1. *Rao Harnarain Singh Sheoji Singh* v. *State*, 1958 Cr LJ 563: AIR 1958 Punj 123: 59 Pun LR 519; followed *In re Kandasami Mudali*, 1960 Cr LJ 930 (Mad) (DB): 1960 Mad LJ 550: AIR 1960 Mad 316.

The provisions contained under section 3(1)(XIII) of the Act could be said to be outcome of creative thinking, because crime created here is an innovation for prevention of atrocities against Scheduled Caste and the Scheduled Tribes.

1. Provisions of Protection of Civil Rights Act, 1955

Under sections 4(iv) and 7(b) of Protection of Civil Rights Act, 1955, it was provided that any person would be liable to punishment who on the ground of 'untouchability' creates any disability in regard to use or access of any river, stream, spring, well, tank, cistern, water-tap, other watering place or any bathing ghat etc.

Variety of cases had come up before courts under the provisions of Protection of Civil Rights Act, 1955, where the Scheduled Castes or Scheduled Tribes' members were prevented or obstructed from taking water from well etc., on such ground[1], or entering temples or hotels.

But 'corrupting' or 'fouling' of water resources which are used by members of Scheduled Castes and Schedule Tribe was a new idea to be put under the list of 'atrocities' against such members.

2. The expression "Less fit"

The expression used in the clause (xiii) of section 3(1) of Act is "less fit" and not 'renders it useless for human consumption', or the like phrases. The expression "less fit" would require a very mitigated or even a slight negligent act "to render" the water source corrupted or polluted. Even washing clothes or utensils with soap in the 'upstream' may render the water of lower 'stream' to be "less fit", though 'not unfit' for human use. The expression may be used for variety of created situations, which may be inadvertent.

3. Similar Offence under section 277 and 278 of IPC

Section 277 of Indian Penal Code 1860 reads as:

"277. *Fouling of water of Public Spring or Reservoir.*—Whoever voluntarily corrupts or fouls the water of any public spring or reservoir, so as to render it less fit for the purpose for which it is ordinarily used, shall be punished with imprisonment of either description for a term which may extend to three months, or with fine which may extend to five hundred rupees, or with both."

The clause (xiii) of sections 3(1) of the Act of 1989 is a *verbatim* copy of first part of the text of section 277 IPC, except deletion of word "voluntarily", and addition of one expression – *viz.*, "or any other source ordinarily used by members of the Scheduled Castes or the Scheduled Tribes".

Therefore to constitute an offence under section 277 IPC, the act of corrupting or fouling the said water must be a voluntary act, while under section 3(1)(XIII) even if the said act has been done by mistake, inadvertently or negligently it becomes an offence. The word "voluntarily" conceives an intention.

---

1. *Behari Lal* v. *State*, AIR 1967 All 130: 1967 Cr LJ 304: 1967 All Cri R 232; *Bendhar Sahu* v. *State*, 157 ILR (1962) Cut 256; *Bisheshwar Prasad* v. *State of Uttar Pradesh*, 1967 Cr LJ 1102: 1967 All WR (HC) 604: 1967 All Cri R 391.

Word "voluntarily" has been defined under section 39 IPC as: "A person is said to cause an effect 'voluntarily' when he causes it by means whereby he intended to cause it, or by means which, at the time of employing those means, he knew or had reason to believe to be likely to cause it.

In deleting the word "voluntarily" from the text of section 3(1)(xiii) of the Act would mean that intention of corrupting or fouling the water, or knowledge of the act being without belief of reason that it would make the water "less fit" becomes immaterial. Perhaps such a situation would not be appreciated by Courts of law, because it hits the cardinal principle of criminal jurisprudence, which stipulates that a criminal act must be done with intention or at least knowledge and belief that the act would cause harm.

The fact that any act has prompted a certain result is not sufficient to constitute an offence, because the act might have been done with any other intention and the knowledge of the effect and consequent result may be lacking. For instance if a person takes bath in a tank (person being a visitor to the area), that person cannot be charged on the ground that the water of the tank was rendered "less fit" for human consumption as it was used for drinking purposes. The said person could be charged only when either the tank displayed any lawful order prohibiting bathing or from other sources the said person gained knowledge that the water of the tank is used for drinking, and bathing will necessarily foul it.

On the other hand fishing or cultivation of paddy in a tank which is known to be a source of drinking water, would certainly contaminate, foul or corrupt the water of the tank, and if it is used by members of Scheduled Caste or Scheduled Tribe, it would certainly be an offence under the present clause.

4. Ingredients

To substantiate a charge under section 3(1)(xiii) of the Act of 1989 it is necessary that three things must be essential—(i) whoever not being a member of a Scheduled Caste or a Scheduled Tribe must foul or contaminate the water intentionally (or even unintentionally), (ii) the water must belong to any spring, reservoir or any other source ordinarily used by members of Scheduled Castes or Scheduled Tribes, and (iii) the act must be such that the fouling or corrupting of such water must render the water 'less fit' for the purpose of its use.

5. Spring, Reservoir or Other Source of Water

For purpose of section 3(1)(xiii) of the Act of 1989, the "spring, reservoir or any other source" of water may or may not be public, as it had been a condition for dealing with the cases under 277 IPC, but these sources must be such that are "ordinarily used by members of the Scheduled Castes or the Scheduled Tribes". The said source may not be *'res communiae'* where a common right is exercised by everyone. The question of ownership of the source of water is not a question in issue, but it may be proved that such source is "ordinarily used by members" of the said class. It may be an Easmentary right. In that way it may be neither a 'public nuisance' nor a 'private nuisance', but a separate kind of offence.

A well is an example of a spring, while a tank or cistern is said to be an example of reservoir. A river is neither considered as spring nor a reservoir thus the provisions could not apply to it[1]. Even the pools formed in the rivers also cannot bc brought under the ambit of reservoirs or springs, but may not be so in cases of "or any sources". A question would arise whether a canal or an artificial lake could be included; or whether a common source of water, commonly used by general public as well as the members of Scheduled Castes or the Scheduled Tribes could be brought under the ambit of section 3(1)(xiii). Public taps in cities, towns and now in villages are commonly been used by all, including such members. Can fouling or corrupting water of such common sources be brought under the ambit of section 3(1)(xiii) exclusively, or in addition to charging the person only under section 277 IPC? Perhaps the provisions of Act of 1989 would not be applicable, but charges could be framed under section 277 IPC or 290.[2]

6. "Ordinarily" used

The expression "ordinarily" may mean "normally", but the said expression must be understood in the context in which it has been used. The expression may mean "solely". When in a common parlance the expression "ordinarily" is used, there may be an option open. It is never used in reference to a case where there is no exception. It never means "primarily".[3]

7. Corrupting or Fouling Necessary

The law enumerated under section 3(1)(xiii) of the Act of 1989 punishes those who try to endanger lives of members of Scheduled Castes and Scheduled Tribes, by contaminating the water supply to them. It is both, – safeguard to their health, as well as a prejudice prevention measure.

The word "corrupt" is a combination of two Latin words, *i.e., cor* (together) and *umpo* (to breach). But in English literature it means to change from a sound to putrid or putrecent state; to cause to rot; deprave; defile or desecrate. While "foul" means to be putrid.

Various kinds of methods may be applied to corrupt or foul the water. A person may foul the water by spitting or washing himself or cattle in it etc. etc. 'Fouling' is fouling and its degree would be immaterial for invoking the provisions of this section.

The fouling or corrupting a source of water used by such members is not confined to drinking water sources, but the use may be for any other purpose. Offence would be complete if the act renders it less fit for use for the purpose of which the source is used.

8. Amount of Relief

The 'Schedule' to 'Annexure I' appended to SC/ST Rules of 1995 [as provided in Rule 12(4)] at Serial No. 13 it is so provided: "upto Rs. 2,50,000 or full cost of restoration of normal facility, including cleaning when the water is fouled. Payment may be made at the stage as deemed fit by District Administration".

The payments are made by the concerned State Government.

---

1. *Nana Ram* v. *State*, 6 Bom LR 52.
2. "Public Nuisance" has been defined under section 268, IPC.
3. *State of Andhra Pradesh* v. *V. Sarma Rao*, 2007 Cr LJ 289 (294) (SC): AIR 2007 SC 137: 2006 AIR SCW 5700; *Kailash Chandra* v. *Union of India*, AIR 1961 SC 1346: ILR (1961) 2 All 195: (1962) 1 SCR 374.

Section 3(1)(xiv) denies a member of a Scheduled Caste or a Scheduled Tribe any customary right of passage to a place of public resort or obstructs such member so as to prevent him from using or having access to a place of public resort to which other members of public or any section thereof have a right to use or access to.

SYNOPSIS

1. Analogous Law
2. Scope
3. Meaning of Words
4. "Place of Public Resort"
5. "Relief Amount" Entitlement

1. Analogous Law

Clause (xiv) of section 3(1) of The Scheduled Castes and the Scheduled Tribes (Prevention of Atrocities) Act, 1989 has consolidated various provisions spread under sections 3, 4, 5 and 7 of Protection of Civil Rights Act, 1955. But under the various said sections, expressions used are as—"place of public" [section 3(b)]; "public restaurant"; "place of public entertainment"; "use of general public" etc. etc. (section 4); "benefit of general public" (section 5) etc.; while, instead section 3(1)(xiv) of the Act of 1989 has used the expression "public resort". This term has been used by Protection of Civil Rights Act, 1955 only once, *i.e.* in section 4(iv).

'Preventing' or the word 'obstruction' in connection of use of "rights" by such members has been made punishable under section 7 of Protection of Civil Rights Act, 1955.

2. Scope

The provisions envisage that no person belonging to such Caste or Tribe should be refused to enter or have an access to a place of public worship where other persons professing same religion are admitted. It was observed that object is not to create any new rights but its intent is put members of Scheduled Caste and the Scheduled Tribe at par with other caste Hindus. It was also observed that where the temple in question was a purely denominational temple confined to Jains alone and the non-Jain Caste Hindus could not enter the temple as of right, because he was a non-Jain.[1]

Similarly if a function is private and it was not a place of public worship a member of Scheduled Caste or a Scheduled Tribe cannot insist to participate.[2]

The act alleged must be proved, such as when it is said that the accused had prevented access to a public well, it must be sufficiently proved that the well was a public well[3]. The provisions do not apply to private wells. The owner of a private well being free to regulate the use of his well. The fact that such owner permitted other co-villagers to draw water from his well, would not prove that every villager has a right to access to the well.[4]

---

1. *State* v. *Puranchand*, 1958 Cr LJ 1398 (DB): AIR 1958 MP 352: 1958 MPC 497.
2. ILR (1963) Cut 455.
3. *State of Orissa* v. *Rengsa*, 1985 Cr LJ 1917: 1985 (59) Cut LT 353: 1985 (1) Ori LR 376.
4. (1962) (28) Cut LT 157; Also see *State of Karnataka* v. *Appa Balu Ingale*, 1993 Cr LJ 1029 (SC): AIR 1993 SC 1126: 1993 AIR SCW 337.

Complainant alleged that the accused proprietor of hotel was keeping separate cups etc., but it was not mentioned that those cups etc., were kept for members of Scheduled Caste or Scheduled Tribes, it was held that acquittal was justified.[1]

In order to attract the rigors of the provisions of the Act, the material ingredients of offences alleged should be established strictly beyond any reasonable doubt.[2]

3. Meaning of Words

To constitute an offence under section 3(1)(xiv) of the Scheduled Castes and the Scheduled Tribes (Prevention of Atrocities) Act, 1989, the place from where such a member is denied or obstructed from using any "right of passage" and "using or having access to a place of public resort" should be proved. Some instances of public places have been mentioned above.

4. "Place of Public Resort"

Grover J. observed: "A public place is one where the public go, no matter whether they have a right to go or not". It was also observed that many shows are exhibited to public on private property, that would not make it public place.[3]

'Place of public resort' is a wider term, taking within its ambit all the places where plurality of people gather. A temple could be such a place where gathering of people takes place

According to Webster "resort" means act of visiting, assembly, meeting concourse, frequent assembly and hence a street or alley adjoining a brewery where beer was sold, not used as a driveway, where from six to twelve persons were in the habit of daily congregating for the purpose of drinking beer for amusement and conversation, was place of 'public resort'.

According to Advanced Law Lexicon by Ramanathan Aiyar, the word "public resort", and 'place of public resort' means:

> "Public resort. A private house and a garden where a sale by public aution takes place is for the timebeing a 'place of public resort'. The place need not be a place of resort all the year around.
>
> "*Public resort, Place of:* A place at which public assembles or to which they retire".

Wharton's Law Lexicon explains the word "resort" as:

> *"Resort:* A court whose decisions is for the particular case before it becomes final and without appeal is, in reference to that case, said to be a Court of Last Resort. The House of Lords has been especially so spoken of."

The same dictionary gives the meaning of the word "public place" as:

> "Public Place: A public place would seem to include a place to which the public are accustomed to resort without being interfered with, though there is no legal right to do so."

---

1. *State* v. *Irappa*, 1981 Cr LJ (NOC) 104 (Kant) (DB); also see 1980 Cr LJ (NOC) 36, *State of Karnataka* v. *Laxminarayana Bhat*, 1991 Cr LJ 2126: 1991 (2) Crimes 251: 1991 (1) Kant LJ 257.
2. (1997) 7 SCC 522: 1997 SCC (Cri) 1110.
3. *Ramekwal Singh* v. *State*, 1954 Cr LJ 998 (Pat): AIR 1954 Pat 309: 1954 BLJR 31, cited the observations of Grove J.

A temple is a place of worship and it is also within the ambit of the expression 'place of public resort'.[1]

But a temple may be private as well. To determine true character of a particular temple, Apex Court has directed that various questions have to be addressed as:

(i) Is the temple built in such imposing manner that it may *prima facie* appear to be a public temple?

(ii) Are the members of the public entitled to worship in that temple as of right?

(iii) Are the temple expenses met from the contributions made by the public?

(iv) Whether the Sevas and Utsavas conducted in the temple are those usually conducted in public temples?

(v) Have the management as well as the devotees been treating that temple as a public temple?[2]

Rule 74 of Order XXI of Civil Procedure Code also mentions the expression 'place of public resort', though, in a different context but meaning could be gathered from there too.

Denial of right of passage to public places, like access to public water tap and other such places are an offence of atrocities as stipulated under section 3(1)(xiv) of the Act of 1989. It was observed that accused are liable to be convicted even on single testimony if the situation demands so, because the lighter punishments would only encourage enhancing instances of atrocities, according to norms prescribed by Supreme Court (State v. *Kashiram*, 2009 Cr LJ 1530).[3]

5. "Relief Amount" Entitlement

Every member of a Scheduled Caste or a Scheduled Tribe who has been subjected to 'denail of customary rights of passage' provided under section 3(1) (xiv) of the Act of 1989, shall be entitled to get "upto Rs. 2,50,000 or full cost of restoration of passage and full compensation of the loss suffered, if any. Payment of 50% when charge-sheet is sent to the court and 50% on conviction in lower Court."

The District Magistrate, Sub-Divisional Magistrate or other Executive Magistrate has been bound under Rule 12(4) of S.C.S.T Rules, 1995 to look after the payment of the said amount has been mentioned in "Annexure I" of Schedule at Serial No. 14.

Section 3(1)(xv) forces or causes a member of a Scheduled Caste or a Scheduled Tribe to leave his house, village or other place of residence.

SYNOPSIS

---

1. *Vennapusa Gangireddy* v. *State of Andhra Pradesh*, 2007 Cr LJ 3230 (AP): 2007 (6) AIR Bom R 1006 (NOC): 2007 (2) ALD (Cri) 167.
2. *Goswami Shri Mahalaxmi Vahuji* v. *Shah Ranchhoddas Kalidas*, AIR 1970 SC 2025: 1970 (2) SCA 143: (1970) 2 SCR 275.
3. *Abaji Shripatrao Tekale* v. *State*, 2011 Cr LJ 2195 (Bom).

1. Scope

Clauses (iv) and (v) of section 3(1) of the Act of 1989 deal with the kinds of atrocity inflicted on a member of a Scheduled Caste or a Scheduled Tribe, who has been dispossessed wrongfully from the land, or premises owned by, or allotted to him, or his right of free enjoyment on the land or premises has been interfered.

Unlawful occupation of agricultural land, owned or allotted to a member of a Scheduled Caste or a Scheduled Tribe [clause (iv)], and dispossession or interference of enjoyment of rights on his land (perhaps open) or premises or water [clause (v)] of such members have already been covered previously, but unlawfully using force to cause such a member to leave his "house, village or other place of residence" has been covered in the present clause. Thus the provisions of clause (xv) are somewhat different from the provisions of clauses (iv) and (v), as the provision stipulate a forceful eviction from his house, village or other place of "residence".

2. Ingredients

Following ingredients must be present to invoke provisions of section 3(1)(xv) of the Act—

(i) "Force" or other kinds of "causes" must be used;

(ii) The aggrieved person must be a member of Scheduled Caste or Scheduled Tribe;

(iii) The person who uses 'forces' or other 'causes' to get such member evicted must not belong to Scheduled Caste or a Scheduled Tribe;

(iv) Such evicted person must hold lawful right or ownership to house or other place of residence (not in case of "village").

3. Meaning of Words

The words "his house........... place of residence" stipulates that the "house" or the "place or residence" is owned by the member of Scheduled Caste or the Scheduled Tribe. In case it was found that such member is unlawfully residing (in house or residence), or in other case the member of the Scheduled Caste or the Scheduled Tribe has been evicted lawfully with due process of law the present provision would not apply. It is so because word "his" cannot mean any other thing than lawful ownership, if not a valid title. It is confirmed by the use of word "Restoration" in the 'Schedule' Annexure 1 to the SC/ST Rules, 1995 at Serial No. 15. (Also see rule 12).

Therefore in absence of any proof of lawful residence in a house, it may not be an offence under the present clause. But sort of eviction or externment from the village which is by 'force' is certainly an offence, as there is no questions involved as to lawful residence in the village.

4. Revision or 482 Cr PC Petition to Drop Charge

The complainant filed a revision against acquittal, where allegations were made against accused that they had forcibly occupied the victim's house and land, besides insulting him and his wife. It was found by the Court in evidence that there had been a dispute regarding the possession of land between the parties. The court did not find any evidence in the statement of witnesses about the manner of incident in the fateful night, worthy of believing, besides there was existing enmity between the parties, thus the revision of the complainant failed.[1]

When a petition was filed in the initial stages under section 482 Cr PC to quash First Information Report lodged under section 3(1)(xv) of the Act, it was held that from the perusal of the FIR it cannot be said that no case is made out and it would be for the investigating agency to collect evidence and find out whether there is a scope for filing a final report in the case. Besides it was also held that there is no prohibition of granting a regular bail since some of the offences under section 3 are not grave and there is "no bar for the Magistrate for granting bail in such cases"[2]

Relief Amount

In 'Annexure I, the Schedule provides at Serial No 15 as: "Restoration of site/ right to stay and compensation of Rs. 60,000 to each victim and reconstruction of the house at Government cost, if destroyed, to be paid in full when charge-sheet is sent to lower court".

Section 3(1) – [After clause (xv)], "shall be punishable with imprisonment for a term which shall not be less than six months but which may extent to five years and with fine."

SYNOPSIS

1. Scope
2. All offences under section 3(1) be Cognizable and Non-Bailable
3. Minimum Punishment
4. Imposition of Fine
5. Sentences by High Court

1. Scope

The word "atrocity" has been defined under section 2(1)(a) of The Scheduled Castes and the Scheduled Tribes (Prevention of Atrocities) Act, 1989, as: "atrocity means an offence punishable under section 3;"

Section 3 of the Act of 1989 has been divided into two sub-sections (1) and (2), thereby creating two categories of offences and punishments arising therefrom.

The legislature has created fifteen different kinds of acts and declared them to be offences, separately mentioned in fifteen clauses and in the last of sub-section (1) had collectively provided punishment which is applicable in uniform manner to each of the acts individually. In other words this last clause would be read with each clause when the Courts are dealing with a case arising out of an atrocitious act done within the ambit of a particular clause and the court has found the accused guilty.

2. All offences under section 3(1) be Cognizable and Non-Bailable

Though, second part (II) of 'First Schedule' of Code of Criminal Procedure 1973 – in respect of "Classification of offences against other laws" provide that

1. *Munsa Kumhar* v. *Brij Kishore*, 2006 Cr LJ (NOC) 395 (MP).
2. *A.M. Ali* v. *State of Kerala*, 2000 Cr LJ 2721 (2722) (Ker): 2000 (1) Ker LJ 802: 2000 (2) Ker LT 280; *Asmathunnisa* v. *State of Andhra Pradesh*, 2011 Cr LJ 2594 (SC).

the offence (other than IPC), "if punishable with imprisonment for 3 years and upwards but not more than 7 years" would be 'cognizable', 'non-bailable' and be triable by court of session. As the punishing clause of sub-section (1) of section 3 of the Act of 1989 provide the punishment with imprisonment "which may extend to five years and with fine", it automatically becomes cognizable and non-bailable, irrespective of the fact that the accused have been roped in under any or many of the offences prescribed in sub-section (1) from clauses (i) to (xv).

The Act of 1989 does not provide that all the offences shall be cognizable in terms of provisions of section 3 of the Act. The punishment may vary from six months to 5 years (with fine), therefore offences under section 3(1) would be cognizable.[1]

3. Minimum Punishment

The clause which provides for punishments when an accused has been found guilty of any of the offences prescribed under section 3(1), additionally provides that the term of imprisonment "shall not be less than six months". In other words the powers and discretion of the courts have been abrogated to take liberties in fixing standards of justice, often awarding minimum possible terms of imprisonments, where courts think that special circumstances under which the crime was committed, considering the age or any other special considerations concerning the accused, or for any other special reason, it was appropriate to do so.

In the present scenario, once the court holds the accused guilty, and calls upon the accused to hear him on the point of sentence under section 235(2) of Cr PC, the court's hand would be tied not to award a sentence of imprisonment for "less than six months", even if it is convinced of special pleas of the accused, for the reason of which provision of section 235(2) Cr PC was legislated. (Question of 'admonition' or release on 'probation' does not arise as it has been barred by section 19 of the Act).

In short, measure of punishment, as minimum punishment, cannot vary in any circumstance.

4. Imposition of Fine

By using the conjunction "and" in-between the provided term of imprisonment and "fine", the punishing clause also makes it mandatory to impose fine, in addition to the awarded term of imprisonment. Whatever be the circumstance the court is bound to impose 'fine' also when the accused has been declared guilty.

Indian Penal Code, 1860, had provided an optional discretion to the courts in most of the provided offences and used the expressions "or fine or both". But the Code has also imposed same kind of mandatory condition in some rare cases for imposition of fine, using the expression "and shall also be liable to fine" (section 380 IPC etc.).

No limitations have been provided in the above punishing clause of section 3(1) of the Act, as to the amount of fine. Therefore, though, it may be presumed that the amount may vary from *Rupee 1* to infinity, but court always use diligence and reason while passing orders.

---

1. 1992 BBCJ 675 (DB) (Pat).

5. Sentences by High Court

Many a times orders of acquittals by lower courts are being challenged before High Courts. The High Courts are empowered to pass sentences on the accused, setting aside the order of acquittal of lower Court. The exercise of this power by High Court has been observed to be regarded and subject to the limitation that the sentence to be passed should not be in excess of the powers of punishment exercisable by the trial Court.[1]

[Please also see under the headlines "Offence" and "Punishment" in early parts of comments on section 3 as well as comments under section 3(2)].

Section 3(2) "Whoever, not being a member of a Scheduled Caste or a Scheduled Tribe,—"

The opening phrase is the verbatim reproduction of words in the same sequence to what has been used in the opening phrase of sub-section (1) of section 3 of the Act.

The explanations and interpretations of words and expressions used in the opening phrase has already been dealt with. [Please see comments under section 3(1)].

Comparison of sub-sections (1) and (2) of section 3

As per the definition of "Atrocity" given under section 2(1)(a) of The Scheduled Castes and the Scheduled Tribes (Prevention of Atrocities) Act, 1989, all offences punishable under section 3 are 'atrocities'. In sub-sections (1) and (2) totally 22 kinds of offences and punishments arising therefrom have been enumerated. These offences and punishments have again been divided into two categories: one, fifteen offences have been specified under sub-section (1) of section 3, and secondly seven offences and punishments have been separately specified in sub-section (2) of the same section.

What is important to note is that in the first category of offences enumerated under sub-section (1) of section 3 of the Act, as a separate clause has been inserted at the fag-end of sub-section (1), which provide collective punishment for all the 15 categories of offences comprising within clause (i) to clause (xv) of sub-section (1); while all the seven clauses of sub-section (2) of section 3 of the Act, provide punishments individually for the offences prescribed in each of the seven clauses.

Secondly, maximum punishments provided collectively for all the fifteen offences specified from clause (i) to clause (xv) of sub-section (1) of section 3, is imprisonment for five years and with fine. But the maximum punishment provided under sub-section (2) of section 3 of the Act is death penalty, life imprisonment and with fine, seven years and with fine etc.

What is common between sub-sections (1) and (2), as far as punishment provisions are concerned, is that courts have been barred to award a sentence of not "less than six months" in each of 21 cases, except under section (3)(2)(vii), the 22nd offence, where the minimum punishment has been provided as: "which shall not be less than one year".

---

1. *Boddepalli Lakshminarayana* v. *Suvvari Sanyasi Appa Rao,* 1959 Cr LJ 1141: AIR 1959 AP 530.

It is specially sub-section (2) of section 3 of the Act which had repeatedly been constitutionally challenged, on the ground of its severity of provided punishments. As the collective punishments provided under sub-section (1) of section could not said to be so severe, it is the punishments provided under sub-section (2) which have become objects of controversy.

Holding the severity of punishments provided under sub-clause (2) of section 3 as constitutional, K.C. Agrawal, C.J. has to observe for pacifying the lot as: "These are however matters left to be judged and decided by Judicial Officer who decides impartially."[1]

Section 3(2)(i) "gives or fabricates false evidence intending thereby to cause, or knowing it to be likely that he will thereby cause, any member of a Scheduled Caste or a Scheduled Tribe to be convicted of a offence which is by the law for the time being in force shall be punished with imprisonment for life and with fine; and if an innocent member of a Scheduled Caste or a Scheduled Tribe be convicted and executed in consequence of such false or fabricated evidence, the person who gives or fabricates such false evidence, shall be punished with death;"

SYNOPSIS

1. Analogous Law

Section 3(2)(i) of the Act is almost *verbatim* reproduction of sections 194, 195 of Indian Penal Code 1860, except that an alternative punishment for imprisonment of life to that of an imprisonment which may extend to ten years. Section 194, of IPC protects public at large from being convicted on false or fabricated evidence in a "capital" offence, while the present clause is restricted to protect members of Scheduled Castes or Scheduled Tribes. Section 194 IPC is an aggravated form

1. *Jai Singh* v. *Union of India*, 1993 Cr LJ 2705 (FB) (Raj): AIR 1993 Raj 177: 1993 (1) Raj LW 157.

of the same offence as has been made punishable under section 193 IPC. The aggravation of punishment has been provided because the risk of life of another is involved.

2. Ingredients

Clause (i) of sub-section (2) of section 3 of the Act of 1989 contain very important provision for protection of members of Scheduled Caste and the Scheduled Tribes from being implicated falsely in offences "which is capital". However, main ingredients of this created offence are as under:

(i) Whoever, himself not being a member of a Scheduled Caste or a Scheduled Tribe, gives or fabricates false evidence;

(ii) Such giving or fabricating false evidence must be against a member of a Scheduled Caste or a Scheduled Tribe;

(iii) Such given or fabricated false evidence must be intentional or with knowledge that it be likely to cause conviction of such member;

(iv) Giving or fabricating false evidence must cause, or likely to cause, conviction of such member "of an offence which is capital by law";

(v) Such member must be "innocent".

3. Punishments

The clause provides two kinds of punishments, *i.e.,* (a) imprisonment for life with fine; and (b) death penalty.

Both the provided punishments are not alternative punishments, but these are independent exclusive punishments to be awarded in two given and prescribed circumstances and conditions,—when the member of a Scheduled Caste or a Scheduled Tribe has been executed in consequence of given or fabricated false evidence, the mandatory punishment is death penalty, but in all other cases the punishment is imprisonment for life with fine. It would mean that intentionally giving or fabricating false evidence against such members in a "capital" case and thereby cause his conviction of any sentence, the giver or fabricator of false evidence would be convicted for at least imprisonment for life, unlike the provisions of sections 194, 195 IPC, where an alternative punishment which may extend to ten years has been provided.

In that sense the prescribing mode of punishment is different from that of Indian Penal Code 1860. For instance under section 302 IPC, 'Punishment for Murder' is "death or imprisonment for life", while under section 3(2)(1) of the Act of 1989 if the member of a Scheduled Caste or a Scheduled Tribe has been executed, the court has no option or discretion but to award death penalty.

4. Sentence of Death

The second part of section 194 IPC also provides a death penalty but power has been given to courts to award alternative punishments as the wording are: "shall be punished either with death or the punishment hereinbefore described". The word "hereinbefore" certainly refers to the two alternative punishments provided in the first part (life or ten years). But under section 3(2)(i) in the provided second condition no alternative punishments, but the only death punishment, has been provided.

When an accused, not being a member of Scheduled Caste or Scheduled Tribe, gives or fabricates false evidence in a "Capital" case and the member of a Scheduled Caste or a Scheduled Tribe has been convicted and executed in consequence of such false evidence, the Special Court has to award the accused the sentence of death. The Special Judges appointed under the provisions of the Act of 1989 are Session Judges, therefore the sentence of death has to be submitted to the High Court for confirmation under section 366 Cr PC, and the sentence shall not be executed unless confirmed by the High Court.

In a series of cases the Courts in India have unanimously developed a rule of caution, stipulating that the death penalty, though in vogue in India, must be awarded in "rarest of rare cases".

It may be said that a non-Scheduled Caste or Tribe person, if gives or fabricates false evidence against a Scheduled Caste or Tribe person in a "capital" case, and if in consequence such member of that community is convicted and executed, the case may be brought under the category of 'rarest of rare cases', because of the fact of the act being atrocities to the highest degree which endangers the life.

Problem

But problems may arise when the High Court, during or at the end of process of confirmation of the death sentence, exercises its powers given under section 368 Cr PC.

In exercise of its powers, the High Court has three options under section 368 Cr PC:

"(a) may confirm the sentence, or pass any other sentence warranted by law, or

(b) may annul the conviction, and convict the accused of any offence of which the court of Session might had convicted him, or order a new trial on the same or amended charge, or

(c) may acquit the accused person:"

In exercise of the powers under section 368 Cr PC, the High Court has only third option open, because their Lordships would be restricted to exercise their powers in passing any other alternate sentence, whatsoever, because there are no option given under section 3(2)(i) of the Act, except extreme penalty in the given situation.

For instance, it may seem to their Lordships, that the charge of 'giving' or 'fabricating' false evidence was not proved beyond doubt, or it is doubtful whether the evidence was actually false (but it may have been true), but if such member was executed in consequence of such evidence, the Court has to confirm death penalty.

The Full Bench of Allahabad High Court had observed: "The punishment prescribed for most of the offences under sub-section (2) of section 3 is more than *minimum punishment*, unfortunately prescribed for the offence under section 3(1). ....The punishment for the offences under clauses (i) to (vii) of section 3(2) vary from six months to death. The punishment being higher under clauses (i) to (viii) of section 3(2), the Parliament discreetly made *mens rea* of such offences a necessary ingredient so that an accused may not unnecessarily be subjected to severe punishment."[1]

Determination of quantum of the sentence is out of question, when it has been proved that the member of the Scheduled Caste or the Scheduled Tribe has already been executed and such execution has taken place on the ground of evidence, which was accordingly false. The falsity or fabrication of evidence has not been defined by the Act of 1989, therefore the interpretations thereof cannot be limited to the defined parameters and may extend to vagueness; or, what the English authors say about the doctrine of transmigration of motive may assume its applicability.

Human Rights Organizations the world over are exerting pressure on UN and the Governments to abolish death penalty and succumbing to such pressure a large number of countries have already abolished death penalty.

Though Indian law has retained death penalty, but Courts have diluted the norms for awarding death sentence and phrases like "rarest of rare cases", have been coined.

In case sometimes in future, if India abolishes the death penalty, it is not likely to create much problems in regard to provisions of section 3(2)(i), because in that case no member of Scheduled Caste or a Scheduled Tribe be executed in consequence of false evidence and thereby attracting a death penalty for the offender giving or fabricating the false evidence would not arise.

No case has been reported in any law Journal of repute yet, but it would be interesting to see how courts react to their curtailed discretionary powers in connection with the death penalty, being the only option open to Courts where a member of the Scheduled Caste or a Scheduled Tribe has been executed as a result of given or fabricated false evidence by the accused.

5. Difference Between Offences under section 3(1)(viii), (ix) and under section 3(2)(i)

Almost similar acts have been declared as atrocity if inflicted on a member of Scheduled Caste or a Scheduled Tribe under section 3(1), clauses (viii) and (ix), where institution of false legal proceedings, civil or criminal and giving false or frivolous informations against such member has been declared as an offence and maximum liability of punishment is five years in prison and with fine. Presence or absence of *mens rea* has not been mentioned as an ingredient of these offences.

But giving or fabricating such false evidence against a member of a Scheduled Caste or a Scheduled Tribe with an intention to get such member convicted "of an offence which is capital by the law or the time being in force", would bring the giver or fabricator of false evidence in the ambit of provisions of section 3(2)(i), with all the implications of severe punishment provided therein.

As such, in the said clauses of section 3(1) the prescribed offences and the punishment is of a general nature, whereas the offence and the punishments in clause (i) of section 3(2) is of a special and graver type.

[Also see comments on clauses (viii) and (ix) of section 3(1)]

1. *Mata Sewak Upadhyay* v. *State of Uttar Pradesh*, 1995 JIC 1168 (All) (FB): 1996 (1) East Cr C 97 (All) (FB).

6. Meaning of Words

6.1 False Evidence

Essential requisite for constituting an offence under this clause is that the evidence must and essentially be false and the prosecution must prove it to be false.

Some very old cases have been cited where the preferred view of various Courts was that the falsity of evidence must be proved by direct evidence, and the view that evidence in question was so improbable that a prudent man would not accept it, was rejected. But such view is opposed to the provisions of Indian Evidence Act. In any case falsity of evidence given must be proved by direct evidence, as the charge attracts very severe punishments under section 3(2)(i) of the Act of 1989. (Position of Contradictory evidence has been explained in foregoing paragraphs).

6.2 "Gives or Fabricates False Evidence

Under English law for giving false evidence has been assigned the name as "perjury". Indian Penal Code 1860 defines the term "Giving false evidence" under sections 191, but the term "perjury" and "giving false evidence" differ on material points.

Webster's Legal Dictionary defines "perjury" as: "the crime of making a false statement under oath or affirmation on a material issue in a judicial or administrative proceeding, other than in the belief that what is being said is true."

On the other hand section 192 of IPC exhaustively define "Fabricating false evidence". Thus both expressions have to be dealt separately.

6.3 "Giving False Evidence"

There is a little difference between the expression and its meaning attributed to it under section 191 IPC, where one of the conditions for the giver of false evidence is, – he must be legally bound by an oath to state the truth, or has a legal obligation to state the truth, then he makes any false statement, which he knows or believes not to be true. But no such condition has been given under section 3(2)(1) of the Act of 1989. A person who "gives" false evidence against such member with the intention to cause or thereby likely to cause a conviction to such member in a "capital" case, he is liable to punishment under the clause.

7. Scope of Falsity or Fabrication

By a general reading of clause (i) of section 3(2) of the Act of 1989, it is clear that giving the false evidence must be related to some judicial or legal proceedings, because the said act should result in conviction in a "capital" offence, which is not possible in any kind of other legal proceedings. Though, absence of mentioning "bound by an oath", renders statements, recorded under section 161 Cr PC, 164 or 313 Cr PC which are found to be based on fabricated false facts may be included, provided such statement has been given during an investigation or trial of a "capital" offence.

As far as 'false evidence' stipulated under section 3(2)(i) is concerned, two essential factors must be present,—

(a) an intentional false evidence has been given; and, (b) the offender must have a belief that the statement is not true. Whoever "gives..........false evidence" cannot strictly be restricted to given statements. The expression is wide enough to include submission of false documents, which by all means a kind of evidence.

But, whether it is a false statement or a document, they cannot be brought under the said clause of section 3(2), if the proceedings are not related to a "capital" offence.

8. Position of contradictory Evidence

In case a witness, who was later charged under section 3(2)(i) gives a contradictory statement or produces a document which looked contradictory to another document on record, in a trial of "capital" offence, against a member of Scheduled Caste or a Scheduled Tribe, question may arise which of the two contradictory statements or produced documents, as the case may be, was "false evidence". The easiest way for prosecution is to prove that two contradictory statements made by the accused were deliberate and were so irreconcilable with each other that both of the statements cannot be possibly true, it was held (in very old cases) that the accused can be convicted of perjury, without the need to prove which of the two statements was false. But this situation must be fool proof as to look both the contradictory statements etc., cannot be true.

But where prosecution charges a person with giving false statement (or document), it has to prove by direct evidence that the statement is false, not considering the other statement. The vagueness of proof would not do. If the two statements are proved, one of which is claimed to be false but it is not certain which one is false, the charge would fail.[1]

For proving falsity, the direct or indirect evidence produced must be sufficient to induce a confidence that the evidence was actually and factually false. It would not be sufficient to produce the purported documents or their certified copies which were claimed by the prosecution to be false evidence, but those records have to be proved by direct evidence. It must be shown conclusively that both the statements, which were claimed to be contradictory were made by the accused.

9. "...intending thereby to cause, or knowing..."

Simply fabricating false evidence against a member of Scheduled Caste or a Scheduled Tribe would not constitute an offence under section 3(2)(i), unless such act of the accused was done with an intention to 'cause' such member convicted "of an offence which is capital by laws". Though, it has not been mentioned under section 3(2)(i) of the Act of 1989 in so many words, but it is presumed that such intentional fabrication of false evidence has been intended to be produced in a judicial proceeding before a court of law, because no other institution is capable of convicting a person in a "Capital" case. Therefore it is a natural inference that fabricated false evidence given in a non-judicial proceedings are not covered under the ambit of provisions of section 3(2)(i).

The other most important implication of "intending" would be that such fabrication of flase evidence must be materially admissible, and the act was not

1. *Umrao Lal* v. *State*, AIR 1954 All 424: 1954 All WR (HC) 10: 1954 Cr LJ 860.

done by mistake, carelessness or inadvertently. Therefore, the subject matter of fabricated false evidence must be capable of affecting the final result of the proceedings against such member. The law declares a false statement punishable when it is intentional and not otherwise.

A statement, though proved to be false and fabricated, but it could have been made with a motive to give more credibility to his story or boastfulness, but it cannot be brought under the criminality and field of section 3(2)(i) of the Act of 1989, unless it is proved that the fabrication and the falsity was with the intention as has been stipulated therein.

"Knowing it to be likely....cause"

Intentional fabrication of false evidence with the sole objective to obtain a conviction of such member of an offence which is 'capital' in nature, while such member was innocent, conceives a knowledge of falsity of such evidence. In normal circumstances it would be very difficult to prove that the accused was within full knowledge about the fabricated false evidence from before that such evidence would cause a conviction to an innocent member of Scheduled Caste or a Scheduled Tribe.

A person may believe a fact not to be true but it cannot be conclusively said that he believd the fact true as well, because the person might not have the conscious knowledge about the said fact, and he might be thinking the fact not to be true by his own inference or analysis. Besides, the knowledge could be based on his delusion. The might have inferred not as a reasonable man but as an unreasonable man.

There are persons who are hasty or reckless by nature in reaching conclusion and despite the fact that they had half knowledge about a fact on the basis of which he had drawn a conclusion in haste and as such believed the fact to be true, which was found later on to be false. Such people in the circumstances could not be punished for fabricating false evidence.

There could be a lot of circumstances and situations under which the observation or inferences drawn at the time of gaining knowledge or at the time of giving evidence, thus it must be proved by defence that the said person was not in a perfect condition to do so. For instance, if a person signs an affidavit, which is a substantial piece of evidence, when he is drunk, though its contents are supposed to have been read over to him, but in fact he does not understand what he is doing, he cannot be charged for giving false evidence. It is so because of absence of intention. [Please also see comments on section 3(2)(ii) for knowledge]

10. "Fabricating false Evidence"

Section 192 IPC defines "fabricating false evidence" stipulating: "whoever causes any circumstance to exist or makes any false entry in any book or record, or makes any document containing a false statement, intending that such circumstance, false entry or false statement may appear in evidence in a judicial proceeding,..... to form an opinion upon the evidence, to entertain an erroneous opinion touching any point material to the result of such proceeding, is said to fabricate false evidence".

The word 'fabricating' would mean manufacturing false evidence. The definition of section 192 IPC defines the expression thereby limiting its scope, as far as offences mentioned in the Code are concerned. But the Scheduled Caste and the Scheduled Tribe (Prevention of Atrocities) Act, 1989 does neither defined the expression nor referred the definition of the Code, therefore its scope is more wider than the Code.

Fabricating false evidence, however in both cases has been declared as an offence, if the intention is to pervert the course of justice, specially under the present clause to obtain a conviction in a "capital" offence of a member of Scheduled Caste or a Scheduled Tribe, by supplying false data or facts to mislead the court in giving an erroneous decision against such member. On one hand the court has been saved from extraneous influences, and on the other, members of the Scheduled Castes and the Scheduled Tribes have been protected from likely atrocity inflicted on them.

The expression 'fabricating evidence' may also be covered in the committal of offence of forgery within the meaning of sections 363 and 364 of Indian Penal Code. But difference for the purpose of section 3(2)(1) of the Act of 1989, as well as of section 192 IPC such as fabricated false evidence or forged document must be with the intention to be presented in evidence in a judicial proceeding; in the present context, such false evidence be presented in a trial against such member when he is being tried for a "Capital" offence.

11. Intention

Simply fabricating or manufacturing certain documents even with the intention of producing in a trial of "capital" offence against a member of Scheduled Caste or a Scheduled Tribe, it would not become an offence unless such fabricated evidence has been produced in such trial with the intention of getting such member convicted of such offence. But intention of fabricating false evidence and production of it before the court is sufficient to constitute other crime. It would not be material in that case that such false evidence finally resulted in the conviction of such member. Likelihood to cause the conviction is sufficient as far as intention is concerned.

12. Distinction Between Giving and Fabricating False Evidence

Simply giving evidence stipulates that a person has given the evidence through his statement; and, if that statement is false, it is called as 'perjury'. While fabrication of documents involves forgery to defraud. Both of these two are the basic elements to constitute a crime under section 3(2)(1) of the Act of 1989.

A person is required to 'give' evidence *in facie curiae,* meaning thereby that law requires that whatever has been stated shall be truth and nothing else, when it is before the Court; while, 'fabrication' takes place behind the back of court.

But in both cases intention of the perpetrator is the cardinal element to constitute a crime under section 3(2)(i) of the Act. Such intention must be proved in either of the cases, to obtain a conviction of a member of a Scheduled Caste or a Scheduled Tribe in a "capital" case.

13. Such False Evidence Must be Admissible

The given or fabricated false evidence must be such that it becomes admissible in the court of trial where the member of Scheduled Caste or a Scheduled Tribes is being tried for a "capital" offence.

For instance, if a person brings in some hearsay evidence, which is false and even stated with the intention of obtaining a conviction of such member, during the recording of his statement during trial, the offence cannot be constituted under section 3(2)(i), on the ground that hearsay evidence is not admissible evidence. Similarly if a statement has not been recorded in accordance with law provided on this behalf, it would not be admissible in evidence.

The subject-matter of false evidence must not only be legal evidence but it must be admissible evidence. This stipulates that a fabricated document which is inadmissible in evidence, cannot be included for charging any person under section 3(2)(i) of the Act of 1989.

Case diaries which are prepared by the investigating officers during investigation of a crime, as they are not admissible in evidence, therefore any false entries therein, found during trial, cannot be brought under the ambit of present section. But on the contrary entries in the General Diaries, if found false and fulfil the requisite of the section may become subject of prosecution. Despite the fact that both kinds of diaries can be used as evidence by the court during a trial, the question of admissibility and the inadmissibility decides the answer.

14. False Statement of Co-accused under section 313 Cr PC

In criminal cases the accused are protected against making false statements, while examined at the end of prosecution evidence, under section 313 Cr PC. They are not under oath [section 313(2)]. Sub-section 313(3) provides that by giving false answers to the question put to accused, he would not render himself for punishment. This rule does not apply to the false answers if given in connection of some co-accused, though, as a rule these answers are not binding on the co-accused, (unless that co-accused has been declared as an approver), but the Court may consider those answers [section 313(4)]. There is one view that the false statement of the accused cannot be used against him till his case is *sub judice*.

But the position will change if the accused puts himself in the witness-box as a witness, which he is free to do. He can become a competent witness in his own defence in disproof of charges levelled against him or any other person who is a co-accused. In such a case the accused would depose as a witness on oath, and if he "gives or fabricates false evidence", he would not only be liable to punishment for perjury in that case, but if such false evidence intentionally given to implicate such member, he may attract provisions of the present section.

15. Abetment for False Evidence Against Such Member

If a person instigates another to make false statement or fabricate evidence against a member of Scheduled Caste or a Scheduled Tribe, and that false evidence has been produced before a court in a "capital" offence, the instigator himself may not be guilty of giving false evidence, but he will be guilty of abetment of the offence. For this purpose the prosecution must prove that the abetment was not only made to make a statement but it should be found to be false.

To answer the question a hypothetical situation may be created: suppose a member of a Scheduled Caste or a Scheduled Tribe instigates a non-Scheduled Caste person to give or fabricate evidence against a member of a Scheduled Caste or a Scheduled Tribe in a trial for "capital" offence, can the abettor be arraigned with the non-Scheduled Caste person as an accused charged under section 3(2)(1) of the Act of 1989? Certainly not, because application of section 3 of the Act of 1989 excludes all such members from the prosecution under the provisions of the Act, though such person may be tried under section 194 IPC, read with other provisions of IPC.

16. Caution for Investigators and Prosecutors

The over-zealous police officer investigating a "capital" offence often introduce padding evidences to establish the charges during investigation which could be found later false or fabricated by the court during trial. Similarly the lawyers responsible for looking after prosecution on behalf of state, introduce or lead evidences in trials which could be later on found to be false by the court.

Such enthusiasm or zeal to succeed in their endeavour to procure conviction of the accused may cost them dearly if the accused belongs to a Scheduled Caste or a Scheduled Tribe and if the trial is for a "capital" offence.

The case diaries prepared during investigation are, though, inadmissible in evidence, but there are a lot of documents prepared during investigation which are admissible evidences. For instance recovery memo of arrest or memos prepared for taking into possession of material evidence are admissible evidences. Even the entries made in the General Diary by the investigating officer (for Rawangi, Wapsi etc.) are also admissible evidences.

It has become a trend that new kind of theories are propounded by the prosecutors (not coinciding with the investigation) and to prove those new kinds of theories, evidences are called by the permission of Court and produced, naturally putting the prosecutor responsible for such adventurism, if later on the evidence is found to be false; the case being a "capital" offence and the accused being a member of Scheduled Caste or a Scheduled Tribe, it is certain that the prosecutor would be in trouble. These acts may be brought under the ambit of section 3(2)(1) of The Scheduled Castes and the Scheduled Tribe (Prevention of Atrocities) Act, 1989, unless the investigator or the prosecutor himself belong to such caste or tribe, as the case may be.

In case an investigator or a prosecutor is charged under section 3(2)(i), it seems half of the job of the prosecutor would be done by the language of section 3(2)(i), as primary intention in both the cases is to procure "conviction". It is provided: "gives or fabricates false evidence intending thereby to cause, or knowing it to be likely cause, any member..........to be convicted.........".

Problem may arise if a complaint case by a relative has been filed, as complaint cases under the Act of 1989 have been held to be legally allowed and can be filed. In such cases protection provided under section 22 of the Act of 1989, or section 197 Cr PC may not be available. It is almost a settled law that protection under section 197 Cr PC is not available when the act was not done in due course of performance of duties. Padding or falsification of evidence cannot be covered under the guise of acts done in due course of duties.

The saving grace or a cogent defense in such a case could be that, besides being primary duty performed, the origin of intention was not on the ground and reason that the accused belonged to a Scheduled Caste or Scheduled Tribe.

17. Proof of False Evidence

Accepting proof of false evidence, whether it is a statement or a document, has already been settled by courts. In each of the cases the original record has to be produced and proved to substantiate the charge of giving or fabricating evidence. In certain cases it was found that it was not possible or practical to produce the original records, then the certified copies were allowed to be produced. But another view was that neither the original records nor the certified copies by itself would be sufficient to prove the falsity of evidence. The opinion said that statement of person be recorded who took down the deposition in question, or at least some person shall be produced who had heard the deposition when it was given. The demands of justice require that the original records must be produced, not only the statement or the document in question, but the entire record file of the trial to understand the nature and the circumstances of the proceedings under which such false evidence was produced. But again it may be said that the records themselves do not prove anything. The person or persons have to be produced who had prepared or on whose presence those records were prepared.

Secondly, the alleged false evidence must be such which was admissible as well as it was taken or recorded in accordance with law. Any defects found in regard to admissibility or recording etc., may render the charge of giving or fabricating false evidence useless.

Thirdly, it is a burden on the prosecution to prove that the alleged evidence was not probably, but necessarily false and the accused knew that fact. A statement may be inaccurate, ambiguous, dubious or uncertain, but it must be false and known to the accused to be so. A contradiction in a statement need not always contain falsity. That contradiction may arise for some other reason, for instance memory. Thus every contradictory statement cannot be made subject matter of prosecution under the present provision of law.

Following points may be proved by the prosecution in support of charge:

(i) As to Giving False Evidence—

(1) That the accused gave the statement in legal proceedings of trial of a SC/ST member in a capital offence (under oath);

(2) that the accused made the statement;

(3) that the accused intentionally made the statement to procure conviction of a ST/ST member;

(4) that the statement was false;

(5) that accused knew or believed the statement to be false.

(ii) As to Fabricating False Evidence—

(1) That the accused caused or made a false document, in part or full;

(2) that such false document or part thereof should appear in a trial of capital offence against a member of SC/ST;

(3) that such false document must be capable of generating an opinion in the mind of Court, which may result in conviction;

(4) that intention of such false fabrication shall be to cause an erroneous opinion which may result in conviction of SC/ST member.

(iii) As to Last Part of Clause (i) of section 3(2)—

In case of last portion of the clause (i), the prosecution has to prove additionally;

(1) that the capital punishment was carried out and member of SC/ST executed,

(2) that the member of SC/ST already executed was innocent.

18. Death of Accused, Complainant and Abatement

It has been provided under section 394 Cr PC that every appeal shall finally abate on the death of appellant. The Proviso of the section says that where the appeal is against a conviction and sentence of death or of imprisonment and the appellant dies during the pendency of the appeal, any of his relative, may apply for special leave, within 30 days of death of such appellant, to continue the appeal and in that case the appeal shall not abate.[1]

The appeal under sections 377 and 378 of Cr PC abates on death of the accused. An appeal against acquittal preferred by the complainant under section 378(4) Cr PC, however, does not abate on the death of complainant.[2]

Appeal against conviction and sentence does not abate even when state concedes the sentence of fine be set aside.[3]

But section 394 Cr PC has no application when the appeal was filed before Supreme Court by seeking special leave under Article 136 and question of abatement of appeal on the death would not be governed by the provisions of Criminal Procedure Code. This position is similarly applicable to the cases of death of the complainant.[4]

When there are many accused in a case, who had appealed and during pendency of appeal only main accused dies, the appeal would abate in regard to him only and for the rest it would continue.[5]

But where two accused were acquitted by the High Court, and the main accused dies during the pendency of the appeal before Supreme Court, naturally the appeal against him would abate. The remaining person left was abettor. It was held that appeal against abettor would become infructious.[6]

1. *S.V. Kameswar Rao* v. *State (A.C.B. Police), Karnool Dist., Andhra Pradesh*, 1992 Cr LJ 118 (SC): AIR 1991 SC 2085: JT 1991 (5) SC 48.
2. *Khelu Mehto* v. *State*, 1991 Crimes 501 (Del).
3. *Lakshmi Shanker Srivastava* v. *State (Delhi Administration)*, AIR 1979 SC 451: 1979 Cr LJ 207 (SC): (1979) 1 SCC 229.
4. *Bhageerathi Amma* v. *Jeevankumar*, 1982 Cr LJ 91 (Ker): ILR (1982) 1 Ker 383: 1981 Ker LT 875.
5. *Ram Ishwar Chaudhary* v. *State of Bihar*, 1986 Cr LJ 1366 (Pat): 1986 BLJ 102: 1986 BLJR 274.
6. *State of Maharashtra* v. *Eknath Yeshwant Pagar*, 1981 Cr LJ 1284: AIR 1981 SC 1571: (1981) 2 SCC 299.

Death of an accused who was involved in crime of conspiracy, would not abate the appeal against others[1].

An appeal filed by the complainant does not abate on complainant's death[2].

Stipulated period of 30 days has been provided for moving the court for substitution and if it has not been affected within limitation period, the appeal would abate.[3]

The rule of abatement of appeals on the death of appellant are not applicable to appeals under section 456(3), and as such substitution is not required in such cases.[4] Therefore, the convicted member of Scheduled Caste or a Scheduled Tribe, as a consequence of fabricated false evidence, dies his natural death before the execution of sentence, the accused would not be liable to the punishment provided under section 3(2)(i), as his execution has been made a condition precedent. The accused may be charged under provision of IPC then.

19. Norms or Relief Amount

Under 'Annexure I, of Schedule attached to the SC/ST Rules, 1995, at serial No.16 it is said [(section 3(2)(i) and (ii)]: "At least Rs. 2,50,000 or full compensation of the loss or harm sustained. 50% to be paid when charge-sheet is sent to court and 50% on conviction by the lower Court."

(Besides at Serial No. 17 different offences prescribed under section 3(2) and the amount of compensation thereof have been dealt with). (Please also see comments under next clause)

Section 3(2)(ii) "gives or fabricates false evidence intending thereby to cause, or knowing it to be likely cause, any member of a Scheduled Caste or a Scheduled Tribe to be convicted of an offence which is not capital but punishable with imprisonment for a term of seven years or upwards, shall be punishable with imprisonment for a term which shall not be less than six months but which may extend to seven years or upwards and with fine;"

SYNOPSIS

1. Analogous Law
2. Comparing Provisions of Clauses (i) and (ii) of section 3(2)
3. Scope
4. The Procedure
5. Element of Knowledge
6. *Locus Paenitentiae* Opportunity to Explain
7. Venial Falsehood
8. Fabrication on Material Points and Facts
9. Measure of Punishment
10. Norms For Relief Amount

1. Analogous Law

Words, phrases and design of section 3(2)(ii) of the Scheduled Castes and the Scheduled Tribes (Prevention of Atrocities) Act, 1989 are a combination of sections 193 and 195 of Indian Penal Code, 1860.

1. *Misri Lal* v. *Tofa Ram*, 1984 Cr LJ 1338: 1984 Raj LR Del 125: 1984 (1) Rec Cri R 319.
2. *Shri Shashi Rout* v. *Gopabandhu*, 1983 Cr LJ (NOC) 189 (Ori).
3. *Union of India* v. *Ghamandiram*, 1995 SCC (Ori) 14.
4. *Ganga* v. *State of Rajasthan*, 1993 Cr LJ 216 (Raj): 1992 (1) Raj LR 202: 1992 (1) Raj LW 442.

The same class of crime has been dealt in the present clause as was prescribed by previous clause (i) of section 3(2) of the Act of 1989, except for the provided respective punishments. The last clause dealt with the perjury and fabrication of evidence in a capital offence, where a member of a Scheduled Caste or a Scheduled Tribe is being tried, convicted and executed.

The last clause of section 3(2)(ii) is similar in criminality and the type but with a less graver punishment. Clause (IX) of section 3(1) of the Act of 1989 can also be put in the present category of offences providing with yet another lessor punishment, therefore a person prosecuted under section 3(2)(ii) may also be convicted under section 3(1)(IX) as well. As such, on point of gravity of the offence prescribed in the present clause takes an intermediate position.

2. Comparing Provisions of Clauses (i) and (ii) of section 3(2)

It was observed that: "A plain reading of the provisions of section 3(2)(i) and 3(2)(ii) of the Scheduled Castes and Scheduled Tribes (Prevention of Atrocities) Act, 1989 it is abundantly clear, although the basic ingredients of the offences punishable under the aforesaid provisions are same but depending on the nature and extent of false evidence given or fabricated and the consequent evils brought or sought to be brought thereby *i.e.,* the severity of the law prescribed two different kinds of punishments and the punishment so prescribed is more harsh in case of former than the latter. While section 3(2)(i) of the Scheduled Castes and Scheduled Tribes (Prevention of Atrocities) Act, 1989 is attracted in a case where by giving and fabricating false evidence the accused intended to cause or knowing it to be likely that he will thereby cause any member of the Scheduled Castes or Scheduled Tribes to be convicted for a capital offence *i.e.,* one which is punishable with death, on the other hand section 3(2)(ii) of the said Act is attracted when by giving and fabricating false evidence the accused intended thereby to cause or knowing it to be likely to cause any person who is a member of Scheduled Castes and Scheduled Tribes be convicted for a non-capital offence punishable with imprisonment for a term of 7 years or upwards."[1]

An important point to be mentioned here is that the provisions of section 3(2)(v), which says that any offence under the Indian Penal Code punishable with imprisonment for a term of ten years or more, against a member of SC or ST (person or property shall be punishable with life imprisonment. In this scenario provisions of sections 193 and 195A IPC, if made applicable would not come into exercise as they provide a punishment which may extend to only seven years, but a prosecution under section 194 IPC would be covered under Act of 1989. In some cases technically other provisions of IPC also may bring prosecution under the Act [Please see notes and comments on section 3(2)(v)].

3. Scope

To constitute an offence under section 3(2)(ii) of the Act of 1989, as well as applicability of the penal provision it is absolutely essential that the false evidence, intending thereby to cause or knowing it to be likely the accused will thereby cause any member of the Scheduled Caste or a Scheduled Tribe to be

1. *S.K. Devanath alias Sampangi* v. *State of West Bengal*, 2008 Cr LJ 2831 (2835-36) (Cal): 2008 (1) Cal Cri LR 591: 2008 (3) Cal HN 474.

convicted for any non-capital offence which is punishable with imprisonment for 7 years or upwards, must be given or fabricated in a criminal trial before a competent court of justice, as without a criminal trial the question of bringing any such conviction of such member for the aforesaid offence does not at all arise.[1]

There is no doubt about it that in order to attract the provisions of the present clause (as well as the previous one), the given or fabricated false evidence, must be given in course of a criminal trial and in consequence thereof a conviction and sentence is warranted.

For instance, where false evidence, whether given or fabricated, has been introduced in a departmental proceedings against such member, the provisions of present clause (or previous one) cannot be made applicable, even if the charge is assumed to be true, for the simple reason that by giving or fabricating false evidence, conviction for imprisonment for seven years upwards is not legally possible in departmental proceedings.

4. The Procedure

Section 195 of Code of Criminal Procedure, 1973 mandates in sub-section (1) (b)(i) that no court shall take cognizance of any offence punishable under any of the following sections of Indian Penal Code (45 of 1860), namely, sections 193 to 196 (both inclusive)....... .... except on the complaint in writing of that court by such officer of the court as that court may authorise in writing in this behalf, or some other court to which that court is subordinate."

This clearly means that no prosecution can be initiated without the complaint of the court concerned, where the given or fabricated false evidence has been produced to procure a conviction. But inevitably the provisions of section 195(1) (b)(i) cover sections 193 to 196 of Indian Penal Code. Provisions of sections 193 to 196 IPC, though analogous to the provisions of section 3(1) and 3(2)(i) and (ii), but it is doubtful whether provision of section 195 Cr PC would also apply in the present case, because it is a special legislation, and it has also been held that complaints by private persons may be filed.

Making of a complaint by the Court concerned is judicial act, hence it is presumed that it would not be performed perfunctorily and also in cases where there is sufficient evidence to justify a finding that the given or fabricated false evidence was produced with only intention or motive to procure conviction of member of a Scheduled Caste or a Scheduled Tribe, and with no other intention.

5. Element of Knowledge

Element of knowledge of the person who gives or fabricates false evidence against a member of Scheduled Caste or a Scheduled Tribe is very material to be proved in prosecution of the accused under section 3(2)(ii) to constitute the crime. This element could be proved by direct evidence, but it is not possible or practical to bring in direct evidence in each case. This evidence may consist of such facts or circumstances which may lead the court to believe that the accused's mind was possessed of the information that the given evidence was false or fabricated. The clear knowledge must be proved and that knowledge need not go beyond the fact that the evidence was false or fabricated.

1. *S.K. Devanath alias Sampangi* v. *State of West Bengal*, 2008 Cr LJ 2831 (2835-36) (Cal): 2008 (1) Cal Cri LR 591: 2008 (3) Cal HN 474.

A mere fact that there was a *prima facie* case made out against the giver of false evidence is not sufficient to prosecute him for perjury. This is so because there can be other circumstances such as concerning to knowledge which may render the prosecution as useless. Hence in cases when finding of acquittal was delivered, it is not possible to prosecute the witnesses of perjury.

6. *Locus Paenitentiae*

The rule of *locus paenitentiae* is based on the desirable principle of observance of interests of justice. It has become a general practice now-a-days that the statement of a witness continues for many days because it cannot be completed on a single date fixed in criminal trials. To compel a witness to repeat the statement given by him on the previous or previous-to-previous date fixed, so that falsity of his statement or contradictions may be brought in would not allow the ends of justice, unless of course the witness has been given an opportunity to explain the anomaly of his statement.

Opportunity to Explain

It is a rule of procedure that at the end of recorded statements, each and every court, without fail, puts down that the statement so recorded was read over and after hearing it the witness has verified it. *("Sun Kar Tasdeeq Kiya")*. Under this phrase the witness is required to sign. Writing such phrase has now become a stereotype exercise and in practice the recorded statements are never read over to the witness and as such verified, at least the presenter of this book in his about forty years of practice in trial courts has never seen this to happen.

In cases where two different or contradictory statements of a person has been brought for prosecution of perjury against him, the conviction cannot stand, if no opportunity has been given to him to explain them. If need arises and the person is called upon later to explain the contradictions, he will not be examined on oath on the ground that in such circumstances the person is not being examined as a witness, but as a prospective accused and the explaining such statement may be used against him later on. Before filing a complaint it must be ascertained that the explanations are plausible, if not probable, as a conviction can only be based on well determined falsity of one of the two statements. In other words there must be reliable evidence to declare one of the statements as false. (Please also see comments on the last clause)

7. Venial Falsehood

Clause (ii) of section 3(2) of The Scheduled Caste and the Scheduled Tribes (Prevention of Atrocities) Act, 1989 [as well as clause (i)] does not require administration of oath, nor the provision stipulates any express legal obligation on the part of 'giver' of the evidence to state the truth. The rule of 'venial falsehood' presumes the first essential element of criminality in relation to 'giving false evidence', as there must be an express provision to state the truth.

In case somebody has been prosecuted under the present clause, he may show that while 'giving' evidence against such member, he was under no legal obligation to state the truth. On the other hand the prosecution has to prove and establish that the accused was under such express legal obligation to state the truth.

Use of such words as: "shall be bound to answer all questions" cannot be said to amount an express provision to speak the truth, but simply signify that these words take away, the option of refusal to answer any question. The express provision must only relate to a legal obligation to speak the truth.

8. Fabrication on Material Points and Facts

Fabricating false evidence as stipulated under section 3(2)(ii) [and also clause (i)] and a charge thereafter for such a created offence would require to fulfil two other ingredients. In the first place the fabricated false evidence must be material to question in issue – *i.e.*, to cause, or knowing it to be likely thereby cause, any member of a Scheduled Caste or a Scheduled Tribe to be convicted; and, secondly the fabrication may be such that it leads the court concerned to form an opinion as to a material point or on a fact which is erroneous because of falsity. Court simply forming an opinion on such fabricated evidence is not enough to constitute the crime. Such erroneous opinion must be directly related to some issue or fact due to which conviction may result. The question of materiality of a piece of evidence must naturally depend on the circumstances of each case.

The fabricated document must also relate to the material point or fact in a particular case. Simply filing a power-of-attorney, which was later on found to be fabricated, by an advocate on behalf of a client would not become evidence on a material point or a fact in any case. Indian law is somewhat different from that of English law on the point of perjury as well as on the point of materiality. Under English law, word 'material' means evidence of such category which affects directly or indirectly the probability of anything. Therefore, a fact may be material though the evidence of existence of the fact may be made admissible improperly. According to Hawkins, he cannot find the matter in question settled or well debated, thus his opinion was to leave the matter to every man's own judgment who would decide, according to the circumstances of each case, whether the perjury was impertinent, idle and insignificant or not.[1]

The question of materiality can be judged from two different angles. In one case a person may accuse another person by creating some falsehood against him, but in the another instance a person may fabricate a falsehood to save his own skin. The second instance is not relevant for the present discussion.

9. Measure of Punishment

Clause (ii) of section 3(2) of the Act of 1989 gives an option to the court to exercise its discretion, unlike the provisions of previous clause of the same section 3(2). Though, the measure of minimum punishment has been fixed, where the discretion of the court is not open (minimum six months), but the upper limits of punishment can be decided by the courts according to the circumstances of each case (with imposition of fine as well)

10. Norms For Relief Amount

Same as has been provided for victims of previous Clause (i) of section 3(2). (Please see notes at the end of the previous clause).

---

1. Hawkins, P.C.C. 27, Secrtion 8.

Section 3(2)(iii) "Commits mischief by fire or any explosive substance intending to cause or knowing it to be likely that he will thereby cause damage to any property belonging to a member of a Scheduled Caste or a Scheduled Tribe, shall be punishable with imprisonment for a term which shall not be less than six months but which may extend to seven years and with fine;"

SYNOPSIS

1. Analogous Law

In fact clause (iii) as well as clause (iv) of sub-section (2) of section 3 of The Scheduled Castes and the Scheduled Tribes (Prevention of Atrocities) Act, 1989 correspond to the provision of section 435 IPC. Few early lines of the said section have been reproduced here for almost a word for a word, except for the value of the damaged property in question.

The idea of declaring "mischief" as an offence has been imported from English Law, where "malicious injury to property" was made an offence according to Digest of the English Criminal Law. A distinction has been made between malice and fraud when committed in the actual sense.

2. "Mischief"

Section 425 of Indian Penal Code, 1860 defines mischief as: "425. Mischief.—Whoever, with intent to cause, or knowing that he is likely to cause, wrongful loss or damage to the public or to any person, causes the destruction of any property, or any such change in any property or in the situation thereof as destroys or diminishes its value or utility, or affects it injuriously, commits 'mischief'."

The concept of 'mischief' being a criminal act is based on rule underlying the maxim *'sie utere tuo ut alieumum non loeads,* which means 'so use your own property so as not to injure your neighbour's". This rule on one hand established preservation of absolute rights of one's property, and on the other makes injury to another's property an offence, besides attracting a civil action.

As has been mentioned above, the mischief correspond to an offence under English criminal law which is being portayed by "malicious injuries to property", where 'malice' has been described as: "some actual intention to cause hurt, damage or injury", and an act which "is maliciously done or omitted to be done where, being prohibited to be done, it is willfully done, or being commanded to be done, it is wilfully omitted to be done without lawful justification or excuse." In short it is an invasion of a legal right.

It is clear from the above mentioned concept of English law that the law contemplates an intention in the act done to attract a punishment.

3. Applicability

For constituting an offence of mischief under section 3(2)(iii) of the Act of 1989, there must be some direct act on the part of the accused, either personally or collectively or through someone else which leads to damage of any property belonging to a member of a Scheduled Caste or a Scheduled Tribe. Secondly that mischief must be by fire or any explosive substance.

Damaging the property of a member of a Scheduled Caste or a Scheduled Tribe through any other means (except by fire or explosive substance) would not come under the ambit of section 3(2)(iii) of the Act.

4. "Arson" – The American Law

For its definition and further details please see comments under the next clause, *i.e.*, section 3(2)(iv) of the Act of 1989.

5. Ingredients

To substantiate the charge under section 3(2)(iii) of the Act of 1989, the prosecution shall prove that the accused had intention to cause or knowing it to be likely that he will thereby cause damage to any property belonging to a member of Scheduled Caste or a Scheduled Tribe, by committing mischief by fire or explosive substance.

Ingredients of the offence are: (i) there must be an intention or knowledge on the part of accused that the act would likely cause damage to any property of such member; (ii) in furtherance of such intention mischief has been committed by fire or explosive substance; (iii) the property must belong or owned by a member of a Scheduled Caste or a Scheduled Tribe; and (iv) the accused does not belong to such caste or the Tribe.

Simple invasion of a civil right would not bring the act of accused under the present clause, even if the damage to the property of such member has already taken place. Additionally the act of mischief has been restricted to be caused by fire or through explosive substance. Mischief of other kinds would be excluded from the ambit of the offence prescribed in the present clause, though, actual damage to the property of such member has taken place.

6. Intention and Knowledge

The phrase – "intending to cause or knowing it……" stipulates not only the intention to cause mischief by fire or any explosive substance, but also to the knowledge of the likelihood of damage to any property belonging to a member of a Scheduled Caste or a Scheduled Tribe.

Under criminal law there can hardly be any offence which has legally not been constituted without *mens rea* (except certain kinds of negligence). When mischief has been committed, two kinds of remedies may arise and co-exist, *i.e.*, a civil remedy and the criminal remedy, because in any way the result of mischief in general is damage or injury to the property (or right as well). In such case both the remedies can be exercisable by the complainant, it would not make any difference, if the accused had the intention or knowledge of the likelihood of the damage caused, the offence would be constituted and criminal proceedings against the culprit would be lawful apart from the civil claim. But such criminal proceedings against the accused would be lawful only when intention or the knowledge has been established.

The word "mischief" used here has a special connotation, if compared with its use in literature, because the offence of "mischief" would not be constituted and brought under the ambit of provisions of Cause (iii) or (iv) of section 3(2) of the Act of 1989, unless a clear intention or knowledge of damage to the property of such member by fire or explosive has been established. As such the presence of intention or the knowledge is most essential requirement.

7. Direct Proof of Intention or Knowledge

The presence of intention in constituting an offence under the said clause is real and cannot be imported through hypothetical means. But the presence of intention or knowledge may be proved through such circumstances and facts where there cannot be any other inference. The situation naturally may differ from case to case. But in this situation it may also be added that presence or absence of intention or knowledge in a particular case is a question of fact and not that of law.

When facts are proved before a court calling upon it to infer an intention or knowledge of the accused to commit the act, circumstances may be created in such a way that these should negate the act being accidental, outcome of carelessness or negligence, or a *bona fide* belief of the accused that he was in such a state of mind that the act was done in exercise of his own right.

To illustrate: where a person was dumping his waste material or garbage at an open space between his house and the house of a member of a Scheduled Caste or a Tribe and such member was also dumping his waste on the same open space though belonging to the other person. The other person tried to burn the garbage because it had gathered unmanageable mass. The garbage was burning with flames, when suddenly winds started blowing and the direction of the wind was towards the house of such member. The inevitable result was that the house of member of the Scheduled Caste caught fire and consequently burnt. Question would arise, whether the person trying to burn the garbage can be prosecuted for an offence under the present clause.

The inevitable answer would be that the person cannot be charged, on the ground that he had no intention to burn the house of such member, nor a prior knowledge could be conceived because he could not have foreseen that winds would suddenly start blowing at the very moment when the flames were at their peak.[1]

Similarly some act of stupidity which may cause some accidental fire or an explosion resulting in and causing damage to the property of such member cannot be brought under the ambit of present clause, because of absence of intention.

---

1. The illustration has been fabricated on the basis of facts as were the facts in:- *Karim Bux* v. *Rex through Karimullah*, 1950 Cr LJ 1242 (All).

On the other hand a legal act may be termed as an offence under the said clause (iii) of section 3(2) of the Act 1989, if the criminal intention could be proved. Suppose a contractor obtains a lease from the government for excavating stone boulders from a hillock and takes due permission to explode some portions of the hillock, at the foot of which some members of Scheduled Caste had built their houses. When the explosion took place some big pieces of stones came down and damaged the property of such members. Later on it was found that explosions were made in such a way that the houses of such members should be damaged. Though the act of explosion etc., was perfectly legal, but as the intention was criminal, the charge can be substantiated on the ground of intention.

8. Meaning of Words

The word "mischief" has already been discussed above.

8.1 "Mischief by fire or any explosive substance"

Clauses (iii) and (iv) of section 3(2) of the Act of 1989 use same words in the expression mentioned but prescribing lessor and enhanced penalty depending on the nature of the property involved and damaged intentionally which belonged to a member of Scheduled Caste or a Scheduled Tribe. But in each case the mischief must have been committed by means of fire or an explosive substance to cause damage to the property in question, which belonged to such member.

A general type of mischief has not been made and declared as an offence, but it must be special kind of mischief which has been restricted to a mischief by fire or any explosive substance. Sections 285 and 286 of Indian Penal Code, 1860 deal with "negligent conduct with respect to fire or combustible matter", and "negligent conduct with respect to explosive substance".

The word "fire" means and includes state of combustion of substance with oxygen, giving out light and heat; and, which also includes anything which generates fire. On the other hand "explosive substance", which is noun means any substance which tend to explode due to its chemical composition tending to react in given circumstances.[1]

The dwelling house of a member of Scheduled Tribe was set on fire, besides the straw heap of brother of the complainant was also set on fire, and as a result the house and the straw heap were destroyed. It was proved by the prosecution that the said house and the straw heap belonged to members of Scheduled Tribe, was within the knowledge of the accused. The accused was also alleged to have made extra-judicial confession before a Ward Member. But the Court acquitted the accused on the ground that the identification of the accused was doubtful and chance of false implication cannot be ruled out.[2]

It is not necessary that the fire should be with flame, it is sufficient that the effect of the fire was to cause damage to the intended property belonging to a member of a Scheduled Caste or a Scheduled Tribe.

---

1. "Explosive" has been defined under section 4(d) of Explosive Act; and "Explosive Substance" has been defined under section 2(a) and (b) of Explosive Substances Act.
2. *Dambaru Gouda* v. *State of Orissa*, 2001 Cr LJ 2993 (Ori) (DB): 2000 (89) Cut LT 702: 2000 (1) Ori LR 454.

8.2 "Damage to any Property"

The term 'damage to any property' contemplates destruction, diminishing in value or the utility or otherwise affect the property injuriously. The ambit of the expression is wide enough to include the entire incidental loss suffered.[1]

But as far as invoking the provisions of section 3(2)(iii) it is necessary that such "damage" must be caused by fire or any explosive substance, while the property must also belong to a member of Scheduled Caste or a Scheduled Tribe.

As far as term "property" is concerned, it should include all kinds of properties, whether movable or immovable. Thus agricultural produce, including grain, chaff *etc.*, or even the standing crop is property. Even non-agricultural property, such as grass, spontaneous growth on the agricultural land or trees would be considered property.

For example: if *A* has rented a piece of agricultural land to *B*, who cultivated it and before the ripe crop could be harvested, *A* entered the land, assaulted *B* and carried away a portion of produce and burnt whatever was left, provisions of clause (iii) of section 3(2) shall be invoked, if *B* was a member of said caste or Tribe. This would be done despite the fact that *A* was owner of the land. As the crop was product of cultivation by *B*, therefore it 'belonged' to him and that property was damaged by *A* 'by fire', therefore *A* was liable to be prosecuted and if proved would be convicted.

The principle contemplated by maxim – *damnum sine injuria* (which means, 'injury without damage') would not be applicable under the offence prescribed under section 3(2)(iii) of the Act of 1989.

8.3 "Member of a Scheduled Caste or a Scheduled Tribe"

Please see comments under section 2(1)(c).

9. Mischief Must Relate to Property

The committed mischief by fire or explosive substance in one way or the other must relate to some property belonging to such member. Where a thing is not property within the meaning of law, then there cannot be any mischief, whatsoever may be consequences of the act done.

Some kinds of properties have been described above, but the 'property' would certainly mean, for the purpose of present discussion, a tangible property, and would not include, for instance an easement or a document. In the similar manner things which are *nulius proprietas* cannot be made subject matter of the contemplated offence under the present clause.

For instance: *A* entered into an illegal and immoral agreement with such a member *B* that his wife would live in adultery, besides *B* was foregoing her claim of maintenance. Later on the accused burnt the document of agreement, which would constitute a property on the ground that the document could be used as evidence of adultery and also cessation of liability of husband to maintain the wife, therefore the destruction of document of agreement by fire would constitute the offence. On the contrary a receipt issued by such member as a result of sale of some goods may be damaged by fire, without constituting any offence.

1. *Babu Lal* v. *State*, 1951 ALJ 558 (All).

In general it could be said that there can be nothing wrong if a *bona fide* right is exercised by a owner of a property, without intention of causing damage to any property belonging to such members. This *bona fide* right may not be capable of separate enjoyment or possession but a common right. For instance: the collector sold a land in execution of some charge on the land and a member of a Scheduled Caste or a Scheduled Tribe purchased the land by depositing purchase-money in accordance with the rules, which provided that the sale would be confirmed on the expiration of sixty days. Before expiration of the said stipulated period the original owner burnt the standing unripe crop sown by him previously. Meanwhile the original owner deposited the required money. Question would arise whether by burning the crop he had committed any offence. The answer should be in the negative because after payment the land had reverted to him.

Similar questions may arise when there is a co-ownership of a property owned by some other person as well as a member of a Scheduled Caste or a Scheduled Tribe.

However, no person can be accused of an offence under the present clause on the basis of vicarious liability, that is an act committed by other person even though that another person was functioning on his or her behalf as an agent etc., unless, of course, an intention has been proved that the agent was functioning on the order of his master.

10. Question of Right of Ownership of Property

As section 3(2)(iii) stipulates "damage to any property belonging to a member of Scheduled Caste or a Scheduled Tribe", therefore absence of fact of ownership of the property in question would negate the exercise of provisions of the said clause. Not only the ownership of property belong to such member should be proved but it should also be in use and possession by such member. A hypothetical situation may be created to explain the question in issue. If a member of a Scheduled Caste or a Scheduled Tribe purchases a land in execution of a decree, whereupon another person had previously unauthorisedly built a house. If such another person set fire to the house built by him on the land in question, he could not be roped in under the provisions of the present section 3(2)(iii) of the Act, despite the fact that the land belonged to such member and he too had obtained symbolic possession of the land by purchasing it in execution of a decree. More so because the destroyed house was the property of another person and only the land in question belonged to such member.

However, the *bona fides* of the accused person may be ascertained from the intention with which stipulated mischief has been allegedly committed. Any person is free to destroy his own property in any way, unless, of course it does not create nuisance or injury to others.

11. Norms for Relief According to Schedule to the Rules of 1995

Please see notes at the end of Clause (iv) of section 3(2) of the Act as provided at item No. 22 in the Schedule.

Section 3(2)(iv).—"Commits mischief by fire or any explosive substance intending to cause or knowing it to be likely that he will thereby cause destruction of any building which is ordinarily used as a place of worship or as a place for human dwelling or as a place for custody of the property by a member of a Scheduled Caste or a Scheduled Tribe, shall be punishable with imprisonment for life and with fine;"

SYNOPSIS

1. Analogous Law
2. Scope
3. Arson
4. Specific Intention
5. Attempt and Actual Burning
6. "Destruction"
7. Knowledge about Caste of Victim
8. Ownership of Destructed Property
9. Punishment
10. Abetment to the Offence
11. Extent of Relief

1. Analogous Law

Clause (iv) of section 3(2) of the Scheduled Castes and the Scheduled Tribes (Prevention of Atrocities) Act, 1989, is verbatim reproduction of section 436 of Indian Penal Code, 1860, except for the inclusion of words "member of a Scheduled Caste or a Scheduled Tribe", thereby restricting the committal of the offence to the properties of a certain class. As far as the provided punishment is concerned, the clause (iv) of section 3(2) of the Act has also restricted the punishment of not less than life imprisonment and with fine. Previously and originally section 436 IPC used words "transportation for life" but Amending Act (26 of 1955) had substituted it for "imprisonment for life", which has been copied here from the said section.

The omission is, words, "or with imprisonment of either description for a term which may extend to ten years", used in section 436 IPC. By deleting these words the discretionary powers of the courts have been abridged while inflicting punishments.

Section 436 of Indian Penal Code has been reproduced:

> *Section "436.—Mischief by Fire or Explosive substance with Intent to Destroy House etc.*—Whoever commits mischief by fire or any explosive substance, intending to cause, or knowing it to be likely that he will thereby cause, the destruction of any building which is ordinarily used as a place of worship or as a human dwelling or as a place for the custody of property, shall be punished with imprisonment for life, or with imprisonment of either description for a term which may extend to ten years, and shall also liable to fine."

Secondly words "place of worship" have been defined in section 2(d) and section 3 of Protection of Civil Rights Act, 1955. (This would be dealt later).

2. Scope

The scope, applicability and provided punishments thereof under the previous clause, *i.e.,* section 3(2)(iii) are quite different from the present clause. Section 3(2)(iii) deals with the offences caused by mischief by fire or by any explosive substance to "any property" belonging to a member of a Scheduled Caste or a Scheduled Tribe, while the present clause makes an offence through same means to "any building who is ordinarily used as a place of worship or as a place of human dwelling or a place for custody of the property," by such members.

In this way three kinds of immovable properties have been made subject matter of offence under the present clause. All kinds of movable properties have been excluded from the scope of section 3(2)(iv), unless, of course such movable properties have also been destroyed in course of or in consequence of such mischief. The words in previous clause [section 3(2)(iii)] deals with "any property" which inevitably deals with movable as well as non-movable properties. (Please also see notes on property under previous clause).

Under the scope of present clause mischief to any allied buildings to the place of worship of such members would be an offence as the clause includes "place for human dwelling", or "place for custody of the property" of such members, besides "place of worship". Thus opinions of Courts previously given in regard to kitchen of the temple (Thidapalli) where Nivedyam is prepared but no worship is performed, were excluded from the scope [ILR (1960) Ker 73].[1]

The other essential requirement for establishing an offence under clause (iv) of section 3(2) of the Act, is that the place of worship, place of human dwelling or place for a custody of the property must belong to members of Scheduled Caste or the Scheduled Tribe. Any snags in ownership of property of such kinds may technically make the accused go scot free. (For damage to such property by mischief, please see notes under previous clause).

3. Arson

Arson has been defined by Webster's Legal Dictionary as: "the crime of intentionally causing a dangerous fire or explosion, especially for purpose of destroying a building of another or of damaging property."

Present clause prescribes a penalty for causing damage, through fire or explosion, to properties belonging to members of the Scheduled Castes or Scheduled Tribes, the buildings may be any of the three kinds – *viz.* (i) building used as a place of worship, (ii) as used for human dwelling, and (iii) the buildings which are being used for custody of property. All the elements of mischief have to be established to constitute an offence under the present clause. The pre-requisite is also to establish that such mischief was caused through fire or explosion essentially to a building of any such kind, which must belong to such members.

Under American common law 'arson' is the malicious and wilful burning of the house or outhouse of another man. In absence of statutory definitions. (as is in the present case), the common-law definition would be relied on.[2] Different American statutes define arson broadly than the others. Some statutes bring in its scope beyond the common definition but simultaneously include all the elements of common definition. For instance, some statutes extend *criminal burning* of buildings and structures which were not subject of arson under common law, by including in its scope burning of one's own building with intention to defraud somebody, like insurer.

1. The said opinion was given by Kerala High Court while dealing with a case under section 2(d) of Protection of Civil Rights Act, 1955.
2. *Williams* v. *State*, 132 So. 186: 100 Fla 1054.

Common law conceptualize the definition of arson and generally regard it as an offence against security of habitation, not considering the rights of property strictly such as title or possession. The statutes try to protect all species of real and personal property against illegal burning or exploding buildings, personal or otherwise. The mischief by fire or explosion or arson of dwelling houses was considered to be heinous felony at common law, because it endangers human life, thus sametimes provided with punishment by death.[1]

4. Specific Intention

Specific intention is essential to constitute a crime under clause (iv) [as well as clause (iii)] of section 3(2) of the Act, as the phrase provides – "intending to cause……. destruction of any building….." Belonging to members of Scheduled Caste or the Scheduled Tribe. The three kinds of building which have been made subject matter of 'destruction' almost cover every kind of building (place of worship, place of human dwelling or a place for custody of property). Thus causing mischief by fire or explosion to any kind of building belonging to such members intentionally, would be an offence covered under the present clause.

Even in other countries the offence of arson could not be constituted without establishing intention to burn a building or other structure under statute or common law. A particular intent or malice against a particular person (or a particular class of persons as in the present case) is sufficient to show that the accused was actuated by a malicious purpose and in consequence he set fire to the building wilfully rather than negligently or accidently.[2] But where an adjoining dwelling building is burnt as a consequence, it could not be covered under the offence because the statute has not made an element of offence as such, on the ground of intention not to burn that adjoining dwelling.[3] It is so because arson must be done willfully or maliciously, and arson not only consists of the fact that the building has been burned, but that it has been willfully (intentionally) and unlawfully fired or exploded.

Therefore acts of negligence or accidents cannot be covered under the provisions of present clause.

On the other hand there can be primary and secondary intent. If a person sets fire to a building while committing some other crime, the case could fall under the secondary intent, because his primary intention was not to commit arson but to commit some other offence, but if the accused has planned and had a clear intention to burn or explode a building from before, the offence would clearly be constituted under the present clause on the basis of intention. Some foreign authorities consider arson constituted irrespective of primary or secondary intentions.[4]

However, motive has not been made an essential element of mischief by fire or explosion, whether the motive is for gain, revenge or any other kind of mischief. But the motive may be shown in evidence to prove the intent for committal of such mischief.

---

1. *Williams* v. *State*, 132 So. 186: 100 Fla 1054.
2. *Crow* v. *State*, 189 SW 687: 136 Tenn 333: 1 ALR 1160.
3. *State* v. *Berowitz*, 29 SW (2d) 150: 325 Mo 519.
4. *Luke* v. *State*, 49 Ala 30: 20 Am. R 269; *Jenkins* v. *State*, 53 Ga 33: 21 Am R 255.

5. Attempt and Actual Burning

The expression, "......... knowing it to be likely that he will thereby cause destruction......." stipulates, *firstly,* that there was clear intention to commit the prescribed offence and, *secondly,* that the act of mischief by fire or explosion was not completed, though it was within the knowledge of the offender that by such act he will thereby cause destruction. The simple inference would be that the prohibited act was attempted with clear intention and knowledge of consequences.

The maxim *incendit at combussit* is applicable only where a building or some part thereof has actually been burnt during the act of arson, but at common law an intent or attempt to commit arson (mischief by fire) would not fall within the meaning of the maxim, unless actual burning of a building or some part thereof takes place. A mere scorching, smoking or discoloration of the building, without the fire being spread thereto if does not take place, would not constitute the offence of arson. Yet, if there is actual ignition of any part of the building, it was held that the offence has been committed, despite the fact that there was no flame, or else the fire goes out immediately by itself, or if some other person extinguishes the fire.[1]

It is not essential for constituting the crime that the building should be completely consumed or materially injured, but it would be sufficient if any part of the building, howsoever small it may be, is consumed by such fire or explosion, or its material has been charred. But in any case there must be burning to constitute the crime.

The foreign authorities are very clear about the presence of intention as well as establishing what would constitute actual burning of the building or its parts as far as common law is concerned relating to arson, but they also except the cases where there are specific statutes creating distinct offences. But under such specific statutes if it has been suggested that the intent of Legislature, creating distinct and separate offence in relation to arson has to be adhered to, irrespective of provisions of common law. The rule of common law requiring actual burning has to be followed in any other case for constituting the crime.

The value of burnt structure is sometimes material and sometimes it is not, because under some statutes value of damaged property has been made material elements of crime of arson and frequently the value has been made basis for determining the grade or degree of offence.

Item number 22 of Annexture 1 to Schedule [Rule 12(4)] providing for relief amount, provided at the end of the Scheduled Castes and the Scheduled Tribes (Prevention of Atrocities) Rules, 1995 mention no specific amount but directs that in cases of "Complete destruction/burnt houses" the house would be constructed at the government cost.

However, the attempt or mere knowledge of probability of damage would not constitute the offence, unless any of the mentioned kinds of buildings (belonging to such members), in fact and actually been set on fire. In short there must be an

1. *State* v. *Schwartz,* 166A. 666: Harr 418; *Woodford* v. *People,* 62 NY 117: 20 Am R 464.

intent plus an overt act, which has to show something more than preparation, but the overt act must be something not falling short of completing the crime. The overt act must be such that it is in immediate process of carrying out intention, and also must be done which would naturally bring the result in ordinary course of crime of mischief by fire which would have burnt the building, if had not been intervened or interrupted in some way.

6. "Destruction"

Two similar offences created by clause (iii) and (iv) of section 3(2) of the Act also use two different words – namely "cause damage" and "cause destruction". It is significant because the used words denote the final outcome of the crime according to which the gravity or degree of crime and consequential punishments vary.

Naturally the 'damage' would include some minor losses due to the criminal act but for proving "destruction" there must be evidence as such. Mere evidence of scorching could not be brought within the meaning of 'destruction' by fire. Neither, perhaps, a small part of damaged building could be said to be as destroyed. Complete charring is required to constitute 'destruction'.

Not every case of mischief by fire has been included under the prescribed offence under section 3(2)(iv), hence use of word "destruction" is significant, because the operation of the prescribed created offence under the clause has been restricted to only those cases where real 'destruction' to the said building has taken place, and mere injury or damage to the building (by fire) would not be sufficient to bring the act under the ambit of this provision.

English Common Law stipulates an inference of intention or possession of knowledge by the accused only when an accused does some definite act from which the court could justifiably infer that intention. Such inference may be reasonably made if the act caused an *actual burning* of the whole or some part of the building, though it is not necessary that the fire should have any continuance or put out immediately or any part of the building had been completely consumed. But without actual burning, at least a part of the building, no such inference can be drawn from a sole intention or actual attempt to fire the building.

7. Knowledge about Caste of Victim

Generally a common plea is being taken by the accused charged under various offences prescribed by section 3 of Act of 1989, that until and unless it is proved that the accused were aware about the fact that the victim or victims belonged to the Scheduled Castes or the Scheduled Tribes, they cannot be held guilty of the offence under the Act. The plea may or may not stand depending on the circumstances and the nature of charges.

For this purpose clause (v) of section 3(2) of the Act of 1989 classifies the offences under Indian Penal Code, 1860, and simultaneously committed against members of Scheduled Castes or the Scheduled Tribes, in two different categories, *i.e.,* those which are punishable with imprisonment for a term of ten years or more; and, those where lessor punishment has been provided. For instance, accused if charged with an offence under section 376 IPC would be covered under section 3(2)(v) of the Act, because the offence is punishable with imprisonment for a term of ten years.[1]

On the basis of above arguments cited by the Apex Court, a Division Bench of the M.P. High Court has held that as Clause (iv) of section 3(2) of the Act of 1989 provides punishment for life imprisonment, "the requirement of knowledge of the accused that a victim is a member of Scheduled Caste and Scheduled Tribe is not in clause 4." It was held that there is "difference between the words mentioned in clause 4 and 5 of sub-section 2 of section 3 of the Act, 1989."[2]

It is submitted that the spirit and the object of the entire Act of 1989 is to protect the person, property and honour of members of Scheduled Castes or the Scheduled Tribes, and if an offence has been committed against such person or his property without knowing that the victim belonged to that special group of the society, the offence cannot be brought under ambit of provisions of the Act, on the ground that the elements of grudge, intentional degradation or revenge *etc.*, cannot be dragged into play. In a case where the accused was charged with an offence under section 302 IPC, where the deceased belonged to Scheduled Caste, it was held by a Division Bench that there was no ground to convict the accused under section 3(2)(v) in absence of any evidence that the accused by his conduct also offended the sensibilities of the deceased in relation to caste to which he belonged.[3]

8. Ownership of Destructed Property

Please see note (i) under section 3(2)(iii).

9. Punishment

The Legislature had provided maximum punishment of imprisonment and in addition a mandatory fine for crimes committed under section 3(2)(iv). Unfortunately nothing was left to the Judge, trying the case, as expression "shall be punishable with imprisonment for life and with fine" has been used, unlike the expression used in section 436 IPC as – "shall be punished with imprisonment, or with imprisonment of either description for a term which may *extend* to ten years.........". The Amending Act 26 of 1955 had substituted "transportation for life" for "imprisonment for life".

When it was pointed out to the Law Commissioners that there is a lot of difference between burning a hut and a valuable dwelling, for which they were providing similar punishment, the learned Law Commissioners stated that it was a matter well left to the discretion of the Judge.[4]

In the present case the said discretion of the Judge has been taken away.

1. *Dinesh* alias *Budha* v. *State of Rajasthan*, (2006) 2 SCC (Cri) 1: 2006 Cr LJ 1679: AIR 2006 SC 1267; *Ramdas* v. *State of Maharashtra*, AIR 2007 SC 155: 2006 AIR SCW 5675: (2007) 2 SCC 170.
2. *Bhupendra* v. *State of Madhya Pradesh*, 2008 Cr LJ 2479 (MP) (DB) (2481): 2008 Cr LR (SC and MP) MPG 457.
3. *Abdul Gafarsab* v. *State of Karnataka*, 1998 Cr LJ 2488 (Kant) (DB): 1998 (3) Crimes 620: 1998 (3) Kant LJ 132; also see *Mata Sewak Upadhyay* v. *State of Uttar Pradesh*, 1995 JIC 1168 (All) (FB): 1996 (1) East Cr C 97 (All) (FB) (1194) *et eq.*
4. First Rep., sections 614, 615.

10. Abetment to the Offence

Section 8 of the Scheduled Castes and the Scheduled Tribes (Prevention of Atrocities) Act, 1989 uses word "Abetted" in connection with the accused who rendered any financial assistance etc., it shall be presumed that such person had abetted the offence. The Rules of 1995 also try to take prescribed measures so that the abetment of offences of atrocities against such mentioned members may not take place.

It is a general rule that if prosecution fails to substantiate the commission of principal offence, there cannot be any conviction for abetment. No doubt there are exceptions to this general rule, which hold good in normal circumstances. In such cases prosecution has to prove through evidence that the abetted offence had been committed, even partly, in consequence of the abetment.

However, as the Act of 1989 did not make separately an offence of abetment, the accused has to be charged under section 109 IPC additionally.

11. Extent of Relief

Annexture 1 to the Schedule [see Rule 12(4)] norms for relief have been made. It has been provided at item No 22 that for "complete destruction/burnt houses", the Government would construct the house with all costs.

Section 3(2)(v) "commits any offence under the Indian Penal Code (45 of 1860) punishable with imprisonment for a term of ten years or more against a person or property on the ground that such person is a member of a Scheduled Caste or a Scheduled Tribe or such property belongs to such member, shall be punishable with imprisonment for life and with fine;"

SYNOPSIS

1. Scope
2. Constitutionality
3. Necessary Ingredients to Attract section 3(2)(v)
4. Grounds for invoking section 3(2)(v)
5. Scope of Sentence under section 3(2)(v)
6. Entire incident has to be Considered as Single Episode
7. Framing of Charges under section 3(2)(v)
8. Quashing of FIR and Compromise
9. "....On Ground that Person is Member of SC or ST" – Sentencing
10. Mentioning Caste in FIR
11. The Relief Amount

1. Scope

Clause (v) of section 3(2) of the Act of 1989 provides an enhanced punishment for offences committed under provision of Indian Penal Code, 1860, where the Code prescribes punishments for ten years or more, the offenders would be subjected to imprisonment for life and fine instead of provided quantum of punishment, in case the offence has been committed against a member of Scheduled Caste or a Scheduled Tribe.

In this way the Special Act of 1989 has categorized the offences and their punishments thereof as has been mentioned in the Indian Penal Code, 1860. The offences providing sentences (maximum) of less than ten years are being excluded from the present clause and the prescribed punishments would remain the same, but every declared offence which provide a maximum sentence of ten years or more, would be (read as) considered by the courts to be "imprisonment of life with fine".

2. Constitutionality

A question was raised before the Full Bench of Allahabad High Court about the minimum and maximum punishments provided under section 3 of the Act of 1989, being arbitrary and violative of Article 14 of the Constitution. The Bench observed that it is for the Legislature to decide the quantum of punishment. Once the Legislature is competent to legislate about offences and punishments depending on the gravity of the offence as considered fit by the Legislature, and no offence can be declared void on the ground of excessive punishment, which is exclusively in the domain of Legislature.

It was further observed that this argument has been forwarded in disregard of Article 35(a)(ii) of the Constitution, which empowers the Parliament alone to prescribe punishment for the acts which are declared to be offences under Part III of the Constitution. These punishments in section 3 of the Act are provided by the Parliament in discharge of constitutional mandate.[1]

3. Necessary Ingredients to Attract section 3(2)(v)

The Scheduled Castes and the Scheduled Tribes (Prevention of Atrocities) Act, 1989 was enacted to prevent atrocities against members of Scheduled Castes and the Scheduled Tribes and also to provide jurisdiction to Special Courts for trial of such offences. 'Atrocity' has been defined in section 2(1)(a) of the Act to mean an offence punishable under section 3, which in turn "creates independent offences relating to such atrocities and they stand by themselves. To attract section 3(2)(v) the following ingredients must be established:

"(1) the offender should not be a member of a Scheduled Caste or a Scheduled Tribe;

(2) he must commit an offence under the Indian Penal Code punishable with imprisonment for a term of 10 years or more;

(3) the commission of such offence must be against a person or property of a member of a Scheduled Caste or a Scheduled Tribe;

(4) the offence must have been committed on the ground that such person is a member of a Scheduled Caste or a Scheduled Tribe."[2]

The Bench further observed that all the above ingredients must be established before it requests the court to enter a conviction under the present section. The burden is on prosecution in this respect as in any other criminal case. In case the caste of the victim is in doubt, the prosecution is duty bound to obtain a certificate from the authorities concerned as to the community to which the victim or the accused belonged and whether he is a member of a Scheduled Caste or a Scheduled Tribe. Evidence has to be produced to show that the victim is a

1. *Mata Sewak Upadhyay* v. *State of Uttar Pradesh*, 1995 JIC 1168 (All) (FB): 1996 (1) East Cr C 97 (All) (FB) (1191-92); *Jai Singh* v. *Union of India*, 1993 Cr LJ 2705 (FB) (Raj): AIR 1993 Raj 177: 1993 (1) Raj LW 157.

2. *M. Ramachandran* v. *State of Kerala*, 1996 Cr LJ 3566 (3567) (Ker) (DB): ILR (1996) 2 Ker 511: 1996 (1) Ker LJ 378.

member of a Scheduled Caste or a Scheduled Tribe. Most importantly the cause for the offence must contain an element of racial prejudice.[1]

In the above mentioned case, which was tried under section 376(2)(f), which is a general section and provides a punishment of minimum imprisonment for 7 years, which may extend to 10 years or for life. In view of the discussions regarding the not-so-established facts and ingredients it was observed that section 3(2)(v) was not attracted and held as such that the conviction under this special provision cannot be sustained.

4. Grounds for Invoking section 3(2)(v)

A single Judge of A.P. High Court, had held that the allegation of rape on the ground that the victim belongs to SC or ST need not be made unless such rape was committed on that very ground. But in case the accused had taken advantage of woman and committed rape, where the woman belonged to SC or ST, need not necessarily be made on a ground to judge applicability of section 3(2)(v). But despite this accepted fact the provisions of Scheduled Castes and the Scheduled Tribes (Prevention of Atrocities) Act, 1989 would be attracted any way. It was additionally observed that if the accused failed to raise the objection at the stage of framing of charges, the inherent jurisdiction of High Court cannot be invoked in appeal.[2]

These above observations of a single Judge Bench were the only one which could be found in a long series of judgments delivered by different courts, including Apex Court in the country. Therefore it cannot be said that there is a difference of opinion, but rather it can be said that there is consensus of opinion which would be evident from following citations.

Almost overruling the above decision and settling the matter finally Supreme Court has held; *"sine qua non"* for application of section 3(2)(v) is that an offence must have been committed against a person on the ground that such person is a member of Scheduled Castes and Scheduled Tribes. In the instant case no evidence has been led to establish this requirement. It is not case of prosecution that the rape was committed on the victim since she was a member of Scheduled Caste. In the absence of evidence to that effect, section 3(2)(v) has no application. Had section 3(2)(v) of the Atrocities Act been applicable then by operation of law, the sentence would have been imprisonment for life and fine."[3]

---

1. *M. Ramachandran* v. *State of Kerala*, 1996 Cr LJ 3566 (3567) (Ker) (DB): ILR (1996) 2 Ker 511: 1996 (1) Ker LJ 378.
2. *Naga Bhixam* alias *Bhixapathi* v. *State of Andhra Pradesh*, 1996 Cr LJ 2400 (AP): 1996 (2) APLJ 239: 1996 APLJ (Cri) 263.
3. *Dinesh alias Buddha* v. *State of Rajasthan*, (2006) 2 SCC (Cri) 1: 2006 Cr LJ 1679 (SC) (1682): AIR 2006 SC 1267; *Hanamath* v. *State of Karnataka*, 2006 Cr LJ 1844 (Kant) (DB): ILR 2006 Kant 1476: 2006 (4) Kant LJ 1; *Bimal Gorai* v. *State of West Bengal*, 2012 Cr LJ 200 (Cal) (DB); Dissented *M.C. Prasannan* v. *State*, 1999 Cr LJ 998 (Cal) (DB): 1999 (1) Cal HN 123: 1999 (1) Cal LT 458 and *M. Ramachandran* v. *State of Kerala*, 1996 Cr LJ 3566 (3569) (Ker) (DB): ILR (1996) 2 Ker 511: 1996 (1) Ker LJ 378; but relied on *Masumsha Hasanasha Musalman* v. *State of Maharashtra*, AIR 2000 SC 1876: 2000 AIR SCW 719: (2000) 3 SCC 557; *Dinesh alias Buddha* v. *State of Rajasthan*, (2006) 2 SCC (Cri) 1: 2006 Cr LJ 1679: AIR 2006 SC 1267 and *State* v. *Chunnilal*, 2009 AIR SCW 5335; *Dharmendra* v. *State of Uttar Pradesh*, 2011 Cr LJ 204 (All) (DB); *Bimal Gorai* v. *State of West Bengal*, 2012 Cr LJ 200 (Cal) (DB).

In the above mentioned cases, the offence committed was rape on the victims belonging to Scheduled Castes or the Scheduled Tribes. In other grave offences committed under the provisions of Indian Penal Code, such as murder or its attempt of the members of Scheduled Castes or the Scheduled Tribes, similar standard was fixed.

The accused was charged with murder punishable under section 302 IPC, and the fact that the deceased belonged to Scheduled Caste, held no ground to convict the accused under section 3(2)(v) of the Act of 1989, in absence of any evidence that by his conduct also offended sensibilities of the deceased in relation to caste to which he belonged. This is no ground on which the accused can be convicted for an offence under section 3(2)(v) of the Act, "unless it is demonstrated that he has by his conduct said or done something that is directed to offend the sensibilities of the deceased".[1]

A Division Bench of Gujarat High Court had observed that even if it is not disputed that victims belonged to Scheduled Caste, but absence of any material that the offence was committed on the ground that victim being a member of Scheduled Caste, a conviction under section 3(2)(v) cannot be sustained and not proper. (case cited in foot-note 1).

Mere knowledge of accused that the victim belonged to Scheduled Caste or a Scheduled Tribe is not sufficient to constitute an offence under section 3(2)(v) of the Act. On the other hand, such knowledge should necessarily be coupled with intention to commit such an offence in order to belittle the person as he/she belongs to Scheduled Caste or Scheduled Tribe community.[2]

Accused person allegedly inflicted injuries on the victim and fled away from the place of occurrence after calling him "Chamar". Court found no evidence on record showing that the injuries were inflicted on the ground that he belonged to the Scheduled Caste community, therefore offence under section 3(2)(v) cannot be said to have been committed. It was held that offence under Penal Code should have been committed on the basis that the victim belongs to a Scheduled Caste or a Scheduled Tribe.[3]

Calling the caste of victim at the time of hot exchange between the victim and the accused offence under section 3(2)(v) would not be constituted because there

1. *Abdul Gafarsab* v. *State of Karnataka*, 1998 Cr LJ 2488 (Kant) (DB): 1998 (3) Crimes 620: 1998 (3) Kant LJ 132; *Lalubha Keshrisinh Garasia* v. *State of Gujarat*, 1997 Cr LJ 3847 (Guj) (DB): 1997 (3) Guj LR 2568: 1997 (2) Guj LH 327; *State of Jharkhand* v. *Amit Chakrabarty*, 2011 Cr LJ (NOC) 339 (Jhar) (DB); *C.T. Raveenran* v. *State of Kerala*, 2011 Cr LJ 1408 (DB).
2. *Mekali Raji Reddy* v. *State of Andhra Pradesh*, 2002 Cr LJ 3407 (AP): 2002 (1) Andh LT (Cri) 306 (AP): 2002 (3) Rec Cri R 6; *Ananda Pangala* v. *T.R. Jagannath*, 2003 Cr LJ 3215 (Kant): 2004 (3) KCCR 1965: 2004 (1) Kant LJ 623.
3. *Masumsha Hasanasha Musalman* v. *State of Maharashtra*, AIR 2000 SC 1876: 2000 AIR SCW 719: (2000) 3 SCC 557; *Amir* v. *State of Madhya Pradesh*, 2004 Cr LJ 3686 (MP) (DB): 2004 (17) All Ind Cas 846: 2005 (1) MPHT 411; *Goverdhan Lal* v. *State*, 2004 Cr LJ 3966 (Raj) (DB): 2004 (4) All Cri LR 624; *Kalasika Prashanta Kumar* v. *State of Andhra Pradesh*, 2004 Cr LJ 1051 (AP) (DB): 2004 (3) Crimes 102: 2004 (3) Rec Cri R 682; *Kumersingh* v. *State of Madhya Pradesh*, 2007 Cr LJ 1349 (MP) (DB): 2007 Cri LR (SC&MP) MP 304: 2007 (4) MPHT 585; *Koki Prabhakara Reddy* v. *State of Andhra Pradesh*, 2007 Cr LJ 263 (AP) (DB): 2007 (2) AIR Jhar (NOC) 534: 2006 (2) ALD (Cri) 501.

is no evidence that the offence was committed because of the fact that victim belonged to Scheduled Caste or Tribe.[1]

But in a case where the accused happened to be a secretary to a Private Institution running for purpose of helping the persons who are mentally and physically abnormal in the local areas and was simultaneously running a Private School under the said Institution. The accused asked the victim Tribal girl to come and work in the said Lok Uthhan Kendra on monthly salary of Rs. 2,000. The victim girl having no other source of income joined the said institute and deputed to do different jobs. She was allotted one room in which she was repeatedly raped by the accused, later on due to which she became pregnant twice which was aborted by a doctor. Neither any money was paid to her as promised salary. It was held that the poor Adivasi girl has been duped, cheated as well as raped by the accused and the court confirmed the conviction.[2]

Rape was committed on a girl aged 6/8 years, who belonged to SC/ST community. But prosecution failed to prove that the offence was committed on the ground that she belonged to such a community. Therefore Court found accused liable for conviction under section 376 IPC and not under section 3(2)(v) of the Act.[3]

A Scheduled Caste girl was threaded on point of knife and raped. The statement of witnesses and report of Forensic Science Laboratory supported the prosecution case. Though, considering the age of the accused at the time of incident sentence was reduced from 12 years to 7 years while confirming the conviction under section 376 IPC, but importantly setting aside the conviction under section 3(2)(v) of Act of 1989, because presence of no evidence that the offence was committed on the ground that the victim belonged to such community.[4]

5. Scope of Sentence under section 3(2)(v)

This provision under section 3(2)(v) of the Act of 1989 "does not prescribe a substantive sentence thus passing separate order of conviction and sentence under the section cannot be said to be legal. Section 3(2)(v) of the Act can be pressed into service only for enabling the Court to pass a sentence of imprisonment for life and a fine when a person has been found guilty of committing an offence under the I.P.C., which is punishable with imprisonment for a term of ten years or more." In the instant the conviction under section 376 IPC and section 3(2)(v) of SC/ST Act was set aside on the reasons mentioned above.[5]

1. *Panchu Yadav* v. *State of Chhattisgarh*, 2008 Cr LJ 4467 (Chha) (DB): 2009 (75) All Ind Cas 709: 2008 (3) Cr LJ 510; *Tutu* alias *Bijaya Kumar Patnaik* v. *State of Orissa*, 2008 Cr LJ 3424 (Ori) (DB).
2. *Harinath Tiwary* v. *State of Jharkhand*, 2009 Cr LJ 3757 (Jhar): 2009 (2) AIR Jhar R 990: 2009 (4) Crimes 672; also see *S. Balaraman* v. *State*, 2009 Cr LJ 3603 (Mad) (DB): 2009 (4) Crimes 8: 2009 (4) Rec Cri R 723; *Gangula Venkateswara Reddy* v. *State of Andhra Pradesh*, 2009 Cr LJ 1958 (AP) (DB): 2009 (1) ALD (Cri) 453.
3. *Lalan Jhaku* v. *State of Bihar*, 2010 Cr LJ 1545 (Jhar) (DB): 2010 (1) AIR Jhar R 444: 2010 (4) Crimes 778; *Katkam Raajanna* v. *State of Andhra Pradesh*, 2010 Cr LJ 3812: 2010 (2) ALD (Cri) 92.
4. *Dharmendra* v. *State of Uttar Pradesh*, 2011 Cr LJ 204 (All) (DB); *C.T. Raveeran* v. *State*, 2011 Cr LJ 1408 (Ker) (DB).
5. *Bachcha* v. *State of Uttar Pradesh*, 2008 Cr LJ 483 (All) (DB): 2007 (6) ALJ 516: 2007 (59) All Cri C 949.

6. Entire incident has to be Considered as Single Episode

Murder and insulting of such a member had taken place and the accused were tried for murder, attempt to murder and under section 3(1)(x) and 3(2)(v) of the Act of 1989. One set of the accused was acquitted on ground of lack and contradictory evidence produced by the prosecution but the other sets were convicted under section 3(2)(v), but again, that set was also acquitted under section 3(1)(x) of the Act on the ground that the witnesses were not reliable. It was observed that, "the entire episode has to be considered as a single incident and the acts cannot be considered as severable from each other and if evidence is not trustworthy to be accepted to constitute offence punishable under section 3(1)(x) of the Atrocities Act, obviously, the offence under section 3(2)(v) could not have been held to have been proved."[1]

7. Framing of Charges under section 3(2)(v)

At the time of framing of charges under sections 227 and 228 of Cr P.C suspicion about commission of offence under section 3(2)(v) of the Act and involvement of the accused in such offence would be sufficient to frame charges. The deceased belonged to Scheduled Caste family and the accused, who had animosity, with the deceased, went to deceased's house and hurled abuses related to caste and threw stones and bricks, one of the bricks hit deceased and as a result of which he died. The accused were aware of the caste of the deceased. It was held that charges framed under section 3(2)(v) of the Act was proper.[2]

On the other hand Jharkhand High Court Commented on the Casual finding of the Special Judge to the effect: "on perusal of the record and case diary it appears that all witnesses supported the case of the prosecution and there is sufficient material to frame charge",— the order does not show that in fact the Special Judge has applied his judicial mind at all on the allegation made or on the points raised by the accused for discharge. The accused and the complainant both were public servants. The High Court found sufficient grounds to discharge the accused from all charges under section 3(1) and 3(2) of the Atrocities Act of 1989.[3]

8. Quashing of FIR and Compromise

The accused was charged under sections 376/328 IPC and section 3 of Scheduled Castes and the Scheduled Tribes (Prevention of Atrocities) Act, 1989. Both the accused and the prosecutrix were under 18 years of age at the time of the incident in question. The matter was compromised by the parties in presence of villagers and the relatives. The prosecutrix was present in the court, who wanted to forget the past and pleaded that for continuing the trial she had made various visits to the Court. Father and brother of the prosecutrix stood by her and pleaded to allow her to move normally on with her life. The court observed that both were minors and needed protection and found the only way to forget it by closing the chapter once for all. Consequently the court allowing the petition,

---

1. *Rasikbhai Gopalbhai Patel* v. *State of Gujarat*, 2008 Cr LJ 34 (Guj) (DB) (42-43): 2007 (2) Guj LH 732: 2008 (2) Guj LR 1009.
2. *Jai Singh* v. *State*, 2011 Cr LJ 3628 (Raj).
3. *Aparajita Jha* v. *State of Jharkhand*, 2009 Cr LJ 3088 (Jhar): 2009 (2) AIR Jhar R 491: 2009 (1) East Cri C 361.

quashed the FIR and the charge-sheet alongwith all the consequental proceedings arising therefrom in the interest of justice.[1]

9. "....On Ground that Person is Member of SC or ST" – Sentencing

Sentencing or invoking the provisions of section 3(2)(v) have been discussed in detail in the above mentioned paragraphs but one specific aspect of the application of the words and its consequental result came up for discussion before a Division Bench.

Accused were not only charged under two different heads *viz.* under section 376(2)(g) of the I.P.C., and under section 3(2)(v) of the Atrocities Act, but the trial court sentenced the accused for two different offences differently *viz.*, R.I. for 10 years for offence under section 376(2)(g) I.P.C., and life imprisonment for the offence punishable under section 3(2)(v) of the Atrocities Act. The Bench observed that these are two distinct offences and as such both have to be proved separately according to the ingredients of the sections involved. The object of clause (v) of section 3(2) of the Act is to punish persons who commit offences, though under the Indian Penal Code, but on the ground that such person belongs to, or such property belongs to such a person.[2]

10. Mentioning Caste in FIR

As far as mentioning the caste of either of the complainant or the accused is concerned, it was held that it need be mentioned in the FIR. The observation was made on the authority of Apex Court judgment (AIR 2009 SC 1973) holding that First Information Report is not expected to be an encyclopedia. It was further suggested that under Rule 7 of the Scheduled Castes and the Scheduled Tribes (Prevention of Atrocities) Rules, 1995, investigation has to be done by officer not the below the rank of Dy. Superintendent of Police and after ascertaining the facts, during the course of investigation, it is open to the Investigation Officer to record that the accused either belongs to or does not belong to Scheduled Caste or Scheduled Tribe. After final opinion is formed, it is open to Court to either accept the same or to take cognizance. Even if charge is framed at trial, materials can be placed to show that the accused belongs to or does not belong to such caste. Hence it is not mandatory to mention the caste in the FIR.[3]

It is submitted that above finding holding caste need not be mentioned in the FIR, may lead to many kinds of confusions, before and after the start of investigation. In a criminal case when FIR is lodged at the police station, the police concerned register a case under the General Diary mentioning not only sections of relevant enactments, but also specifically mention the police officer, usually by name, who would be entrusted with the investigation of the registered case. As Rule 7 of the Rules of 1995 framed under the Act of 1989 provide that investigations under the Act would not be done by a lower rank officer than a Dy S.P., such investigation may be entrusted to a lower rank officer, and if

1. *Chandra Mohan alias Bunti* v. *State of Haryana*, 2011 Cr LJ 898 (P&H).
2. *Hanamath* v. *State of Karnataka*, 2006 Cr LJ 1844 (1848) (Kant) (DB): ILR 2006 Kant 1476: 2006 (4) Kant LJ 1. [please also see note (c) and (d) of this clause.]
3. *Haridas Kisanrao Kharbadkar* v. *State of Maharashtra*, 2010 Cr LJ 3298 (Bom): 2010 (3) AIR Bom R 504: 2010 All MR (Cri) 455.

found later on that the victim or the accused, as the case may be, belonged to the Scheduled Caste or the Scheduled Tribe, a lot of inconvenience and loss of time may become hazardous for the victim or the prosecution, because loss of time may result in loss of relevant evidence. For instance facts of the following case may be perused.

A victim of rape, claimed to be a member of Scheduled Tribe of 'Kondho' caste, but later on it was found that she belonged to 'Telugulu' caste. The victim even did not possess any certificate of Caste. The Court found that she did not belong to the Caste or a Scheduled Tribe as claimed. This had happened at the stage of trial. The FIR did not mention caste hence the investigation was conducted by a Officer-in-charge of a police station and not by Dy. S.P. as required by Rule 7 of rules of 1995, and he submitted the charge-sheet. Despite all these facts regarding investigation the trial court convicted the accused under the provisions of section 3(2)(v) of the Act. The Division Bench had to discuss at length to save the conviction under section 376 IPC only, observing that provisions of Rule 7 were not attracted.[1] Had the correct position been mentioned in the FIR such anomalies could have been avoided.

11. The Relief Amount

In the Annexure I, Schedule, for norms of relief amount, attached to the Rules of 1995, item No. 17 provides at least Rs. 50,000 to the victims.

Section 3(2)(vi) "knowingly or having reason to believe that an offence has been committed under this Chapter, causes any evidence of the commission of that offence to disappear with the intention of screening the offender from legal punishment, or with that intention gives any information respecting the offence which he knows or believes to be false, shall be punishable with the punishment provided for that offence; or"

SYNOPSIS

1. General Comparison
2. Analogous Law
3. Underlying Principle
4. Scope
5. Ingredients
6. The Used Words
   - 6.1 "Offence has been Committed"
   - 6.2 "Reason to Believe"
   - 6.3 "Causes any Evidence......to Disappear"
   - 6.4 "Gives any Information...... Knows or Believes to be False"
7. Concealment of Offence Itself
8. Privileged Communications and Concealment of Informations
9. Primary Offender, if Liable
10. If Homicide was Not Offence by Itself
11. "Disappeared" Material Must be Evidence
12. Evidence Explained
13. Presence of Intention to Screen Offender, Mandatory
14. Knowledge of Committed Offence
15. Punishment and sentence under section 3(2)(vi)
16. Anomaly of Punishment under section 3(2)(vi)

---

1. *Dasarathi Sahukar* v. *State*, 2007 Cr LJ 3445 (Ori) (DB): 2007 (37) OCR 802.

1. General Comparison

Under various clauses of sub-section (1) of section 3 of the Scheduled Castes and the Scheduled Tribes (Prevention of Atrocities) Act, 1989, specially clause (ix), giving false or frivolous information to any public servant and thereby causing such public servant to use his lawful power so that it may result in injury or annoyance to a member of Scheduled Caste or a Scheduled Tribe, has been made an offence. But in the present clause causing 'disappearance of evidence' of already committed offence against a member of a Scheduled Caste or a Scheduled Tribe; or, intentionally or knowingly giving false information with the intention to screen the offender, has been made an offence.

Thus under clause (ix) of section 3(1) of the Act, intentional false information to implicate such a member has been created as an offence, while under section 3(2)(vi) giving false information to save an offender from punishment under the provisions of the act of 1989 has been made an offence. In doing so all aspects of intentional false information, constituting an evidence or an act which renders such evidence to disappear, so that a culprit may be helped and screened from punishment, has been created as an offence by the Special Legislation.

As far as punishment for the offence is concerned, the offender would be liable to a punishment equal to that for which he had caused disappearance of evidence or the false information which was committed by the 'primary' offender, who was intended to be saved, unlike the offence committed under clause (ix) of section 3(1).

2. Analogous Law

English Criminal Law considers aiders and abettors of an offence as accessories to the committed offence. Helping a culprit or offender by causing the evidence against him to disappear and giving intentional false information so that the offender goes scot free, or at least to diminish the criminal deed, has been declared as an offence by itself. In fact 'abettors' come on the scence before the actual commission of a crime, but as such persons who are described by the present clause are those who come to scene when the offence has already been committed, thus the Law Commissioners called this type of offenders as " subsequent abettors".

It is a natural inference that a person helping an offender by an overt act after the offence has been committed, is doing so to aid the offender in some way, hence calling such persons as "subsequent abettors" is appropriate expression. But the drafters of Indian Penal Code did not include the offence in Chapter V naming it as "of Abetment", rather the described offence has been placed under Chapter XI of IPC which is related to false evidence etc..

The clause (vi) reproduces first part and main body of section 201 IPC, which is:

> "201. Whoever, knowing or having reason to believe that an offence has been committed, causes any evidence of the commission of that offence to disappear with the intention of screening the offence from legal punishment or with that intention gives any information respecting the offence which he knows or believes to be false;.......". (Section 201 IPC classified the offences

and punishments accordingly but clause (vi) provided and generalised the punishment).

The other difference being that the words "committed under this Chapter", in the present clause confines the application to offences committed against members of Scheduled Castes or the Scheduled Tribes, while the provisions of IPC (section 201) applies to public at large.

3. Underlying Principle

Lord Hale described or rather defined a "subsequent abettor" or aider of an offence as: "An accessory of the fact may be, where a person knowing a felony to have been committed, receives, relieves, comforts, or assists the felon".[1] Therefore a condition precedent to invoke the provision, it is necessary to prove that such an accessory must know that the offence has already been committed by a particular offender.

4. Scope

As mentioned above, the first requirement for invoking the provisions of section 3(2)(vi) is that the person who causes disappearance the evidence of commission of a crime against a member of Scheduled Caste or a Scheduled Tribe, must know that the offence against such member has already been committed in its final sense, secondly it has to be seen that by causing the evidence against the offender to disappear would assist him in any way to weaken the case of prosecution against him; or, intentionally making public an intentional false information which would help the offender to build his defence etc.

The most essential requirements to exercise the scope of clause (vi) of section 3(2) of the Act are: the offence against a member of Scheduled Caste or Scheduled Tribe must have been committed and the accused must have previous knowledge of already committed offence; what the charged person had made to disappear must be evidence; the charged person must have knowledge that the offence has already been committed; the accused must have clear intention, either for disappearance of evidence or for giving false informations for the object of screening the offender. These positions have been discussed in detail in foregoing paragraphs.

The most important point is that the actual offender, if he violates the provisions cannot be charged for obliterating the traces of his own crime, on the ground that he is not "screening" other offender but himself.[2]

5. Ingredients

The first and foremost condition for invoking the provisions of section 3(2) (vi) is that an offence must have been committed against a member of Scheduled Caste or a Scheduled Tribe and the likely charged person must know, or at least has some reason to believe that such an offence has already been committed against such member.

---

1. 1 Hale, P.C. 618.
2. *State of West Bengal* v. *Hari Ramalu*, 2004 Cr LJ 2659 (Cal) (DB): 2004 (3) All Cri LR 461: 2004 (2) Cal HN 438; *Bhagwan Swarup* v. *State of Rajasthan*, AIR 1991 SC 2062: 1991 Cr LJ 3123: 1991 AIR SCW 2325; *Harishchandrasing Sajjansing Rathod* v. *State of Gujarat*, AIR 1979 SC 1232: 1979 Cr LJ 1025: (1979) 4 SCC 502.

In general, Supreme Court has dealt with the ingredients and applicability of causing disappearance of evidence of offence as:

> To bring home an offence for causing disappearance of evidence, the ingredients to be established are: (i) committal of an offence (against such a member); (ii) person charged with the offence (under the present clause) must have knowledge or reason to believe that an offence has been committed (under the present Chapter); (iii) person charged with the offence should have caused the disappearance of evidence; and, (iv) the act should have been done with the intention of screening the offender from legal punishment or with that intention he should have given information respecting the offence, which he knew or believed to be false. It is plain that the intent to screen the offender committing the offence must be the primary and sole aim of the accused. A mere suspicion is not sufficient. There must be on record cogent evidence to prove that the accused knew or had information sufficient to lead him to believe that the offence had been committed and that the accused has caused the evidence to disappear in order to screen the offender, known or unknown.[1]

6. The Used Words

6.1 "Offence has been Committed"

The application of the present provision for intentional screening of the offender under Chapter II of SC and ST Act, would only start when the offence has actually been committed by the primary offender and within the knowledge of the accused. Mere planning of committing the offence by primary offender would not suffice to invoke the provision. One may have presumed or has a reason to believe that some kind of offence under the Chapter has been committed, though no such actual offence has been committed, and in furtherance thereof disappears something which he believes to be an evidence against the main culprit, no offence under section 3(2)(vi) can be constituted.

But in case when main offence could be established and proved by the prosecution through clinching evidence, it was held that destruction or disappearance of evidence by another, if fully proved, can be established.[2]

When the word "offence" has been referred, it would mean an offence as it appears to the accused, crediting him with knowledge that can reasonably be expected of him.

6.2 "Reason to Believe"

Section 26 of IPC defines the expression as: "A person is said to have 'reason to believe' a thing, if he has sufficient cause to believe that thing but not otherwise."

6.3 "Causes any Evidence......to Disappear"

The evidence may or may not be material to the proof of the primary crime. Neither the evidence need be legally admissible. The meaning to 'evidence' has

1. *Sukhram* v. *State of Maharashtra*, 2007 Cr LJ 4327: AIR 2007 SC 3050: (2007) 7 SCC 5502.
2. *State* v. *Madesha*, 2007 (3) CC SC 703 (SC).

been taken here in its every basic sense. It would mean anything which shows that some crime has been committed evidently, such as blood stains or similar materials indicative of committal of some kind of crime.

The "disappearance" must have been caused with clear intention and primary object to screen the offender, by some overt act and active assistance, from evading punishment. The "disappearance" must have been caused and not merely suffered, nor mere knowledge that the act of such "disappearance" will have the effect of screening, would suffice to constitute an offence under the present clause. For instance, disposing a dead body by removal or concealment would amount to causing "disappearance" of evidence.

6.4 "Gives any Information......Knows or Believes to be False"

Firstly such given information must be false and believed by the giver as such, and secondly the act of giving such false information must be with the sole intention to help or screen the offender.

A question may arise and needs explanation, which is: to whom such false intentional information should be 'given' to constitute the crime under the present provision? In fact the word "gives" can assume various meanings in different circumstances. Whether it would be said that if a person "gives" such false information to an unconcerned person would bring home the charge under this part of section 3 of the Act? The obvious answer would be, no, because that unconcerned person may simply digest the given false information and the object of screening the offender would be defeated. Therefore such a false information must either be given to some authority or any person connected with the authority, who is responsible and interested in bringing the primary offender to justice.

7. Concealment of Offence Itself

Intentionally concealing informations about commission of an offence under Chapter II of the act is one thing, while giving of false information respecting the commission of such offence is another. Both of these acts may be said to be offences prescribed by different laws, because both these acts tend to thwart justice or its administration. Both these acts may be done with different kinds of intentions, such as the commission of offence may be concealed without any intention to screen the actual offender or it may be directing the authorities towards someone else, other than the actual offender.

For constituting an offence under the present provision, the false information must be given to screen the offender from punishment and not beyond, though, it would be immaterial whether such false information was given in an inquiry, during questioning, or has been given voluntarily.

The same expression – "gives any false or frivolous information" used in clause (ix) of section 3(1) of the Act, stipulates similar meaning but in a reversed circumstance.

8. Privileged Communications and Concealment of Informations

Section 122 to section 129 of Indian Evidence Act, 1872 declare certain communications and possession of informations by a certain class of persons as 'privileged communication'. This class cannot be compelled by any authority whatsoever, to divulge the informations received in the course of mentioned communications.

Thus these mentioned class of persons, if deny to divulge any information, such denial cannot be termed as concealment of information. For instance, communication between husband and wife has been protected as a policy of law, and if on that ground a wife refuses to divulge informations which may disclose her husband's crime, no adverse inference could be drawn, neither she can be made responsible for concealment of information. This is one aspect of the matter.

The other aspect is that if such wife causes the evidence 'disappear' she would be undoubtedly liable for such offence as has been prescribed here.

9. Primary Offender, if Liable

Murder of husband of a woman had taken place, while she was lying on the same cot, thus the court believed that she knew the actual offender. The first version given by the woman to police immediately after occurrence was considered by the court to be false and their Lordships believed that the woman knew the given statement to be false. It was observed that "borderline between abetment of the offence and giving false information to screen the offender is rather thin, but it is prudent to err on the safe side, and hold her guilty of an offence" for giving false information to screen the offender. It was also observed that the provision is not restricted to cases to persons screening the offender, but to the person guilty of main offence. But a person cannot be convicted for main offence as well as for giving false information. But as a matter of practice, where a person had been found guilty of the main offence, he should not be convicted both of main offence and for giving false information to screen the offender.[1]

10. If Homicide was Not Offence by Itself

Under the Indian Law suicide, if committed, is no offence, and if a person causes to "disappear" the dead body of such person cannot be made punishable under the provision of section 3 of the Act.

If a thief entered a house and when challenged by the owner of the house, attacked him, the owner in self-defence gave the thief (belonging to SC or ST) a stick blow in the head killing him on the spot, and later disposed off the body with the help of his brother and relatives. The brothers and the relatives cannot be convicted of screening the owner of the house, because the killing was justified by the law and no offence was committed by the owner. As there was neither any offence nor the offender, therefore the relatives cannot be charged under this provision.

11. "Disappeared" Material Must be Evidence

Clause (vi) of section 3(2) provides to penalise a person who caused the 'disappearance' of material which must be evidence of the offence and such 'disappearance' must be made with the intention to screen the offender. Thus

1. *Kalawati* v. *State of Himachal Pradesh*, 1953 Cr LJ 668: AIR 1953 SC 131: 1953 SCR 546 followed in *Ranchhod* v. *State*, 1956 Cr LJ 1401 (DB): AIR 1956 MB 282: ILR (1956) MB 104 etc.

if the 'disappeared' material was not evidence of the offence, then such person causing 'disappearance' has committed no offence under this provision, whatever may have been his act.

The other important point to ponder in the scenario is the meaning of word "disappear", which means "cease to be visible, go missing or cease to exist or be in circulation" (Oxford Dictionary & Thesaurus). Therefore simply removing a dead body from one place to another from where it could easily be found cannot be said to cause it "disappear". Unless an evidence which has been made by some act where it ceases to be visible, go missing or cease to exist, it cannot be said that such evidence or thing has been caused to "disappear". Simply concealing something which is considered an evidence would not constitute an offence, unless such concealed article "disappears".

For example: if two persons murder a person in their field and then removed the dead body from their field and put it in the field owned by the deceased, it would not make the dead body "disappear", hence no offence is committed in the instant provision.

12. Evidence Explained

The word "evidence" used in section 3(2)(vi) of the Act is not the same as has been taken in the Indian Evidence Act, 1872. The word used here has been used in a limited and primary sense. In fact the word 'evidence' used here means anything that is likely to make the crime manifest or evident, or to make it more clear – it would mean that the materials or facts which would lead to the proof of commission of a crime by the primary offender.

Persons cannot be included in the meaning of 'evidence' here in the strict sense, because disappearance of a witness (even eye-witness) could not be included in the stipulated meaning. The value of evidence given by a witness depends on his credibility and he could not therefore said to be evidence.

13. Presence of Intention to Screen Offender, Mandatory

The second most essential requirement is presence of intention of charged person when he causes disappearance of evidence with sole object of screening the offender. This primary and sole object must be proved to bring home the charge under this provision. As said above it may be found that some evidence might have been concealed by the charged person, but if the intention was otherwise than to screen the offender, the provisions of present clause would not be attracted, because it is not the likelihood which has been made an offence under this clause but it speaks of intention to screen the man offender.

The phraseology used here is "with the intention of screening the offender", reflecting a clear intention to do so and nothing less than that. In legal terminology whenever likelihood is intended to be included in the language of criminal legislations, the adopted expression may also mean, "intending or knowing it to be likely", which in the present case is absent. Therefore nothing less than clear intention to screen the offender shall be sufficient to prove the guilt.

For instance, some villagers found a dead body within the limits of the village and removed the body to the limits of a nearby village, with no other intention than to avoid rigours of police harassment during investigations. The removal was obviously not with intention to screen some offender, hence no offence under the provision could be made out.

14. Knowledge of Committed Offence

Section 3(2)(vi) of the Act prescribes to punish only those who knew or has reason to believe that an offence has been committed by somebody known and against a member of Scheduled Caste or a Scheduled Tribe. The concept of an offender stipulates that an offence has already been committed. Though, it is not necessary that the accused should have knowledge of full details of committed offence. A person may believe a certain person to be guilty of the primary offence though he may have no reason for such belief, but simultaneously such person may be said to have some cause to believe a fact. The prosecution is duty bound to prove that such person had cause to believe sufficiently for his belief. This kind of evidence may differ from facts and circumstances of each case. A person who removed a thing, which was later on found to be evidence, by chance without any knowledge of commission of offence, could not be said to have any liability under this provision.

15. Punishment and Sentence under section 3(2)(vi)

Section 3(2)(vi) prescribes the punishment for 'disappearance' of evidence or giving 'false information' intentionally to screen the offender: "shall be punishable with the punishment provided for that offence".

But a situation may arise where same person has been charged for the main committed offence, as well as giving false information or for disappearance of evidence and found guilty for both the acts. Question may arise whether same person may be convicted for both the committed offences. The position contemplated by sections 71 and 72, Indian Penal Code may arise, which says:

> "72. *Punishment of person guilty of one of several offences, the judgment stating that it is doubtful of which.*—In all cases in which judgment is given that a person is guilty of one of several offences specified in the judgment but that it is doubtful of which of these offences, he is guilty, the offender shall be punished for the offence for which the lowest punishment is provided if the same punishment is not provided for all."

Apart from this provision, position contemplated by section 71 IPC would also be interesting to note. It says: "where anything which is an offence is made up of parts, any of which part is itself an offence, the offender shall not be punished with the punishment of more than one of such of his offences.........".

Suppose a person has been found guilty of murder or rape and simultaneously under section 3(2)(vi) of the Act of 1989, then question may arise whether he can be convicted for both the offences separately in light of provisions of sections 71 and 72 of Indian Penal Code. The law has developed gradually and judicial controversy was the theme of such development, *i.e.*, as to whether main offender may be excluded from punishment for disappearance of evidence to screen the offender. In *Kalawati* v. *State*[1] it was observed that the provision "is not restricted

1. *Kalawati* v. *State of Himachal Pradesh*, 1953 Cr LJ 668: AIR 1953 SC 131: 1953 SCR 546 followed in *Ranchhod* v. *State*, 1956 Cr LJ 1401 (DB): AIR 1956 MB 282: ILR (1956) MB 104 etc.

to the case of a person who screens the actual offender. It can be applied even to a person guilty of main offence, though as a matter of practice, a court will not convict a person both of the main offence and the other one. The previous contention that the main offender cannot be convicted, considered not a good law. The stand taken by Supreme Court is a balanced view, implying that if a person is convicted for the main offence, the other offences may be excluded, but where there is no justification for convicting the guilty for the main offence, the person may be convicted for "disappearance" of evidence or giving false information.

Therefore a person can be charged and tried for alternative charges for both the offences and the charges cannot be challenged on the ground of misjoinder, nor it can be declared as irregular or improper. If an alternative charge had been made previously, it may be open to the trial court while delivering judgment holding that person guilty of one of several offences (section 72 IPC), but it is doubtful of which of these offences he is guilty, the court may convict the charged person.[1]

16. Anomaly of Punishment under section 3(2)(vi)

Another eventuality may arise in the present section 3(2)(vi). Suppose a single person has been tried under section 302 IPC, read with section 3(2)(vi) of the Act of 1989, and in the end the court did not find him guilty under section 302 IPC, but there is enough evidence that he caused "disappearance" of evidence to screen himself (the offender); a question may arise as to what extent of punishment he should be convicted, because section 3(2)(vi) provides: "shall be punishable with the punishment provided for that offence". There remain no existence of "that offence".

In the above paragraphs we had discussed opinions of different courts which were given in different cases tried under section 201 IPC, which specifically prescribe different extent of punishments in terms of imprisonments. Section 3(2)(vi) does not prescribe any term of imprisonment, but it has been left to "punishment provided for that offence", and in case 'that (other) offence' cannot be proved, it would be difficult to fix quantum of and extent of imprisonment.

However, the punishment for doing away the evidence would depend entirely upon the nature of "that offence" and punishment provided thereunder, but in any case sentence cannot be awarded without ascertaining the original offence.

"**Section 3(2)(vii)** being a public servant, commits any offence under this section, shall be punishable with imprisonment for a term which shall not be less than one year but which may extend to the punishment provided for that offence."

SYNOPSIS

1. Public Servant
2. Applicability and Scope
3. Principle
4. "Commits any Offence under this section"
5. Relief and Compensation

1. *Mangal Singh* v. *King Emperor*, AIR 1937 PC 179: 64 Ind App 134: 38 Cr LJ 573.

1. Public Servant

Please see notes under section 4 of this presentation.

2. Applicability and Scope

Clause (vii) of section 3(2) of The Scheduled Castes and the Scheduled Tribes (Prevention of Atrocities) Act, 1989 has to be read with the prefixed clause in the start of sub-section (2) as well as sub-section (1), which is: "whoever, not being a member of a Scheduled Caste or a Scheduled Tribe-". Therefore the charged "public servant" under the clause must belong to a caste other than Scheduled Caste/Tribe. With the result for applicability of section 3(2)(vii) three pre-conditions are essential:

(i) the complainant must belong to a Scheduled Caste or Scheduled Tribe; and

(ii) the accused "public servant" must not belong to Scheduled Caste/Tribe.

(iii) the accused "public servant" must have committed any offence prescribed under sub-sections (1) or (2) of section 3.

The caste of a person, whether complainant or the accused, is a question of fact which should be determined on the basis of evidence, when it is disputed. It was observed that there is nothing in the Act to show that where a person claims to belong to a Scheduled Caste or Tribe, the provisions of the Act should be applied. The scheme of the Act shows that if the victim belongs to the Scheduled Caste/ Tribe and the assailant or the offender does not belong to those communities only then the provisions of the Act come into play. In the present system in which we are, no person can shed his caste or community which he or she acquired by birth or marriage, unless he or she converts into another religion.[1]

Accused were public servants who removed the sheds of the *de facto* complainant and abused her in a filthy language touching her caste. It was shown that the *de facto* complainant belonged to a backward caste but married to a scheduled caste person. Even the authorities had cancelled her scheduled caste certificate, despite this fact a petition filed before the court for quashing the complaint was dismissed on the ground that question of fact of caste could only be determined through evidence in a trial.[1]

But other eventualities, such as the committal of an offence against such member and under section 3 of the Act must comply strictly within the norms provided by section 3 of the Act itself. For instance, if the occurrence had taken place within the chamber of the Municipal Commissioner, no offence was found to have been committed under section 3 of the Act, on the ground that chamber of Municipal Commissioner was not a public place and the occurrence had not taken place in "public view" as stipulated under section 3(1)(x) of the Act.[2] [In the present context please see notes under section 3(1)(x)].

---

1. *Bodasingi Satyanarayana* v. *State of Andhra Pradesh*, 2004 Cr LJ 803 (805) (AP); 2004 (1) ALD (Cri) 253: 2004 (2) Rec Cri R 657; also see *Valsamma Paul* v. *Cochin University*, AIR 1996 SC 1011: 1996 AIR SCW 492: (1996) 3 SCC 545.
2. *K. Padma Reddy* v. *Station House Officer, Bellampalli*, 2004 Cr LJ 503 (AP): 2003 (11) All Ind Cas 784: 2003 (5) Andh LD 345.

3. Principle

The present provision deals with the high-handedness of public servants in general and specially shown towards down-trodden people, irrespective of their assigned duty of service. In general, public servants are pregnated with large amount of powers for purposes of exercising their duties. But such exercise of powers must be used subject to limit of certain rules. As long as the powers are exercised within that parameters, the public servant is protected from clutches of criminal (or even civil) law. The line is very thin, therefore it usually becomes a practice to cross that line.

On the other hand State always is inclined to protect its personnel by giving them privilege of "official immunity". The "official immunity" and "sovereign immunity" are two kinds of immunities possessed by all governmental organs, effectively protecting the personnel from criminal or civil action; and for this reason human right organizations, the world over, fight tooth and nail for such immunities as they are the cause of human right violations because of which it becomes difficult for victims to get redressal.

Despite presence of section 3(2)(vii) and section 4 in the body of the Act of 1989, section 22 has been added with its head-line: "Protection of action taken in good faith". In this sense section 3(2)(vii) of the Act of 1989 is an antithesis to the immunity laws generally prevalent, specially in India where it has been retained as a holdover from colonial rule. (Please also see notes under section 4.

4. "Commits any Offence under this section"

Various new kinds of offences have been created by section 3 of the Scheduled Castes and Scheduled Tribes (Prevention of Atrocities) Act, 1989, which are related to the objects of the Act, *viz.*, atrocities on members of Scheduled Caste/ Tribes. But in addition to those newly created offences, offences committed under the provisions of Indian Penal Code, 1860, specially those "punishable, with imprisonment for a term of ten years or more against a person or property on the ground that such person is a member of Scheduled Caste or a Scheduled Tribe" [section 3(2)(v)], have also been included under the expression, "commits any offence under this section". Therefore the said expression not only covers the exclusive offences provided under section 3 of the Act of 1989, but also offences committed under various provisions cf IPC, provided that the said offence has been committed by a non-Scheduled Caste/Tribe public servant against a member of Scheduled Caste/Tribe.

However, section 40 of Indian Penal Code, 1860 defines "offence" as: section 40 "offence" – "Except in the chapters and sections mentioned in clauses 2 and 3 of this section, the word "offence" denotes a thing made punishable by this Code.

In Chapter IV, Chapter VA and in the following sections, namely sections 64, 65, 66, 67, 71, 109, 110, 112, 114, 115, 116, 117, 118, 119, 120, 187, 194, 195, 203, 211, 213, 214, 221, 222, 223, 224, 225, 327, 328, 329, 330, 331, 347, 348, 388, 389 and 445 the word "offence" denotes a thing punishable under the Code, or under any special or local law as hereinafter defined.

And in sections 141, 176, 177, 201, 202, 212, 216 and 441 the word "offence" has the same meaning when the thing punishable under the special or local law is punishable under such law with imprisonment for a term of six months or upwards, whether with or without fine."

It may be noted that above mentioned definition of "offence" by IPC emphatically mention "special or local law", and SC and ST Act, 1989 is a special law, repeatedly held to be so by different Courts in the country.

Therefore it becomes crystal clear that offence committed under various sections of IPC by 'public servants' and against members of Scheduled Castes/ Tribes "shall" be punishable with the imprisonment for a term which shall not be less than one year but which may extend to the punishment provided for that offence. The expression "provided for that offence" stipulates that punishment and extent of imprisonment as has been provided under the appropriate sections of Indian Penal Code, 1860.

One may find that in most of the cases, the minimum punishment provided under section 3 of the Act is a punishment of imprisonment for a period of six months for minor offences, but to deter 'public servants', impregnated with powers and immunity provided by law, section 3(2)(vii) provides minimum punishment "which shall not be less than one year".

5. Relief and Compensation

Item No. 18 provided under Annexture 1 to the SC/ST Rules, 1995 provides that "full compensation on account of damages or loss or harm sustained 50% to be paid when charge-sheet is sent to the court and 50% on conviction by lower court." Though, no provision has been made by the said rules for the cases in which the court finds allegations to be false and acquittal of accused on that ground; what would be the fate of 50% amount paid at the time of filing of the charge-sheet. The U.P. Government had issued an Order that in such cases the already paid amount would not be recovered from the victim or victims.

A 13-year-old tribal girl was arrested under the provisions of TADA Act of 1987, but later on the court found the allegations to be false and ultimately she was acquitted. In addition, the girl was tortured in most inhuman manner by the security agencies while she was in custody. The State was found to cover up the matter instead of punishing concerned Police Officers. The court not only ordered to register cases against concerned officers ('public servants') under section 3(2) (vii) of the Act, but also ordered the state to pay compensation of Rs. 5,00,000 to the victim for the 'atrocities' committed on her.[1]

(For further details please see notes under section 4).

(For 'Procedure and Practices'-please see at the end of Chapter II as well as Appendix II).

4. Punishment for neglect of duties.—Whoever, being a public servant but not being a member of a Scheduled Caste or a Scheduled Tribe, wilfully neglects his duties required to be performed by him

1. *Parbatabai Sakharam Taram* v. *State of Maharashtra*, 2006 Cr LJ 2202 (Bom) (DB): 2006 All MR (Cri) 1018: 2006 (2) Bom CR (Cri) 309.

under this Act, shall be punishable with imprisonment for a term which shall not be less than six months but which may extend to one year.

SYNOPSIS

1. Scope and Applicability
2. Underlying Principles
3. "Public Servant"
4. Exclusion of SC/ST Public Servant
5. Classification, not violative of Article 14
6. Who is 'Public Servant' – A test
7. Alleged Neglected Duty Must be Provided Under the Act
8. Willful Neglect of Duties
9. Section 4 of the Act and section 197 Cr PC
10. Section 4 and Rule 8(ix)
11. Norms of Relief

1. Scope and Applicability

Section 4 of SC/ST Act of 1989 is a generalised extension of class of offences, dealing with the duty of public servants, described and prescribed as offences from sections 217 to 220 of Indian Penal Code, 1860. Though, the Indian Penal Code specifically created offences for a particular disobedience of law concerning a specific circumstance with ill intention by public servants, but section 4 of the Act has made an offence a wilful neglect of duties which the law and the Act expects him to perform.

Section 4 encompasses all the intentional negligence by public servants towards 'prevention of atrocities' on members of Scheduled Castes and the Scheduled Tribes. Indeed, as such, section 4 of the Act is much wider in scope as compared to the class of sections mentioned above (IPC), as this section embraces all cases of intentional neglect.

Section 4 of the Act, thus is more general in its applicability and the liability (criminal) of any lawful authority who is found negligent in exercise of the discretionary powers, specifically vested in him by the provisions of the Act of 1989 or the Rules of 1995 made thereunder. The wilful neglect would expose them to criminal prosecution.

Difference between provisions of section 4 of the Act and section 3(2)(viii) is that the first makes it an offence when the public servant (not being a member of SC/ST) has been found to have committed a wilful negligence towards his mandatory duties, while the other has differentiated general non-SC/ST public and public servants who have committed a specific offence under section 3 of the Act.

"Explanation" attached to section 10 of Protection of Civil Rights Act, 1955 had made "wilful" neglect by public servant of "investigation of any offence punishable under" that Act to be an offence of 'abetment'. Thus the 'wilful neglect' was used only in a limited sphere of investigation.

2. Underlying Principles

The principle incorporated under section 4 of the Act is antithesis to the principle of 'sovereign immunity' which is based on the traditional norm that "the King can do no wrong". An array of different immunity laws have either been directly contained in Constitution of India or been allowed by it to continue.

Article 300(1) specifically provide for sovereign immunity but it is also true that the Constitution does not grant official immunity directly, but it has been so interpreted by the executive that Parliament is allowed to make such laws which fashion direct or *de facto* official immunity. Originally such provisions were made through legislations to immunize the British king, but later on these provisions were retained by 'democratic' independent India. Instances can be seen in sections 45(1), 132(1) and 197 of Criminal Procedure Code 1973 which were almost copied from the Code of 1898. The functionaries of State have been spared from prosecution, except in cases where sanctions have been obtained from respective Governments, which is almost impossible to obtain.

Besides 'sovereign immunity' and 'official immunity', there are other kinds of immunities – such as 'absolute immunity', 'diplomatic immunity', 'judicial immunity', legislative immunity' and 'transactional immunity'.

The said immunity laws, either retained as a British legacy or legislated to contain terrorism etc., have earned widespread criticism of Indian legal system by not only International forums but by various Law Commissions, constituted in this behalf.

In the light of above discussions and existence of various immunity laws in the country, provisions of section 4 of the Act look to be an extreme case of exception – or a very special provision of a 'special Enactment' (Act of 1989).

3. "Public Servant"

There is difference between expressions "servant of Government" and a "public servant". The "servant of Government" stipulates a narrower meaning as it has been defined under section 14 of Indian Penal Code 1860 while "public servant", the subject matter of section 4 of the Act has been defined under section 21 of IPC and section 2(c) of PC Act, 1988 as well. Section 21 of IPC defines "public servant" as:

> 21. *"Public Servant".*—The words "public servant" denotes a person falling under any of the descriptions hereinafter following, namely:—
>
> *First.*—[Omitted by the A.O. 1950;]
>
> *Second.*—Every Commissioned Officer in the Military, Naval or Air Forces of India;
>
> *Third.*—Every Judge including any person empowered by law to discharge, whether by himself or as a member of any body of persons, any adjudicatory functions;
>
> *Fourth.*—Every officer of a court of Justice, (including a liquidator, receiver or commissioner) whose duty it is , as such officer, to investigate or report on any matter of law or fact, or to make, authenticate, or keep any document, or to take charge or dispose of any property, or to execute any judicial process, or to administer any oath, or to interpret, or to preserve order in to Court, and every person specially authorised by a court of justice to perform any of such duties;
>
> *Fifth.*—Every juryman, assessor, or member of a panchayat assisting a court of Justice or public servant;

Sixth.—Every arbitrator or other person to whom any cause or matter has been referred for decision or report by any court of Justice, or by any other competent public authority;

Seventh.—Every person who holds any office by virtue of which he is, empowered to place or keep any person in confinement;

Eighth.—Every officer of the Government whose duty it is, as such officer, to prevent offences, to give information of offences, to bring offenders to justice, or to protect the public health, safety or convenience;

Ninth.—Every officer, whose duty it is, as such officer, to take, receive, keep or expend any property on behalf of the Government, or to make any survey, assessment or contract on behalf of the Government, or to execute any revenue-process, or to investigate, or to report, on any matter affecting the pecuniary interests of the Government, or to make, authenticate or keep any document relating to the pecuniary interests of the Government, or to prevent the infraction of any law for the protection of the pecuniary interests of the Government;

Tenth.—Every officer whose duty it is, as such officer, to take, to receive, keep or expend any property, to make any survey or assessment or to levy any rate of tax for any secular common purpose of any village, town or district or to make, authenticate or keep any document for the ascertaining of the rights of the people of any village, town or district;

Eleventh.—Every person who holds any office by virtue of which he is empowered to prepare, publish, maintain or revise an electoral roll or to conduct an election or part of an election;

Twelfth.—Every person—

(a) in the service or pay of the Government or remunerated by fees or commission for the performance of any public duty by the Government;

(b) in the service or pay of the local authority, or corporation established by or under a Central, Provincial or State Act, or a Government Company as defined in section 617 of the Companies Act, 1956 (1 of 1956).

Illustration

A Municipal Commissioner is a public servant.

Explanation 1.—Persons falling under any of the above descriptions are public servants whether appointed by the Government or not,

Explanation 2.—Wherever the words "public servant" occur, they shall be understood of every person who is in actual possession of the situation of a public servant, whatever legal defect there may be in his right to hold that situation.

Explanation 3.—The word "election" denotes an election for the purpose of selecting members of any legislative, municipal or other public authority, of whatever character, the method of selection to which is by, or under, any law prescribed as by election.

The above definition contained under section 21 of IPC of "public servant" looks to be complete and exhaustive encompassing variety of persons functioning under or on behalf of Government, local legal bodies or otherwise. But it was held that the definition of "public servant" given under section 21 IPC is not exhaustive in specific sense.[1]

For purposes of definition of "public servant", as it has been used in section 4 of the Act, would be construed to be the definition given in section 21 IPC, because section 2(1)(f) of the Act of 1989 says:"words and expressions used but not defined in this Act and defined in the Code or the Indian Penal Code (45 of 1860) shall have the meanings assigned to them respectively in the Code, or as the case may be, in the Indian Penal Code."

Therefore by virtue of the provisions of section 2(1)(f) of the Act of 1989 no other definition given or provided elsewhere would be taken into account. Section 2(c) of Prevention of Corruption Act, 1988 also defines "public servant" somewhat differently and it remains doubtful whether this definition could be taken into account for purposes of section 4 [as well as S 3(2)(VII)] of the Act of 1989.It seems reasonable and cogent proposition that definition of section 2(c) of P.C. Act, 1988 may be considered in situations of doubt, specially where the definition given by section 21 IPC has not been mentioned as a legal authority to be included in such definition.[2]

4. Exclusion of SC/ST Public Servant

The Expression, "but not being a member of Scheduled Castes or the Scheduled Tribes" clearly exclude those public servants who belong to Scheduled Castes or the Scheduled Tribes. This exclusion means that members of SC/ST who are functioning as 'public servants' cannot be brought under the scope or ambit of offence created by section 4 of the Act of 1989. In that sense classification has been done among whole lot of 'public servants' who are otherwise supposed to be considered as one entity.

Due to mandatory 'Reservation' for members of Scheduled Castes and the Scheduled Tribes, a great chunk of such members may be found in existence and functioning in all public offices, without any exception.

Accordingly, the said exclusion of SC/ST members functioning as 'public servant', is not liable to prosecution or any punishment if he "wilfully neglects his duties required to be performed by him under this Act." This rule of exclusion could be based on one of the three reasons: (i) either the Legislature did not expect members of SC/ST functioning as 'public servants', would neglect his duties wilfully because they themselves belonged to same class on whom atrocities are expected to take place; (ii) such 'public servants' (excluded) would themselves be harassed, if included under the ambit of section 4; and (iii) such members are not prone to wilful neglect of duties.

---

1. *Naresh Kumar Madan* v. *State*, (2007) 2 SCC (Cri) 404.
2. Section 2(c) of PC Act, 1988 had widened the scope of the definition of "public servant". Provisions in Clauses (viii), (ix), (xi), and (xii) of section 2(c) of PC Act have added new persons in the said definition with the specific object of preventing widespread corruption. But these added and extended persons perhaps cannot be brought to book under section 4 of the Act of 1989.

5. Classification, not Violative of Article 14

When it was argued before the Full Bench of Allahabad High Court[1] that the Act of 1989 differently treats the accused who is not a member of a Scheduled Caste or a Scheduled Tribe, who would be punished for wilful neglect of duties, while the other class of 'public servants' would not be punished for such created offence. The Bench observed that the argument is wholly misconceived, because the very basis of the offence of atrocities is that, it is committed by a person who is not a member of a Scheduled Caste or a Scheduled Tribe against one who is a member of a Scheduled Caste or a Scheduled Tribe. "Being so, a public servant belonging to a Scheduled Caste or a Scheduled Tribe cannot commit an offence of atrocities and, therefore, his exclusion in section 4 cannot be impugned under Article 14."[2]

It is submitted that the presumption that "a public servant belonging to a Scheduled Caste or a Scheduled Tribe cannot commit offence of atrocities........" against other such members has proved wrong. Much water has flown in the rivers since that observation was made. Many cases have come-up before the Courts showing committal of various offences, including offences which are attributed as 'atrocities', by the same class of persons on their own group or clan, but the said cases were not registered under the provisions of the Act of 1989, because of existence rule of exclusion.

It is true that Supreme Court had held[3] that the offences under the Act of 1989 constitute a separate class and cannot be equated with offence under the Penal Code; or, that what is necessary is that there must be a nexus between the basis of classification and the object of the Act under consideration, for challenging an Act on the ground of hostile discrimination as envisaged under Article 14.[4]

After dealing with the *Maneka Gandhi's* case[5], Supreme Court had started widening the scope of Article 14 from just equality before law. It was observed that an action which is arbitrary or unreasonable is also violative of Article 14 of the Constitution. It was pointed out that 'equality' and the 'arbitrariness' are the sworn enemies, as the first belongs to rule of law while the other belongs to whim and caprice of the absolute monarch. Where an act is arbitrary, it should be understood that it is unequal, both according to political logic and the constitutional law, and therefore it is violative of Article 14.

Now in the light of above observations of Apex Court, question may be raised for treating two groups of 'public servants' differently. For instance, if 'public servants', belonging to SC/ST and not belonging to SC/ST, jointly commit offence of wilful neglect of "duties required to be performed by him under this Act", the later group would be tried by a Special Court for sever punishment while the

1. *Mata Sewak Upadhyay* v. *State of Uttar Pradesh*, 1995 JIC 1168 (All) (FB): 1996 (1) East Cr C 97 (All) (FB) (1185) et eq; also see *Jai Singh* v. *Union of India*, 1993 Cr LJ 2705 (FB) (Raj): AIR 1993 Raj 177: 1993 (1) Raj LW 157.
2. *ibid.*
3. *State of Madhya Pradesh* v. *Ram Kishna Balothia*, 1995 Cr LJ 2076 (SC): AIR 1995 SC 1198: 1995 AIR SCW 1267: JT 1995 (1) SC 310.
4. *Shri Ram Krishna Dalmia* v. *Mr. Justice S.R. Tendolkar*, AIR 1958 SC 538: 1958 SCA 754: 1959 SCJ 147.
5. *Maneka Gandhi* v. *Union of India*, AIR 1978 SC 597: (1978) 1 SCC 248: (1978) 2 SCR 621.

first group would not be tried at all and go scot free. Would that not constitute hostile discrimination or arbitrariness? Importantly here there is no question of severity or lessor punishment, but the question is that section 4 provides specific punishment only on one group (non-SC/ST) and no punishment for same offence for the other group.

6. Who is 'Public Servant' – A test

There is a difference between a private person and a 'public servant'. For determining whether a person is a 'public servant' or not, two essentials should be examined, *viz;* (i) whether the person in question is in service or pay of the Government in any way, and (ii) whether the person in question has been entrusted with performance of any duty by or on behalf of the Government. If these two requirements are present it would be irrelevant what is the nature of office, work or post, low or high. Even a private person who has been entrusted to perform some duties or delegated some work by or on behalf of the Government, he would be considered as 'public servant, within the meaning (definition) of section 21 IPC[1].

A retired person is not a 'public servant'[2], but a 'public servant' on leave remains as such on technical grounds because leave is counted as duty and during leave he is deemed to be a 'public servant'. All the members of statutory public bodies, employees of nationalised banks or insurance companies, railways or road transport corporations or public sector undertakings are 'public servants'.

7. Alleged Neglected Duty Must be Provided Under the Act

Section 4 of the Act creates an offence for wilfully neglecting the duties by public servants (non-SC/ST). Such duties must be provided by the Act itself or the Rules made thereunder. If those duties required to be performed have been provided in some other enactment the 'public servant' cannot be charged under section 4 of Act of 1989.

In a reported case a Magistrate had sent a complaint, filed under section 156(3) Cr PC, to the police for investigation and the police had registered a case under the provisions of Cr PC, the investigation was conducted by Circle Officer and after completion of the investigation he submitted the final report in the case. The learned Magistrate not only rejected the final report, but also took cognizance of offence under section 4 of the Act of 1989 against Circle officer, who submitted the final report alongwith the Superintendent of Police. The matter was agitated before the High Court by the Circle Officer against whom cognizance was taken by the Magistrate.

It was observed that, "a bare reading of section 4 shows that the offences, which are punishable under this section, must have been committed in respect of 'some duty' to be performed under the Scheduled Castes and the Scheduled Tribes (Prevention of Atrocities) Act, 1989. If any duty is to be performed under any other Act (including the Code of Criminal Procedure), then the provisions

---

1. *G.A. Monterio* v. *State of Ajmer*, 1957 Cr LJ 1 (SC): AIR 1957 SC 13: 1956 SCR 682.
2. *Jawahar Lal Kaul* v. *State of Jammu & Kashmir*, 2000 Cr LJ 3581: 2000 (4) Rec Cri R 402.

of section 4 of the Scheduled Castes and the Scheduled Tribes (Prevention of Atrocities) Act, 1989 do not apply".[1]

A crucial question was raised by the Court, as to whether the investigation was conducted under the Act of 1989 and whether the submission of final report was in respect of any duty prescribed under the Scheduled Castes and the Scheduled Tribes (Prevention of Atrocities) Act, 1989. If answer be in the affirmative, it will be said that the offence under section 4 of the Scheduled Castes and the Scheduled Tribes (Prevention of Atrocities) Act, 1989 may be committed. But if the answer be in the negative, then it will have to be said that no offence under section 4 of the Scheduled Castes and the Scheduled Tribes (Prevention of Atrocities) Act, 1989 can be said to have been committed, if any public servant wilfully neglects his duties prescribed by any other law.[1]

Position of law is clear. In the instant case investigation was conducted under section 157 Cr PC and final report was submitted under section 173 Cr PC, in the discharge of duties prescribed therein. Scheduled Castes and the Scheduled Tribes (Prevention of Atrocities) Act, 1989 does not provide any particular procedure for the investigation. In view of the provisions of section 4(2) the offences are required to be investigated, inquired into, tried or otherwise dealt with according to the provisions of Code of Criminal Procedure, except to the extent the general provisions contained in the Code of Criminal Procedure are superseded by any special provision contained in any law, such as Scheduled Castes and the Scheduled Tribes (Prevention of Atrocities) Act, 1989. In such a situation submission of final report under section 173 Code of Criminal Procedure cannot be said to be an act done in exercise of the duty prescribed by or under Scheduled Castes and the Scheduled Tribes (Prevention of Atrocities) Act, 1989. Therefore, it was finally held that even if any neglect of duty in the conduct of investigation was found to have occurred, provisions of section 4 of the Act of 1989 cannot be made applicable or attracted.[1]

In yet another case where it was alleged that the investigation was not conducted in a proper manner, as there was sufficient material which showed that the accused had committed the offences under section 3 of the Act and some materials were also recovered from the accused, but the investigation agency officers had deliberately not included those offences. Thereby the investigating officers wilfully neglected their duties, required by law. It was observed that section 4 of the Act of 1989 fasten criminal liability on the public servants who wilfully neglect their duties required to be performed by them under the Act, and make it punishable with imprisonment for a term not less than six months and which may extend upto one year. In order to invoke section 4 of the Act against the Investigating Officers, there should be necessary and proper averments of facts to the effect that they have wilfully neglected their duties by not properly investigating the offence covered under the SC/ST Act of 1989. There is a failure to take steps on the part of the Investigation Officers is to be clearly stated.

---

1. *Ram Pal* v. *State of Rajasthan*, 1998 Cr LJ 3261 (Raj) (3265): 1998 (1) Raj LR 630: 1998 (1) Raj LW 98.

Consequently, the averments made in the private complaint do not suggest any material present in context of section 4 of the Act of 1989.[1]

8. Willful Neglect of Duties

Webster's Legal Dictionary defines "wilful neglect" as: "intentional, knowing, or reckless failure to fulfil a legal duty", and also defines "wilful (or wanton) negligence" as – "in theory recklessness. In practice these concepts tend to shade into gross negligence. The same Dictionary defines "Criminal negligence" as: (in criminal law) a gross deviation from the standard of care that a reasonable person would observe, under circumstances posing a substantial and unjustifiable risk of which the actor should have been aware, except for relatively rare strict liability offences, this is usually the minimum level of fault that will subject a person to criminal liability".

The word "wilful" can be simply described as wrongful conduct done with intent or knowledge. These acts signify state of mind, which in general terms could be a condition of mind or the element of mind or a degree of fault that accompanies an act or omission; while it particularly can be signified as an additional condition that is required in most crimes, beyond the mere fact that the offender had committed a certain act causing certain result, to make that act a particular crime.

In the body of the Act of 1989 different words have been used for signifying different kinds of 'state of minds', such as knowledge (knowingly), intent and negligence, but these terms have not been defined. Overlapping or poor definition may create difficulties in interpretation or application of a certain provision to a set of facts and the circumstances in each case.

Simple 'negligence' is the breach of a duty caused by omission to do something which a reasonable man guided by regulated conduct of human affairs would do, but this act is opposed to a deliberate act. Simply a negligent act is not done intentionally or designedly. Under English law the word 'negligence' may mean mere neglect of caution, where the mind is not actively but negatively or passively at fault. To such acts they called "inadvertent negligence". But Russell had criticized the term as being misleading and of unhappy verbal innovation.[2]

But here we are concerned with the term "wilfully neglects his duties", which inevitably envisage an intention, knowledge or "foresight of consequences". Where a person intends to do a harm or where that person is content to take the chance of doing something deliberately but in the garb of negligence, to cause harm, that person is responsible for the caused harm or injury. That caused harm or the injury may or may not be direct consequence of his act, but in any case that person should be made responsible criminally, provided the act or omission was done with a certain intention or knowledge that such act or omission would ultimately result in that harm.

If the 'public servant' knows and it is within his knowledge that his wilful neglect of duty would cause some harm or injury to a member of SC/ST, he is responsible to the provided punishment.

1. *Ananda Pangala* v. *T.R. Jagannath*, 2003 Cr LJ 3215 (Kant): 2004 (3) KCCR 1965: 2004 (1) Kant LJ 623; also see (1998) 1 Raj LW 98 (103-104).
2. Russell on Crime p 46-48.

Supreme Court in a recent case has interpreted the word "know" as: "the expression 'know' does not mean a mere possibility, such as might or might not happen."[1] That means the presence of *mens rea* is an essential ingredient in provisions of section 4 of the Act. The test of guilt is that of knowledge ("wilful") and consciousness on the part of 'public servant' that some harm, hurt or damage is likely to result from what he does; his criminality consists in the wilfully incurring the risk of causing loss or suffering on the part of such member of SC/ST.

The accused was appointed by Railway Board for taking care of welfare of the members of Scheduled Castes and the Scheduled Tribe. It was alleged that the accused did not allot a specific railway quarter at a particular place. It was held that there is no material to show that she was appointed by the provisions of the Act of 1989, and she had neglected to perform her duties required to be performed by her under the Act. Therefore order issuing process against the accused was quashed.[2]

The defence of the accused may be built up on the basis of principle of exemption from criminal liability in respect of harmful consequences, that is he should plead and prove not only *bona fide* ignorance from the mere mechanical act, but also "good faith" (as has been provided under section 22 of the Act of 1989).

9. Section 4 of the Act and Section 197 Cr PC

Different kinds of 'public servants" have been protected, through an immunity provided under section 197 of Code of Criminal Procedure, 1973, wherein Courts have been barred from taking cognizance against "Judge or Magistrate or a public servant......", except "with the previous sanction" by the appropriate Government.

Naturally a pertinent question would arise: as to whether a prosecution may be, launched against a 'public servant' under section 4 of the Act of 1989, and the Court can take cognizance against such 'public servant' for wilfully neglecting the duties required, without a previous sanction as required by section 197 Cr PC? The same question may similarly apply to the 'prosecution of public servants' charged under section 3(2)(vii) of the Act of 1989, as well.

The answer to the above mentioned question may be positive as well as negative, depending on the circumstances of each case. Section 197 Cr PC puts two primary conditions for ascertaining the applicability of provisions, *viz*.

(i) "Any person who is or was........a public servant not removable from his office save by or with the sanction of the Government........", and

(ii) "......offence alleged to have been committed by him while acting or purporting to act in the official discharge of his duty......".

While on the other hand requirements for attraction of provisions of section 4 of the Act of 1989 are:

---

1. *Ramchandran* v. *State*, 2011 Cr LJ 4845 (SC) (4850); also see *A.S. Krishnan* v. *State*, 2004 (1) CCSC 872.
2. *Alka A. Misra* v. *J.P. Shoke*, 2003 Cr LJ 1333 (Bom): 2003 (9) All Ind Cas 666: 2003 All MR (Cri) 207.

(i) the charged person must be a 'public servant' not belonging to SC/ST; and,

(ii) such 'public servant' must have wilfully neglected his duties required to be performed by him under the Act of 1989.

Therefore, it was held, "a bare reading of section 4 shows that before an offence under section 4 may be committed, it must be shown that a public servant has wilfully neglected his duties. A *bona fide* action, even though it may be erroneous, cannot be branded as wilful neglect of duty. .... a mere neglect is not punishable under section 4 of the Scheduled Castes and the Scheduled Tribes (Prevention of Atrocities) Act, 1989. ....Submission of a final report under section 173 Cr PC by the petitioner was obviously a duty performed in discharge of his public duties as an Investigating Officer conducting investigation under Code of Criminal Procedure, 1973...........In these circumstances, *prima facie*, the petitioner as well as the Superintendent of Police, Churu both were entitled to protection of section 197, Cr PC and no cognizance of offence could be taken against them without proper sanction."[1]

In the above finding learned Judge of Rajasthan High Court has taken a right and cogent decision, on the ground that the investigation and the consequential 'final report', submitted by the Circle Officer and approved by the Superintendent of Police was not "required to be performed by him under this Act", but the entire proceedings had taken place under the provisions of Code of Criminal Procedure, therefore no offence was found to have been committed under section 4. Besides, the alleged offence had been committed purportedly while they acted "in the official discharge of his duty", hence protection of section 197 Cr PC was available to them.

But in a changed circumstance, the 'public servant' may not claim for the protection of section 197 Cr PC because firstly a 'wilful neglect of duty' by any stretch of imagination can be brought under the meaning of an "act in the official discharge of his duty" (section 197 Cr PC), and, secondly an act of 'wilful neglect of duty' conceives presence of an intention to inflict some harm or injury to a member of a Scheduled Caste or a Scheduled Tribe, stipulated by section 4 of the Act.

In a series of cases Supreme Court has repeatedly held that protection of section 197 Cr PC is available only when alleged act was done by public servants, it has to be reasonably connected with discharge of his official duties, and cannot merely be cloak for doing objectionable or illegal acts. Therefore protection provided has certain limits. If in doing his official duty suppose he had acted in excess of his duty, but there is a reasonable connection between the act and the performance of official duty, the excess will not be a sufficient ground to deprive him from protection, but the act or omission complained could have made him answerable for a charge of dereliction of duty or criminal misconduct.[2]

---

1. *Ram Pal* v. *State of Rajasthan*, 1998 Cr LJ 3261 (Raj) (3265): 1998 (1) Raj LR 630: 1998 (1) Raj LW 98.
2. *State* v. *M.P. Gupta*, 2004 (1) CC SC 172.

'Public servants' are not entitled to indulge in criminal activites[1], and of course intentional (wilful) neglect of duty to injure the interests of SC/ST victims has been made a criminal offence by the provisions of section 4 of the Act.

The allegations against a 'public servant' may come from different fields conceptually, but under section 197 Cr PC substratum and basic feature of the case, should be considered to find out if alleged act has any nexus with discharge of duties.[2]

All acts done by a 'public servant' in purported discharge of his official duties cannot, as a matter of course, be brought under the protective umbrella of section 197. On the other hand, there can be cases of misuse and/or abuse of powers vested in a 'public servant' which can never be said to be part of the official duties required to be performed by him. Therefore abuse of power does not include under the official discharge of duties.[3]

10. Section 4 and Rule 8(ix)

The Scheduled Castes and Scheduled Tribes (Prevention of Atrocities) Rules 1995, framed under the powers provided under section 23 of the Act and accordingly ratified by the Parliament, provide "setting up of the Scheduled Castes and the Scheduled Tribes Protection Cell" under Rule 8. It has been made mandatory under the Rule 8 that State Governments shall set up such "Protection Cells" headed by Director-General of Police of the respective State.

Under sub-rule(1) of Rule 8, it has been provided under Clause (ix): "making enquiries about the wilful negligence by a public servant;" thus the said constituted cell, headed by Director-General or Inspector General of Police, is "responsible for" making enquiries about the wilful negligence by public servants of that particular state.

Though, the 'public servants' belonging to or "being a member of a Scheduled Caste or a Scheduled Tribe" have been excluded from the ambit of punishment provided under section 4 of the Act of 1989, but they may be proceeded against in departmental proceedings for such wilfull neglect of duties in such enquiries conducted by "Protection Cell" constituted under Rule 8(ix). Almost every state in the country has framed Punishment and Appeal Rules for punishing its erring employees who were found for dereliction of duties.

11. Norms of Relief

Annexture 1 of Schedule provide wide-ranging 'norms for relief amount' for the injury, harm or damages suffered by Scheduled Caste or Scheduled Tribe victims. Naturally the victim would be entitled to receive the prescribed amount arising out of and according the caused harm or injury suffered by them as a result of 'wilful neglect' of the 'public servant'.

---

1. *S.K. Zutshi* v. *Bimal Debnath*, 2004 (3) CCSC 1310; *K. Kalimuthu* v. *State*, 2005 (2) CC SC 640; *State* v. *Bhajan Lal*, 1992 Supp (1) SCC 335.
2. *Paul Varghese* v. *State*, (2007) 2 SCC 778.
3. *Choudhury Parveen Sultana* v. *State of West Bengal*, 2009 Cr LJ 1318 (SC): AIR 2009 SC 1404: 2009 AIR SCW 861.

5. Enhanced punishment for subsequent conviction.—Whoever, having already been convicted of an offence under this Chapter is convicted for the second offence or any offence subsequent to the second offence, shall be punishable with imprisonment for a term which shall not be less than one year but which may extend to the punishment provided for that offence.

SYNOPSIS

1. Analogous Law

Section 11 of the Protection of Civil Rights Act, 1955 reads as under:

"11. *Enhanced penalty on subsequent offence.*—Whoever having already been convicted of an offence under this Act or of an abetment of such offence is again convicted of any such offence or abetment, shall on conviction, be punishable-

(a) for the second offence, with imprisonment for a term of not less than six months and not more than one year, and also with fine which shall be not less than two hundred rupees and not more than five hundred rupees;

(b) for the third offence or any offence subsequent to third offence, with imprisonment for a term of not more than one year and not more than two years, and also with fine which shall be not less than five hundred rupees and not more than one thousand rupees."

Section 75 of IPC also deals with "Enhanced punishment......after previous conviction:. The difference in language of section 75 IPC and that of section 5 is that the former section mentions "previous conviction" while the later one uses "subsequent conviction". The other difference is that such previous conviction is restricted to a conviction awarded under Chapter II of the Act of 1989.

2. Considerations of 'Punishment'

While considering the 'object and reasons' for providing "enhanced penalty" under section 11 of the Protection of Civil Rights Act, 1995, the committee observed:

"The Committee considered at length the question of sufficiency of the quantum of punishment provided for in the Bill. It was stressed before the Committee that this being a social legislation, provision for enhanced punishment might lead to disturbance of peace and harmony of the rural life. On the other hand it was feared that without provision for the deterrent punishment, the object of the Bill might be defeated. Provision is therefore considered necessary for making it obligatory upon a court to impose a sentence for both imprisonment and fine in the case of a second or subsequent offence."[1]

In this regard observations of Supreme Court are: "Punishment in criminal cases is both punitive and reformative. The purpose is that the person found guilty of committing the offence is made to realise his fault and is deterred from repeating such acts in future. The reformative aspect is meant to enable the person concerned to relent and repent for his action and make himself acceptable to the society as a useful social being. In determining the question of proper punishment in a criminal case the Court has to weight the degree of culpability of the accused, its effect on others and the desirability of showing any leniency in the matter of punishment in the case. ...... Denying such opportunity (to reform) to a person who has been found to have committed offence in the facts and circumstances placed on record would only have a hardening attitude towards his fellow beings and towards society at large. Such a situation, has to be avoided, again within the permissible limits of law."[2]

The comments made by the Committee (mentioned above) in the year 1954 and ensuing apprehensions regarding "for enhanced punishment might lead to disturbance of peace and harmony of the rural life" could be practically seen in villages, specially of Punjab, Haryana, Rajasthan and Uttar Pradesh, etc. This has become so that the 'attitudes have been hardened towards fellow being. Large scale violence erupts occasionally and atmosphere remain charged.

3. Fixing Minimum Punishment

In most of the created offences under Chapter II of the Scheduled Castes and the Scheduled Tribes (Prevention of Atrocities) Act, 1989, minimum punishment of imprisonment has been provided. Once upon a time the 'Select Committee' at the time of drafting of Indian Penal Code considered the matter for providing minimum sentence limits but after due discussions it was ultimately resolved to fix only the maximum punishments and the apportionment of sentence, in each case, was left to the discretion of the Judge. (But in very exceptional cases the rule was not followed).

However, on the illustrative cases, the principle may be broadly classed into two, *viz.* (i) where Courts are inclined to pass lenient sentences considering the facts and circumstance of each case, and (ii) where courts are inclined to pass deterrent sentences.

The sole object of punishing a person is to prevent him from repeating the offence, besides preventing others from committing similar offence. James J. had observed "No sentence should appear to be vindictive. An excessive sentence defeats its own object and tends to undermine further the respect for law."[3]

"Punishable" carries a meaning which could signify "liable to be punished". The word "punishable" is ordinarily defined as deserving of or capable or

---

1. J.C.R. Gaz. of India, 3-12-1954, Part II, s. 2, Extra., p. 673E.
2. *Karamjit Singh* v. *State (Delhi Admn.)*, 2000 Cr LJ 3178 (3180-81): AIR 2000 SC 3467: 2000 AIR SCW 2217.
3. *Dulla* v. *State*, 1958 Cr LJ 316: AIR 1958 All 198: ILR (1957) 2 All 147.

liable to 'punishment', punishable within a statute. It certainly mean liable to be punished, but cannot mean 'must' be punished.[1]

As an exception it may be mentioned that instead of enhancing the sentence, the Apex Court reduced the sentence, say, in consideration of young age of the accused. The order of reduction of sentence was passed in a case of trial and appeal in a similar provision of law mandating for enhancing the penalty. The facts and reasons were mentioned for reducing the sentence instead of enhancing the penalty.[2]

4. Scope

Following conditions must be fulfilled for bringing a case under the scope of section 5 of the Act of 1989—

(i) the accused must have been previously convicted in an offence under Chapter II of the act of 1989.

(ii) the same previously convicted accused must be convicted for a second offence under Chapter II of the Act.

(iii) Or the same accused must be convicted again after he was convicted for the subsequent offence or "second offence".

It is a condition precedent for application of provisions of section 5 of the Act that the same accused have previously been convicted of an offence under Chapter II of the Act of 1989. That would clearly mean that the accused must have been charged and convicted under any of the sections from section 3 to 9 of the Chapter II of the Scheduled Castes and the Scheduled Tribes (Prevention of Atrocities) Act, 1989, though some of these set of sections do not provide any penalty.

It is noteworthy that the accused might or might not have been tried under provisions provided under Chapter II of the Act. The accused might have been tried in absentia and convicted and that order of conviction remained in existence and not set aside in appeal, could become subject matter under present section.

Secondly, it is not clear, whether a conviction under Chapter II, which has been challenged in appeal which was pending disposal, could become subject matter of or considered to be a previous conviction for purposes of this section and could be considered, at the time of conviction for "enhanced punishment. It may be mentioned here that in general law it is a consensus rule that the appeal is considered to be continuation of proceedings or trial, thus a conviction remains in suspended animation. Question would be whether such suspended convictions could be taken as previous conviction.

But as the specific language of the section denotes, an accused previously convicted under any law for the time being in force, but not under Chapter II of the Act of 1989, shall not be considered for purposes of "enhanced punishment".

5. Question of Double Jeopardy

It means being put in jeopardy twice for the same offence. This is prohibited by law. Law provides that a person who has been tried once for one offence, cannot be tried again for the same offence.

1. *Sube Singh* v. *State of Haryana*, 1989 Cr LJ 297 (SC): AIR 1988 SC 2235: (1989) 1 SCC 235.
2. *Kaka Singh* v. *State*, 1993 Cr LJ 1028 (SC).

'Double jeopardy' has been explained by Webster's Legal Dictionary as: "........ a defendant who has been acquitted may not be tried again in the hope of a conviction, a defendant who has been convicted *may not be tried again to increase the punishment*. ......On the other hand, a defendant may be retried if a conviction is overturned in appeal, if a mistrial is declared at the request of the defendant or because of hung jury or other circumstance beyond the control of the prosecution, or if the same conduct also constitutes an offence in another jurisdiction."

The principle has been based on the maxim: *"Nemo debet bis vexari, is constate quod sit pro una et cadem causa"*, which means no man shall be twice punished, if it appears to the court that it is for one and the same cause. The principle has been embodied under Art. 20 of Constitution, as well as section 300 of Cr PC 1973.

One point is clear from the above definition that a person may be tried for the same conduct when that conduct constitute an offence in another jurisdiction, but he cannot be convicted for both.

Section 26 of the General Clauses Act, 1897 provides:

"26. Provision as to offences punishable under two or more enactments:

Where an act or omission constitute an offence under two or more enactments, then the offender shall be liable to be prosecuted and punished under either or any of those enactments, but shall not be liable to be punished twice for the same offence."

5.1 The Question

A question may come to mind: whether the existence of a previous conviction can be considered at the time of a second conviction for the similar nature of subsequent offence for purposes of enhancing punishment at second or third conviction? And, does this consideration technically hits the principle of double jeopardy?

Article 20(2), section 71 IPC, sections 300, 324, 356 and 427 Cr PC:—

> The protection against double jeopardy has been enshrined in Article 20 of the Constitution and consequently section 71 Indian Penal Code, 1860 and section 300 Cr PC specifically prohibit "person once convicted or acquitted not to be tried for same offence".

It is clear that the law strictly prohibits prosecution or trial etc., of "same" offence twice, but not the "subsequent" similar offence. A subsequent offence may be a similar offence but cannot be the "same" offence.

Section 427 Cr PC also uses expression "subsequent conviction", but in other reference. A person may commit similar offences of same nature but at different times and places and against different persons, but they cannot be branded as "same" offences against which the law has provided protection.

5.2 "Same Offence"

Supreme Court has observed: "Broadly speaking a protection against a second or multiple punishment for the same offence, technical complexities aside, includes a protection against re-prosecution after conviction and a protection against double or multiple punishment for the same offence. ....But the difficulties arise in the application of the principle in the context of what is meant by 'same offence'."[1]

The Court went on, "The expressions 'the same offence', 'substantially the same offence', 'in effect the same offence' or 'practically the same' have not done much to *lessen the difficulty* in applying the tests to identify the legal common denominators of 'same offence." Then the court quoted Friedland in "Double jeopardy" (Oxford 1969) which says at page 108:

> "The trouble with this approach is that it is vague and hazy and conceals the thought processes of the Court. Such an inexact test must depend upon the individual impression of the judges and can give little guidance for future decisions. A more serious consequence is the fact that a decision in one case that two offences are 'substantially the same' may compel the same result in another case involving the same two offences where the circumstances may be such that second prosecution should be permissible......"[1]

Finally the finding was given that the provision of protection cannot be available where the conviction is coming from two distinct offences prescribed by two different enactments, irrespective of the fact that they arise out of the 'same offence'.

To answer the above question, it may be kept in mind that for "enhanced punishment" the convict must have committed and was convicted of an offence under Chapter II of the Act, *i.e.*, "the same offence" or "similar offence" and not the "distinct offence". This may create a technical complexity. But in any way the provisions of section 5 cannot be broadly said to be hitting the principle of double jeopardy.

6. Justification of section 5

Section 5 of the Act provides that persons previously convicted under Chapter II of the Act will be liable to higher punishment, minimum of which shall be, not less than six months, than what they would otherwise be. The last phrase of section 5 is important as it says: "but which may extend to the punishment provided for that offence", because the said section does not provide for any additional sentence on subsequent conviction. Recourse has not been taken for a severe or additional sentence, but has been restricted to "the punishment provided for *that* offence". Here the word "that" certainly denotes the offence for which the accused has been tried and convicted subsequently.

But a slight difference may be found here for consideration of "provided for that offence", which means that maximum limits of imprisonment provided for "that" offence has to be awarded at the subsequent conviction. It may be explained further that as the minimum sentence of six months have been provided under section 5, and it becomes incumbent to consider the previous conviction and the court would be pleased to award a sentence commensurate with the nature of offence.

---

1. *State of Bihar* v. *Murad Ali Khan*, AIR 1989 SC 1: 1989 Cr LJ 1005 (1011): (1988) 4 SCC 655.

It is important that the section 5 of the Act required an 'enhanced punishment' and not a separate sentence. The provision of the section cannot be invoked to enhance sentence enormously in petty offences.

The 'enhanced punishment' for subsequent offence is justified on the ground that repeated offences of the same kind merited more deterrent treatment for such persons. The provision contemplates that a previous conviction had no effect on that person, a more severe sentence becomes a necessity. But the demands of justice require that a rigid and inflexible rule should not be made to be exercised in each and every case. The circumstances of each case should be considered before inflicting enhanced punishment. In the unsettled affairs of the society due to which the present enactment was legislated, and also to check the frequent onslaught on Scheduled Castes and the Scheduled Tribes, the ordinary provisions could be found insufficient and inadequate to deal with the situation. The provisions of section 5 of the Act remains a reserve armoury of Criminal Special Courts which should be suggestively drawn in cases of exceptional urgency.

7. Section 5, Not Itself a Penal Provision

No conviction can legally be awarded independently under section 5 of the Act because an enhanced conviction cannot be passed independently or as a separate sentence. A previous conviction has to be proved under section 54 of Indian Evidence Act as a proof of a previous character and thereafter if the accused is convicted by the Special Court in the ongoing trial, only then present provision may be brought into service for awarding 'enhanced punishment'.

Section 5 of the Act is an enabling provision and merely applies in principle, it does not create a new offence.

8. Charge and Statement under section 313 Cr PC

It is mandatory that at the stage of framing of the charges, the court is required to evaluate the material and documents on record, with a view to find out if there is enough material to frame a particular charge against the accused. Specially when the consequences of framing a charge under section 5 of the Act of 1989, where the provision provides a drastic sentence.

Therefore non-mentioning by the court as to disclose existence of previous conviction or convictions under Chapter II of the Act and existence of all its ingredients, would amount to non-application of mind, hence making the order of framing a charge under section 5 may be declared improper.[1]

Such framing of charge under section 5 would give an opportunity to the accused as well as prosecution to explain and deal with the previous conviction, the previous convictions not being relevant except in cases where the prosecution seek the application of this section.[2] For this purpose it is required that fact, date and place of the previous conviction shall be mentioned. In case any of such statement has been omitted, the court is competent to add it at any stage of the

1. *Premkumar* v. *State of Karnataka*, 1994 Cr LJ 3641 (Kant): 1995 (1) All Cri LR 499: 1994 (2) Crimes 429.
2. *Fatima Bee, In re*, (1954) 2 MLJ 190; also see *Mohammad Ali* v. *State*, 1956 All LJ 611.

trial. But if wrong facts have been mentioned, it may amount to misleading the accused and in that case accused cannot be legally made liable to enhanced punishment.

Similarly when at the end of trial the statement of the accused has to be recorded under section 313 Cr PC then a specific question must be put to him regarding the previous conviction.

6. Application of certain provisions of the Indian Penal Code.—Subject to the other provisions of this Act, the provisions of section 34, Chapter III, Chapter IV, Chapter V, Chapter VA, section 149 and Chapter XXIII of the Indian Penal Code (45 of 1860), shall, so far as may be, apply for the purposes of this Act as they apply for the purposes of the Indian Penal Code.

SYNOPSIS

1. Introduction

It is a general practice that when a special legislation is drafted new kinds of offences are created according to the object of that particular legislation. In addition to the procedure to be adopted by such special legislations, other procedures contained under Code of Criminal Procedure, 1973 are also usually mentioned so that it may become convenient. Section 2 of the Act (Definitions) define "Code" as Cr PC, 1973 in clause (b) and (f) specifically adopted the definitions given in Indian Penal Code and the meanings assigned to the words therein shall be construed to be taken as such under the Act of 1989. Some special legislations may be cited in this context, – for example, Prevention of Corruption Act, 1988, Prevention of Terrorism Act (now repealed), TADA (now repealed) etc.. These special enactments seldom or very rarely adopted the penal or other provisions of Indian Penal Code, 1860 and directed them to become part and parcel of special offences prescribed in those enactments.

But section 6 of The Scheduled Castes and the Scheduled Tribes (Prevention of Atrocities) Act, 1989 provide that, for purposes of this Act provisions of section 34, Chapter III, Chapter IV, Chapter V, Chapter VA, section 149 and Chapter XXIII of Indian Penal Code, 1860 shall *mutatis mutandi* apply only "subject to other provisions of this Act". That means, similar of these offences contained in Indian Penal Code would be considered as if they were offences or otherwise along with their various definitions, explanations and consequential implications would become part and panel of Act of 1989, and in addition to the new offences created by the Act or otherwise.

2. Provisions of Act Extended

Section 34 IPC cover "acts done by several persons in furtherance of common intention" and liability of each of such persons in the manner as if it were done by him alone. [Please see notes under section 8(b)]

Chapter III IPC:—Chapter III of IPC deals with "Of Punishments" generally with certain definitions and various modes of punishments. It is noteworthy to mention section 75 of Chapter III of IPC, which deals with "enhanced punishment.......after previous conviction". This may create problems because section 5 of the Act of 1989 also provides almost same contents. Section 5 of the Act and section 75 IPC contain overlapping but divergent provisions for convicting a person who has been convicted under Chapter II of the Act. Not only section 5 of the Act but section 3(2)(v) of the Act also has made same rules to be followed in regard to offences under Indian Penal Code. (please see notes under section 3(2)(v) and section 5 of the Act)

Chapter IV IPC:—Chapter IV of Indian Penal Code, 1860 deals with "General Exceptions". The provisions of Chapter IV of Indian Penal Code has been designed in such a manner that it does not become necessary to repeat in every penal provision of the Code to mention the limitations or exceptions, provided therein, but they apply uniformally to the whole body of the Code. These specific exceptions have been collectively contained in Chapter IV so that it may not be needed to append these exceptions with every penal section. Some of the limitations are simply related to only one provision, some to a class of provisions, while the rest or whole of them may be common to all the penal provisions of the Code.

By adopting the provisions of Chapter IV of Indian Penal Code, The Scheduled Castes and the Scheduled Tribes (Prevention of Atrocities) Act, 1989, has done favour to the accused, who have been charged under the provisions of the Act of 1989, and who are infants, lunatics, persons who have done some wrong to such member by reason of unsoundness of mind or delirium, persons who have done something in pursuance and direction of law or had done something to the presumed victim with his consent, and, specially, the acts done in exercise of 'self-defence'.

Therefore every penal provision of the Act of 1989 shall be construed subject to the provisions (General Exceptions) contained in Chapter IV of Indian Penal Code. As the Act of 1989 rarely provide such kind of 'exceptions', inclusion of provisions of Chapter IV suffice the norms of justice. But it may also be mentioned here that according to rule of general criminal jurisprudence, burden of proving applicability of any of the said exceptions lies on the person claiming that his case falls under any of such exception.

Chapter V IPC:—Chapter V of Indian Penal Code, 1860 deals with "of Abetment". Sections 107 and 108 of IPC define "Abetment of a thing" and the "Abettor" respectively, and rest of the provisions of Chapter V deals with abetment of various kinds of offences in different circumstances and by different kinds of persons.

Section 10 of Protection of Civil Rights Act, 1955 had made 'abetment' an offence for every act which had been declared an offence by that Act.

Chapter II, specially section 3 of the Scheduled Castes and the Scheduled Tribes (Prevention of Atrocities) Act, 1989, prescribed and had created many offences, providing stringent measures for achieving the object of taking "specific preventive punitive measures to protect the Scheduled Castes and the Scheduled Tribes from being victimsed".[1]

To inflict such kinds of "atrocities", it is not uncommon that some persons try to play some mischief from behind and abet the acts of 'atrocities'. To rope in such persons Chapter V of IPC is expected to play a vital role. Therefore such provisions have been included in the provisions of the Act, and making abetment of each of such offence punishable under the Act of 1989.

Chapter VA of IPC:—The said Chapter VA of IPC deals with "Criminal Conspiracy". (Please see note above).

Section 149 IPC:—Section 149 of Indian Penal Code belongs to Chapter VIII which deals with " of Offences Against the State Tranquility". Out of 21 sections contained in Chapter VIII only section 149 was chosen to be mentioned in section 6 of the Act of 1989. The headnote of section 149 says: "Every member of unlawful assembly guilty of offence committed in prosecution of common object." [Please see notes under section 8(b)]

The basic element in the set of sections contained in Chapter VIII of IPC is an act of 'affray'.[2] Where more than five persons have assembled and created such circumstances which may endanger public peace, the assembly of people are considered as unlawful assembly. Use of force by such unlawful assembly makes, it as riot. There is a difference between 'riot' and 'rout'. Under English law 'rout' is being a disturbance of peace by an assembly of people gathered with an intention to do a thing, which if executed would make the act as 'riot', but the act was not executed.

The object of the Scheduled Castes and the Scheduled Tribes (Prevention of Atrocities) Act, 1989 mention "humiliation and harassment" of member of Scheduled Castes and the Scheduled Tribes by "dominant and mighty" and "more often these people become victims of attacks by the vested interests", therefore section 149 IPC was chosen to be included.

Every person of unlawful assembly is guilty of an offence, who being a member of such assembly, uses threatening, abusive or insulting words or behaviour intentionally which is likely to breach the peace.[3]

Chapter XXIII of IPC:—Chapter XXIII of IPC, which contains only one section 511, which deals with attempts of offences generally as is evident form its head-note: "Punishment for attempting to commit offences punishable with imprisonment for life or other imprisonments". Some attempts of offences have already been made offences specifically, but others have been covered under section 511 IPC.

3. Prosecution under Scheduled Castes and Scheduled Tribes Act and IPC

An accused can be prosecuted under the provisions of the Scheduled Castes and the Scheduled Tribes (Prevention of Atrocities) Act, 1989 as well of offences prescribed by Indian Penal Code, 1860. There is no anomaly in doing so. There

1. Statement of Objects and Reasons of the Act.
2. Defined under section 159 IPC for which punishment provided under section 160 IPC.
3. Halsbury's Laws of England, 3rd Edn., 582, para 1081.

can be overlapping offences but having prescribed with different denominations of periods of punishments, but again that cannot be said to be violative of Article 14 of the Constitution. Hence an accused can be prosecuted under section 3(1) (xii) of the Act of 1989 as well as 376 IPC.

4. Acquittal under Act no Bar for Conviction under IPC

A Special Court constituted under the Act of 1989 is competent to acquit the accused tried jointly under the provisions of IPC, while convicting the same accused under charged section or sections of IPC, legally. But the decision must have come in the same trial. Article 20 of the Constitution or provisions of section 300 Cr PC would not apply in such a case, as principle of double jeopardy would not be applicable. It is so because the accused was not tried and convicted in a subsequent trial, but it has been done in the same trial for the same offence (Many such cases have been cited-please see notes under section 3).

7. Forfeiture of property of certain persons.—(1) Where a person has been convicted of any offence punishable under this Chapter, the Special Court may, in addition to awarding any punishment, by order in writing, declare that any property, movable or immovable or both, belonging to the person, which has been used for the commission of that offence, shall stand forfeited to Government.

(2) Where any person is accused of any offence under this Chapter, it shall be open to the Special Court trying him to pass an order that all or any of the properties, movable or immovable or both, belonging to him, shall, during the period of such trial, be attached, and where such trial ends in conviction, the property so attached shall be liable to forfeiture to the extent it is required for the purpose of realisation of any fine imposed under this Chapter.

SYNOPSIS

1. Legislative History

In the early days of 20th century Colonial British rulers of India wanting to tackle problems of "freedom fighters", designated by the said rulers as German agents and terrorists had legislated Criminal Law Amendment Act, 1908, which was amended later from time-to-time. Section 17E of the said Act provided –

"Power to forfeit funds of an, unlawful association". 'Objects and Reasons' of Amending Act which inserted sections 17A to 17E mention: Mr. Jadhav was of opinion that the provision for forfeiture should be removed altogether. We have decided that it should be retained........." It is noteworthy that Mr. Jadhav was the Indian member while others were British.

This was the first time when a written provision for forfeiture of property of an accused or convict was made, though from antiquity forfeiture of properties of persons, who tried to wage wars against the State or the king, was in vogue.

Later on in the recent past provisions for forfeiture of properties of terrorists was made in TADA, 1987 [section 8(2)] and POTA, 2002 (section 16).

2. Scope

Sub-section (1) of section 7 empowers a Special Court to forfeit movable or immovable properties of a person who has been convicted in an offence, declared as such by Chapter II of the Act of 1989. The Special Court is required to pass an order for such declaration of forfeiture in writing at the time of awarding punishment of imprisonment and forfeiture is in addition to such punishment.

There are two essential requirements for forfeiture of such properties – *viz* (i) the properties must belong to the convicted person and, (ii) the properties must be such that "has been used for the commission of that offence".

Sub-section (2) of section 7 of the Act is applicable to undertrials who have been "accused of any offence under" Chapter II of the Act of 1989. The provision is not for the forfeiture but for attachment and if such trial ends in conviction, only then the attached properties are liable to forfeiture, that too to the extent and purpose of realisation of any fine imposed by the Court.

3. Constitutionality of Section 7

It was argued before a Full Bench of Allahabad High Court that power of forfeiture and attachment of property under section 7 of the Act is unusual and hence arbitrary. It has also been argued (wrongly) that it "has not been provided under any other Act."[1] The Bench observed that under section 1 Special Courts Act upon conviction of the accused may declare forfeiture of his property in addition to the punishment awarded for that offence. Under sub-section (2) of section 7, the Special Court is empowered to order attachment of the property of the accused during the trial. The Act will not become arbitrary on account of such power being conferred on the Special Courts. When the Parliament is empowered to make laws against untouchability it is well entitled to prescribe and add forfeiture and attachment of the property of the accused to the punishment awarded for the offences.[2]

4. Power of Forfeiture, Attachment – Discretionary

Section 7 of the Act of 1989 did not make it mandatory for the Special Courts to make a declaration of forfeiture in each and every case of conviction of accused in

1. The contention was wrong, as many other Acts have similar provisions. Please see Legislative History above.
2. *Mata Sewak Upadhyay* v. *State of Uttar Pradesh*, 1995 JIC 1168 (All) (FB): 1996 (1) East Cr C 97 (All) (FB) (1190).

addition to the sentence of imprisonment; or, in case of every accused brought for trial before it to attach his property. It is purely discretionary power of the Special Court which may be invoked by the prosecution and the Court may, or may not, pass an order for forfeiture or attachment, as the case may be, considering the facts and circumstances of each case.

Such discretion to the Special Court is available to be exercised on its own accord or when requested; only when—

(i) the accused has been finally convicted of an offence specifically committed under the Act of 1989; and (ii) when the trial starts before Special Court [section 7(2)].

In that sense the Special Court has been given dual powers regarding the property, movable and immovable, of the person charged under the provisions of the Act of 1989.

5. Words and Phrases

5.1 Section 7(1) "Convicted of any Offence under this Chapter"

The provisions of section 7(1) of the Act applies to only those cases which have been tried under Chapter II of the Act and none else. For instance if an accused has been tried for offences under section 3 of the Act alongwith some provisions of IPC, and the accused was acquitted from all charges under the Act, but convicted under the provision or provisions of IPC, the Special Court would lose the power of forfeiting the properties of the accused.

5.2 "In Addition to Awarding any Punishment"

The power of declaration of forfeiture of properties of the convict is in addition of punishment, which may be a sentence of imprisonment as well as fine. The word "in addition to" clearly denote an additional punishment to the convict, apart from imprisonment and fine.

5.3 "Belonging to the Person"

The phrase restricts the power of the Special Court to forfeit the properties of any kind which strictly belong to the convicted person. The properties of other family members or others are out of ambit of section 7 and no properties of third parties can be forfeited under this provision.

5.4 "Which has been Used for the Commission of that Offence"

Again the order of forfeiture of any kind of property can be made, which has been used for the commission of "that" offence for which the person is being convicted. That clearly means, other properties belonging to the convict cannot be forfeited at the conviction of the person, because the word "that" specifically indicate that particular property which was "used for the commission of that offence". Other properties of the convict remain outside the ambit of section 7 of the Act.

5.5 Section 7(2). "During the Period of such Trial"

Means as long as the trial lasts since its inception, the properties of the accused may be attached by the Special Court.

5.6 "Liable to Forfeiture to the Extent .... Realisation of any Fine"

The properties attached by the Special Court during trial of the accused, would be liable to forfeiture, in the condition that such trial has ended in conviction. But the said forfeiture would not be total because it may be to the extent of realisation of imposed fine. This provision of forfeiture of properties is independent of provision of forfeiture provided under sub-section (1) of section 7 of the Act. If the amount of forfeited property is higher than the amount of imposed fine, then the difference would be returned to such a convicted person.

Additionally, some condition has been put here as was seen under section 7(1), that of the conviction and fine must be imposed for a committed offence under Chapter II of the Act of 1989.

6. Third Party and Forfeiture or Attachment

A third party to whom belongs the forfeited or attached property of any kind, and against which an order has been passed , may file a suit, appeal or revision, as the case may be.

Such orders are not interlocutory orders, but they are final as far as third party is concerned, because in case they do not get legal redressal their properties may be subjected to trouble for which they may not be responsible or liable.

In such a case Supreme Court had held that a third party against whom order of forfeiture etc., has been passed may file appropriate suit or revision etc. It was observed that such an order would be deemed to be a final order and not an interlocutory one. Interlocutory order in law means, not that which decides the cause but which only settles intervening matter relating to cause. It is made to secure some end and purpose necessary and essential to the progress of the case generally collateral to the cause to be settled by the court in the final judgment.[1]

8. Presumption as to offences.—In a prosecution for an offence under this Chapter, if it is proved that—

(a) the accused rendered any financial assistance to a person accused of, or reasonably suspected of, committing, an offence under this Chapter, the Special Court shall presume, unless the contrary is proved, that such person had abetted the offence;

(b) a group of persons committed an offence under this Chapter and if it is proved that the offence committed was a sequel to any existing dispute regarding land or any other matter, it shall be presumed that the offence was committed in furtherance of the common intention or in prosecution of the common object.

---

1. *Amina Ahmed Dossa* v. *State of Maharashtra*, AIR 2001 SC 656: 2001 Cr LJ 965: 2001 AIR SCW 291.

SYNOPSIS

1. Analogous Law

Section 12 of The Protection of Civil Rights Act 1955 (previously known as Untouchability Act) says:

> "12. *Presumption by Courts in certain cases.*—Where any act constituting an offence under this Act is committed in relation to a member of a Scheduled Caste, the court shall presume, unless contrary is proved, that such act was committed on the ground of 'untouchability'."

Section 12 of Protection of Civil Rights Act, 1955 portrays the general theme of section 8 of the Act of 1989, while section 10 of Protection of Civil Right Act makes "abetment" of the offences committed against Scheduled Castes and Scheduled Tribes as an offence.

Section 8(a) has included the 'abetment' committed under the Chapter II of Act, if the accused had "rendered financial assistance to a person" accused of or even a person suspected of committing such offence. The same phrase had been used under section 21(2) of TADA and section 53(2) of POTA 2002 (now repealed), where "financial assistance" to the main accused was used to draw a presumption.

Section 22 of Maharashtra Control or Organised Crime Act, 1999 also provide for such a presumption.

2. Principle of Presumption

In the old times, and to some extent today as well, under general law no presumption perhaps being more favoured in law than that of presumption of innocence of the accused. On the basis of this presumption, the most fundamental rule of criminal jurisprudence – that prosecution must prove their case and the guilt of the accused beyond all reasonable doubt – had been formulated.

Cardinal principle of criminal law is that it presumes the accused as innocent, unless proved otherwise. Generally a presumption of law is an inference which has derived from the law some arbitrary or artificial effect. The inference is independent of any belief based upon what is probable, because the law declares the effect of a particular state of things and condition of circumstances.

The history of jurisprudence reveals that there had always been a struggle between the courts and the legislature on some principled stand, though, not in the open and not said in so many words. This struggle has been proved to be healthy because through this, uniformity of law has been achieved. The same substantive law is applied to each case of similar nature but they are decided by the Courts on their own facts. When the Courts apply the law to given facts, they simultaneously also consider precedents and through this combination courts deduce rules to determine certain facts which are often found recurring. Such an exercise leads to the development of may rules which were called as presumptions.

Many kinds of presumptions were classified, - such as – 'legal assumption', 'conclusive presumption', irrebuttable presumption', 'mandatory presumption', 'permissive presumption' and 'rebuttable presumption'. (most important being the 'presumption of innocence'). Under this classification, the rules which were found to be arbitrary were discarded, because they tend to detract from the real fact, but on the other hand conclusive kind of presumptive rules were adopted.

Legislature provide guiding principles expecting them to be followed by Courts, but as the Courts have their inherent power of discretion, they use it to the artificial value of these technical rules while dealing with the given facts, the courts remain free to use reason, its commonsense and the experience in judging from given chain of fact and draw its own inferences. On this basis presumptions cannot be drawn at random, because presumption of a fact is only an inference in relation to the existence of some other facts.

It is also important to note here that there must be some connection between facts proved: say, "it is proved that that accused rendered financial assistance to a person accused of" [section 8(a)]; or "a group or persons committed an offence under this Chapter......." [section 8(b)], and the fact which is intended to be inferred.

3. Scope of Section 8

It is clear from general reading of section 8 of the Act, that its operation is confined to the offences committed under Chapter II of the Act. Section 8 of the Act of 1989 raised two presumptions under clauses (a) and (b). Under clause (a) it is stated that in a prosecution for an offence under Chapter II, if it is proved that the accused rendered any financial assistance to a person accused of, or reasonably suspected of committing an offence under the said Chapter, the Special Court shall presume unless contrary is proved, that such person had abetted the offence. Clause (b) in the same manner raises a presumption that if it is proved that a group of persons committed an offence under Chapter II, and that the offence committed was a sequel to any existing dispute regarding land or any other matter, the Special Court will presume that the offence was committed in furtherance of common intention or in prosecution of common object. Raising presumption is a legislative prerogative and no exception can be taken to such provision. It is not uncommon for the legislature to raise presumptions under law. Similar provisions raising presumptions have been made under several statutes. In the perspective of offences of atrocities such presumption cannot be said to be arbitrary. Once the legislature is empowered to raise such presumptions no exception can be taken to them.[1]

Another Division Bench of MP High Court has observed that considering the entire purpose for which the Act has been enacted, the provision in section 8 is necessary for the effective implementation of the provisions in section 3

1. *Mata Sewak Upadhyay* v. *State of Uttar Pradesh*, 1995 JIC 1168 (All) (FB): 1996 (1) East Cr C 97 (All) (FB) (1197).

of the Act. It is necessary to prevent the moneyed persons from encouraging commission of offences under section 3, in indirect way by rendering financial assistance to hired hands to get their work done. On the other hand, it was observed, that the interest of such persons is safeguarded, as the presumption is rebuttable. The Act has further taken care to ensure that the powers are not misused. As the office of Special Public Prosecutors and the Special Courts are manned by experienced persons, their experience, knowledge, professional expertise, judicial discipline and reading of human behaviour, they are well equipped with capacity to decipher truth from falsehood. The provisions of section 8 are not arbitrary, but they are necessary for the effective working of the Act.[1]

4. Limits of Drawing Presumption

Presumption is an inference of a certain fact drawn from other proved facts. Inferring the existence of a fact from another is a process based on intelligent reasoning which the mind of a prudent man would do under similar circumstances. On the other hand presumption is not a final conclusion to be drawn from other facts. But it could be said to be final if it remains undisturbed in the end.

The process of drawing presumption by Court is not automatic but it can only be drawn after certain facts have been proved by evidence.[2]

Section 6 of the Act of 1989 had mandated to include section 34, provisions of Chapter V ('of abetment') and section 149 of the Indian Penal Code, 1860. Clauses (a) and (b) of section 8 of the Act specifically prescribe some conditions under which the Special Court has been empowered to draw a presumption under section 8.

Though, provisions of Indian Penal Code regarding 'common intention', 'abetment' and 'common object' are generally applicable to and included in the charges, whatever the facts be, framed for offences prescribed by Chapter II of the Act of 1989, application of these provisions of IPC is limited for drawing presumptions under section 8 of the Act. This is so because section 8 prescribes certain conditions, such as – "financial assistance" (for (abetment) and the existence of a dispute "regarding land or any other matter", due to which group of persons had committed an offence. Such presumptions cannot be drawn if these pre-conditions do not exist.

Where the story set up by the prosecution inherently militates against or is inconsistent with the fact to be presumed, the presumption will be rendered sterile from its very inception and the plea should be rejected.

5. "Unless the Contrary is Proved" – Rebuttal

Section 8 of the Scheduled Castes and the Scheduled Tribes (Prevention of Atrocities) Act, 1989, provides a statutory presumption to be drawn against the accused by the Special Court specifically under the given situations and conditions.

1. *Dr. Ram Krishna Balothia* v. *Union of India*, 1994 Cr LJ 2658 (MP) (DB) (2663): AIR 1994 MP 143: 1994 MPLJ 644.
2. *Mohd. Iqbal Ahmed* v. *State of* Andhra Pradesh, 1979 Cr LJ 633 (SC): AIR 1979 SC 677 (679): (1979) 4 SCC 172.

This power of Special Court to draw statutory presumption is not absolute, but it is subject to rebuttal. The accused have been given a right of rebuttal by inserting the phrase, "unless the contrary is proved".

For this purpose the prosecution has to prove that the accused had consciously "assisted" the main accused financially; or where the offence committed by a group of persons under Chapter II of the Act it was a sequel to any "existing dispute regarding laud or any other matter", it was committed in furtherance of common intention or of common object.

A five Judge Bench of Supreme Court in such a situation, regarding drawing statutory presumption had observed that the accused in his defense is entitled to prove the non-existence of a fact constituting any of the ingredients. As a part of his defence, he can prove by adducing evidence, the non-existence of fact to rebut the statutory presumption.[1]

Thus, to rebut the presumption mentioned under section 8, a person accused of an offence of 'abetment', may prove that either he did not render any 'financial assistance' to the main accused or in the alternative that, though he had 'rendered financial' assistance but it was for some other purpose, specially not connected with commission of an offence under Chapter II of the Act of 1989. Similarly, the presumption under section 8(b) may be rebutted by producing evidence that either he was not a member of that particular "group of persons" who had committed offence prescribed under Chapter II of the Act; or, or that the said offence was not "a sequel to any existing dispute regarding land or any other matter".

It may be noted here that to invoke the provisions of section 8(b) of the Act and the presumption arising therefrom, the dispute regarding land or other matter must pre-"exist" the time when the actual offence was committed. In case there was no pre-existing dispute between the "group" and the complainants, no such presumption can be drawn. If the said offence was committed, for instance, spontaneously or for any other reason, the situation would abrogate the power of the Special Court to draw presumption under section 8(b).

6. Theme of Presumption

Presumption in Law of Evidence is a rule indicating the stage of shifting the burden of proof. From a certain fact or series of facts, the court may draw an inference and that would remain in existence until it is disproved or dispelled. Until and unless the presumption is disproved through rebuttal process, court is empowered to treat the presumption tantamounting to proof. However, as a caution of prudence it may be unsafe to use that presumption to draw yet another discretionary presumption, unless there is a statutory compulsion. But a presumption cannot be drawn from other presumptions. It can only be drawn from facts and that too by a process of probable and logical reasoning.[2]

Presumption can be drawn from a certain fact or chain of facts which have been legally proved. When the court infers one fact from another, it is through

1. *Sanjay Dutt* v. *State through C.B.I., Bombay*, 1994 AIR SCW 3857: 1995 Cr LJ 477: (1994) 5 SCC 410.
2. *M. Narsinga Rao* v. *State of* Andhra Pradesh, 2001 Cr LJ 515 (SC): AIR 2001 SC 318: 2000 AIR SCW 4427.

the process of intelligent reasoning of an expected prudence. Presumption is not a final inference or conclusion in the intermediary stages, but it would become final if it remains unrebutted at the end. Therefore it becomes an indicator of the stage of shifting the burden of proof.[1]

The process of inferring facts from other facts which is said to be presumption would not apply in a situation where a co-accused has made a confession about the fact that a certain accused has committed the offence; or, where the accused himself has made a confession to a person other than a police officer. In the said situation the normal rule of presumption would be applicable.[2]

7. Proper stage to Draw Presumption is Only Trial, Not Before

Section 8 of the Scheduled Castes and the Scheduled Tribes (Prevention of Atrocities) Act, 1989 opens as: "In a prosecution for an offence under this Chapter, if it is proved that" in a similar manner as the opening phrase was used under section 53 of POTA ,2002 (now repealed), or under section 21 of TADA, 1987 (now repealed) it was observed: "From the aforesaid section it appears: (a) the presumption can only arise at the stage of prosecution *i.e.,* the stage of Trial, and (b) it can arise only after the facts mentioned...... have been proved". It was also observed that at the pre-trial stage presumptions cannot be drawn against the accused, because at this stage prosecution does not commence.[3] That also means that such presumption would not arise during the investigation stage. But the presumption would arise as soon as prosecution has proved the relevant facts as has been stipulated by section 8, because the presumption cannot arise automatically.

8. Word "Proved"

The word "proved" has been used three times in section 8, *i.e.,* in the opening phrase, in clause (a) and in clause (b). The context and meaning of the word in all the three places bear different degrees of its original meaning, because in the opening phrase and clause (b) the word has been used in reference to prosecution, while in clause (a) it has been used in reference to the defense of the accused.

When the word "proved" has been used in reference to both the parties namely the prosecution and the accused, the interpretation given by Supreme Court would show that the burden of proof on the accused is not as onerous as that of prosecution. When it is used in relation to the duty of prosecution, it would mean to be proved beyond the reasonable doubt, whereas when the word "proved" has been used in context to the accused, it would mean that burden of proof on the part of accused would be by preponderance of the probability and it need not be beyond all reasonable doubt.[4]

---

1. *State of Andhra Pradesh* v. *C. Uma Maheswara Rao,* 2004 Cr LJ 2040 (SC): AIR 2004 SC 2042: 2004 AIR SCW 2192; also see *T. Shankar Prasad* v. *State of Andhra Pradesh,* 2004 Cr LJ 884 (SC): AIR 2004 SC 1242: 2004 AIR SCW 262.
2. *State* v. *Nalani J,* JT 1999 (4) SC 106 (400).
3. *Md. Rashid Khan* v. *State of West Bengal,* 1994 Cr LJ 2699 (Cal) (2720): 1995 (1) All Cri LR 191: 1994 Cal Cri LR 278.
4. *State* v. *Duraisami,* 2000 (1) CCR 18 (28).

The words "unless the contrary is proved" make it clear that the presumption has to be rebutted by 'proof' and not by a mere explanation which is simply plausible. A fact is said to be proved when its existence is directly established or when the Court finds on the basis of the material before it, the existence to be so probable that a reasonable and prudent man would act on such supposition that it exists.

9. Difference with Presumption of section 114 Evidence Act

Courts are also empowered to draw a presumption under section 114 of Evidence Act, 1872 for existence of one fact from another, but it is not obligatory on the part of the Court to draw or not to draw such presumption. But if a certain fact has been proved by the prosecution that the accused has committed offence under Chapter II of the Act of 1989; or the offence committed was a sequel to any existing (not past) dispute regarding land or any other matter, the court has no option but to presume the committal of such offence for the limited purposes of 'common intention" or of "common object". Here it may be important to mention that accused is entitled to rebut such allegation by plausible evidence or the explanations, as the case may be.

9. Conferment of powers.—(1) Notwithstanding anything contained in the Code or in any other provision of this Act, the State Government may, if it considers it necessary or expedient so to do,—

(a) for the prevention of and for coping with any offence under this Act, or

(b) for any case or class or group of cases under this Act,

in any district or part thereof, confer, by notification in the Official Gazette, on any officer of the State Government, the powers exercisable by a police officer under the Code in such district or part thereof or, as the case may be, for such case or class or group of cases, and in particular, the powers of arrest, investigation and prosecution of persons before any special court.

(2) All officers of police and all other officers of Government shall assist the officer referred to in sub-section (1) in the execution of the provisions of this Act or any rule, scheme or order made thereunder.

(3) The provisions of the Code shall, so far as may be, apply to the exercise of the powers by an officer under sub-section (1).

SYNOPSIS

2.3 "Any Officer of the State Government"
3. Section 9 and Rule 7
4. Where section 9 is not Applicable
5. Conferring Power of "Arrest"
6. Conferring Power to Investigate
7. Ordering Re-investigation – A Remedy
8. Direction under Rule 7, mandatory or Directory
9. "Prosecution of persons before any Special Court"
10. "Notification"
11. Necessary Requirements under section 9 for issuance of Notification
12. Section 9(3)

1. Scope

While section 23 of the Act of 1989 confers power to Central Government to make Rules "for carrying out the purpose of this Act", section 9 of the Act empowers the State Government, wherever "it considers it necessary or expedient so to do", may confer those powers which are exercisable by a police officer as provided under the Code of Criminal Procedure, 1973, on any officer of the State Government through a notification in the Official Gazette. Thus any officer working under the State Government may be empowered by such Government to have special powers, otherwise only exercisable by a police officer under the law.

Different kinds of powers of police officers have been provided under the Cr PC may be conferred to any State Government officer, but in particular it may relate to "powers of arrest, investigation and prosecution of person before any Special Court".

But importantly such conferment of powers of police officers to any other officer of the State Government, it is limited to two conditions – *viz.* (i) for prevention of and coping with any offence under the Act of 1989; and, (ii) for a particular case or class or group of cases under the Act of 1989.

The Act of 1989 gives a free hand to the State Government to empower its non-police officers to do certain jobs in connection with arrest, investigation or prosecution, where the matter arises out of any offences or atrocities under the provisions of the Act. The Constitution of India conceives a federal structure to the Indian Union and as the Act of 1989 was a Central Act, the Central Government was not empowered to confer such power to State officials, hence this provision was added.

The State Governments are not only empowered to deal with already committed offences under the Act, but it can also use such powers of conferment for "prevention" of or "coping" with any offence which is likely to take place. Therefore State officials may be used by such Government.

When a State Government has to use the powers provided under this section, it has to issue a notification in the Official Gazette to this effect. The notification need not to mention that all police officers and other officers of the government shall have to assist the notified officer, because sub-section (2) of section 9 itself provides so.

Section 9(3) of the Act of 1989 provides that provisions of Cr PC shall apply particularly in matters of power of arrest, investigation and prosecution, to such notified State Government officer who has been appointed as such under the sub-section.

2. The used Phrases in section 9

2.1 "Notwithstanding Anything Contained in the Code or in any other Provision of this Act"

Section 9 of the Act starts with this *non-obstante* clause and in view of the said *non-obstante* clause, a notification issued under section 9 of the Act of 1989 will have an overriding effect, therefore it was observed that effect cannot be held to be *ultra vires*. It was also observed that the rules framed under any act are considered to be part of that Act or enactment. In this view the words-"anything contained in the provisions of the Act will sweep into its embrace the provisions contained in the Rules also. The *non-obstante* clause in section 9 of the Act of 1989 gives an overriding effect to a notification issued by a State Government and that should include section 23 of the Act of 1989 and the Rules made thereunder. Therefore a notification issued in exercise of powers conferred under section 9(1) of the Act cannot be said to be *ultra vires* of the Act or the Rules made thereunder.[1]

(But there is a difference of opinion on the matter mentioned above, which wourld be dealt later).

2.2 "Any Case or Class of Cases"

It necessarily means that the conferment of powers is not restricted to prevention of offences alone but also to deal with the offences already committed. For this reason, if a notification has been issued in reference to a number of cases filed under the Act of 1989, and the said reference, which was made after due and active application of mind to the prevailing circumstances needing early investigation is valid.[1]

2.3 "Any Officer of the State Government"

The given phrase would also include a police officer, according to the Bench. In view of their Lorships, nothing in section 9 of the Act of 1989, restricts the power of the State Government to a district or a part of a district alone. It does enable the State Government to exercise the power conferred by section 9 of the Act of 1989 in respect of a district or a part of a district but that cannot be read to mean that such power cannot be exercised for the whole of the State.[2]

It may be submitted that section 9 of the Act of 1989 itself differentiate between officers who are police officers and "any officer of the State Government", which inevitably means that such other officers were not otherwise empowered to exercise the powers given by the Code. Secondly, had the Legislature was impregnated with an intention as the observation reveal, the phrase—

"powers exercisable by a officer" would not have been used, because it was a non-issue in case of a police officer and there was no need to say so.

3. Section 9 and Rule 7

The Scheduled Castes and the Scheduled Tribes (Prevention of Atrocities) Rules, 1995 was framed by the Central Government in the year 1995 and

1. *Ram Deni Devi* v. *State*, 2011 Cr LJ 2408 (Pat) (DB).

before framing of these Rules, Section 9 of the Act 1989 was used by the State Governments to confer powers of investigation etc., to the police officers of their choice through respective notifications. But after the Rules of 1995 came into force, the position has changed as Rule 7 says:

> *Rule "7. Investigating Officer.*—(1) An offence committed under the Act shall be investigated by a police officer not below the rank of a Deputy Superintendent of Police. The investigating officer shall be appointed by the State Government/Director-General of Police/Superintendent of Police after taking into account his past experience, sense of ability and justice to perceive the implications of the case and investigate it alongwith right lines within the shortest possible time.
>
> (2) The investigating officer so appointed under sub-rule (1) shall complete the investigation on top priority basis within thirty days and submit the report to the Superintendent of Police who in turn will immediately forward the report to the Director-General of Police of the State Government.
>
> (3) The Home Secretary and the Social Welfare Secretary to the State Government, Director of Prosecution, the officer-in-charge of Prosecution and the Director-General of Police shall review by the end of every quarter the position of all investigation done by the investigating officer."

A question was raised before Patna High Court as to whether a notification under section 9 of the Act of 1989 has to be issued, even if the investigation has been conducted by a Dy. S.P. as stipulated under Rule 7, authorising him to conduct such investigation. The State was unable to produce any notification or "no such letter of appointment has been produced in support" of the contention to the effect that the "State Government has appointed Dy. S.P. to investigate into the matter". As a result the plea of State was rejected and the very cognizance of the offence punishable under the Act of 1989, on the basis of charge-sheet submitted by Dy. S.P. was quashed, because such Dy. S.P. was not found by the Court legally authorised to investigated the offence.[1]

Deciding the same question further, a Division Bench of the same High Court has held that a notification issued under section 9 of the Act of 1989 conferring powers of investigation "upon the police officers below the rank of Deputy Superintendent of Police is valid". Its operation with retrospective effect is also valid to the extent that any offence committed prior to the date of the notification, be investigated by a police officer who has been vested with the power of investigation though he may be of the rank below the rank of the Deputy Superintendent of Police. The Bench further went on to observe that to accept such argument "would amount to validating the acts which were unauthorized and invalid from inception. In other words, if an investigation in such crime has been made by a police officer below the rank of the Deputy Superintendent of Police prior to the date of the publication of the impugned notification, such

---

1. *Mohan Choudhary* v. *State of Bihar*, 2000 Cr LJ 1891 (Pat): 2000 (2) BLJ 242: 2000 (1) BLJR 673.

investigation and consequent prosecution which were otherwise invalid cannot stand validated by the impugned notification."[1]

(For further details please see notes below "investigation and cognizance")

4. Where section 9 is not Applicable

In a case where the investigating officer had submitted a final report on the ground that the case was a mistake of fact, the complainant lodged a complaint and an inquiry under section 202 Cr PC was taken up. In the said inquiry five witnesses were examined, including the complainant, and the Special Court was satisfied that a *prima facie* case had been made out in respect of alleged offences. Therefore the Special Judge took cognizance of offences under the Act. Thus it was held that provisions about the investigation has no application.[2]

5. Conferring Power of "Arrest"

Section 9 of the Act of 1989 empowers the State Government to confer power of arrest to "any officer of the State Government" as has been provided under the Code of Criminal Procedure exercisable by police officers, through a notification, to be published in the Official Gazette. Chapter V of Cr PC (Comprising from Section 41 to section 60A) deals with "arrest of persons".

Arrest means: "any significant deprivation of an individual's freedom of action, especially the taking of an individual into custody for the purpose of transporting him to a police station and charging him with a crime".[3] The word 'arrest' is a term of article. It starts with the arrester taking a person into his custody by action or words restraining him from moving anywhere beyond the arrester's control, and it continues until the person so restrained is either released from custody or, having been brought before a Court, but when such person has been remanded by the Court, it becomes Judicial act and not an 'arrest'. In substance 'arrest' is the restraint on an individual's personal liberty by the power or colour of lawful authority. In its natural sense, "arrest" also means the restraint on or deprivation of one's personal liberty. For the same reason, the record of time of arrest is not an index to the actual time of arrest. The 'arrest' commences with the restraint placed on the liberty of the person arrested.[4]

When the word 'arrest' is used in the legal sense, it consists of the taking into custody of another person, having an authority prescribed by law for the purposes of detaining the arrested person to answer a criminal charge or of preventing the commission of a criminal offence. The essential elements to constitute an "arrest" are that there must be an intent to arrest under the authority, accompanied by a seizure or detention of the person in the manner known to law, which is so understood by the arrested person.[5]

---

1. *Ram Deni Devi* v. *State*, 2011 Cr LJ 2408 (Pat) (DB) (2412).
2. *Ramesh Chandra Das* v. *Kasinath Jena*, 2000 Cr LJ 4006 (4008): 2000 (19) OCR 101: 2000 (2) Ori LR 162.
3. Webster's Legal Dictionary.
4. *Ashak Husain Allah Detla* alias *Siddique* v. *Asst. Collector*, 1990 Cr LJ 2201.
5. *Roshan Beevi* v. *Joint Secretary to Government of Tamil Nadu*, 1984 Cr LJ 134 (Mad) (FB): AIR 1984 Mad 103: 1984 (115) ELT 289.

It may be noted here that not every and "any officer of the State Government" has been empowered normally to make arrests of individuals, because they are not generally authorised by law as the Code of Criminal Procedure provide, except the police officers. But section 9 of the Act of 1989 has empowered the State Government to give powers of arrest to "any" of its officers by simply conferring such powers through a notification in the Official Gazette.

6. Conferring Power to Investigate

Section 9 of the Act of 1989 provides conferment of powers by State Government to any of its officers for investigation etc., but Rule 7 of the Scheduled Castes and the Scheduled Tribes (Prevention of Atrocities) Rules, 1995, restricts this power to be conferred to a police officer who is not lower in rank than Deputy Superintendent of Police (Rule 7 has been given under note (c) above, or see the Appendix).

A series of judgments have come up where the cognizance taken by Special Courts were challenged on the basis of charge-sheets filed; the investigations conducted by police officers lower in ranks than Deputy Superintendent of Police, as has been stipulated by Rule 7.

It was held that any investigation conducted by Sub-Inspector or Circle Inspector of Police is illegal because it contravenes the provisions of Rule 7. The question to decide was: "what will be the effect and consequence of carrying out investigation by an unauthorized police officer for the offences and Scheduled Castes and the Scheduled Tribes (Prevention of Atrocities) Act, 1989". In the instant case the investigation was conducted by a sub-inspector of police for the offences committed under the Act of 1989. The investigation was declared invalid and illegal.[1]

The Supreme Court has also considered the point under discussion. The charge-sheet under certain sections of Indian Penal Code and under section 3(1)(x) of the Act of 1989 was submitted on the basis of investigation which was conducted by a police officer not authorised to do so under Rule 7 of 1995. Accused challenged the matter before High Court of Madhya Pradesh and the said High Court had quashed the entire proceedings against the accused persons. The State preferred an appeal before Supreme Court. The Apex Court considered provisions of section 9 of the Act of 1989 and rule 7 and has held that trial of the accused under section 3 of that Act of 1989 cannot proceed. Following observation was made:

> "By virtue of its enabling power, it is the duty and responsibility of the State Government to issue notification conferring power of investigation of cases by notified police officer not below the rank of Deputy Superintendent of Police for different areas in the police districts. Rule 7 of rules provided rank of investigating officer to be not below the rank of Deputy

---

1. *Jwahir Sharma* v. *State of Uttar Pradesh*, 2010 Cr LJ 1528: 2010 (1) ALJ 727: 2010 (2) Crimes 837; *Kailas Govind Wadekar* v. *State of Maharashtra*, 2010 Cr LJ 2752 (Bom): 2010 (3) AIR Bom R 211: 2010 (2) Bom CR (Cri) 709; *Asiskhan Pathan* v. *State*, 2006 (6) AIR Bom R 220; *Uttamlal Yema* v. *State*, 2006 (4) AIR Bom R 20; But also see *Ram Deni Devi* v. *State*, 2011 Cr LJ 2408 (Pat) (DB).

Superintendent of Police. An officer below that rank cannot act as an investigation officer. The provisions in section 9 of the Act, rule 7 of Rules and section 4 of the Code when jointly read lead to an irresistible conclusion that the investigation to an offence under section 3 of the Act by an officer not appointed in terms of rule 7 is illegal and invalid. But when offence complained are both under the I.P.C. and any of the offence enumerated in section 4 of the Act the investigation which is being made by a competent police officer in accordance with the provisions of the Code cannot be quashed for non-investigation of the offence under section 3 of the Act by a competent police officer."[1]

The observations and findings of Hon'ble Supreme Court are final and clear as far as investigation by a proper and authorised police officer is concerned.

7. Ordering Re-investigation – A Remedy

If it is found at the stage of cognizance that the investigation was conducted by an unauthorised police officer, the Court may issue directions to the investigating agency to proceed with proper investigation by a competent person to proceed according to law. It is so because it was held that: "The corollary is that the Court of Sessions or Special Court has no jurisdiction to take cognizance of the offence," where the complaint was filed by an unauthorised officer.[2] In such cases the charge has to be treated as *non est*. In such cases the accused have to be discharged.

But such discharge of the accused could not bar a fresh prosecution of the same matter by an authorised investigating officer and that could not be said to hit by section 300 Cr PC.[3]

As the charge-sheet was filed by an incompetent person, it was held that it was liable to be quashed. But it was also observed that entire proceedings cannot be quashed considering the allegation and objects of the Act. It was further held that, as there was breach of rules, appropriate orders for investigation as may be necessary has to be passed by the Court. Consequently a direction was issued to the investigating agency to proceed with the proper investigation by a competent authority.[4]

But it may also be important to point out here that such fresh investigation could not be directed where the entire trial has ended and the judgment has been delivered and the case has reached at the stage of appeal where it was found that the investigation was conducted by an incompetent officer. It is so because it would hit the principle of 'double jeopardy' enshrined in the constitution as well as section 300 Cr PC.

---

1. *State of Madhya Pradesh*, v. *Chunnilal alias Chunni Singh*, 2009 (65) ACC 652 (SC): 2009 AIR SCW 5335; but also see *Rattiram* v. *State of Madhya Pradesh*, 2012 Cr LJ 1769 (SC).
2. *Prabhakaran* v. *Excise Circle Officer*, 1993 Cr LJ 3599 (Ker) (DB): 1992 (2) KLT 860: ILR (1993) 1 Ker 480.
3. *Joy* v. *State*, 1994 (1) KLT 59.
4. *K. Muhammed* v. *K. Sukumaran*, 2001 Cr LJ 1664 (Ker): ILR (2001) 1 Ker 540: 2001 (1) Ker LJ 154.

In *Ratiram's* case (Supra), the Apex Court has indicated that the objections to the improper or unauthorised investigation has to be raised at the earliest stage of trial or proceedings.

8. Direction under Rule 7, Mandatory or Directory

A question was raised before a Full Bench of Andhra Pradesh High Court: whether the investigation as contemplated under Rule 7 of Rules 1995 is mandatory?

A case was initially registered under sections 447, 427, 354 and 506 IPC and section 7(1)(d) of Protection of Civil Rights Act, 1955 and consequently investigated by a sub-inspector of police. But the Magistrate committed the case under section 3(1)(x) and 3(1)(xi) of Act of 1989 instead of section 7(1)(d) of Protection of Civil Rights Act, 1955. The Special Court framed charges under section 3 of the Act, thus it was challenged on the ground that the committal Magistrate had no jurisdiction to alter the offences on one hand and on the other the investigation was not conducted according to provisions of Rule 7 of the Rules of 1995. A single Judge held that provision of Rule 7 are mandatory thereby making the investigation wholly illegal on the basis of a Division Bench decision on the same question[1]. The Division Bench previously observed, considering two conflicting decisions, that defect or illegality in investigation has no direct bearing on the competence or the procedure relating to cognizance or trial. It was also observed that a valid and legal police report cannot be said to be the foundation of the jurisdiction of the Court to take cognizance under various provisions under the Code (section 190 etc). Therefore illegality committed in investigation (under the code) does not affect competence and jurisdiction of the Court. But the single Judge has rightly observed that a defective investigation under Rule 7 is not a procedural defect, but it is an inherent defect and that would make the entire trial vitiated. In the end the Full Bench, overruling the decision of Division Bench in *Viswanadhula's* (Supra) case, held that the said "Rule is not mandatory but only a directory one[2].

It is submitted that the Act of 1989 is a very 'special' enactment and section 23 of the Act mandates to put the rules so framed before the two Houses of the Parliament in a similar way as is adopted in case of Legislations. The Rules of 1995 have everything of an enactment except the Presidential assent. It would be presumed that the Parliament had considered every aspect and angle, including the aspect of misuse of provisions of the Special Act of 1989 or Rules, therefore mandating a provision relating to investigation of the offences under Rule 7 to be conducted by an officer of police not lower in rank than Deputy Superintendent of Police, who also happen to be the lowest Gazetted Officer in police force. Therefore the Parliament, while giving assent to Rule 7, had an

---

1. *Viswanandhula Chittibabu* v. *State*, 2002 (2) ALD (Cri) 206: 2002 (4) ALT 456 (AP) (DB) (overruled by the FB); also see *State of Madhya Pradesh* v. *Ram Singh*, 2000 Cr LJ 1401 (SC): AIR 2000 SC 870: 2000 AIR SCW 454; *H.N. Rishbud* v. *State of Delhi*, 1955 Cr LJ 526 (SC): AIR 1955 SC 196: ILR (1955) Punj 135.
2. *Yannam Satyanarayan* v. *State of* Andhra Pradesh, 2006 Cr LJ 2320 (AP) (FB): 2006 (4) East Cri C 411: 2006 (3) Rec Cri R 294.

intention to get the offences investigated by a competent officer who is supposed to be professionally efficient and honest. In case an investigation is allowed to be conducted by a lower rank officer, either party may be prejudiced, losing an opportunity to have services of a professionally efficient gazetted officer (Dy. S.P.).

Secondly, the entity of an investigating officer created under the Code of Criminal Procedure cannot be compared with an investigating officer contemplated under Rule 7 of Rules 1995. Though, some of the provisions of the Code are made applicable to the investigations etc. under the Rules of 1995, but the investigating officer prescribed under the Code was conceived to deal with cases or offences under the general law, while an 'special' investigating officer properly authorised under Rule 7 is supposed to deal with 'special offences of atrocities' against members of Scheduled Castes and the Scheduled Tribes. Thus the position of an investigating officer here is quite different.

Different High Courts and the Supreme Court in State of M.P. v. *Chunnilal alias Chuni Singh's* case (Supra) have finally decided the matter. The Apex Court has ruled clearly that an investigation conducted by a police officer lower in rank to Deputy Supritendant of Police is illegal and invalid as far as offences under the Act of 1989 are concerned, but the investigation of offences under the IPC by the same officer in the same case were held to be legal on the basis of which trial could proceed under offences under general law. In that way the Apex Court has clearly differentiated the two kinds of investigating officers, making it mandatory that investigations of offences committed under the Act of 1989 must be conducted by an officer who is not lower in rank than a Deputy Superintendent of Police.

9. "Prosecution of persons before any Special Court"

Section 9 of the Act of 1989 empowers State Government to confer powers of prosecution of persons before any Special Court to "any" officer employed by it. Section 15 of the Act of 1989 specifically provide for appointment of an advocate, having practice of not less than seven years or a P.P. as "Special Public Prosecutor" to conduct cases in Special Court. Section 15 of the Act also stipulates for issuance of a notification to this effect in the Official Gazette, similarly as has been provided under section 9.

Rule 14 of the Rules, 1995, framed under the Act of 1989 provides that the State Government shall review the performance of Special Public Prosecutors, appointed under section 15 twice a year.

Rule 4 of Rules of 1995 provides for preparation etc., of a panel of eminent senior Advocates, their appointments, review of their work and conditions of service, removal or supervision of such Prosecutors.

In any case appointment and supervision etc., of prosecution agency advocates created by section 15, read with Rules 4 and 14, are subject to publication of a specific 'notification' in the Official Gazette for such appointments, but the notification mentioned under section 9 of the Act is somewhat general in nature. (For further details please see notes under section 15 of the Act).

10. "Notification"

Section 9 of the Act has given power to the State Government to "confer" powers to "any officer of State Government", generally exercisable by a police officer under the Code. But such conferring exercise of powers to other officer must be through and by notification in the Official Gazette and by no other means.

'Notification' in common English means and imply a formal announcement of a legally relevant fact or direction. When this word is used in connection with a statute, the meaning would also include its publication in the Official Gazette. 'Notification' is a formal declaration and publication of an order which must be in accordance with the requirements of the statute. Administrative instructions cannot become a substitute for a notification, which stand as a requirement of the statute. Neither the notes attached to rules can substitute a notification.[1]

11. Necessary Requirements under section 9 for issuance of Notification

(i) for prevention of and coping with any offence under Act of 1989,

(ii) for any case or class or group of cases under the Act,

(iii) powers conferred may be exercised in a "district or part thereof",

(iv) the officer on whom powers are conferred must be an officer of the State Government and none else,

(v) conferred powers should relate to arrest, investigation and prosecution

(vi) the powers so conferred be such as are exercisable by police officers provided under the Code.

If the question arises, it would become incumbent on the State Government to show that it considered "it necessary or expedient so to do" to "confer" powers exercisable by a police officer on any other officer.

When an Act empowers the Government to issue notification for appointment of a certain officer to act within a certain area ("district or part thereof"), the officer must be holding certain post as stipulated by the statute. In case a notification has been issued for a particular person the notification could not be deemed to have been issued for another person who takes charge after the transfer of the notified person.[2]

The Rules of 1995 were statutorily made. Supreme Court has observed that notification has no statutory force, hence it cannot override Rules statutorily made governing the conditions of service of the employees (the requirements of section 9).[3]

Courts are not inclined to tolerate any lapse in a notification acquiring an authority which has not been provided, specially in cases where notification was issued in a serious matter. Defects in a notification are not curable.[4]

---

1. *Subhash Ramkumar Bind @ Vakil* v. *State of Maharashtra*, 2003 Cr LJ 443 (SC): AIR 2003 SC 269: 2002 AIR SCW 4732.
2. *Usmanbhai Dawoodbhai Memon* v. *State of Gujarat*, 1988 Cr LJ 938 (SC): AIR 1988 SC 922: (1988) 2 SCC 271.
3. *Union of India* v. *Arun Kumar Roy*, AIR 1986 SC 737 (741): (1986) 1 SCC 675: 1986 (1) SCJ 246.
4. *Narendrajit Singh* v. *State of Uttar Pradesh*, AIR 1971 SC 306: 1971 (1) SCJ 137: (1970) 3 SCR 278.

The notification has to be read in its entirety and not in parts[1]. But the expressions or words which have been used in the notification must be read as such and not in any manner, unless the context requires that the latter course should be followed[2].

12. Section 9(3)

Section 9(3) of the Act of 1989 stipulates that provisions of the Code of Criminal Procedure, 1973 shall, so far as may be, apply to the exercise of the powers by an officer, who has been conferred by a notification in the Official Gazette to exercise powers of a police officer provided under the Code.

Section 9(3) provides independent powers to such officer appointed only subject to Rules of 1995. It is so because it was observed, in the similar conditions, that powers under this section do not depend on the powers provided under the Code of Criminal Procedure, 1973.[3]

---

1. *Grasim Industries Ltd.* v. *State of Madhya Pradesh,* AIR 2000 SC 66: 1999 AIR SCW 4189: (1999) 8 SCC 547.
2. *Hari Chand Aggarwal* v. *Batala Engineering Co. Ltd.*, AIR 1969 SC 483: 1969 Cr LJ 803: (1969) 2 SCR 201.
3. *Moreshwar Savey* v. *State of Uttar Pradesh,* 2001 Cr LJ 1765: 2001 All LJ 638: 2001 (43) All Cri C 73; also see *Major E.G. Barsay* v. *State of Bombay,* 1961 (2) Cr LJ 828 (SC): (1962) 2 SCR 195: AIR 1961 SC 1762.

Chapter III

EXTERNMENT

10. Removal of person likely to commit offence.—(1) Where the Special Court is satisfied, upon a complaint or a police report that a person is likely to commit an offence under Chapter II of this Act in any area included in 'Scheduled Areas' or 'Tribal Areas' as referred to in article 244 of the Constitution, it may, by order in writing, direct such person to remove himself beyond the limits of such area, by such route and within such time as may be specified in the order, and not to return to that area from which he was directed to remove himself for such period, not exceeding two years, as may be specified in the order.

(2) The Special Court shall, along with the order under sub-section (1), communicate to the person directed under that sub-section the grounds on which such order has been made.

(3) The Special Court may revoke or modify the order made under sub-section (1), for the reasons to be recorded in writing, on the representation made by the person against whom such order has been made or by any other person on his behalf within thirty days from the date of the order.

SYNOPSIS

1. Analogous Law
2. History
3. The Kinds
4. Section 10 – A Preventive Measure
5. Intention in Likely Committed Offence
6. The Offences Covered Under Section 10
7. Territorial Application of Section 10
8. Basic Requirements Under section 10 for Order
9. Opportunity of Being Heard
10. Whether an Enquiry Necessary
11. "Satisfaction" of Special Court
12. A Complaint
13. Responsibility for acts of others
14. "Order in Writing"
15. "Order" may be challenged

1. Analogous Law

As law and order is a State subject, hence most of the States in the country have made legislations providing for 'externment' of undesirable professional law breakers with purpose of eliminating disturbing public peace and tranquility of an affected town or area.

There are several enactments, such as UP Control of Goondas Act (8 of 1971), section 3 of which provides for externment of habitual criminals from a district for a limited period so ordered. Similar provisions are also contained under section 3 of Rajasthan Control of Goondas Act, 1975. In Maharashtra such externed persons are called "Tadi-Par".

Difference between such State legislation and provision of section 10 of the Act of 1989, is that under state laws the order of externment is being passed by the Executive Officers, while an order under section 10 of the Act must be passed by Special Court, and as such becomes a judicial order.

2. History

Banishment, which means: condemn to exile, drive out, eject, evict, ex-communicate, expel, expatriate, rusticate or outlaw etc., was a favorite punishment among primitive old and ancient nations. Among Romans and Greeks it was a punishment and the sentence was sanctioned by law, but on some occasions the exile was self-imposed due to political unpopularity or popular displeasure of masses. Some great leaders of Athens were sentenced to externment. In the later years Napolean Bonapart was externed from France. It is purely a form of criminal punishment though, but it had also a place in the civil law.

In ancient India, specially Manu, had prescribed this form of punishment frequently as an approved form, its duration varying with the heinousness of the crime and its rigour with caste of the delinquent. (Please see Manu Smiriti).

Generally punishment in any form has been dealt under branch of adjective law, but now it has become inseparable with the substantive law of crime. In the early days 'banishment' was originally used as punishment by the Penal Code, but subsequently it was abandoned. The law Commissioners deprecated its infliction on an "Indian native" as an "unwarranted severity", thus the legislature had abolished on the ground of it being a duplicate punishment, for the Government of India were by Regulation III of 1818 had given ample powers to depart unwanted persons for reasons of State. Later the sentence of "transportation" was retained as one form of punishment.

3. The Kinds

The bigger form of 'externments' is the punishment of 'transportation' and the 'banishment', which were the methods for expression the punitive reaction to crime. Banishment is closely related to transportation as a part of penalty for certain types of crime. In one of the earliest criminal prosecutions in America, the penalty was inflicted in 1637 AD saying the defendant was to be "banished from out of our jurisdiction as being a woman not fit for our society".[1]

Banishment is of various kinds and which is nearest to process of the "externment" is called in America as "floating", where a person accused of or

1. An Almanc of Liberty,—William O. Douglas (New York: Double day 1954), p 135.

convicted for a crime is ordered to leave the country, city, town or State within specified number of hours. The person so ordered is called "floater".[1]

The other forms being *relegatio, deportatio, exilium* and *lata fuga*. The *relegatio* form of punishment envisage banishment to an island for life, but it is different from 'deportation', which envisages exiled person to be sent to an island which is more pleasant and does not carry with it penalty of confiscation of property. Sometimes *exilium* is being resorted to, but it is either *relegation* or *lata fuga*, which is a residence restricted to a particular town etc., or a prohibition from entering it, and that is nearer to the concept of 'externment', we are interested in.

4. Section 10 – A Preventive Measure

Section 10 stipulates a situation or circumstances where "a person is likely to commit an offence under Chapter II of this Act", which clearly shows that application of the provision does not need actual committal of the offences prescribed under Chapter II of the Act of 1989. Therefore the order of Special Court for 'externment' is not a punishment or sentence, but it is used as a preventive measure, so that the externed person may be deprived of committing an offence of 'atrocity' etc.

The term "crime prevention" has been attributed to the twin methods of *reformation* and an effort to forestall first crimes which is being called *prevention*. It was assumed by Criminologists earlier that severe punishment reforms those who are punished and deters or 'prevents' others from committing first crimes.

Jeremy Bentham, in the first part of the eighteenth century, had given outlines of "indirect methods", other than punishment, which might be used to prevent crime. He suggested such measures as taking away the physical power of injury, diverting the course of dangerous desires, decreasing susceptibility (which means externment to same extent) etc., etc. ("Principles of Penal Law"). Later on scores of other persons have also suggested various such measures but those are out of scope for the present discussion.

Generally the power of 'externment' has been given to Executive Officers, because the basic object is related with law and order situations. But section 10 gives such powers to a Judicial officer presiding a Special Court, who are not supposed to involve themselves generally in controlling law and order situation. This is a general view, but after all the Act of 1989 is a 'Special Act'.

However, section 10 of the Act of 1989 contemplates a stage when the whole project to commit an offence under Chapter II of the Act still lies in the realm of design and intention without any attempt having yet been made to give the committal of intended offence a concrete shape.

"Complaint or a police report".—In a similar situation a Division Bench observed that the power under the Act (Goonda Act, 1970) "can be initiated against a person simply on the basis of a report by the S.H.O. that he is likely to create disturbance." The power can be exercised "on the basis of objective consideration of evidence and material and not on the basis of a report made by S.H.O. which itself is based upon his subjective satisfaction."[2]

1. Principles of Criminology, Sutherland and D.R. Gressey (Sixth Edn.) p 270.
2. *Irfan Khan* v. *State*, 2001 (42) ACC 183 (All) (DB).

Another Division Bench of same Court observed that the police authorities has to exercise powers in sending reports for recommending externment rationally, fairly and without prejudice. Use of such provisions against any citizen should and must be adhered to in most compelling circumstances.[1]

It is presumed that it would be burden on the complainant or the police to prove through solid evidence that the alleged person is likely to commit an offence under Chapter II of the Act. Perhaps it is not easy and that is why no case has been reported.

5. Intention in Likely Committed Offence

The stage contemplated by section 10 of the Act of 1989 is when no offence actually has been committed under the Act. But an allegation made against any person may have been on the basis of simple assumption, presumption or the whim of those complaining the matter to the Special Court. In such circumstances no action can be taken against the alleged person.

If an offender makes some overt act for committing an offence under the Act, he may be roped in for attempting to commit the offence in question, which itself is an offence under the Act. But section 10 stipulates a stage which is before such a stage of overt act because the word "likely" cannot be construed otherwise.

Thus the words "likely to commit" signifies a stage where the alleged person, against whom an 'externment' has been sought, has only intention of committing such an offence. But presence of intention is a difficult matter to decide and prove, because it is always in the mind of such person. The factum of presence of intention with which a crime is likely to be committed can be deduced from the facts and the circumstances of each case.

Where no offence has actually been committed, and the purpose of the alleged person has to be judged, it may be by reference to the conduct and the surrounding circumstances of each case. The proper test to infer an intention for committing a 'likely offence', could be gathered from the conduct and the circumstances sought to be relied upon and that must be consistent with the one and only one for ascertaining presence of intention.

In case facts and the circumstances are susceptible to two interpretations or inferences, one in favour of prosecution and the other in support of alleged person, then the rule which applies to the circumstantial evidence should prevail, meaning thereby—giving benefit of doubt to the alleged person.

6. The Offences Covered Under section 10

The person against whom an order of 'externment' has been sought, must be shown, "likely to commit an offence under Chapter II of this Act". Incidentally Chapter II consist of seven sections, out of which only two sections—3 and 4 prescribe different kinds of offences as has been referred under section 10. The likelihood of any or many of these offences should be mentioned in the complaint to the Special Court, praying for or seeking "externment" of such a person.

---

1. *Kamlendra Pratap Singh* v. *State of Uttar Pradesh*, 2004 Cr LJ 976 (All) (DB): 2003 All LJ 2940: 2003 (3) All Cri R 2947.

It is important to note that section 4 is applicable to "public" servants only and there they have been made liable to be sentenced if they were found wilfully neglecting the duties required by the provisions of the Act to be performed. Though, no such case has been reported yet, but it would be interesting to see, in case such a case comes up before higher Judiciary, what kind of observations comes, when a "public servant" is being proceeded for 'externment' before a Special Court under section 10, because of the fact that section 4, lying in the Chapter II of the Act.

7. Territorial Application of Section 10

Territorial application of Section 10 of the Act of 1989 is limited to only "in any area included in 'Scheduled Areas' or 'Tribal Areas' as referred to in Article 244". Article 244 has been placed in 'Part X' the Chapter being "The Scheduled And Tribal Areas". However Article 244 says:

> "*244. Administration of Scheduled Areas and Tribal Areas.*—(1) The provisions of the Fifth Schedule shall apply to the administration and control of the Scheduled Areas and Scheduled Tribes in any State other than the State of Assam.
>
> (2) The provisions of Sixth Schedule shall apply to the administration of the Tribal Areas in the State of Assam."

Article 244 of the Indian Constitution does not indicate about the territorial limits of "Scheduled Areas" or "Tribal Areas", but refer to "Fifth Schedule" for administration of such 'Areas'. However, "Part c" of the "Fifth Schedule" defines "Scheduled Areas" in paragraph 6 as:

> "*6. Scheduled Area.*—(1) In this Constitution, the expression "Scheduled Areas" means such areas as the President may by order declare to be Scheduled Areas.
>
> (2) The President may at any time by order—
>
> (a) direct that the whole or any specified part of a Scheduled Area shall cease to be Scheduled Area or a part of such an area;
>
> (b) alter, but only by way of rectification of boundaries, any Scheduled Area;
>
> (c) on any alteration of the boundaries of a State or on the admission into the Union or the establishment of a new State, declare any territory not previously included in any State to be, or to form part of, Scheduled Area, and any such order may contain such incidental and consequential provisions as appear to the President to be necessary and proper, but save as aforesaid, the order made under sub-paragraph (1) of this paragraph shall not be varied by any subsequent order."

Paragraph 5 of "Part B" of the "Fifth Schedule" empowers Governor of any State to direct by public notification any particular Act of Parliament not to apply or apply to a Scheduled Area.

All the above discussions clearly shows that each and every inch of Indian territory has not been covered under the expression – the "Scheduled Areas" or the "Tribal Areas", because they are being changed from time-to-time through notifications.

Therefore, unless a proposed 'likely offence' is not being anticipated within a "Scheduled Area" or a "Tribal Area", no proceedings under section 10 of the Act may be drawn.

8. Basic Requirements Under section 10 for Order

Before an order is passed under section 10 of the Act of 1989 for "externment", following requirements must be fulfilled:

(i) the proceeding may be initiated only on "a complaint or a police report";

(ii) the anticipated "likely" offence must belong to Chapter II of the Act;

(iii) the anticipated "likely" offence must be apprehended in "Scheduled Area" or "Tribal Area" and not beyond;

(iv) the order, if passed, to be in writing, and mention the route, time (not exceeding two years) and period of removal;

(v) the order shall mention "the grounds on which such order has been made" [sub-sec (2)].

9. Opportunity of Being Heard

One aspect which has not been mentioned in the body of section 10, is the opportunity, to the person likely to be removed, of being heard, before such order was passed. Besides being a Constitutional guarantee, rules of Natural Justice and Equity require that such person be given an opportunity of being heard before any order is passed against him. Other such laws where there is a provision of externment (such as Uttar Pradesh Control of Goonda Act provide that the authority intending to make an order for removal of a person from a specified area, must be given a show-cause notice to the person concerned, and in that way he gets an opportunity of being heard.

Though, sub-section (3) of section 10 gives powers to Special Court to either "revoke" altogether or "modify" already passed order on the "representation" made by or on behalf of the affected person, it does not justify the order; if passed *ex-parte* or without giving any opportunity of being heard. The law of the land requires that reasonable opportunity of being heard must be given before the order was passed.

10. Whether an Enquiry Necessary

When the Special Court receives a complaint or a police report that a person is likely to commit an offence under Chapter II of the Act, it cannot be conceived that it would pass an order of 'externment' instantly, because a Special Court is a Court functioning under the Rules of Justice, Equity and Good conscience, besides bearing the responsibility to ensure Constitutional guarantees of a citizen. Even a previous conviction of the person may not be taken into account. However, a previous conviction under the Act of 1989 may become relevant in the proceedings under this section, if there is strong evidence against the said person to conceive the likelihood of committal of a crime, but a previous conviction by itself does not prove that the accused is leading a life of crime or hate.

To initiate proceedings under this section the complaint or the police report must disclose a likelihood on the part of the person to commit an offence under Chapter II of the Act. Mere existence of enmity between the groups or factions cannot become a ground to proceed under this section. In order to bring a case within the provisions of section 10, it must be established that committal of an offence under Chapter II of the Act is imminent. Proceedings cannot be initiated against a person on the ground that a dispute is persisting for quite some time, nor there can be a proceeding on the hypothesis that, if certain things happen, the person concerned may commit an offence under the Act.

The informations in the complaint or the police report, as the case may be, must be clear and definite directly connecting the person concerned. A mere *omnibus* statement that some persons have committed various acts is not sufficient ground to proceed. There must be some specific information about the conduct from which a reasonable and immediate inference can be drawn that the person is likely to commit an offence. Therefore it is always safe to judge the credibility of informations in the complaint or the police report.

11. "Satisfaction" of Special Court

Section 10 of the Act of 1989 stipulates that the Special Court shall be satisfied by the information given in the "complaint or a police report" that a "person is likely to commit an offence under Chapter II of this Act". An order of externment could only be passed if the Court is satisfied. Not only that, the Court must be satisfied at the time of drawing up the proceedings that there is existing a likelihood of committal of an offence under the Act. If quite a time has lapsed after the complaint or the police report was made, it would not be safe to proceed in the matter on the strength of such old information, because the 'likelihood' of committing the anticipated offence, or its cause, might have vanished in the meanwhile.

12. A Complaint

A complaint, if moved by a private person (could be a member of SC or ST), the Court may call a report from police as regards the likelihood of committal of an offence under the Act. It is so because the complainant could not be considered from a disinterested person. Even though, in exceptional cases, if the complaint comes from a disinterested person or source, it may be safe to call a report from the police concerned. In any case the Court must be satisfied before proceeding. A statement during a trial may allege that certain person is likely to commit an offence, but such statement cannot become basis for proceeding under section 10.

The word "satisfaction" also includes application of mind by the Court.

13. Responsibility for Acts of Others

In the general law, specially the criminal law, it is the individual who is responsible for his own acts. The only case where a person can be punished for the wrongs done by others is where he tries or actually instigates the offence. Barring that, no person can be foisted with any penalty for acts done by others on whom he has no control or for whose conduct he cannot be held responsible.[1]

---

1. *Reddy Channabasavanna Gouda* v. *State of Mysore*, 1973 Cr LJ 1049: 1972 Mad LJ (Cri) 813.

But on the other hand, proved acts of abetment or instigation by persons which are calculated to cause and commit an offence can hardly be taken out of the category of wrong-doers. But simultaneously it may be said that it would be illegal to take recognizance from one person in order to prevent another from committing an offence under this Act. A non-resident person or for that matter a wealthy or influential member of a party cannot be brought under the ambit of section 10, just because he holds such position, unless there is reasonable substance.

The object of section 10 is to guard against the committal of actual offences against members of Scheduled Castes or the Scheduled Tribes.

14. "Order in Writing"

Unless an order under section 10 has been passed, no proceedings can be drawn under sections 11, 12 and 13. Section 11(2) provides that the order of externment shall be communicated, along with the "grounds on which such order has been made", to the person concerned.

It is important to mention here that an order under section 10 of the Act of 1989 does not amount to be 'conviction', in the sense it is taken generally under the criminal jurisprudence.

15. 'Order' May be Challenged

Section 10(3) of the Act contemplates that the aggrieved person may get the order revoked or modified and that would be done by the Court on the representation made by the person against whom such order was passed. Therefore making of the order of externment is not final, but it may take quite some time, till the final decision on the representation takes place, and in the meantime such person has to leave the said "area", unless the Court itself stays the execution of the order. On the other hand an order passed under section 10 seems to be final and not interlocutory. There is no reported case where such question was raised and decided.

Special Court is a Court of Sessions and its orders can only be challenged before a High Court having jurisdiction. In other remedy a petition under Section 482 C.P.C. or a writ may be filed.

11. Procedure on failure of person to remove himself from area and enter thereon after removal.—(1) If a person to whom a direction has been issued under section 10 to remove himself from any area—

(a) fails to remove himself as directed; or

(b) having so removed himself enters such area within the period specified in the order,

otherwise than with the permission in writing of the Special Court under sub-section (2), the Special Court may cause him to be arrested and removed in police custody to such place outside such area as the Special Court may specify.

(2) The Special Court may, by order in writing, permit any person in respect of whom an order under section 10 has been made, to return to the area from which he was directed to remove himself for such temporary period and subject to such conditions as may be specified in such order and may require him to execute a bond with or without surety for the due observation of the conditions imposed.

(3) The Special Court may at any time revoke any such permission.

(4) Any person who, with such permission, returns to the area from which he was directed to remove himself, shall observe the conditions imposed, and at the expiry of the temporary period for which he was permitted to return, or on the revocation of such permission before the expiry of such temporary period, shall remove himself outside such area and shall not return thereto within the unexpired portion specified under section 10 without a fresh permission.

(5) If a person fails to observe any of the conditions imposed or to remove himself accordingly or having so removed himself enters or returns to such area without fresh permission, the Special Court may cause him to be arrested and removed in police custody to such place outside such area as the Special Court may specify.

SYNOPSIS

1. Analogous Law
2. Scope
3. Warrant of Arrest and Removal
4. Return of Externed Person
5. "Execute a Bond"

1. Analogous Law

Section 11 of the Act of 1989 is a combination of provisions of and contents in various sections of Uttar Pradesh Control of Goondas Act, 1970 or the Rajasthan Control of Goondas Act, 1975. Section 11(1)(a) and (b) the Control of Goondas Act says:

Section 11 (1)..............

(a) has failed to remove himself from the district or part as directed by the order; or

(b) has re-entered the area, from which he was ordered to remove himself during the period of operation of that order, — etc. etc.

Sections 4 and 5 of Goonda Act correspond to sub-sections (2) and (3) of the section 11 of the Act of 1989, etc.

Some of the provisions of Chapter VIII of Code of Criminal Procedure are also applicable.

2. Scope

If a person has been directed to remove himself beyond the limits of ordered area under Section 10 of the Act of 1989, he has to comply with the order instantly. His presence in the "area" becomes illegal. That is why Section 10 (3) provides that the 'representation' may be made "by any other person on his behalf".

Now Section 11 stipulates two situations *viz.*—

(i) he did not remove himself from the area; and

(ii) where in the first instance he removed himself from the area, but re-entered the prohibited area again, without permission of Special Court. Such person defying the order in either of the ways is liable to be arrested and removed from the area in custody. In the first instance the externed person is free to go anywhere he likes beyond the prohibited area. But, in the two described eventualities, it is not clear whether the Special Court would order the police to take such person in custody "to such place outside such area as the Special Court may specify". It is not clear from the body of the section, whether the person has to remain at "such place" where the Court had ordered him to be taken under custody, or he would be free to go anywhere else, he likes.

Sub-section 11(2) empowers the Special Court to permit such externed person to return for a temporary period to the area in question with certain conditions and also may require him to execute a bond with or without surety to observe the conditions. Sub-section (3) also empowers the Court to revoke such temporary permission.

In sub-section (5) also same procedure has been provided to remove such person under custody to "such place" as has been described under sub-section (1) of section 11 of the Act.

Section 11 of the Act is a combination of empowerment of powers to Special Court as well as the procedures adopted in condition of breach of order passed under section 10.

3. Warrant of Arrest and Removal

The arrest and removal of the person contravening the orders under section 10 may be issued by the Special Court. Chapter VI of Code of Criminal Procedure provides for issuance of warrants of different kinds. In case the Special Court receives information that the externed person has not removed himself from the area or has re-entered the area, the Court is required to issue a warrant for his arrest and removal to "such place outside area" as ordered.

Sections 70 to 81 of the Cr PC speculate various kinds of situations under which and to whom Courts may issue warrants. Any technical defect in the issued warrant may render the arrest and removal of the person illegal. There are decisions of various Courts where resisting an illegal warrant was declared to be no offence.

Where such arrested person was to be taken to "such a place" which is outside the area, it may be a place beyond jurisdiction of the Court. Sections 78 to 81 of Cr PC prescribe procedures to be adopted where the execution of warrants have to take place beyond the jurisdiction of the Court issuing the warrant. Sections 74 and 75 of the Cr PC limit the process of execution. The executing police officers have to take such person to the ordered place, which might be beyond jurisdiction of local limits of the Court to release him out of their custody. Secondly it is not clear, whether the police officer executing the warrant would simply let the person go when they reach "such place" so ordered, or for the release they have to take some orders from the Court, exercising jurisdiction in that area.

4. Return of Externed Person

A person who has been ordered to be externed under section 10 of the Act may return to the area when: (i) the ordered period has expired (till or within two years); (ii) the order has been revoked under section 10(3); (iii) when the externed person has been permitted to enter the area by the Special Court, subject to conditions specified in such order and also requiring him to execute a bond with or without 'surety' for the object of observations of the conditions.

The Special Court has been empowered to revoke the temporary permission at any time after such permission was accorded by the Court, before or after such person enters or visiting the prohibited area. Section 11(3) gives such powers to Special Court.

It seems reasonable that the period spent in the area with due permission by the Court, would be counted in the total period of externment.

However, during total period of externment, the person may enter the area with due permission many times, each time taking "fresh permission" as has provided under section 11(5).

5. "Execute a Bond"

Section 11(2) of the Act of 1989 makes it discretionary for the Special Court to require such person, to whom temporary permission has been given to enter the prohibited area, to "execute a bond with or without surety for the due observation of the conditions imposed." It may be safely presumed that power of imposing conditions for according temporary permission is also discretionary. However, if same conditions have been imposed, then ordering to execute a bond, with or without "surety", would become imminent.

In any case, the whole procedure of according temporary permission, imposing conditions and execution of bond etc. completely depend on the satisfaction of the Court. But the bond and surety may be demanded only when the conditions have been imposed.

The basic rule which governs the affairs of the accused and the surety, is that the surety is considered by law to have control over the person for whom a person is standing as a surety. But it is a controversial issue, involving scores of factors, dealt with in various decisions of High Courts. A series of conflicting judgments are available on the point which is out of scope for the present discussion.

Section 11 of the Act of 1989 does not stipulate that the person who has been ordered to be externed from a certain area should be ordered to "execute a bond" *ab initio.* In case the externed person does not seek any permission to enter the prohibited area from the Court, during entire ordered period, such person is not required to execute a bond etc., as has been provided under various provisions of Chapter VIII of Cr PC In general law and practice a person cannot be called upon to provide sureties without ordering him for giving his own bond.

For fixing amounts of surety and the bond, Courts are at consensus that having regard to the circumstances of the case and the means of the party charged, the amount of bond and the surety should be fixed. The character, reputation or the gravity of the likely offence cannot become criterion for fixing the amount for the bond. In short amount should not be excessive or prohibitive.

The bond executed for temporary entry into the prohibited area for due observation of imposed conditions is akin to bond required for keeping peace and good behavior under Chapter VIII of Cr PC. Therefore if questions of breach of conditions and on the basis of which forfeiture of bond arise, it may be decided in the light of opinions devulged by different Courts on the given point. However, the procedure adopted for forfeiture of the bond or the surety may be according to the provisions of section 446 of the Code of Criminal Procedure, 1973.

12. Taking measurements and photographs, etc., of persons against whom order under section 10 is made.—(1) Every person against whom an order has been made under section 10 shall, if so required by the Special Court, allow his measurements and photographs to be taken by a police officer.

(2) If any person referred to in sub-section (1), when required to allow his measurements or photographs to be taken, resists or refuses to allow the taking of such measurements or photographs, it shall be lawful to use all necessary means to secure the taking thereof.

(3) Resistance to or refusal to allow the taking of measurements or photographs under sub-section (2) shall be deemed to be an offence under section 186 of the Indian Penal Code (45 of 1860).

(4) Where an order under section 10 is revoked, all measurements and photographs (including negatives) taken under sub-section (2) shall be destroyed or made over to the person against whom such order is made.

SYNOPSIS

1. Analogous Law

Not exactly the same, but almost similar provisions could be found under section 53A of Cr PC whereas far as use of force by police against the person on refusal, has been allowed. Section 27 of the infamous POTA, 2002 (now repealed) contained similar provisions, providing powers to force a detenue to give samples from his body and other personal information as required.

2. Status of External Person

A person against whom an order has already been passed under section 10 cannot be considered as a convict, nor he is an accused. Criminal jurisprudence only envisage a person to be an accused only when some offence has already been committed but not when it is alleged that there is likelihood that such person would commit some offence. But when no offence has been committed under Chapter II of the Act of 1989, nobody can be alleged to have committed the offence and become, what is called, an accused.

Section 10 stipulates that when "a person is likely to commit an offence", he can be proceeded against under the provision. If all goes well for the prosecution and the Special Court is satisfied, the order of externment would only be passed when it is expected that there is some likelihood of committal of an offence under Chapter II of the Act was probable. Thus the person against whom, an order has been made under section cannot be termed as an accused.

Secondly, the person against whom an order has been passed under section 10 remains a free citizen, unless he contravenes the conditions and get himself arrested under section 11 of the Act. The said person is simply free to go anywhere out of the area so ordered and may travel or reside at any place of his choice, except the prohibited area indicated by the order of the Court.

3. Scope

Sub-section (1).—The person against whom an order of externment has been passed under section 10 of Act is neither a convict nor an accused, as explained above. The order under section 10 is being passed on the basis of a hypothesis that such person is "likely to commit an offence". As soon as a formal accusation has been made against any person for already committed offence, such person becomes entitled to the protections provided under Articles 20 and 21 of the Constitution.

But we have a different situation here, as the alleged person here is neither a convict nor an accused. Therefore a cogent inference may be that constitutional protections are not available to him.

The Special Court, "if so required" by it may allow the measurement and photographs to be taken by a police officer.

Sub-section (2).—If a person who has been directed to give measurement and photograph after an order under section 10, refuses or resists, to follow the direction "it shall be lawful to use all necessary means to secure the taking thereof". The "use of all necessary means" would naturally imply use of force and compulsion against a person who is not a convict, nor an accused.

There cannot be two opinions about the fact that "measurements and photographs etc." are very personal informations of a person. The word "etc." (etcetra) may include finger-prints or blood samples.

Sub-section (3) of section 12 makes such "resistance or refusal" to be an offence under section 186 of IPC.

3.1 Compelling a person to give Personal Informations

A person against whom an order has been passed on a hypothetical ground that he was "likely to commit an offence", finds himself between the devil and the deep sea, as, if he resists or refuses to give his measurements etc., etc., he has to surrender his rights provided by the Constitution, or be prosecuted under section 186 IPC.

The Courts in India feel very repugnant even if an accused is being compelled to give samples of his personal informations, what to say of a free and common citizen. The opinions of courts are alike in Civil Cases. Supreme Court has held in *Kundu's* case that no person can be compelled to give samples from his body.[1] Following *Kundu's* case Andhra Pradesh High Court followed suit.[2] These decisions have come on the ground that every citizen of India has a Constitutional fundamental right which has to be protected against his privacy. At the maximum some "adverse inference" may be drawn against the accused (here such person is not even an accused), if he refuses to give samples of his body by way of measurements, photographs and other things (which word "etc." include).[3]

3.2 Right of Privacy

Fourth Amendment of US Constitution has very clearly put the Right of Privacy as "an essential ingredient of personal liberty", but the said right has not been expressly included under the Fundamental Rights of the India. Despite that Courts in India have adopted the dictum of US Constitution in a series of cases.[4]

Personal liberty is antithesis to personal restraint, coercion and specifically speaking – compulsion. The term "coercion", in words of Subba Rao J.: "the modern age cannot be construed in a narrow sense. In an uncivilized society where there are no inhibitions, only physical restraint may detract from personal liberty, but as a civilization advances the psychological restraints are more effective than physical ones. ..... So also creation of conditions which necessarily endanger inhibitions and fear complexes can be described as physical restraint."[5] Subba Rao J. further observed: "a right of an individual to be free

1. *Goutam Kundu* v. *State of West Bengal*, 1993 Cr LJ 3232 (SC): AIR 1993 SC 2295: 1993 AIR SCW 2325; *Selvi* v. *State of Karnataka*, AIR 2010 SC 1974.
2. *Syed Mohd Ghouse* v. *Noorunnisa*, 2001 Cr LJ 2028: II (2001) DMC 454: 2001 (2) Hindu LR 645.
3. For further details, please see present author's book "DNA Evidence and its Admissibility" Pub. Modern Law House, Alld. And also "Law of Lic Detectors – Narcoanalysis, Polygraphy, Brainmapping, Brain Finger printing", pub. Universal Law Publishing Co., New Delhi.
4. *Kharak Singh* v. *State of Uttar Pradesh.*, AIR 1963 SC 1295: (1963) 2 Cr LJ 329 (340) (SC): (1964) 1 SCR 332, followed by *Maneka Gandhi* v. *Union of India*, AIR 1978 SC 597: (1978) 1 SCC 248: (1978) 2 SCR 621. etc.
5. *Kharak Singh (Supra), also see R. Rajagopal* alias *R.R. Gopal* v. *State of Tamil Nadu.*, AIR 1995 SC 264: 1994 AIR SCW 4420: JT 1994 (6) SC 514.

from restrictions or encroachments on his person, whether those restrictions or encroachments are directly imposed or indirectly brought about by calculated measures", and so defined the ingredients of personal liberty.

The expression used in Article 21 of the Constitution has been given very wide meaning and qualified by the word "personal" indicating thereby that it is only confined to the liberty of the person.[1]

The reason that no cases under section 12(2) have been reported, seem to that the Judicial minds functioning as Special Courts under the Act have not been influenced by the legislation to put the person under restraint and compel them to put themselves in restraint against personal liberty.

Though, sub-section (4) of section 12 directs that when an order under section 10 of the Act is revoked, all the measurements and photographs, including negatives shall be destroyed or be handed over to such person, but such kinds of directions are seldom followed strictly on its own. *Secondly,* sub-section (4) directs to destroy only two kinds of informations, *i.e.,* measurements and the photographs, while the 'heading' of the section 12 uses an additional word etcetra, under which many other things, such as finger prints or blood samples may be taken. There is no direction what would happen to such other personal informations, if taken.

Thirdly it is not clear, whether provisions of sub-section (4) would also be applicable where the said order was not "revoked" and such person returns to the "area" after expiry of ordered period.

4. Resistance or Refusal, a Declared Offence

Section 12(3) of the Act declare it as an offence if the externed person, against whom an order has been passed not only under section 10 and subsequently an order for giving his measurements and photographs etc. to a police officer, refuses or resists to do so. Such resistance or refusal may render such person to be prosecuted under section 186 of IPC.

Section 186 of IPC says:

> "*186. Obstructing public servant in discharge of public functions.*—Whoever voluntarily obstructs any public servant in the discharge of his public functions, shall be punished with imprisonment of either description for a term which may extend to three months, or with fine which may extend to five hundred rupees, or with both."

Mere threat or abusive words would not constitute "obstruction" under this section. To constitute an offence under section 186 IPC threats of violence should be made in such a way that it would prevent public servant from carrying out his functions.[2] A mere offer of passive resistance, opposition or evasion not accompanied by criminal force would not constitute obstruction.

Points to prove a charge under section 186 IPC are: (i) that the accused obstructed; (ii) that he did so voluntarily; (iii) the person obstructed was a

1. For further details, please see present author's book "Law of Lie Detectors"; Published-Universal Law Publishing Co. p 221 et sq.
2. *Abhiram Sahai* v. *State,* (1960) 2 Ori JD 401.

public servant; (iv) the obstruction was made in the official function; and (v) the obstruction was made with use of criminal force and not passively.

13. Penalty for non-compliance of order under section 10.—Any person contravening an order of the Special Court made under section 10 shall be publishable with imprisonment for a term which may extend to one year and with fine.

SYNOPSIS

1. Analogous Law

Section 10 of Uttar Pradesh Control of Goondas Act, 1970, as well as the section marked by the same number of the Rajasthan Control of Goondas Act, 1975, contain same provisions as has been incorporated under Section 13 of the Act of 1989.

2. Scope

Sections 11 and 12 of the Act contain many kinds of contraventions which may originate from an order passed by Special Court under section 10 of the Act of 1989. Such contraventions may be described as:

(i) if ordered person fails to remove himself within specified time and route,
(ii) having so removed, re-enters the prohibited area without permission of Special Court concerned,
(iii) fails to observe any conditions imposed, including surety bond, in the order of permission for temporary period,
(iv) after the temporary allowed period expires enters or return again to such area then the contraventions under section 12 have been made which are punishable under section 186 of IPC.

But if the person is found to be contravening any other condition or orders under sections 11 and 12 of the Act which are not covered under the ambit of those provisions then the said person is not liable for facing the penalty contemplated by section 13, because the provisions itself limit its application to the contraventions of "an order of the Special Court made under section 10".

Section 13 provides a punishment which may extend to one year and with fine. The sentence cannot be passed of only imprisonment, but also some fine has to be imposed, limits of which have not been specific, thus the amount of imposed fine may go to any extent, but should be reasonable.

3. Bail

Section 18 of Act bars application of section 438 Cr PC, but when a person is brought before or surrenders before the Special Judge, he is entitled to bail. It is so that Schedule II of the Code of Criminal Procedure, 1973 makes any offence of other laws other than that of IPC, bailable which are punishable with imprisonment for less than 3 years.

Chapter IV

SPECIAL COURT

14. Special Court.—For the purpose of providing for speedy trial, the State Government shall, with the concurrence of the Chief Justice of the High Court, by notification in the Official Gazette, specify for each district a Court of Session to be a Special Court to try the offences under this Act.

SYNOPSIS

1. Analogous Law

There is a long list of enactments which provide trial or cognizance of offences under those respective enactments to be tried and proceeded against by Special Courts. Some of such enactments have been mentioned below—

(i) Section 6 of the Criminal Law Amendment Act, 1952 empowers the Government to appoint Special Judges by notification in the official Gazette, (the Act was repealed by Central Act, 49 of 1988).

(ii) Section 4 of the Disturbed Area (Special Courts) Act, 1976 empowers the Government to constitute Special Courts.

(iii) Prevention of Corruption Act, 1988 provides for appointment of Special Judges to try offences created therein.

(iv) Repealed Prevention of Terrorism Acts had provisions to constitute Special Courts in Chapter IV of the Act.

(v) Essential Commodity Act as well as Docoity Affected Area Act also bear provisions for constitution of the Special Courts to try offences prescribed under respective enactment.

(vi) Narcotic Drugs & Psychotropic Substances Act, 1985 stipulates that the offences under the Act are triable by Special Court.

The point of distinction between contents of Section 14 of the Act and that of other legislations, is that the body of section 14 of the Act is short, precise and devoid of details as is not the case with other enactments which are found including some provision of constitution of Special Courts. This precision has, though, created some difficulties in the early days to interpret the jurisdiction of Special Courts constituted under the Act of 1989. It took quite some time to settle down the issue of taking cognizance by the Special Courts so constituted under section 14.

2. "Special Courts"

Word "Court" neither has been defined under the Act of 1989, nor it has been defined in the Code of Criminal Procedure. But section 3 of Indian Evidence Act defines Court as: "Court" includes all Judges and Magistrates and all persons, except arbitrators, legally authorized to take evidence. But this definition was held not to be exhaustive. It was observed if a Court has no power either to pass a final order or entertain applications, it cannot be said that it has got authority.[1]

The Court of Session is specified to conduct a trial and no other Court can conduct the trial of offences under the Act. Hence a particular Court of Session, even after being specified as Special Court, would continue to be essentially a Court of Session.

As is evident from the "Statement of Objects and Reasons", the Act of 1989 was enacted as a Special Legislation to check and deter crimes against members of Scheduled Castes and the Scheduled Tribes. A new term "atrocity" was defined for which different kinds of offences were created and special punishments were prescribed. For the speedier trial for those offences constitution of Special Courts became imminent, which have been given exclusive jurisdiction to try the cases arising out of 'atrocities' on such members.

The State Government has been empowered to specify in each district already existing Court of Session to be Special Court for trying offences committed under the Act. The State Government has not been given blatant powers for specifying such Session Courts in each district on its own, but such specification has to be done with concurrence with the Chief Justice of High Court of that State.

3. Object of Constituting Special Courts

The object of establishing the Special Court to try the offences under the Scheduled Castes and the Scheduled Tribes (Prevention of Atrocities) Act, 1989,

1. *Shamsul Haque* v. *Abdul Mabood*, 1987 A Cr R 533 (534); also see, *In re Ramnath Bholgothra (of Jammu)*, 1953 Cr LJ 1737: 1953 Mad WN 488: AIR 1953 Mad 953.

is for the purpose of providing speedy trial. It is for that purpose that the State Government, with the concurrence of the Chief Justice of the High Court, is required, by notification in the Official Gazette, to specify for each district a Court of Session to be a Special Court to try the offences under the present Act.[1]

4. Jurisdiction of Special Court to try Cases under the Act

"The word "trial" is not defined in the Code. 'Trial' according to Stroud's Dictionary means "the conclusion, by a competent tribunal, of question in issue in legal proceedings, whether Civil or Criminal" (Stroud's Judicial Dictionary 3rd Edn. Vol. 4, p. 3092), and according to Wharton's Law Lexicon it means, "the hearing of a cause, civil or criminal, before a judge who has jurisdiction over it, according to the law of the land "(Wharton's Law Lexicon, 14th Edn., p. 1011). The words "tried" and "trial" appear to have no fixed or universal meaning. They are words which must be considered with regard to the particular context in which they are used and with regard to the scheme and purpose of the provisions under considerations.[2]

As seen from the contents of section 14 of the Act of 1989, a Court of Session in each district is specified as a Special Court to try the offences under the Act. Question may arise as to what is meant by "to try" the offence under the Act. Is it also concerned with only actual trial or proceedings prior to it? Whether the word "try" has reference only to the stage of trial? It was held that word "try" in section 14 of the Act is not used in a limited sense. It was observed by Division Bench that, "with due regard to the scheme of the Act particularly in the context of section 14, it is abundantly clear that the word 'try' in section 14 of the Act is not employed in any restricted sense, the same would include every inquiry and trial on the taking cognizance of the offence by the Special Judge."[3]

Though overruled on another point, a Bench of Andhra Pradesh High Court has observed that the word "try" in the phrase "offences for which he is tried" in section 321 of the Code is wide enough to cover inquiry and trial and that the word was not used in a limited sense. It was also observed that Special Courts constituted under section 14 is a Court of original jurisdiction.[4] In the early days, when the Act of 1989 had come into force, two kinds of judicial opinions: one saying that the Special Court under section 14 is a Court of original jurisdiction, and capable of taking direct cognizance, without any committal proceedings, while the other opinion emphasised for a committal proceedings. Both the opinions have been discussed in the following paragraphs. (Finally decided by S.C. in Gangula Ashok's case in the year 2000).

No Jurisdiction Cases

A complaint was brought alleging offences under section 323/506 IPC and under sections 3 of the Act of 1989. It was found that the complainant had not

1. *Hanuman Singh* v. *Union of India*, 1997 Cr LJ 1054 (Raj) (1058): 1997 Cri LR (Raj) RAI 102.
2. *State of Bihar* v. *Ram Naresh Pandey*, AIR 1957 SC 389: 1957 Cr LJ 567 (SC) at 572-73: 1957 SCC 282.
3. *In Re: Director General of Prosecution*, 1993 Cr LJ 760 (Ker) (DB) (767): 1992 (2) Ker LJ 731.
4. *S. Damodar Reddy* v. *State of Andhra Pradesh*, 1996 Cr LJ 3271 (AP): 1996 (2) Andh LD 859: 1996 (4) Cur Cri R 126: 1996 Tab LJ 8: 1996 MPLJ 141 (FB): 1996 AIHC 3527 (AP).

established even by *prima facie* evidence the allegations with regard to the commission of offence under the Act. Therefore it was held that Special Court had no jurisdiction to try the case.[1]

Accused were charge-sheeted for using the atrocious words under section 3 of the Act. The charge-sheet was filed before the Special Court. It was observed that the Special procedure for taking cognizance of offences under the Act has not been laid down, thus the Special Court has to take cognizance of offence only on committal. It was further observed that the complaint was misconceived and filed belatedly after eight months. In these circumstances the Special Court was held to have taken cognizance wrongly and illegally and without jurisdiction, consequently the proceedings were quashed.[2]

A Court of Session, not notified in the Official Gazette under section 14, cannot take cognizance of or try the cases under the Act.[3]

5. Cognizance by Special Courts

In the early days when the Act of 1989 came into force, there was difference of opinion between different High Courts as to whether Special Courts constituted under section 14 of the Act can or cannot take cognizance of offences committed under the Act either directly or only when the case was handed over to it by a committing Magistrate under section 193 or PC. But ultimately Supreme Court intervened and finally decided the matter, holding that Special Courts constituted under section 14 of the Act cannot take direct cognizance of offences under the Act unless the case has been committed to it under section 193 Cr PC.

Many Division and Full Benches were constituted by different High Courts to finally decide the matter but contradictory decisions were delivered, given different reasons and analogies on the matter that whether Special Courts constituted under section 14 of the Act have original criminal jurisdiction to take cognizance of offences under the Act and function as Magistrates as well as Session Courts, or whether they may take cognizance of the offence only when they are committed to it under section 193 Cr PC by Magistrates. Some decisions have been given below.

Decisions Supporting Direct Cognizance

A Division Bench of Kerala High Court citing the decision of Supreme Court in *A.R. Antulay's* case[4] (Full Bench of five Judges) considering the position of Special Court, had observed that Special Court is neither a Court of Session nor a Court of Magistrate. The power of a Special Court under the Act of 1989 is conferred on a Court of Session which is one in hierarchy of Courts envisaged by the Code. The Special Court under the Act is thus to take cognizance of the offences under the Act and proceed with the trial as provided under the Code. But "Section 193 of the Code will not apply to the Special Court".[5]

1. *Raj Mal* v. *Rattan Singh*, 1998 Cr LJ 3922: 1998 (3) All Cri LR 73: 1998 (2) Rec Cri R 791.
2. *Jyoti Arora* v. *State of Haryana*, 1998 Cr LJ 2662 (P&H): 1997 (24) Cri LT 672: 1998 (4) Crimes 643: (1998) 2 All Cr LR 73.
3. (1996) 10 Ori 463 (464): (1996) 81 Cut LJ 746.
4. *A.R. Antulay* v. *Ramdas Sriniwas Nayak*, AIR 1984 SC 718: 1984 Cr LJ 647 (SC): (1984) 2 SCC 500.
5. *In Re: Director-General of Prosecution*, 1993 Cr LJ 760 (Ker) (DB) (763): 1992 (2) Ker LJ 731.

Punjab and Haryana High Court was also of the view that a Special Court while exercising powers to take cognizance, need not be proceeded by committal proceedings by Magistrate.[1]

In yet another case it was observed that: "it is clearly provided in section 14 of the Act that the Special Courts are constituted for the purpose of speedy disposal of cases. Therefore the intention of the Parliament is very clear that the Legislature in its wisdom does not want any delay in disposal of the cases and therefore the intention of the *Legislature is very clear that they want to dispense with the committal procedure.*" The learned Bench had given scores of other reasons (para 14) on the ground of which Special Court can directly take cognizance without the case being committed to it by Magistrate.[2]

6. No Cognizance without Committal – Present Law

A perusal of section 14 shows that a Court of Session in each of the districts is to be specified as a Special Court for trial of cases under the Act. The provision means that the offences under the Act has to be tried by a Court of Sessions, but this provision or others in the Act do not provide for taking cognizance by Special Courts. Section 190 Cr PC provides taking of cognizance by a Magistrate. Additionally section 193 Cr PC provides that Court of Session shall take cognizance of any offence as a Court of original Jurisdiction unless the case has been committed to it by a Court of Magistrate. Special Court under section 14 of the Act is essentially a Court of Session. Therefore it cannot take direct cognizance due to bar of section 193 Cr PC. Additionally it not being a Court of Magistrate, it cannot take cognizance under section 190 Cr PC.[3]

It was argued before a Full Bench that "the Act is a fraud on the Constitution, as no provision enabling the Special Court under the Act to take cognizance of the offence under section 3(1) of the Act has been made to ensure speedy trial ......". The argument was rejected saying it "being bereft of any sound logic". It was further held that committal proceedings under section 193 Cr PC is necessary before the Special Court takes cognizance (paras 66 and 68).[4]

Same finding was given by a Division Bench of Madhya Pradesh High Court.[5]

A Division Bench of Andhra Pradesh High Court has held that Special Court under the Act of 1989 cannot take direct cognizance of offence, but it can deal with the matter only after it was committed to it by Magistrate. Special Court

1. *Raj Mal* v. *Rattan Singh,* 1998 Cr LJ 3922: 1998 (3) All Cri LR 73: 1998 (2) Rec Cri R 791; *S. Damodar Reddy* v. *State of Andhra Pradesh,* 1996 Cr LJ 3271 (AP): 1996 (2) Andh LD 859: 1996 (4) Cur Cri R 126: 1996 Tab LJ 8: 1996 MPLJ 141 (FB): 1996 AI HC 3527 (AP).
2. *Dara Singh* alias *Darbara Singh* v. *Tej Kaur,* 2000 Cr LJ 3145 (P&H) (3149): 2000 (2) CCC 134: ILR (2000) 2 P&H 211; 1995 Cr LJ 2376 (MP) (DB); 1995 AIHC 4542 (FB); (1996) 1 All Cr LR 870 (Ker); 1996 MPLJ 141 (FB); 1998 Mad LJ (Cr) 5—etc.
3. *Pappu Singh* v. *State of Uttar Pradesh,* 1995 Cr LJ 2803 (All) (2804): 1995 All LJ 1037: 1994 (3) Cur CriR 1947.
4. *Mata Sewak Upadhyay* v. *State of Uttar Pradesh,* 1995 JIC 1168 (All) (FB): 1996 (1) East Cr C 97 (All) (FB).
5. *Meera Bai* v. *Bhujbal Singh,* 1995 Cr LJ 2376 (MP) (DB): 1995 (3) Rec Cri R 125; *Jyoti Arora* v. *State of Haryana,* 1998 Cr LJ 2662 (P&H): 1997 (24) Cri LT 672: 1998 (4) Crimes 643: (1998) 2 All Cr LR 73.

cannot act as Court of original jurisdiction contrary to prohibitions contained in section 193 Cr PC. It was further observed that, neither the object of the Act nor the overriding provision contained in section 20 of the Act read with Section 4(2) of Cr PC can be called in aid to hold that the Special Court acts as a Court of original jurisdiction. It cannot be said that the Act excludes the committal proceedings.[1]

Finally overruling Full Bench ruling of Kerala High Court *Hareendran* v. *Sarada,* 1995 AIHC 4542), Supreme Court had held that the particular Court of Session, even after being specified as a Special Court would continue to be essentially a Court of Session and designation of it as a Special Court would not denude it of its character or even powers as a Session Court. Section 193 Cr PC has to be understood in this backdrop. The section imposes an interdict on all Courts of Session against taking cognizance of any offence as a Court of original jurisdiction. It can take cognizance only when the case has been committed to it by a Magistrate. Therefore a charge-sheet or a complaint cannot be straightaway filed before such Special Court.[2]

Andhra Pradesh High Court had later on even declared entire proceedings and judgment of the Special Court as null and void, the Special Court had taken direct cognizance of the tried offence, proceeded with the case and delivered a judgment without the case being committed to it by the concerned Magistrate under section 193 Cr PC.[3]

7. Dual Jurisdiction of Special Court

It was argued before a Full Bench that a Special Court constituted under section 14 of the Act can try only the offences as described under the Act, and if an accused commits offences other than the offences of atrocities in the same transaction, then multiple trials cannot be avoided. It was further pointed out that unlike other enactments where provision for constituting a Special Court has been provided, specific provisions have been given, so that the Special Courts constituted thereof would be empowered to try allied offences as well. But under section 14 or for that matter, nowhere in the Act any such provision has been given, therefore the Act being vague and unworkable, is liable to be struck down. The rule given under section 218(1) of Cr PC is that for every distinct offence there shall be separate charge and every such charge shall be tried separately, but this rule has been diluted through section 220(1) Cr PC which provides that if the acts in the same transaction are so connected together, the same may be charged and tried together in one trial. Section 223(d) Cr PC permits that the persons accused of different offences committed in the same transaction may be charged and tried together. The

1. *Referring Officer, rep. by State* v. *Accused,* 1999 Cr LJ 4173 (All) (DB): 1999 (3) Andh LD 54: 1999 (3) Andh LT 533; *In Re: Referring Officer, Addl. District and Sessions Judge, Srikakulam,* 2000 Cr LJ 3422 (AP) (DB): 2000 (1) Andh LT (Cri) 388; *Nana s/o Narayan Shinde* v. *State of Maharashtra,* 2000 Cr LJ 4778 (Bom): 2001 (1) Ker LJ 365: 2001 (3) Mah LR 381; *Rattiram* v. *State of Madhya Pradesh,* 2012 Cr LJ 1769 (SC).
2. *Gangula Ashok* v. *State of Andhra Pradesh,* 2000 Cr LJ 819 (SC): AIR 2000 SC 740: 2000 AIR SCW 279.
3. *Degumati Hazarath Reddy* v. *State of Andhra Pradesh,* 2001 Cr LJ 4495 (AP): 2002 (3) All Cri LR 406: 2001 (2) Andh LT (Cri) 249.

Special Court designated under section 14 will proceed to take cognizance only when the case has been committed to it by a Magistrate under section 193 Cr PC. There are sufficient guidelines for joinder of charges and for joint trial, and the case once committed, the Special Court may proceed with the trial. Therefore section 14 does not suffer any ambiguity or unworkability.[1]

The Special Court under section 14 of the Act is essentially a Court of Session and that character cannot be denuded.

8. "Specify"

The word "specify" used in the language of section 14 of the Act of 1984 pre-supposes the existence of a Court of Session. It does not take away the powers and jurisdiction of such Court of Session which it had under various provisions of the Code. Various provisions of the Act of 1989 and contained under section 14 are to be so construed as may promote their smooth and harmonious functioning without causing any damage to each other. A Court of an Additional Sessions Judge, exercising the powers as such in a Sessions Division may be 'specified' to be a Special Court for purposes of section 14 of Act of 1989, without in any manner adversely affecting its jurisdiction and powers as a Court of Sessions. Its specification as a Special Court for purposes of Section 14 of the Act would be in addition to and not in derogation of its powers and jurisdiction as a Judge/ Additional Sessions Judge.[2]

The charge-sheet disclosing offences punishable under section 3 of the Act as well as offence under section 376 IPC, the accused can be tried for both offences in the same proceedings and trial. For that no order of commitment by Magistrate for offence under Section 376 IPC is called for.[3] (Later overruled)

Supreme Court had also taken up the matter. It was observed that Sessions Court 'specified' as Special Court under section 14 of the Act of 1989 may also try an offence under section 376 IPC and it would be not without jurisdiction. The Sessions Court continues to be Sessions Court even after being 'specified' as Special Court, therefore may try other offences alongwith the offences under the Act.[4]

Besides it is policy of law that multiplicity of trials and proceedings must be avoided by all means. But in cases where it is found at the earlier stage that no offence under the Act of 1989 is made out, then the case may either be transferred to a Court having jurisdiction or the case may be tried by the same Court as a Court of Sessions and not as a Special Court, provided the remaining offences are exclusively triable by the Court of Session.

It was observed by the Apex Court while dealing with the provisions for the trial of different offences by a Special Court as: "the effort on the part of the legislation is not to have two sets of trial, one under general law and the other

---

1. *Mata Sewak Upadhyay* v. *State of Uttar Pradesh*, 1995 JIC 1168 (All) (FB): 1996 (1) East Cr C 97 (All) (FB) at 1196-97.
2. *Hanuman Singh* v. *Union of India*, 1997 Cr LJ 1054 (Raj) at 1058: 1997 Cri LR (Raj) RAI 102.
3. *In Re: Director-General of Prosecution*, 1993 Cr LJ 760 (Ker) (DB): 1992 (2) Ker LJ 731; *Pratap Chandra Barik* v. *State of Orissa*, 1999 Cr LJ 562 (Ori): 1998 (15) OCR 98.
4. *State of Himachal Pradesh* v. *Gita Ram*, 2000 Cr LJ 4039 (SC): AIR 2000 SC 2940: 2000 AIR SCW 3181.

under Special statute and availability of such a power cannot but be ascribed to be in time with the jurisprudence of the Country."[1]

9. Where Basic Jurisdiction Fails

Though, it has not been provided anywhere in the Act of 1989 (as explained above) that the Special Court may try other offences committed under, say Indian Penal Code, but various findings of Courts justify that such other offences may be tried together, alongwith the offences under the Act of 1989, by the Special Court and the jurisdiction of Special Court would remain unaffected, even if the trial suffered from misjoinder of charges.[2]

But on the other hand, Supreme Court observed that, no doubt the provision (under TADA of 1987) empowers the Special Court to try any offence punishable by any other statute alongwith the offence punishable under the Act, if former is connected with the latter. (a similar situation). That however, does not mean that even when the 'specified' Court comes to the conclusion that there exists no sufficient ground for framing a charge against the accused under section 3 of the Act, *it must* proceed to try the accused for the commission of offences under other statutes. That would tantamount to "usurping jurisdiction". If the Special Court is of the opinion "that the offence is not triable by it (as a Special Court), it shall, notwithstanding that it has no jurisdiction to try such offence, transfer the case for the trial of such offence to any Court having jurisdiction under the Code."[3]

A peculiar situation was found in a very old case. A person was charged under two distinct offences, under sections 161 and 420 IPC, wherein the Special Judge was empowered to try the charge under section 161, IPC only. It was found that the accused was not a public servant, hence he could not be tried under section 161, IPC, while the charge under section 420, IPC remained intact for which the Special Judge observed that it was not open to him to try that charge. The jurisdiction of the Special Judge depended on the fact that the accused must be a public servant. The moment the Special Court found this fact, his jurisdiction to try him ceased and as a consequence his further jurisdiction to try other offence jointly, also ceased. It was held that as the Special Court lacked jurisdiction, the mere circumstance that the charge was framed and evidence recorded cannot create any jurisdiction in it.[4]

The stage for determining the point of jurisdiction is when police submits the charge-sheet after completion of investigation and not during pendency of investigation. But during pendency of investigation, the High Court may exercise its powers to decide the matter, whether a *prima face* case under the Act is made out.[5]

---

1. *Sarwan Singh* v. *State of Punjab,* 2002 (45) ACC 1169 (SC): AIR 2002 SC 3652: 2003 Cr LJ 21.
2. *Prem Shankar Misra* v. *State,* 1957 Cr LJ 108 (All): 1956 All WR (HC) 724: 1956 All LJ 910.
3. *Niranjan Singh Karam Singh Punjabi* v. *Jitendra Bhimraj Bijja,* 1990 Cr LJ 1869 (SC): AIR 1990 SC 1962: (1990) 4 SCC 76; also see *Anil Sanjeev Hegde* v. *State of Maharashra,* 1992 Supp (2) SCC 230: 1992 SCC (Cri) 676.
4. *State* v. *Gulabram,* AIR 1957 MP 224: 1957 Cr LJ 1410: 1957 Jab LJ 449.
5. *Rafiq Abid Patel* v. *Inspector of Police, Kashimira Police Station, Thane,* 1992 Cr LJ 394 (SC) (396-97): 1992 (2) Bom CR 400: 1992 Mah LJ 1612.

When the accused were charge-sheeted for docoity and offences under Special Act but the Special Court discharged the accused for the offences under the Special Act, it was held that Special Court had no jurisdiction to try other offences as Special Court.[1]

10. Ordering Separate Trial

In case separate trials are held for different kinds of offences, it is bound to cause harassment not only to the prosecution but also to the accused, in as much as the prosecution has to examine many witnesses again in second trial. The power has to be exercised to prevent abuse of the process of law. The commission of an offence and the conspiracy to commit the offence should be tried together.[2]

11. Powers as to Investigation

When a normal investigation by police is in progress, the competent Court is kept informed, but when the investigating agency wants to add any section of the Special Act, it was observed that ordinary criminal Courts cannot be allowed to order for such addition, as power of ordinary Criminal Court is confined only to remand of the accused person. Such an order for addition of section of a Special Act can only be passed by a Special Court and not by ordinary criminal Courts.[3]

The Special Court is a creation of a statute and as such enjoys a unique position, which is not known to Code of Criminal Procedure. The Special Court has been clothed with the special authority to take cognizance of offences under the Special Act as well as other laws. It is legal for a Special Court to order for a re-investigation of the case.[4]

But the Special Court has no power to directly entertain an application under section 156(3) and order the police for lodging FIR or investigation, on the ground that the Special Court does not have any original jurisdiction and have to conduct such cases which have been committed to it by a Magistrate.

12. Vagueness as to Multiple Jurisdictions

There is a vagueness and confusion prevailing about deciding final destination of cases where commission of offences reveal, apart from offences under the Act of 1989, other such offences which have to be tried by other Special Courts constituted under other Special Acts. Quite a long time has elapsed since the Act of 1989 was passed and came into force but no measure has yet been taken to remedy the anomaly.

There are plenty of other Special Acts in force in the country, and when the police files a charge-sheet revealing offences exclusively declared by a Special legislation, the case is being sent to the Special Court for trial to which it belongs. In some of the Special legislations provisions are incorporated to deal with the situation at hand, but the Scheduled Castes and the Scheduled Tribes (Prevention of Atrocities) Act,1989 is silent on this point.

1. *Santosh Dattaram More* v. *State of Maharashtra,* 1992 Cr LJ 3409 (Bom) (3414): 1992 (3) Bom CR 292: 1993 (2) Crimes 252.
2. *State of Bihar* v. *Simranjit Singh Mann,* 1987 Cr LJ 999: 1987 East Cri C 337: 1987 Pat LJR 417.
3. *Sampatmall Jain* v. *State of Assam,* 1992 Cr LJ 919: 1992 (1) Cur Cri R 1055: 1991 (2) Gau LR 445.
4. *Parasnath Pande* v. *State,* (1962) 2 Cr LJ 326: AIR 1962 Bom 205: 64 Bom LR 188.

For instance: when a charge-sheet is submitted by police which reveal some offences under the Act of 1989 and some offences are also alleged under the provisions of the Uttar Pradesh Dacoity Affected Areas Act, 1983, or The Maharashtra Control of Organised Crime Act, 1999, etc. etc., under which there are Special Courts constituted and are functioning. An inevitable question would arise – which of the two Special Courts is empowered to take cognizance and try the case?

The offences under the Act of 1989 (SC/ST Act) are exclusively Triable by Special Court constituted under section 14 of the Act and no other Court is empowered to try such offences. In a similar manner the offences committed under the provisions of the said, or for that matter other Special enactments are also triable by Special Courts constituted under the provisions of those respective enactments.

It is not possible, nor practicable that the same case, having same facts and same set of witnesses, be sent for trial to both the Special Courts for charging and trying the same accused separately according to the offences arising out of respective Special legislations. Such multiplicity of trials cannot be allowed by any means and it is against policy of law.

In most of States in the country, including Uttar Pradesh cases are being tried by either of the Special Courts and nobody knows solution of the problem.

But one thing is certain that the Special Court trying offences under a Special legislation for which that particular Special Court was constituted is legal, but trying charges under another Special legislation is out of jurisdiction and illegal. This is so because an ordinary Session Court is not empowered to try a Special case unless the Judge presiding the Court has been notified in the Official Gazette by State Government, and a Special Court constituted under some other Special legislation remains an ordinary Session Court for purposes of the Act of 1989.

One more point could be added here. If an accused who has been charge-sheeted under the Act of 1989, is under 18 years of age, he had to be tried before the Juvenile Court/Board, who cannot assume powers of a Special Court under section 14 of the Act of 1989; neither such Special Court can try a Juvenile accused.

Such anomalies could only be remedied through an amendment in the Act.

13. "Notification in the Official Gazette"

Section 14 of the Act of 1989 mandates and stipulates that the State Government shall with the concurrence of the Chief Justice of the High Court, by notification in the Official Gazette, specify for each district a Court of Session to be a Special Court to try the offences under the Act of 1989.

It is evident that in every district of each State there are many Additional Session Courts, besides the Session Judge (normally called District Judge), and section 14 requires the State Government to "specify" a Court of Session to be a Special Court.

What is clear from the wording of section 14 of the Act of 1989 is that only a particular Session Court has to be specified in the notification, irrespective of the fact who is presiding over the specified Session Court. Presiding Judges may come and go but the 'specified' Session Court would remain a Special Court, competent to try the cases under the Act.

Under other Special legislations, where there is a provision for constituting a Special Court, it has additionally been clarified by a particular special procedure for appointment of Judges for respective Special Courts. Therefore it becomes incumbent on the notifying Government to issue a notification in the name of particular person, who is functioning as a Session or Additional Session Judge.

Sessions Judge includes Additional Session Judge under the Code and he gets all the power and jurisdiction of the Session Judge to try the offence enumerated under the Code. Therefore the notification notifying the Additional Session Judge as Special Court is in a conformity with the requirements of section 14 of the Act of 1989.[1]

Accordingly, when a Session Judge or Additional Session Judge, as the case may be, has to be 'appointed' as a Special Judge to try offences under those respective Special legislations, they are being notified by name of the particular Judge and not *Ex-Officio*. When an Act empowers the Government to issue notification for appointment of a certain Judge to act within the parameters of that particular Act, the Judge must be holding the post of Session or Additional Session Judge. If the notification has been issued for a particular person, such notification could not be deemed to be issued for another person who takes charge after the transfer of such notified person.[2]

No such condition can be attached to the presiding Judges, functioning as a Special Court, because Section 14 of the Act provides that one of the many Session Courts in every district shall be 'specified' as a Special Court under this section. The dictionary meaning of the word "specify" is: "name or mention expressly, identify or list" (also see meaning of 'specify' given previously).

One more point has to be clarified here. The law stipulates that the natural consequence of a notification would presume that formal announcement of legally relevant fact has been published in the Official Gazette. Notification is a formal declaration and publication of an order which must be in accordance with the requirements of the statute. Administrative instructions cannot be a substitute for a notification. The other most essential requirement is publication of the notification in the Official Gazette.[3]

14. Action by a Court, Not 'Notified'

A Session Judge was appointed as Special Judge [Under section 9(8) TADA, 1987 (or POTA under section 23)] by notification. In absence of the Special Judge, another Additional Session Judge passed the impugned order, who was not the notified Judge. The order was related to release of seized money. It was observed that the Additional Session Judge was empowered under section 10 of Cr PC

1. (1997) 1 East Cr C 328: (1997) 2 BL JR 1026 (Pat).
2. *S.K. Sinha* v. *Asstt. Collector of Customs*, 1985 Cr LJ 1137; *Gururaja Joshi* v. *Chief Secretary to Govt. of Karnataka*, 1997 Cr LJ 2830: 1997 (2) Kant LJ 616.
3. *Subhash Ramkumar Bind @ Vakil* v. *State of Maharashtra*, 2003 Cr LJ 443 (SC): AIR 2003 SC 269: 2002 AIR SCW 4732.

for the urgent disposal of applications. When State went to High Court, it was held that Session Judge was not empowered to confer powers to any Additional Session Judge, not being notified Judge, under section 10(3) of the Code because he can only confer powers under section 9, (8) TADA. Hence the order of the Additional Session Judge found to be out of jurisdiction.[1]

There is a total departure from different classes of Criminal Courts enumerated in section 6 of the Code of Criminal Procedure and new hierarchy of Courts (Special Courts) is sought to be established. The Act is a Special Act and creates new classes of offences. The legal fiction contained therein must be restricted to the procedure to be followed.[2]

15. Amended Notification

When a notification issued for specifying a Special Court was found to be defective and was amended subsequently by another notification on a subsequent date, then the original notification as amended takes effect only from the date when the amended notification was issued and not retrospectively. Presentation of a charge-sheet after the amended notification was issued would become valid presentation.[3]

16. Conviction by a Court, Not Notified Under section 14

As has been pointed out under note (12) above, it has become a common practice to send cases under the Act of 1989, to other Special Courts, when two sets of offences are alleged to have been committed by the accused and both are being triable by the Special Courts. In such an eventuality another Special Court (constituted under some other Special legislation), if convicts the accused under offences prescribed by SC/ST Act of 1989, a natural question would arise as to the legality of such conviction.

If a Special Judge who convicts the accused persons, was not notified and appointed as Special Judge (or for that matter not presiding over the notified Court under section 14 of the Act of 1989), the conviction was set aside and instead of ordering a re-trial by a competent Court, let the accused go on the ground of long pendency of the matter.[4]

17. Applicable Procedure

Section 14 read with section 20 of the Act of 1989 leaves no room of doubt that offences under the Act are exclusively triable by the Sessions Court nominated as Special Court under section 14 of the Act. section 20 gives the provisions of the Act of 1989 overriding effect. However, what procedure shall be followed for the investigation and what procedure shall be adopted during the trial, the Act makes no special provisions, except that under section 9, the State Government may by notification confer powers of the police officer on any official of State Government and on such conferment the provisions of the Criminal Procedure

1. *State* v. *P. Narzary*, (1991) 1 Crimes 709.
2. *Usmanbhai Dawoodbhai Memon* v. *State of Gujarat*, 1988 Cr LJ 938 (SC): AIR 1988 SC 922: (1988) 2 SCC 271.
3. *Public Prosecutor* v. *Shaik Sheriff*, (1965) 2 Cr LJ 585 (AP) (DB): AIR 1965 AP 372: (1965) 2 Andh WR 44.
4. *K.M. Kumaraswamy* v. *State*, 2002 Cr LJ 3195: 2002 AIR Kant HCR 1844: 2002 (5) Kant LJ 337.

Code shall apply. (Rule 7 deals with designated power of investigation to a Dy. SP). Thus it is clear that in absence of special provisions made in the special statute making certain acts or omissions as special offences in respect thereof, the same procedure for investigation, inquiry and trial have to be followed as are provided under the Code.

18. The Private Complaint

There are two sets of decisions on the question, whether the Special Court constituted and specified under section 14 is empowered to directly entertain a private complaint or not. The set of judgments which supported the view that Special Court is competent to entertain a complaint filed by a private person, was based on their assumption (which was later found to be erroneous and illegal) that Special Court under section 14 is a Court of original jurisdiction and there was no need to be proceeded by committal of the case by a Magistrate under section 193 Cr PC. Operation of section 193 was presumed to be non-applicable, it was held that private complaints were maintainable before the Special Court. (previous law).

18.1 Previous Decisions

It was observed that power to "try" offences under the Act of 1989, includes power of enquiry which precedes actual trial, as the Special Court is a Court of original jurisdiction. It was left entirely to the discretion of Special Court constituted under section 14 of the Act to consider or not the sworn statements of the complainant, to examine the witnesses on oath under sub-Section (2) of section 202 of the Code. It is not necessary to examine all the witnesses under the Proviso (S 202) is not applicable, because Special Court was considered to have all the powers of a Magistrate.[1] (Now not applicable).

18.2 Present Position

As early as in 1995 a Division Bench held that complaint against offence under the Act cannot be filed in the Court of Special Judge as it has no original jurisdiction and it can only take cognizance of offences only on committal.[2]

However, the matter was finally decided by Supreme Court in *Gangula Ashok* v. *State of Andhra Pradesh*[3], holding that Special Court specified under section 14 of the Act cannot take direct cognizance of offences under the Act, unless the case has been committed to it by a Magistrate under section 193 Cr PC.

It has now become inevitable that the private complaint has to be filed before the Magistrate concerned and after recording statements under sections 200 and 202, Cr PC, the Magistrate may commit the case to Special Court, if it finds it fit to do so. It is also noteworthy that in such case the complainant has to produce all the evidence as required by section 202 Cr PC in cases where the offences

---

1. *S. Damodar Reddy* v. *State of Andhra Pradesh,* 1996 Cr LJ 3271 (AP): 1996 (2) Andh LD 859: 1996 (4) Cur Cri R 126: 1996 Tab LJ 8: 1996 MPLJ 141 (FB): 1996 AIHC 3527 (AP); *Raj Mal* v. *Rattan Singh*, 1998 Cr LJ 3922: 1998 (3) All Cri LR 73: 1998 (2) Rec Cri R 791; *Ramesh Chandra Das* v. *Kasinath Jena*, 2000 Cr LJ 4006 (4008): 2000 (19) OCR 101: 2000 (2) Ori LR 162.
2. *Meera Bai* v. *Bhujbal Singh*, 1995 Cr LJ 2376 (MP) (DB): 1995 (3) Rec Cri R 125.
3. 2000 Cr LJ 819 (SC): AIR 2000 SC 740: 2000 AIR SCW 279.

are triable by Court of Sessions. The Magistrate may reject the complaint under section 303, Cr PC and decline taking any further action in the matter if it finds no credence in the produced evidence under section 202, Cr PC.[1]

19. Power to Grant Bail By Session Court

Under the Act of 1989 the Special Courts are established by the State Government only to ensure speedy trial of cases arising under the said Act. Trial is distinct from inquiry. In that event, there could not be any impediment for a Sessions Court which is not a Special Court and not specially designated under the Act to dispose of a bail petition filed under the provisions of the Code of Criminal Procedure. The bail application filed before the Principal Session Judge, and made over in the usual course to the Additional Sessions Judge for disposal in accordance with law which can be disposed of by Additional Sessions Judge.[2]

The provisions of Code of Criminal Procedure shall apply in matters of moving and disposing applications for bail to the accused charged under the provision of the Act of 1989, because the said Act besides making provisions of Special Courts the purpose is to conduct a speedy trial. No special procedure has been provided by the Act, except barring provision of anticipatory bail, otherwise provided under section 438 Cr PC, application of which has been restricted by section 18 of the Act of 1989.[3]

In normal practice the application for bail is moved in the Court of District and Session Judge, but normally that Court transfers all such applications to the Special Courts specified under section 14 of the Act. But it is no hard and fast rule.

20. Constitutionality of section 14

Section 14 of the Act was challenged on the ground that it violates Articles 14 and 21 of the Constitution as some of the offences which are provided as such in the IPC, but which have been made more heinous, though originally triable by Magistrates only. Other persons committing similar offences will be subjected to different procedure. This classification of offences have been challenged before the Full Bench. But the Bench observed that so long as fair and impartial trial is guaranteed, Articles 14 and 21 would not come into play only because different procedure having been introduced for a particular class of people. Equality prescribed by the Constitution would not be violated if the statute operates equally on all persons who are included in the group and the classification is not arbitrary. The classification is reasonable and has a rational nexus with objects sought to be achieved. Therefore the creation of Special Courts under section 14 is not violative of Article 14. Once it is held that creation of Special Courts is not violative of Article 14, section 14 of the Act cannot be said to be violative of Article 21.[4]

15. Special Public Prosecutor.—For every Special Court, the State Government shall, by notification in the Official Gazette, specify a

1. *Saroj Kumar Ray* v. *Santilata Mallick*, 2004 Cr LJ 5088 (Supp): 2003 (4) Crimes 151: 2003 (96) Cut LT 234.
2. *State* v. *Mahalingu*, 2001 Cr LJ 237 (Kant) (238): ILR 2000 Kant 4499: 2001 (2) Kant LJ 427.
3. (1996) 2 Guj LH 30: (1997) 1 Guj LR 127.
4. *Mata Sewak Upadhyay* v. *State of Uttar Pradesh*, 1995 JIC 1168 (All) (FB): 1996 (1) East Cr C 97 (All) (FB) (1184-85).

Public Prosecutor or appoint an advocate who has been in practice as an advocate for not less than seven years, as a Special Public Prosecutor for the purpose of conducting cases in that court.

SYNOPSIS

1. Analogous Law
2. Scope
3. Appointment of Special Public Prosecutor
4. Procedure for Appointment and Supervision
5. Appointment under Rule 4(5)
6. Notification of Appointment of Special Public Prosecutors
7. Qualifications and "Regular Cadre"
8. Panels of Names
9. Renewal of Term
10. Prosecutors not Part of Investigating Agencies
11. Office of Prosecutor – Independent
12. Basic Functions and Duties of Prosecutor
13. Power of Withdrawal of Cases
14. Importance of Office of Special Public Prosecutor

1. Analogous Law

(i) Section 2(u) of Code of Criminal Procedure 1973, defines a "Public Prosecutor" as: Section 2(4) "Public Prosecutor" means any person appointed under Section 24, and includes any person acting under the directions of a Public Prosecutor;

Section 24 Cr PC contains 9 sub-sections contemplating various kinds of Public Prosecutions, assigned with various functions. It may be added here that States of Bihar, Haryana, Madhya Pradesh, Rajasthan and Uttar Pradesh have made State amendments to this long list of varied provisions.

Section 25 Cr PC deals with "Assistant Public Prosecutors" and Section 25A was inserted accordingly for creating "Directorate of Prosecution".

(ii) Section 13 of TADA, 1987 and Section 28 of erstwhile POTA (now repealed) had similar provisions for appointment of Special Public Prosecutors to conduct cases on behalf of prosecution in Special Courts constituted by those Special legislations. etc., etc.

2. Scope

Section 14 of the Act of 1989 contemplates that State Government shall 'specify' a Court of Session to be a Special Court in each district of the State to try the offences under the Act, and section 15 mandates to 'specify' a "Public Prosecutor" or "appoint an advocate", having provided qualifications, as 'Special Public Prosecutor' in each district. Thus making the two catogaries available for appointment as 'Special Public Prosecutor; It is within the choice of State Government concerned to 'specify' any of the 'Public prosecutors' who have been functioning in "regular Cadre of Prosecuting Officers" [section 24(6) *Explanation* (a)]. The word "specify" has been used in the body of section 15 of the Act and has been so used because State Government has been given powers to pick a suitable person among the "regular Cadre of Prosecuting Officers" and 'specify' him to function as 'Special Public Prosecutor' under Section 15 of the Act of 1989. Such a person is already on the pay-roll of the Government.

But other views also exist. One faction forward arguments that persons belonging to "regular Cadre of Prosecuting Officers" are not advocates within the meaning of Advocates Act, which bar any other kind of employment by advocates, and such member of "regular Cadre of Prosecuting Officers" are Government employees and are on a regular payroll, hence they cannot either be called as advocates or even authorised to appear before Courts of law. They are simply Government servants.

Secondly, section 15 empowers the State Government to "appoint" an advocate who has been in practice as an advocate for not less than seven years, as a Special Public Prosecutor for conducting cases under the Act before the Special Court. However, no length of service of "regular Cadre of Prosecutors" have been made a condition for 'specification', as has been mentioned for members of the Bar (7 years). Therefore a member from "regular Cadre of Prosecutors" may be 'specified' as a Special Prosecutor for the purposes of Section 15, even if he has just been appointed in the 'Cadre' and does not has one day's service.

It is for this reason two separate words—"specify" and "appoint" have been used in section 15.

However, the Special Public Prosecutor may be appointed by the State Government, no consultation with any authority is required.[1] It is the absolute discretion of the Government concerned to appoint or specify a Special Public Prosecutor taking into account the nature of cases and the public interest involved.[2]

3. Appointment of Special Public Prosecutor

Appointment of a Special Public Prosecutor under section 15 of the Act is different to some extent to the position of appointment of a Special Public Prosecutor under section 24 of Cr PC section 24(8) authorises a State Government to appoint Special Public Prosecutor and lays down a specific guideline, namely minimum 10 years of practice as an advocate, and such appointment is made for conducting a case.[3]

The word "appoint" used in section 15 has not been defined. Black's Law Dictionary defines the word as, "to designate, choose, select, assign, ordain, prescribe, constitute or nominate.... To assign authority to a particular use, task, position or office."

Even provisions of Code of Criminal Procedure empower the State Government (or Central Government) to appoint Special Public Prosecutor for conducting either a particular case or particular '*class of cases*'. The cases arising out of offences of 'atrocities' on members of Scheduled Castes or the Scheduled Tribes are certainly can be grouped and called 'class of cases'. Thus power under Section 15 of the Act is similar to the provisions of the Code.

---

1. *Shankar Sinha* v. *State of Bihar*, 1995 Cr LJ 3143 (Pat): 1994 (2) BLJR 966: 1994 (1) Pat LJR 516.
2. *Mary Josa* v. *State of Kerala*, 1997 Cr LJ 4678 (Ker): ILR (1997) 3 Ker 740: 1997 (1) Ker LJ 683.
3. *Vijay Valia* v. *State of Maharashtra*, 1986 Cr LJ 2093: 1986 (88) Bom LR 491.

The term is being used where exclusive power and authority is given to one person, office or body to name persons to hold certain offices. It is usually distinguished from the word 'elect'. As such the appointment order passed for appointing a Special Public Prosecutor to function in a Special Court, has all the powers of a Public Prosecutor to conduct cases.[1]

"What is prohibited is only a back door appointment" and not an appointment of normal nature. The District Magistrate requests Sessions Judge to send names for preparing a panel with bio-data of the candidates. The process was challenged in a writ petition on the ground that Additional Metropolitan Magistrate II was requested to suggest the names for the panel, and as such the Magistrate put up a notice, calling for the applications. It was observed that it is not correct to say that the applications were required to be invited only when somebody intended to join the service. Invitation of applications may be necessary for several purposes, including obtaining the bio-data. The procedure adopted was declared valid.[2]

Power and jurisdiction to prepare a panel for appointment of Public Prosecutor has been vested in the District Magistrate in as much as he would have the overall knowledge, competence and comprehension of the needs of the Courts for which the appointments are to be made, and the professional competence of the counsel for such appointment has to be arrived at by him in consultation with the specified Judicial Officers of the Courts concerned. Under section 24(5) Cr PC, no person can be appointed by the State Government as Public Prosecutor for the district, unless his name appears in the panel of names prepared by the District Magistrate. It was held that the person whose name was not included in the panel has no right to be considered for such appointment.[3]

The law prescribes a particular procedure made for appointment of law officers. Appointment of States Counsel at the behest of political leaders has dangerous potentialities. Interest of the State cannot be safe in the hands of persons appointed on the basis of political desires. In the instant case the appointment was made on the recommendations of three MLAs and one Member of Parliament. It was held that such a procedure was not proper.[4]

A new Government appointed a Special Public Prosecutor in place of another who was looking after the case. The Apex Court disapproved, and held that the proper course for the new Government was that the new Government should

1. *R. Balakrishna Pillai* v. *State of Kerala*, 1999 Cr LJ 1286 (Ker) (1291): ILR (1999) 1 Ker 639: 1999 (1) Ker LJ 383.
2. *B. Rajeswar Reddy* v. *K. Narasimhachari*, 2002 Cr LJ 1 (AP) (FB): 2001 (6) Andh LD 679: 2001 (6) Andh LT 104; also see *Harpal Singh Chauhan* v. *State of Uttar Pradesh*, 1993 Cr LJ 3140 (SC): AIR 1993 SC 2436: 1993 AIR SCW 2843; *State of Uttar Pradesh* v. *Uttar Pradesh State Law Officers' Association*, AIR 1994 SC 1654: 1994 AIR SCW 1389: (1994) 2 SCC 204; *Surapaneni Ram Prasad* v. *Government of Andhra Pradesh*, 1999 Cr LJ 2852: 1999 (3) Andh LD 1; 1998 Cr LJ 1653.
3. *Surapaneni Ram Prasad* v. *Government of Andhra Pradesh*, 2000 Cr LJ 354 (AP): 1999 (4) Andh LD 309: 1999 (2) Andh LT (Cri) 109.
4. *Sangram Keshari Pande* v. *State of Orissa*, 2000 Cr LJ 1625 (Ori): 1999 (17) OCR 391; also see 2000 Cr LJ 1123 (All).

have appointed the Special Public Prosecutor after cancelling the appointment of previously appointed Special Public Prosecutor.[1]

Appointment of Special Prosecutor of the person who was counsel of the complainant was found proper, as it did not hinder the fair trial.[2] But if such appointment touches at the fair trial or devoid of some statutory requirement, the appointment should be declared illegal.[3]

Political leaning of the Advocate is not relevant in his appointment as a Special Public Prosecutor. This is not to say that in every case where one of the parties involved is of a particular political persuasion, no Public Prosecutor, who shares the particular persuasion, should be allowed to conduct the prosecution. To accept such a state of affairs as an invariable rule would not only be contrary to sound practice, but would seriously offend the dignity of the Bar.[4]

4. Procedure for Appointment and Supervision

Section 15 of the Act of 1989 has to be read with Rules 4 and 14 of the Scheduled Castes and the Scheduled Tribes (Prevention of Atrocities) Rules, 1995 for completely understanding the process of appointment, responsibilities and supervision etc., of Special Public Prosecutor.

Rule 4 of the Rules of 1995 says:

> Rule "4. *Supervision of Prosecution and Submission of Report.*—(1) The State Government on the recommendation of the District Magistrate shall prepare for each District a panel of such number of eminent Senior Advocates who have been in practice for not less than seven years, at it may deem necessary for conducting cases in the Special Courts. Similarly, in consultation with the Director of Prosecution/in-charge of the prosecution, a panel of such number of Public Prosecutors as it may deem necessary for conducting cases in the Special Court, shall also be specified. Both these panels shall be notified in the Official Gazette of the State and shall remain in force for a period of three years.
>
> (2) The District Magistrate and the Director of Prosecution/in-charge of the prosecution shall review at least twice in a calendar year, in the months of January and July, the performance of Special Public Prosecutors so specified or appointed and submit a report to the State Government.
>
> (3) If the State Government is satisfied or has reason to believe that a Special Public Prosecutor so appointed or specified has not conducted the case to the best of his ability and due case and caution, his name may be, for reasons to be recorded in writing, denotified.
>
> (4) The District Magistrate and the officer-in-charge of the prosecution at the District level, shall review the position of cases registered under the Act and submit a monthly report on or before 20th day of each subsequent month to the Director of Prosecution and the State Government. This report shall

1. *Sheonandan Paswan* v. *State of Bihar*, 1983 Cr LJ 348 (SC): AIR 1983 SC 194: (1983) 1 SCC 438.
2. *Ajay Kumar* v. *State*, 1986 Cr LJ 932: ILR (1985) 2 Del 40: 1986 Raj LR Del 41.
3. *Rajendra Nigam* v. *State*, 1998 Cr LJ 998 (1001-2): I (1998) DMC 140: 1998 (1) Hindu LR 138.
4. *P.G. Narayanankutty* v. *State of Kerala*, 1982 Cr LJ 2085: 1982 Cri LC 597: 1982 Ker LT 605; but also see *Mary Josa* v. *State of Kerala*, 1997 Cr LJ 4678 (Ker): ILR (1997) 3 Ker 740: 1997 (1) Ker LJ 683.

specify the actions taken/proposed to be taken in respect of investigation and prosecution of each case.

(5) Notwithstanding anything contained in sub-rule (1) the District Magistrate or the Sub-Divisional Magistrate may, if deem necessary or if so desired by the victims of atrocity engage an eminent Senior Advocate for conducting cases in the Special Courts on such payment or fee as he may consider appropriate.

(6) Payment of fee to Special Public Prosecutor shall be fixed by the State Government on a scale higher than the other panel advocates in the State."

Rule 14 of Rules of 1995 says:

Rule "14. Specific responsibility of the State Government.—The State Government shall make necessary provisions in its annual budget for providing relief and rehabilitation facilities to the victims of atrocity. It shall review atleast twice in a calendar year, in the month of January and July the performance of the Special Public Prosecutor specified or appointed under section 15 of the Act, various reports received, investigation made and preventive steps taken by the District Magistrate, Sub-Divisional Magistrate and Superintendent of Police, relief and rehabilitation facilities provided to the victims and the reports in respect of lapses on behalf of the Concerned Officers."

Rule 4(1) prescribes almost similar procedure as has been provided under the Code, *viz.* two panels are being prepared in consultation with relevant authorities, and the two panels may be notified in the Official Gazette by the State Government. But in the meanwhile various kinds of legal and technical problems may arise.

The Act of 1989 is a Special Act which was enacted to prevent the commission of offences of atrocities against the members of Scheduled Castes and the Scheduled Tribes, and Special Courts were established in each district under section 14 for purposes of speedy trial. Section 15, whereas provides that for every Special Court, the State Government shall 'specify' a Public Prosecutor as a Special Public Prosecutor for conducting cases in that Court by notification in the Official Gazette. "In the alternative an advocate who has been in practice as an advocate for not less than 7 years may also be appointed as Special Public Prosecutor for the said purpose. For the said purpose, under Rule 4, the State Government, on the recommendation of the District Magistrate has to prepare a panel of eminent senior advocates who have been in practice for not less than 7 years for conducting cases in the Special Courts. Rule 4 also provides for a specification of a panel of Public Prosecutors to be prepared by the State Government in consultation with the Director of Prosecutions. Both the above said panels shall be notified in the Official Gazette of the State and shall remain in force for a period of 3 years."[1]

The Bench further observed that section 20 of the Act of 1989 provides that the provisions of the Act shall override other laws for the time being in force. Thus it

1. *Jonnakuti Mokshanandam* v. *State of Andhra Pradesh,* 2006 Cr LJ 3034 (3037-38): 2006 (2) ALD (Cri) 430: 2006 (4) Andh LT 155.

is clear that so far as the procedure prescribed under the Act and the rules shall govern the appointment of the Special Public Prosecutor. The State Government is the only authority for such appointment and an appointment, though made by promotion following due process of law, cannot be said to be an appointment by State Government following the prescribed procedure under the rules.[1]

5. Appointment under Rule 4(5)

The provisions regarding appointment of Public Prosecutor are contained in section 24 of the Code and those relating to conduct the trial by Public Prosecutor in a Court of Sessions are contained in sections 225 and 301 of the Code. The provisions relating to appointment of Special Public Prosecutor under section 15, or engagement of an 'eminent senior advocate' under Rule 4(5) are to be read as supplemental to the provisions of the Code. It may be mentioned here that appointment of Public Prosecutor or Special Public Prosecutor—whether under section 24 of the Code or section 15 of the Act of 1989—is for "conducting" cases in the Court of Session or Special Court, as the case may be. Likewise, the engagement of eminent senior advocate under Rule 4(5) of the Rules of 1995 is also for "conducting" cases in the Special Court. The Division Bench did not find any justification in the argument that an advocate engaged under Rule 4(5) can only "aid or assist Special Public Prosecutor and submit written arguments at the end of trial with permission of the Court." This argument was rejected. It was held that there is no conflict between Rule 4(5) and section 15 of the Act, hence same cannot be called in question without challenging the vires of the Rule.[2]

It was observed by a five Judge Bench of Apex Court that when a Special Judge has taken cognizance and the trial has to proceed according to the procedure laid down by the Special Act (The Criminal Law Amendment Act, 1952), "the learned advocate engaged by the complainant to conduct the prosecution will be deemed to be a Public Prosecutor. In such a situation, there is no question of the State appointed Public Prosecutor to conduct the prosecution."[3]

The appointment of a Special Public Prosecutor under Rule 4(5) is almost on the similar footing as has been provided under section 24(8) of the Code. But the complainant cannot be ordered to pay fee of Special Public Prosecutor, even though he had made an application for appointment of Special Public Prosecutor.[4]

6. Notification of Appointment of Special Public Prosecutor

Section 15 empowers the State Government to appoint or specify the two categories of Special Public Prosecutors by notification in the Officer Gazette. That clearly means that the appointment or the specification of such Special

---

1. *Jonnakuti Mokshanandam* v. *State of Andhra Pradesh,* 2006 Cr LJ 3034 (3037-38): 2006 (2) ALD (Cri) 430: 2006 (4) Andh LT 155.
2. *Satki Devi* v. *Tikam Singh,* 2006 Cr LJ 4721 (Raj) (DB) (4727): 2006 (3) Raj LR 706: 2007 (2) Raj LW 1620.
3. *R.S. Nayak* v. *A.R. Antulay,* 1984 Cr LJ 819 (SC) (821): AIR 1984 SC 991: (1984) 3 SCC 86.
4. *Madho Singh* v. *State of Rajasthan,* 2002 Cr LJ 1694 (Raj): 2002 (3) All Cri LR 917: 2002 (2) Raj LR 155; *Navinchandra N. Majithia* v. *State of Meghalaya,* 2000 Cr LJ 4600 (SC): (2000) 8 SCC 323: AIR 2000 SC 3275.

Public Prosecutors could not be complete or legally made till the notification to this effect has already been published in the Official Gazette for each district.

When a question was raised before the Court that, whether the impugned Notification issued by the Government in exercise of its powers under section 24 of the Cr PC and not following the procedure contemplated under Rule 4 and section 15 of the Act, and not publishing the notification in the Official Gazette under the local law, has vitiated the Notification? Answering the question the Court said that by reading Rule 4 of the Rules of 1995 it makes clear that the State Government on the recommendation of the District Magistrate shall prepare the lists of panel to function as Special Public Prosecutors before the Special Courts in each district. The Addendum to Notification issued by the State Government added words and incorporated section 15 and Rule 4, and such Addendum was sent for publication, therefore the plea that there was no notification under section 15 and Rule 4 has to be rejected.[1]

Second point decided in *Gulzar Khan's* case was that, even though the incumbent's name was not there in the panel of senior advocates, prepared by District Magistrate, but he had fulfilled the requisite qualification of having put in 7 years of practice as an advocate, therefore the Notification under challenge cannot be vitiated.[1]

It was further held that the accused have no say in the matter of appointment of prosecutor, and, also that the Publication of Notification appointing prosecutors in the Gazette is directory and not mandatory.[1]

It is submitted that the finding as the notification published in the Official Gazette for the appointment or specification of Special Public Prosecutors is simply directory and not mandatory, cannot be a good law. The finding bases its decision on the basis of a decision of the Apex Court (*Atlas Cycle Industries* v. *State*, AIR 1979 SC 1149). The decision of the Apex Court was given in a case where legal requirements under the Essential Commodities Act, 1955 was that the notification, for the fixation of maximum selling prices of various categories of Iron and Steel, should be put before the Parliament. It is submitted that there is vast difference between a notification issued for fixing prices and appointment of a legal "statutory authority". (Please also see notes under section 14—"Notification").

7. Qualifications and "Regular Cadre"

The expression "Advocate" means a person enrolled as such under the Advocates Act. As per provisions of section 15 (and Rule 4) of the Act, a person who is eligible for appointment as a Special Public Prosecutor, has to be an advocate who has been in practice as an advocate for not less than seven years.[2] When it comes to the question of computing the period of practice, it must be computed from the date when the person was enrolled as an advocate and continued in practice. A pleader or a Judicial Officer, who was not in practice

1. *Gulzar Khan* v. *State of Karnataka*, 2001 Cr LJ 3586 (Kant): 2001 (4) All Cri LR 92: ILR (2001) 2 Kant 3890.
2. *Rajendra Shankar Tripathi* v. *State*, 1979 Cr LJ 243 (All) (247).

for the stipulated period as an advocate cannot be appointed because of lack of qualification.[1]

The Apex Court observed that the power is in subjective terms, still judicial review is permissible if some anomalies in the process of appointment of Public Prosecutors are found as regards to the conditions and the qualifications are concerned. In case of such appointments correct procedure should be followed. In case no names of panel was prepared or there was no consultation with the Judicial Officers (Rule 4), or vague general comments were given by the District Magistrate, it could not be said that the requirements of law were complied with.[2]

The "Public Prosecutor" mentioned in section 15 of the Act, or Rule 4 of the Rules of 1995, are of the same category which has been defined under section 24(6) *Exp.* (a) of the Code as "Regular Cadre of Prosecuting Officers". Rule 4 provides that Director of Prosecution in-charge of prosecution has to be consulted while specifying the names of Public Prosecutors, but there is no condition of length of service of those who have to be 'specified'.

Interpreting the expression, "regular Cadre of Prosecuting Officers" described under the Code, as above said, the Supreme Court has observed that a combined reading of the sections the intention of the Legislature is evident which gives promotional rights of Prosecuting Officers in such of the States where there is already in existence regular Cadre consisting of hierarchy of Prosecuting Officers going to the top level.[3]

It was held that a panel consisting of a single name is no panel in the eyes of law and cannot be considered.[4]

A similar view was given, observing that members not belonging to regular Cadre of Prosecutors are not eligible to be appointed as Special Public Prosecutor, unless they have requisite qualification as has been laid down.[5]

The above discussions and citations clearly show that to be "specified" as a Special Public Prosecutor for purposes of section 15 and Rule 4 of the Rules 1995 a Public Prosecutor must belong to the 'Regular Cadre'. While an advocate must be in practice as such for not less than 7 years.

Secondly, another qualification stipulated by Rule 4 is that the advocate should be an "eminent Senior Advocate". It is noteworthy that any or many advocates who have been in practice for more 7 years may consider himself or herself as "eminent", but there is no tradition, custom or rule at the district level, for preparation of or declaration of a list of "Senior Advocates", as is the practice and even Rule at the Supreme Court Bar.

---

1. *ibid; Mallikarjuna Sharma* v. *State of Andhra Pradesh,* 1978 Cr LJ 1354: 1978 Mad LJ (Cri) 672.
2. *Harpal Singh Chauhan* v. *State of Uttar Pradesh,* 1993 Cr LJ 3140 (SC): AIR 1993 SC 2436: 1993 AIR SCW 2843.
3. *K.J. John, Assistant Public Prosecutor, Grade-I, Palai* v. *State of Kerala,* 1990 Cr LJ 1777 (SC): AIR 1990 SC 1902: (990) SCC 191.
4. *V. Ram Chandran* v. *M.C.J. Gupta,* 1986 Cr LJ 1820 (AP).
5. *Jaidhari Roy* v. *State of Bihar,* 1996 Cr LJ 1498 (Pat): 1994 (2) Pat LJR 558.

8. Panels of Names

Besides the provisions of section 24 of the Code, Rule 4 of the Rules of 1995 stipulates proportion of two panels, *i.e.*—(i) one consisting of "eminent Senior Advocates", and (ii) the other consisting of Public Prosecutors. These panels have to be prepared by the concerned District Magistrate and required to send it with "recommendation" to the State Government.

Rule 4 does not provide the preparation of panel by District Magistrate, from among advocates of the district, with consultation of Judicial Officers or the Session Judge, as is the case mentioned under section 24 of the Code. But as various decisions of the Courts (already mentioned) reveal that section 5 of the Act and Rule 4 has to be read with section 24 of the Code, thus it is presumed that such consultation of Session Judge is being obtained while the District Magistrate prepares the list of advocates, could be drawn on the ground that the ability, efficiency and acumen of advocates of the district are supposedly well-known to the Judicial Officers of the district.

But on the other hand the provisions of the Act of 1989 in this regard clearly mention consultations with Director Prosecution/Officer-in-charge of prosecution only while the District Magistrate prepares the second panel of names from among Public Prosecutors.

However, it was held that the State Government cannot appoint any person as Public Prosecutor, unless his name appears in the panel of names prepared by the District Magistrate.[1]

9. Renewal of Term

Rule 4(1) of the Rules of 1995 prescribe a fixed term of 3 years for appointment or specification, as the case may be, of a Special Public Prosecutor. Rule 4 (2),(3) and Rule 14 provide for the review of performance of such appointed or specified Special Public Prosecutors twice a year, and if the State Government is not "satisfied" with the performance, such specified or appointed officers, their "names may be, for the reasons to be recorded in writing, denotified". Such "denotification" is presumed to be published in the Official Gazette.

But where the performance of such officers are found to be good and "State Government is satisfied", their three years terms may either be extended, or-renewed for the period State Government pleases, though provisions of such extension or renewal has neither been provided in the Act nor the Rules.

But after the expiry of the term of such appointed persons concerned, it requires some statutory exercise in which either new persons are appointed adopting due process of law, or the persons who have been working as Public Prosecutors are again appointed, renewed or extended with a fresh term by the State Government. The procedures prescribed in the Manual are not in conflict with the legislated laws on the subject, therefore deemed to be supplementary to the statutory provisions.

1. *Surapaneni Ram Prasad* v. *Government of Andhra Pradesh*, 2000 Cr LJ 354 (AP): 1999 (4) Andh LD 309: 1999 (2) Andh LT (Cri) 109.

On the other hand, if there is a provision for extension or renewal, it cannot be claimed as a right. The aggrieved persons may certainly make a petition for their grievance on the ground that either they have not received fair treatment by the appointing authority or that the procedure prescribed have not been followed. Courts are competent to review whether there was any infirmity in the decision making process.[1]

Reversing a decision of Allahabad High Court (in the above mentioned case), the Apex Court had held that panel of names should have been prepared by the District Magistrate for extension and renewal of law officers in consultation with the Session Judge. The District Magistrate should have applied his mind in respect of individual cases and should not have made general comments.[1]

Following the above case, it was observed that the prescribed procedure has to be followed while making appointments of Public Prosecutors after completion of their tenures. If the appointment was for a particular tenure (as in the present case), and the tenure has lapsed, then there could again be an appointment of the same person, going through the very same procedure. When the very same incumbent, after the lapse of his previous tenure, gets a fresh appointment once again, it may be called extension or renewal. That must be done in accordance with the law.[2]

It may be presumed that the same norms for extension or renewal would be applicable, if need arises, for a Special Public Prosecutor appointed under Rule 4(5) of the Rules of 1995.

10. Prosecutors not Part of Investigating Agencies

Investigation and prosecution are two different faces in the administration of criminal justice. The role of Public prosecutor is inside the Court, whereas the investigation is outside the Court. Normally the role of Public Prosecutor commences after investigating agency presents the case in the Court on culmination of investigation. Involving the Public Prosecutor in investigation is unjudicious as well as pernicious in law. At any rate no investigating agency can be compelled to seek opinion of a Public Prosecutor under the orders of the Court. The investigating officer cannot be directed to consult Public Prosecutor and submit a charge-sheet in time with the opinion of the Public Prosecutor. The power of the officer-in-charge of the police station is subjected only to the supervision of superior police officers. There is no stage during which the investigating officer is legally obliged to take the opinion of Public Prosecutor or any other authority except superior police officers. Under the Code on the point of formation of opinion, whether or not there is a case to place the accused on trial, has to be that of the officer-in-charge of the police station and none else.[3]

---

1. *Harpal Singh Chauhan* v. *State of Uttar Pradesh*, 1993 Cr LJ 3140 (SC) (3146-47): AIR 1993 SC 2436: 1993 AIR SCW 2843; also see *Smt. Aneeta Khare* v. *State*, 2011 Cr LJ 43 (MP) and *A.K. Ahlavat* v. *State*, 2011 Cr LJ 4708 (P&H) (FB).
2. *Kasu Karthi Seetha Ramulu* v. *Government of Andhra Pradesh*, 1994 Cr LJ 2300 (AP) (2302): 1994 (1) Andh LT 722: 1994 (2) Crimes 778; also add, *A.M. Mahender* v. *State*, 1996 (1) All Cr R 674 (AP).
3. *R. Sarala* v. *T.S. Velu*, 2000 Cr LJ 2453 (SC): AIR 2000 SC 1731: 2000 AIR SCW 1791.

A Public Prosecutor is an officer of Court, thus he is to deal with other field of administration of justice and he is not involved in the investigation. He has no obligation of combined operation of filing the report in the Court. Even when law requires that prosecution could be commenced only with the sanction of some authority concerned, such Sanctioning Authority is not a consulate of the investigating officer. In such a position, it was held that the Investigating Officer cannot be directed to be influenced by the opinion of the Public Prosecutor.[1]

11. Office of Prosecutor – Independent

The engagement of an advocate as Public Prosecutor is not merely a professional engagement. Even if he does not hold a civil post under the State, he carries responsibility and privilege of the public office of great public importance and plays an important role in the administration of criminal justice. Neither his appointment nor removal can be made on the sweet will of the Government, rather the same are guided by public interest, which has always been a paramount consideration in the public administration.[2]

The Government Lawyers cannot be treated as employees but were professional practitioners engaged to do a specific work. Treating them as employees of the Government is not permissible under Rule 49 of the Bar Council of India Rules.[3]

The Public Prosecutor holds a Public Office and the primacy given to him under the provisions of the Code has a social purpose. By virtue of his office certain professional, official obligations and privileges are attached to him. The Public duties given to him are of an "independent and responsible character". Public Prosecutor is not a part of investigating agency, he is an independent "statutory authority", thus he performs statutory functions and duties. Despite the fact that he can withdraw the prosecution of cases on the direction of Government, he holds independent entity.[4]

12. Basic Functions and Duties of Prosecutor

A series of judgments could be cited where the role and duties of the Public Prosecutors have been highlighted and in this regard the pronouncements are unanimous. "There should be on the part of the Public Prosecutor no unseemingly eagerness for or grasping at conviction. His duty as a Public Prosecutor is not merely to secure the conviction of the accused at all costs but to place before the Court whatever evidence is in his possession, whether it be in favour or against the accused and leave it to the Court to decide upon all such evidences whether the accused had or had not committed the offence with which

1. *R. Saral* v. *T.S. Velu,* 2000 Cr LJ 2453 (SC): AIR 2000 SC 1731: 2000 AIR SCW 1791; *Hitendra Vishnu Thakur* v. *State of Maharashtra,* 1995 Cr LJ 517 (SC): AIR 1994 SC 2623: 1994 AIR SCW 3699.
2. *Ram Chandra Joshi* v. *State of Rajasthan,* 2000 Cr LJ 1660 (Raj): 2000 (2) Raj LR 60: 2000 (1) Raj LW 455.
3. *State of Uttar Pradesh* v. *Uttar Pradesh State Law Officers Association,* AIR 1994 SC 1654: 1994 AIR SCW 1389: (1994) 2 SCC 204.
4. *Kanta Kathuria* v. *Manak Chand Surana,* AIR 1970 SC 694: 1970 (2) SCJ 232: (1970) 2 SCR 835; *Mundrika Prasad Sinha* v. *State of Bihar,* AIR 1979 SC 1871: (1979) 4 SCC 701: (1980) 1 SCR 759; *Rabindra Kumar Nayak* v. *Collector, Mayurbhanj, Orissa,* AIR 1999 SC 1120: 1999 AIR SCW 774: (1999) 2 SCC 627.

he stood charged. The Public Prosecutor is not supposed to go out of his way to secure a conviction. He has to be truthful and impartial. A Public Prosecutor is not a mouthpiece for the State. He must not consciously mis-state the facts, nor knowingly conceal the truth. The Public Prosecutor must not suppress or keep back from the Court evidence relevant to the determination of the guilt or innocence of the accused. He must present a complete picture and not be partial. He has to be fair to both sides in the presentation of the case. The ideal Public Prosecutor is not concerned with securing convictions, or with satisfying departments of the State Government, with which he has to be in contact. He must consider himself as an agent of justice."[1]. (Perhaps the findings have fallen on deaf ears).

The above quoted citation is a gist of whatever has been repeatedly observed directions of their Lordships presiding over many Courts. Every word written in the judgment of the Division Bench is truth and nothing else. But unfortunately the observations, assertions and directions of their Lordships are not followed in practice. In that sense the words seem to have gone in vain.

But on the other hand, there are also some factors which force the Prosecutors to remain indifferent, specially in cases where, for instance, under Rule 4(2), (3) and (4), read with Rule 14 of the Rules of 1995, direct that the "performance of Special Public Prosecutors" shall be reviewed twice a year or even monthly and if found "not conducted the case" properly he may be "denotified". The "performance" inevitably presume convictions on the part of Special Public Prosecutors. In such circumstances following the norms would be an idealistic exercise and throwing themselves to the danger of 'denotification'.

13. Power of Withdrawal of Cases

Provision for withdrawal of cases has been provided in section 321 Cr PC and the Public Prosecutor, and in case of Act of 1989 the Special Public Prosecutor appointed under section 15 of that Act, is the person who moves the application for such withdrawal on behalf of the Government. The provisions of section 321 Cr PC are applicable only when the Court is competent and has jurisdiction to try the case. As such a Committing Magistrate has no power to consent for withdrawal.

Section 321 Cr PC provides "the withdrawal from the prosecution" and not the withdrawal of the prosecution. Withdrawal from the prosecution means retiring or stopping back or retracting from a prosecution. But the Public Prosecutor is not expected to act mechanically in the discharge of his duties and statutory function under section 321 Cr PC.

When the Public Prosecutor receives a direction to withdraw a case from prosecution, he has to satisfy himself that it is a fit case for withdrawal from prosecution, before he seeks consent from the Court for that purpose. In this connection Supreme Court had observed in a series of cases that the Court, before such an application of withdrawal has been moved by the Public Prosecutor, the Court too should not act mechanically. It should be decided by Public Prosecutor

1. *Sheshrao* v. *State*, 2001 Cr LJ 3805 (Kant) (DB) (3811): 2002 (2) Hindu LR 344: ILR (2001) 4 Kant 4868; also see *Abdul Kadir* v. *State*, (1993) 1 SCR 346.

as well the Court and after both are satisfired thereof that it is a fit case for withdrawal from the prosecution in accordance with the settled principles indicated in the decisions of the Supreme Court.[1]

It may be a ground for consideration of a Court that when the application for withdrawal is allowed, how far it would help bringing peace and tranquility in the premises of a Temple.[2] However, the withdrawal should be in the interest of administration of justice. The request for withdrawal cannot be given as a necessary formality but the Court would satisfy itself on the basis of material facts placed before it. The grant of consent would serve the administration of justice and that the application was not made covertly with an ulterior purpose unconnected with the vindication of law, which the executive organs are duty bound to perform. That is why it is required that the Court should give reasons while granting permission. A cryptic order, granting such permission is not maintainable.

Some guidelines have been given by the Apex Court for the grounds on which a prosecution may be withdrawn. These are: (i) when the accused was implicated on political or personal vendetta, (ii) in expediency of prosecution, (iii) public interest on lack of success of prosecution, etc. etc.[3]

The application for withdrawal may be moved when the trial has commenced, because before that stage Court cannot give permission to withdraw. It cannot be granted at a stage before the cognizance has been taken after the completion of investigation. The consent may be given before the judgment is signed.

But if the case is withdrawn before framing of charges, the accused would be discharged in respect of the offences involved. When the charge has been framed and the case is allowed to be withdrawn, the accused shall be deemed acquitted, even if the Court passes an order of discharge.[4]

14. Importance of Office of Special Public Prosecutor

The office and post of a Public Prosecutor is not only an Office of State, but in other ways this is a public office of great importance. A person appointed to this office is expected to watch the interest of the office and run it with high degree of efficiency and knowledge of law of crime and the procedures involved. One of the most important trait described is maintaining integrity and character beyond suspicion. He must have sense of duty towards the public and the Court. In case these requirements are lacking, the person holding such an important office is said to be injuring the administration of Criminal Justice System.[5]

---

1. *R.M. Tewari* v. *State (NCT of Delhi)*, 1996 Cr LJ 2872 (SC) (2873-74): 1996 AIR SCW 2454: AIR 1996 SC 2047.
2. *Narayan Nagesh* v. *State*, 1996 Cr LJ 137 (Bom) (1379).
3. *Sheonandan Paswan* v. *State of Bihar*, 1983 Cr LJ 348 (SC): AIR 1983 SC 194: (1983) 1 SCC 438.
4. *State of Karnataka* v. *K.H. Annegowda*, AIR 1977 SC 357: 1977 Cr LJ 220: (1977) 1 SCC 417; *State of Uttar Pradesh* v. *Prabhat Kumar Trivedi*, AIR 1966 All 349: 1966 Cr LJ 737: 1966 All Cri R 281.
5. *A. Mohambaram* v. *M.A. Jayavelu*, AIR 1970 Mad 63: (1969) 1 Mad LJ 261: 1970 Cr LJ 241.

Chapter V

MISCELLANEOUS

16. Power of State Government to impose collective fine.—The provisions of section 10A of the Protection of Civil Right Act, 1955 (22 of 1955) shall, so far as may be, apply for the purposes of imposition and realisation of collective fine and for all other matters connected therewith under this Act.

SYNOPSIS

1. Allied Provision

Section 10A of the Protection of Civil Rights Act, 1955 is as follows:

"*10A. Power of State Government to impose collective fine.*—(1) If, after an inquiry in the prescribed manner, the State Government is satisfied that the inhabitants of an area are concerned in, or abetting the commission of, any offence punishable under this Act, or harbouring persons concerned in the commission of such offence or failing to render all the assistance in their power to discover or apprehend the offender or offenders or suppressing material evidence of the commission of such offence, the State Government may, by notification in the Official Gazette, impose a collective fine on such inhabitants and apportion such fine amongst the inhabitants who are liable collectively to pay it, and such apportionment shall be made according to the State Government's judgment of the respective means of such inhabitants and in making any such apportionment the State Government may assign a portion of such fine to Hindu Undivided Family to be payable by it:

Provided that the fine apportioned to an inhabitant shall not be realized until the petition, if any, filed by him under sub-section (3) is disposed of.

(2) The notification made under sub-section (1) shall be proclaimed in the area by beat of drum or in such other manner as the State Government may think best in the circumstances to bring the imposition of the collective to the notice of the inhabitants of the said area.

(3)(a) Any person aggrieved by the imposition of the collective fine under sub-section (1) or by the order of apportionment, may, within the prescribed period, file a petition before the State Government or such other authority as that Government may specify in this behalf for being exempted from such fine or modification of the order of apportionment:

Provided that no fee shall be charged for filing such petition.

(b) The State Government or the authority specified by it shall, after giving to the petitioner a reasonable opportunity of being heard, pass such order as it may think fit:

Provided that the amount of the fine exempted or reduced under this section shall not be reasonble from any person, and the total fine imposed on the inhabitants of an area under sub-section (1) shall be deemed to have been reduced to that extent.

(4) Notwithstanding anything contained in sub-section (3), the State Government may exempt the victims of any offence punishable under this Act or any person who does not, in its opinion, fall within the category of persons specified in sub-section (1), from the liability to pay collective fine imposed under sub-section (1) or any portion thereof.

(5) The portion of collective fine payable by any person (including a Hindu undivided family) may be recovered in the manner provided by the Code of Criminal Procedure, 1973 (2 of 1974), for the recovery of fines imposed by a Court as if such portion were a fine imposed by a Magistrate."[1]

The Protection of Civil Right Rules, 1977 were framed by the Central Government in exercise of powers conferred by 16B of the Protection of Civil Rights Act, 1955, Rule 3 of Rules of 1977 is being given below:

"3. *Manner of inquiry under sub-section (1) of section 10A.*—(1) The State Government may appoint an officer not below the rank of a Sub-Divisional Magistrate for the purposes of making an inquiry referred to in sub-section (1) of section 10A.

(2) The officer appointed under sub-rule (1) (hereinafter in this Rule referred to as the inquiry officer) shall issue a public notice specifying the date, time, place and purpose of such inquiry and calling upon all the residents of the area in respect of which the inquiry is to be held to furnish such information and materials, including documents in their possession, as may be relevant for the purpose of inquiry.

(3) The public notice referred to in sub-rule (2) shall be in the local language or languages of the area and the same shall be—

(i) published on the notice board in the office of the District Magistrate, the District Superintendent of Police, the Village Panchayat or

1. Inserted by the Untouchability (Offences) Amendment and Miscellaneous Provisions Act, 1976 (106 of 1976), s 13 (19-11-1976).

Municipal Committee of the area and such other places as the inquiry officer deems fit and at least in one daily newspaper circulating in the area; and

(ii) proclaimed in the area by beat of drum or in such other manner as the inquiry officer may think best in the circumstances to bring the contents of the public notice to the notice of the inhabitants of the area.

(4) The inquiry officer, while making such inquiry shall follow as nearly as practicable, the procedure for summary trials including the recording of evidence as laid down in Chapter XII of the Code of Criminal Procedure, 1973 (2 of 1974).

(5) The inquiry officer shall complete the inquiry as expeditiously as possible and submit his report to the State Government within such period, not exceeding six weeks, as may be specified by the State Government in the order appointing the inquiry officer:

Provided that the State Government may, having regard to the nature of the inquiry, extend the period of submission of the report by such period, not exceeding two months in total, as it may consider necessary."

Rule 4 of the Protection of Civil Rights Rules, 1977 provides for filing of a petition under section 10A of the Act of 1955. Rule 4 has been given below:

"4. *Period for filing a petition under sub-section (3) of section 10A.*—(1) Any person aggrieved by the imposition of a collective fine under sub-section (1) of section 10A or by the order of appointment, may within a period of thirty days from the date of proclamation of the notification under sub-section (2) of the section to file a petition before the State Government or the authority specified by it:

Provided that where the State Government or the authority, as the case may be, may entertain the petition after the expiry of the said period if it is satisfied that the petitioner was prevented by sufficient cause from filing the petition in time."

2. Imposition of Fine as Punitive Reaction – A Historical Perspective

The society generally react to law-breaking, and various techniques are used to express punitive reactions. During the history of mankind the methods used varied from time-to-time and place-to-place. But in a given society main methods used for the implementation of punitive policy are: the death, exile, imprisonment, physical torture, social degradation and lastly imposing financial losses as fines or forfeiture of property. These, or combination of these methods cannot be strictly said to be the characteristic of any one historical period or any one society, but certain emphasis may be marked in a given period.

Even in most literate societies imposition of fine, as a financial loss to law-breaker, could be seen as reaction of society and as punitive policy, but there had been great variations on the emphasis of this system. An injured person may claim damages, the amount depending on the gravity of injury and the social position of the injured party. Once upon a time the king claimed a share in this payment on the ground that the State had participated in the entire exercise of damage amount fixation and realization. By twelfth century king's share began to increase and finally the king exacted the entire amount, which ultimately was called a 'fine'. Therefore the concept of 'fine' was developed out of private damage amounts, arising out of civil actions, rather than the criminal law. The method became frequent the world over till the end of 19th century.

Following the general law, the Courts, while enforcing the fines and its realizations from the offenders is through their property or, as law may provide, in case of default the offender is being sent to prison in default of payment of fine.

In philosophical terms, when a fine has been imposed, it tantamounts to a declaration that in fact neither the safety of the community nor the offender's welfare require sending the offender to prison, and also that assumed object of punishment can be achieved without inflicting imprisonment to the offender. The 'fine' becomes a debt to the State and in case of default to pay fine amount, the offender is sent to prison for realization of that debt. The 'fine' is a most economical penalty, from the point of view of the State, as it costs the State nothing practically, if used without imprisonment for a default.

3. Scope

Section 16 of the Act of 1989 provides for imposition of a "collective fine" and refer section 10A of the Protection of Civil Rights Act of 1955, for "purposes of imposition realization of collective fine". Therefore scope of section 16 of the Act includes not only section 10A of the Act of 1955 but also the Rules framed thereunder, specially for the procedure to be adopted. Therefore both the said sections of the two mentioned Acts and Rule 3 and 4 must be read together.

Section 10A of the Civil Rights Protection Act, 1955, provides that the State Government cannot impose a 'collective fine' on the inhabitants all of a sudden or suo moto, but two conditions must precede such an order of imposition of 'collective fine', *viz.:*

(i) appointing an officer not below the rank of Sub-Divisional Magistrate for making an inquiry [section 10A(1) and Rule 3(1)], and submitting his report [Rule 3(5)]

(ii) the State Government is satisfied with the report of such inquiry officer.

The 'satisfaction' of the State Government must be in relation with:

(i) inhabitants of the area are concerned in,

(ii) abetting the commission of offence,

(iii) harbouring person concerned,

(iv) "failing to render all the assistance in their power to discover or apprehend the offenders", and

(v) "suppressing material evidence of commission of such offence."

The word "satified" would inevitably stipulate the subjective satisfaction. For this purpose all the five factors mentioned must be there to complete the subjective satisfaction, which is the settled principle of law relating to 'subjective satisfaction'. If some or many of the above mentioned factors are absent from the report of the inquiry officer so appointed, the law would stipulate that subjective satisfaction was not complete, and if challenged before a Court of law, trouble is bound to occur.

4. Amount of Fine

Section 16 of the Act of 1989, section 10A of the Protection of Civil Rights Act 1955, or the rules framed thereunder did not disclose the maximum or minimum limits of fine to be imposed on the inhabitants of the area collectively by the State Government. Such 'area' may be one that has been identified by the mentioned officers and as has been described under section 17 of the Act of 1989.

Section 63 of the Indian Penal Code deals with such situations. It says:

> *Section "63. Amount of Fine.*—Where no sum is expressed to which a fine may extend the amount of fine to which the offender is liable is unlimited, but shall not be excessive."

Besides, the General Clauses Act (Act X of 1897) contains the provisions to deal with all kinds of fines imposed under the authority of any Enactment, regulation, rule or bye-law, unless the Act, regulation, rule or the bye-law prescribe an express provision to the contrary.

However, when the draft Bill of Indian Penal Code was presented before the committee, a controversy arose even at the draft level. The maximum limits of imposed fine was left to the discretion of the Court (in present case with the State Government), while many systems had already fixed the maximum limits.

Three grounds were forwarded for not fixing the maximum or minimum limits of fine: viz.—

(i) majority of people in Indian society are poor and if a minimum is fixed, it would hamper their families;

(ii) the economic worth of the offender is a consideration for imposing fines, which would naturally differ from case-to-case, and

(iii) in case the offender defaults due to any reasons, for instance it is being excessive, and it had to be realized through his property, it may lead to endless complications.

On the other hand, one clause,—"but shall not be excessive" has been added for the purposes of keeping a balance and putting restraint on the discretion to be abused. A very rational observation of Blackstone J. may be quoted here, "that the quantum of pecuniary fines neither can nor ought to be ascertained by an invariable law. The value of money itself changes from a thousand causes; and, at all events, what is run to one man's fortune, may be matter of indifference to another's; statute law has not, therefore, often ascertained the quality of fine, nor the common law ever."

5. Various Principles Involved

The discretion for imposition of collective fine under section 16 of the Act of 1989 or section 10A of Act of 1955 vests in the State Government. When a situation arises, the discretion has to be used according to some predetermined and well-settled principles.

It is a well-settled principle that a fine cannot be inflicted, the payment of which is very difficult, if not impossible, for the culprit. This assertion is based on the principle that the fine imposed must suit the crime committed in regard to the nature and character of offence. The ultimate object must be kept in mind that the fined class should be pointed out that the mischief they had chosen as the instrument of their vengeance, is also hurtful to the other lot, and not beyond.

The law stipulates a distinction sould be made while passing judgments on sentences like fine etc., on a highway robber and a person committing theft to feed his starving family. Bentham lays down following Rules:

(i) the greater the uncertainty, the greater should be quantum of punishment,

(ii) that it should be sufficient to turn the offender's advantage to a loss, and

(iii) that it should be deterrent.[1]

But it is also true that no hard and fast rules can be framed which are so variable that they can be applied to varied circumstance of each case. For example: the amount of imposed fine may be inconsiderable to rich persons, but it may be hurtfully oppressive for the poor people.

6. The "Collective Fine"

Section 16 of the Act of 1989, section 10A of the Act of 1955 and Rules provide imposition of an unmentioned amount of "collective fine" to be paid by the 'inhabitants' of a certain area in question. The liability to pay such 'collective fine' shall be apportioned amongst the inhabitants of the impugned area "according to State Government's judgment of the *respective means of such inhabitants*...". That would imply that the amount collectively imposed as fine on such inhabitants would not be divided equally to all the inhabitants, because section 10A(1) of Act of 1955 brings in a rider that the State Government cannot simply order a lump sum amount, but obliged to apportion in such a way that the apportionment satisfies the "respective means of such inhabitants".

The Legislature, while enacting section 10A of the Act of 1955, kept in mind the different economic classes among the inhabitants of the area in question, including Hindu Undivided Families. Apportioning equally on all the inhabitants of the area the total notified fine amount, may mean nothing to a rich inhabitants, while for the poor it may become an exorbitant amount, excessive or beyond their "means" to pay. By all means equal distribution or apportionment" of the total amount would be violative of above mentioned principles, besides norms of justice, which comprehend that: magnitude of fine must, in justice be proportioned to the offender's means. That is the reason why the Legislature had followed the policy of not limiting the maximum or minimum limits of fine under section 10A of the Act, 1955. The Legislature had, consequently, left the discretion to the State Government.

One other aspect is also needs attention. It may, in some cases, seem unfair that the Legislature has left the amount of fine to the discretion of the State Government. In the present scenario the caste based politics is in vogue, and nobody can deny this obnoxious truth. The ruling party in a particular Government may be influenced by the factors and use the discretion either ways, unfairly to appease a particular "vote-bank". But, this may be an apprehension

1. Principles of Penal Laws; Bentham, pp. 400 *et sq* (the language used is not easily intelligible).

without any foundation, because, perhaps the Legislature had thought about such eventualities and incorporated sub-section 3 of section 10A of the Act of 1955 and Rule 4 of the Rules 1977 made thereunder. The Act of 1955 and the Rules of 1977 have designed a system where strict monitoring has been provided by "each House of Parliament" twice a year, under Rule 5 of Rules 1977. In that case chances of the State Government taking some arbitrary steps have been negatives almost completely.

If any inhabitant considers the portion of fine inflicted on him as unreasonable or unfair, he may file a petition to this effect, where he would have an opportunity of being heard [section 10A(3)(a) and (b)]. In case the liability of the petitioner is not "reduced" or he is not being "exempted" by the relevant Government authority, he is free to go to Court of law and challenge the order passed. (There are no reported cases). And, according to Proviso of section 10A (1) of the Act of 1955, which provides that the portion of fine slammed on such petitioner would not be realized until his petition is not "disposed of."

7. Right to File Petition

Any person, who is an inhabitant of an area where the State Government, after adopting due process prescribed under section 10A and Rule 3 of the Act of 1955 has by notification imposed a collective fine and apportioned the amount to his extent, may file a petition, within a period of thirty days from the date of proclamation of the notification, before the State Government or any authority specified by such Government, under Rule 4 (1) of the Rules of 1977.

But the period of limitation of thirty days for filing the petition from the date of proclamation of the notification is subject to the conditions provided in the Proviso of such rule. That is, the State Government or the specified authority may entertain the petition even after the stipulated expiry of those thirty days, if such Government or the specified authority is satisfied that the aggrieved person was prevented by sufficient or legitimate cause from filing the petition within the period of limitation.

In any case, Rule 4(2) directs the State Government or the specified authority to dispose of the filed petition as 'expeditiously as possible'.

Rule 5 of the Rules of 1977 provide that the State Government shall take a report before each House of Parliament [section 15A(4)], and naturally the Central Government or the Parliament has been given supervising powers to monitor whether the provisions of the Act and Rules are followed strictly or not.

8. The "Victims" as Inhabitants

The inhabitants of an area would naturally include the victims and the collective fine imposed on the inhabitants collectively may cause prejudice to the victims as well. Sub-section (4) of section 10A of the Act of 1955 empowers the State Government to exempt, firstly any offence committed under the provisions of the Act; and, secondly from the liability to pay the collective fine imposed or any portion thereof. But this power is discretionary as the word "may" has been used. That means, in some exceptional cases the State Government, may include such persons who are called 'victims'.

9. Recovery of Collective Fines

Sub-section (5) of section 10A of the Act of 1955 provides that the collective fine or any portion thereof from the inhabitants of the area, including a Hindu Undivided Family, may be recovered in the manner provided by Code of Criminal Procedure, 1973 for the recovery of fines imposed by a Court, and would be deemed as if such portion were a fine imposed by a Magistrate.

Sections 67, 68 and 69 of Indian Penal Code, respectively provide: "imprisonment for non-payment of fine, when offence punishable with fine only": "imprisonment to terminate on payment of fine"; and "termination of imprisonment on payment of *proportional* part of fine". Importantly these provisions are applicable to the fines imposed by the Court, and as section 10A(5) of the Act of 1955 equates the collective fine or portions thereof as if they were imposed by Court or Magistrate, the provisions are bound to be applicable here.

However, the Code of Criminal Procedure, 1973 provides various circumstances and procedures for recovery of fines. Sections 421, 422, 423, 424, and 431 of the Code provide such circumstances and the procedure for levying of fines.

10. Imposed Fines and Compensation

One of the objects of fine is to compensate the complainant, though the complainant is also free to recover damages as compensation through a civil suit.

Section 357 and 357A of Cr PC provide: "Order to pay compensation"; and, "Victim Compensation Scheme", while section 359 Cr PC empowers the Court to order of payment of costs, in whole or part, while convicting the accused.

Section 10A(5) of the Act of 1955 directs application of provisions of Cr PC for recovery of collective fines, as if such imposition was made by a Court. The said section does not mention or limit the application of the Code in any way, therefore it may be safely presumed that, if the State Government thinks fit, it may order portion or the whole realised collective fine amount to be paid to the victims.

The SC/ST Rules, 1995 also direct under the 'Schedule' annexed to the Rules, specific items for which the victims of 'atrocities' are entitled to the amounts of compensation. But such amount of compensation has to be paid by the State Government itself. Therefore, the portions or the whole amount of 'collective fine', if ordered to be paid to the victims under the provisions of Cr PC would be in addition to the amount of compensation paid under the Rules of 1995.

17. Preventive action to be taken by the law and order machinery.—(1) A District Magistrate or a Sub-divisional Magistrate or any other Executive Magistrate or any police officer not below the rank of a Deputy Superintendent of Police may, on receiving information and after such inquiry as he may thinks necessary, has reason to believe that a person or a group of persons not belonging to the Scheduled Castes or the Scheduled Tribes, residing in or frequenting any place within the local limits of his jurisdiction is likely to commit an offence or has threatened to commit any offence under this Act and is of the opinion that there is sufficient ground for proceeding, declare such an area to be an area prone to atrocities and take necessary action for keeping the peace and good behaviour and maintenance of public order and tranquillity and may take preventive action.

(2) The provisions of Chapters VIII, X and XI of the Code shall, so far as may be, apply for the purposes of sub-section (1).

(3) The State Government may, by notification in the Official Gazette, make one or more schemes specifying the manner in which the officers referred to in sub-section (1) shall take appropriate action specified in such scheme or schemes to prevent atrocities and to restore the feeling of security amongst the members of the Scheduled Castes and the Scheduled Tribes.

SYNOPSIS

1. Analogous Law

Sub-section (2), specially Clause (VI), of section 15A of the Protection of Civil Rights Act, 1955, to some extent initiated the process, which has been incorporated in detail under section 17 of the Act of 1989 and as such analogous to it. Besides Code of Criminal Procedure also contain various provisions which are preventive measures to be enforced in different law and order situations.

2. Scheduled Castes and Scheduled Tribes Rules Elaborate Provisions of section 17

The Scheduled Castes and the Scheduled Tribes (Prevention of Atrocities) rules, 1995, framed by the Central Government under the powers provided by section 23 of the Act of 1989, and much of its space has been covered to extend and elaborate the provisions of section 17 of the Act.

Rule 2(c) defines "identified area" as an area where "atrocity may take place", or "an area prone to atrocity".

Rule 3 prescribes "precautionary and preventive measures" to be taken by the State Government, including ordering District Magistrate and the Superintendent of Police to visit the identified area, cancel arms licences or seize all illegal fire arms of the rest of the population of the 'area', (including their "relations, servants or employees and family friends"); except member's of the Scheduled Castes or Scheduled Tribes; and, instead, provide such member arms licenses;

setting up of various kinds of committees and also deploying "special police force" in the area, etc.[1]

Rules 4, 5, 6 and 7 of the Rules of 1995 are related with 'supervision of prosecution, information to police' regarding offences under the Act, 'spot inspection by officers' and about special 'investigating officer' to investigate the offences of the 'atrocities'. In one way or the other these provisions are special directions to be taken as 'preventive action' by the law and order machinery of the Government.

For continuous monitoring the situation in the 'identified area' Rules 8, 9 and 10 have been framed so that different kinds of cells consisting of high level officers of the State Government may keep a watch on the area.

The most important of the provisions are contained under Rules 12 and 13 for taking drastic "preventive action" in the identified areas and even in individual cases the State Government shall ensure that representation of members of Scheduled Castes and Scheduled Tribes have been made adequately in the administrative staff and police "at all levels, particularly at the level of police posts and police station".

Rule 14 of the Rules of 1995 deals with the "specific responsibility of the State Government", while Rules 15, 16 and 17 deal with plans and Constitution of committees or reports etc.

In that manner the entire skeleton of rules framed specify detail of what had been the real intention of the Legislature when section 17 was legislated.

3. Section 17(2) and the Code

Sub-section (2) of section 17 of the Act of 1989 provides that provisions of Chapters VIII, X and XI of the Code shall apply for implementation of or of taking preventive action in an area where either on the received information or on, an inquiry the appropriate officers mentioned in their reports, as well as law and order machinery has reason to believe that a person or a group of persons, residing or frequenting in the area, is likely to commit offences of atrocities under the Act. The district authorities may proceed and take necessary action for prevention of such offences so that the peace or the tranquility of the area may not be disturbed. These necessary actions may be taken under the provisions of the Code.

Chapter VIII of the Code deals with,—"Security for keeping peace and for good behaviour". Chapter consists of 19 sections from section number 106 to 124. Chapter X of the Code has been attributed to—"maintenance of public order and tranquility", comprising from section 129 to 148; and Chapter XI, starts from section 149 and ends at section 153, which are related with, "preventing action of the Police".

Sub-Section (3) of section 17 stipulates that the State Government would formulate "scheme or schemes" under which such Government shall specify the manner in which officers mentioned under sub-section (1) shall take appropriate action to achieve the objectives.

1. Section 8 of Protection of Civil Rights Act, 1955 provided cancellation of an arm licence on conviction, and that too by the order of the Court, instead of the Government.

4. Section 17 and Chapter VIII of Cr PC

The expressions "keeping peace" or breach of the peace has not been defined, but it would include most of acts which are against or related with the public tranquility, as have been made offences under Chapter VIII of the Indian Penal Code.

According to English law, if a person has a just cause to fear that another will do him some bodily harm, as by killing or beating him, he may demand the security of peace against such person, then it is the duty of 'Justice of Peace' to bind over such person.[1]

The object of the provisions being to prevent an imminent danger of breach of peace, or there must be a likelihood as such, so that a subversive conduct may be prevented before it actually takes dangerous shape. The Executive Magistrates have been invested with discretionary powers for the preservation of order and public peace for an orderly society.

Most of the provisions of the Chapter VIII of Cr PC are preventive and not punitive. But sections 108, 109 and 110 deal with security for good behaviour. The said Chapter also prescribes a definite procedure to deal with such anticipated situations by the Executive.

5. Section 17 and Chapter X of Cr PC

The Chapter deals with and provides powers to Executive Magistrate and the police to handle "unlawful assemblies". Chapter VIII of Indian Penal Code 1860 (from Section 141 to 160) make offences for being a member of unlawful assembly etc., as the headline of the Chapter says, "Of offences against the public tranquility". It is anybody's guess that common object of an unlawful assembly is usually "rioting".

For long the rules as has been framed (under section 129, Cr PC) have been carried from English Law, and was even present in the Code of 1872. Even in more distant past some decisions are indicative of presence of such rules. Tindal, C.J. laid down to the Grand Jury of Bristol, in the year 1832, regarding duties of the soldiers in dispersing rioters etc.[2]

Section 17(2) empowers thus that for disposal of any 'unlawful assembly' or any assembly of five or more persons, the members of which are likely to commit any offence of 'atrocity' under the Act of 1989, may be dispersed by force, by army which may be called for the purpose. This situation may arise when section 17 of the Act and provisions of sections 129, 130, 131 Cr PC are read together.

The expression "preventive action" used under section 17 of the Act also includes removal of nuisance or disposal of the disputes as to immovable property, which is 'likely' to create breach of peace between members of Scheduled Castes and the Scheduled Tribes, and the rest of the population of a certain 'area' or areas.

6. Section 17 and Chapter XI of Cr PC

Chapter XI of Cr PC castes a duty on the police to 'prevent cognizable offences', a 'design' for commission of such offence or arresting persons likely to

---

1. Halsbury's Laws of England Vol. IX, p 414.
2. Please see — Whitley Stokes: Anglo-Indian Codes Vol. II, p 11.

commit such offences etc. These preventive powers of the police provided under the present Chapter are in addition to the powers provided under the Police Act, 1861.

18. Section 438 of the Code not to apply to persons committing an offence under the Act.—Nothing in section 438 of the Code shall apply in relation to any case involving the arrest of any person on an accusation of having committed an offence under this Act.

SYNOPSIS

1. Analogous Law
2. Anticipatory Bail
3. Constitutionality of section 18
4. Bar Under section 18
5. Bar Under section 18 is Not Complete
6. Entitlement to Anticipatory Bail Despite Bar
7. Regular Bail and section 18
8. Section 438 Cr PC and Bailable Offences
9. Other Considerations for Granting Bail
10. Bail Cancellation or Subsequent Application

1. Analogous Law

Present section 18 of the Act of 1989 is a *verbatim* copy of sub-clause (7) of section 20 of TADA Act, 1987 (in fact word for word). Later on, same provision, barring the application of 438 Cr PC was incorporated under section 49(5) of POTA, 2002. (Now both the enactments have been repealed).

Section 15(4) of Terrorist Affected Areas (Special Courts) Act, 1984 (61 of 1984) contains same prohibition.

As could be seen, the provision of prohibition of anticipatory bail was put forward and inserted as a drastic measure for terrorists only. Section 67 of the United Kingdom Terrorism Act, 2000 starts with the headline—"Limitations of Power to Grant Bail".

2. Anticipatory Bail

The Code of Criminal Procedure, 1898 (or the Codes previous to that) did not provide a power to any Court to grant 'anticipatory bail' to the accused who are apprehending arrest. At those times different High Courts had discussed at length regarding the likely powers of the Courts to grant anticipatory bail. In absence of any legislated provision, the majority view was that there was no power with the Court under which it can grant anticipatory bail. Later on Code of Criminal Procedure, 1973 incorporated and inserted section 438.

It was held that it is wrong to say that the power under section 438 Cr PC should be used sparingly. It is not extraordinary to invoke the powers under section 438. Citing report of National Police Commission it was observed that power of arrest is grossly abused etc. The decisions falling on the other side of the fence were held to be not good law.[1]

1. *Rakesh Prahladram Joshi* v. *State,* 2012 Cr LJ 362 (Guj) Followed *Siddharam Sallingappa Mahtre* v. *State of Maharashtra*, AIR 2011 SC 312: (2011) 1 SCC 694: 2011 Cr LJ 3905; *Gurbaksh Singh Sibbia* v. *State of Punjab*, 1980 Cr LJ 1125: AIR 1980 SC 1632: (1980) 2 SCC 565. Not good law: *Yazdi Darabsha Icchaporia* v. *State of Gujarat*, 2003 Cr LJ 2604; *Lilaram L. Revani* v. *R. D. Gandhi*, 1998 Cr LJ 14: 1997 (2) Guj LH 503; *State of Gujarat* v. *Dipak Jaswantlal Sheth*, 1999 Cr LJ 162: 1998 (2) Guj LH 1044: 1998 (3) Guj LR 2240.

The Law Commission in its Forty Eight Report recommended introduction of a provision for grant of 'anticipatory bail'. The recommendations of the Commission were accepted by the Government and Clause 447 was introduced in the draft Bill of the new Code with the purpose of conferring power on a Court of Session or High Court to grant 'anticipatory bail'. The Report observed in paragraph 31 as:

> "The Bill introduces a provision for the grant of anticipatory bail. This is substantially in accordance with the recommendation made by the previous Commission. We agree that this would be a useful addition, though we must add that it is in very exceptional cases that such a power should be exercised.
>
> We are further of the view that in order to ensure that the provision is not put to abuse at the instance of unscrupulous petitioners, the final order should be made only after notice to public prosecutor. The initial order should only be an interim one. Further the relevant section should make it clear that the direction can be issued only for reasons to be recorded, and if the Court is satisfied that such a direction is necessary in the interest of justice."

Consequently Clause 447 was made section 438 when the Code of Criminal Procedure, 1973 was enacted afresh.

But various riders were introduced in the draft Bill and accordingly circumstances prevailing in the State of Uttar Pradesh, applicability of provisions of section 438, providing for 'anticipatory bail', was prohibited (*vide* Uttar Pradesh Act No. 16 of 1976, w.e.f. 28-11-1976).

This State Amending Act of 1976 has made section 18 of the Act of 1989 irrelevant at least in Uttar Pradesh, where, what to say of the Scheduled Castes and the Scheduled Tribes (Prevention of Atrocities) Act, 1989, provisions of section 438, Cr PC is not even applicable under general law.

3. Constitutionality of section 18

It was argued before a Full Bench that founding fathers of the Constitution never thought that State shall exercise its powers in arbitrary manner to take away right to life and liberty of not only citizens of India but of the foreigners as well under Article 21, except in accordance with the procedure established by law. The contention was that every person has right to apply for bail, hence any impediment caused in obtaining the same would contravene Article 21 of the Constitution, though the Bench was dealing with a case arising out of the provisions of the Act of 1989, their Lordships had given the example of sub-section (7) of the Terrorist and Disruptive Activities (Prevention) Act, 1987 (TADA), on the ground that it was also a special enactment passed by the Parliament. It was observed that "the two Acts may be different in their amplitude, but indignity tolerated upto the year 1988 by the Scheduled Castes and the Scheduled Tribes had been felt not to be tolerated any more, consequently the present Act was enacted.

"The right to anticipatory bail did not flow from Article 21 of the Constitution either expressly or impliedly. This right has been conferred by the statute enacted by the Parliament....

"Article 21 is not intended to be a constitutional limitation upon the powers of the legislature. The Parliament had the power to lay down that section 438, Cr PC would not apply to cases arising out or covered by a special Act. What the Constitution has guaranteed under Article 21 is that no person shall be deprived of his life and liberty except in accordance with the procedure established by law."[1]

Therefore Section 18 is not hit by Article 21.

In regard to excluding provisions of section 438 Cr PC, Supreme Court had observed that, it all depends on scheme of the particular Act as to whether the power of the High Court and the Court of Session to grant the bail under sections 438 and 439 exists.[2]

In the similar vein, the Supreme Court, comparing provisions of Section 18 of the Act and section 20(7) of TADA 1987, has held that 'anticipatory bail' cannot be granted as a matter of right. Such right is a statutory right which cannot be considered as an essential ingredient of Article 21; and also cannot be included in the ingredient of Article 21 as right to life. Thus its non-application to a certain special category of offences cannot be considered as violative of Article 21. Holding this, the Apex Court reversed the decision of Madhya Pradesh High Court.[3]

The matter was also brought before a Division Bench of Madras High Court, when section 18 was pleaded to be violative of Articles 14 and 21 of the Constitution. It was observed that having regard to the gravity of offences and the repercussions such acts may have on the society it may be blocked if such persons are to move in the society freely after committing such heinous offences on obtaining 'anticipatory bails'. The offenders under the Act of 1989 and the offenders under the other penal laws of the country fall under different categories. As such they cannot be grouped in "one class". On this ground there is no unreasonable classification when the offenders do not fall within the same category. Thus exclusion of section 438, Cr PC for the offences under the Act of 1989 does not violate Articles 14 or 21 of the Constitution.[4]

4. Bar Under section 18

The accused who were alleged to have committed offences under section 3 of the Act of 1989, besides other offences under the IPC, and applied for 'anticipatory bail', it was observed that according to settled law by the Apex Court that the offences which are enumerated under section 3 (1) of the Act arise out of the practice of "untouchability", and in this context certain special provisions have been made in the Act, including section 18. Exclusion of section

1. *Jai Singh* v. *Union of India*, 1993 Cr LJ 2705 (FB) (Raj) (2712): AIR 1993 Raj 177: 1993 (1) Raj LW 157; also see *Bimal Kaur Khalsa* v. *Union of India*, 1988 Cr LJ 869 (P&H) (FB): AIR 1988 P&H 95 (FB).
2. *Usmanbhai Dawoodbhai Memon* v. *State of Gujarat*, 1988 Cr LJ 938 (SC): AIR 1988 SC 922: (1988) 2 SCC 271.
3. *State of Madhya Pradesh* v. *Ram Kishna Balothia*, 1995 Cr LJ 2076 (SC): AIR 1995 SC 1198: 1995 AIR SCW 1267: JT 1995 (1) SC 310; also see *Kartar Singh* v. *State of Punjab*, 1994 Cr LJ 3139 (SC): (1994) 3 SCC 569: (1994) 2 SCR 375.
4. *Raju Gounder* v. *Union of India*, 1995 Cr LJ 3390 (Mad) (DB): 1995 (2) Mad LW (Cri) 531.

438, Cr PC has to be viewed in the context of prevailing social conditions, and if the offenders are allowed anticipatory bail, the apprehension of intimidation of victims would be inevitable result. Therefore it was held that provisions of section 438, Cr PC are not available to persons committing offences under section 3(1) of the Act.[1]

Taking a balanced view, a Full Bench of Rajasthan High Court, has also observed that it is true that if a person is alleged of accusation of committing an offence under the Act of 1989, the intention of section 18 is clearly to debar him from seeking the remedy of 'anticipatory bail'. But where there are circumstances which reveal no material to infer as to why section 3 of the Act has been applied to implicate the accused, the Courts would be justified in a very limited sphere to examine whether the application can be rejected on the ground of its maintainability. What is intended to be emphasized is that while dealing with an application for 'anticipatory bail', the Court would be justified in examining as to whether there is at all an accusation against a person for registering a case under section 3 of the Act of 1989, and once the ingredients of the offence are available in the FIR or the complaint, the Courts would not be justified in entering into a further inquiry by summoning the case-diary or any other material as to whether the allegations are true or false or whether there is any preponderance of probability of commission of such an offence. Such an exercise is intended to put a complete bar against entertainment of the application of 'anticipatory bail'. The Court at the most would be required to evaluate the facts in the FIR in their face value and not beyond.[2]

5. Bar Under section 18 is Not Complete

When an application for granting pre-arrest bail for the accused was moved and the State counsel objected on the ground that such prayer has been barred by virtue of section 18 of the Act, beside some other preliminary objections, it was held that Section 18 of the Act of 1989 does not create a complete bar for anticipatory bail "and the liberty of a person should not be left to whims of an unscrupulous complaint or a police officer." It was further observed that duty of the Court is to see that the stringent provisions of section 18 of the Act of 1989 are not misused. The said object can be achieved only if judicial scrutiny is made permissible to find out whether an offence under the said Act has been committed by a person or a group of persons before refusing him or them, as the case may be a pre-arrest bail.[3]

A cross-case was registered, wherein one of the mentioned fact was that humiliating words were uttered, therefore section 3(1)(X) of the Act was also invoked. On the scrutiny of facts, court found that those words were alleged to have been uttered inside the shop and which could not be said within "public view". Therefore in absence of ingredients it was found that no case was made

1. *Bapu Gouda* v. *State of Karnataka*, 1996 Cr LJ 1117 (Kant) (1118): ILR 1995 Kant 3586: 1996 (1) Kant LJ 111.
2. *Virendra Singh* v. *State of Rajasthan*, 2000 Cr LJ 2899 (Raj) (FB): 2000 (2) Raj LR 1: 2001 (1) Raj LW 452.
3. *Girdhari Lal* v. *State of Rajasthan*, 1996 Cr LJ 1613: 1996 Cri LR Raj 25; *Rakesh* v. *State*, 1995 Cr LR 472 (Raj).

out under the Act *prima facie*, hence it was held that bar of section 18 of the Act does not apply and the accused were granted bail.[1]

6. Entitlement to Anticipatory Bail Despite Bar

Conclusions drawn by various High Court in regard to exclusion of section 438 Cr. PC, providing a bar under Section 18 for anticipatory bail for an accused, who have been charged under the offences of 'atrocities', various views could be found. (see also above note).

It was argued before the Court that the Court in any case may use its inherent powers and the accused may be admitted to anticipatory bail. A Division Bench of Delhi High Court[2] was referred, where it was held that against threatened or imminent violation of fundamental rights of personal liberty, petition under Article 226 of the Indian Constitution is maintainable. But it was also observed that when there is a specific bar under section 18 of the Act, such power would only be used in exceptional cases. If the court comes to the conclusion that: (i) the process of law is being misused, (ii) the petition is totally *mala fide* and vexations on the basis of which first information report is recorded; "the Court would certainly exercise its inherent powers and even powers under Article 226 of the Constitution." But it would certainly not be exercised to defeat specific provisions namely section 18 of the Act.[3]

It was again observed that the expression "an accusation of having committed an offence under the Act" does not mean that mere registration of the case under the Act would *ipso facto* attract the prohibition contained in section 18.[4]

Section 18 of the Act gives a vision, direction and mandate to the Court to refuse anticipatory bail, but it does not and it certainly cannot whisk away the right of any Court to have *prima facie* judicial scrutiny of the allegations made in the complaint. Nor can it under its hunch permit provisions of law being abused to suit the *mala fide* motivated ends to some unscrupulous complaint.[5]

Another High Court observed that mere mention or non-mention of the provisions of Prevention of Atrocities Act is of no consequence for excluding operation of section 438 Cr PC. The jurisdiction of Court is in no way could be affected by what the Station House Officer does at the time of registering the crime. The crucial question would be what the contents of the complaint or the FIR reveal for attraction of such provisions of the Act. Court's jurisdiction to issue appropriate directions in exercise of its jurisdiction under section 438 Cr PC is in no way be excluded by merely mentioning the said offences under the Act. What is required is a pragmatic assessment of the contents of the complaint. Even if there is a single averment attracting the provisions of the

1. *Mukesh Kumar Saini* v. *State (Delhi Administration)*, 2001 Cr LJ 4587 (Del): 2001 (94) DLT 241: 2001 (60) DRJ 65.
2. *Capt. Satish Kumar Sharma* v. *Delhi Administration*, 1991 Cr LJ 950: 1992 (1) Cur Cri R 708: ILR (1990) 2 Del 203.
3. *Phulla Dass* v. *State of Punjab*, 1998 Cr LJ 157 (P&H) at 159: 1997 (3) All Cri LR 473: 1997 (3) Rec Cri R 212.
4. *Ramesh Prasad Bhanja* v. *State of Orissa*, 1996 Cr LJ 2743 (Ori): 1996 (10) OCR 466.
5. 1991 Raj Cri C 607 (614-15).

Act, it would be enough to exclude the operation of section 438 of the Code. The cumulative effect of the allegations made in the complaint or FIR should be assessed.[1]

Following the above line another High Court has observed that merely because a case has been registered by the police under the Act, an application for anticipatory bail should not be thrown out, without finding out whether there are accusation of commission of offences under that Act. When it is pointed out— (i) that the accusation in FIR do not constitute any offence under the Act; (ii) the complaint is false; (iii) the complaint stems out of *mala fides* to blackmail; (iv) filed to wreck some personal vengeance for settling and scoring personal vendetta; (v) filed by way of some counter blasts; and, (vi) found to be misuse of judicial process,—the duty of the Court is to scrutinize the facts before refusing the application for anticipatory bail on the ground of section 18 of the Act of 1989. In the mentioned circumstances the bar of section 18 does not come into play and accused is entitled to pre-arrest bail.[2]

7. Regular Bail and section 18

A case was registered under section 3(1)(xv) of the Act of 1989, against which the accused went to High Court with twin prayers—*viz.* for quashing the complaint, and for granting the anticipatory bail. The first prayer does not relate to the present discussion.

However, pressing for the second prayer above-mentioned it was argued that as the case is triable by Sessions Court, the Magistrate would not release the accused on bail when they surrender themselves in the Court of the Magistrate, therefore anticipatory bail may be granted. It was observed that an anticipatory bail order is prohibited under section 18, though, there is no prohibition for granting regular bail by the Magistrate at the time when the accused surrenders. The case is triable by Sessions Court but the Magistrate was directed to consider any bail application on merit, when the accused surrenders before the Magistrate, who is looking after the committal proceedings. As such the committing Magistrate is empowered to grant regular bail in cases constituted under the Act.[3]

The persons accused for offences under the Act have been barred from taking benefit of section 438 Cr PC, yet such person can still, by way of alternative remedy can be permitted to invoke the provisions contained in section 439 Cr. P.C. to get himself released on regular ordinary bail, irrespective of the fact that he is not arrested by the Police.[4]

---

1. *K. Mallesham* v. *State of Andhra Pradesh,* 1999 Cr LJ 324 (AP): 1998 (5) Andh LD 120: 1999 (1) Crimes 225.
2. *Somesh Das* v. *State of Chhattisgarh,* 2004 Cr LJ 680 (Chatt): 2004 (13) All Ind Cas 96: 2004 (2) MPHT 17; *Om Prakash Sharma* v. *Union Territory Chandigarh,* (2001) 4 Crimes 208; *Bablu* v. *State,* 1996 (2) MP WN 141; *Ramesh Prasad Bhanja* v. *State of Orissa,* 1996 Cr LJ 2743 (Ori): 1996 (10) OCR 466.
3. *A.M. Ali* v. *State of Kerala,* 2000 Cr LJ 2721 (2722) (Ker): 2000 (1) Ker LJ 802: 2000 (2) Ker LT 280.
4. (1992) 2 Guj LH 492 (498, 499).

8. Section 438 Cr PC and Bailable Offences

When two kinds of offences have been committed under the same special enactment, out of which one is a bailable offence by virtue of the prescribed punishment under two years, and the other, though non-bailable, is not made out from the perusal of the records, Supreme Court held that in such cases anticipatory bail provided under section 438 Cr PC may be allowed.[1]

9. Other Considerations for Granting Bail

Sections 436, 436A, 437, 438 and 439 of Code of Criminal Procedure deal with various kinds of bails, out of which section 18 of the Act of 1989 bars only the provisions of section 438 of the Code to be applicable in cases arising out of the offences under the Act of 1989. As has been discussed in the preceding paragraphs, it is majority opinion of the Courts that where no offence is made out from the complaint, merely mentioning some sections of the Act would not become a prohibition for the Court to grant a bail under the provisions of section 438 Cr PC. Even it was held that if the accusations are found under the Act, the Court may grant a regular bail, without the accused being arrested.

But on the other hand there are well defined considerations for granting bails. Besides various above mentioned sections of the Code there are also imposition of certain conditions to be followed on the release.

Some of the consideration for granting bail have been given and summed up as:

(i) The enormity of the charge or nature of the accusation;
(ii) The severity of punishment which conviction would entail;
(iii) Nature of evidence in support of accusation;
(iv) The danger of applicant's absconding if he is released on bail;
(v) The danger of witnesses for the prosecution being tampered with;
(vi) The protracted nature of trial;
(vii) The period of detention of the accused;
(viii) Character, means and standing of the applicant;
(ix) Previous conduct and behaviour of the accused in Court;
(x) Health, age and sex of the accused;
(xi) Opportunity to the accused for preparation of defense and access to counsel; and
(xii) Danger of repetition of crime.

The Court, while giving list of above mentioned considerations, also mentioned that the list is not exhaustive and there may be other considerations, depending on the facts and circumstances of the each case.[2]

The Supreme Court accepted the plea in granting bail that the applicant has roots in the community as he has landed property, permanent residence, a

1. *R.K. Krishna Kumar* v. *State of Assam*, 1998 Cr LJ 848 (SC): AIR 1998 SC 530: 1998 AIR SCW 119.
2. *Col. Romesh Chandera* v. *State of Himachal Pradesh*, 2002 Cr LJ 1031 (HP) (1032): 2002 (1) Shim LC 272.

married man with two unmarried daughters etc., therefore as such there is no likelihood of his absconding. The bail was granted, thus it became one of the consideration.[1]

10. Bail Cancellation or Subsequent Application

An 'anticipatory bail' might have been granted, despite the prohibition contained in section 18 of the Act of 1989, on the grounds or considerations as have been discussed in the preceding paragraphs, but, for instance, it was found later that the facts or circumstances, as the case may be, were misrepresented, then the prosecution is entitled to move an application for cancellation of such bail.

In other eventuality an accused may prefer to move subsequent application or applications after rejection of his first or previous application for anticipatory bail, which law permits him to do.

A question may arise as to whether this application for cancellation or subsequent application should be moved and which Court is competent to hear such applications. The law on the point has been repeatedly discussed by various Courts, including Supreme Court, and got it settled. On the other hand there are no statutory rules which govern such kinds of applications concerning bails.

Supreme Court clarified the matter observing that long-standing convention and judicial discipline require that subsequent bail application ought to have been placed before the same Judge who had passed earlier orders. Placing of such matter before the same Judge has its roots in principle as it prevents abuse of process of Court inasmuch as an impression is not created that a litigant is shunning or selecting a Court, depending on whether the Court is to his liking or not, and is encouraged to file successive applications without any new factor having cropped up; if successive bail applications on the same subject are permitted to be disposed of by different Judges, there would be conflicting orders. It was further observed that such subsequent applications shall be placed before same Judge, provided he is available for orders. Same principle has to be applicable and followed even for setting aside the orders passed by the Court granting bail on the ground of mis-representation or mis-statement or suppression of some facts.[2]

Further extending the scope of above principle, the Court observed that no Bench can comment on the functioning of a co-ordinate Bench of the same Court, much less sit in the judgment as an appellate Court over its decision. That which could not be done directly could also not be done indirectly. Otherwise a party aggrieved by an order passed by one Bench of the High Court would be tempted to attempt to get the matter reopened before another Bench, and there would not be any end to such attempts. Besides, it was not consistent with the judicial discipline which must be maintained by the Courts both in the interest

---

1. *Hussainara Khatoon* v. *Home Secretary, State of Bihar, Patna,* 1979 Cr LJ 1036: AIR 1979 SC 1360: 1979 Pat LJR 419.
2. *Shahzad Hasan Khan* v. *Ishtiaq Hasan Khan,* (1987) 2 SCC 684: AIR 1987 SC 1613: 1987 Cr LJ 1872; *Harjeet Singh* alias *Seeta* v. *State of Punjab,* 2002 Cr LJ 571 (SC): AIR 2002 SC 281: 2001 AIR SCW 4998.

of administration of justice by assuring the binding nature of an order which becomes final and the faith of the people in the judiciary.[1]

But, successive 'anticipatory bail' applications moved by the accused without any fresh ground was found by the Court to be 'abuse of process of law', and consequently a heavy fine (cost) was also imposed. The accused had moved eight applications for obtaining 'anticipatory bail'.[2]

If the accused had obtained a bail order by misrepresentation or by suppression of facts, it was for the State Government or the aggrieved party to approach the appropriate higher forum. But in this case the matter ought to have been placed before the same Judge. It was not open to the other Judge to sit in appeal against the order passed by the co-ordinate Bench of same Court.[3]

However, cancellation of bail can be ordered by a court which has released the accused only on the grounds that the accused on bail committed misconduct or misused the terms of the bail bond, or that the accused is tampering with the evidence; or is trying to abscond after the charge-sheet has been filed. In the absence of any of such grounds, the Magistrate (Court) is not competent to take the accused in custody, cancelling the bail.[4]

19. Section 360 of the Code or the provisions of the Probation of Offenders Act not to apply to persons guilty of an offence under the Act.—The provisions of section 360 of the Code and the provisions of the Probation of Offenders Act, 1958 (20 of 1958) shall not apply to any person above the age of eighteen years who is found guilty of having committed an offence under this Act.

SYNOPSIS

1. Analogous Law

Section 16A of Protection of Civil Rights Act, 1955 also prohibit provisions of Probation of Offenders Act, 1958 to be applicable on persons found guilty of having committed any offence punishable under that Act.[5] But application of section 360 of the Code has been a new addition of prohibition for applicability under section 19 of the Act of 1989.

2. Scope

Section 19 of the Act of 1989 expressly put two conditions and mention cases where section 360 Cr. P.C. and the entire provisions of the Probations of

---

1. *Vikramjit Singh* v. *State of Madhya Pradesh*, 1992 Supp (3) SCC 62: AIR 1992 SC 474: 1992 Cr LJ 516.
2. *Harish Kathuria* v. *State*, 2012 Cr LJ 425 (Del).
3. *Harjeet Singh* alias *Seeta* v. *State of Punjab*, 2002 Cr LJ 571 (SC): AIR 2002 SC 281: 2001 AIR SCW 4998.
4. *Madaba Ramaiah* v. *State of Andhra Pradesh*, 1992 Cr LJ 676 (AP) (678): 1992 APLJ (Cri) 102: 1991 (2) LS AP 223; *Kallam Chinaiah* v. *State*, (1979) 2 Andh WR 375.
5. Section 16A of the Act was inserted by Act 106 of 1976, (w.e.f. 19-11-1976).

Offenders Act, 1958 shall not be applicable or excluded. These conditions are:

(i) the tried person must have been declared guilty at the end of trial by Special Court, and

(ii) such declared guilty person must be above the age of eighteen years.

The first condition is not relevant for present discussion because provisions of section 360 Cr PC and the provisions of the Probation of Offenders Act cannot be invoked before the trial ends in conviction.

But the second precondition is worth discussing. It clearly means that any person who has not attained eighteen years of age may be given benefit of either section 360 Cr PC or the provisions of Probation of Offenders Act. Perhaps it is so because persons who have not attained eighteen years of age come under the definition of "Juvenile" provided under section (2)(k) of the Juvenile Justice (Care and Protection of Children) Act, 2000, which had repealed Juvenile Justice Act, 1986.

The limit of eighteen years of age, provided by Section 19 of the Act for prohibition of application of provisions of section 360 Cr PC and the Probation of Offenders Act, has been put to discharge various obligations put on the Indian State by Constitutional as well International (UN) legislative provisions. Clause (5) of Article 15, Clauses (e) and (f) of Article 39, Articles 45 and 47 of Indian Constitution impose on the State a primary responsibility that basic needs and human rights are fully protected in regard to children below eighteen years fixed by the Juvenile Act.

United Nations' General Assembly has adopted various Conventions for Protection of Rights of Children with the emphasis specially on reintegration of child victims, to the extent possible, without resorting to judicial proceedings. Indian State was an enthusiastic signatory to these UN Conventions and the last time it was ratified on 11th December, 1992.

3. Juvenile – in Conflict of Law

The Scheduled Castes and the Scheduled Tribes (Prevention of Atrocities) Act, 1989, under section 14 provides that "Special Court to try the offences under this Act," but in case the accused has not attained the age of eighteen years, the case must be tried by "Juvenile Justice Board". Section 7 of the Juvenile Justice Act provides that the Courts not having jurisdiction to try Juveniles, shall without delay forward the Juvenile with records to competent authority (Juvenile Board).

Juvenile Justice Act is a special legislation, as is the Act of 1989. The Act of 1989 restricts any other jurisdiction, except the Special Court constituted under section 14 to try offences of 'atrocities' committed on members of Scheduled Castes and the Scheduled Tribes. Juvenile Justice Act is also a special legislation, exacted to discharge the obligations thrust on the State by International Community. Now suppose a person aged 16 or 17 years commits offences of 'atrocities' on Scheduled Castes or the Scheduled Tribes, a natural question would arise, where the jurisdiction of trial or inquiry lies? Act of 1989 or the Rules of 1995 are silent on the subject. A similar situation arises when the committed offences are within the exclusive jurisdictions of two Special Courts, for instance: a Special Court constituted under section 14 of the Act of 1989 and the Docoity Affected Areas Act etc. (this matter has been discussed in detail previously).

One decision could be found in which the Division Bench received the question through a reference as to whether Juvenile can be tried by the Special Court where various offences have been alleged against him, including some offences under the Act of 1989. It was held that a Juvenile offender should be dealt with by Juvenile Court established under 1986 Act (now Act of 2000).[1]

However, as far as matters relating to Juveniles are concerned, help may also be taken from the phrase used under section 19 of the Act of 1989 which says: "any person found guilty". That would clearly mean that when a person below the age of eighteen years have been found guilty, he may be sent to Juvenile Board, but it must be added here that the Special Court constituted under Section 14 of the Act of 1989 cannot find such a person guilty unless he has been tried by that Court, which, it is not empowered to or have jurisdiction to do. In the end it may be submitted that the problem could only be rectified through amendment.

4. "Found Guilty of having Committed an Offence under this Act"

The phrase used in the end of section 19 of the Act clearly stipulate that the finding of guilt by the Special Court must relate to the offences under the Scheduled Castes and the Scheduled Tribes (Prevention of Atrocities) Act, 1989 and not otherwise. A person might have been tried for offences "under this Act" and some offences punishable under the Indian Penal Code as well, and if the Court finds the accused guilty of offences under the Penal Code only, while acquitting the accused charged under the provisions or offences of Act of 1989, then the prohibition of applicability of section 360 Cr PC or the Probation of Offenders Act would certainly apply, on the ground that the phrase in question limits the said prohibition of applicability to the offence committed "under this Act".

Some young men under the age of 21 years were tried under Section 3 (1)(x) of the Act of 1989 read with sections 323/34 IPC. The Special Court acquitted the accused under section 3 (1)(x) of the Act of 1989, but found them guilty only under section 323 IPC. On this point the guilty persons requested to take benefit of Probation of Offenders Act, 1958, which was denied by the Special Court, without obtaining a report of probation officer. Section 6 of the Probation of Offenders Act stipulates: "when any person under twenty-one years of age is found guilty of having committed an offence punishable with imprisonment but not with imprisonment for life, the Court by which the person is found guilty shall not sentence him to imprisonment unless it is satisfied that, having regard to the circumstances of the case including the nature of the offence and the character of the offender, it would not be desirable to deal with him under section 3 or section 4 and if the Court passes any sentence of imprisonment on the offender, it shall record its reasons for doing so."

The Special Court recorded that the complainant being a member of Scheduled Caste, thus benefit of Probation of Offenders Act cannot be given to the convicted persons, by virtue of section 19 of the Act of 1989. The High Court observed that the convicted persons were entitled to get benefit of Probation of Offenders Act,

1. *In re : Sessions Judge*, 1995 Cr LJ 330 (Ker) (DB): 1994 (2) Ker LJ 122: 1994 (2) Ker LT 157; also see *Antaryami Patra* v. *State of Orissa*, 1993 Cr LJ 1908 (1913): 1993 (75) Cut LT 803: 1993 (1) Ori LR 464.

in the light of acquittal for the offence under the Act, and the conviction was only related to an offence (Section 323) punishable under IPC.[1]

5. Overriding Effect of section 19

All the nine accused were convicted by Special Court in a trial under section 3(1)(XIV) of the Scheduled Castes and the Scheduled Tribes (Prevention of Atrocities) Act, 1989, for preventing the members of Scheduled Caste or Scheduled Tribe to access to the public places. It was argued on behalf of the appellants that they were not convicted for any other offence, therefore the Court may consider to grant the appellants benefit of Probation of Offenders Act or section 360 Cr PC considering the age of the accused. It was held that prayer cannot be entertained in view of the section 19 of the Act of 1989. It was additionally observed that section 20 of the Act of 1989 gives overriding effect to the provisions of the said Act over other laws; and the acts of the appellants being anti-social and great threat to the democratic setup and freedom of individuals. Finally the conviction awarded by the Special Court was confirmed.[2]

There cannot be two opinions about the mandatory exclusion of the benefits of provisions of section 360 Cr PC or the Probation of Offenders Act, but strictly only to those offenders who have been found guilty of the offences under the Act of 1989.

It may be mentioned here that since long the Courts in India were of the view that provisions of section 360 Cr PC (old sections 380, 562 and 564 Cr PC of 1998) are confined to cases where the offender has been declared guilty of offences under the Penal Code and it could not be invoked in cases of offences under other Acts.[3] The benefit could also not be used in cases of defamation. Therefore for bringing in the stringency of punishments provisions of section 19 can be justified.

6. Powers of Appellate Courts

It is inevitable that appeal against the orders of conviction passed by a Special Court lies before High Court and if an offender has been convicted by Special Court (which is also Session Court) under some sections of IPC as well as offences under the Act of 1989,—say section 376 and any clause of section 3 of the Act—and if the appellate Court finds that from the facts and the circumstances offence under the Act of 1989 is not made out, but instead finds the offender guilty of an offence under some other statute the court may pass an appropriate order under section 360(5), (6) Cr PC.[4] In such a case prohibition of section 19 of the SC/ST Act would not be applicable.

---

1. *Manoj Kumar* v. *State of Madhya Pradesh*, 2000 Cr LJ 1997 (MP) (1998-99): 2000 Cri LR (SC&MP) MPJ 125: 2000 (2) Jab LJ 52.
2. *Abaji Shripatrao Takale* v. *State*, 2011 Cr LJ 2195 (Bom) (2203-4).
3. Offences under Motor Vehicles Act — AIR 1927 All 238. Offences under Stamp Act *Emperor* v. *Shankar Dayal*, AIR 1922 Oudh 224. Under Gambling Act — AIR 1952 Pepsu; 1965 Cr LJ 711 etc.
4. *Mayadhar Paik* v. *State*, 1978 Cr LJ 1054: 45 Cut LT 102; *State* v. *Bodya Ramji Patil*, 1978 Cr LJ 411.

In the similar manner, if an order has been passed by the Special Court invoking section 360 Cr PC or the Probation of Offenders Act, the appellate or revisional Court may set aside such order, while invoking the prohibition of section 19.

20. Act to override other laws.—Save as otherwise provided in this Act, the provisions of this Act shall have effect notwithstanding anything inconsistent therewith contained in any other law for the time being in force or any custom or usage or any instrument having effect by virtue of any such law.

SYNOPSIS

1. Analogous Law

(i) Section 16 of the Protection of Civil Rights Act, 1955 reads:

> "*16. Act to override other laws.*—Save as otherwise expressly provided in this Act, the provisions of this Act shall have effect notwithstanding anything inconsistent therewith contained in any other law for the time being in force, or any custom or usage or any instrument having effect by virtue of any such law or any decree of order of any Court or other authority."

It may be marked that except for the last phrase, section 20 of the Act of 1989 has been copied almost word for word from section 16 of Protection of Civil Rights Act, 1955,

(ii) Section 9 of Disturbed Areas (Special Courts) Act, 1976, had given similar provisions, providing that the Act would have an overriding effect on other laws,

(iii) Section 16 of the Terrorist Affected Areas (Special Courts) Act, 1984 contain similar provisions, giving overriding effect to the provisions of that Act,

(iv) Section 22 of the Terrorist and Disruptive Activities (Prevention) Act, 1985 contained a similar provision,

(v) Section 25 of Terrorist and Disruptive Activities (Prevention) Act, 1987, though a bit refined from its previous legislation of 1985, but claimed the same overriding effect.

(vi) Section 56 of Prevention of Terrorism Act, 2002 contained similar provision.[1]

(vii) Some of the provincial legislations like,—The Andhra Pradesh Control of Organised Crimes Act, 2001 etc., contain similar provisions.

2. Scope

A peculiar situation arises when a statute mandates that its provisions shall override the provisions of other statutes. Section 20 of the Act of 1989 mandates and creates a similar situation as one could see under various enactments connected with 'anti-terror laws' (above mentioned).

Many hypothetical situations may be formulated where "notwithstanding anything inconsistent therewith contained in any other law"— may take place between two enactments that may exist; such as: (i) if one is a special law and the other is a general law; (ii) if both are the special enactments but on the different subjects; (iii) where both are special laws on the same subject; (iv) if a latter enactment, which repealed the previous one, but the previous one was having a saving clause that enabled the provisions of previous one to continue some of its provisions, irrespective of its repeal or expiry; (v) if 'inconsistency' is found between natural law and general or special law; and, (vi) if the latter enactment did not repeal the previous enactment on the same subject and let it continue as such (as is the case of Act of 1955 and Act of 1989 under discussion).

Overriding effects in each of the above mentioned situations need some more explanations, as matter comes up before the Courts often, where the Courts are required to decide, as to which of the provisions would prevail and override the other provision, in cases of 'inconsistency'.

2.1 'Inconsistency' between General and Special Acts

It was observed that: "when two Acts are enacted in the same field, one dealing with the general law and the other dealing with special law, then in case of *inconsistency between the two*, the special law will prevail. When two enactments are passed one later than the other, then it becomes a business for the Courts to consider the exact effect of the latter enactment upon the earlier enactment to see whether they can wholly or in part stand together."[2]

An academic question was raised, whether the two "inconsistent" enactments may be read together and the latter one taken as explaining and not repealing the earlier Act. Also where two Acts are "inconsistent" or repugnant to each other, the latter would be read as having impliedly repealed the earlier, the principle being the latest expression of the *Will* of the Parliament must prevail.[3]

As to the question of determination, whether a later statute repeals by implication the earlier one, it is necessary to scrutinize the terms and consider the true meaning and effect of the Act. Where one statute enacts something in general

1. Most of the mentioned Anti-Terrorist legislations have since been repealed, but some of the cases are still pending in the Courts of the Country.
2. *Antaryami Patra* v. *State of Orissa*, 1993 Cr LJ 1908 (1913): 1993 (75) Cut LT 803: 1993 (1) Ori LR 464.
3. *Goodwin* v. *Phillips*, (1907) 7 CLR 1.

terms, and afterwards another statute is made on the same subject, which, though expressed in affirmative language, introduces special conditions and restrictions, the subsequent statute will usually be considered as repealing by implication the former, for affirmative statutes introductive of a new law do imply in negative. The extent to which Special Acts are held to 'override' the general law or create exceptions depend upon the terms of the statute in question.[1] (Note:— question arose before the Court, whether provisions and restrictions of bail under N.D.P.S. Act override the provisions of Juvenile Justice Act, where bail is mandatory).

The above principle is different from the one, where it is said that words used in one enactment may be used for interpretation to the other enactment.[2]

2.2 'Inconsistency' where both are Special Acts

When one special enactment contains a *non-obstante* clause with a view to give previous or continuing Act, in case of conflict inconsistency an "overriding" effect over the other one, where also *non-obstante* clause exists; it was observed that both Juvenile Justice Act and TADA Act are special enactments, and it is also true that Article 15(3) of the Constitution is also a special provision which can be applied in favour of women and children but not against them. Again it was observed that under the provisions of TADA Act terrorism has been treated as a special problem. In the end it was held that provisions of the Juvenile Justice Act cannot "override" the provisions of TADA Act.[3]

However, a Division Bench had held that as far as "overriding" effects of Provisions of The Scheduled Castes and the Scheduled Tribes (Prevention of Atrocities) Act, 1989, mentioned under section 20 of the Act are concerned, it cannot "override" provisions of Juvenile Justice Act. And as such the provisions of Juvenile Justice Act would prevail. It was held that: "the provisions contained in the Scheduled Castes and the Scheduled Tribes (Prevention of Atrocities) Act, 1989 will not have any overriding effect over the provisions contained in the Juvenile Justice Act, 1986."[4]

2.3 'Inconsistency' between two Acts on the Same Subject—latter Repealing Previous

A very good example may be put forward of the two TADA enactments *viz.* TADA Act of 1985 and TADA Act of 1987.

Discussing and interpreting the "inconsistency" in the sentencing scope under the provisions of TADA Act, 1985 and TADA Act, 1987, Supreme Court observed that TADA Act, 1985 had expired on 22-5-1987, but instead of a situation that the statute reaching the stage of expiry by efflux of time, had it had been repealed by

---

1. *Antaryami Patra* v. *State of Orissa,* 1993 Cr LJ 1908 (1913): 1993 (75) Cut LT 803: 1993 (1) Ori LR 464.
2. *Chaparala Krishna Brahman* v. *Guduru Govardhanaiah,* 1954 Cr LJ 1283 (Mad): AIR 1954 Mad 822: 1954 Mad WN 313.
3. *Jagadish Bhuyan* v. *State,* 1992 Cr LJ 3194 (Gau): 1992 (3) Crimes 570: 1992 (2) Gau LR 18 – note – pages of Criminal Law Journal have been intermingled and numbered incorrectly in the said volume.
4. *In re: Sessions Judge,* 1995 Cr LJ 330 (Ker) (DB) (334): 1994 (2) Ker LJ 122: 1994 (2) Ker LT 157; descented 1993 Cr LJ 1908 (Ori): 1993 (75) Cut LT 803: 1993 (1) Ori LR 464.

another statute, nothing would have survived from the repealed statute, unless succeeding statute incorporated necessary provisions to the contrary. TADA Act of 1985 had a saving clause, and it was discussed because its section 3 provided only death sentence, while the latter TADA Act 1987 provided an alternate sentence as imprisonment for life.

The Apex Court found 'inconsistency' between sentencing scopes under the provisions of the two TADA Acts. The expression was used as "in any enactment other than this Act" would encompass even the enactment which, though expired by the efflux of time, was held to continue to operate by virtue of saving clause. It was held that, consequently exclusivity of extreme sentence provided in the previous enactment must stand superseded by the corresponding benevolent provision of the later statute. Hence the death sentence inflicted under TADA Act, 1985 was *altered* to that of alternate punishment, *i.e.,* imprisonment for life.[1]

2.4 *'Inconsistency' between Natural Law and General or Special Law*

The whole structure of criminal law is based on the principle that an accused person has the right to defend himself against the charge.

It was observed that it is well-known rule applicable to the interpretation of statutes that if there is a conflict between a basic natural right guaranteed under the Constitution and the provisions of any general or special law, it is the basic right of natural justice which would prevail and any such provision being in conflict with it must be held to be inapplicable.[2]

But it may be hurriedly mentioned here that Full Bench of Allahabad High Court had upheld all the provisions of the Act 1989 to be Constitutional and not violative of Fundamental Rights. (case mentioned below).

2.5 *Two Special Acts existing on the same subject*

This is the case between Act of 1955 and Act of 1989, presently under discussion. Many of the landmark decisions were given on various points mentioning "untouchability" and atrocities as the crux of the two enactments. [for yet further details please see note (2)(i) above]

3. *Non Obstante* Clause

It was observed that it is well-settled that a *non obstante* clause has doubtless the effect of overriding the provisions of a law or of the laws in which the said clause is inserted. Sarathi in 'Interpretation of Statutes' defines a *non-obstante* clause thus:

> "A section sometimes begins with the phrase 'notwithstanding anything contained etc." Such a clause is called a *non-obstante* clause and its general purpose is to give the provision contained in the *non obstante* clause an over riding effect in the event of a conflict between it and the rest of the section".[3]

1. *State through CBI* v. *Gian Singh,* 1999 Cr LJ 4315 (SC) (4320): 1999 AIR SCW 3433: AIR 1999 SC 3450.
2. *K.C. Sonrexa* v. *State of Uttar Pradesh,* (1963) 1 Cr LJ 38 (All) (42): AIR 1963 All 33; but also see *Mata Sewak Upadhyay* v. *State of Uttar Pradesh,* 1995 JIC 1168 (All) (FB): 1996 (1) East Cr C 97 (All) (FB) etc.
3. *Superintendent and Remembrancer of Legal Affairs, West Bengal* v. *Satyen-Bhowmick,* 1981 Cr LJ 341 (SC) (345): (1981) 2 SCC 109: AIR 1981 SC 917.

Normally a *non-obstante* clause is always expressed in a negative form, that is to say, by using words 'notwithstanding anything contained' or 'anything contained in a previous law shall not affect the provisions of a particular Act and so on. Sastri, C.J. held that *non-obstante* clause cannot reasonably be read as overriding anything contained in any relevant existing law which is "inconsistent" with the new enactment.[1]

Non-obstante clause is of wide amplitude. Such clause not only override provisions of the Act, but also affects overriding provisions of any other law for the time being in force, therefore *non obstante* clause must be given its full effect.[2] It was also observed that *non obstante* clause is no doubt a very potent clause indeed to exclude every consideration arising from other provisions of the same statute or other statute, but for that reason alone "we must determine the scope" of that provision strictly. When the section containing the said clause does not refer to any particular provisions which it intends to override, but refers to the provisions of the statute generally, it is not permissible to hold that it excludes the whole Act and stands all alone by itself.[3] A search has, therefore, to be made with a view for determining which provision answers the description and which does not.[4]

When the phrase "notwithstanding anything contained" is used, the idea is obvious that the provision embraced in the *non obstante* clause will not be an impediment for the operation of the *enactment*.[5]

There should be a close approximation between the *non-obstante* clause and the operative part of the section, the *non obstante* clause need not always be co-extension necessarily with the operative part, so as to have the effect of cutting down the clear provisions of the enactment. A *non obstante* clause cannot cut down the construction and restrict the scope of its operation, if the words of the enactment are clear. In such cases *non obstante* clause has to be read as clarifying the whole position and must be understood to have been incorporated in the enactment by the Legislature in terms of limiting the ambit and scope of the operative part of the enactment.[6]

In another place it was held that *non-obstante* clause has overriding effect only on rules which were in existence when the said rule was brought into force. It could not be construed so as to mean that all future rules and notifications will be subject to such a *non-obstante* clause.[7]

---

1. *Aswini Kumar Ghose* v. *Arabinda Bose*, AIR 1952 SC 369: 1952 SCJ 568: 1953 SCR 1.
2. *Swapan Kumar Achariya* v. *Subhash Chandra Bhattacharjee*, AIR 1998 Cal 271.
3. *H.H. Maharajadhiraja Madhav Rao Jivaji Rao Scindia Bahadur* v. *Union of India*, AIR 1971 SC 530: (1971) 3 SCR 9: 1971 (1) SCJ 295.
4. *A.G. Varadarajulu* v. *State of Tamil Nadu*, AIR 1998 SC 1388: 1998 AIR SCW 1268: (1998) 4 SCC 231.
5. *Benny T.D.* v. *Registrar of Co-operative Society*, AIR 1998 SC 2012: 1998 AIR SCW 1865: (1998) 5 SCC 269.
6. *Maru Ram* v. *Union of India*, AIR 1980 SC 2147: 1980 Cr LJ 1440.
7. *State of West Bengal* v. *Madan Mohan Ghosh*, AIR 2002 SC 2273: 2002 AIR SCW 2393: (2002) 9 SCC 177.

4. Section 20, Investigation, Inquiry and Trial

There cannot be any doubt when section 14 is read with section 20 of the Act of 1989 that offences under the Act have been made exclusively triable by the Sessions Court nominated as Special Court under section 14 of the Act.

Though section 20 gives the provisions of the Act an overriding effect, but the procedure followed for investigation, inquiry and trials, the Act does not provide any special procedure, except that under section 9, the State Government may by notification confer powers of the police officer on any official of the State Government, and after such conferment the provisions of the Criminal Procedure Code has to be applied. Thus it is clear that in absence of special provisions made in the special statute, otherwise making certain acts and omissions as special offences, in respect thereof the same procedure of investigation, inquiry and trial have to be followed as are provided under the Code of Criminal Procedure.[1]

Section 4 of Cr PC provides for trial of offences under the Indian Penal Code as well as other laws. As per sub-section (2) of section 4 all offences under any other law shall be investigated, inquired into, tried or otherwise dealt with according to the provisions of the Code, but subject to any enactment for the time being in force regulating the manner or place of investigation, inquiry into, trying or otherwise dealing with such offences. The conjoint effect of these provisions is that in the absence of specific provision made in the statute indicating that offences will have to be investigated, inquired into, tried and otherwise dealt with according to that statute, the same have to be investigated, inquired into, tried and otherwise dealt with according to the provision of the Code. The Special Act would apply and prevail over the Code, but where Special Act does not prescribe any procedure, the provisions of the Code shall govern the investigation, inquiry and trial. The same position stands by virtue of provisions of section 5 Cr PC.[2]

5. Earlier Cause of Confusions was section 20

In the early days of the Scheduled castes and the Scheduled Tribes (Prevention of Atrocities) Act, 1989, Indian High Courts were holding diverse views on the point, whether the Special Courts constituted under Section 14 of the Act could or could not take congnizance of offences directly, and whether section 193 Cr PC would be applicable.

It was held by a Division Bench that where a Special Court constituted under the Act receives a final report, disclosing offences under section 3 of the Act as well as offences punishable under the Penal Code, provision of section 193 Cr PC need not be followed as the Special Court has got ample power to directly take cognizance, "without any order of commitment by Magistrate..... Further it is worthwhile to note the provisions contained in section 20 of the Act. As per section (20), the provisions contained in the Act have overriding force over any other law for the time being in force. The provisions contained in section 193 of the Code cannot be of any consequence to restrict the jurisdiction of the Special Court."[3]

1. 1995 AI HC 1448 (1451) (Raj); (1977) 3 Chand Cri C 453.
2. *In Re: Director-General of Prosecution*, 1993 Cr LJ 760 (Ker) (DB): 1992 (2) Ker LJ 731.
3. *In Re: Director-General of Prosecution*, 1993 Cr LJ 760 (761) (Ker) (DB): 1992 (2) Ker LJ 731 (Ker) (D.B.).

One Court has ruled that when a complaint is filed before a Magistrate alleging commission of offences under the Act of 1989 and Magistrate is satisfied that *prima facie* material exists, the Magistrate shall return the complaint for presentation to a proper Court with an endorsement.[1] This was so because Section 20 ousts other jurisdictions of prevailing laws.

It was Supreme Court which ultimately settled the confusion and held that section 193 Cr PC is very much applicable. (For other details on the point please see notes under section 14)

6. Whether Special Law Repeals Provisions of IPC and the Punishments

Section 5 of Indian Penal Code reads:

> "5. *Certain laws not to be affected by this Act.*—Nothing in this Act shall affect the provisions of any Act for punishing mutiny and desertion of officers, soldiers, sailors or airmen in the service of the Government of India or the provisions of *any special* or local law."

The saving of special law is based on the principle *generalia specialibus non derogant*, which means that the 'general words do not derogate from special'. General word do not repeal or modify special legislation.[2]

For further clarification of the matter it seems appropriate to mention section 2 of Indian Penal Code, which is:

> "2. *Punishment of offences committed within India.*—Every person shall be liable to punishment under this Code *and not otherwise* for every act or omission contrary to the provisions thereof, of which he shall be guilty within India."

On general reading of sections 2 and 5 of the Indian Penal Code it is evident that these provisions repealed all existing or future penal enactments. But section 5 qualify this general repeal as it declares that notwithstanding, offences defined by other special laws should continue to be punishable and approved by this section, otherwise the expression—"and not otherwise" used under section 2 would have blocked punishing provisions elsewhere.

Sometimes questions are raised, as to whether an offender has to be punished under provisions of Indian Penal Code or a similar prescribed offence under provisions of 'special enactment'.

The answer to be above question has been given by section 26 of the General Clauses Act, 1897, which provides: "where an act or omission constitutes an offence under two or more enactments then the offender shall be liable to be prosecuted and punished under either, or any one of those enactments, but shall not be liable to be punished twice for the same offence."

The usual rule is that where there is a specific punishment provided under a Special Act, it takes precedence of the general punishment under the Penal Code.[3]

1. 1994 Orissa Cri R, 656.
2. *Seward* v. *Vera*, 10 App Cas 68; *Hawkins* v. *Gatherocole*, 6 De M&G 1.
3. *In re: Mrs. B. Gervase*, (1950) 1 MLJ 201.

21. Duty of Government to ensure effective implementation of the Act.—(1) Subject to such rules as the Central Government may make in this behalf, the State Government shall take such measures as may be necessary for the effective implementation of this Act.

(2) In particular, and without prejudice to the generality of the foregoing provisions, such measures may include,—

(i) the provision for adequate facilities, including legal aid, to the persons subjected to atrocities to enable them to avail themselves of justice;

(ii) the provision for travelling and maintenance expenses to witnesses, including the victims of atrocities, during investigation and trial of offences under this Act;

(iii) the provision for the economic and social rehabilitation of the victims of the atrocities;

(iv) the appointment of officers for initiating or exercising supervision over prosecutions for the contravention of the provisions of this Act;

(v) the setting up of committees at such appropriate levels as the State Government may think fit to assist that Government in formulation or implementation of such measures;

(vi) provision for a periodic survey of the working of the provisions of this Act with a view to suggesting measures for the better implementation of the provisions of this Act;

(vii) the identification of the areas where the members of the Scheduled Castes and the Scheduled Tribes are likely to be subjected to atrocities and adoption of such measures so as to ensure safety for such members.

(3) The Central Government shall take such steps as may be necessary to co-ordinate the measures taken by the State Governments under sub-section (1).

(4) The Central Government shall, every year, place on the table of each House of Parliament a report on the measures taken by itself and by the State Governments in pursuance of the provisions of this section.

SYNOPSIS

1. Analogous Law

Section 15A of the Protection of Civil Rights Act, 1955, is closely analogous to Section 21 of the Act of 1989. Section 15A of the Protection of Civil Rights Act, 1955 reads as:

"*15A. Duty of State Government to ensure that the rights accruing from the abolition of 'untouchability' may be availed of by the concerned persons.*—(1) Subject to such rules as the Central Government may make in this behalf, the State Government shall take such measures as may be necessary for ensuring that the rights arising from the abolition of 'untouchability' are made available to, and are availed of by, the persons subjected to any disability arising out of 'untouchability'.

(2) In particular, and without prejudice to the generality of the provisions of sub-section (1), such measures may include—

(i) the provisions of adequate facilities, including legal aid, to the persons subjected to any disability arising out of 'untouchability' to enable them to avail themselves of such rights;

(ii) the appointment of officers for initiating or exercising supervision over prosecutions for the contravention of the provisions of this Act;

(iii) the setting up of special Courts for the trial of offences under this Act;

(iv) the setting up of committees at such appropriate levels as the State Government may think fit to assist the State Government in formulating or implementing such measures;

(v) provision for periodic survey of the working of the provisions of this Act with a view to suggesting measures for the better implementation of the provisions of this Act;

(vi) the identification of the areas where persons are under any disability arising out of 'untouchability' and adoption of such measures as would ensure the removal of such disability from such areas.

(3) The Central Government shall take such steps as may be necessary to co-ordinate the measures taken by the State Government under sub-section (1).

(4) The Central Government shall, every year, place on the Table of each House of Parliament, a report on the measures taken by itself and by the State Government in pursuance of the provisions of this section."[1]

Section 21 of the Act of 1989 has taken very minor modifications, the foremost being substituting the expression—"Subjected to any disability arising out of 'untouchability" (in Section 15A) to "Subjected to atrocities", as throughout the Act of 1989 has used the defined word "atrocities" in place of "disability arising of 'untouchability'."

2. Scope

Contents of sections 21 of the Act of 1989 are neither related with substantive law, nor could be brought under procedural law, but they are directory in nature,

1. Ins. by Act 106 of 1976 (19-11-1976).

which have been subjected to "such rules as the Central Government may make in this behalf." It is noteworthy that the Scheduled Castes and the Scheduled Tribes (Prevention of Atrocities) Rules, 1995 were made six years later after the passage of the Act of 1989 by the Parliament. In fact one of the points raised in challenging the Constitutionality of the Act in *Mata Sewak Upadhaya's* case (Supra) was that no rules had been framed till then, therefore the Act was *ultra vires* (para 89). But the notified Rules were put before the Court at the time of arguments.

Section 21 of the Act stipulates various kinds of "measures" to be taken for the effective implementation of the Act, including legal aid, economic aid to victims and the witnesses, rehabilitation of victims, appointing officers to superwise prosecution, setting up committees at all levels, periodic survey of working and lastly identifying the "areas" where there is likelihood of commission of offences of atrocities. These directions have to be followed by the State Government. While the section puts a responsibility on the Central Government to see that co-ordination between State organs is being followed to implement the "measures" so directed, besides, yearly placement of a report before both Houses of Parliament regarding the taken measures by it and the State Governments.

3. Section 21 and the Rules of 1995

Right from the Rule 3 of the Rules of 1995 (Rule 2 belongs to "Definitions"), the implementation of Clause-wise measures to be taken, by the State Governments, District administration in general and even local administrative machinery, as has been provided by section 21 of the Act of 1989.

To implement the measures and the objects to be achieved as has been directed through the provisions of section 21 of the Act, perfect and detailed procedures have been prescribed by the Rules of 1995. Rule 4 details the provisions of section 21(2)(IV). Rule 6 also incorporates some of the provisions generally contained in the Police Regulations framed long ago. Rules 8, 9, 10, 11, 12, 13 and 16 are explanations and details of the directions of the section. Rule 14, "Specific responsibility of the State Government", is almost akin to the headline, and Rules 15, 16 and 17 contain detailed description of State level monitoring and vigilance of the situation so that appropriate measures may be taken. (Please see the Rules of 1995 in the Appendices).

22. Protection of action taken in good faith.—No suit, prosecution or other legal proceedings shall lie against the Central Government or against the State Government or any officer or authority of Government or any other person for anything which is in good faith done or intended to be done under this Act.

SYNOPSIS

1. Analogous Law
2. Underlying Principles
3. *De Facto* Immunity
4. Scope
5. Scope of section 4 and section 22 of the Act
6. "Good Faith"
   - 6.1 Definition of "good faith"
   - 6.2 Distinction between Negative and Positive Definition of "Good Faith"

1. Analogous Law

(i) Section 14A of the Protection of Civil Rights Act, 1955 is closely analogous to the provisions of section 22 of the Act of 1989. Section 14A of the Protection of Civil Rights Act, 1955 reads as:

> "14A. *Protection of action taken in good faith.*—(1) No suit, prosecution or other legal proceeding shall lie against the Central Government or a State Government for anything which is in good faith done or intended to be done under this Act.
>
> (2) No suit or other legal proceeding shall lie against the Central Government or a State Government for any damage caused or likely to be caused by anything which is in good faith done or intended to be done under this Act."

The difference being that the previous enactment on the same subject also excluded "any damage caused or likely to be caused" against the respective Governments, but section 22 of Act of 1989 does not exclude claims for the damages, as it has not been mentioned in the said body of section.

(ii) Section 138 of The National Security Guards Act, 1986 provides similar security to members of the Security Guards.

(iii) Section 16 of the Unlawful Activities (Prevention) Act, 1967 provides similar protection.

(iv) Section 69 of Narcotic Drugs and Psychotropic Substances Act, 1985 bears same provisions.

(v) Section 24 of TADA Act 1985, and Section 26 of TADA Act, 1987 protected the respective Governments and its officers from being sued for any act done in good faith (Acts now repealed).

(vi) Section 57 of POTA, 2002 (Acts now repealed) had similar provisions of protection.

(vii) Even provincial legislations like—The Maharashtra Prevention of Communal, Anti-Social and Other Dangerous Activities Act, 1980 (Section 16); or, section 22 of Uttar Pradesh Gangsters Anti-Social Activities (Prevention) Act 1986, etc., contain provisions for protection of action if done in good faith.

2. Underlying Principles

Section 22 of the Act of 1989 incorporates the principle of English Law, which envisages the doctrine of sovereign immunity to be taken for granted. The saying goes, that the kind can do no wrong, and also that he cannot be sued or proceeded against in his own Courts. This is a purely English doctrine and concept, which was not recognized in ancient or later Indian legal history.

In the distant past Manu had asserted that it was the duty of the king to protect the law, and also that the king is subject to law as is any other citizen. Not very far away from the period of establishment of British rule in India, Jahangir did not claim immunity and protection from law when he presented himself to be killed by the widow of a common man whose husband was killed by his queen.

However, the Rule of English Law for sovereign immunity was first introduced in India, through the provisions of India Act, to protect British civil servants from any legal action against them. As a colonial legacy the rule arising out of the doctrine was retained by democratic independent India, but it is the irony of fate that the rule has now been modified in England by Crown Proceedings Act, but very much in vogue in this country.

Such a position has been discussed by Supreme Court in one of its judgments, where their Lordships stipulated that the remedy to cure the position lies in the hands of the legislature. While dealing with the question of immunity to State and its officials for the torturous acts, the Court observed that it was borrowed from England where itself now it is not being generally accepted. Besides, Article 300(1) and 34 of the Constitution has provided a very limited scope for immunity to State.[1]

For a long time the perpetrators of Human Rights, including National Human Rights Commission have cried foul against such immunity to State or its officials. Their contention is that the immunity to State and its officials violates Article 2(3) of ICCPR, wherein every State Party is required to undertake "to ensure that any person whose rights or freedoms (....) are violated shall have an effective remedy, notwithstanding that the violation has been committed by persons acting in an official capacity."

National Human Rights Commission has observed that such protective provisions giving them immunity would "adversely affect the already limited jurisdiction of the National Human Rights Commission under section 19 of the Protection of Human Rights Act, 1993 to deal with complaints alleging the violation of Human Rights" by official machinery and in consequence, further militate against the express purpose of that Act, that the Commission should ensure the "better protection" of Human Rights in the country.

Sometimes it is said that in such Special Act enough safeguards have been provided for violation of Human Rights, and if the State or its officials act maliciously (not in good faith) they may be prosecuted, where prime issue to decide would be to prove or disprove the "good faith". It would not be out of order to quote Edmund Buk that, "it is easy to give power, but it is difficult to give wisdom (to exercise the power properly)."

3. *De Facto* Immunity

Apart from various other provisions, section 197 of Cr. P.C. gives an ample discretion to the Government, whether a prosecution may or may not be launched against its servants. It is the sweet will of the Government to give or not to give sanction for such prosecution. Various Courts in India have,

1. *Kasturi Lal Ralia Ram Jain* v. *State of Uttar Pradesh*, AIR 1965 SC 1039: ILR (1965) 2 All 175: (1965) 1 SCR 375.

though, clearly expressed that there is no need to obtain any sanction from the Government if the act done by the servant does not come under the purview of their official duty. The Apex Court has also directed that applied sanction would be taken as granted if it has not been accorded within four months from the date of application.

The Law Commission of India had recommended to enact a law to contain sovereign immunity from restricting the State from "the application of the doctrine of immunity in such a way that the liability of the State becomes the rule and sovereign immunity the exception."

Section 22 of the Act of 1989, though does not conceal anything to be brought under *de facto* immunity, but it certainly gives an open sovereign immunity with a rider "good faith", which is difficult, if not impossible to disprove.

4. Scope

Section 22 of the Act of 1989 in fact suits the jurisdictions of not only Courts but any other tribunal or authority before whom some kind of "legal proceedings" may be initiated against Central Government, State Government, "or any officer or authority of Government and most importantly "any other person", providing that the act done by such persons or "intended to be done" in "good faith" under the provisions of the Act.

The above mentioned persons are protected to be proceeded against in civil as well as criminal prosecutions and though the Courts' jurisdictions would be affected, in such suits, prosecutions or other legal proceedings, but it would be the Courts which are the only statutory bodies where the question of "good faith" would be decided, because if the Court finds, whether the acts done under the provisions of the Act, but exceeded or done maliciously or not in 'good faith', then the respective Court would be competent to proceed and decide the matter finally and the protection so provided under Section 22 would not be available.

5. Scope of section 4 and section 22 of the Act

Section 4 of the Act of 1989, firstly applies to public servants not belonging to Scheduled Castes or the Scheduled Tribes, and secondly a penal liability has been imposed on non-SC/ST public servants who are found "wilfully" neglecting their duties required to be performed by him under the Act under discussion. Inevitably, the 'wilful neglect of duties' excludes the considerations of "good faith".

But, importantly, the protection provided by section 22 of the Act of 1989 applies uniformallly to "officer or authority of Government or any other person", irrespective of whether such person belong to a Scheduled Caste or a Scheduled Tribe, or not. That is to say that non-SC/ST public servants as well as those belonging to that class have been protected, if they are successful in proving "good faith".

It is also important to note here that not only Central Government, State Government, any officer and "authority of the Government" have been protected under the provisions of section 22 of the Act of 1989, but "any other person" has also been included in this list. Such "any other person" has to be interpreted in the given reference and context, which would mean that by the expression "any other person" no common man or even the accused could be brought under the ambit of such expression. The "any other person" must be somebody who, though, not being an officer or the authority functioning under the respective Governments, but may be a person who acting on behalf of Governments might be in a private capacity. A good example may be cited for a person belonging to any of the NGO's, engaged by the Government to promote the objects of the Act, some kind of survey of taking preventive measures etc.

6. "Good Faith"

The application of provisions of section 22 of the Act of 1989 depends exclusively on the question whether the act in question was done in 'good faith' or not. Answer to this question would decide the availability of protection provided by section 22. An aggrieved person may file a suit, initiate a prosecution or other legal proceedings against Central Government, State Government, any officer, any authority of the Government or any other person, only when he is in a position to disprove 'good faith' in the acts done by such entities and which caused such aggrieved person injury or deprivation of rights etc.

Therefore, the expression 'good faith' becomes so important ingredient for purposes of understanding the ambit of Section 22, that it has to be discussed in detail, including ascertaining the meaning of 'good faith'.

6.1 Definition of "Good Faith"

Two different enactments have defined 'good faith' differently,—*viz.* positively and negatively or through exclusion. The General Clauses Act, 1897 gives the positive definition. It defines:

> "3. (22) A thing shall be deemed to be done in 'good faith', where it is in fact done honestly, whether it is done negligently or not."

This definition of 'good faith' provided by General Clauses Act has been copied, word for word, from English Bills of Exchange Act, 1882 and the Sales of Goods Act, 1893.

The negative definition of 'good faith' has been given in Section 52 of Indian Penal Code, 1860, which reads:

> "52. *'Good Faith'.*—Nothing is said to be done or believed in 'good faith' which is done or believed without due care and attention."

The above definition given by section 52, IPC is not perfect definition because it does not reveal what the expression 'good faith' reveals and also what it actually denotes. The definition given under section 52, IPC does not consider moral element to be included in the definition; and that moral element being honesty and right motive. If person had acted negligently, he has not acted "without due care and attention."

The 'good faith' plays a good deal in criminal law and its presence or absence ordinarily decide the result of a criminal charge in many cases. So is the case when it is dealt under section 22 of the Act of 1989.

Interpreting the definition, the Apex Court observed that: "the solitary item included within the purview of the expression 'good faith' is what is done with 'due care and attention'." Due care denotes the degree of reasonableness in the care sought to be exercised. In Black's Law Dictionary "reasonable care" has been explained as: "such a degree of care, precaution, or diligence as may fairly and properly be expected or required, having regard to the nature of the action, or of the subject-matter and the circumstances surrounding the transaction. It is such care as an ordinary prudent person would exercise under the conditions existing at the time he is called upon to act."[1]

6.2 Distinction between Negative and Positive Definition of "Good Faith"

As said above the definition given by General Clauses Act is positive and the one given by Penal Code is negative, and as such both of these definitions come in conflict in more than one ways. If an act has been done negligently but with honesty, it would not be deemed to have been done in 'good faith'. Definition of Penal Code not only require due care and attention but also the honesty and an intention of doing the particular act, while excluding the element of negligence from the ambit of the definition.

However, the common element present in both of these definitions is 'honesty', without which the essence of meaning of 'good faith' would be lost. Lack of diligence has not been appreciated, because diligence is expected from ordinary man which he exercises in ordinary circumstances, is said to be done in 'good faith'.[2]

The moral element of honesty with right motive has a significance to assess 'good faith'. Result is that when an honest blunderer acts in 'good faith' under the definition of General Clauses Act, he cannot be said to be acting with 'good faith' under the definition of Penal Code, because being "negligent", he has not acted with due care and attention. Absence of 'good faith', according to the definition of Penal Code, therefore, is simply carelessness or negligence, want of due care and caution and does not include the element of dishonesty. Thus the Code regards the honesty as immaterial and the only consideration under it is 'care and intention'. In fact the notion adopted by the Penal Code has been derived from English jurisprudence concept of "reasonable and probable cause" or "reasonable and justifiable cause".

In the end it could be safely inferred that while dealing with "good faith" under section 22 of the Act of 1989, the definition of Penal Code has to be followed and not the one given by General Clauses Act, on the ground that the Act, 1989 is a penal statute and if the general definition given by General Clauses Act is adopted, then "due care and intention" has to excluded, whereas the presence of 'intention' is the most basic or fundamental ingredient in all criminal acts (here *mala fide* intention).

6.3 Question of "Good Faith", is a Question of Fact

The question, whether an act was done in 'good faith' or not is dependent on the facts and circumstances of each case. During a trial, the person who has taken

1. *In re: S.K. Sundaram*, 2001 Cr LJ 2932 (SC) (2938-39): AIR 2001 SC 2374: 2001 AIR SCW 2200.
2. *Harbhajan Singh, Accused* v. *State of Punjab*, AIR 1961 Punj 215: (1961) 1 Cr LJ 710: 63 Punj LR 794.

plea of 'good faith', such plea is tested by the proved facts and the circumstances. It is ascertained what he has done, what more he could have done but failed to do or not to do. It is judged, specially under the criminal law, whether the act was done with due care and caution or not, and in this respect it becomes different from the concept followed under civil law.

6.4 Proof of "Good Faith"

As far as criminal law is concerned the moral element is insignificant for consideration of proof in deciding whether the act in question was done in 'good faith' or not. Burden is on the person, who is pleading 'good faith', to prove that he had acted with due care and attention. The proved facts and circumstances must indicate not only due care and attention but also the capacity and intelligence of the person whose conduct is in question.[1]

When the Central Government or the State Government, as the case may be, has been proceeded against under section 22 of the Act of 1989, it is not the Government whose care and attention would be judged but the officers at the helm.

On the other hand, no general principle can be laid down for testing the proof of 'good faith' in a given circumstance, because it is not possible to ascertain finally the variable position generally of due care and intention. But it could be proved that there was lack of care, attention, intention or caution.

Section 111 of Evidence Act deals with one of the aspect of "proof of good faith in transactions where one party is in relation of active confidence". The provision control the civil nature of proceedings, where it is an exception to the general rule relating to burden of proof of 'good faith', because the allegation of 'bad faith' is one which the plaintiff, according to section 101 of Evidence Act, is bound to prove, and then require the defendant to prove 'good faith'.

6.5 Use of "Good Faith" as Defense for Exemption

When the respective Governments, its officers, authority working under it or 'any other person' has been proceeded against, they may very well take plea of 'good faith' in doing the particular act which has been questioned, and seek protection and exemption under section 22 of the Act of 1989.

It is permissible under the law to argue *ex post facto*, which means that there was absence of the requisite care and caution, therefore there was want of 'good faith'. But the accused person taking the plea of 'good faith' may show that he had taken the necessary or required care and the caution, and also that the act was done in 'good faith'. The First Report of Law Commission (section 113) observed:

"He will be required to prove that his conduct was such as to lead fairly to the inference that he acted in good faith as alleged. It is true that he cannot prove directly what was in his mind, but he may be able to prove facts by which this may be sufficiently manifested." "To satisfy the Court of his good faith, he must show at least that he acted advisedly and that he had reasonable ground *prima facie* for believing that he ought to do what he did."

1. *Dhanna* v. *State*, 1964 Raj LW 126.

In a case, arising out of report prepared by some officials, complaint was lodged for defamation on the basis of the report. The officers took a plea of 'good faith', and that basis claimed protection and exemption. It was observed that the accused must prove that he made the enquiry in a reasonable manner considering all the circumstances. The accused is not bound to prove that the enquiry made by him was fool proof or without the possibility of any error or chance of mistake. However, the accused must show that he got the information from proper source and he had reasonable grounds to believe on the facts he acted upon. The accused must prove by preponderance of probability that there was good faith on his part. The accused should also show that there was no malice on his part, that is to say, that there was no ill-will or spite. Finally the accused has to prove his honesty towards the act done.[1]

Under general criminal law, a person is also entitled to seek exemption from criminality if he is successful in establishing 'good faith' in certain acts. Such exemption may be sought as an exception and on ground of 'good faith' as has been provided under the various clauses of the Chapter on "General Exceptions" in the Indian Penal Code.

If an officer etc., trying to seek protection and exemption under section 22 of the Act of 1989, besides proving 'good faith' on his part, also required to prove that such 'good faith' existed while he was acting or purporting to act in the official discharge of his duty. Leading authority on such official discharge of duty could be found in the observations of their Lordships in the following manner:

> "A public servant can only be said to act or to purport to act in the discharge of his official duty, if his act is such as to lie within the scope of his official duty. Thus a Judge neither acts nor purports to act as a Judge in receiving a bribe, though the judgment which he delivers may be such an act; nor does a Government medical officer act or purport to act as a public servant in picking a pocket of a patient whom he is examining, though the examination itself may be such an act. The test may well be whether the public servant, if challenged can reasonably claim that, what he does, he does it by virtue of his office."[2]

The test given by their Lordship can very well be applicable uniformally to most of the similar situations, including one arising out of section 22 of the Act of 1989.

7. Immunity from Action and Departmental Proceedings

Webster's Legal Dictionary defines 'immunity' as: "exemption from civil suit or criminal prosecution for allegedly wrongful acts, granted by law to certain classes of persons—but sometimes it applies only if the wrongful acts were done in the good-faith (albeit erroneous) belief that they were justified". Such type of immunity is called 'qualified immunity' and not the 'absolute immunity'.

---

1. *Damodara Shenoi* v. *Public Prosecutor*, 1989 Cr LJ 2398 (Ker).
2. *H.H.B. Gill* v. *The King*, AIR 1948 PC 128: 49 Cr LJ 503: (1948) 2 Mad LJ 6; also see *Amrik Singh* v. *State of Pepsu*, AIR 1955 SC 309: 1955 SCR 1302: 1955 SCA 368; *Satwant Singh* v. *State of Punjab*, AIR 1960 SC 266: (1960) 2 SCR 89: 1960 Cr LJ 410; *Bauribandhu Patra* v. *Sagar Malla*, AIR 1966 Ori 86: ILR (1965) Cut 558: 32 Cut LT 172.

According to this definition section 22 of the Act of 1989 prescribed qualified immunity, that is to say that presence or of absence of 'good faith' becomes the criteria for deciding whether the suit, proceedings or prosecution would stand or not.

Black Law Dictionary (Sixth Edn.) defines immunity as: "Freedom or exemption from penalty, burden or duty."

Dealing with a similar provision as that of prescribed by section 22, Supreme Court has observed that there is nothing to circumscribe the power of the Central or the State Government to a point of time prior to the commencement of the trial. The plea that the accused was punished previously in a proceeding under Public Servants (Inquiries) Act and he be given protection under Article (20)(2) for tried again for the same offence, cannot stand.[1] Approving both the above mentioned cases, the Supreme Court again held that despite those departmental proceedings, criminal proceedings can be initiated against the very public servant, where he cannot be allowed to claim immunity on such ground.[2]

8. Good Faith – Ignorance of Fact – Diligence

Obviously, if a party to a legal proceedings who has full knowledge of facts cannot rely on 'good faith'. Provisions of Chapter VIII of Evidence Act would tend to stop such person from taking such plea. Good faith is normally regarded as requiring the exercise of reasonable diligence to learn the truth as well as the means to know the truth as from a reference to public records etc. For instance if a property is being taken for public use (say for rehabilitation of members of Scheduled Castes or the Scheduled Tribes for achieving the objects of the Act of 1989), the real condition of the title of the property cannot be claimed to be unknown, and doctrine of estoppel cannot be 'claimed on the ground of ignorance of facts.

Similar to presumption of innocence 'good faith' is also rebuttable. Before declaring an act of the Government as *mala fide*, facts must be established. But the burden of proving the *mala fide* rests on the person alleging it and the other may rebut it on the grounds of 'good faith'.

9. Constitutional Validity of Provision of Protection

A similar provision, as that of section 22 of the Act of 1989, is contained under section 16 of National Security Act, 1980; which was challenged Constitutionally before a Supreme Court Bench, on the ground that such protection confers a wholly unwarranted protection to the officers who may have passed the *mala fide* orders. The said section of the National Security Act provides that—no suit or legal proceedings shall lie against the Central Government or the State Government, and no proceeding or legal action shall lie against any person, for anything done in good faith or intended to be done in pursuance of the Act. The other point of challenge was on the ground of provision of protection being based

1. *S.A. Venkataraman* v. *Union of India*, 1954 Cr LJ 1993 (SC): AIR 1954 SC 375: 1954 SCA 466; *Thomas Dana* v. *State of Punjab*, 1959 Cr LJ 392 (SC): AIR 1959 SC 375: 1959 SCJ 699.
2. *Jasbir Singh* v. *Vipin Kumar Jaggi*, 2001 Cr LJ 3993 (SC) (4001): AIR 2001 SC 2734: 2001 AIR SCW 2958.

on unreasonableness. One of the argument forwarded was that the provisions of General Clauses Act, 1897 are applicable, and according to the Constitution, which stipulates that a suit could be brought on the ground that the act was done carelessly and without application of mind; and, since the General Clauses Act applies, the defending officers could plead and defeat the suit or the other proceeding brought against them by merely showing that the act done had been done honestly.[1]

It was observed on the above contention that if the policy of a law is to protect honest acts, whether they are done with care or not, it cannot be said that the law is unreasonable. In fact, honest acts deserve the highest protection. Then again, the line which divides a dishonest act from a negligent act is often not easy for a defendant to justify his conduct as honest, if it is accompanied by a degree of negligence.[2]

23. Power to make rules.—(1) The Central Government may, by notification in the Official Gazette, make rules for carrying out the purposes of this Act.

(2) Every rule made under this Act shall be laid, as soon as may be after it is made, before each House of Parliament, while it is in session for a total period of thirty days which may be comprised in one session or in two or more successive sessions and if, before the expiry of the session immediately following the session or the successive sessions aforesaid, both Houses agree in making any modification in the rule or both Houses agree that the rule should not be made, the rule shall thereafter have effect only in such modified form or be of no effect, as the case may be; so, however, that any such modification or annulment shall be without prejudice to the validity of anything previously done under that rule.

SYNOPSIS

1. Analogous Law

Most of the enactments, whether Central or State ones, give rule making powers to the respective Governments. In cases of Special Acts, a rule-making

1. *A.K. Roy* v. *Union of India*, 1982 Cr LJ 340 (SC): AIR 1982 SC 710: (1982) 1 SCC 271.
2. *A.K. Roy* v. *Union of India*, 1982 Cr LJ 340 (371): AIR 1982 SC 710: (1982) 1 SCC 271.

power is essentially provided by the statute itself with a view to achieve the objects of the particular enactment. Therefore, all such provisions are analogous to the provisions of section 23 of the Act of 1989.

However, Section 16B of the predecessor Special Act, *viz.* Protection of Civil Rights Act, 1955 reads as follows:

> "*16B. Power to make Rules.*—(1) The Central Government may, by notification in the Official Gazette, make rules to carry out the provisions of this Act.
>
> (2) Every rule made by the Central Government under this Act shall be laid, as soon as may be after it is made, before each House of Parliament while it is in session for a total period of thirty days which may be comprised in one session or in two or more successive sessions, and if, before the expiry of the session immediately following the session or the successive sessions aforesaid, both Houses agree in making any modification in the rule or both Houses agree that the rule should not be made, the rule shall thereafter have effect only in such modified form or be of no effect, as the case may be; so, however, that any such modification or annulment shall be without prejudice to the validity of anything previously done under that rule."

As is evident from the casual perusal of contents of Section 16B of Protection of Civil Rights Act, 1955, the contents of section 23 of the Act of 1989 are *verbatim* reproduction of the said section.

2. Scope

Webster's Legal Dictionary define Rule as: "any of a set of principles and directives formally adopted by or imposed upon a body for its own administration, the governance of those dealing with it, specially, a regulation governing procedures–."

While the same Dictionary define "rulemaking" as: "the enactment by an administrative agency of Regulations governing conduct in those industries or areas of activity over which it has authority; the legislative function of an administrative agency."[1]

The Scheduled Castes and the Scheduled Tribes (Prevention of Activities) Rules, 1995 were framed by the Central Government in exercise of rule-making powers conferred under section 23 of the Act. The Central Government has been authorised under section 23(1) of the Act to make rules for carrying out the purposes and objects of the Act.[2] As such the Central Government had issued a notification in the Official Gazette and the date of such publication the Rules of 1995 had come into force.[3]

This exercise was done by the Central Government according to the powers vested in it by section 23(1) of the Act.

1. *A.K. Roy* v. *Union of India*, 1982 Cr LJ 340: AIR 1982 SC 710: (1982) 1 SCC 271.
2. *D. Ramalinga Reddy @ D. Babu* v. *State of Andhra Pradesh*, 1999 Cr LJ 2918 (AP) (2919): 1999 (2) Andh LD 572: 1999 (2) Crimes 343.
3. *Vide* G.S.R. 316 (E), dated 31st March, 1995, published in the Gazette of India, Extra., Pt II, sec.3 (i), dated 31st March, 1995.

"Every rule made under this Act" have to be put before both Houses of the Parliament in the prescribed sessions stipulated under section 23(2), and these such rules would come into force only when both the Houses of the Parliament finally agree with or without any modifications, if any. That clearly means that the rules so framed by the Central Government assume status of a legislation, only short of taking an assent by the President.

This also means that of the twin powers flowing through section 23 of the Act of 1989, the Central Government is simply made framer of the Rules and the publisher, while the Parliament has been made the approver, after judging the legitimacy, legality and deciding on the point whether such framed rules are capable of achieving and "carrying out the purposes of this Act."

In general practice, the 'rule-making' powers are given to the Central Government, even by some Special Acts, and in this exercise no part is played by the Houses of Parliament. But the involvement and factual or final approval by both the Houses of the Parliament make the rules so framed to assume a special status. This special status of the rules framed under the powers given through section 23 of the Act, must be presumed to be more than 'directory character', if could not be said to be mandatory.

It should also be noted here that unlike presence of such rule-making powers provided under other special enactments to Central Government, the powers given under section 23 of the Act of 1989, are limited. As said above the rules, though framed by the Central Government, but the final authority lie with the both Houses of the Parliament, and they are empowered under section 23 to agree in "modification", or even they "agree that the rule should not be made, the rule shall thereafter have effect only in such modified form or be of no effect." Therefore, irrespective of the fact that whatever has been framed as rule by the Central Government, it may be 'modified' or deleted altogether with the agreement of both the Houses of the Parliament.

3. Rule-Making Powers of Courts

Article 145 of the Constitution empowers Supreme Court to frame rules, and Articles 225 and 227 give powers to High Courts to exercise jurisdiction to make rules, besides being empowered to have powers of superintendence over all Courts and tribunals throughout the territories where they exercise jurisdiction.

It is a settled law that Special Court constituted under section 14 of the Act of 1989 is a Court of Sessions too, besides the orders and decisions of such Special Courts are being challenged before the respective High Courts or the Supreme Court, as the case may be. As neither the Act of 1989 nor the Rules of 1995 prescribe any Special procedure for the functioning of Special Courts in day-to-day business, these rules framed by the High Courts or the Supreme Court are very much applicable.

A reading of the Article 227 of the Constitution in the light of 'antecedent law' on the subject leads one to the irresistible conclusion that the purpose of the Constitution makers was to make the High Court responsible for the entire administration of justice and to vest in the High Court an unlimited reserve of judicial power which could be brought into play at any time when the High Court considered it necessary to draw upon the same.[1]

An example may be cited here. Under the erstwhile TADA Act, 1987 (now expired), there was no powers provided of interference or even of appeal to the High Courts, but many High Courts had held that they had powers to intervene because they derived inherent powers from the Constitution.

Therefore it may safely be assumed that apart from the Rules of 1995, the rules framed by High Courts and the Supreme Court are applicable, though section 23 of the Act of 1989 did not mention such rules.

4. Absence of Rules cannot Abridge Power to be Exercised

A situation may arise, where either the rules might not have been framed as has been mandated, or, though the rules have been framed under certain enactment, but on a certain point, which has come up as an issue, there may be no existing rule.

The SC/ST Act was enacted in the year 1989, but the rules were not framed till six years later, and one of points of its challenge before the Constitutional Full Bench of Allahabad High Court in *Matasewak Upadhyay's* Case (supra), was that no rules had been framed till then, therefore the Act should be declared *ultra vires*. The Rules of 1995 were immediately framed and put before the Court by Mr. Tulsi, the counsel for the State.

An observation of the Supreme Court in this regard would be handy to mention. The Court observed that when an authority is empowered by a statute to act in a certain manner, or to exercise its powers according to rules, such power given by the statute does not depend on the existence of rules, unless the statute itself controls such situation and provide that in absence of rules no powers could be exercised. The existence of rules is not a condition precedent for the statutory exercise of powers. If no rules are framed there is no void and the authority is not restricted from acting or exercising powers provided by the statute. But, of course if rules are in existence the authority has to function within the parameters of those rules.[2]

5. "Make Rules for Carrying out the Purpose of this Act"

Section 23 of the Act of 1989 limits the rule-making powers of the Central Government, as well as both the Houses of the Parliament, who have been empowered to accord final approval of such framed rules by the Central Government after due deliberations, modifications or the "annulment". Such limitation is applicable to the carrying out the purpose of the Act, as has been stipulated in the "Statement of Objects and Reasons", appended to the Act, and not beyond.

The very basic "purpose" of the Act in fact arises not only to abolish "untouchability", as has been provided under Article 17 of the Constitution, but the entire concepts of "disabilities" arising out of "untouchability" and now

1. *Jodhey* v. *State*, 1952 Cr LJ 1282 (All): AIR 1952 All 788: 1952 All LJ 493.
2. *Surinder Singh* v. *Central Government*, AIR 1986 SC 2166: (1986) 4 SCC 667: JT 1986 SC 578.

termed as 'atrocities' by the present Act. Therefore the framed rules have to be within these parameters.

After the completion of the process prescribed by section 23 of the Act, the final and approved Rules would came into force when they were published in the Official Gazette by notification.

6. Positions of Other Rules under the Act

Besides the Scheduled Castes and the Scheduled Tribes (Prevention of Atrocities) Rules, 1995, there are two other rules, which have been purportedly framed by the Central Government to "carry out the purpose of this Act". These Rules are:

(i) The National Commission for the Scheduled Tribes (Specification of Other Functions) Rules, 2005".[1]

(ii) "Rules of Procedure of the National Commission for Scheduled Castes."[2]

There cannot be two opinions about it that the above mentioned two set of rules, framed by the Central Government, does and must come under the ambit of rule-making powers given to the Central Government by section 23 of the Act of 1989. Therefore, the natural consequence would be to follow the procedure prescribed by section 23 of the Act.

Though, the constitution of the National Commission and the framed Rules of 2005, as well as of 2009 were said to have been derived from sub-clause (f) of clause 5 of Article 338A, and Article 338(5) respectively from the Constitution of India and as such the said rules were placed before the President for assent, but in any case the part played by section 23 of the Act of 1989 cannot be ignored or pushed to a back seat.

7. Constitutional Provisions Incorporated in Rules

As mentioned above the Commissions formulated for Scheduled Tribes and the Scheduled Castes, but for the functioning and other affairs of such Commission there must be clear rules.

The duties of the Commission as laid down in the Article 338 (5) of the Constitution are:

"(a) to investigate and monitor all matters relating to the safe guards provided for the Scheduled Castes under the Constitution or under any other law for the time being in force or under any other of the Government and to evaluate the working of such safeguards;

(b) to inquire into specific complaints with respect to the deprivation of rights and safeguards of the Scheduled Castes;

(c) to participate and advise on the planning process of socio-economic development of the Scheduled Castes and to evaluate the progress of their development under the Union and any State;

1. *Vide* S.O. 1175(E), dated 23rd August, 2005, published in the Official Gazette of India, Extra., Pt II, Sec. 3(ii), dated 24th August, 2005.
2. *Vide* G.S.R. 414(E), dated 25th March, 2009, published in the Gazette of India, Extra., Pt II, Sec.3(i), dated 15th June, 2009.

(d) to present to the President, annually and at such other times as the Commission may deem fit, reports upon the working of those safeguards;

(e) to make in such report recommendations as to the measures that should be taken by the Union or any State for the effective implementation of those safeguards and other measures for the protection, welfare and socio-economic development of the Scheduled Castes; and

(f) to discharge such other functions in relation to the protection, welfare and development and advancement of the Scheduled Castes as the President may, subject to the provisions of any law made by Parliament, by rule specify."

Naturally, the terms "any law made by Parliament" indicate the SC/ST Act of 1989 to which the specified Rules 2009 has been subjected to.

Whereas, Article 338A(5)(f) of the Constitution require the Commission to discharge certain functions, Rules of 2005 have been framed to specify other functions of the Commission and the measures to be taken, in regard to the Scheduled Tribes. Such 'Functions' are:

"(i) Measures that need to be taken over conferring ownership rights in respect of minor forest produce to the Scheduled Tribe living in forest area;

(ii) Measures to be taken to safeguard rights of the tribal communities over mineral resources, water resources etc., as per law;

(iii) Measures to be taken for the development of tribals and to work for more viable livelihood strategies;

(iv) Measures to be taken to improve the efficacy of relief and rehabilitation measures for tribal groups displaced by development projects;

(v) Measures to be taken to prevent alienation of tribal people from land and to effectively rehabilitate such people in whose case alienation has already taken place;

(vi) Measures to be taken to elicit maximum co-operation and involvement of tribal communities for protecting forests and undertaking social afforestation;

(vii) Measures to be taken to ensure full implementation of the Provisions of Panchayats (Extension to the Scheduled Areas) Act, 1996 (40 of 1996);

(viii) Measures to be taken to reduce and ultimately eliminate the practice of shifting cultivation by tribals that lead to their continuous disempowerment and degradation of land and environment."

8. Rules Framed must be Consistent with Existing Legislations – Unless Legislation Itself Saves It

Whenever an enactment empowers a Government to make, it is well-accepted principle of law that the rules should be consistent with other existing legislations for the time being in force, of course, unless the statute that is empowering the Government itself saves it by providing that the provisions of the Rules made thereunder or any order shall have effect notwithstanding anything inconsistent therewith.

As an example, some observations of Apex Court may be cited. In a situation a rule framed [Rule 141(2) of Defence of India Rules] was found inconsistent and in conflict of a rule which was provided under section 114 of the Evidence Act, 1872, it was held that the Act under which such rules were framed, saved such inconsistency, on the ground that the saving clause was incorporated in the Act, under which the rule was framed. Hence such inconsistency was not declared as *ultra vires.*[1]

A.N. Mulla J. had observed that if there is a conflict or inconsistency between a basic natural right, even though the said right is has not been specifically recognised by the Constitution or under the provisions of any other General or Special Law, it is the basic right which would prevail, according to the principles of Natural Justice, and such conflicting provision with such right must be held to be inapplicable.[2]

9. Rules of 1995 – Only Applicable when Case Registered Under the Act

Rules framed under any enactment, generally provide rules of procedure. It was observed that the rules of procedure are not the end but the means to achieve ends of justice. Such framed rules are tools and not expected to create hurdles to the path of justice, but to achieve justice. Procedure is meant to serve and not to rule justice. A pragmatic approach should be adopted while constructing a purely procedural provision, otherwise rules of procedure will become mistress instead of continuing the handmaid of justice.[3]

It may be pointed here that the very first step to roll the wheel of justice is when information of committal of an offence is divulged to officer-in-charge of a police station, it is his option to decide whether the Frist Information Report (FIR) has to be recorded under section 154 Cr PC or under Rule 5 of the Rules of 1995. This decision is naturally based on facts and circumstances of each case.

But once the case has been registered under the provisions of the Act of 1989, it would become obligatory on the authorities concerned to follow the procedure prescribed by the Rules of 1995 as to investigation, spot inspection, taking and obtaining mentioned measures or, importantly for payment of different kinds of "relief amounts" to victims etc.

---

1. *Mangi Lal* v. *State,* 1970 Cr LJ 1644 (SC): AIR 1970 SC 1829: (1970) 2 SCR 270.
2. *K.C. Sonrexa* v. *State of Uttar Pradesh,* (1963) 1 Cr LJ 38 (All) (42): AIR 1963 All 33.
3. Owners and Parties interested in *M.V. "V.P."* v. *Farandeo,* AIR 1989 SC 2206.

APPENDIX 1

NOTES ON SOME IMPORTANT RULES OF 1995

Rules of 1995, framed by the Central Government and approved by both the Houses of the Parliament, under the powers provided by section 23, may be broadly divided into two categories,—namely, those which are related with administrative functions of the State machinery and executing to take "preventive measures", so that instances of atrocities may not occur; and, secondly those kinds of rules have been framed which are particularly related with the administration or criminal justice.

The first category of rules provide in essence, besides central theme of "preventive measures", they provide for appointment or various kinds of officers at different levels to monitor the situation in atrocity prone areas, formation of committees for vigilance and monitoring the on-going situation, rehabilitation and monitory helps provided to victims etc. and over all fixing responsibilities on the District or State level executive or the police officers to look after the affairs as has been envisaged by the objects of the Act of 1989. These categories of the rules are self-explanatory and descriptive hence hardly need notes or the comments.

On the other hand variety of situations and circumstances came-up for which the second category of rules become subject-matter of discussion before different Courts. Therefore these rules have been discussed in the foregoing paragraphs.

Notes on Rule 4

Section 15 of the Act of 1989 provides for appointment of "Special Public Prosecutor" by State Government for every Special Court specified according to provisions of section 14 of the Act, for conducting cases in such Courts. section 15 only empowers only two kinds of legal professionals may be appointed as Special Public Prosecutors. (Please see notes under section 15).

Whereas rule 4(1) of Rules of 1995 borrow some of the provisions of section 24 of Cr PC and lay down the procedure for preparation of District panels of the two categories of the legal professionals, as has been mentioned under section 15, but an additional qualification, as being "eminent Senior Advocate" has been added, besides having put in seven years of practice as an advocate. These panels have to be notified by the State Government, which shall remain in force for a period of 3 years.

However, Rule 4 also has added a third category under rule 4(5). Unlike the provisions of section 15 of the Act, where only two categories have been mentioned, who qualify to be appointed as a Special Public Prosecutor, it adds a third kind. Thus following categories are eligible to be appointed as a Special Public Prosecutors to conduct cases before the Special Court at the District. They are: (a) eminent Senior Advocate who have been in practice for not than seven years; (b) from among Public Prosecutors (from "regular cadre of Prosecuting Officers) in consultation of Director of Prosecution; and (c) at the desire of the victim, the District Magistrate or the Sub-Divisional Magistrate may appoint (not the State Government) "an eminent Senior Advocate" for conducting cases in the Special Court [rule 4(5)].

The rest of the provisions of rule 4 of the Rules of 1995 relate to monitoring the performances of such appointed Special Public Prosecutors and "review" their work on the half yearly basis, besides sending reports.

Many kinds of situations arose when the appointments were made of the Special Public Prosecutors to conduct cases before the Special Courts 'specified' by section 14 of the Act of 1989. In such different situations, the Courts had made following observations:

1. Appointments under section 15 read with Rule 4 as well as Section 24 of Cr PC— The trial commenced under various sections of I.P.C. and section 3(2)(v) of the Act of 1989 before a Special Court, and the prosecutor who had been conducting the case was challenged on the ground that he could not be construed as a "Special Prosecutor" because his appointment was not made in conformity with section 15 of the Act or rule 4(1) of rules of 1995. When the matter was agitated, it was found that the person functioning as Special Public Prosecutor was appointed by State Government in exercise of its powers under sub-section (8) of section 24 Cr PC. Therefore such person was holding the post without any legal authority, and also that the State Government had contravened the mandatory and binding made under the Act. At this juncture the State Government had added few words in the notification as Addendum which was not published. The notification of appointment was questioned. The Court formulated two questions for deciding the matter in issue. The questions were:

(i) Whether the notification issued under section 24(8) of Cr PC, and not following the procedure contemplated under rule 4 and section 15 of the Act and not publishing the notification in the Official Gazette to that effect would vitiate the notification; and

(ii) Whether the petitioner was entitled to the sought relief.

It was held that, as the Addendum was sent for publication (but was not published) and was issued, and if even no notification was issued in conformity to section 15 of the Act or rule 4 of the rules of 1995, it would not vitiate the notification in question, as the "publication of the notification is not mandatory, it is only directory". Therefore in view of Section 15 of the Act and having regard to not following Rule 4 would not vitiate the notification.[1]

It is submitted that section 20 of the Act of 1989 makes the provisions of the Act as overriding effect on the general law, for the time being in force. section 24 Cr PC is a provision of general law which cannot override provisions of section 15 of SC/ST Act read with rule 4 of Rules 1995. Unless the procedure is adopted provided in the rule 4, the appointed S.P.P. would not be legally authorized to conduct cases in the Special Courts. The matter could have been sent to a larger Bench because these findings were given by a single Judge.

2. Competent Authority to Appoint S.P.P.—A cogent view has been taken by Andhra Pradesh High Court while dealing with the matter of appointment of Special Public Prosecutor under section 15 read with rule 4 of the rules of 1995. It was observed that it is true that the State Government is competent to appoint Public Prosecutors under section 24 of the Cr PC. However, the Scheduled Castes and the Scheduled Tribes (Prevention of Atrocities) Act, 1989 is a special enactment enacted to prevent the commission of offences of atrocities against the members of the Scheduled Castes and the Scheduled Tribes. Section 15 of the Act provides that the State Government shall specify a Public Prosecutor for purpose of conducting cases, rule 4 also provides for a specification of a panel of Public Prosecutors to be prepared by the State Government. Both the panels shall be notified in the Official Gazette of the State and shall remain in force for three years. It was held that according to the enforcing provisions of section 20 of the Act of 1989, wherein it has been provided that the provisions of the Act shall override the other laws, for the time being in

1. *Gulzar Khan* v. *State of Karnataka*, 2001 Cr LJ 3586 (Kant) (3590): 2001 (4) All Cri LR 92: ILR (2001) 2 Kant 3890.

force. Thus, in the instant case, as the appointment was not made by the State Government and the procedure was not followed prescribed under section 15 read with rule 4, an appointment made by commission of enquiry is illegal as far as Act of 1989 is concerned.[1]

3. Appointment of S.P.P. under Rule 4 (5).—Sub-rule (5) of rule 4 of SC/ST (PA) Rules, 1995 empowers the District Magistrate or a Sub-Divisional Magistrate to engage an advocate to conduct cases in Special Courts with respect to the offences under the Act of 1989, on request of the victims of atrocity. In exercise of such powers a District Magistrate appointed an advocate to conduct the case in question, which was challenged and a single judge declared such appointment not according to law, consequently the matter was sent for disposal to a Division Bench.

It was observed by the Bench that the Act of 1989 is a Special Legislation which overrides any other law for the time being in force. It was argued that District Magistrate is not competent to appoint a Special Public Prosecutor because section 15 empowers only State Government for such appointment and that power cannot be delegated.

It was observed that it is true that rule 4(5) does not lay down any qualifications as to the minimum length of practice, unlike section 15 or rule 4(1), but apparently the framers of Rules did not want to put any restriction on the choice of the victims of atrocity subject to the embargo that the person should be an 'eminent senior advocate', a term which was also used in sub-rule (1) of Rule 4.There is no conflict between sub-rule (5) of rule 4 and section 15 of the Act. On a combined reading of Rule 4, it is manifest that while sub-rule (1) to (4) contain provisions regarding supervision of prosecution through panel prepared under sub-rule (1) etc., sub-rule (5) is an independent provision with a *non-obstante* clause. It was held that the appointment of senior advocate, and who is choice of the victim, under rule 4(5) of the Rules is not guided by the general provisions, and the appointment cannot be called in question, without challenging the vires of the rule.[2]

Notes on Rule 5

Provisions of rules 5 of the Rules of 1995 are related to the "information to Police Officer in-charge of a Police Station", which correspond to the provisions of section 154 Cr PC. In fact rule 5 is a almost verbatim reproduction of contents, spread in three sub-sections, with very minor modification of the language. section 154 Cr PC talks of "commission of a cognizable offence", which is a general term, the information is required to be reduced in writing, but rule 5 confines only the informations relating to the "commission of an offence under this Act" and not beyond. Thus every First Information Report (FIR) which reveal commission of an offence committed under the provisions of the Act of 1989 would be covered under rule 5 and not under Section 154 Cr PC. It is so because rule 5, has an authority of section 23 of the SC/ST (PA) Act, 1989 and by virtue of provisions of section 20 of the Act, this provision has an overriding effect because it has been stipulated impliedly by rule 5 that the said committed offence is related with 'atrocity', though the word has not been used, but it may be safely presumed to be so as rule 5(1) uses the expression "offence under the Act."

If a person fails to get his information to the commission of an offence recorded under the Act of 1989, may send such information to the Superintendent of Police, who on due investigation shall make an order to register the substance of the information in the book, commonly known as General Diary at a police station.

---

1. *Jonnakuti Mokshanandam* v. *State of Andhra Pradesh*, 2006 Cr LJ 3034 (3037-38): 2006 (2) ALD (Cri) 430: 2006 (4) Andh LT 155.
2. *Satki Devi* v. *Tikam Singh*, 2006 Cr LJ 4721 (Raj) (DB): 2006 (3) Raj LR 706: 2007 (2) Raj LW 1620.

The most important modification which has been made under rule 5(3), where the Superintendent of Police is required to investigate the matter himself or by a police officer "not below the rank of Deputy Superintendent of Police", whereas section 154(3) provides such an investigation to be performed by a police officer subordinate to Superintendent of Police.

Mentioning the designated Deputy Superintendent of Police was necessary because rule 7 of Rules of 1995 provides all investigations to be done by police officers not below the rank of Deputy Superintendent of Police. The provision is, thus, a confirmatory provision to the provision of rule 7.

Notes on Rule 7
(Investigation Officer)

Rule 7 of the Scheduled Castes and the Scheduled Tribes (Prevention of Atrocities) rules, 1995 prescribes for the investigation to be conducted by a specific rank of officer, who shall be judged by his "past experience, sense of ability and justice to perceive the implications of the case. The Rules have not only been framed under section 23 of the Act, but also were put before both the houses of the Parliament who, it is safely presumed, have thoroughly examined all aspects and angles of each provision.

Two considerations should have been the reason for fixing responsibility of the investigation of offences under the Act of 1989 on the shoulders of an officer of Police not lower in rank than Deputy Superintendent of Police, and not by sub-inspectors. In the Department of Police, Deputy Superintendent of Police is the lowest ranking officer who is also a Gazetted officer and every officer below that rank is non-gazetted. Therefore diligence and other qualifications related with efficiency, honesty and an ability to reach at the correct decision is naturally expected of such an officer. In addition to these qualifications, rule 7 of the Rules of 1995 also direct some additional qualification—*i.e.* past experience, sense of ability and most importantly justice to perceive the "*implications* of the case". In the normal circumstances these qualifications cannot be expected from a lower non-gazetted police officer.

Aforesaid two reasons for providing the investigation of an offence committed under the Act to be conducted by an officer not below the rank of Deputy Superintendent of Police, are:

(1) A well qualified officer would always keep in mind the objects formulated by the Act of 1989, as it is a social legislation and any slackness on his part may create social problems.

(2) Harsh punishments have been provided for some of the prescribed offences under the Act, and if somebody wanted to misuse the provisions and inclined to settle personal scores or out of grudge, falsely implicate some persons, it may lead to a great social upheavals or disruption, if proper investigations into the matter is not ensured. For this purpose very able, honest and efficient Police officer is required to investigate the matter and truth behind the complaint, that is the reason why Rule 7 prescribes the investigation to be conducted by a police officer not below the rank of Deputy Superintendent of Police (though, it may be conducted by a police officer of even higher rank).

Keeping these views in mind both the Houses of the Parliament had finally decided to assign the investigation for the offences under the Act, to be conducted by an officer not lower in rank than Deputy Superintendent of Police. (In many parts of the country, including Haryana, wrong attitudes by the police officers in investigating cases under the Act, had resulted in what one may call a social/ethnic/class conflicts).

Conflict of Opinions As to Rule 7.—For a long time different High Courts have taken different views on the point that if the provisions of rule 7 of the Rules of 1945 were strictly followed, whether the trial, proceedings or the investigations would be vitiated or not. In fact three views are in existence, *i.e.,*—totally approving strict application of rule 7; totally denying the applicability of the provisions of rule 7; and, thirdly the view of taking a middle course.

(i) Total Approval of Application of Rule 7.—It was observed that since the purpose and objective sought to be attained by the Act is to minimize the offences against Scheduled Castes and the Scheduled Tribes, hence the Act prescribes stringent sentences. In "order to ensure any misuse of the Act, rule 7 of the rules lays down only that the investigation should be done by an Officer not below the rank of Deputy Superintendent of Police but also lays down that such Officer should be specifically appointed by the State Government. It further lays down that, while appointing such officers the Government should take into consideration his past experience, sense of ability and justice." The case was investigated by a sub-inspector, hence the trial was declared as vitiated and the accused were acquitted on this ground.[1]

This view was also being supported by Orissa High Court, a Bench of which had held that competent authority to investigate cases registered under the Act of 1989 is a police officer not below the rank of Deputy Superintendent of Police as provided under rule 7. It clearly indicates intention of Legislature to get the offences investigated by a Officer who is experienced and has sense of ability and justice to perceive implications of case. It was held that non-compliance of rule 7 would render investigation illegal and vitiate the trial.[2]

The same view was taken by Madhya Pradesh High Court. Entire investigation not confirming to the provisions of rule 7 was declared as vitiated.[3]

This view was also given confirmation by Bombay High Court.[4]

(On these mentioned cases please see the next note, where F.B. either Dissented or Overruled.)

(ii) Contrary View on Application of Rule 7. On the basis—Whether Mandatory or Directory.—A Full Bench was constituted by Andhra Pradesh High Court to consider the question whether the provisions of rule 7 were mandatory or directory and also whether a defect in the investigation may, or may not, vitiated the investigation and trial. The Bench discussed the matter at length, including the past findings of that Court, holding that provisions of rule 7 are mandatory and infraction thereof makes the investigation wholly illegal. The constitution of the Full Bench was the result of a reference by the single Judge, whether provisions of the rule 7 are mandatory. As the case was investigated by a sub-inspector and not by the prescribed officer, it was challenged on the basis of decision of a Division Bench of that Court[5], which declared the provision of rule 7 as mandatory.

A reference was made to a Supreme Court decision[6], wherein a principle was laid down that the Code of Criminal Procedure provides for a certain procedure for investigation,

---

1. *D. Ramalinga Reddy @ D. Babu* v. *State of Andhra Pradesh,* 1999 Cr LJ 2918 (AP) (2919): 1999 (2) Andh LD 572: 1999 (2) Crimes 343; *S.M. Kumar* v. *State,* 2004 Cr LJ (NOC) 347 (AP); *M. Niranjan Reddy* v. *State of Andhra Pradesh,* 2000 Cr LJ 3125 (AP): 2000 (2) Andh LT (Cri) 164.
2. *Chandra Sekhar Pani* v. *State of Orissa,* 2004 Cr LJ 2626 (Ori): 2004 (27) OCR 836: 2004 (1) Ori LR 389.
3. *Dhanraj Singh* v. *State of Madhya Pradesh,* 2005 Cr LJ 3782 (MP): 2005 (32) All Ind Cas 555: 2005 (3) MPHT 107.
4. *Uttamlal D. Yerne* v. *State,* 2006 Cr LJ (NOC) 353 (Bom).
5. *Viswanandhula Chittibabu* v. *State,* 2002 (2) ALD (Cri) 206: 2002 (4) ALT 456 (AP) (DB).
6. *H.N. Rishbud* v. *State of Delhi,* 1955 Cr LJ 526 (SC): AIR 1955 SC 196: ILR (1955) Punj 135.

and this procedure is also applicable to the provisions of Special Act, specially referring to sections 190 and 193 Cr. P.C. The Full Bench observed that these decisions of Supreme Court were not considered by the Division Bench, instead the said Bench (DB) referred cases [as has been referred in note (i) above] while considering the same question. It was observed by the Apex Court in *H.N. Rishbud's* case (supra) as follows:

> "If, therefore, cognizance, is in fact taken, on a police report vitiated by the breach of a mandatory provision relating to investigation, there can be no doubt that the result of the trial which follows it cannot be set aside unless the illegality in the investigation can be shown to have brought about a *miscarriage of justice*. Than an illegality committed in the course of investigation does not affect the competence and the jurisdiction of the Court for trial is well-settled."

On the basis of above findings of the Supreme Court, it was held that the competency of the investigating under rule 7 of the rules, has to be seen as a process which will have no bearing on the case, unless and until the accused shows any serious prejudice to him or any right infringed, the trial would not be derailed in any manner. Finally it was held that provisions of the Rule 7 are not mandatory but only directory.[1]

Using the F.B. Decision in Defence.—The Full Bench, though, held provisions of Rule 7 of the Rules only as directory and not mandatory, but at the same time observed firstly, that: "we share the view of the Division Bench only to the extent that the investigation procedure has to be necessarily followed up in the manner as prescribed under the Statute or the rules." And secondly that: "However, it is open to the accused or the party aggrieved at the initial stages to raise such objection on the investigation conducted by any Officer other than the one contemplated under rule 7 of the rules and invite a decision before the commencement of trial itself. It is only where the Court on *either stage* comes to conclusion that the *rights and interests of the accused or the party aggrieved have been substantially affected or prejudiced, necessary benefit has to be extended.*[1]

The Full Bench has not put a blanket ban on raising the point of not properly following the provisions of rule 7, the unauthorisedly investigating a case before the trial starts, or after its conclusion, as the expression "either stage" includes both. But it is most important to note that some prejudice or the infringement of some right of the accused has to be shown as by not assigning the investigation to a proper Officer.

The plea of prejudice or infringement of the right may include inexperience, no sense of ability and absence of justice to perceive the implications of the case on the part of investigating Officer, when he is other than the prescribed one. It is also well-settled law that duty of an investigation officer is not to hook the accused, named by the complainant, by any means including collecting false or irrelevant evidence. The phrase used in rule 7,—"justice to perceive the implications of the case"—signify that the investigating officer must be just, because a biased investigation may lead to social or ethnic conflict to aggravate, and that is what would be ill implication of the case". It is not normally expected from a Deputy Superintendent of Police, who is a Gazetted officer, and changes are more so if such an officer is an experienced and professionally efficient that the investigation would be conducted in an unbaised manner.

However, the Full Bench decision was followed in various other decisions.[2]

---

1. *Yannam Satyanarayan* v. *State of Andhra Pradesh*, 2006 Cr LJ 2320 (2325) (AP) (FB): 2006 (4) East Cri C 411: 2006 (3) Rec Cri R 294.
2. *Vennapusa Gangireddy* v. *State of Andhra Pradesh*, 2007 Cr LJ 3230 (AP): 2007 (6) AIR Bom R (NOC) 1006: 2007 (2) ALD (Cri) 167; *Keshav Singh* v. *State*, 2007 Cr LJ 721: 2007 (49) All Ind Cas 551: 2007 (1) Crimes 58.

(iii) Re-Investigation: If not done by Proper Officer.—When the case was still pending in the Court of Magistrate for committal proceedings, a petition was filed for quashing all the proceedings on the ground that the investigation was conducted by Circle Inspector of Police. It was observed that, "there was a breach of the provisions of the Rules, appropriate order" is needed to be passed. It was not proper to order for the closure of the trial, the Court observed. Therefore it was held that a direction has to be issued to the investigating agency to proceed with the proper investigation by the competent authority and proceed with according to law (rule 7).[1]

A Division Bench also held that in the circumstances where neither trial has commenced nor charges have been framed, and the contention of accused was found correct that the investigation was not done by an officer according to rule 7, re-investigation can be ordered instead of quashing prosecution.[2]

It may be mentioned here that the Full Bench in *Yannam's* case (supra) had allowed the accused to raise the objections, as to investigation not being conducted by proper officer according to rule 7, at either before the trial started—but in that case easy option is to order for a re-investigation; or, even at the end, but in that case accused must show that a prejudice had been caused and legal right was infringed because the investigation was conducted by a lower ranking officer.

Notes on Rule 12 (4), "Scheduled" for "Norms for Relief Amount"

It would be convenient to cite what rule 12(4) says:

"Rule 12.—(4) The District Magistrate or the Sub-Divisional Magistrate or any other Executive Magistrate shall make arrangements for providing immediate relief in cash or kind or both to the victims of atrocity, their family members and dependents according to the scale as in the Schedule annexed to these rules (Annexture I read with Annexture II). Such immediate relief shall also include food, water, clothing, shelter, medical aid, transport facilities and other essential items necessary for human beings."

Sub-rule (4) of Rule 12 of the Rules of 1995 mention for "providing *immediate* relief "to the victims of atrocities; and the "Annexture 1, Schedule" also refer rule 12(4). The headline put to the double columned table also mention "Norms for Relief Amount".

But irony of situation is that among many of the 22 items mentioned expected "*immediate* relief" has to be provided, factually mention "compensation", or even "pension" to be given to such victims, in some cases it being very large amounts.[3] Rule 12(4) did not mention words like 'compensation' or 'pension'.

Irrespective of the above mentioned anomalies (from a legal point of view), there cannot be two openions that victims of atrocities are very much entitled to compensation on the ground of well-settled and accepted principles of 'compensatory Jurisprudence', or victimological science as it is commonly called. Victim compensation is an idea which tries to maintain a balance or equity between, basically the injured and the injurer, or between injured and its protector—the State and the society. The victim must get compensation because:

(i) it is a recompense from the society on the ground that it failed to provide him conducive atmosphere worth living, and protect him during such invasions of his rights;

(ii) the victim must get the recompense from the State because it has failed in its duty to check the deviant behaviour of the injurer and maintain peace and order in the society.

1. *K. Muhammed* v. *K. Sukumaran*, 2001 Cr LJ 1664 (Ker) (1665): ILR (2001) 1 Ker 540: 2001 (1) Ker LJ 154.
2. *Shatrughna Shravan Kamble* v. *State of Maharashtra*, 2003 Cr LJ 790 (Bom) (DB): 2003 (5) All Ind Cas 671: 2003 (1) All MR 420.
3. In item Nos. 14, 15, 16 and 18 "compensations" or "full compensation" has been mentioned, instead of "immediate relief". Whereas item No. 21 makes a provision of "Pension" etc.

This may be said to be the vicarious liability of the State to pay compensation, though the State has not committed any crime directly. Or speaking in terms of SC/ST (PoA) Act of 1989, its machinery and the executive have failed to take "preventive measures" as has been emphatically provided by the statute as well as the Rules.

The other aspect of this process of paying compensations (the 'relief amounts') also need mention. In some cases the provision of paying compensations has been found prone to its misuse. Amounts mentioned in the table are large amount of money, and in most cases half or some portion of mentioned amount are required to be paid at the lodging of the complaint (FIR), and the rest on the filing of charge-sheet or rarely on conviction. The problem for the investigating agency is presence of section 4 of the Act of 1989, where the public servant has been made liable to punishment when found negligent. Therefore, in almost majority of cases charge-sheets are filed and the so-called victims get full payment of the compensation, that amount not being recoverable, even if Court finds the complaint to be false.

Other instructions provide that when an investigation officer files a charge-sheet after completion of the investigation in a case under the Act, he would send a letter to the Harijan Kalyan Officer of the district, mentioning the amount to be paid to the 'victim' which is due according to the category of offence mentioned in the 'Schedule'. One of the situation is that, in case of acquittal by the court concerned, the paid amount would not be taken or realised back from the 'victim'.

Irony of the situation is that in cases where very little or no evidence is required to prove the guilt, as the standard has been fixed by the Courts, – for instance rape etc.[1] The 'Schedule' mentions (item Nos. 11 and 12) a fixed amount to be paid to victim, 50% of which would be paid after medical examination and rest 50% at the conclusion of trial" (irrespective of conviction). It would not be fair and just that genuine cases are not coming up of the real 'atrocities' committed against the protected Castes, but there are also cries of false implications.

One of the most grave problem is presence of section 4 of the Act of 1989. Once a First Information Report is lodged and the investigation is started by a Deputy Superintendant of Police (Rule 7), section 4 of the Act forces him to file a charge-sheet in the case, even if he came to know during investigation that the fact of the case was not genuine, of course if he or she does not himself or herself belong to Scheduled Castes or Scheduled Tribes, as the section 4 stipulates, "being a public servant but not being a member of a Scheduled Castes or Scheduled Tribes." If he files a final report and the victim complains a neglect on the investigator's part, he or she is liable for an "imprisonment for a term which shall not be less than six months but which may extend to one year."

In Uttar Pradesh alone scores of FIRs have been lodged against investigating officers under section 4 of the Act. To save his own skin and service, in majority of cases charge-sheets are being filed in courts. For that reason courts have somewhat tried to dilute the harsher provisions.

Cardinal rule of Nature is to keep balance. In case some safeguards would have been incorporated in the Act and the Rules such anomalies would not have been allowed to occur (Act 15 of 1990). These Orders were made by the President under Articles 341 and 342 of the Constitution.

(Please see comments on section 3 where in the last of each sub-clause amount of relief payable for each offence committed has been mentioned).

---

1. There is a laid down principle by the Courts that only statement of 'prosecutrix' is sufficient to hold the accused guilty. There is no need of any corroborative evidence, including medical evidence.

APPENDIX 2
PRACTICES AND PROCEDURE

(i) A Private Complaint.—The matter has already been dealt to some extent under the comments on section 14 previously. Some larger Benches of Courts had previously held that the Special Court may as well as may not take cognizance of private complaints directly as an original Court of jurisdiction. But after the Supreme Court settled the matter in *Gangula Ashoka's* case (supra) that a Special Court cannot take cognizance directly without following the committal procedure as has been provided under section 193 Cr PC.

Chapter XV of Code of Criminal Procedure deals with the procedure in connection with private complaint, and it should be filed in the Court of a Magistrate only where a complaint may be filed, irrespective of the fact, whether the offences alleged are triable by a Magistrate or a Court of Session. If it appears to the Magistrate that offences are triable by Court of Session, the Magistrate would adopt the procedure provided under section 202 Cr PC.

In another eventuality, if the police concerned after the conclusion of investigation files a 'final-report' instead of a 'charge-sheet' for some reason, the Magistrate concerned is empowered to take cognizance on the evidence produced by the complainant and treat it as private complaint, whether or not the offences are exclusively triable by Court of Session, and in case the Magistrate finds so, he may commit the case after taking all the evidence.

In one such case where the police submitted a 'final report' declaring the case was based on "mistake of fact". The Special Court proceeded and recoded statements of five witnesses, but it was challenged, and the High Court directed that the Special Court was not empowered to proceed under section 202 C. PC and as such ordered the Special Court to return the records to the Court of Magistrate having jurisdiction.[1]

A private complaint filed directly in the Special Court, it was held that it is not empowered to take direct cognizance of the complaint.[2]

Even a Bench of Andhra Pradesh High Court held that after filing of private complaint there was no need for calling a report from the police under section 210 Cr PC, whether an investigation was pending with them. The Bench said that the Magistrate should have proceeded under sections 200 and 202 of Cr PC, and there was no question of quashing the complaint.[3]

(Please also see comments under section 14 for further details).

(ii) Section 156 (3) Cr PC and 'Pre-Trial Stage'.—The matter had come up before the Full Bench of Rajasthan High Court, and it observed that in the context of the SC/ST Act and the Cr PC and on a harmonious construction of the provisions of section 190 Cr PC, and section 14 of the SC/ST Act of 1989, it can be said that the other Magistrate having

---

1. *Ramesh Chandra Das* v. *Kasinath Jena*, 2000 Cr LJ 4006 (4008): 2000 (19) OCR 101: 2000 (2) Ori LR 162.

2. *Jyoti Arora* v. *State of Haryana*, 1998 Cr LJ 2662 (P&H): 1997 (24) Cri LT 672: 1998 (4) Crimes 643: (1998) 2 All Cr LR 73; *Meera Bai* v. *Bhujbal Singh*, 1995 Cr LJ 2376 (MP) (DB): 1995 (3) Rec Cri R 125; *Mangli Prasad* v. *Additional Session Judge-IInd*, 1996 Cr LJ 3596 (All): 1996 All LJ 1251: 1996 (33) All CriC 400.

3. *Vidavaluru Balaramaiah* v. *State of Andhra Pradesh*, 2003 Cr LJ 3192 (AP): 2003 (1) Andh LT (Cri) 420 AP: 2004 (1) Rec Cri R 882; but see *Dinakrushna* v. *Sunanda Behera*, 2003 Cr LJ (Supp) 5102: 2003 (12) All Ind Cas 71: 2003 (2) Ori LR 492; 1996 MPLJ 141 (FB).

jurisdiction over the area do not lose their jurisdiction to deal with the cases involving offences under the SC/ST Act on creation of Special Courts for the area under that Act, even at pre-trial stage. Thus under section 156(3), a Magistrate having jurisdiction over the area could order investigation under sub-section (1) of section 156 of the Code. Therefore the Magistrate having jurisdiction is competent to deal the case upto the pre-trial stages.[1]

(iii) Bail under Offences of the Act.—A correct position as to bail under the offences prescribed by the Act of 1989 is that creation of Special Courts (under section 14) has been made only for the purposes of speedy trial and nothing beyond as far as provisions of granting or rejecting the applications for bails are concerned. The Special Court is also a Court of Session, and additionally the provisions of Code of Criminal Procedure *mutatis mutandi* apply in regard to bails, of course except application of anticipatory bail provided under section 438 Cr PC which has been barred by the Act of 1989. The Special Courts are competent to exercise powers provided under section 437 Cr PC, as are available to any other Court of Sessions, in relation to offences under the Act.[2]

The High Court at Allahabad had directed that when the accused surrenders before the Court his application for bail shall be disposed of the same day.[3] Similarly in other case it was held that the Special Court should pass an appropriate order on bail when the accused surrenders before the Court.[4]

Even though, section 18 bars the application of section 438 Cr PC, but many Courts have taken a view that Courts may entertain such bail applications, in case the FIR did not reveal any offence from its perusal, (Please see comments under section 18 for further details).

(iv) No *De Novo* Trial in Certain Cases.—The expression "a Court of competent jurisdiction" envisaged in section 465 denotes a *validly* Constituted Court conferred with jurisdiction to try the offence or offences. Such a Court will not be denuded of its competence to try the case on account of any procedural lapse and the competence would remain unaffected by non-compliance of the procedural requirement. For instance, inability to take cognizance of an offence without committal proceedings does not mean a duly constituted Court became an incompetent Court for all purposes.

Laying down the principle mentioned above, and distinguishing the Full Bench decision of Madhya Pradesh High Court[5], the Apex Court held that trial held by the Special Court cannot be earned in such situation, on account of such procedural lapse and a *de novo* trial cannot be ordered by appellate Court.[6]

(v) Transfer of Case, if Jurisdiction Lacks.—When it is found that for some technical or other reasoned the Session Court was not empowered to try a Special Case and despite that the Court has proceeded and framed charges, it would not become a ground to quash the entire proceedings. At the worst that may become a ground to transfer the case to a Court which has jurisdiction to try the case or offences. In case no such competent Court of

---

1. *Bhura Lal* v. *State*, 1999 Cr LJ 3552 (Raj) (FB) (3559): 1999 (2) Raj LR 1: 1999 (2) Raj LW 897.
2. (1996) 2 Guj & H 30: (1997) 1 Guj & R 127.
3. *Ram Brich Chaudhary* v. *State*, 1995 ACC 560: JIC 583.
4. *Rakesh Kumar Bajpai* v. *State*, 1993 UP Cr R 586: 1993 JIC 925.
5. *Anand Swaroop* v. *Ram Ratan*, 1996 MPLJ 141.
6. *State of Madhya Pradesh* v. *Bhooraji*, 2001 Cr LJ 4228 (SC): AIR 2001 SC 3372: 2001 AIR SCW 3313.

jurisdiction was empowered till then, the criminal proceedings could be kept in abeyance till the Government issues a notification conferring such powers to a Court.[1]

When a Special Judge not properly appointed as such, passed an order discharging the accused, it was observed that the offences cannot stand abated, and held that if the Special Court had no jurisdiction to try the offence, it had also no jurisdiction to discharge while dismissing the complaint. It was pointed out the proper course for the Court was to return the complaint to the prosecution to be put before proper Court.[2]

(vi) Compromise in the Interest of Justice.—A complaint was lodged by the prosecution under sections 376/328, IPC and section 3 of the Act of 1989, but the police concerned submitted a final report under section 173 Cr PC. Later on a petition was filed under section 482 Cr PC for quashing the F.I.R. on the ground that the matter has been compromised between the parties in presence of relatives etc. The Court held that the FIR and all consequential proceedings has been quashed on the basis of such compromise.[3]

(vii) Probation of Offenders Act.—(Please see notes under section 14 and 3).

(viii) Offences under the Act and Provisions of Central Reserve Police Force Act 1949.—The accused kicked Sh. B.R. Rao, both being members of "Force" consequently injuring the face and a complaint was lodged, which was tried by Assistant Commandant on whom section 16 of Central Reserve Police Force Act, 1949 conferred powers of a Magistrate. The Commandant convicted the accused and that conviction was upheld in appeal by the Special Judge appointed under section 14 of the Act of 1989. The Special Judge upheld the conviction in the said appeal. The decision was challenged in the High Court on the ground that Assistant Commandant was not empowered to try the case, and secondly the Special Court was not empowered to hear the appeal and decided the appeal illegally as there was no provisions of the Act of 1989 were applicable or proved. But both these contentions were rejected by the High Court.[4]

It is submitted that the Assistant Commandant was not in any way empowered to hear a charge under the offences under the Act, if at all these offences were alleged in the complaint, because it is not clear from the mentioned judgment whether offences were alleged in the complaint or the Assistant Commandant (Magistrate) framed any charges to that effect, attracting provisions and offences under the Act of 1989.

(ix) What About a Cross-Case.—It is well-settled that the cross-cases would be tried and disposed of by the same Court, if arising out of same occurrence between the same parties. Therefore if there is a cross-case, it has to be transferred to the Special Court.[5] Till now no such point has been raised before any Court, but naturally a legal question which comes to mind is, what would become of the term "atrocity" as well as of Article 14 etc., of the Constitution, in case the members of SC or ST were found to be agressors.

---

1. *State by Central Bureau of Investigation* v. *S. Bangarappa*, 2001 Cr LJ 111: AIR 2001 SC 222 (225): 2000 AIR SCW 4111.
2. *CBI* v. *K.C. Balasubramanium*, 2006 (3) Cal & T 664.
3. *Chandra Mohan alias Bunti* v. *State of Haryana*, 2011 Cr LJ 898 (P&H).
4. *Hanuman Singh* v. *Union of India*, 1997 Cr LJ 1054 (Raj): 1997 Cri LR (Raj) RAI 102.
5. *Nathilal* v. *State of Uttar Pradesh*, 1990 Supp SCC 145: 1990 SCC (Cr) 638.

APPENDIX 3

THE SCHEDULED CASTES AND THE SCHEDULED TRIBES (PREVENTION OF ATROCITIES) RULES, 1995[1]

In exercise of the powers conferred by sub-section (1) of section 23 of the Scheduled Castes and the Scheduled Tribes (Prevention of Atrocities) Act, 1989 (33 of 1989), the Central Government hereby makes the following rules, namely:—

1. Short title and commencement.—(1) These rules may be called the Scheduled Castes and the Scheduled Tribes (Prevention of Atrocities) Rules, 1995.

(2) They shall come into force on the date of their publication in the Official Gazette.

2. Definitions.—In the rules, unless the context otherwise requires,—

(a) "Act" means the Scheduled Castes and the Scheduled Tribes (Prevention of Atrocities) Act, 1989 (33 of 1989);

(b) "Dependent", with its grammatical variations and cognate expressions, includes wife, children, whether married or unmarried, dependent parents, widowed sister, widow and children of pre-deceased son of a victim of atrocity;

(c) "identified area" means such area where State Government has reason to believe that atrocity may take place or there is an apprehension of reoccurrence of an offence under the Act or an area prone to atrocities;

(d) "Non-Government Organisation" means a voluntary organisation engaged in the welfare activities relating to the Scheduled Castes and the Scheduled Tribes and registered under the Societies Registration Act, 1860 (21 of 1860) or under any law for the registration of documents or such organisation for the time being in force;

(e) "schedule" means the Schedule annexed to these rules;

(f) "section" means section of the Act;

(g) "State Government", in relation to a Union territory, means the Administrator of that Union territory appointed by the President under article 239 of the Constitution;

(h) words and expressions used herein and not defined but defined in the Act shall have the meanings respectively assigned to them in the Act.

3. Precautionary and preventive measures.—With a view to prevent atrocities on the Scheduled Castes and the Scheduled Tribes, the State Government shall:—

(i) identify the area where it has reason to believe that atrocity may take place or there is an apprehension of reoccurrence of an offence under the Act;

(ii) order the District Magistrate and Superintendent of Police or any other officer to visit the identified area and review the law and order situation;

(iii) if deem necessary, in the identified area cancel the arms licences of the persons, not being member of the Scheduled Castes or Scheduled Tribes, their near relations, servants or employees and family friends and get such arms deposited in the Government Armoury;

(iv) seize all illegal fire arms and prohibit any illegal manufacture of fire arms;

---

1. *Vide* G.S.R. 316 (E), dated 31st March, 1995, published in the Gazette of India, Extra., Pt. II, Sec. 3 (i), dated 31st March, 1995.

(v) with a view to ensure the safety of person and property, if deem necessary, provide arms licences to the members of the Scheduled Castes and the Scheduled Tribes;

(vi) constitute a high power State-level committee, district and divisional level committees or such number of other committees as deem proper and necessary for assisting the Government in implementation of the provisions of the Act;

(vii) set-up a vigilance and monitoring committee to suggest effective measures to implement the provisions of the Act;

(viii) set-up Awareness Centres and organise Workshops in the identified area or at some other place to educate the persons belonging to the Scheduled Castes and the Scheduled Tribes about their rights and the protection available to them under the provisions of various Central and State enactments or rules, regulations and schemes framed thereunder;

(ix) encourage Non-Government Organisations for establishing and maintaining Awarenes Centres and organising workshops and provide them necessary financial and other sort of assistance;

(x) deploy special police force in the identified area;

(xi) by the end of every quarter, review the law and order situation, functioning of different committees, performance of Special Public Prosecutors, Investigating Officers and other Officers responsible for implementing the provisions of the Act and the cases registered under the Act.

4. Supervision of Prosecution and Submission of Report.—(1) The State Government on the recommendation of the District Magistrate shall prepare for each District a panel of such number of eminent Senior Advocates who have been in practice for not less than seven years, as it may deem necessary for conducting cases in the Special Courts. Similarly, in consultation with the Director of Prosecution/in-charge of the prosecution, a panel of such number of Public Prosecutors as it may deem necessary for conducting cases in the Special Court, shall also be specified. Both these panels shall be notified in the Official Gazette of the State and shall remain in force for a period of three years.

(2) The District Magistrate and the Director of Prosecution/in-charge of the prosecution shall review at least twice in a calendar year, in the months of January and July, the performance of Special Public Prosecutors so specified or appointed and submit a report to the State Government.

(3) If the State Government is satisfied or has reason to believe that a Special Public Prosecutor so appointed or specified has not conducted the case to the best of his ability and with due care and caution, his name may be, for reasons to be recorded in writing, denotified.

(4) The District Magistrate and the officer-in-charge of the prosecution at the District level, shall review the position of cases registered under the Act and submit a monthly report on or before 20th day of each subsequent month to the Director of Prosecution and the State Government. This report shall specify the actions taken/proposed to be taken in respect of investigation and prosecution of each case.

(5) Notwithstanding anything contained in sub-rule (1) the District Magistrate or the Sub-Divisional Magistrate may, if deem necessary or if so desired by the victims of atrocity engage an eminent Senior Advocate for conducting cases in the Special Courts on such payment of fee as he may consider appropriate.

(6) Payment of fee to the Special Public Prosecutor shall be fixed by the State Government on a scale higher than the other panel advocates in the State.

5. Information to Police Officer in-charge of a Police Station.—(1) Every information relating to the commission of an offence under the Act, if given orally to an officer incharge of a police station shall be reduced to writing by him or under his direction, and be read over to the informant, and every such information, whether given in writing or reduced to writing as aforesaid, shall be signed by the persons giving it, and the substance thereof shall be entered in a book to be maintained by that police station.

(2) A copy of the information as so recorded under sub-rule (1) above shall be given forthwith, free of cost, to the informant.

(3) Any person aggrieved by a refusal on the part of an officer in-charge of a police station to record the information referred to in-sub-rule (1) may send the substance of such information, in writing and by post, to the Superintendent of Police concerned who after investigation either by himself or by a police officer not below the rank of Deputy Superintendent of Police, shall make an order in writing to the officer in-charge of the concerned police station to enter the substance of that information to be entered in the book to be maintained by that police station.

6. Spot inspection by officers.—(1) Whenever the District Magistrate or the Sub-Divisional Magistrate or any other Executive Magistrate or any police officer not below the rank of Deputy Superintendent of Police receives an information from any person or upon his own knowledge that an atrocity has been committed on the members of the Scheduled Castes or the Scheduled Tribes within his jurisdiction, he shall immediately himself visit the place of occurrence to assess the extent of atrocity, loss of life, loss and damage to the property and submit a report forthwith to the State Government.

(2) The District Magistrate or the Sub-District Magistrate or any other Executive Magistrate and the Superintendent of Police/Deputy Superintendent of Police after inspecting the place or area shall on the spot—

(i) draw a list of victims, their family members and dependents entitled for relief;

(ii) prepare a detailed report of the extent of atrocity, loss and damage to the property of the victims;

(iii) order for intensive police patrolling in the area;

(iv) take effective and necessary steps to provide protection to the witnesses and other sympathisers of the victims;

(v) provide immediate relief to the victims.

7. Investigating Officer.—(1) An offence committed under the Act shall be investigated by a police officer not below the rank of a Deputy Superintendent of Police. The investigating officer shall be appointed by the State Government/Director General of Police/Superintendent of Police after taking into account his past experience, sense of ability and justice to perceive the implications of the case and investigate it alongwith right lines within the shortest possible time.

(2) The investigating officer so appointed under sub-rule (1) shall complete the investigation on top priority basis within thirty days and submit the report to the Superintendent of Police who in turn will immediately forward the report to the Director General of Police of the State Government.

(3) The Home Secretary and the Social Welfare Secretary to the State Government, Director of Prosecution, the officer in-charge of Prosecution and the Director General of Police shall review by the end of every quarter the position of all investigations done by the investigating officer.

8. Setting up of the Scheduled Castes and the Scheduled Tribes Protection Cell.—(1) The State Government shall set up a Scheduled Castes and the Scheduled Tribes Protection Cell at the State headquarter under the charge of Director General of Police/ Inspector General of Police. This Cell shall be responsible for—

(i) conducting survey of the identified area;

(ii) maintaining public order and tranquility in the identified area;

(iii) recommending to the State Government for deployment of special police force or establishment of special police post in the identified area;

(iv) making investigations about the probable causes leading to an offence under the Act;

(v) restoring the feeling of security amongst the members of the Scheduled Castes and the Scheduled Tribes;

(vi) informing the nodal officer and special officer about the law and order situation in the identified area;

(vii) making enquiries about the investigation and spot inspections conducted by various officers;

(viii) making enquiries about the action taken by the Superintendent of Police in the cases where an officer in-charge of the police station has refused to enter an information in a book to be maintained by that police station under sub-rule (3) of rule 5;

(ix) making enquiries about the wilful negligence by a public servant;

(x) reviewing the position of cases registered under the Act; and

(xi) submitting a monthly report on or before 20th day of each subsequent month to the State Government/nodal officer about the action taken/proposed to be taken in respect of the above.

9. Nomination of Nodal Officer.—The State Government shall nominate a nodal officer of the level of a Secretary to the State Government preferably belonging to the Scheduled Castes or the Scheduled Tribes, for co-ordinating the functioning of the District Magistrates and Superintendent of Police or other officers authorised by them, investigating officers and other officers responsible for implementing the provisions of the Act. By the end of every quarter, the nodal officer shall review—

(i) the reports received by the State Government under sub-rules (2) and (4) of rule 4, rule 6, clause (xi) of rule 8;

(ii) the position of cases registered under the Act;

(iii) law and order situation in the identified area;

(iv) various kinds of measures adopted for providing immediate relief in cash or kind or both to the victims of atrocity or his or her dependent;

(v) adequacy of immediate facilities like rationing, clothing, shelter, legal aid, travelling allowance, daily allowance and transport facilities provided to the victims of atrocity or his/her dependants;

(vi) performance of Non-Governmental Organisations, the Scheduled Castes and the Scheduled Tribes Protection Cell, various committees and the public servants responsible for implementing the provisions of the Act.

10. Appointment of a Special Officer.—In the identified area a Special Officer not below the rank of a Additional District Magistrate shall be appointed to coordinate with the District Magistrate, Superintendent of Police or other officers responsible for implementing the provisions of the Act, various committees and the Scheduled Castes and the Scheduled Tribes Protection Cell.

The Special Officer shall be responsible for—

(i) providing immediate relief and other facilities to the victims of atrocity and initiate necessary measures to prevent or avoid re-occurrence of atrocity;

(ii) setting up an awareness centre and organising workshop in the identified area or at the district headquarters to educate the persons belonging to the Scheduled Castes and the Scheduled Tribes about their rights and the protection available to them under the provisions of various Central and State enactments or rules and schemes *etc.* framed therein;

(iii) co-ordinating with the Non-Governmental Organisations and providing necessary facilities and financial and other types of assistance to Non-Governmental Organisations for maintaining centres or organising workshops.

11. Travelling allowance, daily allowance, maintenance expenses and transport facilities to the victim of atrocity, his or her dependent and witnesses.—(1) Every victim of atrocity or his/her dependent and witnesses shall be paid to and fro rail fare by second class in express/mail/passenger train or actual bus or taxi fare from his/her place of residence or place of stay to the place of investigation or hearing of trial of an offence under the Act.

(2) The District Magistrate or the Sub-Divisional Magistrate or any other Executive Magistrate shall make necessary arrangements for providing transport facilities or reimbursement of full payment thereof to the victims of atrocity and witnesses for visiting the investigating officer, Superintendent of Police/Deputy Superintendent of Police, District Magistrate or any other Executive Magistrate.

(3) Every woman witness, the victim of atrocity or her dependent being a woman or a minor, a person more than sixty years of age and a person having 40 per cent or more disability shall be entitled to be accompanied by an attendant of her/his choice. The attendant shall also be paid travelling and maintenance expenses as applicable to the witness or the victim of atrocity when called upon during hearing, investigation and trial of an offence under the Act.

(4) The witness, the victim of atrocity or his/her dependent and the attendant shall be paid daily maintenance expenses, for the days he/she is away from the place of his/her residence or stay during investigation, hearing and trial of an offence, at such rates but not less than the minimum wages, as may be fixed by the State Government for the agricultural labourers.

(5) In addition to daily maintenance expenses the witness, the victim of atrocity (or his/her dependant) and the attendant shall also be paid diet expenses at such rates as may be fixed by the State Government from time to time.

(6) The payment of travelling allowance, daily allowance, maintenance expenses and reimbursement of transport facilities shall be made immediately or not later than three days by the District Magistrate or the Sub-Divisional Magistrate or any other Executive Magistrate to the victims, their dependants/attendants and witnessess for the days they visit the investigating officer or in-charge of police station or hospital authorities or Superintendent of Police/Deputy Superintendent of Police or District Magistrate or any other officer concerned or the special court.

(7) When an offence has been committed under section 3 of the Act, the District Magistrate or the Sub-Divisional Magistrate or any other Executive Magistrate shall reimburse the payment of medicines, special medical consultation, blood transfusion, replacement of essential clothing, meals and fruits provided to the victim (s) of atrocity.

12. Measures to be taken by the District Administration.—(1) The District Magistrate and the Superintendent of Police shall visit the place or area where the atrocity has been committed to assess the loss of life and damage to the property and draw a list of victims, their family members and dependents entitled for relief.

(2) Superintendent of Police shall ensure that the First Information Report is registered in the book of the concerned police station and effective measure for apprehending the accused are taken.

(3) The Superintendent of Police, after spot inspection, shall immediately appoint an investigating officer and deploy such police force in the area and take such other preventive measures as he may deem proper and necessary.

(4) The District Magistrate or the Sub-Divisional Magistrate or any other Executive Magistrate shall make arrangements for providing immediate relief in cash or in kind or both to the victims of atrocity, their family members and dependents according to the scale as in the Schedule annexed to these rules (Annexure I read with Annexure II). Such immediate relief shall also include food, water, clothing, shelter, medical aid, transport facilities and other essential items necessary for human beings.

(5) The relief provided to the victim of the atrocity or his/her dependent under sub-rule (4) in respect of death, or injury to, or damage to property shall be in addition to any other right to claim compensation in respect there of under any other law for the time being in force.

(6) The relief and rehabilitation facilities mentioned in sub-rule (4) above shall be provided by the District Magistrate or Sub-Divisional Magistrate or any other Executive Magistrate in accordance with the scales provided in the Schedule annexed to these rules.

(7) A report of the relief and rehabilitation facilities provided to the victims shall also be forwarded to the Special Court by the District Magistrate or the Sub-Divisional Magistrate or the Executive Magistrate of Superintendent of Police. In case the Special Court is satisfied that the payment of relief was not made to the victim or his/her dependent in time or the amount of relief or compensation was not sufficient or only a part of payment of relief or compensation was made it may order for making in full or part the payment of relief or any other kind of assistance.

13. Selection of officers and other staff members for completing the work relating to atrocity.—(1) The State Government shall ensure that the administrative officers and other staff members to be appointed in an area prone to atrocity shall have the right aptitude and understanding of the problems of the Scheduled Castes and the Scheduled Tribes.

(2) It shall also be ensured by the State Government that person from the Scheduled Castes and the Scheduled Tribes are adequately represented in the administration and in the police force at all levels, particularly at the level of police posts and police station.

14. Specific responsibility of the State Government.—The State Government shall make necessary provisions in its annual budget for providing relief and rehabilitation facilities to the victims of atrocity. It shall review atleast twice in a calendar year, in the month of January and July the performance of the Special Public Prosecutor specified or appointed under section 15 of the Act, various reports received, investigation made and preventive steps taken by the District Magistrate, Sub-Divisional Magistrate and Superintendent of Police, relief and rehabilitation facilities provided to the victims and the reports in respect of lapses on behalf of the Concerned officers.

15. Contingency plan by the State Government.—(1) The State Government shall prepare a model contingency plan for implementing the provisions of the Act and notify the same in the Official Gazette of the State Government. It should specify the role and responsibility of various departments and their officers at different levels, the role and responsibility of Rural/Urban Local Bodies and Non-Government Organisations. *Inter alia* this plan shall contain a package of relief measures including the following:—

(a) scheme to provide immediate relief in cash or in kind or both;

(b) allotment of agricultural land and house sites;

(c) the rehabilitation packages;

(d) scheme for employment in Government or Government undertaking to the dependant or one of the family members of the victim;

(e) pension scheme for widows, dependant children of the deceased, handicapped or old age victims of atrocity;

(f) mandatory compensation for the victims;

(g) scheme for strengthening the socio-economic condition of the victim;

(h) provisions for providing brick/stone masonary house to the victims;

(i) such other elements as health care, supply of essential commodities, electrification, adequate drinking water facility, burial/cremation ground and link road to the Scheduled Castes and the Scheduled Tribes habitats.

(2) The State Government shall forward a copy of the contingency plan or a summary thereof and a copy of the scheme, as soon as may be, to the Central Government in the Ministry of Welfare and to all the District Magistrates, Sub-Divisional Magistrates, Inspectors General of Police and Superintendents of Police.

16. Constitution of State-level vigilance and monitoring committee.—(1) The State Government shall constitute a high power vigilance and monitoring committee of not more than 25 members consisting of the following:—

(i) Chief Minister/Administrator—Chairman (in case of a State under President's Rule Governor—Chairman);

(ii) Home Minister, Finance Minister and Welfare Minister—Members (in case of a State under the President's Rule Advisors—Members);

(iii) all elected Members of Parliament and State Legislative Assembly and Legislative Council from the State belonging to the Scheduled Castes and the Scheduled Tribes—Members;

(iv) Chief Secretary, the Home Secretary, the Director-General of Police, [1][representatives of the National Commission for Scheduled Castes and the National Commission for Scheduled Tribes]—Members;

(v) the Secretary in-charge of the welfare and development of the Scheduled Castes and the Scheduled Tribes—Convenor.

(2) The high power vigilance and monitoring committee shall meet at least twice in a calendar year, in the month of January and July to review the implementation of the provisions of the Act, relief and rehabilitation facilities provided to the victims and other matters connected therewith, prosecution of cases under the Act, role of different officers/ agencies responsible for implementing the provisions of the Act and various reports received by the State Government.

17. Constitution of District-level vigilance and monitoring committee.—(1) In each district within the State, the District Magistrate shall set up a vigilance and monitoring committee in his district to review the implementation of the provisions of the Act, relief and rehabilitation facilities provided to the victims and other matters connected

---

1. Subs. by G.S.R. 896(E), dated 23rd December, 2011, for "Director/Deputy Director National Commission for the Scheduled Castes and the Scheduled Tribes" (w.e.f. 23-12-2011).

therewith, prosecution of cases under the Act, role of different officers/agencies responsible for implementing the provisions of the Act and various reports received by the District Administration.

(2) The district-level vigilance and monitoring committee shall consist of the elected Members of the Parliament and State Legislative Assembly and Legislative Council, Superintendent of Police, three group 'A' officers/Gazetted officers of the State Government belonging to the Scheduled Castes and the Scheduled Tribes, not more than 5 non-official members belonging to the Scheduled Castes and the Scheduled Tribes and not more than 3 members from the categories other than the Scheduled Castes and the Scheduled Tribes having association with Non-Government Organizations. The District Magistrate and District Social Welfare Officer shall be Chairman and Member-Secretary respectively.

(3) The district-level committee shall meet at least once in three months.

18. Material for annual report.—The State Government shall every year before the 1st July, forward the report to the Central Government about the measures taken for implementing provisions of the Act and various schemes/plans framed by it during the previous calendar year.

[1][*SCHEDULE*

ANNEXURE I

[*See* rule 12(4)]

NORMS FOR RELIEF AMOUNT

Sl. No.	Name of the offence	Minimum amount of relief
(1)	(2)	(3)
1.	Drink or eat inedible or obnoxious substance [section 3(1)(i)]	Rs. 60,000 or more depending upon the nature and gravity of the offence to each victim and also commensurate with the indignity, insult, injury and defamation suffered by the victim. Payment to be made as follows: I. 25% when the charge-sheet is sent to the Court II. 75% when accused are convicted by the lower court.
2.	Causing injury, insult or annoyance [section 3(1)(ii)]	
3.	Derogatory act [section 3(1)(iii)]	
4.	Wrongful occupation or cultivation of land, etc. [section 3(1)(iv)]	At least Rs. 60,000 or more depending upon the nature and gravity of the offence. The land/premises/water supply shall be restored where necessary at Government cost, Full payment to be made when charge-sheet is sent to the court.
5.	Relating to land, premises and water [section 3(1)(v)]	

1. Subs. by G.S.R. 896(E), dated 23rd December, 2011, for Schedule and Annexure I (w.e.f. 23-12-2011).

(1)	(2)	(3)
6.	Begar or forced or bonded labour [section 3(1)(vi)]	At least Rs. 60,000 to each victim, payment of 25% at FIR stage and 75% on conviction in the lower court.
7.	Relating to right to franchise [section 3(1)(vii)]	Upto Rs. 50,000 to each victim depending upon the nature and gravity of the offence.
8.	False, malicious or vexatious legal proceedings [section 3(1)(viii)]	Rs. 60,000 or reimbursement of actual legal expenses and damages or whichever is less after conclusion of the trial of the accused.
9.	False and frivolous information [section 3(1)(ix)]	
10.	Insult, intimidation and humiliation [section 3(1)(x)]	Upto Rs. 60,000 to each victim depending upon the nature of the offence. Payment of 25% when charge-sheet is sent to the court and rest on conviction.
11.	Outraging the modesty of a woman [section 3(1)(xi)]	Rs. 1,20,000 to each victim of the offence. 50% of the amount may be paid after medical examination and remaining 50% at the conclusion of the trial.
12.	Sexual exploitation of a woman [section 3(1)(xii)]	
13.	Fouling of water [section 3(1)(xiii)]	Upto Rs. 2,50,000 or full cost of restoration of normal facility, including cleaning when the water is fouled. Payment may be made at the stage as deemed fit by District Administration.
14.	Denial of customary rights of passage [section 3(1)(xiv)]	Upto Rs. 2,50,000 or full cost of restoration of right of passage and full compensation of the loss suffered, if any. Payment of 50% when charge-sheet is sent to the court and 50% on conviction in lower-court.
15.	Making one desert place of residence [section 3(1)(xv)]	Restoration of the site/right to stay and compensation of Rs. 60,000 to each victim and reconstruction of the house at Govt. cost, if destroyed, to be paid in full when charge-sheet is sent to the lower court.
16.	Giving false evidence [section 3(2)(i) and (ii)]	At least Rs. 2,50,000 or full compensation of the loss or harm sustained. 50% to be paid when charge-sheet is sent to Court and 50% on conviction by the lower court.

(1)	(2)	(3)
17.	Committing offences under the Indian Penal Code punishable with imprisonment for a term of 10 years or more [section 3(2)]	At least Rs. 1,20,000 depending upon the nature and gravity of the offence to each victim and or his dependents. The amount would vary if specifically otherwise provided in the Schedule.
18.	Victimization at the hands of a public servant [section 3(2)(vii)]	Full compensation on account of damages or loss or harm sustained. 50% to be paid when charge-sheet is sent to the Court and 50% on conviction by lower court.
19.	Disability.—The definition of disability shall be as given in section 2 of the Persons with Disabilities (Equal Opportunities, Protection of Rights and Full Participation) Act, 1995, and guidelines for their assessment shall be as contained in the Ministry of Social Justice & Empowerment, G.O.I. Notification No. 154, dated 1-6-2001, as amended from time-to-time. A copy of the Notification is at Annexure II to the Schedule.	
	(a) 100% incapacitation:	
	(i) Non-earning Member of a family	At least Rs. 2,50,000 to each victim of offence. 50% on FIR and 25% at charge-sheet and 25% on conviction by the lower court.
	(ii) Earning Member of a family	At least Rs. 5,00,000 to each victim of offence, 50% to be paid on FIR/Medical examination stage, 25% when charge-sheet sent to court and 25% at conviction in lower court.
	(b) Where incapacitation is less than 100%	The rates as laid down in a(i) and (ii) above shall be reduced in the same proportion, the stages of payments also being the same. However, not less than Rs. 40,000 to non-earning member and not less than Rs. 80,000 to an earning member of a family.
20.	Murder/Death	
	(a) Non-earning Member of a family	At least Rs. 2,50,000 to each case. Payment of 75% after postmortem and 25% on conviction by the lower court.
	(b) Earning Member of a family	At least Rs. 5,00,000 to each case. Payment of 75% after post-mortem and 25% on conviction by the lower court.

(1)	(2)	(3)
21.	Victim of murder, death, massacre, rape, mass rape and gang rape, permanent incapacitation and dacoity	In addition to relief amounts paid under above, items, relief may be arranged within three months of date of atrocity as follows:— (i) Pension to each widow and/or other dependents of deceased SC and ST @ Rs. 3,000 per month, or Employment to one member of the family of the deceased, or provision of agricultural land, an house, if necessary by outright purchase. (ii) Full cost of the education and maintenance of the children of the victims. Children may be admitted to Ashram Schools/residential schools. (iii) Provision of utensils, rice, wheat, dals, pulses, etc. for a period of three months.
22.	Complete destruction/burnt houses	Brick/stone masonary house to be constructed or provided at Government cost where it has been burnt or destroyed.]

[1][*ANNEXURE II*

[*See* rules 12(4) & 19]

MINISTRY OF SOCIAL JUSTICE AND EMPOWERMENT

NOTIFICATION

New Delhi, the 1st June, 2001

Subject:—Guidelines for evaluation of various disabilities and procedure for certification.

No. 16-18/97-NI. 1.—In order to review the guidelines for evaluation of various disabilities and procedure for certification as given in the Ministry of Welfare's O.M. No. 4-2/83-HW.-III, dated the 6th August, 1986 and to recommend appropriate modifications/alterations keeping in view the Persons with Disabilities (Equal Opportunities, Protection of Rights and Full Participation) Act, 1995, Government of India in the Ministry of Social Justice and Empowerment, *vide* Order No. 16-18/97-NI, I, dated 28-8-1998, set up four committees under the Chairmanships of Director-General of Health Services—one each in the area of mental retardation, Locomotor/Orthopaedic disability, Visual disability and Speech and Hearing disability. Subsequently, another Committee was also constituted on 21-7-1999 for evaluation, assessment of multiple disabilities and categorization and extent of disability and procedures for certification.

2. After having considered the reports of these committees the undersigned is directed to convey the approval of the President to notify the guidelines for evaluation of following disabilities and procedure for certification:—

1. Subs. by G.S.R. 896(E), dated 23rd December, 2011, for Annexure II (w.e.f. 23-12-2011).

1. Visual impairment
2. Locomotor/Orthopaedic disability
3. Speech and hearing disability
4. Mental retardation
5. Multiple Disabilities.

Copy of the Report is enclosed herewith as *Annexure.*

3. The minimum degree of disability should be 40% in order to be eligible for any concessions/benefits.

4. According to the Persons with Disabilities (Equal Opportunities, Protection of Rights and Full Participation) Rules, 1996 notified on 31-12-1996 by the Central Government in exercise of the powers conferred by sub-sections (1) and (2) of section 73 of the Persons with Disabilities (Equal Opportunities, Protection of Rights and Full Participation) Act, 1995 (1 of 1996), authorities to give disability Certificate will be a Medical Board duly constituted by the Central and the State Government. The State Government may constitute a Medical Board consisting of at least three members out of which at least one shall be a specialist in the particular field for assessing locomotor/ Visual including low vision/hearing and speech disability, mental retardation and leprosy cured, as the case may be.

5. Specified test as indicated in *Annexure* should be conducted by the medical board and recorded before a certificate is given.

6. The certificate would be valid for a period of five years for those whose disability is temporary. For those who acquire permanent disability, the validity can be shown as 'Permanent'.

7. The State Government/UT Administrations may constitute the medical boards indicated in para 4 above immediately, if not done so far.

8. The Director-General of Health Services, Ministry of Health and Family Welfare will be the final authority, should there arise any controversy/doubt regarding the interpretation of the definitions/classifications/evaluations tests, etc.

ANNEXURE

Reports of the Committee set up to review the guidelines for evaluation of various disabilities and procedure for certification and to recommend appropriate modifications/alternations keeping in view the Persons with Disabilities (Equal Opportunities. Protection of Rights and Full Participation) Act, 1995.

In order to review the definitions of various types of disability, the guidelines for evaluation of various disabilities and procedure for certification as given in the Ministry of Welfare's O.M. No. 4-2/83-HW.III, dated the 6th August, 1986 and to recommend appropriate modifications/alterations keeping in view the Persons with Disabilities (Equal Opportunities, Protection of Rights and Full Participation) Act, 1995, five Sub-Committees were constituted in the areas of Mental Retardation, Orthopaedic/Locomotor Disability, Visual Disability, Speech and Hearing and Multiple Disabilities, under the Chairmanship of Dr. S.P. Agarwal, Director-General of Health Services, *vide* the Ministry of Social Justice & Empowerment's Order No. 16-18/97-NI.I, dated 28-8-1998 and 21-7-1999. A copy each of the Order is at *Appendix I.*

2. These Sub-Committees, after detailed deliberations, have submitted their reports. List of participants of the meetings taken by the Committee is at *Appendix II.* The reports of the Committees set up to review the guidelines for evaluation of various disabilities and procedure for certification of each of the area of the disabilities are given in *Appendix III.*

APPENDIX I

No. 16-18/97-NI.I

Government of India

Ministry of Social Justice & Empowerment

New Delhi Dated 28th August, 1998

ORDER

In order to review the definitions of various types of disability, the guidelines for evaluation of various disabilities and procedure for certification as given in the Ministry of Welfare's O.M. No. 4-2/83-HW.III, dated the 6th August, 1986 and to recommend appropriate modifications/alterations keeping in view the Persons with Disabilities (Equal Opportunities, Protection of Rights and Full Participation) Act, 1995, the following Sub-Committees are hereby constituted in the areas of Mental Retardation, Orthopedic/ Locomotor-Disability, Visual Disability and Speech & Hearing disability:

I. Sub-Committee on Mental Retardation:

1. Dr. S.P. Aggarwal, Director-General Health Services Ministry of Health and Family Welfare, Nirman Bhawan New Delhi-11 — Chairperson
2. Dr. R. Srinivasa Murthy, Prof. & Head. Deptt. of Psychiatry, NIMHANS, Bangalore-22 — Co-Chairperson
3. Dr. G.G. Prabhu, Workchil Court Mysore — Member
4. Dr. (Mrs.) Neena Vohra, Consultant & HOD, Psychiatry, Dr. R.M.L. Hospital, New Delhi. — Member
5. Dr. Anand Pandit, Hony. Prof & Director KEM Hospital Pune-11 — Member
6. Dr. D.K Menon, Director National lnstt. for Mentally Handicapped Secunderabad — Member-Secretary

II. Sub-Committee on Locomotor/Orthopaedic Disability:

1. Dr. S.P. Aggarwal, D.G.H.S., Ministry of Health, Nirman Bhavan, New Delhi-11 — Chairperson
2. Dr. K.K. Singh, Prof. & Head, AHMS. New Delhi, — Co-Chairperson
3. Dr. Balu Sankaran, FX-DOHS FX-Chairman ALIMCO, New Delhi — Member

4. Dr. Suranjan Bhattacharji, HOD. Deptt. of PMR CMC Hospital, Vellore	Member
5. Dr. R K Srivastava Medical Superintendent Safdarjung Hospital, New Delhi	Member
6. Dr. B.P. Yadav Ex-Chairman Rehab Council of India, New Delhi	Member
7. Dr. B.R. Avadhani Director IPH New Delhi.	Member-Secretary

III. Sub-Committee on Visual Disability:

I. Dr. S.P. Aggarwal D.G.H.S. Ministry of Health, New Delhi	Chairperson
2. Dr. V.K. Dada, Head, Dr. R.P. Centre, AIIMS, New Delhi	Co-Chairperson
3. Dr. Hari Mohan, Director, Mohan Eye Institute, Rajender Nagar, New Delhi	Member
4. Shri Lal Advani Consultant Saket, New Delhi	Member
5. Dr. Bhushan Punani Blind Men's Association, Ahmedabad	Member
6. Shri S.A. Datrange National Association for the Blind, Mumbai	Member
7. Dr. S.R. Shukla Director NIVH, Dehradun.	Member-Secretary

IV. Sub-Committee on Speech & Hearing Disability:

1. Dr. S.P. Aggarwal D.G.H.S. Ministry of Health, New Delhi	Chairperson
2. Dr. S.K. Kacker Ex-Director, AIIMS, New Delhi	Co-Chairperson
3. Dr. S. Nikam Director AIIMS, Mysore	Member
4. Dr. J.M. Hans Sr. ENT Surgeon, Dr. RML Hospital, New Delhi	Member
5. Dr. M Raghunath Professor in Audiology PGIMER, Chandigarh	Member

6. Dr. (Mrs.) Rekha Roy — Member-Secretary
Director
AYJNIHH. Mumbai-400050.

2. The terms of reference for the Committees are as follows:

(a) Providing uniform definitions and categorisation of degree and extent of the disability,

(b) Recommending authorities competent to give certification,

(c) The Committees will submit their report in two months.

3. TA/DA to the members of the Committee will be borne by the concerned Institute whose Director is included as Member-Secretary of the Sub-Committee.

(Gauri Chatterjee)
Joint Secretary to Govt. of India
Tele No. 3381641

To,

All Members of the Committees.

Copy for information to:

PSs to Secretary (SJ&E)/AS(SJ&E),JS(DD)

No. 16-18-97-NI.I

Government of India

Ministry of Social Justice & Empowerment

Shastri Bhavan,
New Delhi, Dated 21st July, 1999

ORDER

It has been decided to constitute a Sub-Committee in the sector of Multiple Disability in order to have standard definitions and guidelines for evaluation and procedure for certification, and to make appropriate recommendations, keeping in view the Persons with Disabilities. (Equal Opportunities, Protection of Rights and Full Participation) Act, 1995. Accordingly, a Sub-Committee is hereby constituted in the sector of multiple disability, with the following Members:

1. Dr. S.P. Aggarwal, — Chairman
Director-General of Hearth Services
Ministry of Health & Family Welfare, Nirman Bhavan,
New Delhi.

2. Smt. Aloka Guha. — Member
Director,
Spastics Society of Tamil Nadu,
Opp. TTTI, Taramani Road,
Chennai-13.

3. Dr. H.C. Goyal, — Member
Consultant,
Rehabilitation Department, Safdarjung Hospital,
New Delhi.

4. Dr. Uma Tuli, — Member
General-Secretary
Amar Jyoti Charitable Trust, N.-192, Greater Kailash-I,
New Delhi–110048.

5. Dr. D.K. Menon, Member-Secretary
Director,
National Institute for the Mentally Handicapped,
Manovikasnagar, Secunderabad-500009.

3. The terms of reference for the Committee are as follows:—

(a) Providing uniform definitions and categorisation of degree and extent of the disabilities.

(b) Recommending authorities competent to give certification.

(c) The Committee will submit its report in two months.

4. TA/DA to the members of the Committee will be borne by the National Institute for the Mentally Handicapped, Secunderabad.

(Gauri Chatterji)
Joint Secretary to the Government of India.
Tele No.338 1641

To:

All Members of the Committees

Copy for information to-:

PSs to Secretary (SJ&E)/ AS (SJ&E)/ JS(DD).

APPENDIX II

List of participants of the meeting held on 29-2-2000 under the Chairmanship of Dr. S.P. Agarwal. Director-General of Health Services with the Members of Sub-committee constituted *vide* Order No. l6-18/96-NI.I (PWD), dated 28-8-1998 of Ministry of Social Justice & Empowerment.

1. Dr. R.K. Srivastava. Addl. Director-General of Health Services.
2. Dr. V.K, Dada, Head, R.P. Centre, AIIMS, New Delhi.
3. Dr. R. Srinivasa Murthy, Prof. & HOD, Deptt. of Psychiatry, NIMHANS, Bangalore.
4. Dr. O.K. Menon, Director, NIMH, Hyderabad.
5. Dr. Rekha Roy, Director, NIHH, Mumbai.
6. Dr. S.R. Shukla, Director, NIVH, Dehradun.
7. Dr. Dharmendra Kumar, Officiating Director, NIRTAR, Cuttack.
8. Dr. A.S. Bais, Deputy Director-General (Medical).
9. Dr. S. Chug, Consultant in Medicine & Chairman, Medical Board, Dr. RML Hospital.
10. Dr. L.S. Chauhan, ADG (IH).
11. Dr. A.N. Sinha, CMO (HA).

List of participants of the meeting held on 17-8-2000 under the Chairmanship of Dr. S.P. Agarwal, Director-General of Health Services with the Members of Sub-Committee constituted vide Order No. 16-18/96-NI.I (PWD). dated 21-7-1999 of Ministry of Social Justice & Empowerment.

1. Dr. R.K. Srivastava, Addl. Director-General of Health Services.
2. Dr. H.C. Goyal, Consultant & HOD, Rehabilitation, S.J. Hospital, New Delhi.
3. Dr. O.K. Menon, Director, National Institute for the Mentally Handicapped, Secunderabad.
4. Smt. Aloka Guha, Director, Spastic Society of Tamil Nadu, Opp. TTTI, Taramani Road, Chennai-13.
5. Dr. A.N. Sinha, CMO (HA).

APPENDIX III

A. MENTAL RETARDATION

1. Definition:—Mental retardation is a condition of arrested or incomplete development of the mind, which is especially characterised by impairment of skills manifested during the development period which contribute to the over all level of intelligence, *i.e.*, cognitive, language, motor and social abilities.

2. Categories of Mental Retardation:—

2.1 *Mild Mental Retardation*:—The range of 50 to 69 (standardised IQ test) is indicative of mild retardation. Understanding and use of language tend to be delayed to a varying degree and executive speech problems that interfere with the development of independence may persist into adult life.

2.2 *Moderate Mental Retardation*:—The IQ is in the range of 35 to 49. Discrepant profiles of abilities are common in this group with some individuals achieving higher levels in visuo-spatial skills than in tasks dependent on language while others are markedly clumsy by enjoying social interaction and simple conversation. The level of development of language is variable: some of those affected can take part in simple conversations while others have only enough language to communicate their basic needs.

2.3 *Severe Mental Retardation*:—The IQ is usually in the range of 20 to 34. In this category, most of the people suffer from a marked degree of motor impairment or other associated deficits indicating the presence of clinically significant damage to or mal-development of the central nervous system.

2.4 *Profound Mental Retardation*:—The IQ in this category estimated to be under 20. The ability to understand or comply with requests or instructions are severally limited. Most of such individuals are immobile or severally restricted in mobility, incontinent and capable at most of only very rudimentary forms of non-verbal communication. They possess little or no ability to care for their own basic needs and require constant help and supervision.

3. Process of Certifications:—

3.1 A disability certificate shall be issued by a Medical Board consisting of three members duly constituted by the Central/State Government. At least, one shall be a Specialist in the area of mental retardation, namely, Psychiatrist, Paediatrician and clinical Psychologist.

3.2 The examination process will consist of three components, namely, clinical assessment, assessment of adaptive behaviour and intellectual functioning.

B. VISUAL DISABILITY

1. Definition:—Blindness refers to a condition where a person suffers from any of the condition, namely,

(i) total absence of sight; or

(ii) visual acuity not exceeding 6/60 or 20/200(snellen) in the better eye with best correcting lenses; or

(iii) limitation of field of vision subtending an angle of 20 degree or worse;

2. Low Vision:—Persons with low vision means a person with impairment of vision of less than 6/18 to 6/60 with best correction in the better eye or impairment of field in any one of the following categories:—

(a) reduction of fields less than 50 degrees

(b) Heminaopia with macular involvement

(c) Altitudinal defect involving lower fields.

3. Categories of Visual Disability:—

All with correction

Category	Better eye	Worse eye	% age impairment
Category 0	6/9-6/18	6/24 to 6/36	20%
Category I	6/18-6/36	6/60 to Nil	40%
Category II	6/40-4/60 or field of vision 10° -20°	3/60 to Nil	75%
Category III	3/60 to 1/60 or field of vision 10°	F.C. at 1 ft. to Nil	100%
Category IV	F. C. at 1 ft. to Nil or field of vision 10°	F.C. at 1 ft. to Nil	100%
One eyed persons	6/6	F. C. at 1 ft. to Nil or field of vision 10°	30%

Note.—F.C. means Finger Count

4. Process of Certification:—A disability certificate shall be issued by a Medical Board duly constituted by the Central/State Government having, at least three members. Out of which, at least one member shall be a specialist in ophthalmology.

C. SPEECH & HEARING DISABILITY

1. Definition of Hearing:—A person with hearing impairment having difficulty of various degrees in hearing sounds is an impaired person.

2. Categories of Hearing Impairment:—

Category	Type of Impairment	D B Level	Speech discrimination	% age of impairment
I	Mild hearing Impairment	DB 26 to 40 dB in better ear	80 to 100% in better ear	Less than 40% to 50%
II (a)	Moderate hearing	41 to 60 dB in better ear	50 to 80% in better ear	40% to 50%
II (b)	Serve hearing Impairment	61 to 70 dB hearing Impairment in better ear	40 to 50% in better ear	51% to 70%
III	(a) Profound hearing Impairment	71 to 90 dB	Less than 40% in better ear	71% to 100%
	(c) Total deafness	91 dB and above/in better ear/to hearing	Very Poor discrimination	100%

(i) Pure tone average of learning in 500, and 2000 HZ, 4000 HZ by conduction (AC and BC) should be taken as basis for consideration as per the test recommendations.

(ii) When there is only as island of hearing present in one or two frequencies in better ear, it should be considered as total loss of hearing.

(iii) Wherever there is no response (NR) at any of the 4 frequencies (500, 1000, 2000 and 4000 HZ), it should be considered as equivalent to 100 dB loss for the purpose of classification of disability and in arriving at the average.

3. Process of Certification:—

A disability certificate shall be issued by a Medical Board duly constituted by the Central and the State Government. Out of which, at least, one member shall be a specialist in the field of ENT.

D. LOCOMOTOR DISABILITY

1. Definition:—

(i) Impairment: An impairment in any loss or abnormality of psychological, physiological or anatomical structure or function in a human being.

(ii) Functional Limitations: Impairment may cause functional limitations which are partial or total inability to perform those activities, necessary for motor, sensory or mental function within the range or manner of which a human being is normally capable.

(iii) Disability: A disability, is any restriction or lack. (resulting from an impairment) of ability to perform an activity in the manner or within the range considered normal for a human being.

(iv) Locomotor Disability: Locomotor disability is defined as a person's inability to execute distinctive activities associated with moving both himself and objects, from place-to-place and such inability resulting from affliction of musculoskeletal and/or nervous system.

2. Categories of Locomotor Disability:—

The categories of locomotor disabilities are enclosed at *Annexure A*.

3. Process of Certification:—

A disability certificate shall be issued by a Medical Board of three members duly constituted by the Central and the State Government, out of which, at least, one member shall be a specialist from either the field of Physical Medicine and Rehabilitation or Orthopaedics.

Two specimen copies of the disability certificate for mental retardation and others (visual disability, speech and hearing disability and locomotor disability) are enclosed at Annexure-B.

It was also decided that whenever required the Chairman of the Board may co-opt other experts including that of the members constituted for the purpose by the Central and the State Government.

On representation by the applicant, the Medical Board may review its decision having regard to all the facts and circumstances of the case and pass such order in the matter as it thinks fit.

ANNEXURE A

LOCOMOTOR DISABILITY REVISED GUIDELINES FOR EVALUATION OF THE PERMANENT PHYSICAL IMPAIRMENT

1.1 GUIDELINES FOR EVALUATION OF PERMANENT PHYSICAL IMPAIRMENT OF UPPER LIMB

1. The estimation of permanent impairment depends upon the measurement of functional impairment and is not expression of a personal opinion.
2. The estimation and measurement should be made when the clinical condition has reached the stage of maximum improvement from the medical treatment. Normally, the time period is to be decided by the medical doctor who is evaluating the case for issuing the PPI Certificate as per standard format of the certificate.
3. The upper limb is divided into two component parts; the arm component and the hand component.

4. Measurement of the loss of function of arm component consists of measuring the loss of motion, muscle strength and co-ordinated activities.
5. Measurement of loss of function of hand component consists of determining the prehension, sensation and strength. For estimation of prehension opposition, lateral pinch cylindrical grasp, spherical grasp and hook grasp have to be assessed as shown in Hand Component of Form A Assessment Proforma for upper extremity.
6. The impairment of the entire extremity depends on the combination of the functional impairments of both components.

1.2 **ARM COMPONENT**

Total value of arm component is 90%.

1.2.1 **Principles of evaluation of range of motion (ROM) of joints**

1. The value of maximum ROM in the arm component is 90%.
2. Each of the three joints of the arm is weighed equally (30%).

Example:

The intra articular fractures of the bones of right shoulder joint may affect range of motion even after healing. The loss of ROM should be calculated in each arc of motion as. envisaged in the Assessment Form A (Assessment Proforma for Upper Extremity).

Arc of ROM	Normal value	Active ROM	Loss of ROM
Shoulder Flexion-	0-220	110	50%
Rotation	0-180	90	50%
Abduction-Adduction	0-180	90	50%

Hence the mean loss of ROM of shoulder will be

$$\frac{50+50+50}{3} = 150/3 = 50\%$$

Shoulder movements constitute 30% of the motion of the arm component, therefore the loss of motion for arm component will be 50 x 0.3d = 15% If more than one joint of the arm is involved the loss of percentage in each joint is calculated separately as above and then added together.

1.2.2 **Principles of evaluation of strength of muscles:**

1. Strength of muscles can be tested by manual method and graded from 0-5 as advocated by Medical Research Council of Great Britain depending upon the strength of the muscles.
2. Loss of muscle power can be given percentages as follows:

Manual muscle Strength grading	Loss of Strength in percentage
0	100%
1	80%
2	60%
3	40%
4	20%
5	0%

3. The mean percentage of loss of muscle strength around a joint is multiplied by 0.30.

4. If loss of muscle strength involves more than one joint the mean loss of percentage in each joint is calculated separately and then added together as has been described for loss of motion.

1.2.3 **Principles of evaluation of coordinated activities:**

1. The total value for coordinated activities is 90%.
2. Ten different coordinated activities should be tested as given in. **Form A. (Appendix I of Annexure A)**
3. Each activity has a value of 9%.

1.2.4 **Combining values for the Arm Component:**

The total value of loss of function of arm component is obtained by combining the value of loss of ROM, muscle strength and coordinated activities, using the combing formula.

$$a+\frac{b\ (90-a)}{90}$$

where a = higher value

b = lower value

Example

Let us assume that an individual with an intra particular fracture of bones of shoulder joint in addition to 16.5% loss of motion in arm has 8.3% loss of strength of muscles and 5% loss of coordination. These values should be combined as follows:

Loss of ROM - 16.5% $16.5+\frac{8.3(90-16.5)}{90}$

Loss of strength of muscles - 8.3% =23.33%

To add

Loss of coordination - 5% $23.3+\frac{5(90-23.3)}{90}$=27 0%

So the total value of loss of function in Arm component will be 27.0%

1.3 **HAND COMPONENT:**

1. Total value of hand component is 90%
2. The functional impairment of hand is expressed as loss of prehension, loss of sensation and loss of strength

1.3.1 **Principles of evaluation of prehension:**

1. Total value of prehension is 30% it includes

(a) Opposition - 8%

Tested against - Index finger -2%

- Middle finger -2%
- Ring -2%
- Little finger -2%

(b) Lateral pinch 5% - Tested by asking the patient to hold a key between the thumb and lateral side of index finger.

(c) Cylindrical grasp - 6% Tested for

(i) Large object of 4 inches size -3%

(ii) Small object of 1 inch size - 3%

(d) Spherical grasp -6% Tested for

(i) Large object of 4 inches size - 3%

(ii) Small object of 1 inch size - 3%

(e) Hook grasp - 5% -Tested by asking the patient to lift a bag

1.3.2. **Principles of Evaluation of sensation:**

1. Total value of sensation in hand is 30%
2. It should be assessed according to the distribution given below:
   (i) Complete loss of sensation
   Thumb ray 9%
   Index finger 6%
   Middle finger 5%
   Ring finger 5%
   Little finger 5%
   (ii) Partial loss of sensation: Assessment should be made according to percentage of loss of sensation in thumb/finger(s)

1.3.3. **Principles of Evaluation of strength**

1. Total value or strength is 30%
2. It includes:
   (i) Grip strength 20%
   (ii) Pinch strength 10%

Strength of hand should be tested with hand dynamo-meter or by clinical method (grip method).

Additional weightage - A total of 10% additional weightage can be given to following accompanying factors if they are continuous and persistent despite treatment.

1. Pam
2. Infection
3. Deformity
4. Mat-alignment
5. Contractures
6. Cosmetic disfiguration
7. Dominant extremity-4%
8. Shortening of upper limb

First 1" - No weightage

For each 1" beyond first 1" -2%

The extra points should not exceed 10% of the total Arm Component and total PPI should not exceed 100% in any case.

1.3.4. **Combining values of hand component:**

The final value of loss of function of hand component is obtained by summing up values of loss of prehension, sensation and strength.

1.3.5. **Combining values for the Extremity:**

Values of impairment of arm component and impairment of hand component should be added by using combining formula:

$$a+b\frac{(90-a)}{90}$$

a= higher value
b= lower value

Example:

Impairment of Arm - 27%

Impairment of hand - 64%

$$64+\frac{27(90-64)}{90}$$

=71.8%

The total value can also be obtained by using the Ready Recknoer table for combining formula given at *Appendix II* of *Annexure A.*

2. Guidelines for Evaluation of permanent physical Impairment in Lower Limb.

The measurement of loss of function in lower extremity is divided into two components: Mobility and standing components

2.1 **Mobility Component:—**

1. Total value of mobility component is 90%
2. It includes range of movement (ROM) and muscle strength

2.1.1. **Principles of Evaluation of Range of Movement:**

1. The value of maximum range of movement in mobility component is 90%
2. Each of three joints *i.e.* hip, knee and foot-ankle component is weighed equally - 30%.

Example:

A fracture of right hip joint bones may affect range of motion of the hip joint. Loss of ROM of the affected hip in different are should be assessed as given in Form B (Assessment Proforma for lower extremity). (*Appendix I of Annexure A*)

Affected Joint - Rt. Hip:

Arc of Movement	Normal ROM	Active ROM	Loss in percentage
Flexion-Extension	0-140	70	50%
Abduction-Adduction	0-90	60	33%
Rotations	0-90	30	66%

Mean loss of ROM of Rt Hip = $\frac{50+33+66}{3}$ = 50%

Since the hip constitute 30% of the total mobility component of the lower limb the loss of motion in relation to the lower limb will be 50 x 0.30=15%

If more than one joint of the limb is involved the mean loss of ROM in percentage should be calculated in relation to individual joint separately and then added together as follows to calculate the loss of mobility component in relation to that particular limb.

For example

Mean loss of ROM of Rt. Hip 50%

Mean loss of ROM Rt. Knee 40%

Loss of mobility component of Rt. Lower Limb will be

(50 x 0.30)+(40 x 0.30) = 27%

2.1.2. **Principle of Evaluation of Muscle Strength:**

1. The value for maximum muscle strength in the limb is 90%
2. Strength of muscles can be tested by Manual Method and graded 0-5 as advocated by MRC of Great Britain depending upon the residual strength in the muscle group.
3. Manual muscle grading can be given percentage like below:

Power Grade of Ms	Loss of strength in percentage
0	100%
1	80%
2	60%
3	40%
4	20%
5	0%.

4. Mean percentage of muscle strength loss around a joint is multiplied by 0.30 to calculate loss in relation to limb.

5. If there has been a loss muscle strength involving more than one joint the values are added as has been described for loss of ROM

2.1.3. **Combining values for mobility component:**

1. The values of loss of ROM and loss of muscle strength should be combined with the help of combining formula: $a+\frac{b(90-a)}{90}$

(a = higher value, b = lower value)

Example: Let us assume that the individual with a fracture of right hip bones has in addition to 16% loss of motion, 8% loss of muscle strength also.

Combined values

Motion-16% $16+\frac{8(90-16)}{90}$

Strength-8% = 22.6%

2.2 **Stability component:**

1. Total value of the stability component is 90%
2. It should be tested by clinical method as given in From B (Assessment Proforma for lower extremity) There are nine activities, which need to be tested, and each activity has a value of ten per cent (10%). The percentage valued in relation to each activity depends upon the percentage of loss stability in relation to each activity.

2.3 **Extra points:**

Extra points have been given for pain, deformities, contractures, loss of sensations and shortening Maximum points to be added are 10% (excluding shortening). Details are as following.

(i) Deformity	In functional position	3%
	In non-functional position	6%
(ii) Pain	Sever (grossly interfering with function)	9%
	Moderate (moderately interfering with function)	6%
	Mild (mildly interfering with function)	3%
(iii) Loss of sensation	Complete Loss	9%
	Partial Loss	6%
(iv) Shortening	First 1/2"	Nil
	Every 1/2" beyond first 1/2"	4%
(v) Complications	Superficial complications	3%

Deep Complications

3. Guidelines for Evaluation of Permanent Physical Impairment of Trunk (Spine) Basic guidelines:

1. As permanent physical impairment caused by spinal deformity tends to change over the years, the certificate issued in relation to spine should be reviewed as per the standard format of the certificate given at *Annexure B of Appendix III.*
2. Permanent physical impairment should be awarded in relation to spine and not in relation to whole body.
3. Permanent physical impairment due to neurological deficit in addition to spinal impairment should be added by combining formula. The local effects of the lesions of the spine can be conventionally divided into traumatic and non-traumatic. The percentage of PPI in relation to each situation should be valued as follows:

3.1 TRAUMATIC LESIONS:

3.1.1 Cervical spine injuries	**Percentage of PPI in relation to Spine**
(i) 25% or more compression of one or two adjacent vertebral bodies with no involvement of posterior elements,	20%
No nerve root involvement, moderate Neck rigidity and persistent	Soreness.
(ii) Posterior element damage with radiological Evidence of moderate parties dislocation/subluxation including whiplash injury.	
(a) With fusion healed. No permanent motor or sensory changes.	10%
(b) Persistent pain with radiologically demonstrable instability.	25%
(iii) Severe Dislocation:	
(a) Fair to good reduction with or without fusion with no residual motor or sensory involvement;	10%
(b) Inadequate reduction with fusion and persistent radicular pain	15%

3.1.2. Cervical Intervertebral Disc Lesions	**Percentage of PPI In relation to Spine**
(i) Treated case of disc lesion with persistent pain and no neurological deficit	10%
(ii) Treated case with pain and instability	15%

3.1.3. Thoracic and Thoracolumbar Spine Injuries:

(i) Compression of less than 50% involving one vertebral body with no neurological manifestation	10%
(ii) Compression of more than 50% involving single vertebra or more with involvement of posterior elements, healed, no neurological manifestations persistent pain, fusion indicated	20%
(iii) Same as (b) with fusion, pain only on heavy use of back	15%
(iv) Radiologically demonstrable instability with fracture or fracture dislocation with persistent pain.	30%

3.1.3. Thoracic and Thoracolumbar Spine Injuries:

(i) Compression of less than 50% involving one vertebral body with no neurological manifestation	10%
(ii) Compression of more than 50% involving singlevertebra or more with involvement of posterior elements, healed, no neurological manifestations persistent pain, fusion indicated	20%
(iii) Same as (b) with fusion, pain only on heavy use of back	15%
(iv) Radiologically demonstrable instability with fracture or fracture dislocation with persistent pain.	30%

3.1.4 Lumbar and Lumbosacral Spine: Fracture

(a)	Compression of 25% or less of one or two adjacent Vertebral bodies, No definite pattern or neurological Deficit	15%

(b)	Compression of more than 25% with disruption of Posterior elements, persistent pain and stiffness, healed with or without fusion, inability to lift more than 10 kgs.	30%
(c)	Radiologically demonstrable instability in low lumbar or Lumbosacral spine with pain.	35%

3.1.5 Disc lesion:

(a)	Treated case with persistent pain	15%
(b)	Treated case with pain and instability	20%
(c)	Treated case of disc disease with pain activities of lifting moderately modified	25%
(d)	Treated case of disc disease with persistent pain and stiffness aggravated by heavy lifting necessitating modification of all activities requiring, heavy weight lifting	30%

3.2 **NON- TRAUMATIC LESIONS:**

3.2.1 Scoliosis:

Basic guidelines – following modification is suggested.

– The largest structural curve should be accounted for while calculating the PPI and not the compensatory curve or both structural curves.

3.2.2 Measurement of Spine Deformity:

Cobb's method for measurement, of angle of curve in the radiograph taken in standing position should be used. The curves have been divided into following groups depending upon the angle of major structural scoliotic deformity.

Group	Cobb's Angle	PPI in relation to Spine
I	0-20	NIL
II	21-50	10%
III	51-100	20%
IV	101 & above	30%

3.2.3 Torso Imbalance:

In addition to the above PPI should also be evaluated in relation the torso imbalance. The torso imbalance should be measured by dropping a plumb line from C7 spine and measuring the distance of plumb line from gluteal crease.

Deviation of Plumb line	**PPI**
Upto 1.5 Cm	4%
1.6 - 3.0 Cm	8%
3.1 - 5.0 Cm	16%
5.1 and above	32%

3.2.4 Head Tilt over C7 spine PPI

Upto 15	4%
More than 15	10%

3.2.5 Cardiopulmonary Test

In cases with scoliosis of severe type cardiopulmonary function tests and percentage deviation from normal should be assessed by one of the following method whichever seems more reliable clinically at the time of assessment. The value thus obtained may be added by combining formula.

a. Chest Expansion	**PPI**
4 - 5 Cm.	Normal
Less than 4 cm reduction in Chest expansion	5% for each cm.
No expansion	25%

b. counting in one breathe:

Breathe Count	PPI
More than 40	Normal
0-40	5%
0-30	10%
0-20	15%
0-10	20%
Less than 5	25%

3.2.6 Associated Problems: To be added directly but the total value of PPI in relation to spine should not exceed 100%.

(a) Pain

–mildly interfering with ADL	4%
–moderately restricting ADL	6%
–severely restricting ADL	10%

(b) Cosmetic-Appearance:

–No obvious disfiguration with clothes on	Nil
–mild disfigurement	2%
–severe disfigurement	4%

(c) Leg Length Discrepancy:

–First ½" shortening	Nil
–Every ½" beyond first ½"	4%

(d) Neurological deficit – Neurological deficit should be calculated as per established method of evaluation of PPI in such cases. Value thus obtained should be added telescopically using combining formula.

3.3 KYPHOSIS

Evaluation should be done on the simitar guidelines as use for scoliosis with the following modifications:

3.3.1 Spinal Deformity	**PPI**
Less than 20	Nil
21-40	10%
41-60	20%
Above 60	30%

3.3.2 Torso Imbalance – Plumb line dropped from external ear normally falls at ankle level. The deviation from normal should be measured from ankle anterior joint line to the plumb line.

Less than 5 cm in front of ankle	4%
5 to 10 cm in front of ankle	8%
10 to 15 cm in front of ankle	16%
More than 15 cm in front of ankle	32%

(Add directly)

Miscellaneous conditions:

Those conditions of the spine which cause stiffness and pain etc. are rated as follows:

	Conditions	*Percentage PPI*
A	Subjective symptoms of pain, no involuntary muscle spasm, not substantiated by demonstrable structural pathology	-0%
B	Pain, persistent muscles spasm and stiffness of spine, substantiated by mild radiological change.	-20%
C	Same as B with moderate radiological changes	-25%
D	Same as B with severe radiological changes involving any one of the regions of spine	-30%
E	Same as D involving whole spine	-40%

4. Guidelines for Evaluation of PPI in cases of Short Stature/Dwarfism:

1. Recumbent length or longitudinal height below 3rd percentile or less than 2 Standard Deviation from the mean is considered to have short stature.
2. The evaluation of a Short Statured person should be considered only when it is of disproportionate variety and is accompanied by an underlying pathological conditions, *e.g.*, Achondroplasia, Chandrodysplasia Punctata, spondyloepiphysical dysplasia, mucopoly and acchrydosis, etc.
3. The ICMR norms as enclosed at Appendix III of Annexure. A should be used as a guideline for the height.
4. Every 1" vertical height reduction should be valued as 4% permanent physical impairment.
5. Associated skeletal deformities should be evaluated, separately and total percentage of both should be added by combining formula.

5. Guideline for Evaluation of Permanent Physical Impairment in Amputees:

Basic Guidelines:

1. In cases of multiple amputees if the total sum of permanent physical impairment is above 100%, it should be taken as 100% only.
2. If the stump is unfit for fitting the prosthesis additional weightage of 5% should be added to the value.
3. In case of amputation in more than one limb percentage of each limb is added by combining formula and another 10% will be added but when only toes or fingers are involved only 5% will be added.
4. Any complication in form of stiffness of proximal joint, neuroma infection, etc., should be given upto a total of 10% additional weightage.
5. Dominant upper extremity should be given 4% additional weightage.

	Upper Limb Amputations	PPI & loss of physical function of each limb
	1	2
1.	Fore-quarter amputations	100%
2.	Shoulder Disarticulation	90%
3.	Above Elbow upto upper 1/3 of arm	85%
4.	Above Elbow upto lower 1/3 of forearm	80%

1				2
5. Elbow disarticulation				75%
6. Below Elbow upto upper 1/3 of forearm				70%
7. Below Elbow upto lower 1/3 of forearm				65%
8. Wrist disarticulation				60%
9. Hand through carpal bones				55%
10. Thumb through CM. or though 1st MC joint				30%
11. Thumb disarticulation through metacarpophalangeal Joint or through proximal phalanx.				25%
12. Thumb disarticulation through inter phalangeal joint or through distal phalanx.				15%
	Index Finger (15%)	Middle Finger (5%)	Ring Finger (3%)	Little Finger (2%)
13. Amputation through Proximal phalanx or Disarticulation through M.P. Joint	15%	5%	3%	2%
14. Amputation through Middle phalanx or Disarticulation through PP joint.	10%	4%	2%	1%
15. Amputation through Distal phalanx or disarticulation through DIP joint.	5%	2%	1%	1%

6. 1.3 Lower Limb Amputations:

1. Hind quarter	100%
2. Hip disarticulation	90%
3. Above knee upto upper 1/3 of thigh	85%
4. Above knee upto lower 1/3 of thigh	80%
5. Through keen	75%
6. B.K. upto 8 cm	70%
7. B.K. upto lower 1/3 of leg	60%
8. Through ankle	55%
9. Syme's	50%
10. Upto mid-foot	40%
11. Upto fore-foot	30%
12. All toes	20%
13. Loss of first toe	10%
14. Loss of second toe	5%
15. Loss of third toe	4%
16. Loss of fourth toe	3%
17. Loss of fifth toe	2%

6. Guidelines for Evaluation of Permanent Physical Impairment of Congenital deficiencies of the limbs:

6.1 Transverse Deficiencies—

1. Functionally congenital transverse limb deficiencies are comparable to acquired amputations and can be called synonymously as congenital

amputation, however, in some cases revision of amputation is required to fit in a prosthesis.

2. The transverse limb deficiencies therefore should be assessed on basis of the guidelines applicable to the evaluation of PPI in cases of amputees as given in the preceding chapter.

For example:	**PPI**
Transverse deficiency Rt. Arm complete (shoulder disarticulation)	90%
Transverse deficiency at thigh complete (hip disarticulation)	90%
Transverse deficiency Proximal Upper arm (Above elbow Amp.)	85%
Transverse deficiency at lower thigh (Above knee Amp. Lower 1/3)	80%
Transverse deficiency forearm complete (elbow disarticulation)	75%
Transverse deficiency lower forearm (Below Elbow Amp.)	65%
Transverse deficiency carpal complete (wrist disarticulation)	60%
Transverse deficiency Metacarpal complete (Disarticulation through carpal bones)	55%

6.2 Longitudinal Deficiencies:

6.2.1 Basic Guidelines

1. In cases of longitudinal deficiencies of limbs due consideration should be given to functional impairment.
2. In upper limb, loss of ROM loss muscular strength and hand functions like prehension, etc. should be tested while assessing the case for PPI.
3. In lower limb clinical method of stability component and shortening of lower limb should be given due weightage.
4. Apart from functional assessment the lost joint/part of body should also be valued as per distribution given in chapter Guidelines for Evaluation of PPI in upper extremity and lower extremity The values so obtained should be added with the help of combing formula.

Example:

Congenital absence of humorous where forearm bones directly articulate with scapula.

There will be miled reduction in ROM and strength of muscles in the existing joints apart from loss of body part.

Loss of shoulder joint can be given - 30%

Loss of ROM of Elbow/Shoulder & wrist

All the components should be added together by the combining formula of

$$a + \frac{b\ (90\text{-}a)}{90}$$

6.2.2 In cases of toss of single bone in forearm the evaluation should be based on the principles of evaluation of Arm component which include Evaluation of ROM, Muscle strength and coordinated activities. The values so obtained should be added together with the help of combining formula.

6.2.3 In case of loss of single bone in leg the evaluation should be based on the principles of evaluation of mobility component and stability components of the lower extremity. The values obtained should be added together with the help of combining formula.

7. Guidelines for Evaluation of Physical Impairments in Neurological conditions.

7.1 Basic Guidelines:

1. Assessment in neurological conditions is not the assessment of disease but the assessment of its effects, *i.e.* clinical manifestations.
2. These guidelines should only be used for central and upper motor neurone lesions.
3. Proformas (form A & B) will be utilized for assessment of lower motor neurone lesions, muscular disorders and other locomotor conditions.
4. Normally any neurological assessment for the purpose of certification has to be done six months after the onset of disease however exact time period is to be decided by the Medical Doctor who is evaluating the case and has to recommend the review of certificate as given in the standard format of certificate.
5. Total percentage of physical impairment in any neurological condition should not exceed 100%
6. In mixed cases the highest score will be taken into consideration. The lower score will be added telescopically to it by the help of combining formula $a+\frac{b(90-a)}{90}$
7. Additional rating of 4% will be given for dominant upper extremity.
8. Additional weightage up to 10% can be given for loss of sensation in each extremity but the total physical impairment should not exceed 100%.

7.2 Table I

Neurological Status	**Physical Impairment**
Altered sensorium	100%

7.3 Table II

Intellectual Impairment (to be assessed by Clinical Psychologist)

Degree of Mental Retardation	IQ Range	Intellectual Impairmant
Border line	70-79	25%
Mild	50-69	50%
Moderate	35-49	75%
Serve	20-34	90%
Profound	Less than 20	100%

7.4 Table III

Speech defect	Physical Impairment
Mild dysarthria	Nil
Moderate dysarthria	25%
Servere dysarthria	50%

7.5 Table IV

Type of Cranial Nerve Involvement	Physical Impairment
Motor cranial nerve	20% for each nerve
Sensory cranial nerve	10% for each nerve

Sensory cranial nerve 10% for each nerve

7.6 Table V

Motor system Disability

Neurological Involvement	**Physical Impairment**
Hemiparesis:—	
- Mild	25%
- Moderate	50%
- Severe	75%

7.7 Table VI

Sensory System Disability

Extent of Sensory Deficit	*Physical Impairment*
Anaesthesia	Upto 10% for each iimb
Hypoaesthesia	Depending upon % of
Paraestheis	Loss of sensation up to 30% depending
Hands/feet sensory loss	Upon % of loss sensation

7.8 Table VII

Bladder disability due to neurogenic Involvement

Bladder Involvement	*Physical Impairment*
Mild (Hesitancy/Frequency)	25%
Moderate (precipitancy)	50%
Severe (occasional but recurrent Incontinence)	75%
Very Severe (Retention/Total Incontinence)	100%

7.9 Table VIII

Post Head Injury Fits and Epileptic Convulsions

Frequency/Severity of Convulsions	*Physical Impairment*
Mild – occurrence of one convulsion only	Nil
Moderate 1-5 Convulsions/month on Adequate – Medication	25%
Severe 6-10 Convulsions/month on Adequate Medication	50%
Very Severe more than 10 fits/months On adequate – Medication	75%

7.10 Table IX

Ataxia (Sensory or Cerebellar)

Severity of Ataxia	*Physical Impairment*
Mild (Detected on examination)	25%
Moderate	50%

Severe	75%
Very Severe	100%.

8. Guidelines for Evaluation of Physical Impairment due to Cardiopulmonary Diseases

8.1 Basic Guidelines:—

1. Modified New York Heart Association subjective classification should be utilised to assess the functional disability.
2. The assessing physician should be alert to the fact that patients who come for disability claims are likely to exaggerate their symptoms. In case of any doubt patients should be referred for detailed physiological evaluation.
3. Disability evaluation of cardiopulmonary patients should be done after full medical, surgical and rehabilitative treatment available, because most of these diseases are potentially treatable.
4. Assessment of cardiopulmonary impairment should also be done in diseases which might have associated cardiopulmonary problems, *e.g.*, amputees, myopathies, etc.
5. For respiratory assessment, routine respiratory functions test should be done, however, in cases of interstitial lung diseases, diffusion studies may be done.
6. In cases of Angina pectoris (chest pain) base line studies in resting ECG should be done. When there is persistence of symptoms, exercise or stress test should be done.

8.2 The proposed classification with loss of function is as follows:—

Group 0: A patient with cardiopulmonary disease who is asymptomatic (*i.e.* has no symptoms of breathlessness, palpitation, fatigue or chest pain).

Group 1: A patient with cardiopulmonary disease who becomes symptomatic during his ordinaty physical activity but has mild restriction (25%) of his physical activities.

Group 2: A patient with cardiopulmonary disease who becomes symptomatic during his ordinary physical activity and has 25-50% restriction of his ordinary physical activities.

Group 3: A patient with cardiopulmonary disease who becomes symptomatic during less than ordinary physical activity so that his ordinary physical activities are 50-75% restricted.

Group 4: A patient with cardiopulmonary disease who is symptomatic even at rest or on mildest exertion so that his ordinary physical activities are severely or completely restricted (75-100%).

Group 5: A patient with cardiopulmonary disease who gets intermittent symptoms at rest (i.e. patients with bronchial asthma, paroxysmal nocturnal dyspnoea, etc.)

1. Definition of Multiple Disabilities:

Multiple disabilities means a combination of two or more disabilities as defined in clause (i) of section (2) of the Persons with Disabilities. (Equal Opportunities, Protection of Rights and Full Participation) Act, 1995, namely—

I. Locomotor disability including leprosy cured
II. Blindness/low vision
III. Speech and hearing impairment
IV. Mental retardation
V. Mental illness.

2. Guidelines for Evaluation:

In order to evaluate the multiple disability, the same guidelines shall be used as have been developed by the respective sub-committees of various single disability, *viz.*, Mental retardation, locomotor disability, visual disability, and speech and hearing disability and recommended in the meeting held on 29-2-2000 under the Chairmanship of Dr. S.P. Agarwal, Director-General of Health Services, Government of India, with reference to Order No. 16-18/96-NI.I, dated 28th August, 1998 and communicated to Ministry of Social Justice & Empowerment, Government of India, *vide* letter No. S-13020/4/98-MH, dated 16th March, 2000.

However, in order to arrive at the total percentage of multiple disability, the combining formula

$a + \frac{b\,(90-a)}{90}$ as given in the "Manual for Doctors to Evaluate

Permanent Physical Impairment, Developed by Expert Group meeting on "Disability Evaluation", shall be used, where "a" will be the higher score and "b" will be the lower score. However, the maximum total percentage of multiple disabilities shall not exceed 100%.

For example, if the percentage of hearing disability is 30% and visual disability is 20%, then by applying the combining formula given above, the total percentage of multiple disability will be calculated as follows:—

$$30 + \frac{20(90-30)}{90} = 43\%$$

3. Procedure for Certification of Multiple Disability:

The procedure will remain the same as has been developed by the respective sub-committees on various single disabilities and finalized in a meeting under the Chairpersonship of Dr. S.P. Agarwal held on 29-2-2000. The final disability certificate for multiple disability will be issued by Disability Board which has given higher score of disability by combining the score of different disabilities using the combining formula, *i.e.*, $a + \frac{b\,(90-a)}{90}$. In case, where two scores of disability are equal, the final certificate of multiple disability will be issued by any one of them as decided by Local authority.

APPENDIX I OF ANNEXURE A

FORM A

ASSESSMENT PERFORMA FOR UPPER EXTERMITY

Name ....Age ....Sex ....Diagnosis..

Address ......................O.P.D. ....Deptt. ....

ARM COMPONENT (Total Value 90%)

Summary value for upper extremity is calculated from component and hand component values Add 4% for dominant extremity 10%. Additional weightage to be given to infection, deformity, malalignment, contracture, cosmetic appearance and abnormal mobility.

APPENDIX I OF ANNEXURE A

FORM B

ASSESSMENT PROFORMA FOR LOWER EXTERMITY

Name ....Age ....Sex ....Diagnosis ....

Address ......................O.P.D. No. .... Deptt. ....

Diagnosis ....

MOBILITY COMPONENT (Total Value (90%)

Joint	Component	Normal Value	Rt. Side	Lt. Side	Loss of % Rt. Side	Loss of % Lt. Side	Mean % Rt. Lt.	Mean 0.30 Rt. Lt.	Combing Value Rt. Lt.	% Summary Value for Mobility Component a+b(90+a) / 90
Range of Movement (Active)	1. Flexion-Extention arc	0-140°								
	2. Abduction	0-90°								
	Adduction	0-90°								
HIP	3. Rotation arc									
Range of Movement (Active) KNEE	1. Flexion Extension arc	0-125°								
Range of Movement	1. Dors flexion Panterlexion arc	0-70°								
(Active) ANKLE & FOOT	2. Invesior Extension	0-60°								

Arm Component	Component	Noamal Value (Degrees)	Rt. Side	Lt. Side	Loss of % Rt. Side	Loss of % Lt. Side	Mean % Loss Rt. Lt.	Sum of % Loss Rt. Lt.	Combining Value Rt. Lt.	% Summary Value for Mobility Component
Range of Movement (Active) Value 90% Elbow	1. Flexion-Extension Arc 2. Rotation Arc 3. Abduction-Adduction Arc	0-220° 0-180° 0-180°								
Shoulder Range of Movement (Active) Value 90% Wrist	1. Flexion-Extension Arc 2. Radial-Ulnaardeviatior Arc	0-160° 0-55°								
Muscle Strength Value 90% Shoulder	1. Flexion 2. Extension 3. Rotation-Ext 4. Rotation Int. 5. Abduction 6. Adduction									
Muscle Strength Value 90%	1. Flexion 2. Extension 3. Pronation 4. Supination									
Muscle Strength Value 90%	1. Dors Flexion 2. Palmar Flexion 3. Radial Deviation 4. Ulnardeviatior									
Coordinated Activities Value 90%	1. Lifting overhead objects remove and placing at the same place 2. Touching nose with end of extremity 3. Eating Indian Style 4. Combing and Plaiting 5. Putting on a shirt/kurta 6. Ablution glass of water 7. Drinking Glass of water 8. Buttoning 9 Tie Nara Dhoti 10. Writing					9% 9% 9% 9% 9% 9% 9% 9% 9% 9%				

HAND COMPONENT	TOTAL VALUE 90%)									
30% prehension	Movement	Normal Value								
1. Hand Component	1. Index	2]								
A.	2. Middle	2]8%								
Opposition (8%)	3. Ring	2]								
	4. Little	2]								
B. Lateral Pinch (5%)	Key Holding									
C. Cylindrical Grasp	a. Large Object (4°)									
	b. Small Object (1°)	5%								
	a. Large Object (4°)									
	b. Small Object (1°)	3)								
	Lifting Bag	3) 6%								
D. Spherical Grasp										
		3)								
		3) 6%								
E. Hook Grasp		5%								
2.										
Sensation 30%	1. Radial Side)	4:1								
	2. Ulnar Side) Thumb									
	3. Radial) Fingers	(4.8:1.2)								
	4. Ulnar)									
3.	Strength 30%	1. Grip Strength	20%							
		2. Pinch Strength	10%							

APPENDIX II OF ANNEXURE A

READY RECKONER TABLE FOR A + $\frac{B(90-A)}{90}$

	B(1)	B(2)	B(3)	B(4)	B(5)	B(6)	B(7)	B(8)	B(9)	B(10)	B(11)	B(12)	B(13)	B(14)	B(15)
A(1)	1.99	3.98	3.97	4.96	5.94	6.93	7.92	8.91	9.90	10.89	11.88	12.87	13.86	14.84	15.83
A(2)	2.98	3.96	4.93	5.91	6.89	7.87	8.84	9.82	10.80	11.78	12.76	13.73	14.71	15.69	16.67
A(3)	3.97	4.93	5.90	6.87	7.83	8.80	9.77	10.73	11.70	12.67	13.63	14.60	15.57	16.53	16.67
A(4)	4.96	5.91	6.87	7.82	8.78	9.73	10.69	11.64	12.65	13.50	14.44	15.39	16.33	17.28	18.33
A(5)	5.94	6.89	7.83	8.78	9.72	10.67	11.61	12.56	13.50	14.44	15.39	16.33	17.28	18.22	19.17
A(6)	6.93	7.87	8.80	9.73	10.67	11.60	12.50	13.46	14.38	15.30	16.27	17.20	18.13	19.07	20.00
A(7)	7.92	8.84	9.77	10.69	11.61	12.53	13.46	14.38	15.29	16.20	17.11	18.07	18.99	19.91	20.83
A(8)	8.91	9.82	10.73	11.64	12.56	13.47	14.38	15.29	16.20	17.10	18.02	18.93	19.84	20.76	21.67
A(9)	9.90	10.80	11.70	12.60	13.50	14.40	15.30	16.20	17.10	18.00	18.90	19.80	20.70	21.60	22.50
A(10)	10.89	11.87	12.67	13.56	14.44	15.33	16.22	17.11	18.00	18.89	19.78	20.67	21.56	22.44	23.33
A(11)	11.88	12.76	13.63	14.51	15.39	16.27	17.14	18.02	18.90	19.78	20.66	21.53	22.41	23.29	24.17
A(12)	12.87	13.73	14.60	15.47	16.33	17.20	18.07	18.93	19.80	20.67	21.53	22.40	23.27	24.13	25.00
A(13)	13.86	14.71	15.57	16.42	17.28	18.13	18.99	19.84	20.70	21.56	22.41	23.27	24.12	24.98	25.83
A(14)	14.84	15.69	16.53	17.38	18.22	19.07	19.91	20.76	21.60	22.44	23.29	24.13	24.98	25.82	26.67
A(15)	15.83	16.67	17.50	18.33	19.17	20.00	20.83	21.67	22.50	23.33	24.17	25.00	25.83	26.67	27.50
A(16)	16.82	17.64	18.47	19.20	20.11	20.93	21.76	22.58	23.40	24.22	25.04	25.87	26.69	27.51	28.33
A(17)	17.81	18.62	19.37	20.24	21.06	21.87	22.68	23.49	24.30	25.11	25.92	26.73	27.54	28.36	29.17
A(18)	18.80	19.60	22.33	21.20	22.00	22.80	23.60	24.40	25.20	26.00	26.80	27.60	28.40	29.20	30.00
A(19)	19.79	20.58	23.30	22.16	22.94	23.73	24.52	25.31	26.10	26.89	27.68	28.47	29.26	30.04	30.83
A(20)	20.78	21.56	24.27	23.11	23.89	24.67	25.44	26.22	27.00	27.78	28.56	29.33	30.11	30.89	31.67
A(21)	21.77	22.53	25.23	24.07	24.83	25.60	26.37	27.13	27.90	28.67	29.43	30.20	30.97	31.73	32.50
A(22)	22.76	23.51	26.20	25.02	25.78	26.33	27.29	28.04	28.80	29.56	30.31	31.07	31.82	32.58	33.33
A(23)	23.44	24.49	27.17	25.08	26.72	27.47	28.21	28.96	29.70	30.44	31.19	31.93	32.68	33.42	34.17
A(24)	24.73	25.47	28.13	26.93	27.67	28.40	29.13	29.87	30.60	31.33	32.07	32.80	33.57	34.27	35.00
A(25)	25.72	26.44	29.10	27.89	28.61	29.33	30.06	30.78	31.50	32.22	32.94	33.67	34.39	35.11	35.83
A(26)	26.71	27.42	30.07	28.84	29.56	30.27	30.98	31.69	32.40	33.11	33.82	34.53	35.21	35.96	36.67
A(27)	27.70	28.40	31.03	29.80	30.50	31.20	31.90	32.60	33.30	34.00	34.40	35.40	36.10	36.80	37.50
A(28)	28.69	29.38	32.00	30.76	31.44	32.13	32.80	33.51	34.40	34.89	35.58	36.27	36.96	37.64	38.33
A(29)	29.68	30.36	32.97	31.71	32.39	33.07	33.74	24.42	35.10	35.78	36.46	37.13	37.81	38.49	39.17
A(30)	30.67	31.33	32.00	32.67	33.33	34.67	35.33	36.00	36.67	36.67	37.33	38.00	38.67	39.33	40.00
A(31)	31.66	32.31	34.97	33.62	34.28	34.93	35.59	36.24	36.90	37.96	38.21	38.87	39.50	40.18	40.83
A(32)	32.64	33.29	33.93	34.58	35.22	35.87	36.51	37.16	37.80	38.44	39.09	39.73	40.38	41.02	41.67
A(33)	33.63	34.27	34.90	35.53	36.17	36.80	37.43	38.07	38.70	39.33	39.97	40.60	41.23	41.87	42.50
A(34)	34.62	35.24	35.87	36.49	37.11	37.73	38.36	38.98	39.60	40.22	40.84	41.47	42.09	42.71	43.33
A(35)	35.61	36.22	36.83	37.44	38.06	38.67	39.28	39.89	40.50	41.11	41.72	42.33	42.94	43.56	44.17
A(36)	36.60	37.20	37.80	38.40	39.00	39.60	40.20	40.80	41.40	42.00	42.60	43.20	43.80	44.40	45.00
A(37)	37.59	38.18	38.77	39.36	39.94	40.53	41.12	41.71	42.30	42.89	43.48	44.07	44.66	45.24	45.83
A(38)	38.58	39.16	39.73	40.31	40.89	41.47	42.04	42.62	43.20	43.78	44.36	44.93	45.51	46.09	46.67
A(39)	39.57	40.13	40.70	41.27	41.83	42.40	42.97	43.53	44.10	44.67	45.23	44.80	46.37	46.93	47.50
A(40)	40.56	41.11	41.67	42.22	42.78	43.33	43.89	44.44	45.00	45.56	46.11	46.67	47.22	47.78	48.33
A(41)	40.54	40.09	42.62	43.18	43.72	44.27	44.81	45.36	45.90	46.44	46.99	47.53	48.08	48.62	49.17
A(42)	42.53	43.07	43.60	44.13	44.67	45.20	45.73	46.27	46.80	47.33	47.87	48.40	48.93	49.47	50.00
A(43)	43.52	44.04	44.57	45.09	45.61	46.13	46.66	47.18	47.70	48.22	48.74	49.24	49.79	50.13	50.83
A(44)	44.51	45.02	44.53	46.04	46.56	47.07	47.58	48.09	48 60	49.11	49.62	50.13	50.64	51.61	51.67
A(45)	45.50	46.00	46.50	47.00	47.50	48.00	48.50	49.00	49.50	50.00	50.50	51.00	51.50	52.00	52.50

READY RECKONER TABLE FOR A + $\frac{B(90-A)}{90}$

	B(1)	B(2)	B(3)	B(4)	B(5)	B(6)	B(7)	B(8)	B(9)	B(10)	B(11)	B(12)	B(13)	B(14)	B(15)
A(46)	46.49	46.98	47.47	47.96	48.44	48.93	49.42	49.91	50.40	50.89	51.38	51.87	52.36	52.84	53.33
A(47)	47.48	47.96	48.43	48.91	49.39	49.87	50.34	50.82	51.30	51.78	52.26	52.73	53.21	53.69	54.17
A(48)	48.47	48.93	49.40	49.87	50.33	50.80	51.27	51.73	52.20	52.67	53.13	53.60	54.07	54.53	55.00
A(49)	49.46	49.91	50.37	50.82	51.28	51.73	52.19	52.64	53.10	53.56	54.01	54.47	54.92	55.38	55.83
A(50)	50.44	50.89	51.33	51.78	52.22	52.67	53.11	53.56	54.00	54.44	54.89	55.33	55.78	56.22	56.67
A(51)	51.43	51.87	52.30	52.73	53.17	53.60	54.03	54.47	54.90	55.33	55.77	56.20	56.63	57.07	57.50
A(52)	52.42	52.84	53.27	53.69	54.11	54.53	54.96	55.38	55.80	56.22	56.64	57.07	57.49	57.91	58.33
A(53)	53.41	53.82	54.23	54.64	55.06	55.47	55.88	56.29	56.70	57.11	57.52	57.93	58.34	58.76	59.17
A(54)	54.40	54.80	55.20	55.60	56.00	56.40	56.80	57.20	57.60	58.00	58.40	58.80	59.20	59.60	60.00
A(55)	55.39	55.78	56.17	56.56	56.94	57.33	57.72	58.11	58.50	58.89	59.28	59.67	60.06	60.44	60.83
A(56)	56.38	56.76	57.13	57.51	57.89	58.27	58.64	59.02	59.40	59.78	60.16	60.53	60.91	61.21	61.67
A(57)	57.37	57.73	58.10	58.47	58.83	59.20	59.57	59.93	60.30	60.67	61.03	61.40	61.77	62.13	62.50
A(58)	58.36	58.71	59.07	59.42	59.78	60.13	60.49	60.84	61.20	61.56	61.91	62.26	62.62	62.98	63.33
A(59)	59.34	59.69	60.03	60.38	60.72	61.07	61.41	61.76	62.10	62.44	62.79	63.13	63.48	63.82	64.17
A(60)	60.33	60.67	61.00	61.33	61.67	62.00	62.33	62.67	63.00	63.00	63.67	64.00	64.33	64.67	65.00
A(61)	61.32	61.64	61.97	62.29	62.61	62.93	63.26	63.58	63.90	64.22	64.54	64.87	65.19	65.51	65.83
A(62)	62.31	62.62	62.93	63.24	63.56	63.87	64.18	64.49	64.80	65.11	65.42	65.73	66.04	66.36	66.67
A(63)	63.30	63.60	63.90	64.20	64.50	64.80	65.10	65.40	65.70	66.00	66.30	66.60	66.90	67.20	67.50
A(64)	64.29	64.58	64.87	65.16	65.44	65.73	66.02	66.31	66.60	66.89	69.18	67.47	67.76	68.04	68.33
A(65)	65.28	65.56	65.83	66.11	66.39	66.67	66.94	67.22	67.50	67.78	68.06	68.33	68.61	68.89	69.17
A(66)	66.27	66.53	66.80	67.07	67.33	67.60	67.87	68.13	68.40	68.67	68.93	69.20	69.47	69.73	70.00
A(67)	67.26	67.51	67.77	68.02	68.28	68.53	68.79	69.04	69.30	69.56	69.81	70.07	70.32	70.58	70.83
A(68)	68.24	68.49	68.73	68.98	69.22	69.47	69.71	69.96	70.20	70.14	70.69	71.93	71.18	71.42	71.67
A(69)	69.23	69.47	69.70	69.93	70.17	70.40	70.63	70.87	71.10	71.33	71.57	71.80	72.03	72.27	72.50
A(70)	70.22	70.44	70.67	70.89	71.11	71.33	71.56	71.78	72.00	72.22	72.44	72.67	72.89	73.11	73.33
A(71)	71.21	71.42	71.63	71.84	72.06	72.27	72.48	72.69	72.90	73.11	73.32	73.53	73.74	73.96	74.17
A(72)	72.20	72.40	72.60	72.80	73.00	73.20	73.40	73.60	73.80	74.00	74.20	74.40	74.60	74.80	75.00
A(73)	73.19	73.38	73.57	73.76	73.94	74.13	74.32	74.51	74.70	74.89	75.08	75.27	75.46	75.64	75.83
A(74)	74.18	74.36	74.53	74.71	74.89	75.07	75.24	75.42	75.60	75.78	75.96	76.13	76.31	76.49	76.67
A(75)	75.17	75.33	75.50	75.67	75.83	76.00	76.17	76.33	76.50	76.67	76.83	77.00	77.17	77.33	77.50
A(76)	76.16	76.31	76.47	76.62	76.78	76.93	77.09	77.24	77.40	77.56	77.71	77.87	78.02	78.18	78.33
A(77)	77.14	77.29	77.43	77.58	77.72	77.87	78.01	78.16	78.30	78.44	78.59	78.73	78.88	79.02	79.17
A(78)	78.13	78.27	78.40	78.53	78.67	78.80	78.93	79.07	79.20	79.33	79.47	79.60	79.73	79.87	80.00
A(79)	79.12	79.24	79.37	79.49	79.61	79.73	79.86	79.98	80.10	80.22	80.34	80.47	80.59	80.71	80.83
A(80)	80.11	80.22	80.33	80.44	80.56	80.67	80.78	80.89	81.00	81.11	81.22	81.33	81.44	81.56	81.67
A(81)	81.10	81.20	81.30	81.40	81.50	81.60	81.70	81.80	81.90	82.00	82.10	82.20	82.30	82.40	82.50
A(82)	82.09	82.18	82.27	82.36	82.44	82.53	82.62	82.71	82.80	82.89	82.98	83.07	83.16	83.24	83.33
A(83)	83.08	83.16	83.23	83.31	83.39	83.47	83.54	83.62	83.70	83.78	83.86	83.93	84.01	84.09	84.17
A(84)	84.07	84.13	84.20	84.27	84.33	84.40	84.47	84.53	84.60	84.67	84.73	84.80	84.87	84.93	85.00
A(85)	85.06	85.11	85.17	85.22	85.28	85.33	85.39	85.44	85.50	85.56	85.61	85.67	85.72	85.78	85.83
A(86)	86.04	86.09	86.13	86.18	86.22	86.27	86.31	86.36	86.40	86.44	86.49	86.53	86.58	86.62	86.67
A(87)	87.03	87.07	87.10	87.13	87.17	87.20	87.23	87.27	87.30	87.33	87.37	87.40	87.43	87.47	87.50
A(88)	88.02	88.04	88.07	88.09	88.11	88.13	88.16	88.18	88.20	88.22	88.24	88.27	88.29	88.13	88.33
A(89)	89.01	89.02	89.03	89.04	89.06	89.07	89.08	89.09	89.10	89.11	89.12	89.13	89.14	89.16	89.17
A(90)	90.00	90.00	90.00	90.00	90.00	90.00	90.00	90.00	90.00	90.00	90.00	90.00	90.00	90.00	90.00

READY RECKONER TABLE FOR A + B(90-A)
90

	B(16)	B(17)	B(18)	B(19)	B(20)	B(21)	B(22)	B(23)	B(24)	B(25)	B(26)	B(27)	B(28)	B(29)	B(30)
A(1)	16.82	17.81	18.80	19.79	20.78	21.77	22.76	23.74	24.73	25.72	26.71	27.70	28.69	29.68	30.67
A(2)	17.64	18.62	19.60	20.58	21.56	22.53	23.51	24.49	25.47	26.44	27.42	28.40	29.38	30.36	31.33
A(3)	18.47	19.43	20.40	21.37	22.33	23.30	24.27	25.23	26.20	27.17	28.13	29.10	30.07	31.03	32.00
A(4)	19.29	20.24	21.20	22.16	23.11	24.07	25.02	25.98	26.93	27.89	28.84	29.80	30.76	31.71	32.67
A(5)	20.11	21.06	22.00	22.94	23.89	24.07	25.78	26.72	27.67	28.61	29.56	30.50	31.44	32.39	33.33
A(6)	20.93	21.87	22.80	23.73	24.67	24.83	26.53	27.47	28.40	29.33	30.27	31.20	32.13	33.07	34.00
A(7)	21.76	22.68	23.60	24.52	25.60	25.60	27.13	28.04	29.13	30.06	30.98	31.90	32.82	33.74	34.67
A(8)	22.58	23.49	24.40	25.31	26.37	26.37	27.90	28.80	29.87	30.78	31.69	32.60	33.51	34.42	35.33
A(9)	23.40	24.30	25.20	26.10	27.00	27.90	28.80	29.70	30.60	31.50	32.40	33.30	34.20	35.10	36.00
A(10)	24.22	25.11	26.00	26.89	27.78	28.67	29.56	30.44	31.33	32.22	33.11	34.00	34.89	35.78	36.67
A(11)	25.04	25.92	26.80	27.68	28.56	29.56	30.31	31.39	32.07	32.94	33.82	34.70	35.58	36.46	37.33
A(12)	25.87	26.73	27.60	28.47	29.33	30.20	31.07	31.93	32.80	33.67	34.53	35.40	36.27	37.13	38.00
A(13)	26.69	27.54	28.40	29.26	30.11	30.97	31.82	32.68	33.53	34.39	35.24	36.10	36.96	37.81	38.67
A(14)	27.51	28.36	29.20	30.04	30.89	31.73	32.58	33.42	34.27	35.11	35.96	36.80	37.64	38.49	39.33
A(15)	28.33	29.17	30.00	30.83	31.67	32.50	33.33	34.17	35.00	35.83	36.67	37.50	38.33	39.17	40.00
A(16)	29.16	29.98	30.80	31.62	32.44	33.27	34.09	34.91	35.73	36.56	37.38	38.20	39.02	39.84	40.67
A(17)	29.98	30.79	31.60	32.41	32.22	34.03	34.84	35.66	36.47	37.28	38.09	38.90	39.71	40.52	41.33
A(18)	30.80	31.60	32.40	32.20	34.00	34.80	35.60	36.40	37.20	38.00	38.80	39.60	40.40	41.20	42.00
A(19)	31.62	32.41	33.20	33.99	34.78	35.57	36.36	37.14	37.93	38.72	39.51	40.30	41.09	41.88	42.67
A(20)	32.44	33.22	34.00	34.78	35.56	36.33	37.11	37.89	38.67	39.44	40.22	41.00	41.78	42.56	43.33
A(21)	33.27	34.03	34.80	35.57	36.33	37.10	37.87	38.63	39.40	40.17	40.93	41.70	42.47	43.23	44.00
A(22)	34.09	34.84	35.60	36.36	37.11	37.87	38.62	39.38	40.13	40.89	41.64	42.40	43.16	43.91	44.67
A(23)	34.91	35.66	36.40	37.14	37.89	38.63	39.38	40.12	40.87	41.61	42.36	43.10	43.84	44.59	45.33
A(24)	35.73	36.47	37.20	37.93	38.67	39.40	40.13	40.87	41.60	42.33	43.07	43.80	44.53	45.27	46.00
A(25)	36.56	37.28	38.00	38.72	39.44	40.17	40.89	41.61	42.33	43.06	43.78	44.50	45.22	45.94	46.67
A(26)	37.38	38.09	38.80	39.51	40.22	40.93	41.64	42.36	43.07	43.78	44.49	45.20	45.91	46.62	47.33
A(27)	38.20	38.90	39.60	40.30	41.00	41.70	42.40	43.10	43.80	44.50	45.20	45.90	46.60	47.30	48.00
A(28)	39.02	39.71	40.40	41.09	41.78	42.47	43.16	43.84	44.53	45.22	45.91	46.60	47.29	47.98	48.67
A(29)	39.84	40.52	41.20	41.88	42.56	43.23	43.91	44.59	45.27	45.94	46.62	47.30	47.98	48.66	49.33
A(30)	40.67	41.33	42.00	42.67	43.33	44.00	44.67	45.33	46.00	46.67	47.33	48.00	48.67	49.33	50.00
A(31)	41.49	42.14	42.80	43.46	44.11	44.77	45.42	46.08	46.73	47.39	48.04	48.70	49.36	50.01	50.67
A(32)	42.31	42.96	43.60	44.24	44.89	45.23	46.18	46.82	47.47	48.11	48.76	49.40	50.04	50.69	51.33
A(33)	43.13	43.77	44.40	45.03	45.67	46.30	46.93	47.57	48.20	48.83	49.47	50.10	50.73	51.37	52.00
A(34)	43.96	44.58	45.20	45.82	46.44	47.07	47.69	48.31	48.93	49.56	50.18	50.80	51.42	52.04	52.67
A(35)	44.78	45.39	46.00	46.61	47.22	47.83	48.44	49.06	49.67	50.28	50.89	51.50	52.11	52.72	53.33
A(36)	45.60	46.20	46.80	47.40	48.00	48.60	49.20	49.80	50.40	51.00	51.60	52.20	52.80	53.40	54.00
A(37)	46.42	47.01	47.60	48.19	48.78	49.37	49.96	50.54	51.13	51.72	52.31	52.90	53.40	54.08	54.67
A(38)	47.24	47.82	48.40	48.98	49.56	50.13	50.71	51.29	51.87	52.44	53.02	53.60	54.18	54.76	55.33
A(39)	48.07	48.63	49.20	49.77	50.33	50.90	51.47	52.03	52.60	53.17	53.73	54.30	54.87	55.43	56.00
A(40)	48.89	49.44	50.00	50.56	51.11	51.67	52.22	52.78	53.33	53.89	54.44	55.00	55.56	56.11	56.67
A(41)	49.71	50.26	50.80	51.34	51.89	52.43	52.98	53.52	54.07	54.61	55.16	55.70	56.24	56.79	57.33
A(42)	50.53	51.07	51.60	52.13	52.67	53.20	53.73	54.27	54.80	55.33	55.87	56.40	56.93	57.47	58.00
A(43)	51.36	51.88	52.40	52.92	53.44	53.97	54.49	55.01	55.53	56.06	56.58	57.10	57.62	58.14	58.67
A(44)	52.18	52.69	53.20	53.71	54.22	54.73	55.24	55.76	56.27	56.78	57.29	57.80	58.31	58.82	59.33
A(45)	53.00	53.50	54.00	54.50	55.00	55.50	56.00	56.50	57.00	57.50	58.00	58.50	59.00	59.50	60.00

READY RECKONER TABLE FOR $A + \frac{B(90\text{-}A)}{90}$

	B(16)	B(17)	B(18)	B(19)	B(20)	B(21)	B(22)	B(23)	B(24)	B(25)	B(26)	B(27)	B(28)	B(29)	B(30)
A(46)	53.82	54.31	54.80	55.29	55.78	56.27	56.76	57.24	57.73	58.22	58.71	59.20	59.69	60.18	60.67
A(47)	54.64	55.12	55.60	56.08	56.56	57.03	57.51	57.99	58.47	58.94	59.42	59.90	60.38	60.86	61.33
A(48)	55.47	55.93	56.40	56.87	57.33	57.80	58.27	58.73	59.20	59.67	60.13	60.60	61.07	61.53	62.00
A(49)	56.29	56.74	57.20	57.66	58.11	58.57	59.02	59.48	59.93	60.39	60.84	61.30	61.76	62.21	62.67
A(50)	57.11	57.56	58.00	58.44	58.89	59.33	59.78	60.22	60.67	61.11	61.56	62.00	62.44	62.89	63.33
A(51)	57.93	58.37	58.80	59.23	59.67	60.10	60.55	60.97	61.40	61.83	62.27	62.70	63.13	63.57	64.00
A(52)	58.76	59.18	59.60	60.02	60.44	60.87	61.29	61.71	62.13	62.56	62.98	63.40	63.82	64.26	64.67
A(53)	59.58	59.99	60.40	60.81	61.22	61.63	62.04	62.46	62.87	63.28	63.69	64.10	64.51	64.92	65.33
A(54)	60.40	60.80	61.20	61.60	62.00	62.40	62.80	63.20	63.60	64.00	64.40	64.80	65.20	65.60	66.00
A(55)	61.22	61.61	62.00	62.39	62.78	63.17	63.56	63.94	64.33	64.72	65.11	65.50	65.89	66.28	66.67
A(56)	62.04	62.42	62.80	63.18	63.56	63.93	64.31	64.69	65.07	65.44	65.82	66.20	66.58	66.96	67.33
A(57)	62.87	63.23	63.60	63.97	64.33	64.70	65.07	65.43	65.80	66.17	66.53	66.90	67.27	67.63	68.00
A(58)	63.69	64.04	64.40	64.76	65.11	65.47	65.82	66.18	66.53	66.89	67.24	67.60	67.96	68.31	68.67
A(59)	64.51	64.86	65.20	65.54	65.89	66.23	66.58	66.92	67.27	67.61	67.96	68.30	68.64	68.99	69.33
A(60)	65.33	65.67	66.00	66.33	66.67	67.00	67.33	67.67	68.00	68.33	68.67	69.00	69.33	69.67	70.00
A(61)	66.16	66.48	66.80	67.12	67.44	67.77	68.09	68.41	68.73	69.06	69.38	69.70	70.02	70.34	70.67
A(62)	66.98	67.29	67.60	67.91	68.22	68.53	68.84	69.16	69.47	69.78	70.09	70.40	70.71	71.02	71.33
A(63)	67.80	68.10	68.40	68.70	69.00	69.30	69.60	69.90	70.20	70.50	70.80	71.10	71.40	71.70	72.00
A(64)	68.62	68.91	69.20	69.49	69.78	70.07	70.36	70.64	70.93	71.22	71.51	71.80	72.09	72.38	72.67
A(65)	69.44	69.72	70.00	70.28	70.56	70.83	71.11	71.39	71.67	71.94	72.22	72.50	72.78	73.06	73.33
A(66)	70.27	70.53	70.80	71.07	71.33	71.60	71.87	72.13	72.40	72.67	72.93	73.20	73.47	73.73	74.00
A(67)	71.09	71.34	71.60	71.86	72.11	72.37	72.62	72.88	73.13	73.39	73.64	73.90	74.16	74.41	74.67
A(68)	71.91	72.16	72.40	72.64	72.89	73.13	73.38	73.62	73.87	74.11	74.36	74.60	74.84	75.09	75.33
A(69)	72.73	72.97	73.20	73.43	73.67	73.90	74.13	74.37	74.60	74.83	75.07	75.30	75.53	75.77	76.00
A(70)	73.56	73.78	74.00	74.22	74.44	74.67	74.89	75.11	75.33	75.56	75.78	76.00	76.22	76.44	76.67
A(71)	74.38	74.59	74.80	75.01	75.22	75.43	75.64	75.86	76.07	76.28	76.49	76.70	76.91	77.12	77.33
A(72)	75.20	75.40	75.60	75.80	76.00	76.20	76.40	76.60	76.80	77.00	77.20	77.40	77.60	77.80	78.00
A(73)	76.02	76.21	76.40	76.59	76.78	76.97	77.16	77.34	77.53	77.72	77.91	78.10	78.29	78.48	78.67
A(74)	76.84	77.02	77.20	77.38	77.56	77.73	77.91	78.09	78.27	78.44	78.62	78.80	78.98	79.16	79.33
A(75)	77.67	77.83	78.00	78.17	78.33	78.50	78.67	78.83	79.00	79.17	79.33	79.50	79.67	79.83	80.00
A(76)	78.49	78.64	78.80	78.96	79.11	79.27	79.42	79.58	79.73	79.89	80.04	80.20	80.36	80.51	80.67
A(77)	79.31	79.46	79.60	79.74	79.89	80.03	80.18	80.32	80.47	80.61	80.76	80.90	81.04	81.19	81.33
A(78)	80.13	80.27	80.27	80.40	80.67	80.80	80.93	81.07	81.20	81.33	81.47	81.60	81.73	81.87	82.00
A(79)	80.96	81.08	81.20	81.32	81.44	81.57	81.69	81.81	81.93	82.06	82.18	82.30	82.42	82.54	82.67
A(80)	81.76	81.89	82.00	82.11	82.22	82.33	82.44	82.56	82.67	82.78	82.89	83.00	83.11	83.22	83.33
A(81)	82.60	82.70	82.80	82.90	83.00	83.10	83.20	83.30	83.40	83.50	83.60	83.70	83.80	83.90	84.00
A(82)	83.42	83.51	83.60	83.69	83.78	83.87	83.96	84.04	84.13	84.22	84.31	81.40	84.90	84.58	84.67
A(83)	84.24	84.24	84.40	84.48	84.56	84.63	84.71	84.79	84.87	84.89	85.02	85.10	85.18	85.26	85.33
A(84)	85.07	85.07	85.20	85.27	85.33	85.40	85.47	85.53	85.60	85.67	85.73	85.80	85.87	85.93	86.00
A(85)	85.89	85.89	86.00	86.06	86.11	86.17	86.22	86.28	86.33	86.39	86.44	86.50	86.56	86.61	86.67
A(86)	86.71	86.76	86.80	86.84	86.89	86.89	86.98	87.02	87.07	87.11	87.16	87.20	87.24	87.29	87.33
A(87)	87.53	87.57	87.57	87.60	87.63	87.67	87.73	87.77	87.80	87.83	87.87	87.90	87.93	87.97	88.00
A(88)	88.36	88.38	88.38	88.40	88.42	88.44	88.49	88.51	88.53	88.56	88.59	88.60	88.62	88.64	88.67
A(89)	89.18	89.13	89.19	89.20	89.21	89.23	89.24	89.26	89.27	89.28	89.29	89.30	89.31	89.32	89.33
A(90)	90.00	90.00	90.00	90.00	90.00	90.00	90.00	90.00	90.00	90.00	90.00	90.00	90.00	90.00	90.00

READY RECKONER TABLE FOR A + B(90-A) / 90

	B(31)	B(32)	B(33)	B(34)	B(35)	B(36)	B(37)	B(38)	B(39)	B(40)	B(41)	B(42)	B(43)	B(44)	B(45)
A(1)	31.66	32.64	33.63	34.62	35.61	36.60	37.59	38.58	39.57	40.56	41.54	42.53	42.52	44.51	45.50
A(2)	32.31	33.29	34.27	35.24	36.22	37.20	38.18	39.16	40.13	41.11	42.09	43.07	44.04	45.02	46.00
A(3)	32.97	33.93	34.90	35.87	36.83	37.80	38.77	39.73	40.70	47.67	42.63	43.60	44.57	45.53	46.50
A(4)	33.62	34.58	35.53	36.49	37.44	38.40	39.36	40.31	41.27	42.22	43.18	44.13	45.09	46.04	47.00
A(5)	34.28	35.22	36.17	37.11	38.06	39.00	39.94	40.89	41.83	42.78	43.72	44.67	45.61	46.56	47.50
A(6)	34.93	35.87	36.80	37.73	38.67	39.60	40.53	41.74	42.40	43.33	44.27	45.20	46.13	47.07	48.00
A(7)	35.59	36.51	37.43	38.36	39.28	40.20	41.12	42.04	42.97	43.89	44.81	45.73	46.66	47.58	48.50
A(8)	36.24	37.16	38.07	38.98	39.89	40.80	41.71	42.62	43.53	44.44	45.36	46.27	47.18	48.09	49.00
A(9)	36.90	37.80	38.70	39.60	40.50	41.40	42.30	43.20	44.10	45.00	45.90	46.80	47.70	48.60	49.50
A(10)	37.56	38.44	38.33	40.22	41.11	42.00	42.89	43.78	44.67	45.56	46.44	47.33	48.22	49.11	50.00
A(11)	38.21	39.09	39.97	40.84	41.72	42.60	43.48	44.36	45.23	46.11	46.99	47.87	48.74	49.62	50.50
A(12)	38.87	39.73	40.60	41.47	42.33	43.20	44.07	44.93	45.80	46.67	47.53	48.40	49.27	50.13	51.00
A(13)	39.52	40.38	41.23	42.94	43.80	44.66	45.51	46.37	47.22	48.08	48.93	49.79	50.64	50.64	51.50
A(15)	40.83	41.67	42.50	43.33	44.17	45.00	45.83	46.67	47.50	48.33	49.17	50.00	50.83	51.67	52.50
A(16)	41.49	42.31	43.13	43.96	44.78	45.60	46.42	47.24	48.07	48.89	49.71	50.53	51.36	52.18	53.00
A(17)	42.14	42.96	43.77	44.58	45.39	46.20	47.01	47.82	48.63	49.44	50.26	51.07	51.88	52.69	53.50
A(18)	42.80	43.60	44.40	45.20	46.00	46.80	47.80	47.60	48.40	49.20	50.00	51.60	52.40	53.20	54.00
A(19)	43.46	44.24	45.03	45.82	46.61	47.40	48.19	48.98	49.77	50.56	51.34	52.13	52.92	53.71	54.50
A(20)	44.11	44.89	45.67	46.44	47.22	48.00	48.78	49.56	50.33	51.11	51.89	52.67	53.44	54.22	55.00
A(21)	44.77	45.53	46.30	47.07	47.83	48.60	49.37	50.13	50.90	51.67	52.43	53.20	53.97	54.73	55.50
A(22)	45.42	46.18	46.93	47.69	48.44	49.20	49.96	50.71	51.47	52.22	52.98	53.73	54.49	55.24	56.00
A(23)	46.08	46.82	47.57	58.31	49.06	49.80	50.54	51.29	52.03	52.78	53.52	54.27	55.01	55.76	56.50
A(24)	46.73	47.47	48.20	48.93	49.67	50.40	51.13	51.87	52.60	53.33	54.07	54.80	55.53	56.27	57.00
A(25)	47.39	48.11	48.83	49.56	50.28	51.00	51.72	52.44	53.17	53.89	54.61	55.33	56.06	56.78	57.50
A(26)	48.04	48.76	49.47	50.18	50.89	51.60	52.31	53.02	53.73	54.44	55.16	55.87	56.58	57.29	58.00
A(27)	48.70	49.40	50.10	50.80	51.50	52.20	52.90	53.50	54.30	55.00	55.70	56.40	57.10	57.80	58.50
A(28)	49.36	50.04	50.73	51.42	52.11	52.80	53.49	54.18	54.87	55.56	56.24	56.93	57.62	58.31	59.00
A(29)	50.01	50.60	51.37	52.04	52.72	53.40	54.08	54.76	55.43	56.11	56.79	57.47	58.14	58.82	59.50
A(30)	50.67	51.33	52.00	53.67	53.33	54.00	54.67	55.33	56.00	56.67	57.33	58.00	58.67	59.33	60.00
A(31)	51.32	51.98	52.63	53.29	53.94	54.60	55.26	55.91	56.57	57.22	57.88	58.53	59.19	59.84	60.50
A(32)	51.98	52.62	53.27	53.91	54.56	55.20	55.84	57.13	57.13	57.78	58.42	59.07	59.71	60.36	61.00
A(33)	52.63	53.27	53.90	54.53	55.17	55.80	56.43	57.07	57.70	58.33	58.97	59.60	60.23	60.87	61.50
A(34)	53.29	53.91	54.53	55.16	55.78	56.40	57.02	57.64	58.27	58.89	59.51	60.13	60.76	61.38	62.00
A(35)	53.94	54.56	55.17	55.78	56.39	57.00	57.61	58.22	58.83	59.44	60.06	60.67	61.28	61.89	62.50
A(36)	54.60	55.20	55.80	56.40	57.00	57.60	58.20	58.80	59.40	60.00	60.60	61.20	61.80	62.40	63.00
A(37)	55.26	55.84	56.43	57.02	57.61	58.20	58.79	59.38	59.97	60.56	61.14	61.73	62.32	62.91	63.50
A(38)	55.91	56.49	57.07	57.64	58.22	58.80	59.38	59.96	60.53	61.11	61.69	62.27	62.84	63.42	64.00
A(39)	56.57	57.13	57.70	58.27	58.83	59.40	59.97	60.53	61.10	61.67	62.23	62.80	63.37	63.93	64.50
A(40)	57.22	57.78	58.33	58.89	59.44	60.00	60.56	61.11	61.67	62.22	62.78	63.33	63.89	64.44	65.00
A(41)	57.88	58.42	58.97	59.51	60.06	60.60	61.14	61.69	62.27	62.78	63.32	63.87	64.41	64.96	65.50
A(42)	58.53	59.07	59.60	60.13	60.67	61.20	61.73	62.27	62.80	63.33	63.87	64.40	64.93	65.47	66.00
A(43)	59.19	59.71	60.23	60.76	61.28	61.80	62.32	63.84	63.37	63.89	64.41	64.93	65.46	65.98	66.50
A(44)	59.84	60.36	60.87	61.38	61.89	62.40	62.91	63.42	63.93	64.44	64.96	65.47	65.98	66.49	67.00
A(45)	60.50	61.00	61.50	62.00	62.50	63.00	63.50	64.00	64.50	65.00	65.50	65.50	65.50	67.00	67.50

READY RECKONER TABLE FOR $A + \frac{B(90-A)}{90}$

	B(31)	B(32)	B(33)	B(34)	B(35)	B(36)	B(37)	B(38)	B(39)	B(40)	B(41)	B(42)	B(43)	B(44)	B(45)
A(46)	61.16	61.64	62.13	62.62	63.13	63.60	64.09	64.58	65.07	65.56	66.04	66.53	67.02	67.51	68.00
A(47)	61.81	62.29	62.77	63.24	63.72	64.20	64.68	65.16	65.63	66.11	66.59	67.07	67.54	68.02	68.50
A(48)	62.47	62.93	63.40	63.87	64.33	64.80	65.27	65.73	66.20	66.67	67.13	67.60	68.07	68.53	69.00
A(49)	63.12	63.58	64.03	64.49	64.94	65.40	65.86	66.3	66.77	67.22	67.68	68.13	68.59	69.04	69.50
A(50)	63.78	64.22	64.67	65.11	65.56	66.00	66.44	66.89	67.33	67.78	68.22	68.67	69.11	69.56	70.00
A(51)	64.43	64.87	65.30	65.73	66.17	66.60	67.03	67.47	67.90	68.33	68.77	69.20	69.63	70.07	70.50
A(52)	65.09	65.51	65.93	66.33	66.78	67.20	67.62	68.40	68.47	68.89	69.31	69.73	70.16	70.58	71.00
A(53)	65.74	66.16	66.57	66.98	67.39	67.80	68.21	68.62	69.03	69.44	69.86	70.27	70.68	71.09	71.50
A(54)	66.40	66.80	67.20	67.60	68.00	68.40	68.80	68.20	69.60	70.00	70.40	70.80	71.20	71.60	72.00
A(55)	67.06	67.44	67.83	68.22	68.61	69.00	69.39	69.78	70.17	70.56	70.94	71.33	71.72	72.11	72.50
A(56)	67.71	68.09	68.47	68.84	69.22	69.60	69.98	70.36	70.73	71.11	71.49	74.87	72.24	72.62	73.00
A(57)	68.37	68.73	69.10	69.47	69.83	70.20	70.57	70.93	71.30	71.67	72.03	72.40	72.77	73.13	73.50
A(58)	69.02	69.38	69.79	70.09	70.44	70.80	71.16	71.51	71.87	72.22	72.58	72.93	73.29	73.64	74.00
A(59)	69.68	70.02	70.37	70.71	71.06	71.40	71.74	72.09	72.43	72.78	73.12	73.47	73.81	74.16	74.50
A(60)	70.33	70.67	71.00	71.33	71.57	72.00	72.33	72.67	73.00	73.33	73.67	74.00	74.33	74.67	75.00
A(61)	70.99	71.31	71.63	71.96	72.28	72.60	72.92	73.24	73.57	73.89	74.21	74.53	74.86	75.18	75.50
A(62)	71.64	71.96	72.27	72.58	72.89	73.20	73.51	73.82	74.13	74.44	74.76	75.07	75.38	75.69	76.00
A(63)	72.30	72.60	72.90	73.20	73.50	73.80	74.10	74.40	74.70	75.00	75.30	75.60	75.90	76.20	76.50
A(64)	72.96	73.24	73.53	73.82	74.11	74.40	74.69	74.98	75.27	75.56	75.84	76.13	76.42	76.71	77.00
A(65)	73.61	73.89	74.17	74.44	74.72	75.00	75.28	75.56	75.83	76.11	76.39	76.67	76.94	77.22	77.50
A(66)	74.27	74.53	74.80	75.07	75.33	75.60	75.87	76.13	76.40	76.67	76.93	77.20	77.47	77.73	78.00
A(67)	74.92	75.18	75.43	75.69	75.94	76.20	76.46	76.71	76.97	77.22	77.48	77.73	77.99	78.24	78.50
A(68)	75.58	75.82	76.07	76.31	76.56	76.80	77.04	77.29	77.53	77.78	78.02	78.27	78.51	78.76	79.00
A(69)	76.23	76.47	76.70	76.93	77.17	77.40	77.63	77.87	78.10	78.33	78.57	78.80	79.03	79.27	79.50
A(70)	76.89	77.11	77.33	77.56	77.78	78.00	78.22	78.44	78.67	78.89	79.11	79.33	79.56	79.78	80.00
A(71)	77.54	77.76	77.97	78.18	78.39	78.60	78.81	79.02	79.23	79.44	79.66	79.87	80.08	80.29	80.50
A(72)	78.20	78.40	78.60	78.80	79.00	79.20	79.40	79.60	79.80	80.00	80.20	80.40	80.60	80.80	81.00
A(73)	78.86	79.04	79.23	79.42	79.61	79.80	79.99	80.18	80.37	80.56	80.74	80.93	81.12	81.31	81.50
A(74)	79.51	79.69	79.87	80.04	80.22	80.40	80.58	80.76	80.93	81.11	81.29	81.47	81.64	81.82	82.00
A(75)	80.17	80.33	80.50	80.67	80.83	81.00	81.17	81.33	81.50	81.67	81.83	82.00	82.17	82.33	82.50
A(76)	80.82	80.98	81.13	81.29	81.44	81.60	81.76	81.91	82.07	82.22	82.38	82.53	82.69	82.84	83.00
A(77)	81.48	81.62	81.77	81.91	82.06	82.20	82.34	82.49	82.63	82.78	82.92	83.07	83.21	83.36	83.50
A(78)	82.13	82.27	82.40	82.53	82.67	82.80	82.93	83.07	83.20	83.33	83.47	83.60	83.73	83.87	84.00
A(79)	82.79	82.91	83.03	83.16	83.28	83.40	83.52	83.64	83.77	83.89	84.01	84.13	84.26	84.38	84.50
A(80)	83.44	83.56	83.67	83.78	86.89	84.00	84.11	84.22	84.33	84.44	84.56	84.67	84.78	78.89	85.00
A(81)	84.10	84.20	84.30	84.40	84.50	84.60	84.70	84.80	84.90	85.00	85.10	85.20	85.30	85.40	85.50
A(82)	84.76	84.84	84.93	85.02	85.11	85.20	85.29	85.38	85.47	85.56	85.64	85.73	85.82	85.91	86.00
A(83)	85.41	85.49	85.57	85.64	85.72	85.80	85.88	85.96	87.03	86.11	86.19	86.27	86.34	86.42	86.50
A(84)	86.07	86.13	86.20	86.27	86.53	86.40	86.47	86.53	87.60	86.67	86.73	86.80	86.87	86.93	87.00
A(85)	86.72	86.78	86.83	86.89	87.94	87.00	87.06	87.11	88.17	87.22	87.28	87.33	87.39	87.44	87.50
A(86)	87.38	87.42	87.47	87.51	88.56	87.60	87.64	87.69	88.73	87.78	87.82	87.87	87.91	87.96	88.00
A(87)	88.03	88.07	88.10	88.13	88.17	88.20	88.23	88.27	88.30	88.33	88.37	88.40	88.43	88.47	88.50
A(88)	88.69	88.71	88.73	88.76	89.78	88.80	88.82	88.84	88.87	88.89	88.91	88.93	88.96	88.98	89.00
A(89)	89.34	89.36	89.37	89.38	89.39	89.40	89.41	89.24	89.43	89.44	89.46	89.44	89.46	89.49	89.50
A(90)	90.00	90.00	90.00	90.00	90.00	90.00	90.00	90.00	90.00	90.00	90.00	90.00	90.00	90.00	90.00

READY RECKONER TABLE FOR A + $\frac{\underline{B(90-A)}}{90}$

	B(46)	B(47)	B(48)	Bf49)	B(50)	B(51)	6(52)	B(53)	B(54)	B(55)	8(56)	B(57)	B(58)	BC59)	B(60)
A(1)	46.49	47.48	48.47	49.46	50.44	51.43	52,42	53.41	54.40	55.39	56,38	57.37	58.36	59.34	60.33
A(2)	46.98	47.96	48.93	49.91	50.89	51.87	52.84	53.82	54.80	55.78	56.76	57.73	58.71	59.69	60.67
A(3)	47.47	48.43	49.40	50.37	51.33	52.30	53.27	54.23	55.20	56.17	57.12	58.10	59.07	60.03	61.00
A(4)	47.96	48.91	49.87	50.82	51.78	52.73	53.69	54.64	55.60	56.56	57.51	58.47	59.42	60.38	61.33
A(5)	48.44	49.39	50.33	51.28	52.22	53,17	54.11	55.06	56.00	56.94	57.89	58.83	59.78	60.72	61.67
A(6)	48.93	49.87	50.80	51.73	52.67	53.60	54.53	55.47	56.40	57.33	58.27	59.20	60.13	61.07	62.00
A(7)	49.42	50.34	51.27	52.19	53.11	54.03	54,96	55.88	56.80	57.72	58.64	59.57	60.49	61.41	62.33
A(8)	49.91	50.82	51.73	52.64	53,56	54.47	55.38	56.20	57.20	58.11	59.02	59.93	60.84	61.76	62.67
A(9)	50.40	51.30	52.20	53.10	54.00	54.90	55.80	56.70	57.60	58.50	59.40	60.30	61.20	62.10	63.00
A(10)	50.89	51.78	52.67	53.56	54.44	55.33	56.22	57.11	58.00	58.89	59.78	60.67	61.56	62.44	63.33
A(11)	51.38	52.26	53.13	54.01	54.83	55.77	56.64	57,52	58.40	59.28	60.16	61.03	61.91	62.79	63.67
A(12)	51.87	52.73	53.60	54.47	55.33	56.20	57.07	57.93	58.80	59.67	60.53	61.40	62.27	63.13	64,00
A(13)	52.36	53.21	54.07	54.92	55.78	56.63	57.49	58.34	59.20	60.06	60.91	61.77	62.62	63.48	64.33
A(14)	52.84	53.69	54.53	55.38	56.22	57.07	57.19	58.76	59.60	60.44	61.29	62.13	62.98	63.82	64.67
A(15)	53.33	54.17	55.00	55.83	56.67	57.50	58.33	59.17	60,00	60.83	61.67	62.50	63.33	64.17	65.00
A(16)	53.82	54.64	55.47	56.29	57.11	57.93	58.76	59.58	60.40	61.22	62.04	62.87'	63,69	64.51	65.33
A(17)	54.31	55.12	55.93	56.74	57.56	58.37	59,18	59.99	60.80	61.61	62.42	63.23	64.04	64.86	65.67
A(18)	54.80	55.60	56.40	57.20	58.00	58.80	59.60	60.40	61.20	62.00	62.80	63.60	64.40	65.20	66.00
A(19)	55.29	56.08	56.87	57.66	58.44	59.23	60.02	60.81	61.60	62.39	63.18	63.97	64.54	65.54	66.33
A(20)	55,78	56.56	57.33	58.11	58.89	59.67	60.44	61.22	62.00	62.78	63.56	64.33	65.11	65.89	66.67
A(21)	56.27	57.03	57.80	58.57	59.33	60.10	60.87	61,63	62.40	63.17	63.93	64.70	65.47	66.23	67.00
A(22)	56.76	57.51	58.27	59.02	59.78	60.53	61.29	62.04	62.80	63.56	64.31	65.07	65.82	66.58	67.33
A(23)	57.24	57.99	58.73	59.48	60.22	60.97	61.71	62.46	63.20	63.94	64.69	65.43	66.18	66.92	67.67
A(24)	57.73	58.47	59.20	59.93	60.67	61.40	62,13	62.87	63.60	64.33	65.07	65.80	66.53	67.27	68.00
A(25)	58.22	58.94	59.67	60.39	61.11	61.83	62.56	63.28	64.00	64.72	65.44	66.17	66.89	67.61	68.33
A(26)	58.71	59.42	60.13	60.84	61.56	62.27	62.98	63.69	64.40	65.11	65.82	66.53	67.24	67.96	68.67
A(27)	59.20	59.90	60.60	61.30	62.00	62.70	63.40	64.10	64.80	65.50	66.20	66.90	67.60	68.30	69.00
A(28)	59.69	60.38	61.07	61.76	62.44	63.13	63.82	64.51	65.20	65.89	66.58	67.27	67.96	68.64	69.33
A(29)	60.18	60.86	61.53	62.21	62.89	63.57	64.24	64.92	65.60	66.28	66.96	67.63	68.31	68.99	69.67
A(30)	60.67	61.33	62.00	62.67	63.33	64.00	64.67	65.33	66.00	66.67	67.33	68.00	68.67	69.33	70.00
A(31)	61.16	61.81	62.47	63.12	63.78	64.43	65.09	65.74	66.40	67.06	67,71	68.37	69.02	69.68	70.33
A(32)	61.64	62.29	62.93	63.58	64.22	64.87	65.51	66.16	66.80	67.44	68.09	68.73	69.38	70.02	70.67
A(33)	62.13	62.77	63.40	64.03	64.67	^65.30	65.93	66,57	67.20	67.83	68.47	69.10	69.73	70.37	71.00
A(34)	62.62	63.24	63.87	64.49	65.11	65.73	66.36	33.98	67.60	68.22	68.84	69.47	70.09	70.71	71.33
A(35)	63.11	63.72	64.33	64.94	65.56	66.17	66.78	67.39	68.00	68.61	69.22	69.83	70.44	71.06	71.67
A(36)	63.90	64.20	64.80	65.40	66.00	66.60	67.20	67.80	68.00	68.61	69.22	70.20	70.80	71.40	72.00
A(37)	64.09	64.68	65.27	65.86	66.44	67.03	67.62	68.04	68.40	69.00	69.60	70.57	71.16	71.74	72.33
A(38)	64.58	65.16	65.73	66.31	66.89	67.47	68.04	68.47	68.80	69.39	69.98	70.93	71.51	72.09	72.33
A(39)	65.07	65.63	66.20	66.27	67.33	67.90	68.47	69.03	69.60	70.17	70.73	71.30	71.87	72.43	73.00
A(40)	65.56	66.11	66.67	67.22	67.78	68.33	68.89	69.44	70.00	70.56	71.11	71.67	72.22	72.78	73.33
A(41)	66.04	66.59	67.13	67.68	68.22	68.77	69.31	69.86	70.40	70.94	71.49	72,03	72.58	73.12	73.67
A(42)	66.53	67.07	67.60	68.13	68.67	69.20	69.73	70.27	70.80	71.33	71.87	72.40	72.93	73.47	74.00
A(43)	67.02	67.54	68.07	68.59	69.11	69.63	70.16	70.68	71.20	71.72	72.24	72.77	73.29	73.81	74.33
A(44)	67.51	68.02	68.53	69.04	69.56	70.07	70.58	71.09	71.60	72.11	72.62	73.13	73.64	74.16	74.67
A(45)	68.00	68.50	69.00	69.50	70.00	70.50	71.00	71.50	72.00	72.50	73.00	73.50	74.00	74.50	75.00

READY RECKONER TABLE FOR $A + \frac{B(90-A)}{90}$

	B(46)	B(47)	B(48)	B(49)	B(50)	B(51)	B(52)	B(53)	B(54)	B(55)	B(56)	B(57)	B(58)	B(59)	B(60)
A(46)	68.49	68.98	69.47	69.96	70.44	70.93	71.42	71.91	72.40	72.89	73.38	73,87	74.36	74.84	75.33
A{47)	68.98	69.46	69.93	70.41	70.89	71.37	71.84	72.32	72.80	73.28	73.76	74.23	74.71	75.19	75.67
A(48)	69.47	69.93	70-40	70.87	71.33	71.80	72.27	72.73	73.20	73.67	74.13	74.60	75.07	75.53	76.00
A(49)	69.96	70.41	70.87	71.32	71.78	72.23	72.69	73.14	73.60	74.06	74.51	74.97	75.42	75.88	76.33
A(50)	70.44	70.89	71.33	71.78	72.22	72.67	73.11	73.56	74.00	74.44	74.89	75.33	75.78	76.22	76.67
A(S1)	70.93	71.37	71.80	72.23	72.67	73.10	73.53	73.97	74.40	74.83	75.27	75.70	76,13	76.57	77.00
A(b2)	71.42	71.84	72.27	72.69	73.11	73.53	73.96	74.38	74,80	75.22	75.64	76.07	76.49	76.91	77.33
A(53)	71.91	72.32	72.73	73.14	73.56	73.97	74.38	74.79	75.20	75.61	76.02	76.43	73.84	77.26	77.67
A(54)	72.40	72.80	73.20	73.60	74.00	74.40	74.80	75.20	75.60	76.00	76.40	76.80	77,20	77.60	78.00
A(55)	72.89	73.28	73.67	74.06	74.44	74.83	75.22	75.61	76.00	76.39	76.78	77.17	77.56	77.94	78.33
A(S6)	73.38	73.76	74.13	74.51	74.89	75.77	75.64	76.02	76.40	76.78	77.14	77,53	77.91	78.29	78.67
A(57)	73.87	74.23	74.60	74.97	75.33	75.70	76.07	76.43	76.80	77.17	77.53	77.90	78.27	78.63	79.00
A(58)	74.36	74.71	75.07	75.42	75.78	76.13	76.49	76.84	77.20	77.56	77.91	78.27	78.62	78.98	79.33
A(59)	74.84	75.19	77.53	75.88	76.22	76.57	76.91	77.26	77.60	77.94	78.29	78.63	78.98	79.32	79.67
A(60)	75.33	75.67	76.00	76.33	76.67	77,00	77.33	77.67	78,00	78.33	78.67	79.00	79.33	79.67	80.00
A(61)	75.82	76.14	76.47	76.79	77.11	77.43	77.76	78.08	78.40	78.72	79.04	79.37	79.69	80.01	80.33
A(62)	76.31	76.62	76.93	77.24	77.56	77.87	78.18	78.40	78,80	79.11	79.42	79.73	80.04	80.36	80.67
A{63)	76.80	77.10	77.40	77.70	78.00	78.30	78.60	78.90	79.20	79.50	79.80	80.10	80.40	80.70	81.00
A(64)	77.29	77.58	77.87	78.16	78.44	78.73	79.02	79.31	79.60	79.89	80.18	80.47	80.76	81.04	81.33
A(65)	77.78	78.06	78.33	78.61	78.89	79.17	79.44	79.72	80.00	80.28	80.56	80.83	81.11	81.39	81.67
A(66)	78.27	78.53	78.80	79.07	79.33	79.60	79.87	80.13	80.40	80.67	80.93	81.20	81.47	81.73	82.00
A(67)	78.76	79.01	79.27	79,52	79.78	80.03	80.29	80.54	80.80	81.06	81.31	81.57	81.82	82.08	82.33
A(68)	79.24	79.49	79.73	79.98	80.22	80.47	80.71	80.96	81.20	81.44	81.69	81.93	82.18	82.42	82.57
A(69)	79.73	79.97	80.20	80.43	80.67	80.90	81.13	81.37	81.60	81.83	82.07	82.30	82.53	82.77	83.00
A(70)	80.22	80.44	80.67	80.89	81.11	81.33	81.56	81.78	82.00	82.22	82.44	82.67	82.89	83.11	83.33
A(71)	80.71	80.92	81.13	81.34	81.56	81.77	81.98	82.19	82.40	82.61	82.82	83.03	83.24	83.46	83.67
A(72)	81.20	81.40	81.60	81.80	82.00	82.20	82.40	82.60	82.80	83.00	83.20	83.40	83.60	83.80	84.00
A(73)	81.69	81.88	82.07	82.26	82.44	82.63	82.82	83.01	83.20	83.39	83.58	83.77	83.96	84.14	84.33
A(74)	82.18	82.36	82.53	82.71	82.89	83.07	83,24	83.42	83.60	83.78	83.96	84.13	84.31	84.49	84.67
A(75)	82.67	82.83	83.00	33.17	83.33	83.50	83.67	83.83	84.00	84.17	84.33	84.50	84.67	84.83	85.00
A(76)	83.16	83.31	83.47	83.62	83.78	83.93	84.09	84.24	84.40	84.56	84.71	84.87	85.02	85.18	85.33
A(77)	83.64	83.79	83.93	84.08	84.22	84.37	84.51	84.66	84.80	84.94	85.09	85.23	85.38	85.52	85.67
A(78)	84.13	84.27	84.40	84.53	84.67	84.80	84.93	85.07	85.20	85.33	85.47	85.60	85.73	85.87	86.00
A(79)	84.62	84.74	84.87	84.99	85.11	55.23	85.36	85.48	85.60	85.72	85.84	85.97	86,09	86,21	86.33
A(80)	85.11	85.22	85.33	85.44	85.56	85.67	85.78	85.89	86.00	86.11	86.22	86.33	86.44	86.56	86.67
A(81)	85.60	85.70	85.80	85.90	86.00	86.10	86.20	86.30	86.40	86.50	86.60	86.70	86.80	86.90	87.00
A(82)	86.09	86.18	86.27	86.36	86.44	86.53	86.62	86.71	86.80	86.89	86.98	87.07	87.16	87.24	87.33
A(83)	86.58	86.66	86.73	86.81	86.89	86.97	87.04	87.12	87.20	87.28	87.36	87.43	87.51	87.59	87.67
A(84)	87.07	87.13	87.20	87.27	87.33	87.40	87.47	87.53	87.60	87.67	87.73	87.80	87.87	87.93	88.00
A(85)	87.56	87.61	87.67	87.72	87.78	87.83	87.89	87.94	88.00	88.06	88.11	88.17	88.22	88.28	88.33
A(86)	88.04	88.09	88.13	88.18	88.22	88.27	88.31	88,36	88.40	88.44	88.49	88,53	88,58	88.62	88.67
A(87)	88.53	88.57	88.60	88.63	88.67	88.70	88.73	88.77	88.80	88.83	88.87	88.90	88.93	88.97	89.00
A(88)	89.02	89.04	89.07	89.09	89.11	89.13	89.16	89.18	89.20	89.22	89.24	89.27	89.29	89.31	89.33
A(89)	89.51	89.52	89.53	89.54	89.56	89.57	89.58	89.59	89.60	89.61	89.62	89.63	89.64	89.66	89.67
A(90)	90.00	90.00	90.00	90.00	90.00	90.00	90.00	90.00	90.00	90.00	90.00	90.00	90.00	90.00	90.00

READY RECKONER TABLE FOR

$$\frac{A + B(90\text{-}A)}{90}$$

	B(61)	B(62)	B(63)	B(64)	B(65)	B(66)	B(67)	B(68)	B(69)	B(70)	B(71)	B(72)	B(73)	B(74)	B(75)
A(1)	61.32	62.31	63.30	64.29	65.28	66.27	67.26	68.24	69.23	70.22	71.21	72.20	73.19	74.18	75.17
A(2)	61.64	62.62	63.60	64.58	65.56	66.53	67.51	68.49	69.47	70.44	71.42	72.40	73.38	74.36	75.33
A(3)	61.97	62.93	63.90	64.87	65.83	66.80	67.77	68.73	69.70	70.67	71.63	72.60	73.57	74.53	75.50
A(4)	62.29	63.24	64.20	65.16	66.11	67.07	68.02	68.98	69.93	70.89	71.84	72.80	73.76	74.71	75.67
A(5)	62.61	63.56	64.50	65.44	66.39	67.33	68.28	69.22	70.17	71.11	72.06	73.00	73.94	74.89	75.83
A(6)	62.93	63.87	64.80	65.73	66.67	67.60	68.53	69.47	70.40	71.33	72.27	73.20	74.13	75.07	76.00
A(7)	63.26	64.18	65.10	66.02	66.94	67.87	68.79	69.71	70.63	71.56	72.48	73.40	74.32	75.24	76.17
A(8)	63.58	64.49	65.40	66.31	67.22	68.13	69.04	69.96	70.87	71.78	72.69	73.60	74.51	75.42	76.33
A(9)	63.90	64.80	65.70	66.60	67.50	68.40	69.30	70.20	72.10	72.00	72.90	73.80	74.70	75.60	76.50
A(10)	64.22	65.11	66.00	66.89	67.78	68.67	69.56	70.44	71.33	72.22	73.11	74.00	74.89	75.78	76.67
A(11)	64.54	65.42	66.30	67.18	68.06	68.93	69.81	70.69	71.57	72.44	73.32	74.20	75.08	75.96	76.83
A(12)	64.87	65.73	66.60	67.47	68.33	69.20	70.07	70.93	71.80	72.67	73.53	74.40	75.27	76.13	77.17
A(13)	65.19	66.04	66.90	67.78	68.61	69.47	70.32	71.18	72.03	72.89	73.74	74.60	75.46	76.49	77.33
A(14)	65.51	66.36	67.20	68.04	68.89	69.73	70.58	71.42	72.27	73.11	73.96	74.80	75.83	76.67	77.50
A(15)	65.83	66.67	67.50	68.33	69.17	70.00	70.83	71.67	72.50	73.33	74.17	75.00	76.02	76.84	77.67
A(16)	66.16	66.98	67.80	68.62	69.44	70.27	71.09	71.91	72.73	73.56	74.38	75.20	76.21	77.02	77.83
A(17)	66.68	67.29	68.10	68.91	69.72	70.53	71.34	72.16	72.97	73.78	74.59	75.40	76.40	77.20	78.00
A(18)	66.80	67.60	68.40	69.20	70.00	70.80	71.60	72.40	73.20	74.00	74.80	75.60	76.59	77.36	78.17
A(19)	67.12	67.91	68.70	69.49	70.28	71.07	71.86	72.64	73.43	74.22	75.01	75.80	76.78	77.56	78.33
A(20)	67.44	68.22	69.00	69.78	70.56	71.33	72.11	72.89	73.67	74.44	75.22	76.00	76.78	77.56	78.33
A(21)	67.77	68.53	69.30	70.07	70.80	71.60	72.37	73.13	73.90	74.67	75.43	76.20	76.97	77.73	78.50
A(22)	68.09	68.84	69.60	70.36	71.11	71.87	72.62	73.38	74.13	74.89	75.64	76.40	77.16	77.91	78.67
A(23)	68.14	69.10	69.90	70.64	71.39	72.13	72.88	73.62	74.37	75.11	75.86	76.60	77.34	78.09	78.83
A(24)	68.73	69.47	70.20	70.93	71.67	72.40	73.13	73.87	74.60	75.33	76.07	76.80	77.53	78.27	79.00
A(25)	69.06	69.78	70.50	71.22	71.94	72.67	73.39	74.11	74.83	75.56	76.28	77.00	77.72	78.44	79.17
A(26)	69.38	70.00	70.80	71.51	72.22	72.93	73.64	74.36	75.07	75.78	76.49	77.20	77.91	78.62	79.33
A(27)	69.07	75.40	71.10	71.80	72.50	73.20	73.90	74.60	75.30	76.00	76.70	77.40	78.10	78.80	79.50
A(28)	70.02	70.71	71.40	72.09	72.78	73.47	74.16	74.84	75.53	76.22	76.91	76.60	78.29	78.98	79.67
A(29)	70.34	71.02	71.70	72.38	73.06	73.73	74.41	75.09	75.77	76.44	77.12	77.80	78.48	79.6	79.83
A(30)	70.67	71.33	72.00	72.67	73.33	74.00	74.67	75.33	76.00	76.67	77.33	78.00	78.67	79.33	80.00
A(31)	70.99	71.64	72.30	72.96	73.61	74.27	74.92	75.58	76.23	76.89	77.54	78.20	78.86	79.51	80.17
A(32)	71.31	71.96	72.60	73.24	73.89	74.53	75.82	75.18	76.47	77.11	77.76	78.40	79.04	79.69	80.33
A(33)	71.69	72.27	72.90	73.53	74.17	74.80	75.43	76.07	76.70	77.33	77.97	78.60	79.23	79.87	80.50
A(34)	71.96	72.58	73.20	73.82	74.44	75.07	75.69	76.31	76.93	77.56	78.18	78.80	79.42	80.04	80.67
A(35)	72.28	72.89	73.50	74.11	74.72	75.33	75.94	76.56	77.17	77.78	78.39	79.00	79.61	80.22	80.83
A(36)	72.60	73.20	73.80	74.40	75.00	75.60	76.20	76.80	77.40	78.00	78.60	78.20	79.80	80.40	81.00
A(37)	72.92	73.51	74.10	70.69	75.28	75.87	76.46	77.04	77.63	78.22	78.81	79.40	79.99	80.58	81.17
A(38)	73.24	73.82	74.40	74.99	75.56	76.13	76.71	77.29	77.87	78.44	79.02	79.60	80.18	80.76	81.33
A(39)	73.57	74.13	74.70	75.27	75.83	76.40	76.97	77.53	78.10	78.67	79.23	79.80	80.37	80.93	81.50
A(40)	73.89	74.44	75.00	75.56	76.11	76.67	77.22	77.78	78.33	78.89	79.44	80.00	80.56	81.11	81.67
A(41)	74.21	74.76	75.30	75.84	76.39	76.93	77.48	78.02	78.57	79.11	79.66	80.20	80.74	81.29	81.83
A(42)	74.43	75.07	75.60	76.13	76.67	77.20	77.73	78.27	78.80	79.33	79.87	80.40	80.93	81.47	82.00
A(43)	74.86	75.38	75.90	76.42	76.94	77.47	77.99	78.51	79.03	79.56	80.08	80.60	81.12	81.64	82.17
A(44)	75.18	75.69	76.20	76.71	77.22	77.73	78.24	78.76	79.27	79.78	80.29	80.80	81.31	81.82	82.33
A(45)	75.50	76.00	76.50	77.00	75.50	78.00	78.50	79.00	79.50	80.00	80.50	81.00	81.50	82.00	82.50

READY RECKONER TABLE FOR

A + B (90-A) / 90

	B(61)	B(62)	B(63)	B(64)	B(65)	B(66)	B(67)	B(68)	B(69)	B(70)	B(71)	B(72)	B(73)	B(74)	B(75)
A(46)	75.82	76.31	76.80	77.29	77.78	78.27	78.76	79.24	79.73	80.22	80.71	81.20	81.69	82.18	82.67
A(47)	76.14	76.62	77.10	77.58	78.06	78.53	79.01	79.49	79.97	80.44	80.92	81.40	81.88	82.36	82.83
A(48)	76.47	76.93	77.40	77.87	78.33	78.80	79.27	79.73	80.20	80.67	81.13	81.60	82.07	82.53	83.00
A(49)	76.79	77.24	77.70	78.16	78.61	79.07	79.52	79.98	80.43	80.89	81.34	81.80	82.26	82.71	83.17
A(50)	77.11	77.56	78.00	78.44	78.89	79.33	79.78	80.22	80.67	81.11	81.56	82.00	82.44	82.89	83.33
A(51)	77.43	77.87	78.30	78.73	79.17	79.60	80.03	80.47	80.90	81.33	81.77	82.20	82.63	83.07	83.50
A(52)	77.76	78.18	78.60	79.02	79.44	79.87	80.29	80.71	81.13	81.56	81.98	82.40	82.82	83.24	83.67
A(53)	78.08	78.49	78.90	79.31	79.72	80.13	80.54	80.96	81.37	81.78	82.19	82.60	83.01	83.42	83.83
A(54)	78.40	78.80	79.20	79.60	80.00	80.40	80.80	81.20	81.60	82.00	82.40	82.80	83.20	83.60	84.00
A(55)	78.72	79.11	79.50	79.60	80.28	80.67	81.06	81.44	81.83	82.22	82.61	83.00	83.39	83.78	84.17
A(56)	79.04	79.42	79.80	80.18	80.56	80.93	81.33	81.69	82.07	82.44	82.82	83.20	83.58	83.96	84.33
A(57)	79.37	79.73	80.10	80.47	80.83	81.20	81.57	81.93	82.30	82.67	83.03	83.40	83.77	84.13	84.50
A(58)	79.69	80.04	80.40	80.76	81.11	81.47	81.82	82.18	82.53	82.89	83.24	83.60	83.96	84.31	84.67
A(59)	80.01	80.36	80.70	81.04	81.39	81.73	82.08	82.42	82.77	83.11	83.46	83.80	84.14	84.49	84.83
A(60)	80.33	80.67	81.00	81.33	81.67	82.00	82.33	82.67	83.00	83.33	83.67	84.00	84.33	84.67	85.00
A(61)	80.66	80.98	81.30	81.62	81.94	82.27	82.59	82.91	83.23	83.56	83.88	84.20	84.52	84.84	85.17
A(62)	80.98	81.29	81.60	81.91	82.22	82.53	82.84	83.16	83.47	83.78	84.09	84.40	84.71	85.02	85.33
A(63)	81.30	81.60	81.90	82.20	82.50	82.80	83.10	82.40	83.70	84.00	84.30	84.60	84.90	85.20	85.50
A(64)	81.62	81.91	82.20	82.49	82.78	83.07	83.36	83.64	83.93	84.22	84.51	84.80	85.09	85.38	85.67
A(65)	81.94	82.22	82.50	82.78	83.06	83.33	83.61	83.89	84.17	84.44	84.72	85.00	85.28	85.56	85.83
A(66)	82.27	82.53	82.80	83.07	83.33	83.60	83.87	84.13	84.40	84.67	84.93	85.20	85.47	85.73	86.00
A(67)	82.59	82.84	83.10	83.36	83.61	83.87	84.12	84.38	84.63	84.89	85.14	85.40	85.66	85.91	86.17
A(68)	82.91	83.16	83.40	83.64	83.89	84.13	84.38	84.62	84.87	85.11	85.36	85.60	85.84	86.09	86.33
A(69)	83.73	83.47	83.70	83.93	84.17	84.40	84.63	84.87	85.10	85.33	85.57	85.80	86.03	86.27	86.50
A(70)	73.56	83.78	84.00	84.22	84.44	84.67	84.89	85.11	85.33	85.56	85.78	86.00	86.22	86.44	86.67
A(71)	83.88	84.09	84.30	84.51	84.72	84.93	85.14	85.36	85.57	85.78	85.99	86.20	86.41	86.62	86.83
A(72)	84.20	84.40	84.60	84.80	85.00	85.20	85.40	85.60	85.80	86.00	86.20	86.40	86.60	86.80	87.00
A(73)	84.52	84.71	84.90	85.09	85.28	85.47	85.66	85.84	86.03	86.22	86.41	86.60	86.79	86.98	87.17
A(74)	84.84	85.02	85.20	85.38	85.56	85.73	85.91	86.09	86.27	86.44	86.62	86.80	86.98	87.16	87.33
A(75)	85.17	85.33	85.50	85.67	85.83	86.00	86.17	86.33	86.50	86.67	86.83	87.00	87.17	87.33	87.50
A(76)	85.49	85.64	85.80	85.96	86.11	86.27	86.42	86.58	86.73	86.89	87.04	87.20	87.36	87.51	87.67
A(77)	85.81	85.96	86.10	86.24	86.39	86.53	86.68	86.82	86.97	87.11	87.26	87.04	87.54	87.69	87.83
A(78)	86.13	86.27	86.40	86.53	86.67	86.80	86.93	87.07	87.20	87.33	87.47	87.60	87.43	87.87	88.00
A(79)	86.16	86.58	86.70	86.82	86.94	87.07	87.19	87.31	87.73	87.56	87.68	87.80	87.92	88.04	88.17
A(80)	86.78	86.89	87.00	87.11	87.22	87.33	87.44	87.56	87.67	87.78	87.89	88.00	88.11	88.22	88.33
A(81)	87.10	87.20	87.30	87.40	87.50	87.60	87.70	87.80	87.90	88.00	88.10	88.20	88.30	88.40	88.50
A(82)	87.42	87.51	87.60	87.69	87.78	87.87	87.96	88.04	88.13	88.22	88.31	88.40	88.49	88.58	88.67
A(83)	87.74	87.82	87.90	87.98	88.06	88.13	88.21	88.29	88.37	88.44	88.52	88.60	88.68	88.76	88.83
A(84)	88.07	88.13	88.20	88.27	88.33	88.40	88.47	88.53	88.60	88.67	88.73	88.80	88.87	88.93	89.00
A(85)	88.39	88.44	88.50	88.56	88.61	88.67	88.72	88.78	88.83	88.89	88.94	89.00	89.06	89.11	89.17
A(86)	88.71	88.76	88.80	88.84	88.89	88.93	88.98	89.02	89.07	89.11	89.16	89.20	89.24	89.29	89.33
A(87)	89.03	89.07	89.10	89.13	89.17	89.20	89.23	89.27	89.30	89.33	89.37	89.40	89.43	89.47	89.50
A(88)	89.36	89.38	89.40	89.42	89.44	89.47	89.49	89.51	89.53	89.56	89.58	89.60	89.62	89.64	89.67
A(89)	89.68	89.69	89.70	89.71	89.72	89.73	89.74	89.76	89.77	89.78	89.79	89.80	89.81	89.82	89.83
A(90)	90.00	90.00	90.00	90.00	90.00	90.00	90.00	90.00	90.00	90.00	90.00	90.00	90.00	90.00	90.00

READY RECKONER TABLE FOR

A + B (90-A)
90

	B(76)	B(77)	B(78)	B(79)	B(80)	B(81)	B(82)	B(83)	B(84)	B(85)	B(86)	B(87)	B(88)	B(89)	B(90)
A(1)	76.16	77.14	78.13	79.12	80.11	81.10	82.09	83.08	84.07	85.06	86.04	87.03	88.02	89.01	90.00
A(2)	76.31	77.29	78.27	79.24	80.22	81.20	82.18	83.16	84.13	85.11	86.09	87.07	88.04	89.02	90.00
A(3)	76.47	77.43	78.40	79.37	80.33	81.30	82.27	83.23	84.20	85.17	86.13	87.10	88.07	89.03	90.00
A(4)	76.62	77.58	78.53	79.49	80.44	81.40	82.36	83.31	84.27	85.22	86.18	87.13	88.09	89.04	90.00
A(5)	76.78	77.72	78.67	79.61	80.56	81.50	82.44	83.39	84.33	85.28	86.22	87.17	88.11	89.06	90.00
A(6)	76.93	77.87	78.80	79.73	80.67	81.60	82.53	83.47	84.40	85.33	86.27	87.20	88.13	89.07	90.00
A(7)	77.09	78.01	78.93	79.86	80.78	81.70	82.62	83.54	84.47	85.39	86.31	87.23	88.16	89.09	90.00
A(8)	77.24	78.16	79.07	79.98	80.89	81.80	82.71	83.62	84.53	85.44	86.36	87.27	88.18	89.09	90.00
A(9)	77.40	78.30	79.20	80.10	81.00	81.90	82.80	83.70	84.60	85.50	86.40	87.30	88.20	89.10	90.00
A(10)	77.56	78.44	79.33	80.22	81.11	82.00	82.89	83.78	84.67	85.56	86.44	87.33	88.22	89.11	90.00
A(11)	77.71	78.59	79.47	80.34	81.22	82.10	82.98	83.86	84.73	85.61	86.49	87.37	88.24	89.12	90.00
A(12)	77.87	78.73	79.60	80.47	81.33	82.20	83.07	83.93	84.80	85.67	86.53	87.40	88.27	89.13	90.00
A(13)	78.02	78.88	79.73	80.59	81.44	82.30	83.16	84.01	84.87	85.72	86.18	87.43	88.29	89.16	90.00
A(14)	78.18	79.02	79.87	80.71	81.56	82.40	83.24	84.09	84.93	85.78	86.02	87.47	88.31	89.16	90.00
A(15)	78.33	79.17	80.00	80.83	81.67	82.50	83.33	84.17	85.00	85.83	86.61	87.50	88.33	89.17	90.00
A(16)	78.49	79.31	80.13	80.96	81.78	82.60	83.42	84.24	85.07	85.89	86.71	87.53	88.36	89.81	90.00
A(17)	78.64	79.46	80.27	81.08	81.89	82.70	83.51	84.32	85.13	85.94	86.76	87.57	88.38	89.19	90.00
A(18)	78.80	79.60	80.40	81.20	82.00	82.80	83.60	84.40	85.20	86.00	86.80	87.60	88.40	89.20	90.00
A(19)	78.96	79.74	80.53	81.32	82.71	82.90	83.69	84.48	85.27	86.06	86.84	87.63	88.42	89.21	90.00
A(20)	79.11	79.89	80.67	81.44	82.22	83.00	83.78	84.56	85.33	86.11	86.89	87.67	88.44	89.22	90.00
A(21)	79.27	80.03	80.80	81.57	82.33	83.10	83.87	84.63	85.40	86.17	86.93	87.70	88.47	89.23	90.00
A(22)	79.42	80.18	81.93	81.69	82.44	83.20	83.96	84.71	85.47	86.22	86.98	87.73	88.49	89.24	90.00
A(23)	79.58	80.32	81.07	81.81	82.56	83.30	84.04	84.79	85.53	86.28	87.02	87.77	88.51	89.26	90.00
A(24)	79.73	80.47	81.20	81.93	82.67	83.40	84.13	84.87	85.60	86.33	87.07	87.80	88.53	89.27	90.00
A(25)	79.89	80.61	81.33	82.06	82.78	83.50	84.22	84.94	85.67	86.39	87.11	87.80	88.56	89.28	90.00
A(26)	80.04	80.76	81.47	82.18	82.89	83.60	84.31	85.02	85.73	86.44	87.16	87.89	88.58	89.29	90.00
A(27)	80.20	80.90	81.60	82.30	83.00	83.70	84.40	85.10	85.80	86.50	87.20	87.90	88.60	89.30	90.00
A(28)	80.36	81.04	81.73	82.42	83.11	83.80	84.49	85.18	58.87	86.56	87.24	87.93	88.62	89.31	90.00
A(29)	80.51	81.19	81.87	82.54	83.22	83.90	84.58	85.26	85.93	86.61	87.29	87.97	88.64	89.32	90.00
A(30)	80.67	81.33	82.00	82.67	83.33	84.00	84.67	85.33	86.00	86.67	87.33	88.00	88.67	89.33	90.00
A(31)	80.82	81.48	82.13	82.79	83.44	84.10	84.76	85.41	86.07	86.72	87.38	88.03	88.69	89.34	90.00
A(32)	80.98	81.62	82.27	82.91	83.56	84.20	84.84	85.49	86.13	86.78	87.42	88.07	88.70	89.36	90.00
A(33)	81.13	81.77	82.40	83.03	83.67	84.30	84.93	85.57	86.20	86.83	87.47	88.10	88.73	89.37	90.00
A(34)	81.29	81.91	82.53	83.16	83.78	84.40	85.02	85.64	86.27	86.89	87.51	88.13	88.67	89.38	90.00
A(35)	81.44	82.06	82.67	83.28	83.89	84.50	85.11	85.72	86.33	86.94	87.56	88.17	88.78	89.39	90.00
A(36)	81.60	82.20	82.80	83.40	84.00	84.60	85.20	85.80	86.40	87.00	87.60	88.20	88.80	89.40	90.00
A(37)	81.76	82.34	82.93	83.53	84.11	84.70	85.29	85.88	86.47	87.06	87.64	88.23	88.82	89.41	90.00
A(38)	81.91	82.49	83.07	83.64	84.22	84.80	85.38	85.96	86.53	87.11	87.69	88.27	88.84	89.42	90.00
A(39)	82.07	82.63	83.20	83.77	84.33	84.90	85.47	86.03	86.60	87.17	87.73	88.30	88.87	89.43	90.00
A(40)	82.22	82.78	83.33	83.89	84.44	85.00	85.56	86.11	86.67	87.22	87.78	88.33	88.89	89.44	90.00
A(41)	82.38	82.92	83.47	84.01	84.56	85.10	85.64	86.19	86.73	87.82	87.28	87.82	88.37	88.91	90.00
A(42)	82.53	83.07	83.60	84.13	84.67	85.20	85.73	86.27	86.80	87.33	87.87	88.40	88.93	89.46	90.00
A(43)	83.69	83.21	83.73	84.26	84.78	85.30	85.82	86.34	86.87	87.39	87.91	88.43	88.96	89.67	90.00
A(44)	82.84	83.36	83.87	84.38	84.89	85.40	85.91	86.42	86.93	87.44	87.96	88.47	88.98	89.84	90.00
A(45)	83.00	83.50	84.00	84.50	85.00	85.50	86.00	86.50	87.00	87.50	88.00	88.50	89.00	89.50	90.00

READY RECKONER TABLE FOR
A + B (90-A)
90

	B(76)	B(77)	B(78)	B(79)	B(80)	B(81)	B(82)	B(83)	B(84)	B(85)	B(86)	B(87)	B(88)	B(89)	B(90)
A(46)	83.16	83.64	84.13	84.62	85.11	85.60	86.09	86.58	87.07	87.56	88.04	88.53	89.02	89.51	90.00
A(47)	83.31	83.79	84.27	84.74	85.22	85.70	86.18	86.66	87.13	87.61	88.09	88.57	89.04	89.52	90.00
A(48)	83.47	83.93	84.40	84.87	85.33	85.80	86.27	86.73	87.20	87.67	88.13	88.60	89.07	89.53	90.00
A(49)	83.62	84.08	84.53	84.99	85.44	85.90	86.36	86.81	87.27	87.72	88.18	88.63	89.09	89.54	90.00
A(50)	83.78	84.22	84.67	85.11	85.56	86.00	86.44	86.89	87.33	87.78	88.22	87.67	89.11	89.56	90.00
A(51)	83.93	84.37	84.80	85.23	85.67	86.10	86.53	86.97	87.40	87.83	88.27	88.70	89.13	89.57	90.00
A(52)	84.09	84.66	84.93	85.36	85.78	86.20	86.62	87.04	87.47	87.89	88.31	88.73	89.16	89.58	90.00
A(53)	84.24	84.66	85.07	85.48	85.89	86.30	86.71	87.12	87.53	87.94	88.36	88.77	89.18	89.59	90.00
A(54)	84.40	84.80	85.20	85.60	86.00	86.40	86.80	87.20	87.60	88.00	88.40	88.80	89.20	89.60	90.00
A(55)	84.56	84.94	85.33	85.72	86.11	86.50	86.89	87.28	87.67	88.06	88.44	88.83	89.22	89.61	90.00
A(56)	84.71	85.09	85.47	85.84	86.22	86.60	86.98	87.36	87.73	88.11	88.49	88.87	89.24	89.62	90.00
A(57)	84.87	85.23	85.60	85.97	86.33	86.70	87.07	87.43	87.80	88.17	88.53	88.90	89.27	89.63	90.00
A(58)	85.02	85.38	85.73	86.09	86.44	86.80	87.16	87.51	87.87	88.22	88.58	88.93	88.29	89.64	90.00
A(59)	85.18	85.52	85.87	86.21	86.56	86.90	87.24	87.59	87.93	88.28	88.62	88.97	89.31	89.66	90.00
A(60)	85.33	85.67	86.00	86.33	86.67	87.00	87.33	87.67	88.00	88.33	88.67	89.00	89.67	89.67	90.00
A(61)	85.49	85.81	86.13	86.46	86.78	87.10	87.42	87.74	88.07	88.39	88.71	89.03	89.36	89.68	90.00
A(62)	85.64	85.96	86.27	86.58	86.89	87.20	87.51	87.82	88.13	88.44	88.76	89.07	89.38	89.69	90.00
A(63)	85.80	86.10	86.40	86.70	87.00	87.30	87.60	87.90	88.20	88.50	88.80	89.10	89.40	89.70	90.00
A(64)	85.96	86.24	86.53	86.82	87.11	87.40	87.69	87.98	88.27	88.56	88.84	89.13	89.42	89.71	90.00
A(65)	86.11	86.39	86.67	86.94	87.22	87.50	87.78	88.06	88.33	88.61	88.89	89.17	89.44	89.72	90.00
A(66)	86.27	86.53	86.80	87.07	87.33	87.60	87.87	88.13	88.40	88.67	88.93	89.20	89.47	89.73	90.00
A(67)	86.42	86.68	86.93	87.19	87.44	87.70	87.96	88.21	88.47	88.72	88.98	89.23	89.49	89.74	90.00
A(68)	86.58	86.87	87.07	87.31	87.56	87.80	88.04	88.29	88.53	88.78	89.02	89.27	89.51	89.76	90.00
A(69)	86.73	86.97	87.20	87.43	87.67	87.90	88.13	88.37	88.60	88.83	89.07	89.30	89.53	89.77	90.00
A(70)	86.89	87.41	87.33	87.56	87.78	88.00	88.22	88.44	88.67	88.89	89.11	89.33	89.56	89.78	90.00
A(71)	87.04	87.18	87.47	87.68	87.89	88.10	88.31	88.52	88.73	88.94	89.16	89.37	89.58	89.79	90.00
A(72)	87.20	87.40	87.60	87.80	88.00	88.20	88.40	88.60	88.80	89.00	89.20	89.40	89.60	89.80	90.00
A(73)	87.36	87.54	87.73	87.92	88.11	88.30	88.49	88.68	88.87	89.06	89.24	89.43	89.62	89.81	90.00
A(74)	87.51	87.69	87.87	88.04	88.17	88.33	88.50	88.67	88.93	89.11	89.29	89.47	89.64	89.82	90.00
A(75)	87.67	87.83	88.00	88.17	88.33	88.50	88.67	88.83	89.00	89.17	89.33	89.50	89.67	89.83	90.00
A(76)	87.82	87.98	88.13	88.29	88.44	88.60	88.76	88.91	89.07	89.22	89.38	89.53	89.69	89.84	90.00
A(77)	87.98	88.12	88.27	88.41	88.56	88.70	88.84	88.99	89.13	89.28	89.42	89.57	89.71	89.86	90.00
A(78)	88.13	88.27	88.40	88.53	88.67	88.80	88.93	89.07	89.20	89.33	89.47	89.60	89.73	89.87	90.00
A(79)	89.29	88.41	88.53	88.66	88.78	88.90	89.02	89.14	89.27	89.39	89.51	89.63	89.76	89.88	90.00
A(80)	88.45	88.56	88.67	88.78	88.89	89.00	89.11	89.22	89.33	89.44	89.56	89.67	89.78	89.89	90.00
A(81)	88.60	88.70	88.80	88.90	89.00	89.10	89.20	89.30	89.40	89.50	89.60	89.70	89.80	89.90	90.00
A(82)	88.76	88.84	88.93	89.02	89.11	89.20	89.29	89.38	89.47	89.56	89.64	89.73	89.82	89.91	90.00
A(83)	88.91	88.99	89.07	89.14	89.22	89.30	89.38	89.46	89.53	89.61	89.69	89.77	89.84	89.92	90.00
A(84)	89.07	89.13	89.20	89.27	89.33	89.40	89.47	89.53	89.60	89.67	89.73	89.80	89.87	89.93	90.00
A(85)	89.22	89.28	89.33	89.39	89.44	89.50	89.56	89.61	89.67	89.72	89.78	89.83	89.89	89.94	90.00
A(86)	89.38	89.42	89.47	89.51	89.56	89.60	89.64	89.69	89.73	89.78	89.82	89.87	89.91	89.96	90.00
A(87)	89.53	89.57	89.60	89.63	89.67	89.70	89.73	89.77	89.80	89.83	89.87	89.90	89.93	89.97	90.00
A(88)	89.69	89.71	89.73	89.76	89.78	89.80	89.82	89.84	89.87	89.89	89.91	89.93	89.96	89.98	90.00
A(89)	89.47	89.86	89.87	89.88	89.89	89.90	89.91	89.92	89.93	89.94	89.96	89.97	89.98	89.99	90.00
A(90)	90.00	90.00	90.00	90.00	90.00	90.00	90.00	90.00	90.00	90.00	90.00	90.00	90.00	90.00	90.00

APPENDIX III OF ANNEXURE A

STANDING HEIGHTS FOR INDIAN POPULATION (IN INCHES) MEAN AND STANDARD DEVIATIONS

Age	Mean	S.D.	-2S.D.	Mean	S.D.	-2S.D.
Less than 3 months	22.13	2.32	17.49	21.65	2.13	17.39
3 months,+	24.68	1.58	21.52	23.98	2.40	21.80
6 months +	25.55	3.19	19.17	25.35	1.43	22.49
9 months +	27.36	1.77	23.82	26.26	1.52	23.22
1 year +	29.09	2.07	24.95	28.54	2.04	24.46
2 year -f	32.13	2.10	27.93	31.53	2.28	26.97
3 year +	34.96	2.58	29.80	34.33	2.50	29.33
4 year"+	37.80	2.65	32.50	37.20	2.50	32.20
5 year +	40.19	3.16	33.84	39.92	2.90	34.12
6 year +	42.71	2.81	37.09	42.28	3.41	35.46
7 year +	44.84	3.41	38.02	44.04	3.34	37.72
8 year +	46.96	2.89	41.18	46.53	3.03	40.47
9 year +	48.70	3.65	.41.40	48.38	2.96	42.46
10 year +	48.97	3.93	41.11	50.55	3.15	44.25
11 year +	52.51	3.83	44.86	52.60	3.73	45.14
12 year +	54.45	3.99	46.47	54.80	4.03	46.74
13 year +	56.93	3.84	49.25	56.65	3.63	49.39
14 year +	59.10	3.95	51.20	58.07	3.82	50.43
15 year +	61.22	3.94	53.34	58.89	3.27	52.35
16 year +	62.79	3.84	55.11	59.44	2.80	53.84
17 year +	63.54	4.11	55.32	59.64	2.95	53.74
18 year +	64.21	3.76	56.69	59.72	2.31	55.10
19 year +	64.37	3.79	56.79	59.72	2.31	55.10
20 year +	64.60	2.75	59.10	59.72	2.32	55.08
21 year +	64.64	2.40	59.84	60.24	2.24	55.76

ANNEXURE B

CERTIFICATE OF MENTAL RETARDATION FOR GOVERNMENT BENEFITS

This is to certify that Shri/Smt./Kum...

Son/Daughter of................................of Village/Town/City................................with particulars given below:—

(a) Age

(b) Sex

(c) Signature/Thumb-impression

CATEGORISATION OF MENTAL RETARDATION

Mild/Moderate/Server/Profound

Validity of the Certificate : Permanent

Signature of the Government
Doctor/Hospital with seal

Chairperson Mental Retardation
Certification Board

Recent Attested Photograph, showing the disability affixed here.

Dated....................
Place....................

ANNEXURE B

STANDARD FORMAT OF THE CERTIFICATE

Certificate No.....................
Date....................

CERTIFICATE FOR THE PERSONS WITH DISABILITIES

This is to certify that Shri/Smt/Kum.. Son/wife/daughter of Shri..Age............................old male/female, Registration No. ....is a case of .... He/She is physically disabled/visual disabled/speech & hearing disabled and has....................% (.................... per cent) permanent (physical impairment/visual impairment/speech & hearing impairment) in relation to his/her.......................................

Note.—

1. This condition is progressive/non-progressive/likely to improve/not likely improve.

2. Re-assessment is not recommended/is recommended after a period of.. months/years.*

*Strike out which is not applicable.

Sd/- Sd/- Sd/-
(DOCTOR) (DOCTOR) (DOCTOR)
Seal Seal Seal

Signature/Thumb-impression of the patient.

Counter-signed by the
Medical Superintendent/CMO/Head of
Hospital (with seal)
Recent Attested Photograph showing the disability affixed here]

APPENDIX 4

THE NATIONAL COMMISSION FOR THE SCHEDULED TRIBES (SPECIFICATION OF OTHER FUNCTIONS) RULES, 2005[1]

In exercise of the powers conferred by sub-clause (f) of clause 5 of Article 338A of the Constitution, the President hereby makes the following rules to specify the other functions of the National Commission for the Scheduled Tribes, namely:—

1. Short title and commencement.—(1) These rules may be called the National Commission for the Scheduled Tribe (Specification of Other Functions) Rules, 2005.

(2) They shall come into force on the date of their publication in the Official Gazette.

2. The Commission shall discharge the following other functions in relation to the protection, welfare and development and advancement of the Scheduled Tribes, namely:—

(i) Measures that need to be taken over conferring ownership rights in respect of minor forest produce to the Scheduled Tribes living in forest areas;

(ii) Measures to be taken to safeguard rights of the tribal communities over mineral resources, water resources etc. as per law;

(iii) Measures to be taken for the development of tribals and to work for more viable livelihood strategies;

(iv) Measures to be taken to improve the efficacy of relief and rehabilitation measures for tribal groups displaced by development projects;

(v) Measures to be taken to prevent alienation of tribal people from land and to effectively rehabilitate such people in whose case alienation has already taken place;

(vi) Measures to be taken to elicit maximum cooperation and involvement of tribal communities for protecting forests and undertaking social afforestation;

(vii) Measures to be taken to ensure full implementation of the Provisions of Panchayats (Extension to the Scheduled Areas) Act, 1996 (40 of 1996);

(viii) Measures to be taken to reduce and ultimately eliminate the practice of shifting cultivation by tribals that lead to their continuous disempowerment and degradation of land and the environment.

---

1. *Vide* S.O. 1175(E), dated 23rd August, 2005, published in the Gazette of India, Extra., Pt. II, Sec. 3(ii), dated 24th August, 2005.

APPENDIX 5

RULES OF PROCEDURE OF THE NATIONAL COMMISSION FOR SCHEDULED CASTES[1]

CHAPTER I

GENERAL

1. Constitutional Provisions

The duties of the Commission as laid down in the Article 338(5) of the Constitution are:

(a) to investigate and monitor all matters relating to the safeguards provided for the Scheduled Castes under the Constitution or under any other law for the time being in force or under any order of the Government and to evaluate the working of such safeguards;

(b) to inquire into specific complaints with respect to the deprivation of rights and safeguards of the Scheduled Castes;

(c) to participate and advise on the planning process of socio-economic development of the Scheduled Castes and to evaluate the progress of their development under the Union and any State;

(d) to present to the President, annually and at such other times as the Commission may deem fit, reports upon the working of those safeguards;

(e) to make in such report recommendations as to the measures that should be taken by the Union or any State for the effective implementation of those safeguards and other measures for the protection, welfare and socio-economic development of the Scheduled Castes; and

(f) to discharge such other functions in relation to the protection, welfare and development and advancement of the Scheduled Castes as the President may, subject to the provisions of any law made by Parliament, by rule specify.

CHAPTER II

DIVISION OF RESPONSIBILITIES AND ALLOCATION OF WORK

2.0 Chairperson

2.1 The Chairperson shall be the head of the Commission and shall have powers to decide on all questions and matters pertaining to the Commission.

2.2 The Chairperson shall allocate subjects and responsibilities among the Members of the Commission. The Orders allocating the subjects and responsibilities shall be notified to all concerned by the Secretariat of the Commission.

2.3 The Chairperson shall be the authority to sanction leave and approve tours of the Members, Secretary, Joint Secretary and Directors.

2.4 The Chairperson shall preside over the meetings of the Commission.

2.5 All important decisions in the Commission about its functioning shall be taken with the approval of the Chairperson.

2.6. All important administrative matter like appointments, promotions, transfers, posting, deputation and sanction of leave, etc. shall be placed before the Chairperson wherein he/she may pass general or specific order on such matter.

---

1. *Vide* G.S.R. 414(E), dated 25th March, 2009, published in the Gazette of India, Extra., Pt. II, Sec. 3(i), dated 15th June, 2009.

2.7 The Chairperson may call for any records on any matter which he/she considers important and may take a decision on it himself/herself or, if necessary, place it at the meeting of the Commission.

2.8 The Chairperson shall be authority to approve Annual Report, Special Report, and communicate to the Ministries/Departments of the Government of India/State Governments/Media.

2.9 The Chairperson shall take decision to conduct specific studies in the areas of the safeguards provided to SCs and shall sanction the budget required for such studies.

3.0 Vice-Chairperson

3.1 The Vice-Chairperson shall preside over the meetings of the Commission in the absence of the Chairperson.

3.2 The Vice-Chairperson shall perform such functions as are entrusted to him/her by the Chairperson.

3.3 All important administrative matters like appointments, promotions, transfers, posting, deputation and sanction of leave, etc. to other than Secretary, Joint Secretary and Directors shall be place before the Vice-Chairperson wherein he/she may pass general or specific order on such matter.

4.0 Members

4.1 The Members of the Commission shall have collective responsibility and shall function by participating in the 'meetings' and 'sittings' of the Commission and looking after the subjects allocated to them. Important actions and decisions of a Member may be brought at a meeting of the Commission which may review the same.

4.2 Any Member may suggest items for inclusion in the agenda of a meeting of the Commission and the same shall be so included after obtaining the consent of the Chairperson.

4.3 Each Member shall have overall responsibility of subjects and/or regions or State(s) as may be allocated to him.

4.4 The Members shall play the role of advising the State Governments under their jurisdiction on matters of planning and development relating to the welfare of Scheduled Castes in accordance with the decision taken in the meetings of the Commission/with approval of the Chairman. The Commission's Secretariat at Headquarters and the State Offices shall assist the Members in keeping them fully informed of the problems and activities of the States and subjects under their respective charge.

4.5 One or more Members may, in accordance with the procedure specified in the rules elsewhere, hold sittings of the Commission to give hearing to the cases or to collect evidence or information on any matter, issue or case under investigation or inquiry of the Commission.

4.6 The Members shall communicate their tour programmes through the Secretariat of the Commission well in advance to the State Offices indicating in detail the purpose of the visit and to the State Government Department and other concerned for discussions/inquiry, etc., during the tour/visit and shall be responsible to submit tour/visit report before commencing next tour/visit or within a week of the tour/visit concerned.

4.7 The Member will observe the norms laid down by the State Governments regarding security/travel/accommodation, etc., during such tours.

5.0 Secretary

5.1 The Secretary shall be the administrative head of the secretariat of the Commission and shall assist the Chairperson/Commission in the discharge of its functions with the assistance of the officers of the Commission.

5.2 All important administrative matters shall be placed before the Secretary who may pass general or specific orders on such matters with the approval of the Chairperson only.

5.3 The Secretary shall be responsible for having the agenda prepared for the meetings of the Commission and for circulating the minutes with prior approval of the Chairperson.

5.4 The Secretary shall be responsible to assist and monitor preparation of Annual Report, Special Reports, and ensure proper liaison with the Ministries/Departments of GOI/State Governments/UTs.

5.5. The Secretary shall be accountable to the Commission and shall responsible to update the Commission with all relevant information relating to safeguards provided for the Scheduled Castes under the Constitution, under any other law for the time being in force or under any order of the Government.

5.6. The Secretary may, in his discretion, delegate any of his functions or authority to a subordinate officer of the Secretariat.

5.7 The Secretary shall be the authority to sanction leave to all Group "A" officers excluding himself and Joint Secretary of the Commission.

5.8 The Secretary shall be Chief Vigilance Officer of the Commission and shall report all important matters to the Chairperson pertaining to vigilance cases.

6.0 Joint Secretary

6.1 The Joint Secretary shall be responsible to monitor working of the Officials of the Commission including State Offices of the Commission.

6.2 All important administrative matters shall be placed before the Joint Secretary who may pass general or specific orders on such matters with the approval of the Chairperson/Secretary.

6.3 The Joint Secretary shall be responsible for having the agenda prepared for the meetings of the Commission.

6.4 The Joint Secretary shall be the authority to sanction leave to all officers of the Commission other than Director and above.

6.5 The Joint Secretary shall be accountable to the Commission and shall responsible to update the Commission with all relevant information relating to safeguards provided for the Scheduled Castes under the Constitution, under any other law for the time being in force or under any order of the Government.

6.6. The Joint Secretary may, in his discretion, delegate any of his functions or authority to a subordinate officer of the Secretariat.

6.7 The Joint Secretary shall be responsible for updating the website of the Commission and shall function as a Appellate Authority for disposal of cases relating to the Right to Information Act.

6.8 The Joint Secretary shall also function as Vigilance Officer of the Commission and may act as Chief Vigilance Officer in absence of the Secretary of the Commission and shall report to the Chairperson/Secretary on vigilance matter.

CHAPTER III

7.0 Investigation and Inquiry by the Commission

7.1 The Commission shall function by holding 'sittings' and 'meetings' at any place within the country and also through its officers at the Headquarters and in the State Offices. The Members of the Commission including the Chairperson and the Vice-Chairperson shall function in accordance with the procedure prescribed under these rules.

7.1.1 The Commission may adopt any one or more of the following methods for investigating for inquiring into the matters falling within its authority:

(a) by the Commission directly;

(b) by an Investigating Team constituted at the Headquarters of the Commission;

(c) through its State Offices;

(d) by the State Agencies; and

(e) by any other institution/Deptt. funded by Central Government and its statutory bodies.

7.2 (a) Investigation and Inquiry by the Commission directly

7.2(a) (i) The Commission may hold sittings for investigation into matters relating to safeguards, protection, welfare and development of the Scheduled Castes for inquiry into specific complaints for which the Commission decided to take up investigation or inquiry directly. Such sittings may be held either at the Headquarters of the Commission or at any other place within the country.

7.2(a) (ii) The sitting(s) of the Commission would be held after giving due notice to the parties intended to be heard and also due publicity/notice to the general public. Care will be taken to see that the members of the Scheduled Castes who are affected in the matter under investigation or inquiry are given due information through notice or publicity.

7.2(a) (iii) When a decision for direct investigation is taken, an officer not below the rank of Investigator/Research Officer/Section Officer along with necessary staff may be attached to the Member(s) entrusted with such investigation or enquiry and they shall take all steps to arrange such sittings.

7.2(a) (iv) The Commission shall convene meeting of all the Chief Secretaries, Secy. (Home), Secy. (Social Welfare), DGPs of the State and Secretaries of the Government of India, who may be considered accountable for the implementation of the programme of the safeguards as enumerated under Article 338(5)(a) once in a year for monitoring the safeguards and development.

7.2(a) (v) In accordance with Clause (8) of Article 338 of the Constitution, while investigating in a matter referred to in sub-clause (a) or in inquiring into any complaint referred to in sub-clause (b) of clause (5) of Article 338, the Commission shall have all the powers of civil court trying a suit and in particular in respect of the following matters, namely:—

(a) summoning and enforcing the attendance of any person from any part of India and examining him on oath;

(b) requiring the discovery and production of any document;

(c) receiving evidence on affidavits;

(d) requisitioning any public record or copy thereof from any court or office;

(e) issuing commissions for the examination of witnesses and documents;

(f) any other matter which the President may, by rule, determine.

7.2(a) (vi) The Commission for the purpose of taking evidence in the investigation or inquiry, requires the presence of any person and when considered necessary may issue summons to him/her with the approval of the Chairman. The summons for enforcing attendance of any person from any part of India and examining him/her during the course of investigation and inquiry by the Commission shall provide at least 15 days' notice to the person directed to be present before the Commission from the date of receipt of the summons. In serious cases of atrocities, three days' notice will be given to the person directed to be present before the Commission from the date of receipt of the summons by him/her.

7.2(a) (vii) Where the property, service/employment of Scheduled Castes and other related matters are under immediate threat and prompt attention of the Commission is required, the matter shall be taken cognizance by issue of telex/fax to the concerned authority for making it known to them that the Commission is seized of the issue and that authority will be prohibited to take any action till the completion of the enquiry in the matter by the NCSC. Urgent reply by telegram or fax shall be called from the concerned authority. In case no reply is received within three working days, the authority concerned may be required to appear before the Commission at a three days' notice for enquiry.

7.2(a) (viii) The Commission may issue commission/under Clause 8(e) of Article 338 of the Constitution to take evidence in any matter under investigation or inquiry and for this purpose appoint any person by an order in writing. The Commission may make further rules for payment of fee and travelling and other allowances to persons appointed to take evidence on commission.

7.2(a) (ix) After holding the required sittings, the Member(s) who conducted the investigation shall make a report, which shall be sent to the enquiry officer appointed under Rule, 34 or any other officer authorized by the Commission to receive the report. The report received in the Commission shall be submitted within 3 days to the Chairperson for inspections. After examination, action may be initiated on the report with the approval of the Chairperson.

7.2(b) Investigation or inquiry by an Investigation Team constituted at the Headquarters of the Commission

7.2(b) (i) The Commission may decide about the matter that is to be investigated or enquired into by an Investigating Team of officials of the Commission, provided that in case the matter is urgent, the decision for such investigation or inquiry may be taken by the Chairperson.

7.2.(b) (ii) The Investigating Team shall hold the investigation or inquiry, as the case may be, promptly and for this purpose, may initiate necessary correspondence including issuance of notices for production of documents in Form I, appended to these rules.

7.2(b) (iii) The Investigating Team may visit the area concerned after observing due formalities for obtaining approval of tours and other administrative requirements and after giving information to the concerned local authorities regarding the matter, purpose, scope and procedure of the investigation or inquiry. The Investigating Team may enlist the help of the officers and staff of the concerned State Office but the responsibility of preparing and presenting the report shall rest with the head of the Investigating Team.

7.2(b) (iv) The Investigating Team shall submit the report of the investigation or inquiry, as the case may be, to the Chairman/Secretary or a subordinate officer of the Commission as may be directed by general or specific orders by the Chairperson within the stipulated time, if any. If the time limit stipulated is likely to be exceeded, the head of the Investigating Team shall obtain the orders of the Chairperson through the Officer-in-charge of the matter. The report shall be examined and put upto the Chairperson for a decision regarding the action to be taken on the report.

7.2(b) (v) The decision of the report shall be sent to the Secy Joint Secy/Officer-in-charge placed before the Chairperson of the Commission who will take appropriate action in the matter.

7.2(c) Investigation and inquiry through the State Offices

7.2(c) (i) The Chairperson, the Vice-Chairperson, the Members having jurisdiction over the subject may decide about an investigation or inquiry that may be carried out through the State Offices of the Commission. The decision will be conveyed to the Officer-in-Charge of the concerned State Office who will be asked to get the matter investigated or inquired into within a stipulated time and send the report. The State Office shall conduct the investigation or inquiry through interrogation, on the spot visit, discussions and correspondence and examination of documents as may be necessary in the case and shall follow any special or general instructions issued in the matter by the Chairperson/ V.C./Member through the officials of the Commission from time-to-time.

7.2(c) (ii) If the investigation or inquiry cannot be completed within the stipulated time, the officer-in-charge of the State Office may send a communication to the Secretariat of the Commission before the expiry of the stipulated time and explain the circumstances and reasons for non-completion of the investigation or inquiry, as the case may be, within the stipulated time. The Secretary to the Commission or the Member under delegated functions may consider the request and communicate a revised date after taking approval of the Chairperson for the completion of the investigation or inquiry.

7.2(c) (iii) If during the course of investigation or inquiry, the Head of the State Office feels that it is necessary to invoke the powers of the Commission to require the production of any document or compelling the attendance of a person, he may make a special report with full facts to the Secretariat of the Commission. On receipt of such special report, the matter shall be placed before the Chairperson/Member in-charge of the subject/State/UT who may make an order that necessary legal processes to compel attendance or to require production of any document may be issued. The summons and warrants issued for the purpose may be served on the person concerned either directly or through the officer-in-charge of the State Office as may be directed by the Chairperson authorizing issue of such legal process.

7.2(c) (iv) After completion of the investigation or inquiry, as the case may be, the head of the State Office shall submit the report to the Secretary of the Commission suggesting the course of action that could be followed in the matter. The gist or findings of the report may be placed before the Chairperson with specific proposals by the Secretary/Joint Secretary who may decide about further action in the matter.

7.2(d) Investigation by the State Agencies

The Chairperson may decide about an investigation or inquiry that may be carried out through the State Agencies. The decision will be conveyed to the Chief Secretary/ Officer-in-Charge of the concerned State/State Agency(s) who will be asked to get the matter investigated or inquired into within a stipulated time and send the report.

7.2(e) Investigation by any other institution/Deptt funded by Central Government and its statutory bodies.

7.3 Procedure for inquiry

7.4 Inquiry into specific complaints

The Commission is required to inquire into specific complaints with respect to the deprivation of rights and safeguards of Scheduled Castes. In order to enable the Commission to perform this function effectively and efficiently, the Commission would like the members of Scheduled Castes to know that it will be helpful to inquire into their grievances if they substantiate their complaints with supporting documents and quote the relevant provisions of the Act or Rules or directions which have been violated.

7.4.1 The following aspect may be kept in mind while filing complaints before the Commission—

(a) The complaint should be directly addressed to the Chairman/Vice-Chairman/Secretary, National Commission for Scheduled Castes, New Delhi or the heads of its State Offices.

(b) The complainants should disclose his full identity and give his full address and should sign the representation.

(c) Complaints should be legibly written or typed and, where necessary, supported by authenticated documents.

(d) Complaints should clearly disclose the violation of Reservation policy, DOPT OMs, Government of India Orders, State Government Orders, PSUs and Autonomous Bodies orders or any other violation Rules of Reservation.

(e) No action will be taken on matters, which are subjudice. Hence subjudice matter need not be referred to the Commission as complaint(s).

(f) Cases pending in courts or cases in which a court has already given its final verdict may not be taken up afresh with the Commission.

(g) The cases of Administrative nature like transfer/posting/grading of ACRs will not be taken up by the Commission unless there is caste based harassment of petitioner.

(h) No action will be taken on the matters where there is no mention of violation of Reservation policy, DOPT OMs, Government of India Orders, State Government Orders, PSUs and Autonomous Bodies orders or any other violation of Rules of Reservation. Hence the matters where there is no mention of violation of above Rules need not be referred to the Commission as complaints.

7.5 Inquiry into cases of atrocities

7.5.1 Whenever information is received in the Commission about any incident of atrocity against a person belonging to Scheduled Castes, the Commission would immediately get in touch with the law enforcing and administrative machinery of the State and the district to ascertain the details of incident and the action taken by the district administration. If after detailed inquiry/investigation; the Commission finds substance in the allegation/complaint regarding atrocity, the Commission may recommend to file an FIR against the accused with the concerned law-enforcing agency of the State/District. In such cases, the State Government/District Administration/Police Personnel may be called within three days through the summons.

7.5.2 The Commission ensures the following while by monitoring and issuing instruction to the concerned authorities—

(i) Whether the scene of occurrence of the crime has been visited immediately by Collector and Supdt. of Police of the district on receipt of information.

(ii) Whether proper FIR is registered in local Police Station.

(iii) Whether names of all the persons involved/cited by the complainant has been included in the FIR.

(iv) Whether investigation has been taken up by a Senior Police Officer as per provisions of the SCs & STs (POA) Act, 1989.

(v) Whether culprits have been apprehended and booked without loss of time.

(vi) Whether proper charge sheet has been filed mentioning the relevant sections of IPC together with the PCR Act, 1955 and SCs & STs (POA) Act, 1989 in Court.

(vii) Whether the cases are tried by the Special Courts.

(viii) Whether special Public Prosecutors are appointed to handle these cases.

(ix) Whether Police assists the courts in bringing forward witnesses and see that the culprits are suitably punished by the courts.

7.5.3 The Commission will also monitor that—

(i) the victims are provided with suitable medical assistance and on time;

(ii) adequate protection is arranged for the victims of such incidents by providing police protection by stationing a police party, by patrolling, etc;

(iii) to see that proper compensation is paid to the victims as per provisions of law.

7.5.4 The Commission will, wherever possible depending upon the gravity and circumstances of the case, visit the place of incident to oversee the arrangements and to console and infuse confidence among the victims.

7.5.5 The Commission may laid down detailed procedure for conducting such inquiries and monitoring at all levels. Such inquiries can be conduced by the Members of the Commission or Teams of Investigators from Headquarters or State office of the Commission or any other officer(s)/agency duly appointed authorized by the Chairman.

7.5.6 When any offence as is described as an atrocity in the relevant acts for the time being in force, is committed in the view or presence of the Commission or has been found to have been taken cognizance by the Commission, in pursuance of the enquiry/investigation conducted by it in the discharge of its functions, the Commission may, after recording the facts constituting the offence, forward the case to a Magistrate having jurisdiction to try the same.

7.6 Confidentiality of certain reports

The Chairperson/Commission may, through a decision at a meeting or otherwise, direct that the contents of any report made on any matter shall be kept confidential and shall not be revealed to any person other than those who have been authorized access to such report.

7.7 Legal processes

All summons and warrants that are required to be issued in pursuance of the exercise of the powers of a civil court by the Commission shall be written in the prescribed form and shall bear the seal of the Commission. The legal process shall be issued from the Legal Cell of the Commission and shall bear its seal. The provisions of the Code of Civil Procedure applicable for the service of the legal processes shall be followed by the Commission.

7.8 Issue of letters and notices

Letters and notices requiring production of documents which are issued without exercising the powers of the civil court by the Commission may be signed by an officer not below the rank of Research Officer/Section Officer/Senior Investigator.

7.9 Form of summons and warrants

The summons and warrants shall be as provided in Forms II and III respectively, appended to these rules.

CHAPTER IV

8.0 Meetings of the Commission

8.1 Frequency of meetings

The Commission shall meet at least once in a month. The notice for a meeting shall normally be issued two weeks in advance. Emergent meetings may also be called by the Chairperson either on his own or on the request of a Member or the Secretary for disposing of important matters requiring urgent consideration by the Commission.

8.2 Quorum

Presence of at least three members including the Chairperson and/or Vice-Chairperson shall constitute the quorum for holding meeting of the Commission.

8.3 Matters requiring decisions by the Commission at its meetings

The following matters shall be brought up before the Commission at a meeting for consideration and decision:

(i) any amendment to these Rules of Procedure;

(ii) matters to be investigated by the Commission directly;

(iii) all the reports that are required to be considered by the Commission as provided in these rules;

(iv) any matters that a Member may like to bring to the meeting, with the approval of the Chairperson;

(v) important matters relating to planning and development for the welfare and advancement of the Scheduled Castes and specially references received under Article 338(9) of the Constitution; and

(vi) any matter that the Chairperson may direct to be placed at a meeting of the Commission.

8.4 Agenda for the meeting

The agenda will normally be circulated to all the Members at least seven days before the date of the meeting, provided that for an Emergent Meeting, this time limit may not apply.

8.5 The minutes of a meeting shall be circulated as soon as possible to all the Members.

8.6 Place of meeting of the Commission

Normally the place of meeting of the Commission shall be the Headquarter of the Commission at New Delhi. The Commission may, however, decide to hold a meeting at any other place in India.

8.7 Fee

The Chairperson, the Vice-Chairperson and the Members shall not be entitled to any fee for sitting in the meeting of the Commission. However, the entitlement of part-time Members, if any, may be determined by the terms of appointment of such Members.

CHAPTER V

9.0 Sittings of the Commission

9.1 Need for sittings

Whenever a matter is to be investigated into directly by the Commission it may do so by holding sittings of the Commission. In the case of such sittings, the presence of all the Member may not be necessary.

9.2 Officers to be present

Whenever a Member(s) is holding a sitting, an officer of the Commission, not below the rank of Research Officer/Section Officer, duly deputed for the purpose, shall be present to assist the Member(s) holding the sitting to discharge the functions properly and promptly. It shall be the duty of the officer to assist the Member(s) in preparing the report if called upon to do so by the Member(s). The officer shall also be responsible for assisting the Member(s) in following the prescribed procedure.

9.3 Frequency of sitting(s)

Sittings of the Commission may be held as and when necessary. The Commission may hold more than one sitting simultaneously in different parts of the country with different Members functioning separately.

9.4 Programme of the sittings

The programme of the sittings both at the Headquarters and at other places, would normally be worked out each month in advance and duly circulated.

9.5 Defraying expenses to witnesses

The Commission may defray travelling expenses to persons who have been called through summons to appear before the Commission in a sitting, provided that the place of residence of one person is more than 8 kms. from the place of the sitting of the Commission. The amount so defrayed shall be limited to the actual travelling expenses plus Daily Allowance for the number of days that the person has appeared before the Commission in its sitting, provided that the person is not entitled to travelling and daily allowance from any other source. Persons who are employees of the Government/Public Sector Undertaking shall be deemed to be on duty if they are summoned to depose before the Commission or produce documents. The limit of travelling expenses shall be determined on the basis of the rail fare and road mileage calculated on the basis of the rates that may be prescribed by the Commission. In the case of any doubt regarding the entitlement of the person, the decision of the Secretary of the Commission shall be final.

9.6 The officer attached to the Member for the purposes of the sitting shall take steps to ensure that sufficient cash amount is carried if the sitting is held at a place other than the Headquarters of the Commission. The Secretariat of the Commission may devise a suitable procedure to ensure that such claims as above are paid on the spot and in cash to the person(s) so appearing.

9.7 The claim for travelling expenses as above shall not be admissible in the case of a person who appears before the Commission during any investigation or enquiry on his own accord or in response to a communication or notice which is not a summon issued by the Commission.

CHAPTER VI

10.0 Duties of the State Offices of the Commission

It shall be the duty of the State Offices of the Commission:

(i) To act as the "eyes and ears" of the Commission in the State(s) under their jurisdiction.

(ii) To maintain effective interaction and liaison with State Government/UT Administration on behalf of the Commission.

(iii) To serve on State Level Advisory Councils/Committees/Corporations, etc. on behalf of the Commission.

(iv) To provide information and documentation about the policies and programmes of the Union Government for the welfare and advancement of Scheduled Castes to the States, NGOs, Media in their respective jurisdiction, and obtain similar information and documentation from such organizations and provide to the Headquarters of the Commission information/documentation about important developments, social movements, policy changes, etc. in the State(s) affecting the interest of Scheduled Castes.

(v) To monitor and assist the working of voluntary and other non-governmental organizations receiving grant-in-aid from the Ministry of Social Justice and Empowerment as also other Ministries/Departments of the Central Government and the concerned State Governments, Foreign Aid Agencies etc., for Research Studies and any other development work relating to Scheduled Castes.

(vi) To conduct Research Studies, Seminars, Conferences, Surveys, etc. either on their own or as entrusted to them by Headquarters from time- to-time.

(vii) To conduct on-the-spot inquiries into cases of atrocities on Scheduled Castes either on their own or as entrusted to them by Headquarters and interact with the concerned Administrative/Police authorities having jurisdiction and report to the Headquarters.

(viii) To deal with complaints/representations from individuals, Scheduled Castes Welfare Associations, etc., on various matters.

(ix) To participate and advise in the planning process for socio-economic development of Scheduled Castes as envisaged under Clause (5) of Article 338 of the Constitution of India.

(x) To collect, compile, analyse and monitor issues pertaining to development of Scheduled Castes in the states especially with reference to Special Component Plan (SCP) and Special Central Assistance (SCA) and prepare drafts of Reports pertaining to the State(s)/UT(s) under their jurisdiction.

(xi) To prepare and maintain a comprehensive and up-to-date database of Scheduled Castes population, education, development, etc. in the State(s)/UT(s); and

(xii) To perform any other duty specifically assigned/entrusted to the State Office(s) by the Commission or the Secretary or any other officer empowered in this regard.

CHAPTER VII

11.0 Advisory Role of the Commission

Interaction of the Commission with the State Governments

11.1 The Commission shall interact with the State Governments through its Members, Secretariat and the State Offices.

11.2 The Members in-charge of the State/UT would interact with the State Government/UT Administration through meetings, personal contacts, visits and correspondence. The information in this regard may be sent to the concerned Deptt./Organizations well in advance and the State Offices should also be informed about the same. For this purpose, detailed guidelines may be formulated by the Commission. The Secretariat of the Commission through its concerned Wing(s) would provide necessary assistance and information to the Member for enabling him to discharge his functions effectively. The State Governments should provide facilities for transport, security, accommodation, etc. to the Member as per his entitlement.

12.0 Interaction with the Planning Commission

12.1 The Commission shall interact with the Planning Commission at appropriate levels through representation in the various Committees, Working Groups or other such bodies set up by the Planning Commission. The Commission shall indicate this requirement through general or specific communication to the Planning Commission.

12.2. The Commission may request the Planning Commission to forward copies of all the documents concerning the process of planning and development and evaluation of all programmes and schemes touching upon the Scheduled Castes.

12.3 The Commission may decide about the manner of interaction between the Chairperson/Members of the Commission and the Deputy Chairman/Members of the Planning Commission.

13.0 Interaction of the State Offices with the State Governments

13.1 The State Offices of the Commission shall work in a manner so as to provide a regular and effective link between the State Governments concerned and the Commission. For this purpose, the Commission may send communications to the State Governments suggesting that the officers-in-charge of the State Offices of the Commission may be taken on important Planning, Evaluation and Advisory bodies including Corporations concerned with the welfare, protection and development of the Scheduled Castes.

13.2 The officers-in-charge of the State Offices may be directed or authorized by the Commission to convey to any State authority the formal views, opinion or approach of the Commission on any specific or general matter or issue arising at any meeting or deliberation.

14.0 Research/Studies/Surveys/Evaluation

14.1 The Commission may undertake studies to evaluate the impact of the development schemes on the socio-economic development of the Scheduled Castes taken up by the Union or State Governments. For this purpose, the Commission may constitute Study Teams either at the Headquarters or at the State Offices. The Study Teams may undertake investigations, surveys or studies either in collaboration with Central or State Government authorities or Universities or Research Bodies, as the case may be, or may do so independently.

14.2 The Commission may entrust surveys or evaluation studies to any professional body or person considered suitable and competent to undertake such work and, for this purpose, may make any reasonable payment to such body or person towards the cost of the study by way of fee or grant.

14.3 The studies so undertaken or their gist may form part of the Annual or Special Report of the Commission to be presented to the President or may be published separately by the Commission.

14.4 The Commission may forward a copy of such a study report to the Union or the State Government concerned, as the case may be, asking for their comments, if any. The comments or action taken reports by the Union/State Government may also form part of the Annual Report of the Commission.

CHAPTER VIII

15.0 Monitoring Functions of the Commission

15.1 The Commission to determine subjects for monitoring

The Commission may determine from time to time the subjects or matters and areas that it would monitor relating to safeguards and other socio-economic development measures provided for the Scheduled Castes under the Constitution or under any other law for the time being in force or under any order of the Government.

15.2 Prescribing returns and reports

15.2.1 The Commission may prescribe periodical returns or reports to be furnished by any authority responsible for or having control of the subject-matter of which monitoring is being done by the Commission.

15.2.2 The Commission may from time to time issue instructions to its State Offices to collect information and data on any particular subject or matter from the State Governments, Local bodies, Corporate Bodies or any other authorities which is charged with the implementation of the safeguards provided for the Scheduled Castes.

15.2.3 The Commission may direct its State Offices to process the information of data in the State Offices with a view to arriving at conclusions with regard to the deficiencies/shortcomings discovered through such processing or analysis of the data and to bring these to the notice of the concerned authority for comments and rectification, where necessary.

15.2.4 The Commission may have data relating to the subjects monitored, collected at the headquarters and may prescribe returns and reports for the purpose to be sent directly to its Headquarters by the Ministries/Departments of the Central Government or a State Government or Public Sector Undertaking or any other body or authority which is charged with the responsibility of implementing safeguards relating to the Scheduled Castes.

16.0 Follow-up action

16.1 In order to ensure that monitoring is done effectively, the Commission, after getting the information as prescribed in the above rules and after reaching conclusions may as early as possible send out communications to the concerned authority describing the shortcomings that have been noticed in the implementation of the safeguards and suggesting corrective steps. Decisions on sending out such a communication may be taken at a level not lower than that of Joint Secretary/Secretary at Headquarters. Directors-in-Charge of State Offices may take decisions on routine matter whereas they will seek approval of the Secretary and the concerned Member on complete and important matters affecting the interest of Scheduled Castes as a group.

16.2 The Commission may ask for the comments of the concerned authority on the action taken in pursuance of the communications sent under Rule 76.

16.3 The Commission may include in its Annual Report or any Special Report, findings and conclusions arrived at through the process of monitoring of the subjects relating to the safeguards and socio-economic development measures provided for the Scheduled Castes under the Constitution or under any other law for the time being in force or under any order of the Union/State Government.

CHAPTER IX

17.0 Non-formal actions by the Commission

17.1 The Commission may initiate correspondence in special cases in matters which are not strictly covered under the law if the matter is such that the welfare of an individual person belonging to Scheduled Castes or that of a group of such persons is involved and it is necessary for the Commission in its inherent capacity as the protector of the interests of these classes of persons, to take action. The decision for correspondence on such matter shall be taken at the level of Director or above.

17.2 All routine formal communications from the Commission shall be issued under the signatures of an Officer not below the rank of Research Officer/Section Officer.

17.3 The Commission can sue or be sued through its Secretary.

17.4 The Scheduled Castes in these rules will have the same connotation as is given in Clause (10) of Article 338 of the Constitution.

18.0 Applicability of rules, etc., of the Central Government

18.1 All rules, regulations and orders issued by the Central Government and applicable in the Ministries/Departments will also apply in the Commission.

18.2 The provisions relating to the delegation of financial powers in the Government of India shall apply to the corresponding officers in the Commission.

19.0 Use of Staff cars

The Staff Car Rules of the Government of India shall apply for the purposes of utilization of staff cars in the Commission.

20.0 Decision on matters not specified in these rules

If a question arises regarding any such matter for which no provision exists in these rules, the decision of the Chairperson shall be sought. The Chairperson may, if he deems fit, direct that the matter may be considered at a meeting of the Commission.

FORM I

NATIONAL COMMISSION FOR SCHEDULED CASTES

(A Constitutional body exercising powers of Civil Courts under
Article 338 of the Constitution of India)

5th Floor, Loknayak Bhawan
New Delhi-110 003.

(Notice for collecting basic facts)

To

....

....

....

Whereas a Petition/complaint/information has been received by the National Commission for Scheduled Castes from.............................. or press news under caption.............................. appearing in .... dated.............................. as enclosed and the Commission has decided to investigate/inquire into the matter in pursuance of the powers conferred upon it under Article 338 of the Constitution of India. You are hereby requested to submit the facts and information pertaining to the said allegations/matters to the undersigned within 3/7/15/30 days of receipt of this notice either by post or in person or by any other means of communication.

Please take notice that in case the Commission does not receive reply from you within the stipulated time, the Commission may exercise the powers of Civil Courts conferred on it under Article 338 of the Constitution of India and issue summons for your appearance in person or by a representative before the Commission.

Signature

Director/Dy. Secretary/Under Secretary/Dy. Director/Assistant Director/
Research Officer/Section Officer
National Commission for Scheduled Castes

Dated........................

FORM II

BEFORE THE NATIONAL COMMISSION FOR SCHEDULED CASTES

(A Constitutional body exercising powers of Civil Courts under
Article 338 of the Constitution of India)

SUMMONS

File No.:

5th Floor, Loknayak Bhawan
New Delhi-110 003

To

....

....

....

Whereas the National Commission has decided to investigate into the following matter in pursuance of powers conferred upon it under Article 338 of the Constitution of India, your attendance is hereby required in person to appear before the National Commission on the.............................. of.............................. 20......... at.............................. hours at.............................. You are required to bring with you the connected documents for examination by the National Commission.

Case reference

If you fail to comply with this order without lawful excuse, you shall be subjected to the consequences of non-attendance laid down in Rule 12 of Order XVI of Code of Civil Procedure, 1908.

Given under my hand and seal of the National Commission for Scheduled Castes exercising powers of Civil Court this................ of.................... 20.............

Signature

Chairman/Vice-Chairman/Member.

Seal

FORM III

(Warrant of arrest of witness)

NATIONAL COMMISSION FOR SCHEDULED CASTES

(A Constitutional body exercising powers of Civil Courts under Article 338 of the Constitution of India)

Loknayak Bhawan (Floor V)
New Delhi-110 003.

To

....

....

....

Whereas...................... r/o...................... was duly served with a summons but has failed to attend (absconds and keeps out of the way for the purpose of avoiding service of a summons), the National Commission for Scheduled Castes exercising powers of a Civil Court under Article 338(8) of the Constitution of India hereby order you to arrest and bring the said...................... before the National Commission at New Delhi.

You are further ordered to return this warrant on or before the...................... day of .... 20............. with an endorsement certifying the day and the manner in which it has been executed, or the reason why it has not been executed.

Given under my hand and the seal of the National Commission exercising powers of Civil Court, this...................... of.......... 20...............

Signature
Chairman/Vice-Chairman/Member

SEAL

APPENDIX 6

THE PROTECTION OF CIVIL RIGHTS ACT, 1955

(22 of 1955)

[*8th May, 1955*]

An Act to prescribe punishment for the [1]*[preaching and practice of "Untouchability"] for the enforcement of any disability arising therefrom and for matters connected therewith.*

BE it enacted by Parliament in the Sixth Year of the Republic of India as follows:—

1. Short title, extent and commencement.—(1) This Act may be called [2][the Protection of Civil Rights Act], 1955.

(2) It extends[3] to the whole of India.

(3) It shall come into force on such date[4] as the Central Government may, by notification in the Official Gazette, appoint.

2. Definitions.—In this Act, unless the context otherwise requires,—

[5][(a) "civil rights" means any right accruing to a person by reason of the abolition of "untouchability" by article 17 of the Constitution;]

[6][(aa)] "hotel" includes a refreshment room, a boarding house, a lodging house, a coffee house and a cafe;

[7][(b) "place" includes a house, building and other structure and premises; and also includes a tent, vehicle and vessel;]

(c) "place of public entertainment" includes any place to which the public are admitted and in which an entertainment is provided or held.

Explanation—"Entertainment" includes any exhibition, performance, game, sport and any other form of amusement;

(d) "place of public worship" means a place, by whatever name known, which is used as a place of public religious worship or which is dedicated generally to, or is used generally by persons professing any religion or belonging to any religious denomination or any section thereof, for the performance of any religious service, or for offering prayers therein, [8][and includes—

(i) all lands and subsidiary shrines appurtenant or attached to any such place;

(ii) a privately owned place of worship which is, in fact, allowed by the owner thereof to be used as a place of public worship; and

---

1. Subs. by Act 106 of 1976, sec. 2, for "practice of Untouchability" (w.e.f. 19-11-1976).
2. Subs. by Act 106 of 1976, sec. 3, for "the Untouchability (Offences) Act" (w.e.f. 19-11-1976).
3. Extended to Goa, Daman and Diu with modification by Regulation 12 of 1962, sec. 3 and Sch.; to Dadra and Nagar Haveli by Regulation 6 of 1963, sec. 2 and Sch. I (w.e.f. 1st July, 1965) and to Pondicherry by Regulation 7 of 1963, sec. 3 and Sch. I (w.e.f. 1-10-1963).
4. Came into force on 1-6-1955, *vide* S.R.O. 1109, dated the 23rd May, 1955, Gazette of India, 1955, Extra., Pt. II, Sec. 3.
5. Ins. by Act 106 of 1976, sec. 4 (w.e.f. 19-11-1976).
6. Clause (a) re-lettered as clause (aa) by Act 106 of 1976, sec. 4 (w.e.f. 19-11-1976).
7. Subs. by Act 106 of 1976, sec. 4, for clause (b) (w.e.f. 19-11-1976).
8. Ins. by Act 106 of 1976, sec. 4 (w.e.f. 19-11-1976).

(iii) such land or subsidiary shrine appurtenant to such privately owned place of worship as is allowed by the owner thereof to be used as a place of public religious worship;]

[1][(da) "prescribed" means prescribed by rules made under this Act;

(db) "Scheduled Castes" has the meaning assigned to it in clause (24) of article 366 of the Constitution;]

(e) "shop" means any premises where goods are sold either wholesale or by retail or both wholesale and by retail [2][and includes—

(i) any place from where goods are sold by a hawker or vendor or from a mobile van or cart;

(ii) a laundry and a hair cutting saloon;

(iii) any other place where services are rendered to customers].

3. Punishment for enforcing religious disabilities.—Whoever on the ground of "untouchability" prevents any person—

(a) from entering any place of public worship which is open to other persons professing the same religion [3][***] or any section thereof, as such person; or

(b) from worshipping or offering prayers or performing any religious service in any place of public worship, or bathing in, or using the waters of, any sacred tank, well, spring or water-course [4][river or lake or bathing at any ghat of such tank, water-course, river or lake] in the same manner and to the same extent as is permissible to the other persons professing the same religion [3][***] or any section thereof, as such person,

[5][shall be punishable with imprisonment for a term of not less than one month and not more than six months and also with fine which shall be not less than one hundred rupees and not more than five hundred rupees].

Explanation.—For the purposes of this section and section 4 persons professing the Buddhist, Sikh or Jaina religion or persons professing the Hindu religion in any of its forms or developments including Virashaivas, Lingayats, Adivassis, followers of Brahmo, Prarthana, Arya Samaj and the Swaminarayan Sampraday shall be deemed to be Hindus.

The object of this section is to keep the untouchables at par with other caste Hindus and not to create any new rights in favour of them, while the object of the *explanation* attached to the section is to bring the Act within the ambit of Article 25(2)(b) and *Explanation II* of the Constitution; *State* v. *Puranchand,* AIR 1958 M P 352: 1958 Cr LJ 1398.

4. Punishment for enforcing social disabilities.—Whoever on the ground of "untouchability" enforces against any person any disability with regard to—

(i) access to any shop, public restaurant, hotel or place of public entertainment; or

(ii) the use of any utensils, and other articles kept in any public restaurant, hotel, *dharamshala, sarai* or *musafirkhana* for the use of the general public or of [6][any section thereof]; or

(iii) the practice of any profession or the carrying on of any occupation, trade or business [7][or employment in any job]; or

---

1. Ins. by Act 106 of 1976, sec. 4 (w.e.f. 19-11-1976).
2. Subs. by Act 106 of 1976, sec. 4, for certain words (w.e.f. 19-11-1976).
3. The words "or belonging to the same religious denomination" omitted by Act 106 of 1976, sec. 5 (w.e.f. 19-11-1976).
4. Ins. by Act 106 of 1976, sec. 5 (w.e.f 19-11-1976).
5. Subs. by Act 106 of 1976, sec. 5, for certain words (w.e.f. 19-11-1976).
6. Subs. by Act 106 of 1976, sec. 6, for certain words (w.e.f. 19-11-1976).
7. Ins. by Act 106 of 1976, sec. 6 (w.e.f. 19-11-1976).

(iv) the use of, or access to, any river, stream, spring, well, tank, cistern, water-tap or other watering place, or any bathing ghat, burial or cremation ground, any sanitary convenience, any road, or passage, or any other place of public resort which other members of the public, or [1][any section thereof], have a right to use or have access to; or

(v) the use of, or access to, any place used for a charitable or a public purpose maintained wholly or partly out of State funds or dedicated to the use of the general public or [1][any section thereof]; or

(vi) the enjoyment of any benefit under a charitable trust created for the benefit of the general public or of [1][any section thereof]; or

(vii) the use of, or access to, any public conveyance; or

(viii) the construction, acquisition, or occupation of any residential premises in any locality, whatsoever; or

(ix) the use of any *dharamshala, sarai* or *musafirkhana* which is open to the general public, or to [1][any section thereof]; or

(x) the observance of any social or religious custom, usage or ceremony or [2][taking part in, or taking out, any religious, social or cultural procession]; or

(xi) the use of jewellery and finery,

[3][shall be punishable with imprisonment for a term of not less than one month and not more than six months and also with fine which shall be not less than one hundred rupees and not more than five hundred rupees].

[4][*Explanation.*—For the purposes of this section, "enforcement of any disability" includes any discrimination on the ground of "untouchability".]

5. Punishment for refusing to admit person to hospitals, etc.—Whoever on the ground of "untouchability"—

(a) refuses admission to any person to any hospital, dispensary, educational institution or any hostel [5][***], if such hospital, dispensary, educational institution or hostel is established or maintained for the benefit of the general public or any section thereof; or

(b) does any act which discriminates against any such person after admission to any of the aforesaid institutions,

[6][shall be punishable with imprisonment for a term of not less than one month and not more than six months and also with fine which shall be not less than one hundred rupees and not more than five hundred rupees].

6. Punishment for refusing to sell goods or render services.—Whoever on the ground of "untouchability" refuses to sell any goods or refuses to render any service to any person at the same time and place and on the same terms and conditions at or which such goods are sold or services are rendered to other persons in the ordinary course of business [7][shall be punishable with imprisonment for a term of not less than one month

---

1. Subs. by Act 106 of 1976, sec. 6, for certain words (w.e.f. 19-11-1976).
2. Subs. by Act 106 of 1976, sec. 6, for "taking part in any religious procession" (w.e.f. 19-11-1976).
3. Subs. by Act 106 of 1976, sec. 6 (w.e.f. 19-11-1976).
4. Ins. by Act 106 of 1976, sec. 6 (w.e.f 19-11-1976).
5. The words "attached thereto" omitted by Act 106 of 1976, sec. 7 (w.e.f. 19-11-1976).
6. Subs. by Act 106 of 1976, sec. 7, for certain words (w.e.f. 19-11-1976).
7. Subs. by Act 106 of 1976, sec. 8, for certain words (w.e.f. 19-11-1976).

and not more than six months and also with fine which shall be not less than one hundred rupees and not more than five hundred rupees].

7. Punishment for other offences arising out of "untouchability".—(1) Whoever—

(a) prevents any person from exercising any right accruing to him by reason of the abolition of "untouchability" under Article 17 of the Constitution; or

(b) molests, injures, annoys, obstructs or causes or attempts to cause obstruction to any person in the exercise of any such right or molests, injures, annoys or boycotts any person by reason of his having exercised any such right; or

(c) by words, either spoken or written, or by signs or by visible representations or otherwise, incites or encourages any person or class of persons or the public generally to practice "untouchability" in any form whatsoever; [1][or]

[1][(d) insults or attempts to insult, on the ground of "untouchability", a member of a Scheduled Caste;]

[1][shall be punishable with imprisonment for a term of not less than one month and not more than six months, and also with fine which shall be not less than one hundred rupees and not more than five hundred rupees].

[2][*Explanation I*].—A person shall be deemed to boycott another person who—

(a) refuses to let to such other person or refuses to permit such other person, to use or occupy any house or land or refuses to deal with, work for hire for or do business with, such other person or to render to him or receive from him any customary service, or refuses to do any of the said things on the terms on which such things would be commonly done in the ordinary course of business; or

(b) abstains from such social, professional or business relations as he would ordinarily maintain with such other person.

[1][*Explanation II*.—For the purpose of clause (c) a person shall be deemed to incite or encourage the practice of "untouchability"—

(i) if he, directly or indirectly, preaches "untouchability" or its practice in any form; or

(ii) if he justifies, whether on historical, philosophical or religious grounds or on the ground of any tradition of the caste system or on any other ground, the practice of "untouchability" in any form.]

[1][(1A) Whoever commits any offence against the person or property of any individual as a repraisal or revenge for his having exercised any right accruing to him by reason of the abolition of "untouchability" under article 17 of the Constitution, shall, where the offence is punishable with imprisonment for a term exceeding two years, be punishable with imprisonment for a term which shall not be less than two years and also with fine.]

(2) Whoever—

(i) denies to any person belonging to his community or any section thereof any right or privilege to which such person would be entitled as a member of such community or section, or

(ii) takes any part in the ex-communication of such person, on the ground that such person has refused to practice 'untouchability' that such person has done any act in furtherance of the objects of this Act,

---

1. Ins. by Act 106 of 1976, sec. 9 (w.e.f. 19-11-1976).
2. *Explanation* re-numbered as *Explanation I* by Act 106 of 1976, sec. 9 (w.e.f. 19-11-1976).

[1][shall be punishable with imprisonment for a term of not less than one month and not more than six months and also with fine which shall be not less than one hundred rupees and not more than five hundred rupees.]

[2][**7A. Unlawful compulsory labour when to be deemed to be a practice of "untouchability".**—(1) Whoever compels any person, on the ground of "untouchability", to do any scavenging or sweeping or to remove any carcass or to flay any animal, or to remove the umbilical cord or to do any other job of a similar nature shall be deemed to have enforced a disability arising out of "untouchability".

(2) Whoever is deemed under sub-section (1) to have enforced a disability arising out of "untouchability" shall be punishable with imprisonment for a term which shall not be less than three months and not more than six months and also with fine which shall not be less than one hundred rupees and not more than five hundred rupees.

Explanation.— For the purposes of this section, "compulsion" includes a threat of social or economic boycott.]

8. Cancellation or suspension of licences in certain cases.—When a person who is convicted of an offence under section 6 holds any licence under any law for the time being in force in respect of any profession, trade, calling or employment in relation to which the offence is committed, the court trying the offence may without prejudice to any other penalty to which such person may be liable under that section, direct that the licence shall stand cancelled or be suspended for such period as the court may deem fit, and every order of the court so cancelling or suspending a licence shall have effect as if it had been passed by the authority competent to cancel or suspend the licence under any such law.

Explanation—In this section, "licence" includes a permit or a permission.

9. Resumption or suspension of grants made by Government.—Where the manager or trustee of a place of public worship [3][or any educational institution or hostel] which is in receipt of a grant of land or money from the Government is convicted of an offence under this Act and such conviction is not reversed or quashed in any appeal or revision, the Government may, if in its opinion the circumstances of the case warrant such a course, direct the supension or resumption of the whole or any part of such grant.

10. Abetment of offence.—Whoever abets any offence under this Act shall be punishable with the punishment provided for the offence.

[4][*Explanation.*—A public servant who wilfully neglects the investigation of any offence punishable under this Act shall be deemed to have abetted an offence punishable under this Act.]

[5][**10A. Power of State Government to impose collective fine.**—(1) If, after an inquiry in the prescribed manner, the State Government is satisfied that the inhabitants of an area are concerned in, or abetting the commission of, any offence punishable under this Act, or harbouring persons concerned in the commission of such offence or failing to render all the assistance in their power to discover or apprehend the offender or offenders or suppressing material evidence of the commission of such offence, the State Government may, by notification in the Official Gazette, impose a collective fine on such inhabitants and apportion such fine amongst the inhabitants who are liable collectively to pay it, and such apportionment shall be made according to the State Government's judgment of the

---

1. Subs. by Act 106 of 1976, sec. 9, for certain words (w.e.f. 19-11-1976).
2. Ins. by Act 106 of 1976, sec. 10 (w.e.f. 19-11-1976).
3. Ins. by Act 106 of 1976, sec. 11 (w.e.f. 19-11-1976).
4. Ins. by Act 106 of 1976, sec. 12 (w.e.f. 19-11-1976).
5. Ins. by Act 106 of 1976, sec. 13 (w.e.f. 19-11-1976).

respective means of such inhabitants and in making any such apportionment the State Government may assign a portion of such fine to a Hindu undivided family to be payable by it:

Provided that the fine apportioned to an inhabitant shall not be realised until the petition, if any, filed by him under sub-section (3), is disposed of.

(2) The notification made under sub-section (1) shall be proclaimed in the area by beat of drum or in such other manner as the State Government may think best in the circumstances to bring the imposition of the collective fine to the notice of the inhabitants of the said area.

(3) (a) Any person aggrieved by the imposition of the collective fine under sub-section (1) or by the order of apportionment, may, within the prescribed period, file a petition before the State Government or such other authority as that Government may specify in this behalf for being exempted from such fine or for modification of the order of apportionment:

Provided that no fee shall be charged for filing such petition.

(b) The State Government or the authority specified by it shall, after giving to the petitioner a reasonable opportunity of being heard, pass such order as it may think fit:

Provided that the amount of the fine exempted or reduced under this section shall not be realisable from any person, and the total fine imposed on the inhabitants of an area under sub-section (1) shall be deemed to have been reduced to that extent.

(4) Notwithstanding anything contained in sub-section (3), the State Government may exempt the victims of any offence punishable under this Act or any person who does not, in its opinion, fall within the category of persons specified in sub-section (1) from the liability to pay the collective fine imposed under sub-section (1) or any portion thereof.

(5) The portion of collective fine payable by any person (including a Hindu undivided family) may be recovered in the manner provided by the Code of Criminal Procedure, 1973 (2 of 1974), for the recovery of fines imposed by a Court as if such portion were a fine imposed by a Magistrate.]

11. Enhanced penalty on subsequent conviction.—Whoever having already been convicted of an offence under this Act or of an abetment of such offence is again convicted of any such offence or abetment, [1][shall, on conviction, be punishable—

(a) for the second offence, with imprisonment for a term of not less than six months and not more than one year, and also with fine which shall be not less than two hundred rupees and not more than five hundred rupees;

(b) for the third offence or any offence subsequent to the third offence with imprisonment for a term of not less than one year and not more than two years, and also with fine which shall be not less than five hundred rupees and not more than one thousand rupees].

12. Presumption by Courts in certain cases.—Where any act constituting an offence under this Act is committed in relation to a member of a Scheduled Caste [2][***], the Court shall presume, unless the contrary is proved, that such act was committed on the ground of "untouchability".

13. Limitation of Jurisdiction of Civil Courts.—(1) No Civil Court shall entertain or continue any suit or proceeding or shall pass any decree or order if the claim involved

---

1. Subs. by Act 106 of 1976, sec. 14, for certain words (w.e.f. 19-11-1976).
2. The words "as defined in clause (24) of article 366 of the Constitution" omitted by Act 106 of 1976, sec. 15 (w.e.f. 19-11-1976).

in such suit or proceeding or if the passing of such decree or order or if such execution would in any way be contrary to the provisions of this Act.

(2) No Court shall, in adjudicating any matter or executing any decree or order, recognise any custom or usage imposing any disability on any person on the ground of "untouchability".

14. Offences by companies.—(1) If the person committing an offence under this Act is a company, every person who at the time the offence was committed was in charge of, and was responsible to the company for the conduct of the business of the company, shall be deemed to be guilty of the offence and shall be liable to be proceeded against and punished accordingly:

Provided that nothing contained in this sub-section shall render any such person liable to any punishment, if he proves that the offence was committed without his knowledge or that he exercised all due diligence to prevent the commission of such offence.

(2) Notwithstanding anything contained in sub-section (1), where an offence under this Act has been committed with the consent of any director or manager, secretary or other officer of the company, such director, manager, secretary or other officer shall also be deemed to be guilty of that offence and shall be liable to be proceeded against and punished accordingly.

Explanation.—For the purposes of this section,—

(a) "company" means any body corporate and includes a firm or other association of individuals; and

(b) "director" in relation to a firm means a partner in the firm.

[1][**14A. Protection of action taken in good faith.**—(1) No suit, prosecution or other legal proceeding shall lie against the Central Government or a State Government for anything which is in good faith done or intended to be done under this Act.

(2) No suit or other legal proceeding shall lie against the Central Government or a State Government for any damage caused or likely to be caused by anything which is in good faith done or intended to be done under this Act.]

[2][**15. Offences to be cognizable and triable summarily.**—(1) Notwithstanding anything contained in the Code of Criminal Procedure, 1973 (2 of 1974), every offence punishable under this Act shall be cognizable and every such offence, except where its punishable with imprisonment for a minimum term exceeding three months, may be tried summarily by a Judicial Magistrate of the first class or in a metropolitan area by a Metropolitan Magistrate in accordance with the procedure specified in the said Code.

(2) Notwithstanding anything contained in the Code of Criminal Procedure, 1973 (2 of 1974), when any public servant is alleged to have committed the offence of abetment of an offence punishable under this Act, while acting or purporting to act in the discharge of his official duty, no Court shall take cognizance of such offence of abetment except with the previous sanction—

(a) of the Central Government, in the case of a person employed in connection with the affairs of the Union; and

(b) of the State Government, in the case of a person employed in connection with the affairs of a State.]

[2][**15A. Duty of State Government to ensure that the rights accruing from the abolition of "untouchability" may be availed of by the concerned persons.**—(1) Subject

---

1. Ins. by Act 106 of 1976, sec. 16 (w.e.f. 19-11-1976).
2. Sections 15 and 15A subs. by Act 106 of 1976, sec. 17, for section 15 (w.e.f. 19-11-1976).

to such rules as the Central Government may make in this behalf, the State Government shall take such measures as may be necessary for ensuring that the rights arising from the abolition of "untouchability" are made available to, and are availed of by the persons subjected to any disability arising out of "untouchability".

(2) In particular, and without prejudice to the generality of the provisions of sub-section (1), such measures may include—

(i) the provision of adequate facilities, including legal aid, to the persons subjected to any disability arising out of "untouchability" to enable them to avail themselves of such rights;

(ii) the appointment of officers for initiating or exercising supervision over prosecutions for the contravention of the provisions of this Act;

(iii) the setting up of special courts for the trial of offences under this Act;

(iv) the setting up of Committees at such appropriate levels as the State Government may think fit to assist the State Government in formulating or implementing such measures;

(v) provision for a periodic survey of the working of the provisions of this Act with a view to suggesting measures for the better implementation of the provisions of this Act;

(vi) the identification of the areas where persons are under any disability arising out of "untouchability" and adoption of such measures as would ensure the removal of such disability from such areas.

(3) The Central Government shall take such steps as may be necessary to co-ordinate the measures taken by the State Government under sub-section (1).

(4) The Central Government shall, every year, place on the Table of each House of Parliament a report on the measures taken by itself and by the State Governments in pursuance of the provision of this section.]

16. Act to override other laws.—Save as otherwise expressly provided in this Act, the provision of this Act shall have effect notwithstanding anything inconsistent therewith contained in any other law for the time being in force, or any custom or usage or any instrument having effect by virtue of any such law or any decree or order of any Court or other authority.

[1][**16A. Probation of Offenders Act, 1958, not to apply to persons above the age of fourteen years.**—The provisions of the Probation of Offenders Act, 1958 (20 of 1958), shall not apply to any person above the age of fourteen years who is found guilty of having committed any offence punishable under this Act.]

[1][**16B. Power to make rules.**—(1) The Central Government may, by notification in the Official Gazette, make rules to carry out the provisions of this Act.

(2) Every rule made by the Central Government under this Act shall be laid, as soon as may be after it is made, before each House of Parliament while it is in session for a total period of thirty days which may be comprised in one session or in two or more successive sessions, and if, before the expiry of the session immediately following the session or the successive sessions aforesaid, both Houses agree in making any modification in the rule or both Houses agree that the rule should not be made, the rule shall thereafter have effect only in such modified form or be of no effect, as the case may be; so, however, that any such modification or annulment shall be without prejudice to the validity of anything previously done under that rule.]

1. Ins. by Act 106 of 1976, sec. 18 (w.e.f. 19-11-1976).

17. Repeal.—The enactments specified in the Schedule are hereby repealed to the extent to which they or any of the provisions contained therein correspond or are repugnant to this Act or to any of the provisions contained therein.

THE SCHEDULE

(*See* section 17)

1. The Bihar Harijan (Removal of Civil Disabilities) Act, 1949 (Bihar Act XIX of 1949).
2. The Bombay Harijan (Removal of Social Disabilities) Act, 1946 (Bombay Act X of 1947).
3. The Bombay Harijan Temple Entry Act, 1947 (Bombay Act XXXV of 1947).
4. The Central Provinces and Berar Scheduled Castes (Removal of Civil Disabilities) Act, 1947 (Central Provinces and Berar Act XXIV of 1947).
5. The Central Provinces and Berar Temple Entry Authorisation Act, 1947 (Central Provinces and Berar Act XLI of 1947).
6. The East Punjab (Removal of Religious and Social Disabilities) Act, 1948 (East Punjab Act XVI of 1948).
7. The Madras Removal of Civil Disabilities Act, 1938 (Madras Act XXI of 1938).
8. The Orissa Removal of Civil Disabilities Act, 1946 (Orissa Act XI of 1946).
9. The Orissa Temple Entry Authorisation Act, 1948 (Orissa Act XI of 1948).
10. The United Provinces Removal of Social Disabilities Act, 1947 (U.P. Act XIV of 1947).
11. The West Bengal Hindu Social Disabilities Removal Act, 1948 (West Bengal Act XXXVII of 1948).
12. The Hyderabad Harijan Temple Entry Regulations, 1358 F (No. LV of 1358 Fasli).
13. The Hyderabad Harijan (Removal of Social Disabilities) Regulation, 1358F (No. LVI of 1385 Fasli).
14. The Madhya Bharat Harijan Ayogta Nivaran Vidhan, Samvat 2005 (Madhya Bharat Act No. 15 of 1949).
15. The Removal of Civil Disabilities Act, 1943 (Mysore Act XLII of 1943).
16. The Mysore Temple Entry Authorisation Act, 1948 (Mysore Act XIV of 1948).
17. The Saurashtra Harijan (Removal of Social Disabilities) Ordinance (No. XL of 1948).
18. The Travancore-Cochin Removal of Social Disabilities Act, 1125K (Travancore-Cochin Act VIII of 1125).
19. The Travancore-Cochin Temple Entry (Removal of Disabilities) Act, 1950 (Travancore-Cochin Act XXVII of 1950).
20. The Coorg Scheduled Castes (Removal of Civil and Social Disabilities) Act, 1949 (Coorg Act I of 1949).
21. The Coorg Temple Entry Authorisation Act, 1949 (Coorg Act II of 1949).

APPENDIX 7

THE PROTECTION OF CIVIL RIGHTS RULES, 1977[1]

In exercise of the powers conferred by section 16B of the Protection of Civil Rights Act, 1955 (22 of 1955), the Central Government hereby makes the following rules namely:—

1. Short title and commencement.—(1) These rules may be called the Protection of Civil Rights Rules, 1977.

(2) They shall come into force on the date of their publication in the Official Gazette.

2. Definitions— In these rules, unless the context otherwise requires,—

(a) "Act" means the Protection of Civil Rights Act, 1955 (22 of 1955).

(b) "section" means a section of the Act.

3. Manner of inquiry under sub-section (1) of section 10A.—(1) The State Government may appoint an officer not below the rank of a Sub-divisional Magistrate for the purpose of making an inquiry referred to in sub-section (1) of section 10A.

(2) The officer appointed under sub-rule (1) (hereinafter in this rule referred to as the inquiry officer) shall issue a public notice specifying the date, time, place and the purpose of such inquiry and calling upon all the residents of the area in respect of which the inquiry is to be held to furnish such information and materials, including documents in their possession, as may be relevant for the purposes of the inquiry.

(3) The public notice referred to in sub-rule (2) shall be in the local language or languages of the area and the same shall be,—

(i) published on the notice board in the offices of the District Magistrate, the District Superintendent of Police, the Village Panchayat or Municipal Committee of the area and such other places as the inquiry officer deems fit and at least in one daily newspaper circulating in the area; and

(ii) proclaimed in the area by beat of drum or in such other manner as the inquiry officer may think best in the circumstances to bring the contents of the public notice to the notice of the inhabitants of the area.

(4) The inquiry officer, while making such inquiry shall follow as nearly as practicable, the procedure for summary trials including the recording of evidence as laid down in Chapter XXI of Code of Criminal Procedure, 1973 (2 of 1974).

(5) The inquiry officer shall complete the inquiry as expeditiously as possible and submit his report to the State Government within such period, not exceeding six weeks, as may be specified by the State Government in the order appointing the inquiry officer:

Provided that the State Government may, having regard to the nature of the inquiry, extend the period of submission of the report by such period not exceeding two months in total as it may consider necessary.

4. Period for filing a petition under sub-section (3) of section 10A.—Any person aggrieved by the imposition of a collective fine under sub-section (1) of section 10A or by the order of apportionment, may within a period of thirty days from the date of proclamation of the notification under sub-section (2) of that section file a petition before the State Government or the authority specified by it:

---

1. *Vide* S.O. 3006, dated 15th September, 1977, published in the Gazette of India, Pt. II, Sec. 3 (ii), dated 1st October, 1977.

Provided that where the State Government or the authority, as the case may be, may entertain the petition after the expiry of the said period if it is satisfied that the petitioner was prevented by sufficient cause from filing the petition in time.

(2) The State Government or the authority before which the petition is filed shall dispose of the petition as expeditiously as possible.

5. Report by the State Government.—Every State Government shall, for the purpose of enabling the Central Government, place the report referred to in sub-section (4) of section 15A, on the Table of each House of Parliament, furnish to the Government before the 15th day of February each year, a summary of the measures taken by it under sub-sections (1) and (2) of that section during the preceding calendar year and shall also furnish such other information as may be required by the Central Government from time to time.

APPENDIX 8

THE CONSTITUTION OF INDIA

(Relevant Provisions)

15. Prohibition of discrimination on grounds of religion, race, caste, sex or place of birth.—(1) The State shall not discriminate against any citizen on grounds only of religion, race, caste, sex, place of birth or any of them.

(2) No citizen shall, on grounds only of religion, race, caste, sex, place of birth or any of them, be subject to any disability, liability, restriction or condition with regard to—

(a) access to shops, public restaurants, hotels and places of public entertainment; or

(b) the use of wells, tanks, bathing ghats, roads and places of public resort maintained wholly or partly out of State funds or dedicated to the use of general public.

(3) Nothing in this article shall prevent the State from making any special provision for women and children.

(4) Nothing in this article or in clause (2) of article 29 shall prevent the State from making any special provision for the advancement of any socially and educationally backward classes of citizens or for the Scheduled Castes and the Scheduled Tribes.

(5) Nothing in this article or in sub-clause (g) of clause (1) of article 19 shall prevent the State from making any special provision, by law, for the advancement of any socially and educationally backward classes of citizens or for the Scheduled Castes or the Scheduled Tribes in so far as such special provisions relate to their admission to educational institutions including private educational institutions, whether aided or unaided by the State, other than the minority educational institutions referred to in clause (1) of article 30.

17. Abolition of untouchability.—"Untouchability" is abolished and its practice in any form is forbidden. The enforcement of any disability arising out of "Untouchability" shall be an offence punishable in accordance with law.

PART XVI

SPECIAL PROVISIONS RELATING TO CERTAIN CLASSES

330. Reservation of seats for Scheduled Castes and Scheduled Tribes in the House of the People.—(1) Seats shall be reserved in the House of the People for—

(a) the Scheduled Castes;

(b) the Scheduled Tribes except the Scheduled Tribes in the autonomous districts of Assam; and

(c) the Scheduled Tribes in the autonomous districts of Assam.

(2) The number of seats reserved in any State or Union territory for the Scheduled Castes or the Scheduled Tribes under clause (1) shall bear, as nearly as may be, the same proportion to the total number of seats allotted to that State or Union territory in the House of the People as the population of the Scheduled Castes in the State or Union territory or of the Scheduled Tribes in the State or Union territory or part of the State or Union territory, as the case may be, in respect of which seats are so reserved, bears to the total population of the State or Union territory.

(3) Notwithstanding anything contained in clause (2), the number of seats reserved in the House of the People for the Scheduled Tribes in the autonomous districts of Assam

shall bear to the total number of seats allotted to that State a proportion not less than the population of the Scheduled Tribes in the said autonomous districts bears to the total population of the State.

Explanation.—In this article and in article 332, the expression "population" means the population as ascertained at the last preceding census of which the relevant figures have been published:

Provided that the reference in this *Explanation* to the last preceding census of which the relevant figures have been published shall, until the relevant figures for the first census taken after the year 2026 have been published, be construed as a reference to the 2001 census.

331. Representation of the Anglo-Indian community in the House of the People.—Notwithstanding anything in article 81, the President may, if he is of opinion that the Anglo-Indian community is not adequately represented in the House of the people, nominate not more than two members of that community to the House of the People.

332. Reservation of seats for Scheduled Castes and Scheduled Tribes in the Legislative Assemblies of the States.—(1) Seats shall be reserved for the Scheduled Castes and the Scheduled Tribes, except the Scheduled Tribes in the autonomous districts of Assam, in the Legislative Assembly of every State.

(2) Seats shall be reserved also for the autonomous districts in the Legislative Assembly of the State of Assam.

(3) The number of seats reserved for the Scheduled Castes or the Scheduled Tribes in the Legislative Assembly of any State under clause (1) shall bear, as nearly as may be, the same proportion to the total number of seats in the Assembly as the population of the Scheduled Castes in the State or of the Scheduled Tribes in the State or part of the State, as the case may be, in respect of which seats are so reserved bears to the total population of the State.

(3A) Notwithstanding anything contained in clause (3), until the taking effect, under article 170, of the re-adjustment, on the basis of the first census after the year 2026, of the number of seats in the Legislative Assemblies of the States of Arunachal Pradesh, Meghalaya, Mizoram and Nagaland, the seats which shall be reserved for the Scheduled Tribes in the Legislative Assembly of any such State shall be,—

(a) if all the seats in the Legislative Assembly of such State in existence on the date of coming into force of the Constitution (Fifty-seventh Amendment) Act, 1987 (hereafter in this clause referred to as the existing Assembly) are held by members of the Scheduled Tribes, all the seats except one;

(b) in any other case, such number of seats as bears to the total number of seats, a proportion not less than the number (as on the said date) of members belonging to the Scheduled Tribes in the existing Assembly bears to the total number of seats in existing Assembly.

(3B) Notwithstanding anything contained in clause (3), until the re-adjustment, under article 170, takes effect on the basis of the first census after the year [4][2026], of the number of seats in the Legislative Assembly of the State of Tripura, the seats which shall be reserved for the Scheduled Tribes in the Legislative Assembly shall be, such number of seats as bears to the total number of seats, a proportion not less than the number, as on the date of coming into force of the Constitution (Seventy-second Amendment) Act, 1992, of members belonging to the Scheduled Tribes in the Legislative Assembly in existence on the said date bears to the total number of seats in that Assembly.

(4) The number of seats reserved for an autonomous district in the Legislative Assembly of the State of Assam shall bear to the total number of seats in that Assembly

a proportion not less than the population of the district bears to the total population of the State.

(5) The constituencies for the seats reserved for any autonomous district of Assam shall not comprise any area outside that district.

(6) No person who is not a member of a Scheduled Tribe of any autonomous district of the State of Assam shall be eligible for election to the Legislative Assembly of the State from any constituency of that district:

Provided that for elections to the Legislative Assembly of the State of Assam, the representation of the Scheduled Tribes and non-Scheduled Tribes in the constituencies included in the Bodoland Territorial Areas District, so notified, and existing prior to the constitution of the Bodoland Territorial Areas District, shall be maintained.

333. Representation of the Anglo-Indian community in the Legislative Assemblies of the States.—Notwithstanding anything in article 170, the Governor of a State may, if he is of opinion that the Anglo-Indian community needs representation in the Legislative Assembly of the State and is not adequately represented therein, nominate one member of that community to the Assembly.

334. Reservation of seats and special representation to cease after seventy years.—Notwithstanding anything in the foregoing provisions of this Part, the provisions of this Constitution relating to—

(a) the reservation of seats for the Scheduled Castes and the Scheduled Tribes in the House of the People and in the Legislative Assemblies of the States; and

(b) the representation of the Anglo-Indian community in the House of the People and in the Legislative Assemblies of the States by nomination,

shall cease to have effect on the expiration of a period of seventy years from the commencement of this Constitution:

Provided that nothing in this article shall affect any representation in the House of the People or in the Legislative Assembly of a State until the dissolution of the then existing House or Assembly, as the case may be.

335. Claims of Scheduled Castes and Scheduled Tribes to services and posts.—The claims of the members of the Scheduled Castes and the Scheduled Tribes shall be taken into consideration, consistently with the maintenance of efficiency of administration, in the making of appointments to services and posts in connection with the affairs of the Union or of a State:

Provided that nothing in this article shall prevent in making of any provision in favour of the members of the Scheduled Castes and the Scheduled Tribes for relaxation in qualifying marks in any examination or lowering the standards of evaluation, for reservation in matters of promotion to any class or classes of services or posts in connection with the affairs of the Union or of a State.

336. Special provision for Anglo-Indian community in certain services.—(1) During the first two years after the commencement of this Constitution, appointments of members of the Anglo-Indian community to posts in the railway, customs, postal and telegraph services of the Union shall be made on the same basis as immediately before the fifteenth day of August, 1947.

During every succeeding period of two years, the number of posts reserved for the members of the said community in the said services shall, as nearly as possible, be less by ten per cent. than the numbers so reserved during the immediately preceding period of two years:

Provided that at the end of ten years from the commencement of this Constitution all such reservations shall cease.

(2) Nothing in clause (1) shall bar the appointment of members of the Anglo-Indian community to posts other than, or in addition to, those reserved for the community under that clause if such members are found qualified for appointment on merit as compared with the members of other communities.

337. Special provision with respect to educational grants for the benefit of Anglo-Indian community.—During the first three financial years after the commencement of this Constitution, the same grants, if any, shall be made by the Union and by each State for the benefit of the Anglo-Indian community in respect of education as were made in the financial year ending on the thirty-first day of March, 1948.

During every succeeding period of three years the grants may be less by ten per cent. than those for the immediately preceding period of three years:

Provided that at the end of ten years from the commencement of this Constitution such grants, to the extent to which they are a special concession to the Anglo-Indian community, shall cease:

Provided further that no educational institution shall be entitled to receive any grant under this article unless at least forty per cent. of annual admissions therein are made available to members of communities other than the Anglo-Indian community.

338. National Commission for Scheduled Castes.—(1) There shall be a Commission for the Scheduled Castes to be known as the National Commission for the Scheduled Castes.

(2) Subject to the provisions of any law made in this behalf by Parliament, the Commission shall consist of a Chairperson, Vice-Chairperson and three other Members and the conditions of service and tenure of office of the Chairperson, Vice-Chairperson and other Members so appointed shall be such as the President may by rule determine.]

(3) The Chairperson, Vice-Chairperson and other Members of the Commission shall be appointed by the President by warrant under his hand and seal.

(4) The Commission shall have the power to regulate its own procedure.

(5) It shall be the duty of the Commission—

(a) to investigate and monitor all matters relating to the safeguards provided for the Scheduled Castes under this Constitution or under any other law for the time being in force or under any order of the Government and to evaluate the working of such safeguards;

(b) to inquire into specific complaints with respect to the deprivation of rights and safeguards of the Scheduled Castes;

(c) to participate and advise on the planning process of socio-economic development of the Scheduled Castes and to evaluate the progress of their development under the Union and any State;

(d) to present to the President, annually and at such other times as the Commission may deem fit, reports upon the working of those safeguards;

(e) to make in such reports recommendations as to the measures that should be taken by the Union or any State for the effective implementation of those safeguards and other measures for the protection, welfare and socio-economic development of the Scheduled Castes; and

(f) to discharge such other functions in relation to the protection, welfare and development and advancement of the Scheduled Castes as the President may, subject to the provisions of any law made by Parliament, by the rule specify.

(6) The President shall cause all such reports to be laid before each House of Parliament along with a memorandum explaining the action taken or proposed to be taken on the recommendations relating to the Union and the reasons for the non-acceptance, if any, of any of such recommendations.

(7) Where any such report, or any part thereof, relates to any matter with which any State Government is concerned, a copy of such report shall be forwarded to the Governor of the State who shall cause it to be laid before the Legislature of the State along with a memorandum explaining the action taken or proposed to be taken on the recommendations relating to the State and the reasons for the non-acceptance, if any, of any of such recommendations.

(8) The Commission shall, while investigating any matter referred to in sub-clause (a) or inquiring into any complaint referred to in sub-clause (b) of clause (5), have all the powers of a civil court trying a suit and in particular in respect of the following matters, namely:—

(a) summoning and enforcing the attendance of any person from any part of India and examining him on oath;

(b) requiring the discovery and production of any documents;

(c) receiving evidence on affidavits;

(d) requisitioning any public record or copy thereof from any court or office;

(e) issuing commissions for the examination of witnesses and documents;

(f) any other matter which the President may, by rule, determine.

(9) The Union and every State Government shall consult the Commission on all major policy matters affecting Scheduled Castes.

(10) In this article, references to the Scheduled Castes shall be construed as including references to such other backward classes as the President may, on receipt of the report of a Commission appointed under clause (1) of article 340 by order specify and also to the Anglo-Indian community.

338A. National Commission for Scheduled Tribes.—(1) There shall be a Commission for the Scheduled Tribes to be known as the National Commission for the Scheduled Tribes.

(2) Subject to the provisions of any law made in this behalf by Parliament, the Commission shall consist of a Chairperson, Vice-Chairperson and three other Members and the conditions of service and tenure of office of the Chairperson, Vice-Chairperson and other Members so appointed shall be such as the President may be rule determine.

(3) The Chairperson, Vice-Chairperson and other Members of the Commission shall be appointed by the President by warrant under his hand and seal.

(4) The Commission shall have the power to regulate its own procedure.

(5) It shall be the duty of the Commission—

(a) to investigate and monitor all matters relating to the safeguards provided for the Scheduled Tribes under this Constitution or under any other law for the time being in force or under any order of the Government and to evaluate the working of such safeguards;

(b) to inquire into specific complaints with respect to the deprivation of rights and safeguards of the Scheduled Tribes;

(c) to participate and advise on the planning process of socio-economic development of the Scheduled Tribes and to evaluate the progress of their development under the Union and any State;

(d) to present to the President, annually and at such other times as the Commission may deem fit, reports upon the working of those safeguards;

(e) to make in such reports recommendations as to the measures that should be taken by the Union or any State for the effective implementation of those safeguards and other measures for the protection, welfare and socio-economic development of the Scheduled Tribes; and

(f) to discharge such other functions in relation to the protection, welfare and development and advancement of the Scheduled Tribes as the President may, subject to the provisions of any law made by Parliament, by rule specify.

(6) The President shall cause all such reports to be laid before each House of Parliament along with a memorandum explaining the action taken or proposed to be taken on the recommendations relating to the Union and the reasons for the non-acceptance, if any, of any of such recommendations.

(7) Where any such report, or any part thereof, relates to any matter with which any State Government is concerned, a copy of such report shall be forwarded to the Governor of the State who shall cause it to be laid before the Legislature of the State along with a memorandum explaining the action taken or proposed to be taken on the recommendations relating to the State and the reasons for the non-accpetance, if any, of any such recommendations.

(8) The Commission shall, while investigating any matter referred to in sub-clause (a) or inquiring into any complaint referred to in sub-clause (b) of clause (5), have all the powers of a civil court trying a suit and in particular in respect of the following matters, namely:—

(a) summoning and enforcing the attendance of any person from any part of India and examining him on oath;

(b) requiring the discovery and production of any document;

(c) receiving evidence on affidavits;

(d) requisitioning any public record or copy thereof from any court of office;

(e) issuing commissions for the examination of witnesses and documents;

(f) any other matter which the President may, by rule, determine.

(9) The Union and every State Government shall consult the Commission on all major policy matters affecting Scheduled Tribes.

339. Control of the Union over the administration of Scheduled Areas and the welfare of Scheduled Tribes.—(1) The President may at any time and shall, at the expiration of ten years from the commencement of this Constitution by order appoint a Commission to report on the administration of the Scheduled Areas and the welfare of the Scheduled Tribes in the States.

The order may define the composition, powers and procedure of the Commission and may contain such incidental or ancillary provisions as the President may consider necessary or desirable.

(2) The executive power of the Union shall extend to the giving of directions to a State as to the drawing up and execution of schemes specified in the direction to be essential for the welfare of the Scheduled Tribes in the State.

340. Appointment of a Commission to investigate the conditions of backward classes.—(1) The President may by order appoint a Commission consisting of such persons as he thinks fit to investigate the conditions of socially and educationally backward classes within the territory of India and the difficulties under which they labour and to make recommendations as to the steps that should be taken by the Union or any State to remove such difficulties and to improve their condition and as to the grants that should be made for the purpose by the Union or any State and the conditions subject to which such grants should be made, and the order appointing such Commission shall define the procedure to be followed by the Commission.

(2) A Commission so appointed shall investigate the matters referred to them and present to the President a report setting out the facts as found by them and making such recommendations as they think proper.

(3) The President shall cause a copy of the report so presented together with a memorandum explaining the action taken thereon to be laid before each House of Parliament.

341. Scheduled Castes.—(1) The President may with respect to any State or Union territory, and where it is a State, after consultation with the Governor thereof, by public notification, specify the castes, races or tribes or parts of or groups within castes, races or tribes which shall for the purposes of this Constitution be deemed to be Scheduled Castes in relation to that State or Union territory, as the case may be.

(2) Parliament may by law include in or exclude from the list of Scheduled Castes specified in a notification issued under clause (1) any caste, race or tribe or part of or group within any caste, race or tribe, but save as aforesaid a notification issued under the said clause shall not be varied by any subsequent notification.

342. Scheduled Tribes.—(1) The President may with respect to any State or Union territory, and where it is a State, after consultation with the Governor thereof, by public notification, specify the tribes or tribal communities or parts of or groups within tribes or tribal communities which shall for the purposes of this Constitution be deemed to be Scheduled Tribes in relation to that State or Union territory, as the case may be.

(2) Parliament may by law include in or exclude from the list of Scheduled Tribes specified in a notification issued under clause (1) any tribe or tribal community or part of or group within any tribe or tribal community, but save as aforesaid a notification issued under the said clause shall not be varied by any subsequent notification.

APPENDIX 9

THE LEGAL SERVICES AUTHORITIES ACT, 1987

(39 of 1987)

[11th October, 1987]

An Act to constitute legal services authorities to provide free and competent legal service to the weaker sections of the society to ensure that opportunities for securing justice are not denied to any citizen by reason of economic or other disabilities, and to organise Lok Adalats to secure that the operation of the legal system promotes justice on a basis of equal opportunity.

Be it enacted by Parliament in the Thirty-eighth Year of the Republic of India as follows:—

CHAPTER I

PRELIMINARY

1. Short title, extent and commencement.—(1) This Act may be called the Legal Services Authorities Act, 1987.

(2) It extends to the whole of India, except the State of Jammu and Kashmir.

(3) It shall come into force on such date as the Central Government may, by notification, appoint; and different dates[1] may be appointed for different provisions of this Act and for different States, and any reference to commencement in any provision of this Act in relation to any State shall be construed as a reference to the commencement of that provision in that State.

2. Definitions.—(1) In this Act, unless the context otherwise requires,—

[2][(a) "case" includes a suit or any proceeding before a court;

(aa) "Central Authority" means the National Legal Services Authority constituted under section 3;

(aaa) "court" means a civil, criminal or revenue court and includes any tribunal or any other authority constituted under any law for the time being in force, to exercise judicial or quasi-Judicial functions;]

(b) "District Authority" means a District Legal Services Authority constituted under section 9;

[3][(bb) "High Court Legal Services Committee" means a High Court Legal Services Committee constituted under section 8A;]

(c) "legal service" includes the rendering of any service in the conduct of any case or other legal proceeding before any court or other authority or tribunal and the giving of advice on any legal matter;

(d) "Lok Adalat" means a Lok Adalat organised under Chapter VI;

(e) "notification" means a notification published in the Official Gazette;

(f) "prescribed" means prescribed by rules made under this Act;

[4][(ff) "regulations" means regulations made under this Act;]

---

1. Whole Act except Chapter III came into force on 9-11-1995, *vide* S.O. 893(E), dated 9th Novembre, 1995. Details of enforcement of the provisions of Chapter III have been given in the Appendix.
2. Subs. by Act 59 of 1994, sec. 2, for clause (a) (w.e.f. 29-10-1994).
3. Ins. by Act 59 of 1994, sec. 2 (w.e.f. 29-10-1994).
4. Ins. by Act 59 of 1994, sec. 2 (w.e.f. 29-10-1994).

(g) "scheme" means any scheme framed by the Central Authority, a State Authority or a District Authority for the purpose of giving effect to any of the provisions of this Act;

(h) "State Authority" means a State Legal Services Authority constituted under section 6;

(i) "State Government" includes the administrator of a Union Territory appointed by the President under Article 239 of the Constitution;

[1][(j) "Supreme Court Legal Services Committee" means the Supreme Court Legal Services Committee constituted under section 3A;

(k) "Taluk Legal Services Committee" means a Taluk Legal Services Committee constituted under section 11A.]

(2) Any reference in this Act to any other enactment or any provision thereof shall, in relation to an area in which such enactment or provision is not in force, be construed as a reference to the corresponding law or the relevant provision of the corresponding law, if any, in force in that area.

CHAPTER II

THE NATIONAL LEGAL SERVICES AUTHORITY

[2][3. **Constitution of the National Legal Services Authority.**—(1) The Central Government shall constitute a body to be called the National Legal Services Authority to exercise the powers and perform the functions conferred on, or assigned to, the Central Authority under this Act.

(2) The Central Authority shall consist of—

(a) the Chief Justice of India who shall be the Patron-in-Chief;

(b) a serving or retired Judge of the Supreme Court to be nominated by the President, in consultation with the Chief Justice of India, who shall be the Executive Chairman; and

(c) such number of other members, possessing such experience and qualifications, as may be prescribed by the Central Government, to be nominated by that Government in consultation with the Chief Justice of India.

(3) The Central Government shall, in consultation with the Chief Justice of India, appoint a person to be the Member-Secretary of the Central Authority, possessing such experience and qualifications as may be prescribed by that Government, to exercise such powers and perform such duties under the Executive Chairman of the Central Authority as may be prescribed by that Government or as may be assigned to him by the Executive Chairman of that Authority.

(4) The terms of office and other conditions relating thereto, of members and the Member-Secretary of the Central Authority shall be such as may be prescribed by the Central Government in consultation with the Chief Justice of India.

(5) The Central Authority may appoint such number of officers and other employees as may be prescribed by the Central Government, in consultation with the Chief Justice of India, for the efficient discharge of its functions under this Act.

(6) The officers and other employees of the Central Authority shall be entitled to such salary and allowances and shall be subject to such other conditions of service as may be prescribed by the Central Government in consultation with the Chief Justice of India.

1. Ins. by Act 59 of 1994, sec. 2 (w.e.f. 29-10-1994).
2. Subs. by Act 59 of 1994, sec. 3, for section 3 (w.e.f. 29-10-1994).

(7) The administrative expenses of the Central Authority, including the salaries, allowances and pensions payable to the Member- Secretary, officers and other employees of the Central Authority, shall be defrayed out of the Consolidated Fund of India.

(8) All orders and decisions of the Central Authority shall be authenticated by the Member-Secretary or any other officer of the Central Authority duly authorised by the Executive Chairman of that Authority.

(9) No act or proceeding of the Central Authority shall be invalid merely on the ground of the existence of any vacancy in, or any defect in the constitution of the Central Authority.

3A. Supreme Court Legal Services Committee.—(1) The Central Authority shall constitute a committee to be called the Supreme Court Legal Services Committee for the purpose of exercising such powers and performing such functions as may be determined by regulations made by the Central Authority.

(2) The Committee shall consist of—

(a) a sitting Judge of the Supreme Court who shall be the Chairman; and

(b) such number of other members possessing such experience and qualifications as may be prescribed by the Central Government,

to be nominated by the Chief Justice of India.

(3) The Chief Justice of India shall appoint a person to be the Secretary to the Committee, possessing such experience and qualifications as may be prescribed by the Central Government.

(4) The terms of Office and other conditions relating thereto, of the members and Secretary of the Committee shall be such as may be determined by regulations made by the Central Authority.

(5) The Committee may appoint such number of officers and other employees as may be prescribed by the Central Government, in consultation with the Chief Justice of India, for the efficient discharge of its functions.

(6) The officers and other employees of the Committee shall be entitled to such salary and allowances and shall be subject to such other conditions of service as may be prescribed by the Central Government in consultation with the Chief Justice of India.]

4. Functions of the Central Authority.—The Central Authority shall [1][***] perform all or any of the following functions, namely:—

(a) lay down policies and principles for making legal services available under the provisions of this Act;

(b) frame the most effective and economical schemes for the purpose of making legal services available under the provisions of this Act;

(c) utilise the funds at its disposal and make appropriate allocations of funds to the State Authorities and District Authorities;

(d) take necessary steps by way of social justice litigation with regard to consumer protection, environmental protection or any other matter of special concern to the weaker sections, of the society and for this purpose, give training to social workers in legal skills;

(e) organise legal aid camps, especially in rural areas, slums or labour colonies with the dual purpose of educating the weaker sections of the society as to

---

1. The words " subject to the general directions of the Central Government" omitted by Act 59 of 1994 sec. 4, (w.e.f. 29-10-1994).

their rights as well as encouraging the settlement of disputes through Lok Adalats;

(f) encourage the settlement of disputes by way of negotiations, arbitration and conciliation;

(g) undertake and promote research in the field of legal services with special reference to the need for such services among the poor;

(h) to do all things necessary for the purpose of ensuring commitment to the fundamental duties of citizens under Part IVA of the Constitution;

(i) monitor and evaluate implementation of the legal aid programmes at periodic intervals and provide for independent evaluation of programmes and schemes implemented in whole or in part by funds provided under this Act;

[1][(j) provide grants-in-aid for specific schemes to various voluntary social service institutions and the State and District Authorities, from out of the amounts placed at its disposal for the implementation of legal services schemes under the provisions of this Act;]

(k) develop, in consultation with the Bar Council of India, programmes for clinical legal education and, promote guidance and supervise the establishment and working of legal services clinics in universities, law colleges and other institutions;

(l) take appropriate measures for spreading legal literacy and legal awareness amongst the people and, in particular, to educate weaker sections of the society about the rights, benefits and privileges guaranteed by social welfare legislations and other enactments as well as administrative programmes and measures;

(m) make special efforts to enlist the support of voluntary social welfare institutions, working at the grass-root level, particularly among the Scheduled Castes and the Scheduled Tribes, women and rural and urban labour; and

(n) coordinate and monitor the functioning of [2][State Authorities, District Authorities, Supreme Court Legal Services Committee, High Court Legal Services Committees, Taluk Legal Services Committees and voluntary social service institutions] and other legal services organisations and give general directions for the proper implementation of the legal services programmes.

5. Central Authority to work in coordination with other agencies.—In the discharge of its function under this Act, the Central Authority shall, wherever appropriate, act in coordination with other governmental and non-governmental agencies, universities and others engaged in the work of promoting the cause of legal services to the poor.

CHAPTER III

STATE LEGAL SERVICES AUTHORITY

[3][**6. Constitution of State Legal Services Authority.**—(1) Every State Government shall constitute a body to be called the Legal Services Authority for the State to exercise the powers and perform the functions conferred on, or assigned to, a State Authority under this Act.

1. Subs. by Act 59 of 1994 sec. 4, for clause (j) (w.e.f. 29-10-1994).
2. Subs. by Act 59 of 1994, sec. 4, for "State and District Authorities and other voluntary social welfare institution" (w.e.f. 29-10-1994).
3. Subs. by Act 59 of 1994, sec. 5, for section 6 (w.e.f. 29-10-1994).

(2) A State Authority shall consist of—

(a) the Chief Justice of the High Court who shall be the Patron-in-Chief;

(b) a serving or retired Judge of the High Court, to be nominated by the Governor, in consultation with the Chief Justice of the High Court, who shall be the Executive Chairman; and

(c) such number of other members, possessing such experience and qualifications as may be prescribed by the State Government, to be nominated by that Government in consultation with the Chief Justice of the High Court.

(3) The State Government shall, in consultation with the Chief Justice of the High Court, appoint a person belonging to the State Higher Judicial Service, not lower in rank than that of a District Judge, as the Member-Secretary of the State Authority, to exercise such powers and perform such duties under the Executive Chairman of the State Authority as may be prescribed by that Government or as may be assigned to him by the Executive Chairman of that Authority:

Provided that a person functioning as Secretary of a State Legal Aid and Advice Board immediately before the date of constitution of the State Authority may be appointed as Member-Secretary of that Authority, even if he is not qualified to be appointed as such under this sub-section, for a period not exceeding five years.

(4) The terms of Office and other conditions relating thereto, of members and the Member-Secretary of the State Authority shall be such as may be prescribed by the State Government in consultation with the Chief Justice of the High Court.

(5) The State Authority may appoint such number of officers and other employees as may be prescribed by the State Government, in consultation with the Chief Justice of the High Court, for the efficient discharge of its functions under this Act.

(6) The officers and other employees of the State Authority shall be entitled to such salary and allowances and shall be subject to such other conditions of service as may be prescribed by the State Government in consultation with the Chief Justice of the High Court.

(7) The administrative expenses of the State Authority, including the salaries, allowances and pensions payable to the Member-Secretary, officers and other employees of the State Authority shall be defrayed out of the Consolidated Fund of the State.

(8) All orders and decisions of the State Authority shall be authenticated by the Member-Secretary or any other officer of the State Authority duly authorised by the Executive Chairman of the State Authority.

(9) No act or proceeding of a State Authority shall be invalid merely on the ground of the existence of any vacancy in, or any defect in the constitution of, the State Authority.

7. Functions of the State Authority—(1) It shall be the duty of the State Authority to give effect to the policy and directions of the Central Authority.

(2) Without prejudice to the generality of the functions referred to in sub-section (1), the State Authority shall perform all or any of the following functions, namely:—

(a) give legal service to persons who satisfy the criteria laid down under this Act;

(b) conduct [1][Lok Adalats; including Lok Adalats for High Court cases];

(c) undertake preventive and strategic legal aid programmes; and

(d) perform such other functions as the State Authority may, in consultation with the [2][Central Authority,] fix by regulations.

1. Subs. by Act 59 of 1994, sec 6, for "Lok Adalats" (w.e.f. 29-10-1994).
2. Subs. by Act 59 of 1994, sec. 6, for "Central Government" (w.e.f. 29-10-1994).

[1][**8. State Authority to act in coordination with other agencies etc., and be subject to directions given by Central Authority.**—In the discharge of its functions the State Authority shall appropriately act in coordination with other governmental agencies, non-governmental voluntary social service institutions, universities and other bodies engaged in the work of promoting the cause of legal services to the poor and shall also be guided by such directions as the Central Authority may give to it in writing.

8A. High Court Legal Services Committee.—(1) The State Authority shall constitute a Committee to be called the High Court Legal Services Committee for every High Court, for the purpose of exercising such powers and performing such functions as may be determined by regulations made by the State Authority.

(2) The Committee shall consist of—

(a) a sitting Judge of the High Court who shall be the Chairman; and

(b) such number of other members possessing such experience and qualifications as may be determined by regulations made by the State Authority,

to be nominated by the Chief Justice of the High Court.

(3) The Chief Justice of the High Court shall appoint a Secretary to the Committee possessing such experience and qualifications as may be prescribed by the StateGovernment.

(4) The terms of office and other conditions relating thereto, of the members and Secretary of the Committee shall be such as may be determined by regulations made by the State Authority.

(5) The Committee may appoint such number of officers and other employees as may be prescribed by the State Government in consultation with the Chief Justice of the High Court for the efficient discharge of its functions.

(6) The officers and other employees of the Committee shall be entitled to such salary and allowances and shall be subject to such other conditions of service as may be prescribed by the State Government in consultation with the Chief Justice of the High Court.]

[2][**9. District Legal Services Authority**—(1) The State Government shall, in consultation with the Chief Justice of the High Court, constitute a body to be called the District Legal Services Authority for every district in the State to exercise the powers and perform the functions conferred on, or assigned to, the District Authority under this Act.

(2) A District Authority shall consist of—

(a) the District Judge who shall be its Chairman; and

(b) such number of other members, possessing such experience and qualifications, as may be prescribed by the State Government, to be nominated by that Government in consultation with the Chief Justice of the High Court.

(3) The State Authority shall, in consultation with the Chairman of the District Authority, appoint a person belonging to the State Judicial Service not lower in rank than that of a Subordinate Judge or Civil Judge posted at the seat of the District Judiciary as Secretary of the District Authority to exercise such powers and perform such duties under Chairman of that Committee as may be assigned to him by such Chairman.

(4) The terms of office and other conditions relating thereto, of members and Secretary of the District Authority shall be such as may be determined by regulations made by the State Authority in consultation with the Chief Justice of the High Court.

1. Subs. by Act 59 of 1994, sec. 7, for section 8 (w.e.f. 29-10-1994).
2. Subs. by Act 59 of 1994, sec. 7, for section 9 (w.e.f. 29-10-1994).

(5) The District Authority may appoint such number of officers and other employees as may be prescribed by the State Government in consultation with the Chief Justice of the High Court for the efficient discharge of its functions.

(6) The officers and other employees of the District Authority shall be entitled to such salary and allowances and shall be subject to such other conditions of service as may be prescribed by the State Government in consultation with the Chief Justice of the High Court.

(7) The administrative expenses of every District Authority, including the salaries, allowances and pensions payable to the Secretary, officers and other employees of the District Authority shall be defrayed out of the Consolidated Fund of the State.

(8) All orders and decisions of the District Authority shall be authenticated by the Secretary or by any other officer of the District Authority duly authorised by the Chairman of that Authority.

(9) No act or proceeding of a District Authority shall be invalid merely on the ground of the existence of any vacancy in, or any defect in the Constitution of, the District Authority.]

10. Functions of District Authority.—(1) It shall be the duty of every District Authority to perform such of the functions of the State Authority in the District as may be delegated to it from time to time by the State Authority.

(2) Without prejudice to the generality of the functions referred to in sub-section (1), the District Authority may perform all or any of the following functions, namely:—

[1][(a) co-ordinate the activities of the Taluk Legal Services Committee and other Legal Services in the District;]

(b) organise Lok Adalats within the District; and

(c) perform such other functions as the State Authority may [2][***] fix by regulations.

11. District Authority to act in coordination with other agencies and be subject to directions given by the Central Authority, etc.—In the discharge of its functions under this Act, the District Authority shall, wherever appropriate, act in coordination with other governmental and non-governmental institutions, universities and others engaged in the work of promoting the cause of legal services to the poor and shall also be guided by such directions as the Central Authority or the State Authority may give to it in writing.

[3]**[11A. Taluk Legal Services Committee.**—(1) The State Authority may constitute a Committee, to be called the Taluk Legal Services Committee, for each taluk or mandal or for group of taluks or mandals.

(2) The Committee shall consist of—

(a) The [4][Senior-most Judicial Officer] operating within the jurisdiction of the Committee who shall be the *ex officio* Chairman; and

(b) such number of other members, possessing such experience and qualifications, as may be prescribed by the State Government, to be nominated by that Government in consultation with the Chief Justice of the High Court.

---

1. Subs. by Act 59 of 1994, sec. 8, for clause (a) (w.e.f. 29-10-1994).
2. The words "in consultations with the State Government", omitted by Act 59 of 1994, sec. 8 (w.e.f. 29-10-1994).
3. Ins. by Act 59 of 1994, sec. 9 (w.e.f. 29-10-1994).
4. Subs. by Act 37 of 2002, sec. 2, for "Senior Civil Judge" (w.e.f. 11-6-2002).

(3) The Committee may appoint such number of officers and other employees as may be prescribed by the State Government in consultation with the Chief Justice of the High Court for the efficient discharge of its functions.

(4) The officers and other employees of the Committee shall be entitled to such salary and allowances and shall be subject to such other conditions of service as may be prescribed by the State Government in consultation with the Chief Justice of the High Court.

(5) The administrative expenses of the Committee shall be defrayed out of the District Legal Aid Fund by the District Authority.

11B. Functions of Taluk Legal Services Committee.—The Taluk Legal Services Committee may perform all or any of the following functions, namely:—

(a) coordinate the activities of legal services in the taluk;

(b) organise Lok Adalats within the taluk; and

(c) perform such other functions as the District Authority may assign to it.]

CHAPTER IV

ENTITLEMENT TO LEGAL SERVICES

12. Criteria for giving legal services.—Every person who has to file or defend a case shall be entitled to legal services under this Act if that person, is—

(a) a member of a Scheduled Caste or Scheduled Tribe;

(b) a victim of trafficking in human beings or beggar as referred to in Article 23 of the Constitution;

(c) a women or a child;

[1][(d) a person with disability as defined in clause (i) of section 2 of the Persons with Disabilities (Equal Opportunities, Protection of Rights and Full Participation) Act, 1995 (1 of 1996);]

(e) a person under circumstances of undeserved want such as being a victim of a mass disaster, ethnic violence, caste atrocity, flood, drought, earthquake or industrial disaster; or

(f) an industrial workman; or

(g) in custody, including custody in a protective home within the meaning of clause (g) of section 2 of the Immoral Traffic (Prevention) Act, 1956 (104 of 1956) or in a juvenile home within the meaning of clause (j) of section 2 of the Juvenile Justice Act, 1986 (53 of 1986) or in a psychiatric hospital or psychiatric nursing home within the meaning of clause (g) of section 2 of the Mental Health Act, 1987 (14 of 1987); or

[2][(h) in receipt of annual income less than rupees nine thousand or such other higher amount as may be prescribed by the State Government, if the case is before a court other than the Supreme Court, and less than rupees twelve thousand or such other higher amount as may be prescribed by the Central Government, if the case is before the Supreme Court.]

13. Entitlement to legal services.—(1) Persons who satisfy all or any of the criteria specified in section 12 shall be entitled to receive legal services provided that the concerned Authority is satisfied that such person has a *prima facie* case to prosecute or to defend.

---

1. Subs. by Act 1 of 1996, sec. 74, for clause (d) (w.e.f. 7-2-1996).
2. Subs. by Act 59 of 1994, sec. 10, for clause (h) (w.e.f. 29-10-1994).

(2) An affidavit made by a person as to his income may be regarded as sufficient for making him eligible to the entitlement of legal services under this Act unless the concerned Authority has reason to disbelieve such affidavit.

CHAPTER V

FINANCE, ACCOUNTS AND AUDIT

14. Grants by Central Government.—The Central Government shall, after due appropriation made by Parliament by law in this behalf pay to the Central Authority, by way of grants, such sums of money as the Central Government may think fit for being utilised for the purposes of this Act.

15. National Legal Aid Fund.—(1) The Central Authority shall establish a fund to be called the National Legal Aid Fund and there shall be credited thereto—

(a) all sums of money given as grants by the Central Government under section 14;

(b) any grants or donations that may be made to the Central Authority by any other person for the purposes of this Act;

(c) any amount received by the Central Authority under the orders of any court or from any other source.

(2) The National Legal Aid Fund shall be applied for meeting—

(a) the cost of legal services provided under this Act including grants made to State Authorities;

[1][(b) the cost of legal services provided by the Supreme Court Legal Services Committee;

(c) any other expenses which are required to be met by the Central Authority.]

16. State Legal Aid Fund.—A State Authority shall establish a fund to be called the State Legal Aid Fund and there shall be credited thereto—

(a) all sums of money paid to it or any grants made by the Central Authority for the purposes of this Act;

(b) any grants or donations that may be made to the State Authority by the State Government or by any person for the purposes of this Act;

(c) any other amount received by the State Authority under the orders of any court or from any other source.

(2) A State Legal Aid Fund shall be applied for meeting—

(a) the cost of functions referred to in section 7;

[2][(b) the cost of legal services provided by the High Court Legal Services Committees;

(c) any other expenses which are required to be met by the State Authority.]

17. District Legal Aid Fund.—(1) Every District Authority shall establish a fund to be called the District Legal Aid Fund and there shall be credited thereto—

(a) all sums of money paid or any grants made by the State Authority to the District Authority for the purposes of this Act;

[3][(b) any grants or donations that may be made to the District Authority by any person, with the prior approval of the State Authority, for the purposes of this Act;

---

1. Subs. by Act 59 of 1994, sec. 11, for clause (b) (w.e.f. 29-10-1994).
2. Subs. by Act 59 of 1994, sec. 12, for clause (b) (w.e.f. 29-10-1994).
3. Subs. by Act 59 of 1994, sec. 13, for clause (b) (w.e.f. 29-10-1994).

(c) any other amount received by the District Authority under the orders of any court or from any other source.]

(2) The District Legal Aid Fund shall be applied for meeting—

(a) the cost of functions referred to in section 10 [1][and 11B];

(b) any other expenses which are required to be met by the District Authority.

18. Accounts and audit.—(1) The Central Authority, State Authority or the District Authority (hereinafter referred to in this section as 'the Authority'), as the case may be, shall maintain proper accounts and other relevant records and prepare an annual statement of accounts including the income and expenditure account and the balance-sheet in such form and in such manner as may be prescribed by the Central Government in consultation with the Comptroller and Auditor-General of India.

(2) The accounts of the Authorities shall be audited by the Comptroller and Auditor-General of India at such intervals as may be specified by him and any expenditure incurred in connection with such audit shall be payable by the Authority concerned to the Comptroller and Auditor-General of India.

(3) The Comptroller and Auditor-General of India and any other person appointed by him in connection with the auditing of the accounts of an Authority under this Act shall have the same rights and privileges and authority in connection with such audit as the Comptroller and Auditor-General of India has in connection with the auditing of the Government accounts and, in particular, shall have the right to demand the production of books, accounts, connected vouchers and other documents and papers and to inspect any of the offices of the Authorities under this Act.

(4) The accounts of the Authorities, as certified by the Comptroller and Auditor-General of India or any other person appointed by him in this behalf together with the audit report thereon, shall be forwarded annually by the Authorities to the Central Government or the State Governments as the case may be.

[2][(5) The Central Government shall cause the accounts and the audit report received by it under sub-section (4) to be laid, as soon as may be after they are received, before each House of Parliament.

(6) The State Government shall cause the accounts and the audit report received by it under sub-section (4) to be laid, as soon as may be after they are received, before the State Legislature.]

CHAPTER VI
LOK ADALATS

[3][**19. Organisation of Lok Adalats.**—(1) Every State Authority or District Authority or the Supreme Court Legal Services Committee or every High Court Legal Services Committee or, as the case may be, Taluk Legal Services Committee may organise Lok Adalats at such intervals and places and for exercising such jurisdiction and for such areas as it thinks fit.

(2) Every Lok Adalat organised for an area shall consist of such number of—

(a) serving or retired judicial officers; and

(b) other persons,

of the area as may be specified by the State Authority or the District Authority or the Supreme Court Legal Services Committee or the High Court Legal Services Committee, or as the case may be, the Taluk Legal Services Committee, organising such Lok Adalat.

1. Ins. by Act 59 of 1994, sec. 13. (w.e.f. 29-10-1994).
2. Ins. by Act 59 of 1994, sec. 14 (w.e.f. 29-10-1994).
3. Subs. by Act 59 of 1994, sec. 15, for section 19 (w.e.f. 29-10-1994).

(3) The experience and qualifications of other persons referred to in clause (b) of sub-section (2) for Lok Adalats organised by the Supreme Court Legal Services Committee shall be such as may be prescribed by the Central Government in consultation with the Chief Justice of India.

(4) The experience and qualifications of other persons referred to in clause (b) of sub-section (2) for Lok Adalats other than referred to in sub-section (3) shall be such as may be prescribed by the State Government in consultation with the Chief Justice of the High Court.

(5) A Lok Adalat shall have jurisdiction to determine and to arrive at a compromise or settlement between the parties to a dispute in respect of—

(i) any case pending before; or

(ii) any matter which is falling within the jurisdiction of, and is not brought before,

any court for which the Lok Adalat is organised:

Provided that the Lok Adalat shall have no jurisdiction in respect of any case or matter relating to an offence not compoundable under any law.]

[1][**20. Cognizance of cases by Lok Adalats.**—(1) Where in any case referred to in clause (i) of sub-section (5) of section 19—

(i) (a) the parties thereof agree; or

(b) one of the parties thereof makes an application to the court,

for referring the case to the Lok Adalat for settlement and if such court is *prima facie* satisfied that there are chances of such settlement; or

(ii) the court is satisfied that the matter is an appropriate one to be taken cognizance of by the Lok Adalat,

the court shall refer the case to the Lok Adalat:

Provided that no case shall be referred to the Lok Adalat under sub-clause (b) of clause (i) or clause (ii) by such court except after giving a reasonable opportunity of being heard to the parties.

(2) Notwithstanding anything contained in any other law for the time being in force, the Authority or Committee organising the Lok Adalat under sub-section (1) of section 19 may, on receipt of an application from any one of the parties to any matter referred to in clause (ii) of sub-section (5) of section 19 that such matter needs to be determined by a Lok Adalat, refer such matter to the Lok Adalat, for determination:

Provided that no matter shall be referred to the Lok Adalat except after giving a reasonable opportunity of being heard to the other party.

(3) Where any case is referred to a Lok Adalat under sub-section (1) or where a reference has been made to it under sub-section (2), the Lok Adalat shall proceed to dispose of the case or matter and arrive at a compromise or settlement between the parties.

(4) Every Lok Adalat shall, while determining any reference before it under this Act, act with utmost expedition to arrive at a compromise or settlement between the parties and shall be guided by the principles of justice, equity, fair play and other legal principles.

(5) Where no award is made by the Lok Adalat on the ground that no compromise or settlement could be arrived at between the parties, the record of the case shall be returned by it to the court, from which the reference has been received under sub-section (1) for disposal in accordance with law.

---

1. Subs. by Act 59 of 1994, sec. 15, for section 20 (w.e.f. 29-10-1994).

(6) Where no award is made by the Lok Adalat on the ground that no compromise or settlement could be arrived at between the parties, in a matter referred to in sub-section (2), that Lok Adalat shall advice the parties to seek remedy in a court.

(7) Where the record of the case is returned under sub-section (5) to the court, such court shall proceed to deal with such case from the stage which was reached before such reference under sub-section (1).]

21. Award of Lok Adalat.—[1][(1) Every award of the Lok Adalat shall be deemed to be a decree of a civil court or, as the case may be, an order of any other court and where a compromise or settlement has been arrived at, by a Lok Adalat in a case referred to it under sub-section (1) of section 20, the court-free paid in such case shall be refunded in the manner provided under the Court Fees Act, 1870 (7 of 1870).]

(2) Every award made by a Lok Adalat shall be final and binding on all the parties to the dispute, and no appeal shall lie to any court against the award.

22. Powers of [2][Lok Adalat or Permanent Lok Adalat].—(1) The [2][Lok Adalat or Permanent Lok Adalat] shall, for the purposes of holding any determination under this Act, have the same powers as are vested in a civil court under the Code of Civil Procedure, 1908 (5 of 1908) while trying a suit in respect of the following matters, namely:—

(a) the summoning and enforcing the attendance of any witness and examining him on oath;

(b) the discovery and production of any document;

(c) the reception of evidence on affidavits;

(d) the requisitioning of any public record or document or copy of such record or document from any court or office; and

(e) such other matters as may be prescribed.

(2) Without prejudice to the generality of the powers contained in sub-section (1), every [3][Lok Adalat or Permanent Lok Adalat] shall have the requisite powers to specify its own procedure for the determination of any dispute coming before it.

(3) All proceedings before a [3][Lok Adalat or Permanent Lok Adalat] shall be deemed to be judicial proceedings within the meaning of sections 193, 219 and 228 of the Indian Penal Code (45 of 1860) and every [3][Lok Adalat or Permanent Lok Adalat] shall be deemed to be a civil court for the purpose of section 195 and Chapter XXVI of the Code of Criminal Procedure, 1973 (2 of 1974).

[4][*CHAPTER VIA*

PRE-LITIGATION CONCILIATION AND SETTLEMENT

22A. Definitions.—In this Chapter and for the purposes of sections 22 and 23, unless the context otherwise requires,—

(a) "Permanent Lok Adalat" means a Permanent Lok Adalat established under sub-section (1) of section 22B.

(b) "public utility service" means any—

(i) transport service for the carriage of passengers or goods by air, road or water; or

(ii) postal, telegraph or telephone service; or

1. Subs. by Act 59 of 1994, sec. 16, for sub-section (1) (w.e.f. 29-10-1994).
2. Subs. by Act 37 of 2002, sec. 3, for "Lok Adalat" (w.e.f. 11-6-2002).
3. Subs. by Act 37 of 2002, sec. 3, for "Lok Adalat" (w.e.f. 11-6-2002).
4. Chapter VIA (containing sections 22A to 22E) ins. by Act 37 of 2002, sec. 4 (w.e.f. 11-6-2002).

(iii) supply of power, light or water to the public by any establishment; or

(iv) system of public conservancy or sanitation; or

(v) service in hospital or dispensary; or

(vi) insurance service,

and includes any service which the Central Government or the State Government, as the case may be, may, in the public interest, by notification, declare to be a public utility service for the purposes of this Chapter.

22B. Establishment of Permanent Lok Adalats.—(1) Notwithstanding anything contained in section 19, the Central Authority or, as the case may be, every State Authority shall, by notification, establish Permanent Lok Adalats at such places and for exercising such jurisdiction in respect of one or more public utility services and for such areas as may be specified in the notification.

(2) Every Permanent Lok Adalat established for an area notified under sub-section (1) shall consist of—

(a) a person who is, or has been, a district judge or additional district judge or has held judicial office higher in rank than that of a district judge, shall be the Chairman of the Permanent Lok Adalat; and

(b) two other persons having adequate experience in public utility service to be nominated by the Central Government or, as the case may be, the State Government on the recommendation of the Central Authority or, as the case may be, the State Authority,

appointed by the Central Authority or, as the case may be, the State Authority, establishing such Permanent Lok Adalat and the other terms and conditions of the appointment of the Chairman and other persons referred to in clause (b) shall be such as may be prescribed by the Central Government.

22C. Cognizance of cases by Permanent Lok Adalat.—(1) Any party to a dispute may, before the dispute is brought before any court, make an application to the Permanent Lok Adalat for the settlement of dispute:

Provided that the Permanent Lok Adalat shall not have jurisdiction in respect of any matter relating to an offence not compoundable under any law:

Provided further that the Permanent Lok Adalat shall also not have jurisdiction in the matter where the value of the property in dispute exceeds ten lakh rupees:

Provided also that the Central Government, may, by notification, increase the limit of ten lakh rupees specified in the second proviso in consultation with the Central Authority.

(2) After an application is made under sub-section (1) to the Permanent Lok Adalat, no party to that application shall invoke jurisdiction of any court in the same dispute.

(3) Where an application is made to a Permanent Lok Adalat under sub-section (1), it—

(a) shall direct each party to the application to file before it a written statement, stating therein the facts and nature of dispute under the application points or issues in such dispute and grounds relied in support of, or in opposition to, such points or issues, as the case may be, and such party may supplement such statement with any document and other evidence which such party deems appropriate in proof of such facts and grounds and shall send a copy of such statement together with a copy of such document and other evidence, if any, to each of the parties to the application;

(b) may require any party to the application to file additional statement before it at any stage of the conciliation proceedings;

(c) shall communicate any document or statement received by it from any party to the application to the other party, to enable such other party to present reply thereto.

(4) When statement, additional statement and reply, if any, have been filed under sub-section (3), to the satisfaction of the Permanent Lok Adalat, it shall conduct conciliation proceedings between the parties to the application in such manner as it thinks appropriate taking into account the circumstances of the dispute.

(5) The Permanent Lok Adalat shall, during conduct of conciliation proceedings under sub-section (4), assist the parties in their attempt to reach an amicable settlement of the dispute in an independent and impartial manner.

(6) It shall be the duty of every party to the application to cooperate in good faith with the Permanent Lok Adalat in conciliation of the dispute relating to the application and to comply with the direction of the Permanent Lok Adalat to produce evidence and other related documents before it.

(7) When a Permanent Lok Adalat, in the aforesaid conciliation proceedings, is of opinion that there exist elements of settlement in such proceedings which may be acceptable to the parties, it may formulate the terms of a possible settlement of the dispute and give to the parties concerned for their observations and in case the parties reach at an agreement on the settlement of the dispute, they shall sign the settlement agreement and the Permanent Lok Adalat shall pass an award in terms thereof and furnish a copy of the same to each of the parties concerned.

(8) Where the parties fail to reach at an agreement under sub-section (7), the Permanent Lok Adalat shall, if the dispute does not relate to any offence, decide the dispute.

22D. Procedure of Permanent Lok Adalat.—The Permanent Lok Adalat shall, while conducting conciliation proceedings or deciding a dispute on merit under this Act, be guided by the principles of natural justice, objectivity, fair play, equity and other principles of justice, and shall not be bound by the Code of Civil Procedure, 1908 (5 of 1908) and the Indian Evidence Act, 1872 (1 of 1872).

22E. Award of Permanent Lok Adalat to be final.—(1) Every award of the Permanent Lok Adalat under this Act made either on merit or in terms of a settlement agreement shall be final and binding on all the parties thereto and on persons claiming under them.

(2) Every award of the Permanent Lok Adalat under this Act shall be deemed to be a decree of a civil court.

(3) The award made by the Permanent Lok Adalat under this Act shall be by a majority of the persons constituting the Permanent Lok Adalat.

(4) Every award made by the Permanent Lok Adalat under this Act shall be final and shall not be called in question in any original suit, application or execution proceeding.

(5) The Permanent Lok Adalat may transmit any award made by it to a civil court having local jurisdiction and such civil court shall execute the order as if it were a decree made by that court.]

CHAPTER VII
MISCELLANEOUS

[1][**23. Members and staff of Authorities, Committees and Lok Adalats to be public servants.**—The members including Member-Secretary or, as the case may be, Secretary of Central Authority, the State Authorities, the District Authorities, the Supreme Court Legal Services Committee, High Court Legal Services Committees, Taluk Legal Services

1. Subs. by Act 59 of 1994, sec. 17, for sections 23 and 24 (w.e.f. 29-10-1994).

Committees and officers and other employees of such Authorities, Committees and the [1][members of the Lok Adalats or persons constituting Permanent Lok Adalats] shall be deemed to be public servants within the meaning of section 21 of the Indian Penal Code (45 of 1860).

24. Protection of action taken in good faith.—No suit, prosecution or other legal proceedings shall lie against—

(a) the Central Government or the State Government;

(b) the Patron-in-Chief, Executive Chairman, members of, Members-Secretary or officers or other employees of the Central Authority;

(c) Patron-in-Chief, Executive Chairman, Member, Member-Secretary or officers or other employees of the State Authority;

(d) Chairman, Secretary, members or officers or other employees of the Supreme Court Legal Services Committee, High Court Legal Services Committees, Taluk Legal Services Committees or the District Authority; or

(e) any other person authorised by any of the Patron-in-Chief, Executive Chairman, Chairman, members, Member-Secretary referred to in sub-clauses (b) to (d),

for anything which is in good faith done or intended to be done under the provisions of this Act or any rule or regulation made thereunder.]

25. Act to have overriding effect.—The provisions of this Act shall have effect notwithstanding anything inconsistent therewith contained in any other law for the time being in force or in any instrument having effect by virtue of any law other than this Act.

26. Power to remove difficulties.—(1) If any difficulty arises in giving effect to the provision of this Act, the Central Government may, by order published in the Official Gazette, make such provisions not inconsistent with the provisions of this Act as appear to it to be necessary or expedient for removing the difficulty:

Provided that no such order shall be made after the expiry of a period of two years from the date on which this Act receives the assent of the President.

(2) Every order made under this section shall, as soon as may be after it is made, be laid before each House of Parliament.

[2][**27. Power of Central Government to make rules.**—(1) The Central Government in consultation with the Chief Justice of India may, by notification, make rules to carry out the provisions of this Act.

(2) In particular, and without prejudice to the generality of the foregoing power, such rules may provide for all or any of the following matters, namely:—

(a) the number, experience and qualifications of other members of the Central Authority under clause (c) of sub-section (2) of section 3;

(b) the experience and qualifications of the Member-Secretary of the Central Authority and his powers and functions under sub-section (3) of section 3;

(c) the terms of office and other conditions relating thereto, of members and Member-Secretary of the Central Authority under sub-section (4) of section 3;

(d) the number of officers and other employees of the Central Authority under sub-section (5) of section 3;

---

1. Subs. by Act 37 of 2002, sec. 5, for "members of the Lok Adalats" (w.e.f. 11-6-2002).
2. Subs. by Act 59 of 1994, sec. 18, for sections 27, 28 and 29 (w.e.f. 29-10-1994).

(e) the conditions of service and the salary and allowances of officers and other employees of the Central Authority under sub-section (6) of section 3;

(f) the number, experience and qualifications of members of the Supreme Court Legal Services Committee under clause (b) of sub-section (2) of section 3A;

(g) the experience and qualifications of Secretary of the Supreme Court Legal Services Committee under sub-section (3) of section 3A;

(h) the number of officers and other employees of the Supreme Court Legal Services Committee under sub-section (5) of section 3A and the conditions of service and the salary and allowances payable to them under sub-section (6) of that section;

(i) the upper limit of annual income of a person entitling him to legal services under clause (h) of section 12, if the case is before the Supreme Court;

(j) the manner in which the accounts of the Central Authority, the State Authority or the District Authority shall be maintained under section 18;

(k) the experience and qualifications of other persons of the Lok Adalats organised by the Supreme Court Legal Services Committee specified in sub-section (3) of section 19;

(l) other matters under clause (e) of sub-section (1) of section 22;

[1][(la) the other terms and conditions of appointment of the Chairman and other persons under sub-section (2) of section 22B;]

(m) any other matter which is to be, or may be prescribed.

28. Power of State Government to make rules.—(1) The State Government in consultation with the Chief Justice of the High Court may, by notification, make rules to carry out the provisions of this Act.

(2) In particular and without prejudice to the generality of the foregoing powers, such rules may provide for all or any of the following matters, namely:—

(a) the number, experience and qualifications of other members of the State Authority under clause (c) of sub-section (2) of section 6;

(b) the powers and functions of the Member-Secretary of the State Authority under sub-section (3) of section 6;

(c) the terms of office and other conditions relating thereto, of members and Member-Secretary of the State Authority under sub-section (4) of section 6;

(d) the number of officers and other employees of the State Authority under sub-section (5) of section 6;

(e) the conditions of service and the salary and allowances of officers and other employees of the State Authority under sub-section (6) of section 6;

(f) the experience and qualifications of Secretary of the High Court Legal Services Committee under sub-section (3) of section 8A;

(g) the number of officers and other employees of the High Court Legal Services Committee under sub-section (5) of section 8A and the conditions of service and the salary and allowances payable to them under sub-section (6) of that section;

(h) the number, experience and qualifications of members of the District Authority under clause (b) of sub-section (2) of section 9;

1. Ins. by Act 37 of 2002, sec. 6 (w.e.f. 11-6-2002).

(i) the number of officers and other employees of the District Authority under sub-section (5) of section 9;

(j) the conditions of service and the salary and allowances of the officers and other employees of the District Authority under sub-section (6) of section 9;

(k) the number, experience and qualifications of members of the Taluk Legal Services Committee under clause (b) of sub-section (2) of section 11A;

(l) the number of officers and other employees of the Taluk Legal Services Committee under sub-section (3) of section 11A;

(m) the conditions of service and the salary and allowances of officers and other employees of the Taluk Legal Services Committee under sub-section (4) of section 11A;

(n) the upper limit of annual income of a person entitling him to legal services under clause (h) of section 12, if the case is before a court, other than the Supreme Court;

(o) the experience and qualifications of other persons of the Lok Adalats other than referred to in sub-section (4) of section 19;

(p) any other matter which is to be, or may be, prescribed.

29. Power of Central Authority to make regulations.—(1) The Central Authority may, by notification, make regulations not inconsistent with the provisions of this Act and the rules made thereunder, to provide for all matters for which provision is necessary or expedient for the purposes of giving effect to the provisions of this Act.

(2) In particular and without prejudice to the generality of the foregoing power, such regulations may provide for all or any of the following matters, namely:—

(a) the powers and functions of the Supreme Court Legal Services Committee under sub-section (1) of section 3A;

(b) the terms of office and other conditions relating thereto, of the members and Secretary of the Supreme Court Legal Services Committee under sub-section (4) of section 3A.

29A. Power of State Authority to make regulations.—(1) The State Authority may, by notification, make regulations not inconsistent with the provisions of this Act and the rules made thereunder, to provide for all matters for which provision is necessary or expedient for the purposes of giving effect to the provisions of this Act.

(2) In particular, and without prejudice to the generality of the foregoing power, such regulations may provide for all or any of the following matters, namely:—

(a) the other functions to be performed by the State Authority under clause (d) of sub-section (2) of section 7;

(b) the powers and functions of the High Court Legal Services Committee under sub-section (1) of section 8A;

(c) the number, experience and qualifications of members of the High Court Legal Services Committee under clause (b) of sub-section (2) of section 8A;

(d) the terms of office and other conditions relating thereto, of the members and Secretary of the High Court Legal Services Committee under sub-section (4) of section 8A;

(e) the terms of office and other conditions relating thereto, of the members and Secretary of the District Authority under sub-section (4) of section 9;

(f) the number, experience and qualifications of members of the High Court Legal Services Committee under clause (b) of sub-section (2) of section 8A;

(g) other functions to be performed by the District Authority under clause (c) of sub-section (2) of section 10;

(h) the terms of office and other conditions relating thereto, of members and Secretary of the Taluk Legal Services Committee under sub-section (3) of section 11A.]

30. Laying of rules and regulations.—(1) Every rule made under this Act by the Central Government and every regulation made by the Central Authority thereunder shall be laid, as soon as may be after it is made, before each House of Parliament, while it is in session, for a total period of thirty days which may be comprised in one session or in two or more successive sessions, and if, before the expiry of the session immediately following the session or the successive sessions aforesaid, both Houses agree in making any modification in the rule or regulation, or both Houses agree that the rule or regulation should not be made, the rule or regulation shall thereafter have effect only in such modified form or be of no effect, as the case may be; so, however, that any such modification or annulment shall be without prejudice to the validity of anything previously done under that rule or regulation.

(2) Every rule made under this Act by a State Government and every regulation made by a State authority thereunder shall be laid, as soon as may be after it is made, before the State Legislature.

APPENDIX 10

DECLARATION OF BASIC PRINCIPLES OF JUSTICE FOR VICTIMS OF CRIME AND ABUSE OF POWER*

THE GENERAL ASSEMBLY

Recalling that the Sixth United Nations Congress on the Prevention of Crime and the Treatment of Offenders recommended that the United Nations should continue its present work on the development of guidelines and standards regarding abuse of economic and political power,

Cognizant that millions of people throughout the world suffer harm as a result of crime and the abuse of power and that the rights of these victims have not been adequately recognized,

Recognizing that the victims of crime and the victims of abuse of power, and also frequently their families, witnesses and others who aid them, are unjustly subjected to loss, damage or injury and that they may, in addition, suffer hardship when assisting in the prosecution of offenders,

1. Affirms the necessity of adopting national and international measures in order to secure the universal and effective recognition of, and respect for, the rights of victims of crime and of abuse of power.
2. Stresses the need to promote progress by all States in their efforts to that end, without prejudice to the rights of suspects or offenders.
3. Adopts the Declaration of Basic Principles of Justice for Victims of Crime and Abuse of Power, annexed to the present resolution, which is designed to assist Governments and the international community in their efforts to secure justice and assistance for victims of crime and victims of abuse of power.
4. Calls upon Member States to take the necessary steps to give effect to the provisions contained in the Declaration and, in order to curtail victimization as referred to hereinafter, endeavour:
   (a) To implement social, health, including mental health, educational, economic and specific crime prevention policies to reduce victimization and encourage assistance to victims in distress;
   (b) To promote community efforts and public participation in crime prevention;
   (c) To review periodically their existing legislation and practices in order to ensure responsiveness to changing circumstances, and to enact and enforce legislation proscribing acts that violate internationally recognized norms relating to human rights, corporate conduct, and other abuses of power;
   (d) To establish and strengthen the means of detecting, prosecuting and sentencing those guilty of crimes;
   (e) To promote disclosure of relevant information to expose official and corporate conduct to public scrutiny, and other ways of increasing responsiveness to public concerns;

---

* A/RES/40/34 29 November 1985, 96th plenary meeting.

(f) To promote the observance of codes of conduct and ethical norms, in particular international standards, by public servants, including law enforcement, correctional, medical, social service and military personnel, as well as the staff of economic enterprises;

(g) To prohibit practices and procedures conducive to abuse, such as secret places of detention and incommunicado detention;

(h) To co-operate with other States, through mutual judicial and administrative assistance, in such matters as the detection and pursuit of offenders, their extradition and the seizure of their assets, to be used for restitution to the victims.

5. Recommends that, at the international and regional levels, all appropriate measures should be taken:

(a) To promote training activities designed to foster adherence to United Nations standards and norms and to curtail possible abuses;

(b) To sponsor collaborative action-research on ways in which victimization can be reduced and victims aided, and to promote information exchanges on the most effective means of so doing;

(c) To render direct aid to requesting Governments designed to help them curtail victimization and alleviate the plight of victims;

(d) To develop ways and means of providing recourse for victims where national channels may be insufficient.

6. Requests the Secretary-General to invite Member States to report periodically to the General Assembly on the implementation of the Declaration, as well as on measures taken by them to this effect.

7. Also requests the Secretary-General to make use of the opportunities, which all relevant bodies and organizations within the United Nations system offer, to assist Member States, whenever necessary, in improving ways and means of protecting victims both at the national level and through international co-operation.

8. Further requests the Secretary-General to promote the objectives of the Declaration, in particular by ensuring its widest possible dissemination.

9. Urges the specialized agencies and other entities and bodies of the United Nations system, other relevant intergovernmental and non-governmental organizations and the public to co-operate in the implementation of the provisions of the Declaration.

ANNEXURE

DECLARATION OF BASIC PRINCIPLES OF JUSTICE FOR VICTIMS OF CRIME AND ABUSE OF POWER

A. VICTIMS OF CRIME

1. "Victims" means persons who, individually or collectively, have suffered harm, including physical or mental injury, emotional suffering, economic loss or substantial impairment of their fundamental rights, through acts or omissions that are in violation of criminal laws operative within Member States, including those laws proscribing criminal abuse of power.

2. A person may be considered a victim, under this Declaration, regardless of whether the perpetrator is identified, apprehended, prosecuted or convicted and regardless of the familial relationship between the perpetrator and the victim. The term "victim" also includes, where appropriate, the immediate family or dependants of the direct victim and persons who have suffered harm in intervening to assist victims in distress or to prevent victimization.

3. The provisions contained herein shall be applicable to all, without distinction of any kind, such as race, colour, sex, age, language, religion, nationality, political or other opinion, cultural beliefs or practices, property, birth or family status, ethnic or social origin, and disability.

Access to justice and fair treatment

4. Victims should be treated with compassion and respect for their dignity. They are entitled to access to the mechanisms of justice and to prompt redress, as provided for by national legislation, for the harm that they have suffered.

5. Judicial and administrative mechanisms should be established and strengthened where necessary to enable victims to obtain redress through formal or informal procedures that are expeditious, fair, inexpensive and accessible. Victims should be informed of their rights in seeking redress through such mechanisms.

6. The responsiveness of judicial and administrative processes to the needs of victims should be facilitated by:

(a) Informing victims of their role and the scope, timing and progress of the proceedings and of the disposition of their cases, especially where serious crimes are involved and where they have requested such information;

(b) Allowing the views and concerns of victims to be presented and considered at appropriate stages of the proceedings where their personal interests are affected, without prejudice to the accused and consistent with the relevant national criminal justice system;

(c) Providing proper assistance to victims throughout the legal process;

(d) Taking measures to minimize inconvenience to victims, protect their privacy, when necessary, and ensure their safety, as well as that of their families and witnesses on their behalf, from intimidation and retaliation;

(e) Avoiding unnecessary delay in the disposition of cases and the execution of orders or decrees granting awards to victims.

7. Informal mechanisms for the resolution of disputes, including mediation, arbitration and customary justice or indigenous practices, should be utilized where appropriate to facilitate conciliation and redress for victims.

Restitution

8. Offenders or third parties responsible for their behaviour should, where appropriate, make fair restitution to victims, their families or dependants. Such restitution should include the return of property or payment for the harm or loss suffered, reimbursement of expenses incurred as a result of the victimization, the provision of services and the restoration of rights.

9. Governments should review their practices, regulations and laws to consider restitution as an available sentencing option in criminal cases, in addition to other criminal sanctions.

10. In cases of substantial harm to the environment, restitution, if ordered, should include, as far as possible, restoration of the environment, reconstruction of the infrastructure, replacement of community facilities and reimbursement of the expenses of relocation, whenever such harm results in the dislocation of a community.

11. Where public officials or other agents acting in an official or *quasi*-official capacity have violated national criminal laws, the victims should receive restitution from the State whose officials or agents were responsible for the harm inflicted. In cases where the Government under whose authority the victimizing act or omission occurred is no longer in existence, the State or Government successor in title should provide restitution to the victims.

Compensation

12. When compensation is not fully available from the offender or other sources, States should endeavour to provide financial compensation to:

(a) Victims who have sustained significant bodily injury or impairment of physical or mental health as a result of serious crimes;

(b) The family, in particular dependants of persons who have died or become physically or mentally incapacitated as a result of such victimization.

13. The establishment, strengthening and expansion of national funds for compensation to victims should be encouraged. Where appropriate, other funds may also be established for this purpose, including those cases where the State of which the victim is a national is not in a position to compensate the victim for the harm.

Assistance

14. Victims should receive the necessary material, medical, psychological and social assistance through governmental, voluntary, community-based and indigenous means.

15. Victims should be informed of the availability of health and social services and other relevant assistance and be readily afforded access to them.

16. Police, justice, health, social service and other personnel concerned should receive training to sensitize them to the needs of victims, and guidelines to ensure proper and prompt aid.

17. In providing services and assistance to victims, attention should be given to those who have special needs because of the nature of the harm inflicted or because of factors such as those mentioned in paragraph 3 above.

B. VICTIMS OF ABUSE OF POWER

18. "Victims" means persons who, individually or collectively, have suffered harm, including physical or mental injury, emotional suffering, economic loss or substantial impairment of their fundamental rights, through acts or omissions that do not yet constitute violations of national criminal laws but of internationally recognized norms relating to human rights.

19. States should consider incorporating into the national law norms proscribing abuses of power and providing remedies to victims of such abuses. In particular, such remedies should include restitution and/or compensation, and necessary material, medical, psychological and social assistance and support.

20. States should consider negotiating multilateral international treaties relating to victims, as defined in paragraph 18.

21. States should periodically review existing legislation and practices to ensure their responsiveness to changing circumstances, should enact and enforce, if necessary, legislation proscribing acts that constitute serious abuses of political or economic power, as well as promoting policies and mechanisms for the prevention of such acts, and should develop and make readily available appropriate rights and remedies for victims of such acts.

APPENDIX 11

CRIME AND DISORDER ACT, 1998 (UK)

PART I

PREVENTION OF CRIME AND DISORDER

CHAPTER I

ENGLAND AND WALES

1. Anti-social behaviour orders.—(1) An application for an order under this section may be made by a relevant authority if it appears to the authority that the following conditions are fulfilled with respect to any person aged 10 or over, namely—

(a) that the person has acted, since the commencement date, in an anti-social manner, that is to say, in a manner that caused or was likely to cause harassment, alarm or distress to one or more persons not of the same household as himself; and

(b) that such an order is necessary to protect relevant persons from further anti-social acts by him.

(1A) in this section and sections 1B and 1E "relevant authority" means—

(a) the council for a local government area;

(b) the chief officer of police of any police force maintained for a police area;

(c) the chief constable of the British Transport Police Force; or

(d) any person registered under section 1 of the Housing Act, 1996 (c. 52) as a social landlord who provides or manages any houses or hostel in a local government area.

(1B) In this section "relevant persons" means—

(a) in relation to a relevant authority falling within paragraph (a) of sub-section (1A), persons within the local government area of that council;

(b) in relation to a relevant authority falling within paragraph (b) of that sub-section, persons within the police area;

(c) in relation to a relevant authority falling within paragraph (c) of that sub-section—

(i) persons who are on or likely to be on policed premises in a local government area; or

(ii) persons who are in the vicinity of or likely to be in the vicinity of such premises;

(d) in relation to a relevant authority falling within paragraph (d) of that sub-section—

(i) persons who are residing in or who are otherwise on or likely to be on premises provided or managed by that authority; or

(ii) persons who are in the vicinity of or likely to be in the vicinity of such premises.

***

(3) Such an application shall be made by complaint to the magistrates' court whose commission area includes the local government area or police area concerned.

(4) If, on such an application, it is proved that the conditions mentioned in sub-section (1) above are fulfilled, the magistrates' court may make an order under this section (an "anti-social behaviour order") which prohibits the defendant from doing anything described in the order.

(5) For the purpose of determining whether the condition mentioned in sub-section (1)(a) above is fulfilled, the court shall disregard any act of the defendant which he shows was reasonable in the circumstances.

(6) The prohibitions that may be imposed by an anti-social behaviour order are those necessary for the purpose of protecting persons (whether relevant persons or persons elsewhere in England and Wales) from further anti-social acts by the defendant.

(7) An anti-social behaviour order shall have effect for a period (not less than two years) specified in the order or until further order.

(8) Subject to sub-section (9) below, the applicant or the defendant may apply by complaint to the court which made an anti-social behaviour order for it to be varied or discharged by a further order.

(9) Except with the consent of both parties, no anti-social behaviour order shall be discharged before the end of the period of two years beginning with the date of service of the order.

(10) If without reasonable excuse a person does anything which he is prohibited from doing by an anti-social behaviour order, he is guilty of an offence and liable—

(a) on summary conviction, to imprisonment for a term not exceeding six months or to a fine not exceeding the statutory maximum, or to both; or

(b) on conviction on indictment, to imprisonment for a term not exceeding five years or to a fine, or to both.

(11) Where a person is convicted of an offence under sub-section (10) above, it shall not be open to the court by or before which he is so convicted to make an order under sub-section (1)(b) (conditional discharge) of section 12 of the Powers of Criminal Courts (Sentencing) Act, 2000 in respect of the offence.

(12) In this section—

"British Transport Police Force" means the force of constables appointed under section 53 of the British Transport Commission Act, 1949 (c. xxix);

"the commencement date" means the date of the commencement of this section;

"local government area" means—

(a) in relation to England, a district or London borough, the City of London, the Isle of Wight and the Isles of Scilly;

(b) in relation to Wales, a county or county borough.

"policed premises" has the meaning given by section 53(3) of the British Transport Commission Act, 1949.

1A. Power of Secretary of State to add to relevant authorities.—The Secretary of State may by order provide that the chief officer of a body of constables maintained otherwise than by a police authority is, in such cases and circumstances as may be prescribed by the order, to be a relevant authority for the purposes of section 1 above.

1C. Orders on conviction in criminal proceedings.—(1) This section applies where a person (the "offender") is convicted of a relevant offence.

(2) If the court considers—

(a) that the offender has acted, at any time since the commencement date, in an anti-social manner, that is to say in a manner that caused or was likely to cause harassment, alarm or distress to one or more persons not of the same household as himself, and

(b) that an order under this section is necessary to protect persons in any place in England and Wales from further anti-social acts by him, it may make an order which prohibits the offender from doing anything described in the order.

(3) The court may make an order under this section whether or not an application has been made for such an order.

(4) An order under this section shall not be made except—

(a) in addition to a sentence imposed in respect of the relevant offence; or

(b) in addition to an order discharging him conditionally.

(5) An order under this section takes effect on the day on which it is made, but the court may provide in any such order that such requirements of the order as it may specify shall, during any period when the offender is detained in legal custody, be suspended until his release from that custody.

(6) An offender subject to an order under this section may apply to the court which made it for it to be varied or discharged.

(7) In the case of an order under this section made by a magistrates' court, the reference in sub-section (6) to the court by which the order was made includes a reference to any magistrates' court acting for the same petty sessions area as that court.

(8) No application may be made under sub-section (6) for the discharge of an order before the end of the period of two years beginning with the day on which the order takes effect.

(9) Sub-sections (7), (10) and (11) of section 1 apply for the purposes of the making and effect of orders made by virtue of this section as they apply for the purposes of the making and effect of anti-social behaviour orders.

(10) In this section—

"the commencement date" has the same meaning as in section 1 above;

"the court" in relation to an offender means—

(a) the court by or before which he is convicted of the relevant offence; or

(b) if he is committed to the Crown Court to be dealt with for that offence, the Crown Court, and

"relevant offence" means an offence committed after the coming into force of section 64 of the Police Reform Act, 2002 (c. 30).

1D. Interim orders.—(1) The applications to which this section applies are—

(a) an application for an anti-social behaviour order; and

(b) an application for an order under section 1B.

(2) If, before determining an application to which this section applies, the court considers that it is just to make an order under this section pending the determination of that application ("the main application"), it may make such an order.

(3) An order under this section is an order which prohibits the defendant from doing anything described in the order.

(4) An order under this section—

(a) shall be for a fixed period;

(b) may be varied, renewed or discharged;

(c) shall, if it has not previously ceased to have effect, cease to have effect on the determination of the main application.

(5) Sub-sections (6), (8) and (10) to (12) of section 1 apply for the purposes of the making and effect of orders under this section as they apply for the purposes of the making and effect of anti-social behaviour orders.

1E. Consultation requirements.—(1) This section applies to—

(a) applications for an anti-social behaviour order; and

(b) applications for an order under section 1B.

(2) Before making an application to which this section applies, the council for a local government area shall consult the chief officer of police of the police force maintained for the police area within which that local government area lies.

(3) Before making an application to which this section applies, a chief officer of police shall consult the council for the local government area in which the person in relation to whom the application is to be made resides or appears to reside.

(4) Before making an application to which this section applies, a relevant authority other than a council for a local government area or a chief officer of police shall consult—

(a) the council for the local government area in which the person in relation to whom the application is to be made resides or appears to reside; and

(b) the chief officer of police of the police force maintained for the police area within which that local government area lies.

2. Sex offender orders.—(1) If it appears to a chief officer of police that the following conditions are fulfilled with respect to any person who he believes is in, or is intending to come to, his police area, namely:—

(a) that the person is a sex offender; and

(b) that the person has acted, since the relevant date, in such a way as to give reasonable cause to believe that an order under this section is necessary to protect the public in the United Kingdom, or any particular members of that public, from serious harm from him,

the chief officer may apply for an order under this section to be made in respect of the person.

(2) Such an application shall be made by complaint to—

(a) any magistrates' court; or

(b) any magistrates' court whose commission area includes any part of the applicant's police area,

whose commission area includes any place where it is alleged that the defendant acted in such a way as is mentioned in sub-section (1)(b) above.

(3) If, on such an application, it is proved that the conditions mentioned in sub-section (1) above are fulfilled, the magistrates' court may make an order under this section (a "sex offender order") which prohibits the defendant from doing anything described in the order.

(4) The prohibitions that may be imposed by a sex offender order are those necessary for the purpose of protecting the public in the United Kingdom, or any particular members of that public, from serious harm from the defendant.

(5) A sex offender order shall have effect for a period (not less than five years) specified in the order or until further order; and while such an order has effect, Part I of the Sex Offenders Act, 1997 shall have effect as if—

(a) the defendant were subject to the notification requirements of that Part; and

(b) in relation to the defendant, the relevant date (within the meaning of that Part) were the date of service of the order.

(6) Subject to sub-section (7) below, the applicant any other relevant chief officer of police or the defendant may apply by complaint to the appropriate court for the sex offender order to be varied or discharged by a further order.

(6A) In sub-section (6) above—

"the appropriate court" means—

(a) the court which made the sex offender order; or

(b) any magistrates' court whose commission area includes any part of the police area of the applicant or of any other relevant chief officer of police,

"relevant chief officer of police" means a chief officer of police who believes that the defendant is in, or is intending to come to, his police area.

(7) Except with the consent of both parties and subject to sub-section (7A) below, no sex offender order shall be discharged before the end of the period of five years beginning with the date of service of the order.

(7A) Where any magistrates' court makes a sex offender order in relation to a person who is already subject to such an order (whether made by that court or another), the earlier order is discharged by the making of the subsequent one.

(8) If without reasonable excuse a person does anything which he is prohibited from doing by a sex offender order, he is guilty of an offence and liable—

(a) on summary conviction, to imprisonment for a term not exceeding six months or to a fine not exceeding the statutory maximum, or to both; or

(b) on conviction on indictment, to imprisonment for a term not exceeding five years or to a fine, or to both.

(9) Where a person is convicted of an offence under sub-section (8) above, it shall not be open to the court by or before which he is so convicted to make an order under sub-section (1)(b) (conditional discharge) of section 12 of the Powers of Criminal Courts (Sentencing) Act, 2000 in respect of the offence.

2A. Interim orders: sex offenders.—(1) This section applies where an application for a sex offender order ("the main application") to a magistrates' court has not been determined.

(2) The applicant may apply by complaint to the court for an interim order, pending the determination of the main application.

(3) The court may make an interim order prohibiting the defendant from doing anything described in the order if it considers that it is appropriate to do so.

(4) An interim order—

(a) shall have effect for the period specified in the order;

(b) shall (if still in force) cease to have effect on the determination of the main application.

(5) While an interim order is in force, Part 1 of the Sex Offenders Act, 1997 (c. 51) shall have effect as if—

(a) the defendant were subject to the notification requirements of that Part; and

(b) in relation to him, the relevant date (within the meaning of that Part) were the date of service of the order.

(6) The applicant or the defendant may apply by complaint to the court which made the interim order for it to be varied or discharged by a further order.

(7) If without reasonable excuse a person does anything which he is prohibited from doing by an interim order, he is guilty of an offence.

(8) A person guilty of an offence under sub-section (7) above shall be liable—

(a) on summary conviction, to imprisonment for a term not exceeding six months or to a fine not exceeding the statutory maximum, or to both; or

(b) on conviction on indictment, to imprisonment for a term not exceeding five years or to a fine, or to both.

(9) Where a person is convicted of an offence under sub-section (7) above, it shall not be open to the court by or before which he is convicted to make an order under sub-section (1)(b) (conditional discharge) of section 12 of the Powers of Criminal Courts (Sentencing) Act, 2000 (c. 6) in respect of the offence.

2B. Sex offender orders made in Scotland or Northern Ireland.—(1) If without reasonable excuse a person does anything in England and Wales which he is prohibited from doing there by—

(a) an order under section 20(4) below; or

(b) an order under Article 6 or 6A of the Criminal Justice (Northern Ireland) Order 1998 (S.I. 1998/2839 (N.I. 20)),

he is guilty of an offence.

(2) A person who is guilty of an offence under sub-section (1) above shall be liable—

(a) on summary conviction, to imprisonment for a term not exceeding six months or to a fine not exceeding the statutory maximum, or to both; or

(b) on conviction on indictment, to imprisonment for a term not exceeding five years or to a fine, or to both.

(3) Where a person is convicted of an offence under sub-section (1) above, it shall not be open to the court by or before which he is convicted to make an order under sub-section (1)(b) (conditional discharge) of section 12 of the Powers of Criminal Courts (Sentencing) Act, 2000 in respect of the offence.

3. Sex offender orders: supplemental.—(1) In section 2 above and this section "sex offender" means a person who—

(a) has been convicted of a sexual offence to which Part I of the M2Sex Offenders Act, 1997 applies;

(b) has been found not guilty of such an offence by reason of insanity, or found to be under a disability and to have done the act charged against him in respect of such an offence;

(c) has been cautioned by a constable, in England and Wales or Northern Ireland, in respect of such an offence which, at the time when the caution was given, he had admitted; or

(d) has been punished under the law in force in a country or territory outside the United Kingdom for an act which—

(i) constituted an offence under that law; and

(ii) would have constituted a sexual offence to which that Part applies if it had been done in any part of the United Kingdom.

(2) In sub-section (1) of section 2 above "the relevant date", in relation to a sex offender, means—

(a) the date or, as the case may be, the latest date on which he has been convicted, found, cautioned or punished as mentioned in sub-section (1) above; or

(b) if later, the date of the commencement of that section.

(3) Sub-sections (2) and (3) of section 6 of the Sex Offenders Act, 1997 apply for the construction of references in sub-sections (1) and (2) above as they apply for the construction of references in Part I of that Act.

(4) In sub-sections (1) and (2) above, any reference to a person having been cautioned shall be construed as including a reference to his having been reprimanded or warned (under section 65 below) as a child or young person.

(5) An act punishable under the law in force in any country or territory outside the United Kingdom constitutes an offence under that law for the purposes of sub-section (1) above, however it is described in that law.

(6) Subject to sub-section (7) below, the condition in sub-section (1)(d)(i) above shall be taken to be satisfied unless, not later than rules of court may provide, the defendant serves on the applicant a notice—

(a) stating that, on the facts as alleged with respect to the act in question, the condition is not in his opinion satisfied;

(b) showing his grounds for that opinion; and

(c) requiring the applicant to show that it is satisfied.

(7) The court, if it thinks fit, may permit the defendant to require the applicant to show that the condition is satisfied without the prior service of a notice under sub-section (6) above.

4. Appeals against orders.—(1) An appeal shall lie to the Crown Court against the making by a magistrates' court of an anti-social behaviour order an order under section 1D above, a sex offender order or an order under section 2A above.

(2) On such an appeal the Crown Court—

(a) may make such orders as may be necessary to give effect to its determination of the appeal; and

(b) may also make such incidental or consequential orders as appear to it to be just.

(3) Any order of the Crown Court made on an appeal under this section (other than one directing that an application be re-heard by a magistrates' court) shall, for the purposes of section 1(8) or 2(6) above, be treated as if it were an order of the magistrates' court from which the appeal was brought and not an order of the Crown Court.

5. Authorities responsible for strategies.—(1) Subject to the provisions of this section, the functions conferred by section 6 below shall be exercisable in relation to each local government area by the responsible authorities, that is to say—

(a) the council for the area and, where the area is a district and the council is not a unitary authority, the council for the county which includes the district; and

(b) every chief officer of police any part of whose police area lies within the area.

(1A) The Secretary of State may by order provide in relation to any two or more local government areas in England—

(a) that the functions conferred by sections 6 to 7 below are to be carried out in relation to those areas taken together as if they constituted only one area; and

(b) that the persons who for the purposes of this Chapter are to be taken to be responsible authorities in relation to the combined area are the persons who comprise every person who (apart from the order) would be a responsible authority in relation to any one or more of the areas included in the combined area.

(1B) The Secretary of State shall not make an order under sub-section (1A) above unless—

(a) an application for the order has been made jointly by all the persons who would be the responsible authorities in relation to the combined area or the Secretary of State has first consulted those persons; and

(b) he considers it would be in the interests of reducing crime and disorder, or of combatting the misuse of drugs, to make the order.

(2) In exercising those functions, the responsible authorities shall act in co-operation with the following persons and bodies, namely—

(b) every local probation board any part of whose area lies within the area;

(c) every person or body of a description which is for the time being prescribed by order of the Secretary of State under this sub-section; and

(d) where they are acting in relation to an area in Wales, every person or body which is of a description which is for the time being prescribed by an order under this sub-section of the National Assembly for Wales,

and it shall be the duty of those persons and bodies to co-operate in the exercise by the responsible authorities of those functions.

(3) The responsible authorities shall also invite the participation in their exercise of those functions of at least one person or body of each description which is for the time being prescribed by order of the Secretary of State under this sub-section.

(4) In this section and sections 6 and 7 below "local government area" means—

(a) in relation to England, each district or London borough, the City of London, the Isle of Wight and the Isles of Scilly;

(b) in relation to Wales, each county or county borough.

6. Formulation and implementation of strategies.—(1) The responsible authorities for a local government area shall, in accordance with the provisions of section 5 above and this section, formulate and implement, for each relevant period,

(a) in the case of an area in England—

(i) a strategy for the reduction of crime and disorder in the area, and

(ii) a strategy for combatting the misuse of drugs in the area; and

(b) in the case of an area in Wales—

(i) a strategy for the reduction of crime and disorder in the area, and

(ii) a strategy for combatting substance misuse in the area.

(2) Before formulating a strategy, the responsible authorities shall—

(a) carry out, taking due account of the knowledge and experience of persons in the area, a review—

(i) in the case of an area in England, of the levels and patterns of crime and disorder in the area and of the level and patterns of the misuse of drugs in the area, and

(ii) in the case of an area in Wales, of the levels and patterns of crime and disorder in the area and of the level and patterns of substance misuse in the area;

(b) prepare an analysis of the results of that review;

(c) publish in the area a report of that analysis; and

(d) obtain the views on that report of persons or bodies in the area (including those of a description prescribed by order under section 5(3) above), whether by holding public meetings or otherwise.

(3) In formulating a strategy, the responsible authorities shall have regard to the analysis prepared under sub-section (2)(b) above and the views obtained under sub-section (2)(d) above.

(4) A strategy shall include—

(a) objectives to be pursued by the responsible authorities, by co-operating persons or bodies or, under agreements with the responsible authorities, by other persons or bodies; and

(b) long-term and short-term performance targets for measuring the extent to which such objectives are achieved.

(5) After formulating a strategy, the responsible authorities shall publish in the area a document which includes details of—

(a) co-operating persons and bodies;

(b) the review carried out under sub-section (2)(a) above;

(c) the report published under sub-section (2)(c) above; and

(d) the strategy, including in particular—

(i) the objectives mentioned in sub-section (4)(a) above and, in each case, the authorities, persons or bodies by whom they are to be pursued, and

(ii) the performance targets mentioned in sub-section (4)(b) above.

(6) While implementing a strategy, the responsible authorities shall keep it under review with a view to monitoring its effectiveness and making any changes to it that appear necessary or expedient.

(6A) Within one month of the end of each reporting period, the responsible authorities shall submit a report on the implementation of their strategies during that period—

(a) in the case of a report relating to the strategies for an area in England, to the Secretary of State; and

(b) in the case of a report relating to the strategies for an area in Wales, to the Secretary of State and to the National Assembly for Wales.

(7) In this section—

"co-operating persons or bodies" means persons or bodies co-operating in the exercise of the responsible authorities' functions under this section;

"relevant period" means—

(a) the period of three years beginning with such day as the Secretary of State may by order appoint; and

(b) each subsequent period of three years;

"reporting period" means every period of one year which falls within a relevant period and which begins—

(a) in the case of the first reporting period in the relevant period, with the day on which the relevant period begins; and

(b) in any other case, with the day after the day on which the previous reporting period ends;

"substance misuse" includes the misuse of drugs or alcohol.

6A. Powers of the Secretary of State and National Assembly for Wales.—(1) The Secretary of State may, by order, require—

(a) the responsible authorities for local government areas to formulate any section 6 strategy of theirs for the reduction of crime and disorder so as to include, in particular, provision for the reduction of—

(i) crime of a description specified in the order, or

(ii) disorder of a description so specified;

(b) the responsible authorities for local government areas in England to prepare any section 6 strategy of theirs for combatting the misuse of drugs so as to include in it a strategy for combatting, in the area in question, such other forms of substance misuse as may be specified or described in the order.

(2) After formulating any section 6 strategy (whether in a case in which there has been an order under sub-section or in any other case), the responsible authorities for a local government area shall send both—

(a) a copy of the strategy; and

(b) a copy of the document which they propose to publish under section 6(5), to the Secretary of State.

(3) It shall be the duty of the responsible authorities, when preparing any document to be published under section 6(5), to have regard to any guidance issued by the Secretary of State as to the form and content of the documents to be so published.

(4) If the responsible authorities for a local government area propose to make any changes to a section 6 strategy of theirs, they shall send copies of the proposed changes to the Secretary of State.

(5) In sub-sections (2) to (4)—

(a) references to the Secretary of State, in relation to responsible authorities for local government areas in Wales shall have effect as references to the Secretary of State and the National Assembly for Wales; and

(b) accordingly, guidance issued for the purposes of sub-section (3) in relation to local government areas in Wales must be issued by the Secretary of State and that Assembly acting jointly.

(6) In this section—

"responsible authorities" and "local government area" have same meanings as in sections 5 and 6;

"section 6 strategy" means a strategy required to be formulated under section 6(1); and

"substance misuse" has the same meaning as in section 6.

7. Supplemental.—(1) The responsible authorities for a local government area shall, whenever so required by the Secretary of State, submit to the Secretary of State a report on such matters connected with the exercise of their functions under section 6 above as may be specified in the requirement.

(2) A requirement under sub-section (1) above may specify the form in which a report is to be given.

(3) The Secretary of State may arrange, or require the responsible authorities to arrange, for a report under sub-section (1) above to be published in such manner as appears to him to be appropriate.

8. Parenting orders.—(1) This section applies where, in any court proceedings—

(a) a child safety order is made in respect of a child;

(b) an anti-social behaviour order or sex offender order is made in respect of a child or young person;

(c) a child or young person is convicted of an offence; or

(d) a person is convicted of an offence under section 443 (failure to comply with school attendance order) or section 444 (failure to secure regular attendance at school of registered pupil) of the Education Act, 1996.

(2) Subject to sub-section (3) and section 9(1) below [and to section 19(5) of, and paragraph 13(5) of Schedule 1 to, the Powers of Criminal Courts (Sentencing) Act, 2000], if in the proceedings the court is satisfied that the relevant condition is fulfilled, it may make a parenting order in respect of a person who is a parent or guardian of the child or young person or, as the case may be, the person convicted of the offence under section 443 or 444 ("the parent").

(3) A court shall not make a parenting order unless it has been notified by the Secretary of State that arrangements for implementing such orders are available in the area in which it appears to the court that the parent resides or will reside and the notice has not been withdrawn.

(4) A parenting order is an order which requires the parent—

(a) to comply, for a period not exceeding twelve months, with such requirements as are specified in the order; and

(b) subject to sub-section (5) below, to attend, for a concurrent period not exceeding three months and not more than once in any week, such counselling or guidance sessions as may be specified in directions given by the responsible officer,

and in this sub-section "week" means a period of seven days beginning with a Sunday.

(5) A parenting order may, but need not, include such a requirement as is mentioned in sub-section (4)(b) above in any case where such an order has been made in respect of the parent on a previous occasion.

(6) The relevant condition is that the parenting order would be desirable in the interests of preventing—

(a) in a case falling within paragraph (a) or (b) of sub-section (1) above, any repetition of the kind of behaviour which led to the child safety order, anti-social behaviour order or sex offender order being made;

(b) in a case falling within paragraph (c) of that sub-section, the commission of any further offence by the child or young person;

(c) in a case falling within paragraph (d) of that sub-section, the commission of any further offence under section 443 or 444 of the Education Act, 1996.

(7) The requirements that may be specified under sub-section (4)(a) above are those which the court considers desirable in the interests of preventing any such repetition or, as the case may be, the commission of any such further offence.

(8) In this section and section 9 below "responsible officer", in relation to a parenting order, means one of the following who is specified in the order, namely—

(a) an officer of a local probation board;

(b) a social worker of a local authority social services department; and

(bb) a person nominated by a person appointed as chief education officer under section 532 of the Education Act, 1996.

(c) a member of a youth offending team

9. Parenting orders: supplemental.—(1) Where a person under the age of 16 is convicted of an offence, the court by or before which he is so convicted—

(a) if it is satisfied that the relevant condition is fulfilled, shall make a parenting order; and

(b) if it is not so satisfied, shall state in open court that it is not and why it is not.

(1A) Sub-section (1) above has effect subject to section 19(5) of, and paragraph 13(5) of Schedule 1 to, the Powers of Criminal Courts (Sentencing) Act, 2000.

(2) Before making a parenting order—

(a) in a case falling within paragraph (a) of sub-section (1) of section 8 above;

(b) in a case falling within paragraph (b) or (c) of that sub-section, where the person concerned is under the age of 16; or

(c) in a case falling within paragraph (d) of that sub-section, where the person to whom the offence related is under that age, a court shall obtain and consider information about the person's family circumstances and the likely effect of the order on those circumstances.

(3) Before making a parenting order, a court shall explain to the parent in ordinary language—

(a) the effect of the order and of the requirements proposed to be included in it;

(b) the consequences which may follow (under sub-section (7) below) if he fails to comply with any of those requirements; and

(c) that the court has power (under sub-section (5) below) to review the order on the application either of the parent or of the responsible officer.

(4) Requirements specified in, and directions given under, a parenting order shall, as far as practicable, be such as to avoid—

(a) any conflict with the parent's religious beliefs; and

(b) any interference with the times, if any, at which he normally works or attends an educational establishment.

(5) If while a parenting order is in force it appears to the court which made it, on the application of the responsible officer or the parent, that it is appropriate to make an order under this sub-section, the court may make an order discharging the parenting order or varying it—

(a) by cancelling any provision included in it; or

(b) by inserting in it (either in addition to or in substitution for any of its provisions) any provision that could have been included in the order if the court had then had power to make it and were exercising the power.

(6) Where an application under sub-section (5) above for the discharge of a parenting order is dismissed, no further application for its discharge shall be made under that sub-section by any person except with the consent of the court which made the order.

(7) If while a parenting order is in force the parent without reasonable excuse fails to comply with any requirement included in the order, or specified in directions given by the responsible officer, he shall be liable on summary conviction to a fine not exceeding level 3 on the standard scale.

10. Appeals against parenting orders.—(1) An appeal shall lie—

(a) to the High Court against the making of a parenting order by virtue of paragraph (a) of sub-section (1) of section 8 above; and

(b) to the Crown Court against the making of a parenting order by virtue of paragraph (b) of that sub-section.

(2) On an appeal under sub-section (1) above the High Court or the Crown Court—

(a) may make such orders as may be necessary to give effect to its determination of the appeal; and

(b) may also make such incidental or consequential orders as appear to it to be just.

(3) Any order of the High Court or the Crown Court made on an appeal under sub-section (1) above (other than one directing that an application be re-heard by a magistrates' court) shall, for the purposes of sub-sections (5) to (7) of section 9 above, be treated as if it were an order of the court from which the appeal was brought and not an order of the High Court or the Crown Court.

(4) A person in respect of whom a parenting order is made by virtue of section 8(1)(c) above shall have the same right of appeal against the making of the order as if—

(a) the offence that led to the making of the order were an offence committed by him; and

(b) the order were a sentence passed on him for the offence.

(5) A person in respect of whom a parenting order is made by virtue of section 8(1)(d) above shall have the same right of appeal against the making of the order as if the order were a sentence passed on him for the offence that led to the making of the order.

(6) The Lord Chancellor may by order make provision as to the circumstances in which appeals under sub-section (1)(a) above may be made against decisions taken by courts on questions arising in connection with the transfer, or proposed transfer, of proceedings by virtue of any order under paragraph 2 of Schedule 11 (jurisdiction) to the Children Act, 1989 ("the 1989 Act").

(7) Except to the extent provided for in any order made under sub-section (6) above, no appeal may be made against any decision of a kind mentioned in that sub-section.

11. Child safety orders.—(1) Subject to sub-section (2) below, if a magistrates' court, on the application of a local authority, is satisfied that one or more of the conditions specified in sub-section (3) below are fulfilled with respect to a child under the age of 10, it may make an order (a "child safety order") which—

(a) places the child, for a period (not exceeding the permitted maximum) specified in the order, under the supervision of the responsible officer; and

(b) requires the child to comply with such requirements as are so specified.

(2) A court shall not make a child safety order unless it has been notified by the Secretary of State that arrangements for implementing such orders are available in the area in which it appears that the child resides or will reside and the notice has not been withdrawn.

(3) The conditions are—

(a) that the child has committed an act which, if he had been aged 10 or over, would have constituted an offence;

(b) that a child safety order is necessary for the purpose of preventing the commission by the child of such an act as is mentioned in paragraph (a) above;

(c) that the child has contravened a ban imposed by a curfew notice; and

(d) that the child has acted in a manner that caused or was likely to cause harassment, alarm or distress to one or more persons not of the same household as himself.

(4) The maximum period permitted for the purposes of sub-section (1)(a) above is three months or, where the court is satisfied that the circumstances of the case are exceptional, 12 months.

(5) The requirements that may be specified under sub-section (1)(b) above are those which the court considers desirable in the interests of—

(a) securing that the child receives appropriate care, protection and support and is subject to proper control; or

(b) preventing any repetition of the kind of behaviour which led to the child safety order being made.

(6) Proceedings under this section or section 12 below shall be family proceedings for the purposes of the 1989 Act or section 65 of the M8Magistrates' Courts Act, 1980 ("the 1980 Act"); and the standard of proof applicable to such proceedings shall be that applicable to civil proceedings.

(7) In this section "local authority" has the same meaning as in the 1989 Act.

(8) In this section and section 12 below, "responsible officer", in relation to a child safety order, means one of the following who is specified in the order, namely—

(a) a social worker of a local authority social services department; and

(b) a member of a youth offending team.

12. Child safety orders: supplemental.—(1) Before making a child safety order, a magistrates' court shall obtain and consider information about the child's family circumstances and the likely effect of the order on those circumstances.

(2) Before making a child safety order, a magistrates' court shall explain to the parent or guardian of the child in ordinary language—

(a) the effect of the order and of the requirements proposed to be included in it;

(b) the consequences which may follow (under sub-section (6) below) if the child fails to comply with any of those requirements; and

(c) that the court has power (under sub-section (4) below) to review the order on the application either of the parent or guardian or of the responsible officer.

(3) Requirements included in a child safety order shall, as far as practicable, be such as to avoid—

(a) any conflict with the parent's religious beliefs; and

(b) any interference with the times, if any, at which the child normally attends school.

(4) If while a child safety order is in force in respect of a child it appears to the court which made it, on the application of the responsible officer or a parent or guardian of the child, that it is appropriate to make an order under this sub-section, the court may make an order discharging the child safety order or varying it—

(a) by cancelling any provision included in it; or

(b) by inserting in it (either in addition to or in substitution for any of its provisions) any provision that could have been included in the order if the court had then had power to make it and were exercising the power.

(5) Where an application under sub-section (4) above for the discharge of a child safety order is dismissed, no further application for its discharge shall be made under that sub-section by any person except with the consent of the court which made the order.

(6) Where a child safety order is in force and it is proved to the satisfaction of the court which made it or another magistrates' court acting for the same petty sessions area, on the application of the responsible officer, that the child has failed to comply with any requirement included in the order, the court—

(a) may discharge the order and make in respect of him a care order under sub-section (1)(a) of section 31 of the 1989 Act; or

(b) may make an order varying the order—

(i) by cancelling any provision included in it, or

(ii) by inserting in it (either in addition to or in substitution for any of its provisions) any provision that could have been included in the order if the court had then had power to make it and were exercising the power.

(7) Sub-section (6)(a) above applies whether or not the court is satisfied that the conditions mentioned in section 31(2) of the 1989 Act are fulfilled.

13. Appeals against child safety orders.—(1) An appeal shall lie to the High Court against the making by a magistrates' court of a child safety order; and on such an appeal the High Court—

(a) may make such orders as may be necessary to give effect to its determination of the appeal; and

(b) may also make such incidental or consequential orders as appear to it to be just.

(2) Any order of the High Court made on an appeal under this section (other than one directing that an application be re-heard by a magistrates' court) shall, for the purposes of sub-sections (4) to (6) of section 12 above, be treated as if it were an order of the magistrates' court from which the appeal was brought and not an order of the High Court.

(3) Subsections (6) and (7) of section 10 above shall apply for the purposes of sub-section (1) above as they apply for the purposes of sub-section (1)(a) of that section.

14. Local child curfew schemes.—(1) A local authority or a chief officer of police] may make a scheme (a "local child curfew scheme") for enabling the authority or (as the case may be) the officer]—

(a) subject to and in accordance with the provisions of the scheme; and

(b) if, after such consultation as is required by the scheme, the authority or (as the case may be) the officer] considers it necessary to do so for the purpose of maintaining order,

to give a notice imposing, for a specified period (not exceeding 90 days), a ban to which sub-section (2) below applies.

(2) This sub-section applies to a ban on children of specified ages under being in a public place within a specified area—

(a) during specified hours (between 9 pm and 6 am); and

(b) otherwise than under the effective control of a parent or a responsible person aged 18 or over.

(3) Before making a local child curfew scheme, a local authority shall consult—

(a) every chief officer of police any part of whose police area lies within its area; and

(b) such other persons or bodies as it considers appropriate.

(3A) Before making a local child curfew scheme, a chief officer of police shall consult—

(a) every local authority any part of whose area lies within the area to be specified; and

(b) such other persons or bodies as he considers appropriate.

(4) A local child curfew scheme shall, if made by a local authority, be made under the common seal of the authority.

(4A) A local child curfew scheme shall not have effect until it is confirmed by the Secretary of State.

(5) The Secretary of State—

(a) may confirm, or refuse to confirm, a local child curfew scheme submitted under this section for confirmation; and

(b) may fix the date on which such a scheme is to come into operation,

and if no date is so fixed, the scheme shall come into operation at the end of the period of one month beginning with the date of its confirmation.

(6) A notice given under a local child curfew scheme (a "curfew notice") may specify different hours in relation to children of different ages.

(7) A curfew notice shall be given—

(a) by posting the notice in some conspicuous place or places within the specified area; and

(b) in such other manner, if any, as appears to the local authority or (as the case may be) the chief officer of police to be desirable for giving publicity to the notice.

(8) In this section—

"local authority" means—

(a) in relation to England, the council of a district or London borough, the Common Council of the City of London, the Council of the Isle of Wight and the Council of the Isles of Scilly;

(b) in relation to Wales, the council of a county or county borough;

"public place" has the same meaning as in Part II of the M9Public Order Act, 1986.

15. Contravention of curfew notices.—(1) Sub-sections (2) and (3) below apply where a constable has reasonable cause to believe that a child is in contravention of a ban imposed by a curfew notice.

(2) The constable shall, as soon as practicable, inform the local authority for the area that the child has contravened the ban.

(3) The constable may remove the child to the child's place of residence unless he has reasonable cause to believe that the child would, if removed to that place, be likely to suffer significant harm.

(4) In sub-section (1) of section 47 of the 1989 Act (local authority's duty to investigate)—

(a) in paragraph (a), after sub-paragraph (ii) there shall be inserted the following sub-paragraph—

"(iii) has contravened a ban imposed by a curfew notice within the meaning of Chapter I of Part I of the Crime and Disorder Act, 1998; or"; and

(b) at the end there shall be inserted the following paragraph—" In the case of a child falling within paragraph (a)(iii) above, the enquiries shall be commenced as soon as practicable and, in any event, within 48 hours of the authority receiving the information."

16. Removal of truants to designated premises etc.—(1) This section applies where a local authority—

(a) designates premises in a police area ("designated premises") as premises to which children and young persons of compulsory school age may be removed under this section; and

(b) notifies the chief officer of police for that area of the designation.

(2) A police officer of or above the rank of superintendent may direct that the powers conferred on a constable by sub-section (3) below—

(a) shall be exercisable as respects any area falling within the police area and specified in the direction; and

(b) shall be so exercisable during a period so specified,

and references in that sub-section to a specified area and a specified period shall be construed accordingly.

(3) If a constable has reasonable cause to believe that a child or young person found by him in a public place in a specified area during a specified period—

(a) is of compulsory school age; and

(b) is absent from a school without lawful authority,

the constable may remove the child or young person to designated premises, or to the school from which he is so absent.

(3A) The power of a police officer of or above the rank of superintendent under sub-section (2) to specify any area falling within a police area shall be exercisable by such an officer who is a member of the British Transport Police as if the reference in that sub-section to an area in the police area were a reference to—

(a) any area in or in the vicinity of any policed premises; or

(b) the whole or any part of any such premises,

and references in sub-section (3) to the specified area shall have effect accordingly.

(4) A child's or young person's absence from a school shall be taken to be without lawful authority unless it falls within sub-section (3) (leave, sickness, unavoidable cause or day set apart for religious observance) of section 444 of the M10Education Act, 1996.

(5) In this section—

"British Transport Police" means the force of constables appointed under section 53 of the British Transport Commission Act, 1949 (c. xxix);

"local authority" means—

(a) in relation to England, a county council, a district council whose district does not form part of an area that has a county council, a London borough council or the Common Council of the City of London,

(b) in relation to Wales, a county council or a county borough council;

"policed premises" has the meaning given by section 53(3) of the British Transport Commission Act, 1949;

"public place" has the same meaning as in section 14 above;

"school" has the same meaning as in the Education Act, 1996.

17. Duty to consider crime and disorder implications.—(1) Without prejudice to any other obligation imposed on it, it shall be the duty of each authority to which this section applies to exercise its various functions with due regard to the likely effect of the exercise of those functions on, and the need to do all that it reasonably can to prevent, crime and disorder in its area.

(2) This section applies to a local authority, a joint authority, the London Fire and Emergency Planning Authority, a police authority, a National Park authority and the Broads Authority.

(3) In this section—

"local authority" means a local authority within the meaning given by section 270(1) of the Local Government Act, 1972 or the Common Council of the City of London;

"joint authority" has the same meaning as in the Local Government Act, 1985;

"National Park authority" means an authority established under section 63 of the Environment Act, 1995.

18. Interpretation etc., of Chapter.—(1) In this Chapter—

"anti-social behaviour order" has the meaning given by section 1(4) above;

"chief officer of police" has the meaning given by section 101(1) of the Police Act, 1996;

"child safety order" has the meaning given by section 11(1) above;

"curfew notice" has the meaning given by section 14(6) above;

"local child curfew scheme" has the meaning given by section 14(1) above;

"parenting order" has the meaning given by section 8(4) above;

"police area" has the meaning given by section 1(2) of the Police Act, 1996;

"police authority" has the meaning given by section 101(1) of that Act;

"responsible officer"—

(a) in relation to a parenting order, has the meaning given by section 8(8) above;

(b) in relation to a child safety order, has the meaning given by section 11(8) above,

"sex offender order" has the meaning given by section 2(3) above.

(2) In this Chapter, "protecting the public from serious harm" shall be construed in accordance with section 161(4) of the Powers of Criminal Courts (Sentencing) Act, 2000.

(3) Where directions under a parenting order are to be given by an officer of a local probation board, the officer of a local probation board shall be an officer appointed for or assigned to the petty sessions area within which it appears to the court that the child or, as the case may be, the parent resides or will reside.

(4) Where the supervision under a child safety order is to be provided, or directions under a parenting order are to be given, by—

(a) a social worker of a local authority social services department; or

(b) a member of a youth offending team,

the social worker or member shall be a social worker of, or a member of a youth offending team established by, the local authority within whose area it appears to the court that the child or, as the case may be, the parent resides or will reside.

(5) For the purposes of this Chapter the Inner Temple and the Middle Temple form part of the City of London.

CHAPTER II
SCOTLAND

19. Anti-social behaviour orders.—(1) A local authority may make an application for an order under this section if it appears to the authority that the following conditions are fulfilled with respect to any person of or over the age of 16, namely—

(a) that the person has—

(i) acted in an anti-social manner, that is to say, in a manner that caused or was likely to cause alarm or distress, or

(ii) pursued a course of anti-social conduct, that is to say, pursued a course of conduct that caused or was likely to cause alarm or distress,

to one or more persons not of the same household as himself in the authority's area (and in this section "anti-social acts" and "anti-social conduct" shall be construed accordingly); and

(b) that such an order is necessary to protect persons in the authority's area from further anti-social acts or conduct by him.

(2) An application under sub-section (1) above shall be made by summary application to the sheriff within whose sheriffdom the alarm or distress was alleged to have been caused or to have been likely to be caused.

(3) On an application under sub-section (1) above, the sheriff may, if he is satisfied that the conditions mentioned in that sub-section are fulfilled, make an order under this section (an "anti-social behaviour order") which, for the purpose of protecting persons in the area of the local authority from further anti-social acts or conduct by the person against whom the order is sought, prohibits him from doing anything described in the order.

(4) For the purpose of determining whether the condition mentioned in sub-section (1)(a) is fulfilled, the sheriff shall disregard any act of the person in respect of whom the application is made which that person shows was reasonable in the circumstances.

(5) This section does not apply in relation to anything done before the commencement of this section.

(6) Nothing in this section shall prevent a local authority from instituting any legal proceedings otherwise than under this section against any person in relation to any anti-social act or conduct.

(7) In this section "conduct" includes speech and a course of conduct must involve conduct on at least two occasions.

(8) In this section and section 21 below "local authority" means a council constituted under section 2 of the Local Government etc., (Scotland) Act, 1994 and any reference to the area of such an authority is a reference to the local government area within the meaning of that Act for which it is so constituted.

20. Sex offender orders.—(1) An application for an order under this section may be made by a chief constable if it appears to him that the conditions mentioned in sub-section (2) below are fulfilled with respect to any person who he believes is in, or is intending to come to, the area of his police force.

(2) The conditions are—

(a) that the person in respect of whom the application for the order is made is—

(i) of or over the age of 16 years, and

(ii) a sex offender; and

(b) that the person has acted, since the relevant date, in such a way as to give reasonable cause to believe that an order under this section is necessary to protect the public in the United Kingdom, or any particular members of that public from serious harm from him.

(3) An application under sub-section (1) above shall be made by summary application to—

(a) the sheriff within whose sheriffdom the person is alleged to have acted as mentioned in sub-section (2)(b) above; or

(b) the sheriff whose sheriffdom includes any part of the area of the applicant's police force.

(4) On an application under sub-section (1) above the sheriff may—

(a) pending the determination of the application, make any such interim order as he considers appropriate; and

(b) if he is satisfied that the conditions mentioned in sub-section (2) above are fulfilled, make an order under this section ("a sex offender order") which prohibits the person in respect of whom it is made from doing anything described in the order.

(5) The prohibitions that may be imposed by an order made under sub-section (4) above are those necessary for the purpose of protecting the public in the United Kingdom, or any particular members of that public, from serious harm from the person in respect of whom the order is made.

(6) While a sex offender order has effect, Part I of the Sex Offenders Act, 1997 shall have effect as if—

(a) the person in respect of whom the order has been obtained were subject to the notification requirements of that Part; and

(b) in relation to that person, the relevant date (within the meaning of that Part) were the date on which the copy of the order was given or delivered to that person in accordance with sub-sections (8) and (9) of section 21 below.

(7) Section 3 above applies for the purposes of this section as it applies for the purposes of section 2 above with the following modifications—

(a) any reference in that section to the defendant shall be construed as a reference to the person in respect of whom the order is sought; and

(b) in sub-section (2) of that section, the reference to sub-section (1) of the said section 2 shall be construed as a reference to sub-section (2)(b) of this section.

(8) A constable may arrest without warrant a person whom he reasonably suspects of doing, or having done, anything prohibited by an order under sub-section (4)(a) above or a sex offender order.

21. Procedural provisions with respect to orders.—(1) Before making an application under—

(a) section 19(1) above;

(b) sub-section (7)(b)(i) below,

the local authority shall consult the relevant chief constable.

(2) Before making an application under section 20(1) above or sub-section (7)(b)(i) below, the chief constable shall consult the local authority within whose area the person in respect of whom the order is sought is for the time being.

(3) In sub-section (1) above "relevant chief constable" means the chief constable of the police force maintained under the Police (Scotland) Act, 1967 the area of which includes the area of the local authority making the application.

(4) A failure to comply with sub-section (1) or (2) above shall not affect the validity of an order made on any application to which either of those sub-sections applies.

(5) A record of evidence shall be kept on any summary application under section 19 or 20 above or sub-section (7)(b) below.

(6) Sub-sections (7) to (9) below apply to anti-social behaviour orders and sex offender orders and sub-sections (8) and (9) below apply to an order made under section 20(4)(a) above.

(7) An order to which this sub-section applies—

(a) shall have effect for a period specified in the order or indefinitely; and

(b) smay at any time be varied or revoked (in the case of a sex offender order, by the appropriate court for that order) on a summary application by—

(i) the local authority or, as the case may be, chief constable who obtained the order or, in the case of a sex offender order, any other relevant chief constable; or

(ii) the person subject to the order.

(7A) In sub-section (7) above—

"the appropriate court" means—

(a) the sheriff who made the sex offender order; or

(b) the sheriff whose sheriffdom includes any part of the area of the applicant's police force or of the police force of any other relevant chief constable;

"relevant chief constable" means a chief constable who believes that the accused is in, or is intending to come to, the area of his police force.

(7B) Where a sheriff makes a sex offender order in relation to a person who is already subject to such an order (whether made by that court or another), the earlier order is discharged by the making of the subsequent one.

(8) The clerk of the court by which an order to which this sub-section applies is made or varied shall cause a copy of the order as so made or varied to be—

(a) given to the person named in the order; or

(b) sent to the person so named by registered post or by the recorded delivery service.

(9) An acknowledgement or certificate of delivery of a letter sent under sub-section (8)(b) above issued by the Post Office shall be sufficient evidence of the delivery of the letter on the day specified in such acknowledgement or certificate.

(10) Where an appeal is lodged against the determination of an application under section 19 or 20 above or sub-section (7)(b) above, any order made on the application shall, without prejudice to the determination of an application under sub-section (7)(b) above made after the lodging of the appeal, continue to have effect pending the disposal of the appeal.

21A Sex offender orders made in England and Wales or Northern Ireland.—(1) If without reasonable excuse a person does anything in Scotland which he is prohibited from doing there by—

(a) an order under section 2(3) or 2A above; or

(b) an order under Article 6 or 6A of the Criminal Justice (Northern Ireland) Order, 1998 [(S.I. 1998/ 2839 (N.I. 20)],

he is guilty of an offence.

(2) A person who is guilty of an offence under sub-section (1) above shall be liable—

(a) on summary conviction, to imprisonment for a term not exceeding six months or to a fine not exceeding the statutory maximum, or to both; or

(b) on conviction on indictment, to imprisonment for a term not exceeding five years or to a fine, or to both.

22. Offences in connection with breach of orders.—(1) Subject to sub-section (3) below, if without reasonable excuse a person breaches an anti-social behaviour order by doing anything which he is prohibited from doing by the order, he shall be guilty of an offence and shall be liable—

(a) on summary conviction, to a term of imprisonment not exceeding six months or to a fine not exceeding the statutory maximum or to both; or

(b) on conviction on indictment, to imprisonment for a term not exceeding five years or to a fine or to both.

(2) Sub-section (3) applies where—

(a) the breach of the anti-social behaviour order referred to in sub-section (1) above consists in the accused having acted in a manner prohibited by the order which constitutes a separate offence (in this section referred to as the "separate offence"); and

(b) the accused has been charged with that separate offence.

(3) Where this sub-section applies, the accused shall not be liable to be proceeded against for an offence under sub-section (1) above but, subject to sub-section (4) below, the court which sentences him for that separate offence shall, in determining the appropriate sentence or disposal for that offence, have regard to—

(a) the fact that the offence was committed by him while subject to an anti-social behaviour order;

(b) the number of such orders to which he was subject at the time of the commission of the offence;

(c) any previous conviction of the accused of an offence under sub-section (1) above; and

(d) the extent to which the sentence or disposal in respect of any such previous conviction of the accused differed, by virtue of this sub-section, from that which the court would have imposed but for this sub-section.

(4) The court shall not, under sub-section (3) above, have regard to the fact that the separate offence was committed while the accused was subject to an anti-social behaviour order unless that fact is libelled in the indictment or, as the case may be, specified in the complaint.

(5) The fact that the separate offence was committed while the accused was subject to an anti-social behaviour order shall, unless challenged—

(a) in the case of proceedings on indictment, by giving notice of a preliminary objection under paragraph (b) of section 72 of the Criminal Procedure (Scotland) Act, 1995 ("the 1995 Act") or under that paragraph as applied by section 71(2) of that Act; or

(b) in summary proceedings, by preliminary objection before his plea is recorded,

be held as admitted.

(6) Subject to sub-section (7) below, sub-sections (1) to (5) above apply in relation to an order under section 20(4)(a) above and to a sex offender order as they apply in relation to an anti-social behaviour order.

(7) Sub-section (2) above as applied for the purposes of sub-section (6) above shall have effect with the substitution of the words "at the time at which he committed" for the words "which constitutes".

23. Anti-social behaviour as ground of eviction.—(1) ***

(2) ***

(3) ***

(4) For Ground 15 in Schedule 5 to the Housing (Scotland) Act, 1988 (eviction on ground of use of premises for immoral or illegal purposes etc.) there shall be substituted the following—

"Ground 15

The tenant, a person residing or lodging in the house with the tenant or a person visiting the house has—

(a) been convicted of—

(i) using or allowing the house to be used for immoral or illegal purposes; or

(ii) an offence punishable by imprisonment committed in, or in the locality of, the house; or

(b) acted in an anti-social manner in relation to a person residing, visiting or otherwise engaging in lawful activity in the locality; or

(c) pursued a course of anti-social conduct in relation to such a person as is mentioned in head (b) above.

In this Ground 'anti-social', in relation to an action or course of conduct, means causing or likely to cause alarm, distress, nuisance or annoyance, 'conduct' includes speech and a course of conduct must involve conduct on at least two occasions and 'tenant' includes any one of joint tenants."

(5) No person shall be liable to eviction under paragraph 2 or 7 of Schedule 3 to the Housing (Scotland) Act, 1987 or Ground 15 in Schedule 5 to the Housing (Scotland) Act, 1988 as substituted respectively by sub-sections (2), (3) and (4) above in respect of any act or conduct before the commencement of this section unless he would have been liable to be evicted under those paragraphs or, as the case may be, that Ground as they had effect before that substitution.

24. Noise-making equipment: police power of seizure.—(1) The Civic Government (Scotland) Act, 1982 shall be amended in accordance with this section.

(2) In section 54 (offence of playing instruments, etc.), after sub-section (2) there shall be inserted the following sub-sections—

"(2A) Where a constable reasonably suspects that an offence under sub-section (1) above has been committed in relation to a musical instrument or in relation to such a device as is mentioned in paragraph (c) of that sub-section, he may enter any premises on which he reasonably suspects that instrument or device to be and seize any such instrument or device he finds there.

(2B) A constable may use reasonable force in the exercise of the power conferred by sub-section (2A) above.

(2C) Schedule 2A to this Act (which makes provision in relation to the retention and disposal of property seized under sub-section (2A) above) shall have effect."

(3) In section 60 (powers of search and seizure)—

(a) in sub-section (5)—

(i) after the words "Nothing in" there shall be inserted the words "section 54(2A) of this Act or"; and

(ii) for the words from "which" to the end there shall be substituted the words "which is otherwise exercisable by a constable"; and

(b) in sub-section (6)—

(i) in paragraph (a), for the words from "in pursuance" to the word "vessel" there shall be substituted the words—"to enter and search—

(i) any premises in pursuance of section 54(2A) of this Act or of sub-section (1) above; or

(ii) any vehicle or vessel in pursuance of the said sub-section (1),"; and

(ii) in paragraph (c), after "under" there shall be inserted the words "section 54(2A) of this Act or".

(4) After Schedule 2 there shall be inserted the Schedule set out in Schedule 1 to this Act.

CHAPTER III
GREAT BRITAIN

25. Powers to require removal of masks etc.—(1) After sub-section (4) of section 60 (powers to stop and search in anticipation of violence) of the Criminal Justice and Public Order Act, 1994 ("the 1994 Act") there shall be inserted the following sub-section—

"(4A) This section also confers on any constable in uniform power—

(a) to require any person to remove any item which the constable reasonably believes that person is wearing wholly or mainly for the purpose of concealing his identity;

(b) to seize any item which the constable reasonably believes any person intends to wear wholly or mainly for that purpose."

(2) In sub-section (5) of that section, for the words "those powers" there shall be substituted the words "the powers conferred by sub-section (4) above".

(3) In sub-section (8) of that section, for the words "to stop or (as the case may be) to stop the vehicle" there shall be substituted the following paragraphs—

"(a) to stop, or to stop a vehicle; or

(b) to remove an item worn by him,".

26. Retention and disposal of things seized.—After section 60 of the 1994 Act there shall be inserted the following section—

"60A Retention and disposal of things seized under section 60.

(1) Any things seized by a constable under section 60 may be retained in accordance with regulations made by the Secretary of State under this section.

(2) The Secretary of State may make regulations regulating the retention and safe keeping, and the disposal and destruction in prescribed circumstances, of such things.

(3) Regulations under this section may make different provisions for different classes of things or for different circumstances.

(4) The power to make regulations under this section shall be exercisable by statutory instrument which shall be subject to annulment in pursuance of a resolution of either House of Parliament."

27. Power of arrest for failure to comply with requirement.—(1) In section 24(2) (arrestable offences) of the Police and Criminal Evidence Act, 1984 ("the 1984 Act"), after paragraph (n) there shall be inserted—

"(o) an offence under section 60(8)(b) of the Criminal Justice and Public Order Act, 1994 (failing to comply with requirement to remove mask etc.);".

(2) After section 60A of the 1994 Act there shall be inserted the following section—

"60B Arrest without warrant for offences under section 60: Scotland.—In Scotland, where a constable reasonably believes that a person has committed or is committing an offence under section 60(8) he may arrest that person without warrant."

PART II

CRIMINAL LAW

28. Meaning of.—"racially or religiously aggravated."

(1) An offence is racially or religiously aggravated for the purposes of sections 29 to 32 below if—

(a) at the time of committing the offence, or immediately before or after doing so, the offender demonstrates towards the victim of the offence hostility based on the victim's membership (or presumed membership) of a racial or religious group; or

(b) the offence is motivated (wholly or partly) by hostility towards members of a racial or religious group based on their membership of that group.

(2) In sub-section (1)(a) above—

"membership", in relation to a racial or religious group, includes association with members of that group;

"presumed" means presumed by the offender.

(3) It is immaterial for the purposes of paragraph (a) or (b) of sub-section (1) above whether or not the offender's hostility is also based, to any extent, on any other factor not mentioned in that paragraph.

(4) In this section "racial group" means a group of persons defined by reference to race, colour, nationality (including citizenship) or ethnic or national origins.

(5) In this section "religious group" means a group of persons defined by reference to religious belief or lack of religious belief.

29. Racially or religiously aggravated assaults.—(1) A person is guilty of an offence under this section if he commits—

(a) an offence under section 20 of the Offences Against the Person Act, 1861 (malicious wounding or grievous bodily harm);

(b) an offence under section 47 of that Act (actual bodily harm); or

(c) common assault,

which is racially or religiously aggravated for the purposes of this section.

(2) A person guilty of an offence falling within sub-section (1)(a) or (b) above shall be liable—

(a) on summary conviction, to imprisonment for a term not exceeding six months or to a fine not exceeding the statutory maximum, or to both;

(b) on conviction on indictment, to imprisonment for a term not exceeding seven years or to a fine, or to both.

(3) A person guilty of an offence falling within sub-section (1)(c) above shall be liable—

(a) on summary conviction, to imprisonment for a term not exceeding six months or to a fine not exceeding the statutory maximum, or to both;

(b) on conviction on indictment, to imprisonment for a term not exceeding two years or to a fine, or to both.

30. Racially or religiously aggravated criminal damage.—(1) A person is guilty of an offence under this section if he commits an offence under section 1(1) of the Criminal Damage Act, 1971 (destroying or damaging property belonging to another) which is racially or religiously aggravated for the purposes of this section.

(2) A person guilty of an offence under this section shall be liable—

(a) on summary conviction, to imprisonment for a term not exceeding six months or to a fine not exceeding the statutory maximum, or to both;

(b) on conviction on indictment, to imprisonment for a term not exceeding fourteen years or to a fine, or to both.

(3) For the purposes of this section, section 28(1)(a) above shall have effect as if the person to whom the property belongs or is treated as belonging for the purposes of that Act were the victim of the offence.

31. Racially or religiously aggravated public order offences.—(1) A person is guilty of an offence under this section if he commits—

(a) an offence under section 4 of the Public Order Act, 1986 (fear or provocation of violence);

(b) an offence under section 4A of that Act (intentional harassment, alarm or distress); or

(c) an offence under section 5 of that Act (harassment, alarm or distress),

which is racially or religiously aggravated for the purposes of this section.

(2) A constable may arrest without warrant anyone whom he reasonably suspects to be committing an offence falling within sub-section (1)(a) or (b) above.

(3) A constable may arrest a person without warrant if—

(a) he engages in conduct which a constable reasonably suspects to constitute an offence falling within sub-section (1)(c) above;

(b) he is warned by that constable to stop; and

(c) he engages in further such conduct immediately or shortly after the warning.

The conduct mentioned in paragraph (a) above and the further conduct need not be of the same nature.

(4) A person guilty of an offence falling within sub-section (1)(a) or (b) above shall be liable—

(a) on summary conviction, to imprisonment for a term not exceeding six months or to a fine not exceeding the statutory maximum, or to both;

(b) on conviction on indictment, to imprisonment for a term not exceeding two years or to a fine, or to both.

(5) A person guilty of an offence falling within sub-section (1)(c) above shall be liable on summary conviction to a fine not exceeding level 4 on the standard scale.

(6) If, on the trial on indictment of a person charged with an offence falling within sub-section (1)(a) or (b) above, the jury find him not guilty of the offence charged, they may find him guilty of the basic offence mentioned in that provision.

(7) For the purposes of sub-section (1)(c) above, section 28(1)(a) above shall have effect as if the person likely to be caused harassment, alarm or distress were the victim of the offence.

32. Racially or religiously aggravated harassment etc.—(1) A person is guilty of an offence under this section if he commits—

(a) an offence under section 2 of the M4Protection from Harassment Act, 1997 (offence of harassment); or

(b) an offence under section 4 of that Act (putting people in fear of violence),

which is racially or religiously aggravated for the purposes of this section.

(2) ***

(3) A person guilty of an offence falling within sub-section (1)(a) above shall be liable—

(a) on summary conviction, to imprisonment for a term not exceeding six months or to a fine not exceeding the statutory maximum, or to both;

(b) on conviction on indictment, to imprisonment for a term not exceeding two years or to a fine, or to both.

(4) A person guilty of an offence falling within sub-section (1)(b) above shall be liable—

(a) on summary conviction, to imprisonment for a term not exceeding six months or to a fine not exceeding the statutory maximum, or to both;

(b) on conviction on indictment, to imprisonment for a term not exceeding seven years or to a fine, or to both.

(5) If, on the trial on indictment of a person charged with an offence falling within sub-section (1)(a) above, the jury find him not guilty of the offence charged, they may find him guilty of the basic offence mentioned in that provision.

(6) If, on the trial on indictment of a person charged with an offence falling within sub-section (1)(b) above, the jury find him not guilty of the offence charged, they may find him guilty of an offence falling within sub-section (1)(a) above.

(7) Section 5 of the Protection from Harassment Act, 1997 (restraining orders) shall have effect in relation to a person convicted of an offence under this section as if the reference in sub-section (1) of that section to an offence under section 2 or 4 included a reference to an offence under this section.

Racially-aggravated offences: Scotland

33. Racially-aggravated offences.—After section 50 of the Criminal Law (Consolidation) (Scotland) Act, 1995 there shall be inserted the following section—

"Racially-aggravated harassment

50A. Racially-aggravated harassment.—(1) A person is guilty of an offence under this section if he—

(a) pursues a racially-aggravated course of conduct which amounts to harassment of a person and—

(i) is intended to amount to harassment of that person; or

(ii) occurs in circumstances where it would appear to a reasonable person that it would amount to harassment of that person; or

(b) acts in a manner which is racially aggravated and which causes, or is intended to cause, a person alarm or distress.

(2) For the purposes of this section a course of conduct or an action is racially aggravated if—

(a) immediately before, during or immediately after carrying out the course of conduct or action the offender evinces towards the person affected malice and ill-will based on that person's membership (or presumed membership) of a racial group; or

(b) the course of conduct or action is motivated (wholly or partly) by malice and ill-will towards members of a racial group based on their membership of that group.

(3) In sub-section (2)(a) above—

"membership", in relation to a racial group, includes association with members of that group;

"presumed" means presumed by the offender.

(4) It is immaterial for the purposes of paragraph (a) or (b) of sub-section (2) above whether or not the offender's malice and ill-will is also based, to any extent, on—

(a) the fact or presumption that any person or group of persons belongs to any religious group; or

(b) any other factor not mentioned in that paragraph.

(5) A person who is guilty of an offence under this section shall—

(a) on summary conviction, be liable to a fine not exceeding the statutory maximum, or imprisonment for a period not exceeding six months, or both such fine and such imprisonment; and

(b) on conviction on indictment, be liable to a fine or to imprisonment for a period not exceeding seven years, or both such fine and such imprisonment.

(6) In this section—

"conduct" includes speech;

"harassment" of a person includes causing the person alarm or distress;

"racial group" means a group of persons defined by reference to race, colour, nationality (including citizenship) or ethnic or national origins,

and a course of conduct must involve conduct on at least two occasions."

Miscellaneous.

34. Abolition of rebuttable presumption that a child is *doli incapax*.—The rebuttable presumption of criminal law that a child aged 10 or over is incapable of committing an offence is hereby abolished.

35. Effect of child's silence at trial.—In section 35 of the 1994 Act (effect of accused's silence at trial), the following provisions shall cease to have effect, namely—

(a) in sub-section (1), the words "who has attained the age of fourteen years"; and

(b) sub-section (6).

36. Abolition of death penalty for treason and piracy.—(1) In section 1 of the Treason Act (Ireland) 1537 (practising any harm etc., to, or slandering, the King, Queen or heirs apparent punishable as high treason), for the words "have and suffer such pains of death and" there shall be substituted the words "be liable to imprisonment for life and to such ".

(2) In the following enactments, namely—

(a) section II of the Crown of Ireland Act, 1542 (occasioning disturbance etc., to the Crown of Ireland punishable as high treason);

(b) section XII of the Act of Supremacy (Ireland) 1560 (penalties for maintaining or defending foreign authority);

(c) section 3 of the Reason Act, 1702 (endeavouring to hinder the succession to the Crown etc., punishable as high treason);

(d) section I of the Reason Act (Ireland) 1703 (which makes corresponding provision),

for the words "suffer pains of death" there shall be substituted the words "be liable to imprisonment for life".

(3) The following enactments shall cease to have effect, namely—

(a) the Treason Act, 1790;

(b) the Treason Act, 1795.

(4) In section 1 of the Treason Act, 1814 (form of sentence in case of high treason), for the words "such person shall be hanged by the neck until such person be dead", there shall be substituted the words "such person shall be liable to imprisonment for life".

(5) In section 2 of the Piracy Act, 1837 (punishment of piracy when murder is attempted), for the words "and being convicted thereof shall suffer death" there shall be substituted the words "and being convicted thereof shall be liable to imprisonment for life".

(6) The following enactments shall cease to have effect, namely—

(a) the Sentence of Death (Expectant Mothers) Act, 1931; and

(b) sections 32 and 33 of the Criminal Justice Act Northern Ireland 1945 (which make corresponding provision).

PART III

CRIMINAL JUSTICE SYSTEM

Youth justice

37. Aim of the youth justice system.—(1) It shall be the principal aim of the youth justice system to prevent offending by children and young persons.

(2) In addition to any other duty to which they are subject, it shall be the duty of all persons and bodies carrying out functions in relation to the youth justice system to have regard to that aim.

38. Local provision of youth justice services.—(1) It shall be the duty of each local authority, acting in co-operation with the persons and bodies mentioned in sub-section (2) below, to secure that, to such extent as is appropriate for their area, all youth justice services are available there.

(2) It shall be the duty of—

(a) every chief officer of police or police authority any part of whose police area lies within the local authority's area; and

(b) every local probation board Strategic Health Authority, or health authority any part of whose area lies within that area,

to co-operate in the discharge by the local authority of their duty under sub-section (1) above.

(3) The local authority and every person or body mentioned in sub-section (2) above shall have power to make payments towards expenditure incurred in the provision of youth justice services—

(a) by making the payments directly; or

(b) by contributing to a fund, established and maintained by the local authority, out of which the payments may be made.

(4) In this section and sections 39 to 41 below "youth justice services" means any of the following, namely—

(a) the provision of persons to act as appropriate adults to safeguard the interests of children and young persons detained or questioned by police officers;

(b) the assessment of children and young persons, and the provision for them of rehabilitation programmes, for the purposes of section 66(2) below;

(c) the provision of support for children and young persons remanded or committed on bail while awaiting trial or sentence;

(d) the placement in local authority accommodation of children and young persons remanded or committed to such accommodation under section 23 of the Children and Young Persons Act, 1969 ("the 1969 Act");

(e) the provision of reports or other information required by courts in criminal proceedings against children and young persons;

(f) the provision of persons to act as responsible officers in relation to parenting orders, child safety orders, reparation orders and action plan orders;

(g) the supervision of young persons sentenced to a probation order, a community service order or a combination order;

(h) the supervision of children and young persons sentenced to a detention and training order or a supervision order;

(i) the post-release supervision of children and young persons under section 37(4A) or 65 of the 1991 Act or section 31 of the Crime (Sentences) Act, 1997 ("the 1997 Act");

(j) the performance of functions under sub-section (1) of section 102 of the Powers of Criminal Courts (Sentencing) Act, 2000 (period of detention and training under detention and training orders) by such persons as may be authorised by the Secretary of State under that sub-section;

(k) the implementation of referral orders within the meaning of the Powers of Criminal Courts (sentencing) Act, 2000.

(5) The Secretary of State may by order amend sub-section (4) above so as to extend, restrict or otherwise alter the definition of "youth justice services" for the time being specified in that sub-section.

39. Youth offending teams.—(1) Subject to sub-section (2) below, it shall be the duty of each local authority, acting in co-operation with the persons and bodies mentioned in sub-section (3) below, to establish for their area one or more youth offending teams.

(2) Two (or more) local authorities acting together may establish one or more youth offending teams for both (or all) their areas; and where they do so—

(a) any reference in the following provisions of this section (except sub-section (4)(b)) to, or to the area of, the local authority or a particular local authority shall be construed accordingly; and

(b) the reference in sub-section (4)(b) to the local authority shall be construed as a reference to one of the authorities.

(3) It shall be the duty of—

(a) every chief officer of police any part of whose police area lies within the local authority's area; and

(b) every local probation board Strategic Health Authority, or health authority any part of whose area lies within that area,

to co-operate in the discharge by the local authority of their duty under sub-section (1) above.

(4) The local authority and every person or body mentioned in sub-section (3) above shall have power to make payments towards expenditure incurred by, or for purposes connected with, youth offending teams—

(a) by making the payments directly; or

(b) by contributing to a fund, established and maintained by the local authority, out of which the payments may be made.

(5) A youth offending team shall include at least one of each of the following, namely—

(a) an officer of a local probation board;

(b) a social worker of a local authority social services department;

(c) a police officer;

(d) a person nominated by a Primary Care Trust or a health authority any part of whose area lies within the local authority's area;

(e) a person nominated by the chief education officer appointed by the local authority under section 532 of the Education Act, 1996.

(6) A youth offending team may also include such other persons as the local authority thinks appropriate after consulting the persons and bodies mentioned in sub-section (3) above.

(7) It shall be the duty of the youth offending team or teams established by a particular local authority—

(a) to co-ordinate the provision of youth justice services for all those in the authority's area who need them; and

(b) to carry out such functions as are assigned to the team or teams in the youth justice plan formulated by the authority under section 40(1) below.

40. Youth justice plans.—(1) It shall be the duty of each local authority, after consultation with the relevant persons and bodies, to formulate and implement for each year a plan (a "youth justice plan") setting out—

(a) how youth justice services in their area are to be provided and funded; and

(b) how the youth offending team or teams established by them (whether alone or jointly with one or more other local authorities) are to be composed and funded, how they are to operate, and what functions they are to carry out.

(2) In sub-section (1) above "the relevant persons and bodies" means the persons and bodies mentioned in section 38(2) above and, where the local authority is a county council, any district councils whose districts form part of its area.

(3) The functions assigned to a youth offending team under sub-section (1)(b) above may include, in particular, functions under paragraph 7(b) of Schedule 2 to the 1989 Act (local authority's duty to take reasonable steps designed to encourage children and young persons not to commit offences).

(4) A local authority shall submit their youth justice plan to the Board established under section 41 below, and shall publish it in such manner and by such date as the Secretary of State may direct.

41. The Youth Justice Board.—(1) There shall be a body corporate to be known as the Youth Justice Board for England and Wales ("the Board").

(2) The Board shall not be regarded as the servant or agent of the Crown or as enjoying any status, immunity or privilege of the Crown; and the Board's property shall not be regarded as property of, or held on behalf of, the Crown.

(3) The Board shall consist of 10, 11 or 12 members appointed by the Secretary of State.

(4) The members of the Board shall include persons who appear to the Secretary of State to have extensive recent experience of the youth justice system.

(5) The Board shall have the following functions, namely—

(a) to monitor the operation of the youth justice system and the provision of youth justice services;

(b) to advise the Secretary of State on the following matters, namely—

(i) the operation of that system and the provision of such services,

(ii) how the principal aim of that system might most effectively be pursued,

(iii) the content of any national standards he may see fit to set with respect to the provision of such services, or the accommodation in which children and young persons are kept in custody; and

(iv) the steps that might be taken to prevent offending by children and young persons;

(c) to monitor the extent to which that aim is being achieved and any such standards met;

(d) for the purposes of paragraphs (a), (b) and (c) above, to obtain information from relevant authorities;

(e) to publish information so obtained;

(f) to identify, to make known and to promote good practice in the following matters, namely—

(i) the operation of the youth justice system and the provision of youth justice services,

(ii) the prevention of offending by children and young persons, and

(iii) working with children and young persons who are or are at risk of becoming offenders;

(g) to make grants, with the approval of the Secretary of State, to local authorities or other bodies for them to develop such practice, or to commission research in connection with such practice;

(h) themselves to commission research in connection with such practice.

(i) to enter into agreements for the provision of—

(i) secure accommodation within the meaning of section 75(7) below for the purpose of detaining persons in respect of whom a detention and training order is made under section 73 below or an order is made under section 77(3)(a) or 78(2) below,

(ii) accommodation which is or may be used for the purpose of detaining persons sentenced under section 53(1) or (3) of the 1933 Act,

(iii accommodation which is or may be used for the purpose of detaining persons dealt with under sub-section (4)(c) of section 23 of the 1969 Act, as that section has effect in relation to persons described in section 98(1) below,

(iv) accommodation which is or may be used for the purpose of detaining persons who are under the age of 18 when remanded in custody under section 128 of the 1980 Act,

(v) accommodation which is or may be used for the purpose of detaining persons sentenced when under the age of 18 and before 1st April 2000 to detention in a young offender institution under section 1A of the 1982 Act, and

(vi) accommodation which is or may be used for the purpose of detaining persons subject to secure training orders made before 1st April 2000 under section 1 of the 1994 Act;

but no agreement shall be made under this paragraph in relation to accommodation for persons who have attained the age of 18 unless it appears to the Board that it is expedient to enter into such an agreement for the operation of the youth justice system;

(j) to facilitate arrangements between the Secretary of State and any person providing—

(i) secure accommodation within the meaning of section 75(7) below to be used for detaining a person in accordance with a determination under section 75(1), 77(3)(a) or 78(2) below, or

(ii) accommodation to be used for detaining a person in accordance with a direction by the Secretary of State under section 53(1)(a) or (3)(a) of the 1933 Act;

(k) to offer assistance to local authorities in discharging their duty under section 61 of the 1991 Act, whether by acting as the agent of a local authority or facilitating arrangements under section 61(2), or otherwise; and

(l) annually—

(i) to assess future demand for secure accommodation for remanded and sentenced children and young persons,

(ii) to prepare a plan setting out how they intend to exercise, in the following three years, the functions described in paragraphs (i) and (k) above, and any function for the time being exercisable by the Board concurrently with the Secretary of State by virtue of sub-section (6)(b) below which relates to securing the provision of such accommodation, and

(iii) to submit the plan to the Secretary of State for approval.

(6) The Secretary of State may by order—

(a) amend sub-section (5) above so as to add to, subtract from or alter any of the functions of the Board for the time being specified in that sub-section; or

(b) provide that any function of his which is exercisable in relation to the youth justice system shall be exercisable concurrently with the Board.

(7) In carrying out their functions, the Board shall comply with any directions given by the Secretary of State and act in accordance with any guidance given by him.

(8) A relevant authority—

(a) shall furnish to the Board any information required for the purposes of sub-section (5)(a), (b) or (c) above; and

(b) whenever so required by the Board, shall submit to the Board a report on such matters connected with the discharge of their duties under the foregoing provisions of this Part as may be specified in the requirement,

A requirement under paragraph (b) above may specify the form in which a report is to be given.

(9) The Board may arrange, or require the relevant authority to arrange, for a report under sub-section (8)(b) above to be published in such manner as appears to the Board to be appropriate.

(10) In this section "relevant authority" means a local authority, a chief officer of police, a police authority, a local probation board a Strategic Health Authority, and a health authority.

(11) Schedule 2 to this Act (which makes further provision with respect to the Board) shall have effect.

42. Supplementary provisions.—(1) In the foregoing provisions of this Part and this section—

"chief officer of police" has the meaning given by section 101(1) of the Police Act, 1996;

"local authority" means—

(a) in relation to England, a county council, a district council whose district does not form part of an area that has a county council, a London borough council or the Common Council of the City of London,

(b) in relation to Wales, a county council or a county borough council;

"police authority" has the meaning given by section 101(1) of the Police Act, 1996;

"youth justice system" means the system of criminal justice in so far as it relates to children and young persons.

(2) For the purposes of those provisions, the Isles of Scilly form part of the county of Cornwall and the Inner Temple and the Middle Temple form part of the City of London.

(3) In carrying out any of their duties under those provisions, a local authority, a police authority, a local probation board a Strategic Health Authority, or a health authority shall act in accordance with any guidance given by the Secretary of State.

Time limits etc.

43. Time limits.—(1) In sub-section (2) of section 22 (time limits in relation to criminal proceedings) of the Prosecution of Offences Act, 1985 ("the 1985 Act"), for paragraphs (a) and (b) there shall be substituted the following paragraphs—

"(a) be made so as to apply only in relation to proceedings instituted in specified areas, or proceedings of, or against persons of, specified classes or descriptions;

(b) make different provision with respect to proceedings instituted in different areas, or different provision with respect to proceedings of, or against persons of, different classes or descriptions;".

(2) For sub-section (3) of that section there shall be substituted the following sub-section—

"(3) The appropriate court may, at any time before the expiry of a time limit imposed by the regulations, extend, or further extend, that limit; but the court shall not do so unless it is satisfied—

(a) that the need for the extension is due to—

(i) the illness or absence of the accused, a necessary witness, a judge or a magistrate,

(ii) a postponement which is occasioned by the ordering by the court of separate trials in the case of two or more accused or two or more offences, or

(iii) some other good and sufficient cause; and

(b) that the prosecution has acted with all due diligence and expedition."

(3) In sub-section (4) of that section, for the words from "the accused" to the end there shall be substituted the words "the appropriate court shall stay the proceedings".

(4) In sub-section (6) of that section—

(a) for the word "Where" there shall be substituted the words "Sub-section (6A) below applies where"; and

(b) for the words from "the overall time limit" to the end there shall be substituted the words "and is accordingly unlawfully at large for any period."

(5) After that sub-section there shall be inserted the following sub-section—

"(6A) The following, namely—

(a) the period for which the person is unlawfully at large; and

(b) such additional period (if any) as the appropriate court may direct, having regard to the disruption of the prosecution occasioned by—

(i) the person's escape or failure to surrender; and

(ii) the length of the period mentioned in paragraph (a) above,

shall be disregarded, so far as the offence in question is concerned, for the purposes of the overall time limit which applies in his case in relation to the stage which the proceedings have reached at the time of the escape or, as the case may be, at the appointed time."

(6) In sub-section (7) of that section, after the words "time limit," there shall be inserted the words "or to give a direction under sub-section (6A) above,".

(7) In sub-section (8) of that section, after the words "time limit" there shall be inserted the words "or to give a direction under sub-section (6A) above,".

(8) After sub-section (11) of that section there shall be inserted the following sub-section—

"(11ZA) For the purposes of this section, proceedings for an offence shall be taken to begin when the accused is charged with the offence or, as the case may be, an information is laid charging him with the offence."

44. Additional time limits for persons under 18.—After section 22 of the 1985 Act there shall be inserted the following section—

"22A Additional time limits for persons under 18—

(1) The Secretary of State may by regulations make provision—

(a) with respect to a person under the age of 18 at the time of his arrest in connection with an offence, as to the maximum period to be allowed for the completion of the stage beginning with his arrest and ending with the date fixed for his first appearance in court in connection with the offence ("the initial stage");

(b) with respect to a person convicted of an offence who was under that age at the time of his arrest for the offence or (where he was not arrested for it) the laying of the information charging him with it, as to the period within which the stage between his conviction and his being sentenced for the offence should be completed.

(2) Sub-section (2) of section 22 above applies for the purposes of regulations under sub-section (1) above as if—

(a) the reference in paragraph (d) to custody or overall time limits were a reference to time limits imposed by the regulations; and

(b) the reference in paragraph (e) to proceedings instituted before the commencement of any provisions of the regulations were a reference to a stage begun before that commencement.

(3) A magistrates' court may, at any time before the expiry of the time limit imposed by the regulations under sub-section (1)(a) above ("the initial stage time limit"), extend, or further extend, that limit; but the court shall not do so unless it is satisfied—

(a) that the need for the extension is due to some good and sufficient cause; and

(b) that the investigation has been conducted, and (where applicable) the prosecution has acted, with all due diligence and expedition.

(4) Where the initial stage time limit (whether as originally imposed or as extended or further extended under sub-section (3) above) expires before the person arrested is charged with the offence, he shall not be charged with it unless further evidence relating to it is obtained, and—

(a) if he is then under arrest, he shall be released;

(b) if he is then on bail under Part IV of the Police and Criminal Evidence Act, 1984, his bail (and any duty or conditions to which it is subject) shall be discharged.

(5) Where the initial stage time limit (whether as originally imposed or as extended or further extended under sub-section (3) above) expires after the person arrested is charged with the offence but before the date fixed for his first appearance in court in connection with it, the court shall stay the proceedings.

(6) Where—

(a) a person escapes from arrest; or

(b) a person who has been released on bail under Part IV of the Police and Criminal Evidence Act, 1984 fails to surrender himself at the appointed time,

and is accordingly unlawfully at large for any period, that period shall be disregarded, so far as the offence in question is concerned, for the purposes of the initial stage time limit.

(7) Sub-sections (7) to (9) of section 22 above apply for the purposes of this section, at any time after the person arrested has been charged with the offence in question, as if any reference (however expressed) to a custody or overall time limit were a reference to the initial stage time limit.

(8) Where a person is convicted of an offence in any proceedings, the exercise of the power conferred by sub-section (3) above shall not be called into question in any appeal against that conviction.

(9) Any reference in this section (however expressed) to a person being charged with an offence includes a reference to the laying of an information charging him with it."

45. Re-institution of stayed proceedings.—After section 22A of the 1985 Act there shall be inserted the following section—

"22B Re-institution of proceedings stayed under section 22(4) or 22A(5).

(1) This section applies where proceedings for an offence ("the original proceedings") are stayed by a court under section 22(4) or 22A(5) of this Act.

(2) If—

(a) in the case of proceedings conducted by the Director, the Director or a Chief Crown Prosecutor so directs;

(b) in the case of proceedings conducted by the Director of the Serious Fraud Office, the Commissioners of Inland Revenue or the Commissioners of Customs and Excise, that Director or those Commissioners so direct; or

(c) in the case of proceedings not conducted as mentioned in paragraph (a) or (b) above, a person designated for the purpose by the Secretary of State so directs,

fresh proceedings for the offence may be instituted within a period of three months (or such longer period as the court may allow) after the date on which the original proceedings were stayed by the court.

(3) Fresh proceedings shall be instituted as follows—

(a) where the original proceedings were stayed by the Crown Court, by preferring a bill of indictment;

(b) where the original proceedings were stayed by a magistrates' court, by laying an information.

(4) Fresh proceedings may be instituted in accordance with sub-sections (2) and (3)(b) above notwithstanding anything in section 127(1) of the Magistrates' Courts Act, 1980 (limitation of time).

(5) Where fresh proceedings are instituted, anything done in relation to the original proceedings shall be treated as done in relation to the fresh proceedings if the court so directs or it was done—

(a) by the prosecutor in compliance or purported compliance with section 3, 4, 7 or 9 of the Criminal Procedure and Investigations Act, 1996; or

(b) by the accused in compliance or purported compliance with section 5 or 6 of that Act.

(6) Where a person is convicted of an offence in fresh proceedings under this section, the institution of those proceedings shall not be called into question in any appeal against that conviction."

46. Date of first court appearance in bail cases.—(1) In sub-section (3) of section 47 of the 1984 Act (bail after arrest), for the words "sub-section (4)" there shall be substituted the words "sub-sections (3A) and (4)".

(2) After that sub-section there shall be inserted the following sub-section:—

"(3A) Where a custody officer grants bail to a person subject to a duty to appear before a magistrates' court, he shall appoint for the appearance—

(a) a date which is not later than the first sitting of the court after the person is charged with the offence; or

(b) where he is informed by the clerk to the justices for the relevant petty sessions area that the appearance cannot be accommodated until a later date, that later date."

Functions of courts etc.

47. Powers of youth courts.—(1) Where a person who appears or is brought before a youth court charged with an offence subsequently attains the age of 18, the youth court may, at any time—

(a) before the start of the trial;. . .

(b) . . . .

remit the person for trial F17. . . to a magistrates' court (other than a youth court) acting for the same petty sessions area as the youth court.

In this sub-section "the start of the trial" shall be construed in accordance with section 22(11B) of the 1985 Act.

(2) Where a person is remitted under sub-section (1) above—

(a) he shall have no right of appeal against the order of remission;

(b) the remitting court shall adjourn proceedings in relation to the offence; and

(c) sub-sections (3) and (4) below shall apply.

(3) The following, namely—

(a) section 128 of the 1980 Act; and

(b) all other enactments (whenever passed) relating to remand or the granting of bail in criminal proceedings,

shall have effect in relation to the remitting court's power or duty to remand the person on the adjournment as if any reference to the court to or before which the person remanded is to be brought or appear after remand were a reference to the court to which he is being remitted ("the other court").

(4) The other court may deal with the case in any way in which it would have power to deal with it if all proceedings relating to the offence which took place before the remitting court had taken place before the other court.

(5) After sub-section (3) of section 10 of the 1980 Act (adjournment of trial) there shall be inserted the following sub-section—

"(3A) A youth court shall not be required to adjourn any proceedings for an offence at any stage by reason only of the fact—

(a) that the court commits the accused for trial for another offence; or

(b) that the accused is charged with another offence."

(6) After sub-section (1) of section 24 of the 1980 Act (summary trial of information against child or young person for indictable offence) there shall be inserted the following sub-section—

"(1A) Where a magistrates' court—

(a) commits a person under the age of 18 for trial for an offence of homicide; or

(b) in a case falling within sub-section (1)(a) above, commits such a person for trial for an offence,

the court may also commit him for trial for any other indictable offence with which he is charged at the same time if the charges for both offences could be joined in the same indictment."

(7) In sub-section (2) of section 47 (procedure in youth courts) of the Children and Young Persons Act, 1933 ("the 1933 Act"), the words from the beginning to "court; and" shall cease to have effect.

48. Youth courts: power of stipendiary magistrates to sit alone.—(1) In paragraph 15 of Schedule 2 to the 1933 Act (constitution of youth courts)—

(a) in paragraph (a), after the word "shall", in the first place where it occurs, there shall be inserted the words "either consist of a metropolitan stipendiary magistrate sitting alone or" and the word "shall", in the other place where it occurs, shall cease to have effect;

(b) in paragraph (b), after the words "the chairman" there shall be inserted the words "(where applicable"; and

(c) in paragraph (c), after the words "the other members" there shall be inserted the words "(where applicable) ".

(2) In paragraph 17 of that Schedule, the words "or, if a metropolitan stipendiary magistrate, may sit alone" shall cease to have effect.

49. Powers of magistrates' courts exercisable by single justice etc.—(1) The following powers of a magistrates' court for any area may be exercised by a single justice of the peace for that area, namely—

(a) to extend bail or to impose or vary conditions of bail;

(b) to mark an information as withdrawn;

(c) to dismiss an information, or to discharge an accused in respect of an information, where no evidence is offered by the prosecution;

(d) to make an order for the payment of defence costs out of central funds;

(e) to request a pre-sentence report following a plea of guilty and, for that purpose, to give an indication of the seriousness of the offence;

(f) to request a medical report and, for that purpose, to remand the accused in custody or on bail;

(g) to remit an offender to another court for sentence;

(h) where a person has been granted police bail to appear at a magistrates' court, to appoint an earlier time for his appearance;

(i) to extend, with the consent of the accused, a custody time limit or an overall time limit;

(j) . . . .

(k) where an accused has been convicted of an offence, to order him to produce his driving licence;

(l) to give a direction prohibiting the publication of matters disclosed or exempted from disclosure in court;

(m) to give, vary or revoke directions for the conduct of a trial, including directions as to the following matters, namely—

(i) the timetable for the proceedings,

(ii) the attendance of the parties,

(iii) the service of documents (including summaries of any legal arguments relied on by the parties)

(iv) the manner in which evidence is to be given; and

(n) to give, vary or revoke orders for separate or joint trials in the case of two or more accused or two or more informations.

(2) Without prejudice to the generality of sub-section (1) of section 144 of the 1980 Act (rules of procedure)—

(a) rules under that section may, subject to sub-section (3) below, provide that any of the things which, by virtue of sub-section (1) above, are authorised to be done by a single justice of the peace for any area may, subject to any specified restrictions or conditions, be done by a justices' clerk for that area; and

(b) rules under that section which make such provision as is mentioned in paragraph (a) above may make different provision for different areas.

(3) Rules under that section which make such provision as is mentioned in sub-section (2) above shall not authorise a justices' clerk—

(a) without the consent of the prosecutor and the accused, to extend bail on conditions other than those (if any) previously imposed, or to impose or vary conditions of bail;

(b) to give an indication of the seriousness of an offence for the purposes of a pre-sentence report;

(c) to remand the accused in custody for the purposes of a medical report or, without the consent of the prosecutor and the accused, to remand the accused on bail for those purposes on conditions other than those (if any) previously imposed;

(d) to give a direction prohibiting the publication of matters disclosed or exempted from disclosure in court; or

(e) without the consent of the parties, to give, vary or revoke orders for separate or joint trials in the case of two or more accused or two or more informations.

(4) Before making any rules under that section which make such provision as is mentioned in sub-section (2) above in relation to any area, the Lord Chancellor shall consult justices of the peace and justices' clerks for that area.

(5) In this section and section 50 below "justices' clerk" has the same meaning as in section 144 of the 1980 Act.

50. Early administrative hearings.—(1) Where a person ("the accused") has been charged with an offence at a police station, the magistrates' court before whom he appears or is brought for the first time in relation to the charge may, unless the accused falls to be dealt with under section 51 below, consist of a single justice.

(2) At a hearing conducted by a single justice under this section – the accused shall be asked whether he wishes to be granted a right to representation funded by the Legal Services Commission as part of the Criminal Defence Service and, if he does, the justice shall decide whether or not to grant him such a right.

(3) At such a hearing the single justice—

(a) may exercise, subject to sub-section (2) above, such of his powers as a single justice as he thinks fit; and

(b) on adjourning the hearing, may remand the accused in custody or on bail.

(4) This section applies in relation to a justices' clerk as it applies in relation to a single justice; but nothing in sub-section (3)(b) above authorises such a clerk to remand the accused in custody or, without the consent of the prosecutor and the accused, to remand the accused on bail on conditions other than those (if any) previously imposed.

(5) ***

51. No committal proceedings for indictable-only offences.—(1) Where an adult appears or is brought before a magistrates' court ("the court") charged with an offence triable only on indictment ("the indictable-only offence"), the court shall send him forthwith to the Crown Court for trial—

(a) for that offence; and

(b) for any either-way or summary offence with which he is charged which fulfils the requisite conditions (as set out in sub-section (11) below).

(2) Where an adult who has been sent for trial under sub-section (1) above subsequently appears or is brought before a magistrates' court charged with an either-

way or summary offence which fulfils the requisite conditions, the court may send him forthwith to the Crown Court for trial for the either-way or summary offence.

(3) Where—

(a) the court sends an adult for trial under sub-section (1) above;

(b) another adult appears or is brought before the court on the same or a subsequent occasion charged jointly with him with an either-way offence; and

(c) that offence appears to the court to be related to the indictable-only offence,

the court shall where it is the same occasion, and may where it is a subsequent occasion, send the other adult forthwith to the Crown Court for trial for the either-way offence.

(4) Where a court sends an adult for trial under sub-section (3) above, it shall at the same time send him to the Crown Court for trial for any either-way or summary offence with which he is charged which fulfils the requisite conditions.

(5) Where—

(a) the court sends an adult for trial under sub-section (1) or (3) above; and

(b) a child or young person appears or is brought before the court on the same or a subsequent occasion charged jointly with the adult with an indictable offence for which the adult is sent for trial,

the court shall, if it considers it necessary in the interests of justice to do so, send the child or young person forthwith to the Crown Court for trial for the indictable offence.

(6) Where a court sends a child or young person for trial under sub-section (5) above, it may at the same time send him to the Crown Court for trial for any either-way or summary offence with which he is charged which fulfils the requisite conditions.

(7) The court shall specify in a notice the offence or offences for which a person is sent for trial under this section and the place at which he is to be tried; and a copy of the notice shall be served on the accused and given to the Crown Court sitting at that place.

(8) In a case where there is more than one indictable-only offence and the court includes an either-way or a summary offence in the notice under sub-section (7) above, the court shall specify in that notice the indictable-only offence to which the either-way offence or, as the case may be, the summary offence appears to the court to be related.

(9) The trial of the information charging any summary offence for which a person is sent for trial under this section shall be treated as if the court had adjourned it under section 10 of the 1980 Act and had not fixed the time and place for its resumption.

(10) In selecting the place of trial for the purpose of sub-section (7) above, the court shall have regard to—

(a) the convenience of the defence, the prosecution and the witnesses;

(b) the desirability of expediting the trial; and

(c) any direction given by or on behalf of the Lord Chief Justice with the concurrence of the Lord Chancellor under section 75(1) of the Supreme Court Act, 1981.

(11) An offence fulfils the requisite conditions if—

(a) it appears to the court to be related to the indictable-only offence; and

(b) in the case of a summary offence, it is punishable with imprisonment or involves obligatory or discretionary disqualification from driving.

(12) For the purposes of this section—

(a) "adult" means a person aged 18 or over, and references to an adult include references to a corporation;

(b) "either-way offence" means an offence which, if committed by an adult, is triable either on indictment or summarily;

(c) an either-way offence is related to an indictable-only offence if the charge for the either-way offence could be joined in the same indictment as the charge for the indictable-only offence;

(d) a summary offence is related to an indictable-only offence if it arises out of circumstances which are the same as or connected with those giving rise to the indictable-only offence.

52. Provisions supplementing section 51.—(1) Subject to section 4 of the Bail Act, 1976, section 41 of the 1980 Act, regulations under section 22 of the 1985 Act and section 25 of the 1994 Act, the court may send a person for trial under section 51 above—

(a) in custody, that is to say, by committing him to custody there to be safely kept until delivered in due course of law; or

(b) on bail in accordance with the Bail Act, 1976, that is to say, by directing him to appear before the Crown Court for trial.

(2) Where—

(a) the person's release on bail under sub-section (1)(b) above is conditional on his providing one or more sureties; and

(b) in accordance with sub-section (3) of section 8 of the Bail Act, 1976, the court fixes the amount in which a surety is to be bound with a view to his entering into his recognisance subsequently in accordance with sub-sections (4) and (5) or (6) of that section,

the court shall in the meantime make an order such as is mentioned in sub-section (1)(a) above.

(3) The court shall treat as an indictable offence for the purposes of section 51 above an offence which is mentioned in the first column of Schedule 2 to the 1980 Act (offences for which the value involved is relevant to the mode of trial) unless it is clear to the court, having regard to any representations made by the prosecutor or the accused, that the value involved does not exceed the relevant sum.

(4) In sub-section (3) above "the value involved" and "the relevant sum" have the same meanings as in section 22 of the 1980 Act (certain offences triable either way to be tried summarily if value involved is small).

(5) A magistrates' court may adjourn any proceedings under section 51 above, and if it does so shall remand the accused.

(6) Schedule 3 to this Act (which makes further provision in relation to persons sent to the Crown Court for trial under section 51 above) shall have effect.

Miscellaneous

53. Crown Prosecution Service: powers of non-legal staff.—For section 7A of the 1985 Act there shall be substituted the following section—

"7A. ***Powers of non-legal staff***—

(1) The Director may designate, for the purposes of this section, members of the staff of the Crown Prosecution Service who are not Crown Prosecutors.

(2) Subject to such exceptions (if any) as may be specified in the designation, a person so designated shall have such of the following as may be so specified, namely—

(a) the powers and rights of audience of a Crown Prosecutor in relation to—

(i) applications for, or relating to, bail in criminal proceedings,

(ii) the conduct of criminal proceedings in magistrates' courts other than trials;

(b) the powers of such a Prosecutor in relation to the conduct of criminal proceedings not falling within paragraph (a)(ii) above.

(3) A person so designated shall exercise any such powers subject to instructions given to him by the Director.

(4) Any such instructions may be given so as to apply generally.

(5) For the purposes of this section—

(a) "bail in criminal proceedings" has the same meaning as it would have in the Bail Act, 1976 by virtue of the definition in section 1 of that Act if in that section "offence" did not include an offence to which sub-section (6) below applies;

(b) "criminal proceedings" does not include proceedings for an offence to which sub-section (6) below applies; and

(c) a trial begins with the opening of the prosecution case after the entry of a plea of not guilty and ends with the conviction or acquittal of the accused.

(6) This sub-section applies to an offence if it is triable only on indictment, or is an offence—

(a) for which the accused has elected to be tried by a jury;

(b) which a magistrates' court has decided is more suitable to be so tried; or

(c) in respect of which a notice of transfer has been given under section 4 of the Criminal Justice Act, 1987 or section 53 of the Criminal Justice Act, 1991.

(7) Details of the following for any year, namely—

(a) the criteria applied by the Director in determining whether to designate persons under this section;

(b) the training undergone by persons so designated; and

(c) any general instructions given by the Director under sub-section (4) above,

shall be set out in the Director's report under section 9 of this Act for that year."

54. Bail: increased powers to require security or impose conditions.—(1) In sub-section (5) of section 3 of the Bail Act, 1976 (general provisions as to bail), the words "If it appears that he is unlikely to remain in Great Britain until the time appointed for him to surrender to custody" shall cease to have effect.

(2) In sub-section (6) of that section, after paragraph (d) there shall be inserted the following paragraph—

"(e) before the time appointed for him to surrender to custody, he attends an interview with an authorised advocate or authorised litigator, as defined by section 119(1) of the Courts and Legal Services Act, 1990;".

(3) In sub-section (2) of section 3A of that Act (conditions of bail in the case of police bail), for the words "paragraph (d)" there shall be substituted the words "paragraph (d) or (e)".

55. Forfeiture of recognizances.—For sub-sections (1) and (2) of section 120 of the 1980 Act (forfeiture of recognizances) there shall be substituted the following sub-sections—

"(1) This section applies where—

(a) a recognizance to keep the peace or to be of good behaviour has been entered into before a magistrates' court; or

(b) any recognizance is conditioned for the appearance of a person before a magistrates' court, or for his doing any other thing connected with a proceeding before a magistrates' court.

(1A) If, in the case of a recognizance which is conditioned for the appearance of an accused before a magistrates' court, the accused fails to appear in accordance with the condition, the court shall—

(a) declare the recognizance to be forfeited;

(b) issue a summons directed to each person bound by the recognizance as surety, requiring him to appear before the court on a date specified in the summons to show cause why he should not be adjudged to pay the sum in which he is bound,

and on that date the court may proceed in the absence of any surety if it is satisfied that he has been served with the summons.

(2) If, in any other case falling within sub-section (1) above, the recognizance appears to the magistrates' court to be forfeited, the court may—

(a) declare the recognizance to be forfeited; and

(b) adjudge each person bound by it, whether as principal or surety, to pay the sum in which he is bound,

but in a case falling within sub-section (1)(a) above, the court shall not declare the recognizance to be forfeited except by order made on complaint."

56. Bail: restrictions in certain cases of homicide or rape.—In sub-section (1) of section 25 of the 1994 Act (no bail for defendants charged with or convicted of homicide or rape after previous conviction of such offences), for the words "shall not be granted bail in those proceedings" there shall be substituted the words "shall be granted bail in those proceedings only if the court or, as the case may be, the constable considering the grant of bail is satisfied that there are exceptional circumstances which justify it".

57. Use of live television links at preliminary hearings.—(1) In any proceedings for an offence, a court may, after hearing representations from the parties, direct that the accused shall be treated as being present in the court for any particular hearing before the start of the trial if, during that hearing—

(a) he is held in custody in a prison or other institution; and

(b) whether by means of a live television link or otherwise, he is able to see and hear the court and to be seen and heard by it.

(2) A court shall not give a direction under sub-section (1) above unless—

(a) it has been notified by the Secretary of State that facilities are available for enabling persons held in custody in the institution in which the accused is or is to be so held to see and hear the court and to be seen and heard by it; and

(b) the notice has not been withdrawn.

(3) If in a case where it has power to do so a magistrates' court decides not to give a direction under sub-section (1) above, it shall give its reasons for not doing so.

(4) In this section "the start of the trial" has the meaning given by sub-section (11A) or (11B) of section 22 of the 1985 Act.

PART IV
DEALING WITH OFFENDERS
CHAPTER I
ENGLAND AND WALES
Sexual or violent offenders

58. ***

59. Effect of extended sentences.—For section 44 of the 1991 Act there shall be substituted the following section—

"44 Extended sentences for sexual or violent offenders—

(1) This section applies to a prisoner serving an extended sentence within the meaning of section 58 of the Crime and Disorder Act, 1998.

(2) Subject to the provisions of this section and section 51(2D) below, this Part, except sections 40 and 40A, shall have effect as if the term of the extended sentence did not include the extension period.

(3) Where the prisoner is released on licence under this Part, the licence shall, subject to any revocation under section 39(1) or (2) above, remain in force until the end of the extension period.

(4) Where, apart from this sub-section, the prisoner would be released unconditionally—

(a) he shall be released on licence; and

(b) the licence shall, subject to any revocation under section 39(1) or (2) above, remain in force until the end of the extension period.

(5) The extension period shall be taken to begin as follows—

(a) for the purposes of sub-section (3) above, on the date given by section 37(1) above;

(b) for the purposes of sub-section (4) above, on the date on which, apart from that sub-section, the prisoner would have been released unconditionally.

(6) Sections 33(3) and 33A(1) above and section 46 below shall not apply in relation to the prisoner.

(7) For the purposes of sections 37(5) and 39(1) and (2) above the question whether the prisoner is a long-term or short-term prisoner shall be determined by reference to the term of the extended sentence.

(8) In this section "extension period" has the same meaning as in section 58 of the Crime and Disorder Act, 1998."

60. Re-release of prisoners serving extended sentences.—After section 44 of the 1991 Act there shall be inserted the following section—

"44A Re-release of prisoners serving extended sentences—

(1) This section applies to a prisoner serving an extended sentence within the meaning of section 58 of the Crime and Disorder Act, 1998 who is recalled to prison under section 39(1) or (2) above.

(2) Subject to sub-section (3) below, the prisoner may require the Secretary of State to refer his case to the Board at any time.

(3) Where there has been a previous reference of the prisoner's case to the Board (whether under this section or section 39(4) above), the Secretary of State shall not be required to refer the case until after the end of the period of one year beginning with the disposal of that reference.

(4) On a reference—

(a) under this section; or

(b) under section 39(4) above,

the Board shall direct the prisoner's release if satisfied that it is no longer necessary for the protection of the public that he should be confined (but not otherwise).

(5) If the Board gives a direction under sub-section (4) above it shall be the duty of the Secretary of State to release the prisoner on licence."

Offenders dependent etc., on drugs

61. ***

62. ***

63. ***

64. ***

Young offenders: reprimands and warnings

65. Reprimands and warnings.—(1) Sub-sections (2) to (5) below apply where—

(a) a constable has evidence that a child or young person ("the offender") has committed an offence;

(b) the constable considers that the evidence is such that, if the offender were prosecuted for the offence, there would be a realistic prospect of his being convicted;

(c) the offender admits to the constable that he committed the offence;

(d) the offender has not previously been convicted of an offence; and

(e) the constable is satisfied that it would not be in the public interest for the offender to be prosecuted.

(2) Subject to sub-section (4) below, the constable may reprimand the offender if the offender has not previously been reprimanded or warned.

(3) The constable may warn the offender if—

(a) the offender has not previously been warned; or

(b) where the offender has previously been warned, the offence was committed more than two years after the date of the previous warning and the constable considers the offence to be not so serious as to require a charge to be brought;

but no person may be warned under paragraph (b) above more than once.

(4) Where the offender has not been previously reprimanded, the constable shall warn rather than reprimand the offender if he considers the offence to be so serious as to require a warning.

(5) The constable shall—

(a) where the offender is under the age of 17, give any reprimand or warning in the presence of an appropriate adult; and

(b) explain to the offender and, where he is under that age, the appropriate adult in ordinary language—

(i) in the case of a reprimand, the effect of sub-section (5)(a) of section 66 below,

(ii) in the case of a warning, the effect of sub-sections (1), (2), (4) and (5)(b) and (c) of that section, and any guidance issued under sub-section (3) of that section.

(6) The Secretary of State shall publish, in such manner as he considers appropriate, guidance as to—

(a) the circumstances in which it is appropriate to give reprimands or warnings, including criteria for determining—

(i) for the purposes of sub-section (3)(b) above, whether an offence is not so serious as to require a charge to be brought, and

(ii) for the purposes of sub-section (4) above, whether an offence is so serious as to require a warning;

(aa) the places where reprimands and warnings may be given;

(b) the category of constable by whom reprimands and warnings may be given; and

(c) the form which reprimands and warnings are to take and the manner in which they are to be given and recorded.

(7) In this section "appropriate adult", in relation to a child or young person, means—

(a) his parent or guardian or, if he is in the care of a local authority or voluntary organisation, a person representing that authority or organisation;

(b) a social worker of a local authority social services department;

(c) if no person falling within paragraph (a) or (b) above is available, any responsible person aged 18 or over who is not a police officer or a person employed by the police.

(8) No caution shall be given to a child or young person after the commencement of this section.

(9) Any reference (however expressed) in any enactment passed before or in the same Session as this Act to a person being cautioned shall be construed, in relation to any time after that commencement, as including a reference to a child or young person being reprimanded or warned.

66. Effect of reprimands and warnings.—(1) Where a constable warns a person under section 65 above, he shall as soon as practicable refer the person to a youth offending team.

(2) A youth offending team—

(a) shall assess any person referred to them under sub-section (1) above; and

(b) unless they consider it inappropriate to do so, shall arrange for him to participate in a rehabilitation programme.

(3) The Secretary of State shall publish, in such manner as he considers appropriate, guidance as to—

(a) what should be included in a rehabilitation programme arranged for a person under sub-section (2) above;

(b) the manner in which any failure by a person to participate in such a programme is to be recorded; and

(c) the persons to whom any such failure is to be notified.

(4) Where a person who has been warned under section 65 above is convicted of an offence committed within two years of the warning, the court by or before which he is so convicted—

(a) shall not make an order under sub-section (1)(b) (conditional discharge) of section 12 of the Powers of Criminal Courts (Sentencing) Act, 2000, in respect of the offence unless it is of the opinion that there are exceptional circumstances relating to the offence or the offender which justify its doing so; and

(b) where it does so, shall state in open court that it is of that opinion and why it is.

(5) The following, namely—

(a) any reprimand of a person under section 65 above;

(b) any warning of a person under that section; and

(c) any report on a failure by a person to participate in a rehabilitation programme arranged for him under sub-section (2) above,

may be cited in criminal proceedings in the same circumstances as a conviction of the person may be cited.

(6) In this section "rehabilitation programme" means a programme the purpose of which is to rehabilitate participants and to prevent them from re-offending.

Young offenders: non-custodial orders

67. ***

68. ***

69. ***

70. ***

71. ***

72. ***

73. ***

74. ***

75. ***

76. ***

77. ***

78. ***

79. ***

Sentencing: general

80. Sentencing guidelines.—(1) This section applies where the Court—

(a) is seised of an appeal against, or a reference under section 36 of the Criminal Justice Act, 1988 with respect to, the sentence passed for an offence; or

(b) receives a proposal under section 81 below in respect of a particular category of offence,

and in this section "the relevant category" means any category within which the offence falls or, as the case may be, the category to which the proposal relates.

(2) The Court shall consider—

(a) whether to frame guidelines as to the sentencing of offenders for offences of the relevant category; or

(b) where such guidelines already exist, whether it would be appropriate to review them.

(3) Where the Court decides to frame or revise such guidelines, the Court shall have regard to—

(a) the need to promote consistency in sentencing;

(b) the sentences imposed by courts in England and Wales for offences of the relevant category;

(c) the cost of different sentences and their relative effectiveness in preventing re-offending;

(d) the need to promote public confidence in the criminal justice system; and

(e) the views communicated to the Court, in accordance with section 81(4)(b) below, by the Sentencing Advisory Panel.

(4) Guidelines framed or revised under this section shall include criteria for determining the seriousness of offences, including (where appropriate) criteria for determining the weight to be given to any previous convictions of offenders or any failures of theirs to respond to previous sentences.

(5) In a case falling within sub-section (1)(a) above, guidelines framed or revised under this section shall, if practicable, be included in the Court's judgment in the appeal.

(6) Subject to sub-section (5) above, guidelines framed or revised under this section shall be included in a judgment of the Court at the next appropriate opportunity (having regard to the relevant category of offence).

(7) For the purposes of this section, the Court is seised of an appeal against a sentence if—

(a) the Court or a single judge has granted leave to appeal against the sentence under section 9 or 10 of the Criminal Appeal Act, 1968; or

(b) in a case where the judge who passed the sentence granted a certificate of fitness for appeal under section 9 or 10 of that Act, notice of appeal has been given,

and (in either case) the appeal has not been abandoned or disposed of.

(8) For the purposes of this section, the Court is seised of a reference under section 36 of the Criminal Justice Act, 1988 if it has given leave under sub-section (1) of that section and the reference has not been disposed of.

(9) In this section and section 81 below—

"the Court" means the criminal division of the Court of Appeal;

"offence" means an indictable offence.

81. The Sentencing Advisory Panel.—(1) The Lord Chancellor, after consultation with the Secretary of State and the Lord Chief Justice, shall constitute a sentencing panel to be known as the Sentencing Advisory Panel ("the Panel") and appoint one of the members of the Panel to be its chairman.

(2) Where, in a case falling within sub-section (1)(a) of section 80 above, the Court decides to frame or revise guidelines under that section for a particular category of offence, the Court shall notify the Panel.

(3) The Panel may at any time, and shall if directed to do so by the Secretary of State, propose to the Court that guidelines be framed or revised under section 80 above for a particular category of offence.

(4) Where the Panel receives a notification under sub-section (2) above or makes a proposal under sub-section (3) above, the Panel shall—

(a) obtain and consider the views on the matters in issue of such persons or bodies as may be determined, after consultation with the Secretary of State and the Lord Chief Justice, by the Lord Chancellor;

(b) formulate its own views on those matters and communicate them to the Court; and

(c) furnish information to the Court as to the matters mentioned in section 80(3)(b) and (c) above.

(5) The Lord Chancellor may pay to any member of the Panel such remuneration as he may determine.

82. ***

Miscellaneous and supplemental

83. Power to make confiscation orders on committal for sentence.—After sub-section (9) of section 71 of the Criminal Justice Act, 1988 (confiscation orders) there shall be inserted the following sub-section—

"(9A) Where an offender is committed by a magistrates' court for sentence under section 38 or 38A of the Magistrates' Courts Act, 1980 or section 56 of the M6Criminal Justice Act, 1967, this section and sections 72 to 74C below shall have effect as if the offender had been convicted of the offence in the proceedings before the Crown Court and not in the proceedings before the magistrates' court."

84. ***

85. ***

CHAPTER II

SCOTLAND

Sexual or violent offenders

86. Extended sentences for sex and violent offenders.—(1) After section 210 of the 1995 Act there shall be inserted the following section—

"210A Extended sentences for sex and violent offenders—

(1) Where a person is convicted on indictment of a sexual or violent offence, the court may, if it—

(a) intends, in relation to—

(i) a sexual offence, to pass a determinate sentence of imprisonment, or

(ii) a violent offence, to pass such a sentence for a term of four years or more; and

(b) considers that the period (if any) for which the offender would, apart from this section, be subject to a licence would not be adequate for the purpose of protecting the public from serious harm from the offender,

pass an extended sentence on the offender.

(2) An extended sentence is a sentence of imprisonment which is the aggregate of—

(a) the term of imprisonment ("the custodial term") which the court would have passed on the offender otherwise than by virtue of this section; and

(b) a further period ("the extension period") for which the offender is to be subject to a licence and which is, subject to the provisions of this section, of such length as the court considers necessary for the purpose mentioned in sub-section (1)(b) above.

(3) The extension period shall not exceed, in the case of—

(a) a sexual offence, ten years; and

(b) a violent offence, five years.

(4) A court shall, before passing an extended sentence, consider a report by a relevant officer of a local authority about the offender and his circumstances and, if the court thinks it necessary, hear that officer.

(5) The term of an extended sentence passed for a statutory offence shall not exceed the maximum term of imprisonment provided for in the statute in respect of that offence.

(6) Subject to sub-section (5) above, a sheriff may pass an extended sentence which is the aggregate of a custodial term not exceeding the maximum term

of imprisonment which he may impose and an extension period not exceeding three years.

(7) The Secretary of State may by order—

(a) amend paragraph (b) of sub-section (3) above by substituting a different period, not exceeding ten years, for the period for the time being specified in that paragraph; and

(b) make such transitional provision as appears to him to be necessary or expedient in connection with the amendment.

(8) The power to make an order under sub-section (7) above shall be exercisable by statutory instrument; but no such order shall be made unless a draft of the order has been laid before, and approved by a resolution of, each House of Parliament.

(9) An extended sentence shall not be imposed where the sexual or violent offence was committed before the commencement of section 86 of the Crime and Disorder Act, 1998.

(10) For the purposes of this section—

"licence" and "relevant officer" have the same meaning as in Part I of the Prisoners and Criminal Proceedings (Scotland) Act, 1993;

"sexual offence" means—

(i) rape;

(ii) clandestine injury to women;

(iii) abduction of a woman or girl with intent to rape or ravish;

(iv) assault with intent to rape or ravish;

(v) indecent assault;

(vi) lewd, indecent or libidinous behaviour or practices;

(vii) shameless indecency;

(viii) sodomy;

(ix) an offence under section 170 of the Customs and Excise Management Act, 1979 in relation to goods prohibited to be imported under section 42 of the Customs Consolidation Act, 1876, but only where the prohibited goods include indecent photographs of persons;

(x) an offence under section 52 of the Civic Government (Scotland) Act, 1982 (taking and distribution of indecent images of children);

(xi) an offence under section 52A of that Act (possession of indecent images of children);

(xii) an offence under section 1 of the Criminal Law (Consolidation) (Scotland) Act, 1995 (incest);

(xiii) an offence under section 2 of that Act (intercourse with a step-child);

(xiv) an offence under section 3 of that Act (intercourse with child under 16 by person in position of trust);

(xv) an offence under section 5 of that Act (unlawful intercourse with girl under 16);

(xvi) an offence under section 6 of that Act (indecent behaviour towards girl between 12 and 16);

(xvii) an offence under section 8 of that Act (abduction of girl under 18 for purposes of unlawful intercourse);

(xviii) an offence under section 10 of that Act (person having parental responsibilities causing or encouraging sexual activity in relation to a girl under 16); and

(xix) an offence under sub-section (5) of section 13 of that Act (homosexual offences);

"imprisonment" includes—

(i) detention under section 207 of this Act, and

(ii) detention under section 208 of this Act; and

"violent offence" means any offence (other than an offence which is a sexual offence within the meaning of this section) inferring personal violence.

(11) Any reference in sub-section (10) above to a sexual offence includes—

(a) a reference to any attempt, conspiracy or incitement to commit that offence; and

(b) except in the case of an offence in paragraphs (i) to (viii) of the definition of "sexual offence" in that sub-section, a reference to aiding and abetting, counselling or procuring the commission of that offence."

(2) In section 209 of the 1995 Act (supervised release orders), in sub-section (1)—

(a) after the word "convicted" there shall be inserted the words "on indictment";

(b) after the words "an offence" there shall be inserted the words "other than a sexual offence within the meaning of section 210A of this Act,"; and

(c) the words "not less than twelve months but" shall cease to have effect.

87. Further provision as to extended sentences.—After section 26 of the Prisoners and Criminal Proceedings (Scotland) Act, 1993 ("the 1993 Act") there shall be inserted the following section—

"Extended sentences

26A. Extended sentences.—(1) This section applies to a prisoner who, on or after the date on which section 87 of the Crime and Disorder Act, 1998 comes into force, has been made subject to an extended sentence within the meaning of section 210A of the 1995 Act (extended sentences).

(2) Subject to the provisions of this section, this Part of this Act, except section 1A, shall apply in relation to extended sentences as if any reference to a sentence or term of imprisonment was a reference to the custodial term of an extended sentence.

(3) Where a prisoner subject to an extended sentence is released on licence under this Part the licence shall, subject to any revocation under section 17 of this Act, remain in force until the end of the extension period.

(4) Where, apart from this sub-section, a prisoner subject to an extended sentence would be released unconditionally—

(a) he shall be released on licence; and

(b) the licence shall, subject to any revocation under section 17 of this Act, remain in force until the end of the extension period.

(5) The extension period shall be taken to begin as follows—

(a) for the purposes of sub-section (3) above, on the day following the date on which, had there been no extension period, the prisoner would have ceased to be on licence in respect of the custodial term;

(b) for the purposes of sub-section (4) above, on the date on which, apart from that sub-section, he would have been released unconditionally.

(6) Subject to section 1A(c) of this Act and section 210A(3) of the 1995 Act and to any direction by the court which imposes an extended sentence, where a prisoner is subject to two or more extended sentences, the extension period which is taken to begin in accordance with sub-section (5) above shall be the aggregate of the extension period of each of those sentences.

(7) For the purposes of sections 12(3) and 17(1) of this Act, and subject to sub-section (8) below, the question whether a prisoner is a long-term or short-term prisoner shall be determined by reference to the extended sentence.

(8) Where a short-term prisoner serving an extended sentence in respect of a sexual offence is released on licence under sub-section (4)(a) above, the provisions of section 17 of this Act shall apply to him as if he was a long-term prisoner.

(9)In relation to a prisoner subject to an extended sentence, the reference in section 17(5) of this Act to his sentence shall be construed as a reference to the extended sentence.

(10) For the purposes of this section "custodial term", "extension period" and "imprisonment" shall have the same meaning as in section 210A of the 1995 Act.

(11) In section 1A(c) and section 16(1)(a) of this Act, the reference to the date on which a prisoner would have served his sentence in full shall mean, in relation to a prisoner subject to an extended sentence, the date on which the extended sentence, as originally imposed by the court, would expire."

88. Re-release of prisoners serving extended sentences.—After section 3 of the 1993 Act there shall be inserted the following section—

"3A Re-release of prisoners serving extended sentences.

(1) This section applies to a prisoner serving an extended sentence within the meaning of section 210A of the 1995 Act (extended sentences) who has been recalled to prison under section 17(1) of this Act.

(2) Subject to sub-section (3) below, a prisoner to whom this section applies may require the Secretary of State to refer his case to the Parole Board—

(a) where his case has previously been referred to the Parole Board under this section or section 17(3) of this Act, not less than one year following the disposal of that referral;

(b) in any other case, at any time.

(3) Where a prisoner to whom this section applies is subject to another sentence which is not treated as a single sentence with the extended sentence, the Secretary of State shall not be required to refer his case to the Parole Board before he has served one half of that other sentence.

(4) Where the case of a prisoner to whom this section applies is referred to the Parole Board under this section or section 17(3) of this Act, the Board shall, if it is satisfied that it is no longer necessary for the protection of the public from serious harm that the prisoner should be confined (but not otherwise), direct that he should be released.

(5) If the Parole Board gives a direction under sub-section (4) above, the Secretary of State shall release the prisoner on licence."

Offenders dependent etc., on drugs

89. Drug treatment and testing orders.—After section 234A of the 1995 Act there shall be inserted the following section—

"234B. Drug treatment and testing order—

(1) This section applies where a person of 16 years of age or more is convicted of an offence, other than one for which the sentence is fixed by law,

committed on or after the date on which section 89 of the Crime and Disorder Act, 1998 comes into force.

(2) Subject to the provisions of this section, the court by or before which the offender is convicted may, if it is of the opinion that it is expedient to do so instead of sentencing him, make an order (a "drug treatment and testing order") which shall—

(a) have effect for a period specified in the order of not less than six months nor more than three years ("the treatment and testing period"); and

(b) include the requirements and provisions mentioned in section 234C of this Act.

(3) A court shall not make a drug treatment and testing order unless it—

(a) has been notified by the Secretary of State that arrangements for implementing such orders are available in the area of the local authority proposed to be specified in the order under section 234C(6) of this Act and the notice has not been withdrawn;

(b) has obtained a report by, and if necessary heard evidence from, an officer of the local authority in whose area the offender is resident about the offender and his circumstances; and

(c) is satisfied that—

(i) the offender is dependent on, or has a propensity to misuse, drugs;

(ii) his dependency or propensity is such as requires and is susceptible to treatment; and

(iii he is a suitable person to be subject to such an order.

(4) For the purpose of determining for the purposes of sub-section (3)(c) above whether the offender has any drug in his body, the court may by order require him to provide samples of such description as it may specify.

(5) A drug treatment and testing order or an order under sub-section (4) above shall not be made unless the offender expresses his willingness to comply with its requirements.

(6) The Secretary of State may by order—

(a) amend paragraph (a) of sub-section (2) above by substituting a different period for the minimum or the maximum period for the time being specified in that paragraph; and

(b) make such transitional provisions as appear to him necessary or expedient in connection with any such amendment.

(7) The power to make an order under sub-section (6) above shall be exercisable by statutory instrument; but no such order shall be made unless a draft of the order has been laid before and approved by resolution of each House of Parliament.

(8) A drug treatment and testing order shall be as nearly as may be in the form prescribed by Act of Adjournal."

90. Requirements and provisions to be included in drug treatment and testing orders.—After section 234B of the 1995 Act there shall be inserted the following section—

"234C. Requirements and provisions of drug treatment and testing orders—

(1) A drug treatment and testing order shall include a requirement ("the treatment requirement") that the offender shall submit, during the whole of the treatment and testing period, to treatment by or under the direction of a specified person having the necessary qualifications or experience ("the treatment provider") with a view to the reduction or

elimination of the offender's dependency on or propensity to misuse drugs.

(2) The required treatment for any particular period shall be—

(a) treatment as a resident in such institution or place as may be specified in the order; or

(b) treatment as a non-resident in or at such institution or place, and at such intervals, as may be so specified,

but the nature of the treatment shall not be specified in the order except as mentioned in paragraph (a) or (b) above.

(3) A court shall not make a drug treatment and testing order unless it is satisfied that arrangements have been made for the treatment intended to be specified in the order (including arrangements for the reception of the offender where he is required to submit to treatment as a resident).

(4) A drug treatment and testing order shall include a requirement ("the testing requirement") that, for the purpose of ascertaining whether he has any drug in his body during the treatment and testing period, the offender shall provide during that period, at such times and in such circumstances as may (subject to the provisions of the order) be determined by the treatment provider, samples of such description as may be so determined.

(5) The testing requirement shall specify for each month the minimum number of occasions on which samples are to be provided.

(6) A drug treatment and testing order shall specify the local authority in whose area the offender will reside when the order is in force and require that authority to appoint or assign an officer (a "supervising officer") for the purposes of sub-sections (7) and (8) below.

(7) A drug treatment and testing order shall—

(a) provide that, for the treatment and testing period, the offender shall be under the supervision of a supervising officer;

(b) require the offender to keep in touch with the supervising officer in accordance with such instructions as he may from time to time be given by that officer, and to notify him of any change of address; and

(c) provide that the results of the tests carried out on the samples provided by the offender in pursuance of the testing requirement shall be communicated to the supervising officer.

(8) Supervision by the supervising officer shall be carried out to such extent only as may be necessary for the purpose of enabling him—

(a) to report on the offender's progress to the appropriate court;

(b) to report to that court any failure by the offender to comply with the requirements of the order; and

(c) to determine whether the circumstances are such that he should apply to that court for the variation or revocation of the order."

91. Procedural matters relating to drug treatment and testing orders.—After section 234C of the 1995 Act there shall be inserted the following section—

"234D Procedural matters relating to drug treatment and testing orders—

(1) Before making a drug treatment and testing order, a court shall explain to the offender in ordinary language—

(a) the effect of the order and of the requirements proposed to be included in it;

(b) the consequences which may follow under section 234G of this Act if he fails to comply with any of those requirements;

(c) that the court has power under section 234E of this Act to vary or revoke the order on the application of either the offender or the supervising officer; and

(d) that the order will be periodically reviewed at intervals provided for in the order.

(2) Upon making a drug treatment and testing order the court shall—

(a) give, or send by registered post or the recorded delivery service, a copy of the order to the offender;

(b) send a copy of the order to the treatment provider;

(c) send a copy of the order to the chief social work officer of the local authority specified in the order in accordance with section 234C(6) of this Act; and

(d) where it is not the appropriate court, send a copy of the order (together with such documents and information relating to the case as are considered useful) to the clerk of the appropriate court.

(3) Where a copy of a drug treatment and testing order has under sub-section (2)(a) been sent by registered post or by the recorded delivery service, an acknowledgment or certificate of delivery of a letter containing a copy order issued by the Post Office shall be sufficient evidence of the delivery of the letter on the day specified in such acknowledgement or certificate."

92. Amendment and periodic review of drug treatment and testing orders.—After section 234D of the 1995 Act there shall be inserted the following sections—

"*234E. Amendment of drug treatment and testing order.*—(1) Where a drug treatment and testing order is in force either the offender or the supervising officer may apply to the appropriate court for variation or revocation of the order.

(2) Where an application is made under sub-section (1) above by the supervising officer, the court shall issue a citation requiring the offender to appear before the court.

(3) On an application made under sub-section (1) above and after hearing both the offender and the supervising officer, the court may by order, if it appears to it in the interests of justice to do so—

(a) vary the order by—

(i) amending or deleting any of its requirements or provisions,

(ii) inserting further requirements or provisions, or

(iii) subject to sub-section (4) below, increasing or decreasing the treatment and testing period; or

(b) revoke the order.

(4) The power conferred by sub-section (3)(a)(iii) above shall not be exercised so as to increase the treatment and testing period above the maximum for the time being specified in section 234B(2)(a) of this Act, or to decrease it below the minimum so specified.

(5) Where the court, on the application of the supervising officer, proposes to vary (otherwise than by deleting a requirement or provision) a drug treatment and testing order, sections 234B(5) and 234D(1) of this Act shall apply to the variation of such an order as they apply to the making of such an order.

(6) If an offender fails to appear before the court after having been cited in accordance with sub-section (2) above, the court may issue a warrant for his arrest.

234F. Periodic review of drug treatment and testing order.—(1) A drug treatment and testing order shall—

(a) provide for the order to be reviewed periodically at intervals of not less than one month;

(b) provide for each review of the order to be made, subject to sub-section (5) below, at a hearing held for the purpose by the appropriate court (a "review hearing");

(c) require the offender to attend each review hearing;

(d) provide for the supervising officer to make to the court, before each review, a report in writing on the offender's progress under the order; and

(e) provide for each such report to include the test results communicated to the supervising officer under section 234C(7)(c) of this Act and the views of the treatment provider as to the treatment and testing of the offender.

(2) At a review hearing the court, after considering the supervising officer's report, may amend any requirement or provision of the order.

(3) The court—

(a) shall not amend the treatment or testing requirement unless the offender expresses his willingness to comply with the requirement as amended;

(b) shall not amend any provision of the order so as reduce the treatment and testing period below the minimum specified in section 234B(2)(a) of this Act or to increase it above the maximum so specified; and

(c) except with the consent of the offender, shall not amend any requirement or provision of the order while an appeal against the order is pending.

(4) If the offender fails to express his willingness to comply with the treatment or testing requirement as proposed to be amended by the court, the court may revoke the order.

(5) If at a review hearing the court, after considering the supervising officer's report, is of the opinion that the offender's progress under the order is satisfactory, the court may so amend the order as to provide for each subsequent review to be made without a hearing.

(6) A review without a hearing shall take place in chambers without the parties being present.

(7) If at a review without a hearing the court, after considering the supervising officer's report, is of the opinion that the offender's progress is no longer satisfactory, the court may issue a warrant for the arrest of the offender or may, if it thinks fit, instead of issuing a warrant in the first instance, issue a citation requiring the offender to appear before that court as such time as may be specified in the citation.

(8) Where an offender fails to attend—

(a) a review hearing in accordance with a requirement contained in a drug treatment and testing order; or

(b) a court at the time specified in a citation under sub-section (7) above,

the court may issue a warrant for his arrest.

(9) Where an offender attends the court at a time specified by a citation issued under sub-section (7) above—

(a) the court may exercise the powers conferred by this section as if the court were conducting a review hearing; and

(b) so amend the order as to provide for each subsequent review to be made at a review hearing."

93. Consequences of breach of drug treatment and testing order.—After section 234F of the 1995 Act there shall be inserted the following sections—

"234G. Breach of drug treatment testing order.—(1) If at any time when a drug treatment and testing order is in force it appears to the appropriate court that the offender has failed to comply with any requirement of the order, the court may issue a citation requiring the offender to appear before the court at such time as may be specified in the citation or, if it appears to the court to be appropriate, it may issue a warrant for the arrest of the offender.

(2) If it is proved to the satisfaction of the appropriate court that the offender has failed without reasonable excuse to comply with any requirement of the order, the court may by order—

(a) without prejudice to the continuation in force of the order, impose a fine not exceeding level 3 on the standard scale;

(b) vary the order; or

(c) revoke the order.

(3) For the purposes of sub-section (2) above, the evidence of one witness shall be sufficient evidence.

(4) A fine imposed under this section in respect of a failure to comply with the requirements of a drug treatment and testing order shall be deemed for the purposes of any enactment to be a sum adjudged to be paid by or in respect of a conviction or a penalty imposed on a person summarily convicted.

234H. Disposal on revocation of drugs treatment and testing order.—(1) Where the court revokes a drugs treatment and testing order under section 234E(3)(b), 234F(4) or 234G(2)(c) of this Act, it may dispose of the offender in any way which would have been competent at the time when the order was made.

(2) In disposing of an offender under sub-section (1) above, the court shall have regard to the time for which the order has been in operation.

(3) Where the court revokes a drug treatment and testing order as mentioned in sub-section (1) above and the offender is subject to—

(a) a probation order, by virtue of section 234J of this Act; or

(b) a restriction of liberty order, by virtue of section 245D of this Act; or

(c) a restriction of liberty order and a probation order, by virtue of the said section 245D,

the court shall, before disposing of the offender under sub-section (1) above—

(i) where he is subject to a probation order, discharge that order;

(ii) where he is subject to a restriction of liberty order, revoke that order; and

(iii) where he is subject to both such orders, discharge the probation order and revoke the restriction of liberty order."

94. Combination of orders.—(1) After section 234H of the 1995 Act there shall be inserted the following section—

"234J. Concurrent drug treatment and testing and probation orders.—(1) Notwithstanding sections 228(1) and 234B(2) of this Act, where the court considers it expedient that the offender should be subject to a drug treatment and testing order and to a probation order, it may make both such orders in respect of the offender.

(2) In deciding whether it is expedient for it to exercise the power conferred by sub-section (1) above, the court shall have regard to the circumstances, including the nature of the offence and the character of the offender and to the report submitted to it under section 234B(3)(b) of this Act.

(3) Where the court makes both a drug treatment and testing order and a probation order by virtue of sub-section (1) above, the clerk of the court shall send a copy of each of the orders to the following—

(a) the treatment provider within the meaning of section 234C(1);

(b) the officer of the local authority who is appointed or assigned to be the supervising officer under section 234C(6) of this Act; and

(c) if he would not otherwise receive a copy of the order, the officer of the local authority who is to supervise the probationer.

(4) Where the offender by an act or omission fails to comply with a requirement of an order made by virtue of sub-section (1) above—

(a) if the failure relates to a requirement contained in a probation order and is dealt with under section 232(2)(c) of this Act, the court may, in addition, exercise the power conferred by section 234G(2)(b) of this Act in relation to the drug treatment and testing order; and

(b) if the failure relates to a requirement contained in a drug treatment and testing order and is dealt with under section 234G(2)(b) of this Act, the court may, in addition, exercise the power conferred by section 232(2)(c) of this Act in relation to the probation order.

(5) Where an offender by an act or omission fails to comply with both a requirement contained in a drug treatment and testing order and in a probation order to which he is subject by virtue of sub-section (1) above, he may, without prejudice to sub-section (4) above, be dealt with as respects that act or omission either under section 232(2) of this Act or under section 234G(2) of this Act but he shall not be liable to be otherwise dealt with in respect of that act or omission."

(2) Schedule 6 to this Act (Part I of which makes further provision in relation to the combination of drug treatment and testing orders with other orders and Part II of which makes provision in relation to appeals) shall have effect.

95. Interpretation provision in relation to drug treatment and testing orders.—(1) After section 234J of the 1995 Act there shall be inserted the following section—

"234K. Drug treatment and testing orders: interpretation.—In sections 234B to 234J of this Act—

"the appropriate court" means—

(a) where the drug treatment and testing order has been made by the High Court, that court;

(b) in any other case, the court having jurisdiction in the area of the local authority for the time being specified in the order under section 234C(6) of this Act, being a sheriff or district court according to whether the order has been made by a sheriff or district court, but in a case where an order has been made by a district court and there is no district court in that area, the sheriff court; and

"local authority" means a council constituted under section 2 of the;

Local Government etc. (Scotland) Act, 1994 and any reference to the area of such an authority is a reference to the local government area within the meaning of that Act for which it is so constituted."

(2) In section 307(1) of the 1995 Act (interpretation), after the definition of "diet" there shall be inserted the following definition—

"drug treatment and testing order" has the meaning assigned to it in section 234B(2) of this Act;".

Racial aggravation

96. Offences racially aggravated.—(1) The provisions of this section shall apply where it is—

(a) libelled in an indictment; or

(b) specified in a complaint,

and, in either case, proved that an offence has been racially aggravated.

(2) An offence is racially aggravated for the purposes of this section if—

(a) at the time of committing the offence, or immediately before or after doing so, the offender evinces towards the victim (if any) of the offence malice and ill-will based on the victim's membership (or presumed membership) of a racial group; or

(b) the offence is motivated (wholly or partly) by malice and ill-will towards members of a racial group based on their membership of that group,

and evidence from a single source shall be sufficient evidence to establish, for the purposes of this sub-section, that an offence is racially aggravated.

(3) In sub-section (2)(a) above—

"membership", in relation to a racial group, includes association with members of that group;

"presumed" means presumed by the offender.

(4) It is immaterial for the purposes of paragraph (a) or (b) of sub-section (2) above whether or not the offender's malice and ill-will is also based, to any extent, on—

(a) the fact or presumption that any person or group of persons belongs to any religious group; or

(b) any other factor not mentioned in that paragraph.

(5) Where this section applies, the court shall, on convicting a person, take the aggravation into account in determining the appropriate sentence.

(6) In this section "racial group" means a group of persons defined by reference to race, colour, nationality (including citizenship) or ethnic or national origins.

PART V

MISCELLANEOUS AND SUPPLEMENTAL

Remands and committals

97. Remands and committals of children and young persons.—(1) In sub-section (4) of section 23 of the 1969 Act (remands and committals to local authority accommodation), for the words "Subject to sub-section (5) below," there shall be substituted the words" Subject to sub-sections (5) and (5A) below,".

(2)In sub-section (5) of that section, for the words "a young person who has attained the age of fifteen" there shall be substituted the words "a child who has attained the age of twelve, or a young person, who (in either case) is of a prescribed description".

(3) After that sub-section there shall be inserted the following sub-section—

"(5A) A court shall not impose a security requirement in respect of a child or young person who is not legally represented in the court unless—

(a) he applied for legal aid and the application was refused on the ground that it did not appear his means were such that he required assistance; or

(b) having been informed of his right to apply for legal aid and had the opportunity to do so, he refused or failed to apply."

(4) In sub-section (12) of that section, after the definition of "imprisonable offence" there shall be inserted the following definition—

"prescribed description" means a description prescribed by reference to age or sex or both by an order of the Secretary of State;".

(5) Section 20 of the 1994 Act (which has not been brought into force and is superseded by this section) is hereby repealed.

98. Remands and committals: alternative provision for 15 or 16 year old boys.—(1) Section 23 of the 1969 Act shall have effect with the modifications specified in sub-sections (2) to (6) below in relation to any male person who—

(a) is of the age of 15 or 16; and

(b) is not of a description prescribed for the purposes of sub-section (5) of that section.

(2) In sub-section (1), immediately before the words "the remand" there shall be inserted the words "then, unless he is remanded to a remand centre or a prison in pursuance of sub-section (4)(b) or (c) below,".

(3) For sub-sections (4) to (5A) there shall be substituted the following sub-sections—

"(4) Where a court, after consultation with a probation officer, a social worker of a local authority social services department or a member of a youth offending team, declares a person to be one to whom sub-section (5) below applies—

(a) it shall remand him to local authority accommodation and require him to be placed and kept in secure accommodation, if—

(i) it also, after such consultation, declares him to be a person to whom sub-section (5A) below applies, and

(ii) it has been notified that secure accommodation is available for him;

(b) it shall remand him to a remand centre, if paragraph (a) above does not apply and it has been notified that such a centre is available for the reception from the court of persons to whom sub-section (5) below applies; and

(c) it shall remand him to a prison, if neither paragraph (a) nor paragraph (b) above applies.

(4A) A court shall not declare a person who is not legally represented in the court to be a person to whom sub-section (5) below applies unless—

(a) he applied for legal aid and the application was refused on the ground that it did not appear his means were such that he required assistance; or

(b) having been informed of his right to apply for legal aid and had the opportunity to do so, he refused or failed to apply.

(5) This sub-section applies to a person who—

(a) is charged with or has been convicted of a violent or sexual offence, or an offence punishable in the case of an adult with imprisonment for a term of fourteen years or more; or

(b) has a recent history of absconding while remanded to local authority accommodation, and is charged with or has been convicted of an imprisonable offence alleged or found to have been committed while he was so remanded,

if (in either case) the court is of opinion that only remanding him to a remand centre or prison, or to local authority accommodation with a requirement that he be placed and kept in secure accommodation, would be adequate to protect the public from serious harm from him.

(5A) This sub-section applies to a person if the court is of opinion that, by reason of his physical or emotional immaturity or a propensity of his to harm himself, it would be undesirable for him to be remanded to a remand centre or a prison."

(4) In sub-section (6)—

(a) for the words "imposes a security requirement in respect of a young person" there shall be substituted the words "declares a person to be one to whom sub-section (5) above applies"; and

(b) for the words "sub-section (5) above" there shall be substituted the words "that sub-section".

(5) In sub-section (7), after the words "a security requirement" there shall be inserted the words "(that is to say, a requirement imposed under sub-section (4)(a) above that the person be placed and kept in secure accommodation)".

(6) After sub-section (9) there shall be inserted the following sub-section—

"(9A) Where a person is remanded to local authority accommodation without the imposition of a security requirement, a relevant court may, on the application of the designated authority, declare him to be a person to whom sub-section (5) above applies; and on its doing so, sub-section (4) above shall apply."

(7) Section 62 of the 1991 Act (which is superseded by this section) shall cease to have effect.

Release and recall of prisoners

99. Power to release short-term prisoners on licence.—Immediately before section 35 of the 1991 Act there shall be inserted the following section—

"34A. Power to release short-term prisoners on licence.—(1) Subject to sub-section (2) below, sub-section (3) below applies where a short-term prisoner aged 18 or over is serving a sentence of imprisonment for a term of three months or more.

(2) Sub-section (3) below does not apply where—

(a) the sentence is an extended sentence within the meaning of section 58 of the Crime and Disorder Act, 1998;

(b) the sentence is for an offence under section 1 of the M1Prisoners (Return to Custody) Act, 1995;

(c) the sentence was imposed under paragraph 3(1)(d) or 4(1)(d) of Schedule 2 to this Act in a case where the prisoner had failed to comply with a requirement of a curfew order;

(d) the prisoner is subject to a hospital order, hospital direction or transfer direction under section 37, 45A or 47 of the Mental Health Act, 1983;

(e) the prisoner is liable to removal from the United Kingdom for the purposes of section 46 below;

(f) the prisoner has been released on licence under this section at any time and has been recalled to prison under section 38A(1)(a) below;

(g) the prisoner has been released on licence under this section or section 36 below during the currency of the sentence, and has been recalled to prison under section 39(1) or (2) below;

(h) the prisoner has been returned to prison under section 40 below at any time; or

(j) the interval between—

(i) the date on which the prisoner will have served the requisite period for the term of the sentence, and

(ii) the date on which he will have served one-half of the sentence,

is less than 14 days.

(3) After the prisoner has served the requisite period for the term of his sentence, the Secretary of State may, subject to section 37A below, release him on licence.

(4) In this section "the requisite period" means—

(a) for a term of three months or more but less than four months, a period of 30 days;

(b) for a term of four months or more but less than eight months, a period equal to one-quarter of the term;

(c) for a term of eight months or more, a period that is 60 days less than one-half of the term.

(5) The Secretary of State may by order made by statutory instrument—

(a) repeal the words "aged 18 or over" in sub-section (1) above;

(b) amend the definition of "the requisite period" in sub-section (4) above; and

(c) make such transitional provision as appears to him necessary or expedient in connection with the repeal or amendment.

(6) No order shall be made under sub-section (5) above unless a draft of the order has been laid before and approved by a resolution of each House of Parliament."

100. Curfew condition to be included in licence.—(1) After section 37 of the 1991 Act there shall be inserted the following section—

"37A. Curfew condition to be included in licence under section 34A.—(1) A person shall not be released under section 34A(3) above unless the licence includes a condition ("the curfew condition") which—

(a) requires the released person to remain, for periods for the time being specified in the condition, at a place for the time being so specified (which may be an approved probation hostel); and

(b) includes requirements for securing the electronic monitoring of his whereabouts during the periods for the time being so specified.

(2) The curfew condition may specify different places or different periods for different days, but shall not specify periods which amount to less than 9 hours in any one day (excluding for this purpose the first and last days of the period for which the condition is in force).

(3) The curfew condition shall remain in force until the date when the released person would (but for his release) have served one-half of his sentence.

(4) The curfew condition shall include provision for making a person responsible for monitoring the released person's whereabouts during the periods

for the time being specified in the condition; and a person who is made so responsible shall be of a description specified in an order made by the Secretary of State.

(5) The power conferred by sub-section (4) above—

(a) shall be exercisable by statutory instrument; and

(b) shall include power to make different provision for different cases or classes of case or for different areas.

(6) Nothing in this section shall be taken to require the Secretary of State to ensure that arrangements are made for the electronic monitoring of released persons' whereabouts in any particular part of England and Wales;

(7) In this section "approved probation hostel" has the same meaning as in the Probation Service Act, 1993."

(2) Immediately before section 39 of the 1991 Act there shall be inserted the following section—

"*38A. Breach of curfew condition.*—(1) If it appears to the Secretary of State, as regards a person released on licence under section 34A(3) above—

(a) that he has failed to comply with the curfew condition;

(b) that his whereabouts can no longer be electronically monitored at the place for the time being specified in that condition; or

(c) that it is necessary to do so in order to protect the public from serious harm from him,

the Secretary of State may, if the curfew condition is still in force, revoke the licence and recall the person to prison.

(2) A person whose licence under section 34A(3) above is revoked under this section—

(a) may make representations in writing with respect to the revocation;

(b) on his return to prison, shall be informed of the reasons for the revocation and of his right to make representations.

(3) The Secretary of State, after considering any representations made under sub-section (2)(b) above or any other matters, may cancel a revocation under this section.

(4) Where the revocation of a person's licence is cancelled under sub-section (3) above, the person shall be treated for the purposes of sections 34A(2)(f) and 37(1B) above as if he had not been recalled to prison under this section.

(5) On the revocation under this section of a person's licence under section 34A(3) above, he shall be liable to be detained in pursuance of his sentence and, if at large, shall be deemed to be unlawfully at large.

(6) In this section "the curfew condition" has the same meaning as in section 37A above."

101. Early release: two or more sentences.—(1) For sub-section (2) of section 51 of the 1991 Act (interpretation of Part II) there shall be substituted the following sub-sections—

"(2) For the purposes of any reference in this Part, however expressed, to the term of imprisonment to which a person has been sentenced or which, or part of which, he has served, consecutive terms and terms which are wholly or partly concurrent shall be treated as a single term if—

(a) the sentences were passed on the same occasion; or

(b) where they were passed on different occasions, the person has not been released under this Part at any time during the period beginning with the first and ending with the last of those occasions.

(2A) Where a suspended sentence of imprisonment is ordered to take effect, with or without any variation of the original term, the occasion on which that order is made shall be treated for the purposes of sub-section (2) above as the occasion on which the sentence is passed.

(2B) Where a person has been sentenced to two or more terms of imprisonment which are wholly or partly concurrent and do not fall to be treated as a single term—

(a) nothing in this Part shall require the Secretary of State to release him in respect of any of the terms unless and until the Secretary of State is required to release him in respect of each of the others;

(b) nothing in this Part shall require the Secretary of State or the Board to consider his release in respect of any of the terms unless and until the Secretary of State or the Board is required to consider his release, or the Secretary of State is required to release him, in respect of each of the others;

(c) on and after his release under this Part he shall be on licence for so long, and subject to such conditions, as is required by this Part in respect of any of the sentences; and

(d) the date mentioned in section 40(1) above shall be taken to be that on which he would (but for his release) have served each of the sentences in full.

(2C) Where a person has been sentenced to one or more terms of imprisonment and to one or more life sentences (within the meaning of section 34 of the M3Crime (Sentences) Act, 1997), nothing in this Part shall—

(a) require the Secretary of State to release the person in respect of any of the terms unless and until the Secretary of State is required to release him in respect of each of the life sentences; or

(b) require the Secretary of State or the Board to consider the person's release in respect of any of the terms unless and until the Secretary of State or the Board is required to consider his release in respect of each of the life sentences.

(2D) Sub-sections (2B) and (2C) above shall have effect as if the term of an extended sentence (within the meaning of section 58 of the Crime and Disorder Act, 1998) included the extension period (within the meaning of that section)."

(2) After sub-section (3) of section 34 of the 1997 Act (interpretation of Chapter II) there shall be inserted the following sub-section—

"(4) Where a person has been sentenced to one or more life sentences and to one or more terms of imprisonment, nothing in this Chapter shall require the Secretary of State to release the person in respect of any of the life sentences unless and until the Secretary of State is required to release him in respect of each of the terms."

102. ***

103. Recall to prison of short-term prisoners.—(1) This section has effect for the purpose of securing that, subject to section 100(2) above, the circumstances in which prisoners released on licence under Part II of the 1991 Act may be recalled to prison are the same for short-term prisoners as for long-term prisoners.

(2) Section 38 of the 1991 Act (breach of licence conditions by short-term prisoners) shall cease to have effect.

(3) In sub-section (1) of section 39 of the 1991 Act (recall of long-term prisoners while on licence), after the words "in the case of a" there shall be inserted the words "short-term or".

104. Release on licence following recall to prison.—(1) In sub-section (3) of section 33 of the 1991 Act (duty to release short-term and long-term prisoners), for the word "unconditionally" there shall be substituted the words "on licence".

(2) After sub-section (1) of section 37 of that Act (duration and conditions of licences) there shall be inserted the following sub-section—

"(1A) Where a prisoner is released on licence under section 33(3) or (3A) above, sub-section (1) above shall have effect as if for the reference to three-quarters of his sentence there were substituted a reference to the whole of that sentence."

105. Release on licence following return to prison.—After section 40 of the 1991 Act there shall be inserted the following section—

"40A. Release on licence following return to prison.—(1) This section applies (in place of sections 33, 33A, 37(1) and 39 above) where a court passes on a person a sentence of imprisonment which—

(a) includes, or consists of, an order under section 40 above; and

(b) is for a term of twelve months or less.

(2) As soon as the person has served one-half of the sentence, it shall be the duty of the Secretary of State to release him on licence.

(3) Where the person is so released, the licence shall remain in force for a period of three months.

(4) If the person fails to comply with such conditions as may for the time being be specified in the licence, he shall be liable on summary conviction—

(a) to a fine not exceeding level 3 on the standard scale; or

(b) to a sentence of imprisonment for a term not exceeding the relevant period,

but not liable to be dealt with in any other way.

(5) In sub-section (4) above "the relevant period" means a period which is equal in length to the period between the date on which the failure occurred or began and the date of the expiry of the licence.

(6) As soon as a person has served one-half of a sentence passed under sub-section (4) above, it shall be the duty of the Secretary of State to release him, subject to the licence if it is still subsisting."

Miscellaneous

106. Pre-consolidation amendments.—The enactments mentioned in Schedule 7 to this Act shall have effect subject to the amendments there specified, being amendments designed to facilitate, or otherwise desirable in connection with, the consolidation of certain enactments relating to the powers of courts to deal with offenders or defaulters.

107. Amendments to Chapter I of Part II of 1997 Act.—(1) Chapter I of Part II of the 1997 Act (which relates to the effect of determinate custodial sentences) shall be amended as follows.

(2) Sections 8 and 10 to 27 are hereby repealed.

(3) ***

(4) ***

(5) ***

108. Repeal of Chapter I of Part III of Crime and Punishment (Scotland) Act, 1997.—Chapter I of Part III of the Crime and Punishment (Scotland) Act, 1997 (early release of prisoners) shall cease to have effect.

109. Transitional provisions in relation to certain life prisoners.—(1) Section 16 of the Crime and Punishment (Scotland) Act, 1997 (designated life prisoners) shall have effect and shall be deemed always to have had effect with the amendments made by sub-sections (2) and (3) below.

(2) In sub-section (2), at the beginning there shall be inserted the words "Except in a case to which sub-section (3A) or (3B) below applies,".

(3) After sub-section (3) there shall be inserted the following sub-sections—

"(3A) This sub-section applies in a case where a person—

(a) was sentenced, prior to 20 October 1997, in respect of a murder committed by him before he attained the age of 18 years; and

(b) has been released on licence, other than under section 3 of the 1993 Act, whether before or on that date.

(3B) This sub-section applies in a case where a person—

(a) was sentenced, prior to 20 October 1997, in respect of a murder committed by him before he attained the age of 18 years; and

(b) has been released on licence, other than under section 3 of the 1993 Act, after that date without his case having been considered under sub-section (2) above.

(3C) In a case to which sub-section (3A) or (3B) applies, Part I of the 1993 Act shall apply as if the person were a designated life prisoner, within the meaning of section 2 of that Act, whose licence had been granted under sub-section (4) of that section on his having served the designated part of his sentence."

(4) Where, prior to the commencement of this section, a certificate has been issued under sub-section (2) of section 16 of the Crime and Punishment (Scotland) Act, 1997 in respect of a case to which sub-section (3A) of that section applies, the certificate shall be disregarded.

110. Calculation of period of detention at customs office etc., where person previously detained.—In section 24 of the Criminal Law (Consolidation) (Scotland) Act, 1995 (detention and questioning by customs officers), in sub-section (4)—

(a) for the words from "he" to "be" there shall be substituted the words "and is"; and

(b) after the word "detention" there shall be inserted the words, "the period of six hours mentioned in sub-section (2) above shall be reduced by the length of that earlier detention".

111. Early release in Scotland: two or more sentences.—(1) After section 1 of the 1993 Act there shall be inserted the following section—

"1A. Application to persons serving more than one sentence—

Where a prisoner has been sentenced to two or more terms of imprisonment which are wholly or partly concurrent and do not fall to be treated as a single term by virtue of section 27(5) of this Act—

(a) nothing in this Part of this Act shall require the Secretary of State to release him in respect of any of the terms unless and until the Secretary of State is required to release him in respect of each of the other terms;

(b) nothing in this Part of this Act shall require the Secretary of State or the Parole Board to consider his release in respect of any of the terms unless and until the Secretary of State or the Parole Board is required to consider his release, or the Secretary of State is required to release him, in respect of each of the other terms; and

(c) where he is released on licence under this Part of this Act, he shall be on a single licence which—

(i) shall (unless revoked) remain in force until the date on which he would (but for his release) have served in full all the sentences in respect of which he has been so released, and

(ii) shall be subject to such conditions as may be specified or required by this Part of this Act in respect of any of the sentences."

(2) After sub-section (7) of section 16 of the 1993 Act (orders for return to prison on commission of further offence) there shall be inserted the following sub-section—

"(8) Where a prisoner has been sentenced to two or more terms of imprisonment which are wholly or partly concurrent and do not fall to be treated as a single term by virtue of section 27(5) of this Act, the date mentioned in sub-section (1)(a) above shall be taken to be that on which he would (but for his release) have served all of the sentences in full."

(3) For sub-section (5) of section 27 of the 1993 Act (interpretation of Part I) there shall be substituted the following sub-section—

"(5) For the purposes of any reference, however expressed, in this Part of this Act to the term of imprisonment or other detention to which a person has been sentenced or which, or any part of which, he has served, consecutive terms and terms which are wholly or partly concurrent shall be treated as a single term if—

(a) the sentences were passed at the same time; or

(b) where the sentences were passed at different times, the person has not been released under this Part of this Act at any time during the period beginning with the passing of the first sentence and ending with the passing of the last."

(4) In sub-paragraph (1) of paragraph 6B of Schedule 6 to the 1993 Act (aggregation of old and new sentences)—

(a) for the words "a prisoner" there shall be substituted the words "an existing prisoner";

(b) the word "and" after head (a) shall cease to have effect;

(c) in head (b), for the words "that date" there shall be inserted the words "the date on which section 111 of the Crime and Disorder Act, 1998 comes into force"; and

(d) after head (b) there shall be inserted the following—"; and

(c) he has not at any time prior to the passing of the sentence or sentences mentioned in head (b) above been released from the sentence or sentences mentioned in head (a) above under the existing provisions."

(5) After that paragraph there shall be inserted the following paragraph—

"6C(1) This paragraph applies where—

(a) an existing prisoner was, at the relevant date, serving a sentence or sentences of imprisonment, on conviction of an offence, passed before that date;

(b) on or after the date on which section 111 of the Crime and Disorder Act, 1998 comes into force he is, or has been, sentenced to a further term or terms of imprisonment on conviction of an offence, to be served wholly or partly concurrently with the sentence or sentences mentioned in head (a); and

(c) the sentences do not fall to be treated as a single term by virtue of paragraph 6B(2)(a) above.

(2) In a case to which this paragraph applies the Secretary of State shall not release, or be required to consider the release of, the prisoner unless and until the requirements for release, or for consideration of his release, of the new and the existing provisions are satisfied in relation to each sentence to which they respectively apply.

(3) In a case to which this paragraph applies the Parole Board shall not be required to consider the release of the prisoner unless and until the requirements for release, or for consideration for release, of the new and the existing provisions are satisfied in relation to each sentence to which they respectively apply.

(4) In a case to which this paragraph applies, where the prisoner is released on licence, he shall be on a single licence which—

(a) shall (unless revoked) remain in force until the later of—

(i) the date on which he would have been discharged from prison on remission of part of his sentence or sentences under the existing provisions if, after his release, he had not forfeited remission of any part of that sentence under those provisions; or

(ii) the date on which he would (but for his release) have served in full all the sentences in respect of which he was released on licence and which were imposed after the relevant date; and

(b) shall be deemed to be granted under the new provisions and, subject to sub-paragraph (5) below, those provisions so far as relating to conditions of licences, and recall or return to prison, shall apply as they apply in respect of a prisoner on licence in respect of a sentence passed after the relevant date.

(5) In the application of section 16 to a person whose licence is deemed to be granted under the new provisions by virtue of sub-paragraph (4)(b) above, the reference to the original sentence (within the meaning of that section) shall be construed as a reference to the further term or terms mentioned in head (b) of sub-paragraph (1) above."

(6) Subject to sub-section (7) below, the amendments made by sub-sections (1) to (5) above apply where one or more of the sentences concerned was passed after the commencement of this section.

(7) Where the terms of two or more sentences passed before the commencement of this section have been treated, by virtue of section 27(5) of, or paragraph 6B of Schedule 6 to, the 1993 Act, as a single term for the purposes of Part I of that Act, they shall continue to be so treated after that commencement.

(8) In relation to a prisoner released on licence at any time under section 16(7)(b) of the 1993 Act, section 17(1)(a) of that Act shall have effect as if after the word "Act" there were inserted the words "or a short term prisoner has been released on licence by virtue of section 16(7)(b) of this Act".

112. Restriction on consecutive sentences for released prisoners: Scotland.—After section 204 of the 1995 Act there shall be inserted the following section—

"204A Restriction on consecutive sentences for released prisoners—

A court sentencing a person to imprisonment or other detention shall not order or direct that the term of imprisonment or detention shall commence on the expiration of any other such sentence from which he has been released at any time under the existing or new provisions within the meaning of Schedule 6 to the Prisoners and Criminal Proceedings (Scotland) Act, 1993."

113. Deputy authorising officer under Part III of Police Act, 1997.—(1). . . . .

(2) In sub-section (3) of that section, for paragraphs (a) and (b) there shall be substituted the words "he holds the rank of assistant chief constable in that Service or Squad".

(3) . . . .

Supplemental

114. Orders and regulations.—(1) Any power of a Minister of the Crown or of the National Assembly for Wales to make an order or regulations under this Act—

(a) is exercisable by statutory instrument; and

(b) includes power to make such transitional provision as appears to him necessary or expedient in connection with any provision made by the order or regulations.

(2) A statutory instrument containing an order under section 1A, 5(1A), (2) or (3), 6A(1) or 10(6) above (other than one made by the National Assembly for Wales), or containing regulations under paragraph 1 of Schedule 3 to this Act, shall be subject to annulment in pursuance of a resolution of either House of Parliament.

(3) No order under section 38(5) or 41(6) above shall be made unless a draft of the order has been laid before and approved by a resolution of each House of Parliament.

115. Disclosure of information—(1) Any person who, apart from this sub-section, would not have power to disclose information—

(a) to a relevant authority; or

(b) to a person acting on behalf of such an authority,

shall have power to do so in any case where the disclosure is necessary or expedient for the purposes of any provision of this Act.

(2) In sub-section (1) above "relevant authority" means—

(a) the chief officer of police for a police area in England and Wales;

(b) the chief constable of a police force maintained under the Police (Scotland) Act, 1967;

(c) a police authority within the meaning given by section 101(1) of the Police Act, 1996;

(d) a local authority, that is to say—

(i) in relation to England, a county council, a district council, a London borough council, a parish council or the Common Council of the City of London,

(ii) in relation to Wales, a county council, a county borough council or a community council,

(iii) in relation to Scotland, a council constituted under section 2 of the Local Government etc. (Scotland) Act, 1994;

(e) a local probation board in England and Wales;

(ea) a Strategic Health Authority;

(f) a health authority.

116. Transitory provisions.—(1) The Secretary of State may by order provide that, in relation to any time before the commencement of section 73 above, a court shall not make an order under—

(a) section 1 of the 1994 Act (secure training orders); or

(b) sub-section (3)(a) of section 4 of that Act (breaches of supervision requirements),

unless it has been notified by the Secretary of State that accommodation at a secure training centre, or accommodation provided by a local authority for the purpose of restricting the liberty of children and young persons, is immediately available for the offender, and the notice has not been withdrawn.

(2) An order under this section may provide that sections 2 and 4 of the 1994 Act shall have effect, in relation to any such time, as if—

(a) for sub-sections (2) and (3) of section 2 there were substituted the following sub-section—

"(2) Where accommodation for the offender at a secure training centre is not immediately available—

(a) the court shall commit the offender to accommodation provided by a local authority for the purpose of restricting the liberty of children and young persons until such time as accommodation for him at such a centre is available; and

(b) the period of detention in the centre under the order shall be reduced by the period spent by the offender in the accommodation so provided.";

(b) in sub-section (5) of that section, for the words "sub-sections (2)(a)(ii) and (4)(b) apply" there were substituted the words "sub-section (4)(b) applies";

(c) for sub-section (8) of that section there were substituted the following sub-section—

"(8) In this section "local authority" has the same meaning as in the Children Act, 1989."; and

(d) in sub-section (4) of section 4, for the words "paragraphs (a), (b) and (c) of sub-section (2) and sub-sections (5), (7) and (8) of section 2" there were substituted the words "paragraphs (a) and (b) of sub-section (2) and sub-sections (7) and (8) of section 2".

(3) In relation to any time before the commencement of section 73 above, section 4 of the 1994 Act shall have effect as if after sub-section (4) there were inserted the following sub-section—

"(4A) A fine imposed under sub-section (3)(b) above shall be deemed, for the purposes of any enactment, to be a sum adjudged to be paid by a conviction."

(4) In relation to any time before the commencement of section 73 above, section 1B of the 1982 Act (special provision for offenders under 18) shall have effect as if—

(a) in sub-section (4), immediately before the words "a total term" there were inserted the words "a term or (in the case of an offender to whom sub-section (6) below applies)";

(b) in sub-section (5)—

(i) immediately before the words "total term" there were inserted the words "term or (as the case may be", and

(ii) for the words "the term" there were substituted the word "it"; and

(c) for sub-section (6) there were substituted the following sub-section—

"(6) This sub-section applies to an offender sentenced to two or more terms of detention in a young offender institution which are consecutive or wholly or partly concurrent if—

(a) the sentences were passed on the same occasion; or

(b) where they were passed on different occasions, the offender has not been released under Part II of the Criminal Justice Act, 1991 at any time during the period beginning with the first and ending with the last of those occasions,

and in sub-sections (4) and (5) above "the total term", in relation to such an offender, means the aggregate of those terms."

(5) In this section "local authority" has the same meaning as in the 1989 Act.

117. General interpretation.—(1) In this Act—

"the 1933 Act" means the Children and Young Persons Act, 1933;

"the 1969 Act" means the Children and Young Persons Act, 1969;

"the 1973 Act" means the Powers of Criminal Courts Act, 1973;

"the 1980 Act" means the Magistrates' Courts Act, 1980;

"the 1982 Act" means the Criminal Justice Act, 1982;

"the 1984 Act" means the Police and Criminal Evidence Act, 1984;

"the 1985 Act" means the Prosecution of Offences Act, 1985;

"the 1989 Act" means the Children Act, 1989;

"the 1991 Act" means the Criminal Justice Act, 1991;

"the 1994 Act" means the Criminal Justice and Public Order Act, 1994;

"the 1997 Act" means the Crime (Sentences) Act, 1997;

"caution" has the same meaning as in Part V of the Police Act, 1997;

"child" means a person under the age of 14;

"commission area" has the same meaning as in the Justices of the Peace Act, 1997;

"custodial sentence" has the same meaning as in the Powers of Criminal Courts (Sentencing) Act, 2000;

"guardian" has the same meaning as in the 1933 Act;

"local probation board" means a local probation board established under section 4 of the Criminal Justice and Court Services Act, 2000;

"prescribed" means prescribed by an order made by the Secretary of State;

"young person" means a person who has attained the age of 14 and is under the age of 18;

"youth offending team" means a team established under section 39 above.

(2) In this Act—

"the 1993 Act" means the Prisoners and Criminal Proceedings (Scotland) Act, 1993; and

"the 1995 Act" means the Criminal Procedure (Scotland) Act, 1995.

(3) For the purposes of this Act, the age of a person shall be deemed to be that which it appears to the court to be after considering any available evidence.

118. Provision for Northern Ireland.—An Order in Council under paragraph 1(1)(b) of Schedule 1 to the Northern Ireland Act, 1974 (legislation for Northern Ireland in the interim period) which contains a statement that it is made only for purposes corresponding to those of sections 2 to 4, 34, 47(5), 57, 61 to 64 and 85 above—

(a) shall not be subject to paragraph 1(4) and (5) of that Schedule (affirmative resolution of both Houses of Parliament); but

(b) shall be subject to annulment in pursuance of a resolution of either House of Parliament.

119. Minor and consequential amendments.—The enactments mentioned in Schedule 8 to this Act shall have effect subject to the amendments there specified, being minor amendments and amendments consequential on the provisions of this Act.

120. Transitional provisions, savings and repeals.—(1) The transitional provisions and savings contained in Schedule 9 to this Act shall have effect; but nothing in this sub-section shall be taken as prejudicing the operation of sections 16 and 17 of the Interpretation Act, 1978 (which relate to the effect of repeals).

(2) The enactments specified in Schedule 10 to this Act, which include some that are spent, are hereby repealed to the extent specified in the third column of that Schedule.

121. Short title, commencement and extent.—(1) This Act may be cited as the Crime and Disorder Act, 1998.

(2) This Act, except this section, sections 109 and 111(8) above and paragraphs 55, 99 and 117 of Schedule 8 to this Act, shall come into force on such day as the Secretary of State may by order appoint; and different days may be appointed for different purposes or different areas.

(3) Without prejudice to the provisions of Schedule 9 to this Act, an order under sub-section (2) above may make such transitional provisions and savings as appear to the Secretary of State necessary or expedient in connection with any provision brought into force by the order.

(4) Subject to sub-sections (5) to (12) below, this Act extends to England and Wales only.

(5) The following provisions extend to Scotland only, namely—

(a) Chapter II of Part I;

(b) section 33;

(c) Chapter II of Part IV;

(d) sections 108 to 112 and 117(2); and

(e) paragraphs 55, 70, 71, 98 to 108, 115 to 124 and 140 to 143 of Schedule 8 and section 119 above so far as relating to those paragraphs.

(6) The following provisions also extend to Scotland, namely—

(a) Chapter III of Part I;

(b) section 36(3) to (5);

(c) section 65(9);

(d) section 115;

(e) paragraph 3 of Schedule 3 to this Act and section 52(6) above so far as relating to that paragraph;

(f) . . . .

(g) paragraphs 1, 7(1) and (3), 14(1) and (2), 35, 36, 45, 135, 136 and 138 of Schedule 8 to this Act and section 119 above so far as relating to those paragraphs; and

(h) this section.

(7) Sections 36(1), (2)(a), (b) and (d) and (6)(b) and section 118 above extend to Northern Ireland only.

(8) Section 36(3)(b), (4) and (5) above, paragraphs 7(1) and (3), 45, 135 and 138 of Schedule 8 to this Act, section 119 above so far as relating to those paragraphs and this section also extend to Northern Ireland.

(9) Section 36(5) above, paragraphs 7(1) and (3), 45 and 134 of Schedule 8 to this Act, section 119 above so far as relating to those paragraphs and this section also extend to the Isle of Man.

(10) Section 36(5) above, paragraphs 7(1) and (3), 45 and 135 of Schedule 8 to this Act, section 119 above so far as relating to those paragraphs and this section also extend to the Channel Islands.

(11) The repeals in Schedule 10 to this Act, and section 120(2) above so far as relating to those repeals, have the same extent as the enactments on which the repeals operate.

(12) Section 9(4) of the Repatriation of Prisoners Act, 1984 (power to extend Act to Channel Islands and Isle of Man) applies to the amendments of that Act made by paragraphs 56 to 60 of Schedule 8 to this Act; and in Schedule 1 to the 1997 Act—

(a) paragraph 14 (restricted transfers between the United Kingdom and the Channel Islands) as applied in relation to the Isle of Man; and

(b) paragraph 19 (application of Schedule in relation to the Isle of Man),

apply to the amendments of that Schedule made by paragraph 135 of Schedule 8 to this Act.

SCHEDULE 1

Section 24(4)

SCHEDULE 2A TO THE CIVIC GOVERNMENT (SCOTLAND) ACT, 1982

"SCHEDULE 2A

RETENTION AND DISPOSAL OF PROPERTY SEIZED UNDER SECTION 54(2A) OF THIS ACT

Section 54(2C).

"Schedule 2AS Retention and disposal of property seized under section 54(2A) of this Act

Application

1. This schedule applies to property seized under section 54(2A) of this Act.

Retention

2. (1) Subject to sub-paragraph (2) below, property to which this Schedule applies may be retained for a period of twenty-eight days beginning with the day on which it was seized.

(2) Where proceedings for an offence are instituted within the period specified in sub-paragraph (1) above against any person, the property may be retained for a period beginning on the day on which it was seized and ending on the day when—

(a) the prosecutor certifies that the property is not, or is no longer, required as a production in criminal proceedings or for any purpose relating to such proceedings;

(b) the accused in such proceedings—

(i) is sentenced or otherwise dealt with for the offence, or

(ii) is acquitted of the offence; or

(c) the proceedings are expressly abandoned by the prosecutor or are desertedsimpliciter.

Arrangements for custody of property

3. (1) Subject to the proviso to section 17(3)(b) of the Police (Scotland) Act, 1967 (duty to comply with instructions received from prosecutor), the chief constable shall, in accordance with the provisions of this Schedule, make such arrangements as he considers appropriate for the care, custody, return or disposal of property to which this Schedule applies.

(2) Any reference in this Schedule to property being in the possession of, delivered by or disposed of by, the chief constable includes a reference to its being in the possession of, delivered by or disposed of by, another person under arrangements made under sub-paragraph (1) above.

Disposal

4. Where the period of retention permitted by paragraph 2 above expires and the chief constable has reason to believe that the person from whom the property was seized is not the owner or the person having right to possession of it, he shall take reasonable steps to ascertain the identity of the owner or of the person with that right and to notify him of the procedures determined under paragraph 5(1) below.

5. (1) Subject to sub-paragraphs (5) and (6) below, the owner or any person having right to possession of any property to which this Schedule applies and which, at the expiry of the period of retention permitted by paragraph 2 above, is in the possession of the chief constable may at any time prior to its disposal under paragraph 6 below claim that property in accordance with such procedure as the chief constable may determine.

(2) Subject to sub-paragraphs (3), (5) and (6) below, where the chief constable considers that the person making a claim in accordance with the procedure determined under sub-paragraph (1) above is the owner of the property or has a right to possession of it, he shall deliver the property to the claimant.

(3) Subject to sub-paragraph (4) below, the chief constable may impose such conditions connected with the delivery to the claimant of property under sub-paragraph (2) above as he thinks fit and, without prejudice to that generality, such conditions may relate to the payment of such reasonable charges (including any reasonable expenses incurred in relation to the property by or on behalf of him) as he may determine.

(4) No condition relating to the payment of any charge shall be imposed by the chief constable on the owner or person having right of possession of the property where he is satisfied that that person did not know, and had no reason to suspect, that the property to which this Schedule applies was likely to be used in a manner which gave rise to its seizure.

(5) This paragraph does not apply where the period of retention expires in such manner as is mentioned in paragraph 2(2)(b)(i) above and the court by which he was convicted has made a suspended forfeiture order or a restraint order in respect of the property to which this Schedule applies.

(6) This paragraph shall cease to apply where at any time—

(a) the property to which this Schedule applies—

(i) is seized under any other power available to a constable, or

(ii) passes into the possession of the prosecutor; or

(b) proceedings for an offence are instituted, where the property to which this Schedule applies is required as a production.

6. (1)Where this sub-paragraph applies, the chief constable may—

(a) sell property to which this Schedule applies; or

(b) if in his opinion it would be impracticable to sell such property, dispose of it.

(2) Sub-paragraph (1) above applies—

(a) at any time after the expiry of the relevant period where, within that period—

(i) no claim has been made under paragraph 5 above, or

(ii) any such a claim which has been made has been rejected by the chief constable; and

(b) where a claim has been made under paragraph 5 above and not determined within the relevant period, at any time after the rejection of that claim by the chief constable.

(3) In sub-paragraph (2) above, the "relevant period" means a period of six months beginning with the day on which the period of retention permitted by paragraph 2 above expired.

(4) Sections 71, 72 and 77(1) of this Act shall apply to a disposal under this paragraph as they apply to a disposal under section 68 of this Act.

Appeals

7. (1) A claimant under sub-paragraph (2) of paragraph 5 above may appeal to the sheriff against any decision of the chief constable made under that paragraph as respects the claim.

(2) The previous owner of any property disposed of for value under paragraph 6 above may appeal to the sheriff against any decision of the chief constable made under section 72 of this Act as applied by sub-paragraph (4) of that paragraph.

(3) Sub-sections (3) to (5) of section 76 of this Act shall apply to an appeal under this paragraph as they apply to an appeal under that section.

Interpretation

8. In this Schedule—

"chief constable" means the chief constable for the police area in which the property to which this Schedule applies was seized, and includes a constable acting under the direction of the chief constable for the purposes of this Schedule;

"restraint order" shall be construed in accordance with section 28(1) of the Proceeds of Crime (Scotland) Act, 1995;

"suspended forfeiture order" shall be construed in accordance with section 21(2) of that Act."

SCHEDULE 2

Section 41(11)

THE YOUTH JUSTICE BOARD: FURTHER PROVISIONS

Membership

1. The Secretary of State shall appoint one of the members of the Board to be their chairman.

2. (1) Subject to the following provisions of this paragraph, a person shall hold and vacate office as a member of the Board, or as chairman of the Board, in accordance with the terms of his appointment.

(2) An appointment as a member of the Board may be full-time or part-time.

(3) The appointment of a person as a member of the Board, or as chairman of the Board, shall be for a fixed period of not longer than five years.

(4) Subject to sub-paragraph (5) below, a person whose term of appointment as a member of the Board, or as chairman of the Board, expires shall be eligible for re-appointment.

(5) No person may hold office as a member of the Board for a continuous period which is longer than ten years.

(6) A person may at any time resign his office as a member of the Board, or as chairman of the Board, by notice in writing addressed to the Secretary of State.

(7) The terms of appointment of a member of the Board, or the chairman of the Board, may provide for his removal from office (without cause being assigned) on notice from the Secretary of State of such length as may be specified in those terms, subject (if those terms so provide) to compensation from the Secretary of State; and in any such case the Secretary of State may remove that member from office in accordance with those terms.

(8) Where—

(a) the terms of appointment of a member of the Board, or the chairman of the Board, provide for compensation on his removal from office in pursuance of sub-paragraph (7) above; and

(b) the member or chairman is removed from office in pursuance of that sub-paragraph,

the Board shall pay to him compensation of such amount, and on such terms, as the Secretary of State may with the approval of the Treasury determine.

(9) The Secretary of State may also at any time remove a person from office as a member of the Board if satisfied—

(a) that he has without reasonable excuse failed to discharge his functions as a member for a continuous period of three months beginning not earlier than six months before that time;

(b) that he has been convicted of a criminal offence;

(c) that a bankruptcy order has been made against him, or his estate has been sequestrated, or he has made a composition or arrangement with, or granted a trust deed for, his creditors; or

(d) that he is unable or unfit to discharge his functions as a member.

(10) The Secretary of State shall remove a member of the Board, or the chairman of the Board, from office in pursuance of this paragraph by declaring his office as a member of the Board to be vacant and notifying that fact in such manner as the Secretary of State thinks fit; and the office shall then become vacant.

(11) If the chairman of the Board ceases to be a member of the Board he shall also cease to be chairman.

Members and employees

3. (1) The Board shall—

(a) pay to members of the Board such remuneration;

(b) pay to or in respect of members of the Board any such allowances, fees, expenses and gratuities; and

(c) pay towards the provision of pensions to or in respect of members of the Board any such sums,

as the Board are required to pay by or in accordance with directions given by the Secretary of State.

(2) Where a member of the Board was, immediately before becoming a member, a participant in a scheme under section 1 of the M1Superannuation Act, 1972, the Minister for the Civil Service may determine that his term of office as a member shall be treated for the purposes of the scheme as if it were service in the employment or office by reference to which he was a participant in the scheme; and his rights under the scheme shall not be affected by sub-paragraph (1)(c) above.

(3) Where—

(a) a person ceases to hold office as a member of the Board otherwise than on the expiry of his term of appointment; and

(b) it appears to the Secretary of State that there are special circumstances which make it right for him to receive compensation,

the Secretary of State may direct the Board to make to the person a payment of such amount as the Secretary of State may determine.

4. (1) The Board may appoint a chief executive and such other employees as the Board think fit, subject to the consent of the Secretary of State as to their number and terms and conditions of service.

(2) The Board shall—

(a) pay to employees of the Board such remuneration; and

(b) pay to or in respect of employees of the Board any such allowances, fees, expenses and gratuities,

as the Board may, with the consent of the Secretary of State, determine.

(3) Employment by the Board shall be included among the kinds of employment to which a scheme under section 1 of the Superannuation Act, 1972 may apply.

5. The Board shall pay to the Minister for the Civil Service, at such times as he may direct, such sums as he may determine in respect of any increase attributable to paragraph 3(2) or 4(3) above in the sums payable out of money provided by Parliament under the Superannuation Act, 1972.

House of Commons disqualification

6. In Part II of Schedule 1 to the House of Commons Disqualification Act, 1975 (bodies of which all members are disqualified), there shall be inserted at the appropriate place the following entry—"The Youth Justice Board for England and Wales".

Procedure

7. (1) The arrangements for the procedure of the Board (including the quorum for meetings) shall be such as the Board may determine.

(2) The validity of any proceedings of the Board (or of any committee of the Board) shall not be affected by—

(a) any vacancy among the members of the Board or in the office of chairman of the Board; or

(b) any defect in the appointment of any person as a member of the Board or as chairman of the Board.

Annual reports and accounts

8. (1) As soon as possible after the end of each financial year of the Board, the Board shall send to the Secretary of State a report on the discharge of their functions during that year.

(2) The Secretary of State shall lay before each House of Parliament, and cause to be published, a copy of every report sent to him under this paragraph.

9. (1) The Board shall—

(a) keep proper accounts and proper records in relation to the accounts; and

(b) prepare a statement of accounts in respect of each financial year of the Board.

(2) The statement of accounts shall contain such information and shall be in such form as the Secretary of State may, with the consent of the Treasury, direct.

(3) The Board shall send a copy of the statement of accounts to the Secretary of State and to the Comptroller and Auditor General within such period after the end of the financial year to which the statement relates as the Secretary of State may direct.

(4) The Comptroller and Auditor General shall—

(a) examine, certify and report on the statement of accounts; and

(b) lay a copy of the statement of accounts and of his report before each House of Parliament.

10. For the purposes of this Schedule the Board's financial year shall be the period of twelve months ending with 31st March; but the first financial year of the Board shall be the period beginning with the date of establishment of the Board and ending with the first 31st March which falls at least six months after that date.

Expenses

11. The Secretary of State shall out of money provided by Parliament pay to the Board such sums towards their expenses as he may determine.

SCHEDULE 3

PROCEDURE WHERE PERSONS ARE SENT FOR TRIAL UNDER SECTION 51

Regulations

1. The Attorney General shall by regulations provide that, where a person is sent for trial under section 51 of this Act on any charge or charges, copies of the documents containing the evidence on which the charge or charges are based shall,

(a) be served on that person; and

(b) be given to the Crown Court sitting at the place specified in the notice under sub-section (7) of that section before the expiry of the period prescribed by the regulations; but the judge may at his discretion extend or further extend that period.

(2) The regulations may make provision as to the procedure to be followed on an application for the extension or further extension of a period under sub-paragraph (1) above.

Applications for dismissal

2. (1) A person who is sent for trial under section 51 of this Act on any charge or charges may, at any time—

(a) after he is served with copies of the documents containing the evidence on which the charge or charges are based; and

(b) before he is arraigned (and whether or not an indictment has been preferred against him),

apply orally or in writing to the Crown Court sitting at the place specified in the notice under sub-section (7) of that section for the charge, or any of the charges, in the case to be dismissed.

(2) The judge shall dismiss a charge (and accordingly quash any count relating to it in any indictment preferred against the applicant) which is the subject of any such application if it appears to him that the evidence against the applicant would not be sufficient for a jury properly to convict him.

(3) No oral application may be made under sub-paragraph (1) above unless the applicant has given to the Crown Court sitting at the place in question written notice of his intention to make the application.

(4) Oral evidence may be given on such an application only with the leave of the judge or by his order; and the judge shall give leave or make an order only if it appears to him, having regard to any matters stated in the application for leave, that the interests of justice require him to do so.

(5) If the judge gives leave permitting, or makes an order requiring, a person to give oral evidence, but that person does not do so, the judge may disregard any document indicating the evidence that he might have given.

(6) If the charge, or any of the charges, against the applicant is dismissed—

(a) no further proceedings may be brought on the dismissed charge or charges except by means of the preferment of a voluntary bill of indictment; and

(b) unless the applicant is in custody otherwise than on the dismissed charge or charges, he shall be discharged.

(7) Crown Court Rules may make provision for the purposes of this paragraph and, without prejudice to the generality of this sub-paragraph, may make provision—

(a) as to the time or stage in the proceedings at which anything required to be done is to be done (unless the court grants leave to do it at some other time or stage);

(b) as to the contents and form of notices or other documents;

(c) as to the manner in which evidence is to be submitted; and

(d) as to persons to be served with notices or other material.

Reporting restrictions

3. (1) Except as provided by this paragraph, it shall not be lawful—

(a) to publish in Great Britain a written report of an application under paragraph 2(1) above; or

(b) to include in a relevant programme for reception in Great Britain a report of such an application,

if (in either case) the report contains any matter other than that permitted by this paragraph.

(2) An order that sub-paragraph (1) above shall not apply to reports of an application under paragraph 2(1) above may be made by the judge dealing with the application.

(3) Where in the case of two or more accused one of them objects to the making of an order under sub-paragraph (2) above, the judge shall make the order if, and only if, he is satisfied, after hearing the representations of the accused, that it is in the interests of justice to do so.

(4) An order under sub-paragraph (2) above shall not apply to reports of proceedings under sub-paragraph (3) above, but any decision of the court to make or not to make such an order may be contained in reports published or included in a relevant programme before the time authorised by sub-paragraph (5) below.

(5) It shall not be unlawful under this paragraph to publish or include in a relevant programme a report of an application under paragraph 2(1) above containing any matter other than that permitted by sub-paragraph (8) below where the application is successful.

(6) Where—

(a) two or more persons were jointly charged; and

(b) applications under paragraph 2(1) above are made by more than one of them,

sub-paragraph (5) above shall have effect as if for the words "the application is" there were substituted the words "all the applications are".

(7) It shall not be unlawful under this paragraph to publish or include in a relevant programme a report of an unsuccessful application at the conclusion of the trial of the person charged, or of the last of the persons charged to be tried.

(8) The following matters may be contained in a report published or included in a relevant programme without an order under sub-paragraph (2) above before the time authorised by sub-paragraphs (5) and (6) above, that is to say—

(a) the identity of the court and the name of the judge;

(b) the names, ages, home addresses and occupations of the accused and witnesses;

(c) the offence or offences, or a summary of them, with which the accused is or are charged;

(d) the names of counsel and solicitors engaged in the proceedings;

(e) where the proceedings are adjourned, the date and place to which they are adjourned;

(f) the arrangements as to bail;

(g) whether a right to representation funded by the Legal Services Commission as part of the Criminal Defence Service was granted to the accused or any of the accused.

(9) The addresses that may be published or included in a relevant programme under sub-paragraph (8) above are addresses—

(a) at any relevant time; and

(b) at the time of their publication or inclusion in a relevant programme.

(10) If a report is published or included in a relevant programme in contravention of this paragraph, the following persons, that is to say—

(a) in the case of a publication of a written report as part of a newspaper or periodical, any proprietor, editor or publisher of the newspaper or periodical;

(b) in the case of a publication of a written report otherwise than as part of a newspaper or periodical, the person who publishes it;

(c) in the case of the inclusion of a report in a relevant programme, any body corporate which is engaged in providing the service in which the programme is included and any person having functions in relation to the programme corresponding to those of the editor of a newspaper;

shall be liable on summary conviction to a fine not exceeding level 5 on the standard scale.

(11) Proceedings for an offence under this paragraph shall not, in England and Wales, be instituted otherwise than by or with the consent of the Attorney General.

(12) Sub-paragraph (1) above shall be in addition to, and not in derogation from, the provisions of any other enactment with respect to the publication of reports of court proceedings.

(13) In this paragraph—

"publish", in relation to a report, means publish the report, either by itself or as part of a newspaper or periodical, for distribution to the public;

"relevant programme" means a programme included in a programme service (within the meaning of the Broadcasting Act, 1990);

"relevant time" means a time when events giving rise to the charges to which the proceedings relate occurred.

Power of justice to take depositions etc.

4. (1) Sub-paragraph (2) below applies where a justice of the peace for any commission area is satisfied that—

(a) any person in England and Wales ("the witness") is likely to be able to make on behalf of the prosecutor a written statement containing material evidence, or produce on behalf of the prosecutor a document or other exhibit likely to be material evidence, for the purposes of proceedings for an offence for which a person has been sent for trial under section 51 of this Act by a magistrates' court for that area; and

(b) the witness will not voluntarily make the statement or produce the document or other exhibit.

(2) In such a case the justice shall issue a summons directed to the witness requiring him to attend before a justice at the time and place appointed in the summons, and to have his evidence taken as a deposition or to produce the document or other exhibit.

(3) If a justice of the peace is satisfied by evidence on oath of the matters mentioned in sub-paragraph (1) above, and also that it is probable that a summons under sub-paragraph (2) above would not procure the result required by it, the justice may instead of issuing a summons issue a warrant to arrest the witness and to bring him before a justice at the time and place specified in the warrant.

(4) A summons may also be issued under sub-paragraph (2) above if the justice is satisfied that the witness is outside the British Islands, but no warrant may be issued under sub-paragraph (3) above unless the justice is satisfied by evidence on oath that the witness is in England and Wales.

(5) If—

(a) the witness fails to attend before a justice in answer to a summons under this paragraph;

(b) the justice is satisfied by evidence on oath that the witness is likely to be able to make a statement or produce a document or other exhibit as mentioned in sub-paragraph (1)(a) above;

(c) it is proved on oath, or in such other manner as may be prescribed, that he has been duly served with the summons and that a reasonable sum has been paid or tendered to him for costs and expenses; and

(d) it appears to the justice that there is no just excuse for the failure,

the justice may issue a warrant to arrest the witness and to bring him before a justice at the time and place specified in the warrant.

(6) Where—

(a) a summons is issued under sub-paragraph (2) above or a warrant is issued under sub-paragraph (3) or (5) above; and

(b) the summons or warrant is issued with a view to securing that the witness has his evidence taken as a deposition,

the time appointed in the summons or specified in the warrant shall be such as to enable the evidence to be taken as a deposition before the relevant date.

(7) If any person attending or brought before a justice in pursuance of this paragraph refuses without just excuse to have his evidence taken as a deposition, or to produce the document or other exhibit, the justice may do one or both of the following—

(a) commit him to custody until the expiration of such period not exceeding one month as may be specified in the summons or warrant or until he sooner has his evidence taken as a deposition or produces the document or other exhibit;

(b) impose on him a fine not exceeding £2,500.

(8) A fine imposed under sub-paragraph (7) above shall be deemed, for the purposes of any enactment, to be a sum adjudged to be paid by a conviction.

(9) If in pursuance of this paragraph a person has his evidence taken as a deposition, the chief executive to the justice concerned shall as soon as is reasonably practicable send a copy of the deposition to the prosecutor and the Crown Court.

(10) If in pursuance of this paragraph a person produces an exhibit which is a document, the chief executive to the justice concerned shall as soon as is reasonably practicable send a copy of the document to the prosecutor and the Crown Court.

(11) If in pursuance of this paragraph a person produces an exhibit which is not a document, the chief executive to the justice concerned shall as soon as is reasonably practicable inform the prosecutor and the Crown Court of that fact and of the nature of the exhibit.

(12) In this paragraph—

"prescribed" means prescribed by rules made under section 144 of the 1980 Act;

"the relevant date" has the meaning given by paragraph 1(2) above.

Use of depositions as evidence

5. (1) Subject to sub-paragraph (3) below, sub-paragraph (2) below applies where in pursuance of paragraph 4 above a person has his evidence taken as a deposition.

(2) Where this sub-paragraph applies the deposition may without further proof be read as evidence on the trial of the accused, whether for an offence for which he was sent for trial under section 51 of this Act or for any other offence arising out of the same transaction or set of circumstances.

(3) Sub-paragraph (2) above does not apply if—

(a) it is proved that the deposition was not signed by the justice by whom it purports to have been signed;

(b) the court of trial at its discretion orders that sub-paragraph (2) above shall not apply; or

(c) a party to the proceedings objects to sub-paragraph (2) above applying.

(4) If a party to the proceedings objects to sub-paragraph (2) applying the court of trial may order that the objection shall have no effect if the court considers it to be in the interests of justice so to order.

Power of Crown Court to deal with summary offence

6. (1) This paragraph applies where a magistrates' court has sent a person for trial under section 51 of this Act for offences which include a summary offence.

(2) If the person is convicted on the indictment, the Crown Court shall consider whether the summary offence is related to the offence that is triable only on indictment or, as the case may be, any of the offences that are so triable.

(3) If it considers that the summary offence is so related, the court shall state to the person the substance of the offence and ask him whether he pleads guilty or not guilty.

(4) If the person pleads guilty, the Crown Court shall convict him, but may deal with him in respect of the summary offence only in a manner in which a magistrates' court could have dealt with him.

(5) If he does not plead guilty, the powers of the Crown Court shall cease in respect of the summary offence except as provided by sub-paragraph (6) below.

(6) If the prosecution inform the court that they would not desire to submit evidence on the charge relating to the summary offence, the court shall dismiss it.

(7) The Crown Court shall inform the justices' chief executive for the magistrates' court of the outcome of any proceedings under this paragraph.

(8) If the summary offence is one to which section 40 of the Criminal Justice Act, 1988 applies, the Crown Court may exercise in relation to the offence the power conferred by that section; but where the person is tried on indictment for such an offence, the functions of the Crown Court under this paragraph in relation to the offence shall cease.

(9) Where the Court of Appeal allows an appeal against conviction of an indictable-only offence which is related to a summary offence of which the appellant was convicted under this paragraph—

(a) it shall set aside his conviction of the summary offence and give the clerk of the magistrates' court notice that it has done so; and

(b) it may direct that no further proceedings in relation to the offence are to be undertaken,

and the proceedings before the Crown Court in relation to the offence shall thereafter be disregarded for all purposes.

(10) A notice under sub-paragraph (9) above shall include particulars of any direction given under paragraph (b) of that sub-paragraph in relation to the offence.

(11). . . . .

(12) An offence is related to another offence for the purposes of this paragraph if it arises out of circumstances which are the same as or connected with those giving rise to the other offence.

Procedure where no indictable-only offence remains

7. (1) Subject to paragraph 13 below, this paragraph applies where—

(a) a person has been sent for trial under section 51 of this Act but has not been arraigned; and

(b) the person is charged on an indictment which (following amendment of the indictment, or as a result of an application under paragraph 2 above, or for any other reason) includes no offence that is triable only on indictment.

(2) Everything that the Crown Court is required to do under the following provisions of this paragraph must be done with the accused present in court.

(3) The court shall cause to be read to the accused each count of the indictment that charges an offence triable either way.

(4) The court shall then explain to the accused in ordinary language that, in relation to each of those offences, he may indicate whether (if it were to proceed to trial) he would plead guilty or not guilty, and that if he indicates that he would plead guilty the court must proceed as mentioned in sub-paragraph (6) below.

(5) The court shall then ask the accused whether (if the offence in question were to proceed to trial) he would plead guilty or not guilty.

(6) If the accused indicates that he would plead guilty the court shall proceed as if he had been arraigned on the count in question and had pleaded guilty.

(7) If the accused indicates that he would plead not guilty, or fails to indicate how he would plead, the court shall consider whether the offence is more suitable for summary trial or for trial on indictment.

(8) Subject to sub-paragraph (6) above, the following shall not for any purpose be taken to constitute the taking of a plea—

(a) asking the accused under this paragraph whether (if the offence were to proceed to trial) he would plead guilty or not guilty;

(b) an indication by the accused under this paragraph of how he would plead.

8. (1) Subject to paragraph 13 below, this paragraph applies in a case where—

(a) a person has been sent for trial under section 51 of this Act but has not been arraigned;

(b) he is charged on an indictment which (following amendment of the indictment, or as a result of an application under paragraph 2 above, or for any other reason) includes no offence that is triable only on indictment;

(c) he is represented by a legal representative;

(d) the Crown Court considers that by reason of his disorderly conduct before the court it is not practicable for proceedings under paragraph 7 above to be conducted in his presence; and

(e) the court considers that it should proceed in his absence.

(2) In such a case—

(a) the court shall cause to be read to the representative each count of the indictment that charges an offence triable either way;

(b) the court shall ask the representative whether (if the offence in question were to proceed to trial) the accused would plead guilty or not guilty;

(c) if the representative indicates that the accused would plead guilty the court shall proceed as if the accused had been arraigned on the count in question and had pleaded guilty;

(d) if the representative indicates that the accused would plead not guilty, or fails to indicate how the accused would plead, the court shall consider whether the offence is more suitable for summary trial or for trial on indictment.

(3) Subject to sub-paragraph (2)(c) above, the following shall not for any purpose be taken to constitute the taking of a plea—

(a) asking the representative under this section whether (if the offence were to proceed to trial) the accused would plead guilty or not guilty;

(b) an indication by the representative under this paragraph of how the accused would plead.

9. (1) This paragraph applies where the Crown Court is required by paragraph 7(7) or 8(2)(d) above to consider the question whether an offence is more suitable for summary trial or for trial on indictment.

(2) Before considering the question, the court shall afford first the prosecutor and then the accused an opportunity to make representations as to which mode of trial would be more suitable.

(3) In considering the question, the court shall have regard to—

(a) any representations made by the prosecutor or the accused;

(b) the nature of the case;

(c) whether the circumstances make the offence one of a serious character;

(d) whether the punishment which a magistrates' court would have power to impose for it would be adequate; and

(e) any other circumstances which appear to the court to make it more suitable for the offence to be dealt tried in one way rather than the other.

10. (1) This paragraph applies (unless excluded by paragraph 15 below) where the Crown Court considers that an offence is more suitable for summary trial.

(2) The court shall explain to the accused in ordinary language—

(a) that it appears to the court more suitable for him to be tried summarily for the offence, and that he can either consent to be so tried or, of he wishes, be tried by a jury; and

(b) that if he is tried summarily and is convicted by the magistrates' court, he may be committed for sentence to the crown court under section 3 of the Powers of Criminal Courts (Sentencing) Act, 2000 if the convicting court is of such opinion as is mentioned in sub-section (2) of that section.

(3) After explaining to the accused as provided by sub-paragraph (2) above the court shall ask him whether he wishes to be tried summarily or by a jury, and—

(a) if he indicates that he wishes to be tried summarily, shall remit him for trial to a magistrates' court acting for the place where he was sent to the Crown Court for trial;

(b) if he does not give such an indication, shall retain its functions in relation to the offence and proceed accordingly.

11. If the Crown Court considers that an offence is more suitable for trial on indictment, the court—

(a) shall tell the accused that it has decided that it is more suitable for him to be tried for the offence by a jury; and

(b) shall retain its functions in relation to the offence and proceed accordingly.

12. (1) Where the prosecution is being carried on by the Attorney General, the Solicitor General or the Director of Public Prosecutions and he applies for an offence which may be tried on indictment to be so tried—

(a) sub-paragraphs (4) to (8) of paragraph 7, sub-paragraphs (2)(b) to (d) and (3) of paragraph 8 and paragraphs 9 to 11 above shall not apply; and

(b) the Crown Court shall retain its functions in relation to the offence and proceed accordingly.

(2) The power of the Director of Public Prosecutions under this paragraph to apply for an offence to be tried on indictment shall not be exercised except with the consent of the Attorney General.

13. (1) This paragraph applies, in place of paragraphs 7 to 12 above, in the case of a child or young person who—

(a) has been sent for trial under section 51 of this Act but has not been arraigned; and

(b) is charged on an indictment which (following amendment of the indictment, or as a result of an application under paragraph 2 above, or for any other reason) includes no offence that is triable only on indictment.

(2) The Crown Court shall remit the child or young person for trial to a magistrates' court acting for the place where he was sent to the Crown Court for trial unless—

(a) he is charged with such an offence as is mentioned in sub-section (1) or (2) of section 91 of the Powers of Criminal Courts (Sentencing) Act, 2000 (punishment of certain grave crimes) and the Crown Court considers that if he is found guilty of the offence it ought to be possible to sentence him in pursuance of sub-section (3) of that section; or

(b) he is charged jointly with an adult with an offence triable either way and the Crown Court considers it necessary in the interests of justice that they both be tried for the offence in the Crown Court.

(3) In sub-paragraph (2) above "adult" has the same meaning as in section 51 of this Act.

Procedure for determining whether offences of criminal damage etc., are summary offences

14. (1) This paragraph applies where the Crown Court has to determine, for the purposes of this Schedule, whether an offence which is listed in the first column of Schedule 2 to the 1980 Act (offences for which the value involved is relevant to the mode of trial) is a summary offence.

(2) The court shall have regard to any representations made by the prosecutor or the accused.

(3) If it appears clear to the court that the value involved does not exceed the relevant sum, it shall treat the offence as a summary offence.

(4) If it appears clear to the court that the value involved exceeds the relevant sum, it shall treat the offence as an indictable offence.

(5) If it appears to the court for any reason not clear whether the value involved does or does not exceed the relevant sum, the court shall ask the accused whether he wishes the offence to be treated as a summary offence.

(6) Where sub-paragraph (5) above applies—

(a) if the accused indicates that he wishes the offence to be treated as a summary offence, the court shall so treat it;

(b) if the accused does not give such an indication, the court shall treat the offence as an indictable offence.

(7) In this paragraph "the value involved" and "the relevant sum" have the same meanings as in section 22 of the 1980 Act (certain offences triable either way to be tried summarily if value involved is small).

Power of Crown Court, with consent of legally-represented accused, to proceed in his absence

15. (1) The Crown Court may proceed in the absence of the accused in accordance with such of the provisions of paragraphs 9 to 14 above as are applicable in the circumstances if—

(a) the accused is represented by a legal representative who signifies to the court the accused's consent to the proceedings in question being conducted in his absence; and

(b) the court is satisfied that there is good reason for proceeding in the absence of the accused.

(2) Sub-paragraph (1) above is subject to the following provisions of this paragraph which apply where the court exercises the power conferred by that sub-paragraph.

(3) If, where the court has considered as required by paragraph 7(7) or 8(2)(d) above, it appears to the court that an offence is more suitable for summary trial, paragraph 10 above shall not apply and—

(a) if the legal representative indicates that the accused wishes to be tried summarily, the court shall remit the accused for trial to a magistrates' court acting for the place where he was sent to the Crown Court for trial;

(b) if the legal representative does not give such an indication, the court shall retain its functions and proceed accordingly.

(4) If, where the court has considered as required by paragraph 7(7) or 8(2)(d) above, it appears to the court that an offence is more suitable for trial on indictment, paragraph 11 above shall apply with the omission of paragraph (a).

(5) Where paragraph 14 above applies and it appears to the court for any reason not clear whether the value involved does or does not exceed the relevant sum, sub-paragraphs (5) and (6) of that paragraph shall not apply and—

(a) the court shall ask the legal representative whether the accused wishes the offence to be treated as a summary offence;

(b) if the legal representative indicates that the accused wishes the offence to be treated as a summary offence, the court shall so treat it;

(c) if the legal representative does not give such an indication, the court shall treat the offence as an indictable offence.

SUBJECT INDEX

M

P

•••